TO WIN THE WINTER SKY

The Air War over the Ardennes 1944-1945

PREVIOUS PAGE: The Big Show. Luftwaffe pilots of *I/JG 77*, the "Red Hearts," head out for their waiting Messerschmitt G-14s for *"Operation Bodenplatte,"* the New Year's Day surprise attack on Allied airfields. Ten pilots of the hundred *"Herzas"* pilots taking part would not return. With merely 214 German aircrew lost in the 900 plane operation, January 1, 1945 witnessed the largest single-day Luftwaffe losses of the entire war. *(Pieper via Roba)*

TO WIN THE WINTER SKY

The Air War over the Ardennes
1944-1945

Danny S. Parker

COMBINED BOOKS
Pennsylvania

Contents

Maps

Acknowledgments

The author wishes to thank the numerous individuals who helped with this effort. Dr. James H. Kitchens at the U.S.A.F. Historical Research Center (HRC) at Maxwell AFB deserves special recognition for his help with many sources, both German and Allied. Of yeoman assistance at the "point" were HRC Archivists Marvin L. Fisher and Joseph D. Caver and Technicians Essie G. Roberts, Sandi D. Smith and Ann D. Webb. Special thanks to the Ninth Air Force Association and their help in locating the various veterans organizations. Donald Caldwell, the author of the excellent history on *Jagdgeschwader 26*, provided a review of the manuscript and was instrumental in pointing out important sources for my research. At the National Archives the usual skill of John E. Taylor and Robin E. Cookson in locating the obscure is most appreciated. In the Still Pictures Branch, Sharon Culley and Jonathan Heller provided help with their photographic collection. Mr. Mark Ridley at the Air Force Historical Center at Bolling AFB was able to provide other assistance. The USAF photo collection is now maintained at the National Air and Space Museum Archives. Melissa Keiser and Allan Janus were instrumental in assisting with the review of several thousand photographs to select many of those appearing in this volumne. Two Belgian WWII aviation experts, Mr. Jean-Louis Roba and Mr. Cynrik De Decker provided considerable unique information including specific monographs prepared for the author's research. Similar assistance was provided from England by Dr. Alfred Price and from Germany by Ulf Balke and Axel Paul. Mr. Jim Bowman translated a number of lengthy German documents. Richard Signore and Lisa Shepperd assisted with the edit of the initial drafts. Wanda Dutton provided word processing assistance. Bob Pigeon and Ken Gallagher at Combined Books kept the project on track. And last, but not least, the cooperative staff at the Cocoa Beach Library, particularly Ms. Maggie Leonicio and Ms. JoAnne McIntosh have been instrumental in pursuing my lengthy interlibrary loan requests. My sincere gratitude to all involved.

For
Shep

The Unknown Bulge

In December, 1944 and January, 1945 one of the great battles of World War II was fought in the skies over the Ardennes Forest of Germany, Belgium and Luxembourg. This battle is virtually unknown. Unlike the famous Battle of the Bulge, the air war overhead was almost completely one-sided— the Allied air forces won the campaign decisively. Moreover, the magnitude of this victory had a profound influence on the outcome of the ground battle below. For the U.S. and British air forces had not only menaced the German enemy on the battlefield, blasting their troops and tanks, but they also starved their armies by lancing their sources of supply. So decisive was the impact, that the outcome of the battle in the Ardennes was virtually predestined.

The use of Allied air power against the German Ardennes Offensive was historic. Never before had air power blunted an enemy's surprise counter-offensive from the sky. Until that winter, air power providing ground support had only been used in mass to support attacking armies. Although Adolf Hitler had carefully selected the time and circumstances under which his great operation would be launched, it was the first time Germany had embarked on a major offensive without assurance of air superiority. Indeed, so dubious was Hitler of his Luftwaffe's capabilities, that he forbade the opening of the attack without a forecast of poor weather to keep the Allied planes on the tarmac. At first, the weather promised Hitler success. The fog, mist and snows grounded most aircraft for the initial days of the great German offensive. Afterwards, however, the veil of clouds lifted and Allied air power was given a task unprecedented in modern warfare: to strangle the enemy's armored spearheads by attack from the air while friendly forces reeled under a vigorous assault below. The Allied air forces rose magnificently to the challenge.

But if the Luftwaffe failed in this great battle, it was not for lack of effort. Most conventional accounts off-handedly discount the threat of the German air force in late 1944, dismissing its ability to counter the Allied control of the air or intervene in the ground battle. The German air force is portrayed as a paper tiger. Nothing could be further from the truth. The Luftwaffe, although driven from European air space that summer, was husbanding its strength for a final all-out effort to reclaim the initiative in the air. By late fall, the swelling enemy fighter force loomed as a dangerous threat to the Allied air forces in the west. With increasing numbers, the German air leaders prepared to redress the remaining imbalance with unparalleled developments in aeronautical technology. The Allied air leaders worried about this most of all. What if their bomber fleets suddenly encountered hundreds of the new enemy jets? They would have been even more troubled had they known that the Germans possessed a shrewd plan to turn the tables on air superiority with one great blow. Three hundred heavy bombers were to be shot down in a single day!

That the Luftwaffe was never able to carry out the operation as originally envisioned, nor use its force effectively is part of our story. The Germans fought valiantly for the skies over Europe in an unequal aerial contest; some of the largest air battles of World War II were fought that Christmas of 1944. And on New Year's Day, 1945, the Luftwaffe staged one of the most spectacular air operations in history— a massive thousand plane surprise air strike on Allied airfields. But just how did all this come about? We must first set the stage...

Prologue

The Reichsmarschall

Hermann Wilhelm Göring, the rotund head of the German air force in World War II, had an altogether unlikely appearance for the second most powerful man in Adolf Hitler's Third Reich. As the Führer's designated successor and the head of the Luftwaffe, Göring's influence was enormous. Simply recounting his lengthy titles is onerous: Reichsminister for Air, Supreme Commander of the German Air Force, Prime Minister of Prussia, President of the State Council, President of the *Reichstag*, Reichsminister of Forestry and Game, President of the Scientific Research Council and so on. But the apex came in the summer of 1940 when Hitler made him a six star general after Germany's conquest of France. The *Reichsmarschall* became the highest ranking officer in Europe, or for that matter, the world. Only one other in German history, Prince Eugen, had reached that heady mark.

Most of the characters and charlatans who peopled Hitler's draconian domain were cold, spartan and menacing in appearance— Himmler, Bormann and Goebbels to name just a few. All fit the Third Reich's mold of sacrificial fanatics. Beyond other worldly concerns they shared a devotion to National Socialism, its aims and the Zarathustrian persona of Adolf Hitler himself. Against this backdrop of monotonous misanthropes and political misfits, Hermann Göring stood as an unlikely successor to Adolf Hitler. The *Reichsmarschall's* appearance immediately suggested caricature. He festooned himself with gaudy diamond-studded belts and his fingers were ringed with jewels. For his uniform he often wore a cloak over luxuriant silks and waddled along in ballooning riding pants to cover his bloated 264-pound frame. Polished jackboots, an ornate baton or a studded dagger and a chest of brilliant medals decorated the Reichmarschall's garish hulk.

The *Reichsmarschall* was vain and corrupt, being totally obsessed with personal wealth and power. Raised in a medieval castle in the dark forests

11

of the Franconia countryside around Nuremberg— Veldenstein— young Göring grew up seeing himself as a triumphant knight of old. Family and friends did little to inspire young Göring; they taught him that money and power could buy all; morality was more a convenience than an imperative. "I have no conscience," he once proclaimed, "Adolf Hitler is my conscience!" Faithfully following this path during the course of the war, Hermann Göring had indulged himself in a sybaritic lifestyle. The experience, as he professed after the war, "had been a good run for my money."

In the early years of the Third Reich, "Hermann," as he was known to the German public, enjoyed a reputation second only to Hitler himself. The public had bestowed upon him his favorite epithets: "Ironman" and "the most faithful paladin of the Führer." He endeared himself to the German people as a sort of avuncular vaudevillian figure. Strangely, the Germans loved his flashy demeanor and exaggerated flourish, perhaps for the contrast with the otherwise drab countenance of the others with which the Führer surrounded himself.

Hermann Göring's physical demeanor was nearly obscene, his gluttony and love of fine food and drink having left him flabby and egg-shaped. Göring was the object of continual jokes— even the public called him *der Dicke*— the "fat one."

But Göring did more than put on aristocratic airs: professing a love of art and beauty, he used his position to acquire enormous spoils of conquest. Beginning his "shopping expeditions" in Amsterdam in 1940, Göring amassed incredible wealth by confiscating works of art while pandering his insatiable lust for gold, precious jewels and other finery. His Luftwaffe ground troops sent him trainloads of "appropriated" art treasures from France and Italy. The European art community would take decades to locate most of the goods seized by his Nazi "Art Protection Commission." Some are still missing.

There were even darker perils from his epicurean lifestyle: after the First World War Göring had become seriously addicted to morphine. His *Eukodal* problem, along with other mental anguish brought on by the troubles of the National Socialist Party in 1925, saw the need for Göring to dry out at Langbro Asylum in Sweden. Göring said he had broken the habit after this experience, but his colleagues remained unconvinced. By the time the war was in full swing he was consuming up to thirty capsules of paracodeine a day.

The *Reichsmarschall* obviously preferred the palatial splendor of Karinhall, his home deep in the woods near the Baltic Coast northeast of Berlin. Named for his first wife, Baroness Karin von Fock-Kantzow, the 100,000 acre estate's huge main building was his ostentatious copy of a Swedish hunting lodge. Its huge Norse stone walls housed some of the more spectacular pieces of his art "collection" (including Rembrandt's "Bearded Man" and da

Vinci's Spirdon Leda) along with huge chandeliers and taxidermic mementos of his passion for hunting. The spacious compound was even outfitted with Göring's beloved pet lions; a terrific surprise to the host's uninitiated guests. As the war's devastation progressed, Göring grew to prefer the sanctuary of his family and lavish accommodations to the chilly, prison-like atmosphere at Hitler *Wolfschanze* (Wolf's Lair). Karinhall was Hermann Göring's vision of a Nazi Camelot.

But there were other reasons than luxury for residing at Karinhall: only the jangling telephone could transmit the ever increasing vitriol spewing from Hitler and his aides. By late 1944 the theme of these phone conversations had become monotonously repetitive: the city of such-and-such had been smashed by another deadly rain of explosives or incendiaries from hundreds of Allied bombers; so many were dead and the factories, which had been urgently manufacturing (guns, tanks, planes, oil, etc.) were destroyed. Only the numbers and names changed from week to week. But the one recurring theme from Hitler was the "failure of the Luftwaffe." Göring's standing as head of the Luftwaffe was anchored first and foremost in his devotion to the German leader. From the beginning Göring had been Hitler's right-hand man. Behind an outward varnish of avuncular joviality, Göring was ruthless. He brutally arranged the killings of National Socialism's insurgents during the murderous "Night of the Long Knives." During the early years of Hitler's rise he also had the dubious honor of not only establishing the Storm Troopers and the penal system that would later harbor the concentration camps, but also of creating the Gestapo— the dreaded Nazi secret police. To crown Hitler's seizure of power, Göring had been a principal in the murderous Röhm affair. In July of 1934, after the bloody deeds were done, Göring returned late from a hunting trip to attend a state dinner with British Ambassador Sir Eric Philips. Göring apologized profusely, explaining that he had only just gotten back from shooting. "Animals, I hope," Sir Eric dryly remarked. After the war Göring attempted to portray himself less maliciously— "an upright soldier with the heart of a child," he once said. At Nuremberg, he constantly reiterated that he was unaware of the concentration camps, but regardless of this convenient memory lapse and care to not inquire into goings-on at places like Dachau, his guilt in the "final solution" seems undeniable.

In choosing Göring as his principal lieutenant and head of his air force, Hitler recognized more than his personal devotion and proper *Aryan* outlook. Göring's experience extended beyond politics— in World War I he was a courageous flier who was the last commander of the legendary Richthofen Squadron and was credited with 22 victories from 1915 - 1918. As a captain he became the head of Civil Aviation in Germany in 1933, and was appointed as General and Commander-in-Chief of the Luftwaffe. As Göring's star rose, so did those of his former flying comrades, although there were never

enough of the "Old Eagles" to fill the top leadership position in the embryonic Luftwaffe. Many officers ended up being drawn from the Army and
had no practical flying experience. The auspicious debut of the Luftwaffe in
1939 owed more to the technical genius of the German aviation engineers
and pre-war training than it did to the foresight of its leaders.

As the 1930s drew to a close, Hitler's desire for conquest became increasingly evident. Göring's dread of another World War was equal to Hitler's
lust for another go at Germany's old foes. Under Hitler's resolve the prospect of war seemed unavoidable; through the mid-thirties the German
leader constantly lectured those in his company on the need for *Lebensraum*,
or living space, "which we are going to have to seize by force." For his part,
Göring complained to his aviation experts that he and his Luftwaffe was not
yet ready. He also worried about the potential involvement of the United
States in any coming conflict.

By mid-1939, Göring's coolness to the winds of war had cost the
Reichsmarschall credibility in Hitler's eyes. Sensitive to his master's scorn,
Göring bade his subordinates organize a grand display of the most advanced
Luftwaffe projects in progress. "Show everything achieved up to now," he
told his chief of armaments Ernst Udet. Pull out all the stops. The dazzling
display of aviation technology was scheduled for Hitler's visit to Rechlin
research station on July 3, 1939. The collection was indeed breathtaking:
Ernst Heinkel brought along two astonishing marvels, a Heinkel 176 rocket-
powered fighter with a fantastic rate of climb, and the experimental He-178
jet fighter. There were glittering rows of other modern piston aircraft, but a
gushing test pilot, Erich Warsitz, told Hitler and Göring "In a few years you
won't see many propeller driven planes in the skies." Hitler was agog at the
wizardry and futuristic engineering. The Luftwaffe was further along than
he had dared hope!

Later in the war Hermann Göring would point to Rechlin as the foun-
tainhead of many of Hitler's misconceptions regarding the Luftwaffe's
technological superiority. "They put on such a demonstration for me that I
can only say this now: what bunglers our finest magicians are in comparison!
We're still waiting for the things they conjured up there before my very
eyes— and worse still, the Führer's." Göring was right. Although advanced,
all of these planes were far from proven designs capable of mass production.

But when war actually began in 1939 and 1940 it all seemed so easy. In
campaigns lasting mere weeks, Hitler's panzer armies conquered Western
Europe under the paralyzing bombardment of Göring's air force. Göring
himself had provided detailed planning for *Case Yellow*, the attack on France
and the Low Countries. He called for an important surprise attack on Dutch
and Belgian fortifications to take them out of the battle in the early going
while his fighters shot the French air force out of the skies. The Luftwaffe's
participation was to be so important that Hitler delayed the attack at

Göring's request until the forecast predicted at least four days of perfect flying weather. On the morning of May 10th Göring's colossal war machine rose over French skies. In all, his armada comprised 1,482 bombers, 1,016 single-engined and 248 twin-engined bombers. By afternoon the obsolete French air force had suffered tremendous losses and Fort Eben Emael had been captured by a contingent of Luftwaffe paratroopers. This daring raid opened the floodgates to the German panzers.

While his entourage fawned over the *Reichsmarschall*, Luftwaffe Stuka dive bombers were pounding the French into headlong retreat at Sedan. By the evening of May 15th the aircraft-led German tanks were pushing across the Meuse River into the open French countryside. In a matter of days they would arrive at the channel coast and the defense of France would be in ruins. The only blemish had been the British escape at Dunkirk. Bad weather had grounded much of the German air operation and allowed 300,000 British and French soldiers to escape. Still Hermann Göring was jubilant; the war, he thought, was nearly over.

That the dramatic collapse of the dynasties of Poland and France was, in part, due to the German air onslaught seems undeniable. The hallmark of the *Blitzkrieg*, the shrieking dive bombing Ju-87 Stukas, seemed to validate the pre-war logic of a tactical air force to support ground armies. Göring was so impressed with himself and his omnipotent Luftwaffe that he quickly lost sight of one of the most important maxims of war: do not underestimate your enemy. "The Luftwaffe's advantage was assured for all time," he proclaimed, "its start could never be overtaken, whatever might happen."

Such visions of grandeur came tumbling down a few weeks later when Göring opened the Battle of Britain. Between July and October, the Luftwaffe endured grievous losses in vicious fighting with a tenacious and determined enemy. The twin-engined Me-110 proved too slow to win against the more agile British fighters and the Me-109s did not have the endurance to fight for long over southern England. Worse still, the Ju-87 Stukas, which had proven so deadly in France, were sitting ducks without fighter cover. Due to the disorganized and indecisive Luftwaffe strategic planning that was to dog all its future operations, the German strategic aims for the Battle of Britain were constantly shifting; one week it was elimination of British fighters in the air, on another it was destruction of airdromes and plane manufacture. Finally there was the misguided terror bombing of London which gave the RAF the respite it needed to rebuild. With both numerical and qualitative superiority of the Luftwaffe dwindling towards mere parity, the incompetent and often indifferent command at the yoke of the Luftwaffe was at last exposed. By the end of October, 1940, the cost of the bungled operation had become so critical (1,700 German planes and many valuable pilots) that Göring was forced to call a halt to his daylight attack. The

Reichsmarschall's reputation was tarnished; the Luftwaffe had suffered its first irrefutable defeat.

The following year saw increasing tension between Hitler and Göring. Having failed to eliminate the British, the Führer turned his attention to the east and the Bolsheviks. Göring abhorred the idea of an attack on Soviet Russia. He was sure it would lead to disaster. In January of 1941 he had nearly convinced Hitler to take another course, but the German leader claimed *Führerprinzip* and changed his mind. Göring pleaded with Hitler to remember Napoleon and his great Armageddon in the Russian steppes. But Hitler dismissed this concerns, flushed from his colossal defeat of France. Napoleon, he said, "did not have great panzer armies or the strongest air force in the world." With his vanity so stroked, the *Reichsmarschall* resigned himself to Hitler's dangerous course. "We will smash the Russians before winter," Hitler declared.

Throughout the spring of 1941, the retaliatory terror bombing of London and Berlin escalated as Hitler and his generals planned *Operation Barbarossa*. In May, Göring's air force took the island of Crete in a daring paratroop assault. But losses made it a pyrrhic victory and the Germans worried that somehow the British had learned the precise time of the German operation. Four thousand paratroopers became casualties in the first assault wave. Göring's subordinates should have followed their suspicions, for this was precisely the case. ULTRA, the top-secret Allied deciphering system, was faithfully decoding Luftwaffe radio transmissions as they were made. By the time the units in the field had their flying orders, it would usually be less than 24 hours before senior Allied commanders knew the same. But as summer approached, Göring fretted increasingly of Russia and *Barbarossa*.

At first it looked like France all over again. When at last the great campaign began in Russia, on June 22, 1941 Göring's Luftwaffe flung itself at the Soviet enemy with such reckless abandon that the *Reichsmarschall* himself was dubious of the claims coming from the front. Some 1,800 planes were said to be destroyed on the first day, and by the end of June *OKW* reported the destruction of 4,017 aircraft at a cost of only 150 of their own. But later that summer the vastness of Russia and the enormity of the Soviet resources became more apparent. In October, upon almost reaching the suburbs of Moscow, the rains and mud transformed the unpaved roads to molasses. Hitler's armies mired to a halt. It was only weeks later that the severe Russian winter caught the summer-minded German army ill prepared. It was clear that the war in Russia would be a long one.

As the curtain opened on 1942, the German situation in Russia had reached great peril. Although mere pinpricks in 1940, the Allied air attacks were growing in violence. Late on the evening of May 30, 1942, while Göring was entertaining guests, the phone at Vedelstein castle jangled nosily. Word came from the *Gauleiter* of Cologne that an incredibly destructive British bombing attack was in progress. Göring protested loudly: the raid must only be a small raid. He slammed down the receiver. But soon the irksome phone rang again. On picking it up Göring fell silent; it was Hitler this time. As he always did when speaking to the German leader, Göring stood at attention. Hitler informed him that "hundreds" of bombers were attacking. That, Göring insisted, was impossible. A tally the next day showed incredible destruction in the city with some 500 killed; the Germans themselves had shot down 40 bombers. The next day, an embarrassed *Reichsmarschall* learned from the BBC that over a thousand bombers had taken part. Göring said it was a lie, but Hitler knew otherwise: "It is out of the question that only 70 or 80 bombers attacked," the German leader professed. And then he exaggerated, "I never capitulate to an unpleasant truth. I must see clearly if I am to draw the proper conclusion." The truth was that the air war was now out of control.

Göring never really freed himself from convictions spawned by his experiences in the previous war and his youthful dreams of knighthood. Even though his early successes had won him the coveted *Pour le Mérite* the memories served later as limitations. In the glory days of the bi-plane, Göring had seen pilot skill and determination as the end-all to winning dogfights over the trenches of World War 1. He relegated technical superiority in aeronautical matters to a back seat. An aircraft's technical limitations could be overcome by a pilot's brash, bold attacks without regard to personal safety. The kernel of this conviction would plague him to the end of the war. Göring, the self-proclaimed Renaissance Man, fancied that aerial warfare decided by ramming was really "the most dignified way of fighting." He even actively pursued this as a fighter tactic for the Luftwaffe, enjoining the development of the *Sturmböcke* ("Battering-Ram") fighter tactics which involved flying into the path of enemy bombers and closing within jousting distance to either shoot them down or destroy them by ramming. A heavily armored version of the Fw-190 with a big 3-cm cannon in place of the jousting lance was even produced to pursue these desperate tactics. To those who disapproved, he had nothing but disdain. "You are all cowards!" he scowled. Later, when his own nephew, flying for the Luftwaffe, was killed while attempting to ram an enemy bomber over France, Göring shed not a tear.

The *Reichsmarschall* saw most developments in aviation technology as scientific gadgets over which to marvel, rather than vital turning points which would decide the fate of the Luftwaffe and perhaps of Germany herself. Before the war Göring was fortunate to have those like General Walther Wever, in charge of the Luftwaffe's technical department, who saw the truth. "Perhaps in no other arm in the service," Werver drilled those under him," is the mutual dependence of tactics and technology and their inter-working so great as in the Luftwaffe." But Wever's sagacity was not to guide the Luftwaffe for long; in 1936 he was killed in a flying accident. Wever's permanent replacement, Gen. Hans Jeschonnek, was short-sighted and inordinately influenced both by Göring, who had little vision or even interest in such details, and Gen. Ernst Udet, the influential Director of Air Armaments.

Even though a gifted flyer and a dependable crony from Göring's Richthofen days, Udet was miscast at his post. Göring was dedicated to his wartime companions and slow to realize Udet's shortcomings. Supreme advocates of precision dive bombing, Udet and Jeschonnek were obsessed with the concept. Dive bombing, they said, would be the wave of the future; it was more effective and less wasteful. Even new medium German bombers must dive, Jeschonnek ordered in 1938. Moreover, the "offensive spirit" of the early days of the war called for the bombers to be as fast as the enemy fighters. The aviation designers like Heinkel and Messerschmitt were dumbfounded: it was a hopeless objective. While the potentially revolutionary discoveries of jet and rocket propulsion tantalized the Germans with the possibility of tremendous German technical superiority, the Luftwaffe leadership languished under Göring, Udet and Jeschonnek. The trio complained that all of this new aviation technology was too expensive and unnecessary— in just a year the war would be over!

In spite of doing his best to ignore the war at Karinhall, by the summer of 1941 it was clear even to the *Reichsmarschall* that he must do something about the dawdling Udet. Regardless of numerous promises otherwise, his World War I comrade had failed to increase German aircraft output since the beginning of the war. At the front, shortages of combat aircraft crippled operations and retarded the training of pilots— facts that had not escaped Hitler's attention. Meanwhile, Udet was avoiding the reality of his failure by a steady abuse of drugs and alcohol. The mental torment was finally too much for the Director of Air Armaments. On November 17, 1941, Ernst Udet shot himself, the first in a line of Luftwaffe chiefs who could find no other way out.

Within days Göring appointed Field Marshal Erhard Milch as Udet's successor. But the damage had already been done. Jeschonnek and Udet had previously concluded that Germany lacked the need or industrial base to support a strategic air force. Regarding improved fighter types, both men were equally damning. Why bother? The short campaigns of the new "lightning war" made such long term planning investments unnecessary. "The further development of air power must take economy as its motto," he told those around him. His lack of vision would also claim him. On August 18, 1943 Jeschonnek also took his own life, but not before squandering any advantage the Luftwaffe might have enjoyed later in the war.

The 1939 Luftwaffe had been organized for a short, offensive war. It was widely believed by Göring and others that protection of the German homeland could be left to the anti-aircraft flak guns in conjunction with a few fighter wings. The flak guns with their precision sighting and fire-control systems would make such raids too costly to be risked. In any case, they believed that German air attacks against enemy aerodromes would make concentrated enemy operations against Germany impossible. Before the war Göring had boasted that "If any enemy bomber penetrates to Germany, my name is no longer Hermann Göring. You can call me Meier." He chose an obviously ordinary Jewish name for his witticism. Later he would even announce that he would "eat a broomstick" should enemy bombers get through.

But in the late summer of 1940 the unthinkable happened. On the night of August 26th, the British Bomber Command bombed Berlin in retaliation for the Luftwaffe's strangle hold in the Battle of Britain. There were those who whispered of "Meier the broom," but the public was generally sympathetic. In spite of increasing scorn from the top members of the Nazi hierarchy, Göring remained popular with the people of Germany. The *Gauleiters* heaped obloquy on Göring for his posh life style, while the public was strangely tolerant of the constant air raids and food shortages. Touring the devastation in the industrial Ruhr valley in October of 1943, Hermann found that the common folk slapped him on the back and cheered his entourage as he continually professed his sympathy. Albert Speer, who was along for the tour of the wreckage, was amazed at their continence. "His face was beaming in the reflection of their evident admiration. He was only too obviously their great hero. And after he had left them, I heard them say to each other: He's a good fellow, *der Dicke*. He cares." But Speer and the others in the procession were unconvinced.

His credibility was further damaged by the failure of his Luftwaffe to deliver on its promises in January, 1943, to buttress the surrounded *Sixth Armee* in Russia. Unable to fly in enough supplies to the frostbitten Stalingrad garrison, the German army capitulated. Then, too, the Luftwaffe had been cast out of North Africa along with Rommel. And with these pivotal turns of fortune Göring's lot fell to rock bottom with Hitler and the others.

Early the following summer, the Germans shot down one of the new American Boeing B-17 Flying Fortresses. This huge four-engined strategic bomber was not only quick and able to operate at great altitude, but it was considerably more advanced than any offensive aircraft in the German arsenal. Moreover, it looked dangerous to attack, bristling with machine guns. So menacing was the plane's armament, particularly from the rear, that later Göring would have to pay morale-boosting visits to the various fighter squadrons to encourage them to continue with their successful tactics of attacking Allied bombers from the tail. The Allies claimed that soon they would be flying thousand plane raids with this aircraft to destroy the heart of Germany. But for now, Göring dismissed the plane and Churchill's "bluff." Jeschonnek cheerfully agreed.

Of those in the National Socialist hierarchy, only Milch appreciated the magnitude of the Allied threat. He pointed out that the Allies had dropped twice as many tons of bombs on Germany that year as in the previous two years.

On January 27, 1943 a large group of unescorted Flying Fortresses from the U.S. Eighth Air Force launched a bold daylight bombing attack on the Wilhelmshaven Naval Base. It was the first daylight attack on a German city and so surprised was the Luftwaffe high command that it was forced to fruitlessly use night fighter units to contest the heavy bombers. Further insult arrived on January 30th as Göring prepared to broadcast over German radio. It was the tenth anniversary of the "Thousand Year Reich" and Göring was to spout his accolades over the airwaves at 11 AM. Just then, however, a swarm of RAF Mosquito bombers swooped over Berlin. Along with all the rest, Göring spent a good part of the day in an air raid shelter.

At the high command's behest, Göring beat a hasty path back to the *Wolfschanze* on March 11th. Hitler dressed him down— perform or else. Göring understood an ultimatum. He quickly drew together the chief aircraft designers and respected Luftwaffe experts to plan a new stratagem. Gen. Adolf Galland, his chief of fighter forces, was emphatic in his conviction that the new jet and rocket interceptor aircraft could give Germany a technological edge. "If the enemy sticks to the piston engine," Galland told Göring with relish, "the Me-262 is going to give us an unimaginable lead." Milch agreed and asked Göring to dump the piston powered Me-209 to "turn out every 262 we can, as a matter of urgency." But the current polemic demanded a scapegoat for the Luftwaffe's troubles. Since Udet was dead, Göring affixed the blame on the chief designers of German war aircraft. Assembling them together, Göring railed against Professors Messerschmitt, Heinkel and Dornier. The German aircraft designers left the meeting with unusually direct orders from Göring to bring their technological promises to fruition. With Karinhall and his art treasures on the line, Hermann Göring was anxious. On June 1, 1943, he signed the Me-262 jet fighter into mass production. The party might be over, he mused. "It's not quite clear to me how we are going to end this war."

Although German objectives lay muddled and confused, Allied intentions in the air war were becoming ever more obvious. In the spring of 1943 the raids over Berlin and the industrial Ruhr began to reach a savagery heretofore unknown. On May 4th the Luftwaffe met the sturdy P-47s escorting the heavy bombers to pulverize Antwerp. A new and exceedingly dangerous era was introduced where German fighters would have to take on the tenacious P-47s before even getting a shot at the Fortresses and Liberators of the Eighth Air Force. Then, on May 26th, RAF Bomber Command blasted Dusseldorf with some 2,000 tons of high explosives. The same treatment over the next week would leave the town of Wuppertal with nearly 2,500 dead and over 100,000 homeless. Even distant locations in Central Germany, like the city of Jena, were no longer safe; the Zeiss Optical works there was wasted.

Sensing grave trouble, Göring at last was shaken out of his luxury-loving revelry. Reclaiming something of the dynamic of the old *Reichsmarschall*, he threw himself into resuscitating the Luftwaffe and with it, he hoped, his fortunes. With surprising aplomb, he directed his air operations officers to study new ways that the problem-ridden He-177 bombers could be used to hit back at Britain. He also commanded that more flak defenses be erected around sensitive German targets. Above all, he commanded, "we need new fighter tactics against the big fighter-escorted bomber formations." Göring was particularly encouraged by development of the so-called "secret weapons." The V1 pilotless robot bomb would soon be available. Its pulse-jet missile could carry a one-ton bomb nearly 300 miles. Perhaps, Göring thought, he would finally have some way to counter England's blows. At the very least, his deputy Milch ventured, "The enemy air force will be obliged to attack these launching sites, and our fighter planes and flak will have wonderful opportunities to inflict annihilating damage on them." Later that summer, in spite of the merciless Allied pounding from the air, Göring and Milch witnessed the impressive flight of the fourth production jet Me-262 from Rechlin. At last, both men thought, here was the plane that could save the war!

The summer of 1943 showed little evidence of a turning point in Germany's fortunes in the air. While Hitler's great Kursk tank offensive foundered on Russia's thorny defenses and the Western Allies stormed ashore at Sicily, the RAF continued its devastating night attacks on the Ruhr valley. A series of savage fire raids ravaged Mühlheim, Gelsenkirchen and Oberhausen. The towns were pitiful piles of smoking ruins; thousands of civilians died. But an equally severe economic blow came late in June when the Americans hit the crucial oil refinery at Hüls.

The hated phone at Karinhall rang almost nightly now. Increasingly, Göring struggled to understand why his air force could no longer establish superiority over European skies. "Technology-numbers-morale-officers," he pondered in his diary, "Basically our wafer-thin resources are to blame. We don't concentrate anywhere. We are inferior. So we are pushed back all along the line. Air power holds the key— as witness the efforts of our enemies... My present task: overhauling the air force. Clear technological objectives. Revive flagging spirits." The attention to detail was beginning to pay off. Under Milch's tutelage the factories were now producing more than a thousand planes a month and newer aircraft types with more deadly armaments were becoming available. But after visiting the devastation in the

Ruhr, Milch recommended doubling the German fighter production once again. Göring scowled.

Milch's counsel did not seem so extreme after July 28th, 1943. On that fair day a massive RAF incendiary bombing raid created a "fire storm" in the ancient Germany port of Hamburg. In minutes, huge sections of the urban center were engulfed by a conflagration so horrible that perhaps only the atomic bomb could exceed it. So hot was the fire cyclone, that even the asphalt streets ignited. By morning, 26,000 charred bodies had been counted. Hitler vowed revenge. How, he demanded of the Luftwaffe, had this happened? The British had neutralized the German radar defenses of the Kammhuber Line by the use of "chaff"— strips of metal foil which obscured the echoes made by the bombers. It was this catastrophe which finally seemed to light a fire under Göring. He convened an emergency meeting of his top generals to study alternatives. The overwhelming conclusion was that the Luftwaffe should immediately refocus on defensive efforts against the Allied air forces. Offensive air weapons would be sacrificed to produce the increased fighter forces. Even Dietrich Peltz, the General in charge of the German bomber forces, agreed. Remembered Adolf Galland:

> "Never before and never again did I witness such determination and agreement among the circle of those responsible for the leadership of the Luftwaffe. It was as though under the impact of the Hamburg catastrophe everyone put aside either personal or departmental ambitions. There was no conflict between the General Staff and the war industry, no rivalry between bombers and fighters; only the one common will to do everything in this critical hour for the defense of the Reich..."

But it was Göring who had to go before Hitler to get the okay to proceed with the drastic measures. Leaving the others behind, Göring met with Hitler for over an hour. When the large sullen figure emerged from the Führer's headquarters, Galland and Gen. Dietrich Peltz joined the *Reichsmarschall* to see how it had gone:

> "We were met with a shattering picture. Göring had completely broken down. With his head buried in his arms on the table, he moaned some indistinguishable words. We stood there for some time in embarrassment until at last he pulled himself together and said that we were witnessing his deepest moments of despair. The Führer had lost faith in him. All the suggestions from which he had expected a radical change in the situation of the war in the air had been rejected; the Führer had announced that the Luftwaffe had disappointed him too often, and a changeover from offensive to defensive in the air against the West was out of the question."

After a time, Göring cleared the tears from his eyes and straightened up. "The Führer has made me realize our mistake— the Führer is always right." To Galland and Peltz, he seemed almost like a chastised schoolboy. "We must deal such mighty blows to our enemy in the West that he will never dare to risk another raid like Hamburg." Then he turned away from Galland.

"General Peltz," he began, "I herewith appoint you assault leader against England." It was the birth of *Operation Capricorn*. The tables had turned: another mindless and wasteful attack against London. But Göring was rationalizing his fate; even he recognized the foolishness of allowing the Allied terror bombing to take them away from militarily meaningful targets. As expected, Peltz's "mini-blitz" on London accomplished little other than to increase the soaring Luftwaffe pilot and aircraft losses and again escalate the terror bombing. Fifty seven bombers and crews were lost in the first week.

Meanwhile, so spread out were the Luftwaffe forces in the East, in France and the Mediterranean, that the U.S. Eighth Air Force was now making bombing runs with 200 to 300 B-17s, still unescorted, and theoretically vulnerable. On August 17th the Americans plastered the Messerschmitt works at Regensberg and the ball bearing factories at Schweinfurt. Again Göring's telephone jangled. And once more it was Hitler. An agitated Führer gave the *Reichsmarschall* an earful. Time for a new scapegoat. Göring complained that the growing travesty was due to Jeschonnek's ineptitude. The next night the British blasted Peenemünde, the top-secret missile research site. The project to produce the V2 rocket, capable of an unstoppable revenge on London, sustained a severe setback. A German brain-trust of over 700 scientists and workers were killed. Hitler phoned Jeschonnek the following morning. By noon a tersely worded telegram arrived at Göring's headquarters. Jeschonnek had blown his brains out.

Next in line, and not without understandable reservations, was Gen. Günther Korten. He took over on August 20th, 1943, and along with his new Bavarian deputy, Lt. Gen. Karl Koller, the new command began to set things straight. They called fighter squadrons back from Russia and Italy to defend the Reich. New electronic countermeasures and tactics were instituted to subdue the RAF night bomber fighter force. Thousands of murderously effective anti-aircraft guns were sited around Germany. And it was all not a moment too soon. Berlin came under attack again three days after his appointment. By now 100,000 German civilians were in graves and there was an air of desperation creeping into Luftwaffe planning.

Göring's reputation, while still passable with the public and the lower Luftwaffe ranks, reached a new low with Hitler and his staff. Speer blamed him for the years of inept aircraft manufacture and others, like Rommel, were quick to ascribe their battlefield defeats to the *Reichsmarschall*'s indifference to their plight. Hitler raged at Göring at every opportunity. As conditions worsened, people in the street became bitter. During the day the German fighters were seldom seen when the B-17s were out. "Göring's fighters have arrived," a citizen caustically observed, "so the raid must be over."

But finally in the fall, things began to change. Using their innovative SN-2

Lichtenstein radar and new night-fighter tactics the Germans raked the British Bomber Command. So grievous were the British losses that the RAF was forced to call off its attacks on Berlin. But it was Göring himself who orchestrated the greatest Luftwaffe victory against the Eighth Air Force. In early October, while nervously flying to Obersalzberg, and imagining himself as a gunner in one of the hated American B-17s, Göring happened on a tactic that might cripple the bombers. A nearly constant attack, he divined from his fantasy, would rob the Americans of ammunition. Stripped of their means of self-defense and without fighter escort they would be sitting ducks! His Luftwaffe fighters could engage the enemy, then land, refuel and attack three times more in a four- hour bomber mission.

On October 14th, 300 B-17s of the Eighth Air Force once again attacked the ball bearing factories at Schweinfurt and Regensburg. Göring and Galland were ready with the new stratagem. As soon as the P-47 escort headed for home, the first wave of German fighters hove in, pummeling the bomber formations with machine gun, rocket and cannon fire. As Göring had ordered, his fighters landed all over Germany, refueling and rearming. Soon another wave of 160 German fighters lashed out at the bombers as they completed their bomb run. Just as the *Reichsmarschall* had imagined, they were able to blast away at the bombers with near impunity. For a loss of only 14 planes the Germans would claim 121 American B-17s. It was a shocking loss, and one that the Allied air commanders could not sustain. For the time being, all unescorted bomber missions into Germany ceased.

Still unable to see any future ability to compete in numbers, Göring increasingly placed his faith in the new technically superior aircraft. In November, he visited the jet aircraft plants at Regensberg where he met with Dr. Messerschmitt. He was apprehensive of the slow progress of the project and urged the professor to get things moving. "I don't want to come up with the 262 half a year too late," he worried. Messerschmitt showed him the sixth prototype Me-262 and a new top-secret rocket intercepter the Me-163. Göring was impressed, but production of the vital jet only increased at a modest rate. It would be mid-1944 before mass production began. Continuing his tour, he stopped by Dessau to inspect the Junkers production of the Jumo-004B jet engine. There he inspected the large swept-wing prototype Ju-287 jet bomber. Lastly, he made a quick circuit through Brandenburg where Dr. Walter Blume had assembled five prototypes of the Ar-234 jet bomber. Professor Blume's sleek aircraft could reach 500 mph and had a 600 mile range with a bomb load. Plans were to manufacture a thousand by mid-1945. Göring relished what he could accomplish with a fleet of these. Meantime Korten informed Hitler of the rapid progress of the V2 rocket and the V1 flying bomb. Within weeks the "buzz bomb" would be catapulting towards London from launching sites in France.

In November, 1943, Göring traveled about Berlin after a heavy air raid on the German capital. Looking over the wreckage someone in the entourage spoke of the need for more thorough air raid preparations. "Air raid precautions?" Göring protested, "What we need is fighters. Fighters!" Not only did the *Reichsmarschall* ask for more fighters, but he demanded more heavily armed machines able to take down a four-engined bomber in a single blow. As ordered, the arsenal aboard Galland's fighter aircraft was now more impressive than ever before. The *Jagdflieger* was also in the process of creating elite squadrons of heavily armored Fw-190s, the *Stürmbock*, that would close to within pointblank range of the Allied bombers before unleashing their devastating cannon fire.

But even with an enemy bent on their destruction, the Allied bomber forces could not be stilled. RAF Bomber Command resumed its offensive against Berlin in November, killing thousands and razing the capital buildings, including Hitler's Chancellery. Göring attempted to prop up his falling prestige with another display of advanced aircraft at Insterburg air base on November 26th. But this time Hitler recalled the similar ruse at Rechlin before the war. Rather than acclamation, Göring left with admonishment. Where were the squadrons of heavy Me-410 fighters with the 50mm cannon? Why would the Fi-103 Flying Bomb not be ready as promised to bombard London on New Years? And why was he shown the Me-262 without bombs. "I'm not interested in this plane as a fighter," he sputtered, "I order this plane built as a bomber." On December 16, 1943 Hitler cast this command in stone. He was thinking of the inevitable invasion in the west, "the vital thing is to rain bombs down on the enemy the moment he invades." Göring, in spite of his new found energy, was sick of the war. He retired to Karinhall to spend Christmas away from Berlin and the bombs. There, to his great delight, he found that his paratroopers in Italy had thoughtfully sent him a fantastic cache of confiscated art.

I

Enemy Number One...

The new year of 1944 offered little to cheer the *Reichsmarschall*. At night, the Luftwaffe was winning, inflicting such grievous losses on the British that their nightly bombings were momentarily suspended. But the savage daytime pounding by the American air force was a different matter. On January 11th the Eighth Air Force streamed over Brunswick and Oschersleben to pound the aircraft factories there. The move met stout opposition; some 64 B-17s were lost, but the head-butting contest cost the Luftwaffe dearly. Forty German fighters failed to return and the targets were blasted into non-production. As Galland had darkly warned, the long-range American fighters appeared in the form of the P-51 Mustang. Without a doubt, this was a clear turning point in the air war. No longer did the bombers have to hold back from targets deep in Germany. Now, the Flying Fortresses would be escorted by "little friends" of great danger to the older, less nimble German Me-109s and Fw-190s. And not only did the Mustangs protect and cosset their bombers, but now they put out "fighter sweeps" venturing ahead of the bombers to hunt down the German fighters. Luftwaffe losses soared.

In February, 1944, the Eighth Air Force began the "Big Week" where B-17 bombers plunked down thousands of tons of bombs on every important aircraft factory in Germany. So incredible was the devastation that it appeared that Luftwaffe aircraft manufacture was finished. And in another sop to Albert Speer's rising star, and Göring's fall from grace, Hitler assigned responsibility for German fighter aircraft manufacture to Karl-Otto Saur, Speer's nebbish action- oriented deputy. The powers of the new *Jägerstab* were sweeping.

Though despised by Göring, Speer and Saur got results: a 72-hour work-week was instituted at the aircraft factories; all the facilities were hardened against further air assault, dispersed around the countryside and strict production targets were set. Construction of new bombers was discontinued while greatly expanding production of Me-109 and Fw-190 fighters. Critical production, like that of the Junkers jet engines and the jet aircraft, was moved to underground factories impervious to bombardment. Foreign workers and convict laborers were impressed into the factories by the thousands. The extreme measures paid off; fighter aircraft production surged almost immediately. That Hitler saw the air war as decisive was obvious; in the spring of 1944 he gave top priority to aircraft production, even above that of tanks and submarines. Taking a mountain stroll with Karl-Otto Saur on April 7th Hitler announced that, provided a critical need was met, he could still win the war:

> "The prerequisite for that is the 100% fulfillment of the air force program to clear the skies over Germany this year. I need tanks and assault guns in deadly earnest. But first of all we've got to have a fighter umbrella over the Reich. That's the alpha and omega of it all."

Meanwhile, the British resumed their night attacks on Germany. But now Göring was ready with his new tactics. Over Nuremberg on the night of March 31st, the Germans counter-punched the British with nearly 250 night fighters. They destroyed 96 English bombers in a decisive victory that halted the RAF's nightly bombing raids for some six months. But the situation during the daytime hours had taken on a new gravity. Having added fuel drop tanks to increase the range of the P-51 Mustang fighter, the Americans in April of 1944 had fighter escort into the deepest reaches of Germany. By May of 1944 the sacrifice of the German fighter forces was reaching a crisis level. *I Jagdkorps* recorded that it had shot down 530 Allied aircraft for a loss of 384 of their own. This represented nearly 11% of the home defense fighter sorties flown.

Since March, daytime attacks on Berlin had become commonplace. Göring was stunned, "I would have thought it impossible that so many four-engined bombers could fly around for hours over German territory." With the long range fighter escort that he had so long professed to be impossible, Göring knew that "the end would be tragic." Göring estimated that after the American fighter escort began to support the bombers deep into Germany his ratio of pilots to aircraft lost increased from 1 in 5 to near parity. Before that, he claimed, a large number of planes were lost to non-combat causes; many bailed out after draining their fuel tanks trying vainly to reach their home base after an aerial scrap rather than landing at the nearest airfield. "A fighter pilot wants to sleep in his own bed," he surmised. In spite of the grim developments, the non-stop bombing was effecting a result contrary to that intended by the Allied air commanders: it hardened the resolve of the German people. They saw no alternative but to fight on to the bitter end.

While the Allies established air superiority over Germany, Göring was imagining fanciful means to salvage his flagging reputation. He would smite the Allied invasion force as soon as it attempted to land in France! The idea consumed Göring; it was certainly a pleasant alternative to contemplating his current situation. The skies over Germany were populated almost exclusively by Allied aircraft; the urban landscape of the Third Reich below was progressively chipping away into ruins. Göring ruminated over his tactics for nearly a year, convinced that the expected Allied invasion would be the deciding contest. If only he could serve the Allies a great blow on the French beaches, he opined, his standing and that of the Luftwaffe would be quickly restored. He ordered that a thousand plane reserve be created for the purpose. "The invasion must be defeated even if there's no German air force at the end of it."

Göring got the fight he had longed for on June 6, 1944, when word arrived from *II Jagdkorps* that the Allies were landing in Normandy. At first Hitler was ebullient: "They are landing here— and here," the German leader said pointing to a map, "just where we expected them!" But almost immediately, Göring's plan to rapidly concentrate his fighters in France went awry. Göring himself that Tuesday was game hunting in the Schorfheide forest. Meanwhile, for critical hours Hitler was asleep. No one dared wake him. Even after arising, Hitler and *OKW* could not determine whether Normandy was the real invasion or a feint, and it would be 24 additional hours before the high command would authorize Göring to begin transferring his fighters to France. During this lapse the Allies flew 14,000 sorties. Against this crushing weight, the Germans could assemble less than a hundred aircraft over Normandy.

Faced with a total debacle in the west, reckless personalities in Hitler's crumbling Reich advocated extreme proposals. The Führer's fanatical female test pilot, Hanna Reitsch, was now talking of a suicide force of at least a thousand volunteers who would pilot explosive laden aircraft into the invasion force at sea. "Though their deaths, thousands of soldiers and civilians can be saved," she claimed. Reitsch stood ace-high with her Führer. She approached her leader with the idea of German *kamikazes* on February 28th, but Hitler could not bring himself to such a desperate course— at least not yet. "It is not in keeping with the German character," the Führer told her. Heinrich Himmler, the SS leader who was always ready with ideas for total sacrifice, had another juicy scheme: use condemned criminals for the pilots. They would fly the experimental Me-328 flying bomb (a dangerously unstable twin-engined piloted version of the Fi-103) with a 2,000 pound warhead which would explode upon hitting its troopship. But upon approaching Göring and Korten, Reitsch was disgusted to find no enthusiasm at all. "We need strong leadership tempered with an idealism to match our own," she protested.

With Allied domination of the skies, the German fighter pilots became the butt of jokes and official reproach. The *Jagdflieger* pointed out that their fliers were usually outclassed in aircraft— they mainly flew the same old types, the Me-109s and Fw-190s, throughout the war. They were also under the threat of being destroyed piecemeal, with their great dispersal over the wide-ranging Eastern and Western fronts. When the Allied bombers approached Germany, they would do so with significant local numerical superiority. Until later in the war, there was no large and coherent home defense force within Germany. Losses, in turn, increased drastically and the cadre of trained pilots dipped proportionately. "It is true," Galland acknowledged, "that the Luftwaffe as a whole has sixty to seventy thousand officers; but this same air force has never gotten beyond the figure of 7,000 aircrew." Whereas the total monthly losses on the Allied side remained with few exceptions less than 1% of the sorties flown, the comparative figures for the *Jagdwaffe* was reached 10-20% during the chaotic months of 1944. By that September, the German fighters charged with the defense of the air space over the Reich could only report a dismal accounting: 307 Allied planes destroyed for the loss of 371 of their own. The truth was certainly worse since both sides nearly always inflated claims on their opponent.

Meanwhile, Hitler's mania over the Me-262 reached a new level.   In reviewing the latest aircraft production figures on May 23rd, Hitler saw the few produced planes listed under the *fighter* category. "Who obeys my orders!" he exploded. Had he not ordered the 262 produced only as a bomber? Never a sycophant, Erhard Milch spoke his mind. "Mein Führer," he piped up, "even the smallest child could see that this is a fighter and not a bomber aircraft." But rather than casting Milch out on his ear, he vented his venom on Göring. Those around Hitler said he "nearly had a stroke." Later even Speer, who Hitler afforded special respect, met with the German leader to change his mind on the issue. As a bomber, Speer reasoned, the 262 could drop but half a ton of bombs on the enemy, but as a fighter it could handily shoot down four-engined bombers which were dropping thousands of tons of bombs on Germany every day. But Hitler's prejudices on the matter were insuperable. Even Speer could not change his mind.

In spite of all these setbacks, Göring was finally able to open the V1 bombardment of London on June 15th, when some 244 of the pilotless robot bombs were launched. Terrible fires raged in London. But most important of all, the V-1 launching sites, which were mobile and capable of easily shifting, began to distract the huge bombing effort that had been pulverizing German cities only a few weeks before. Allied fighter resources had to be moved from escort duty to intercepting the buzz bombs.

However, the Allies renewed their attacks on German oil manufacture. With the stakes so high, the air battle that summer had all the appearances of Armageddon. Fuel production collapsed, posing a most serious threat to the German ability to continue the war. Fuel reserves plummeted. In April,

175,000 tons of fuel had been available, but by July barely 35,000 tons were produced and ULTRA noted the increasingly desperate orders from Göring and his staff to conserve the paltry stocks remaining. Little petrol was now available for the vital task of training pilots or testing aircraft. The gravity of their situation became clear when Allied code-breakers overheard Göring's orders to acquire horse-drawn vehicles to tow the Me-262 units to the runway since each jet consumed fifty gallons of fuel taxiing out under its own power.

While the German army struggled in Normandy under almost constant air attack (another Luftwaffe failure) a group of army officers and civilians plotted to kill Hitler and end the increasingly pointless war. They made their move on July 20th at Hitler's headquarters in East Prussia. It was an oppressively hot day at *Wolfschanze* and the windows to the various bunkers were open to catch any breeze to provide relief. Göring was in a building not far from Hitler arguing with his subordinates about the delays in an air attack on Soviet power plants. Suddenly the stifling air was jarred by a muffled roar. The acrid smell of cordite hung in the air amid a cacophony of alarms. Hitler's adjutant phoned Göring excitedly. An attempt had been made on the Führer's life, he explained: a bomb had exploded under the oaken conference table. Although shaken, Hitler was alive and well, but Bodenschatz and Korten had been seriously injured. Korten's injuries would later prove to be fatal.

Strangely, the failed assassination buoyed Göring and Hitler. Both men were gripped by a conviction that divine providence had spared them. After the glow of divine providence faded, Hitler raged for vengeance. He and Göring assigned the stodgy Gen. Werner Kreipe to replace Korten and the witchhunt for the assassins began. Dozens were rounded up and shot the first week— even Rommel would later succumb to involvement in the plot.

Even Speer caught Hitler's wrath. In mid-August he and Galland lobbied Hitler in Berlin to move more of the fighter force from the tottering Western Front to the defense of the Reich. Speer made a long-winded case for the troubled armaments industry and how the war would falter unless the fighters could protect it. It was obviously convincing, for Hitler flew into a violent outburst:

> I want no more planes produced at all. The fighter arm is to be dissolved. Stop aircraft production! Stop it at once, understand? You're always complaining about the shortage of skilled workers aren't you? Put them into flak production at once. Let all the workers produce anti-aircraft guns. Use all the material for that too! Now that's an order...Every day I read in the foreign press reports how dangerous flak is. They still have some respect for that, but not for our fighters.

All through the summer of 1944, the Allied air forces owned the skies over Europe. Almost daily, bomber fleets prowled the European skies, often in hunt for the means of German war production. Allied tactical fighter groups buzzed the air space over France, bombing exposed German positions at will and machine gunning troops and columns of fuel and supply vehicles caught hapless on the country-roads. The Luftwaffe was seldom seen and even planes sent to hit the Allies on the beaches found a numerically superior enemy fighter force waiting. *III Gruppe/Schlachtgeschwader 4* (*SG 4*) was assigned to attack the Allied lodgement on June 7th, the day after the landings. On June 6th, the *Gruppe* lost four pilots and four mechanics flying with them to stalking U.S. fighters. And these losses were sustained while in the process of simply transferring its Fw-190Fs from St. Quentin to Laval!

"From 0600 hrs four operations were mounted, in which 24 aircraft were sent against landings and troop concentrations in the area of the River Orne. Because of the strong fighter defenses, three of the operations had to be broken off before reaching the target and the bombs jettisoned..."

Without friendly air support, the Germans were forced to flee France under the scornful eyes of Allied fighter-bombers "It would have been hard to shoot at the road in any place and not hit a German car or truck," remembered Lt. John A. Neely of Col. Anthony Grosetta's 406th Fighter Group (FG).[1] His P-47s severely cut up the Germans in the Argentan pocket in August of that summer. "We followed the roads right down, over hills and around corners until we ran out of ammunition. When we looked back, fires were flicking all along the roads." The view from the enemy side of the hill was even less encouraging to German aims. "The American fliers are chasing us like hares," one German soldier wrote home from Normandy. Gen. Fritz Bayerlein, of the vaunted *Panzer Lehr Division*, sarcastically described his march route from Vire on June 8th as *"Jabo Rennstrecke"*— a fighter-bomber racecourse![2] Later the Allies would drop over 4,000 tons of high explosives in a carpet bombing directly on the heads his tankers. Bayerlein estimated that *Panzer Lehr* was reduced in combat strength by over 70%, Gen. George S. Patton's armor ran roughshod over his dazed division the following day,

---

1 A U.S. fighter group consisted of three fighter squadrons each with about 25 operational aircraft. Each squadron had about 80 fighter pilots along with the necessary ground crew, administrative and service personnel. For the average combat mission, each squadron supplied four flights of four aircraft each with an extra flight of four aircraft on standby status. During the Bulge, however, combat losses and wear and tear typically reduced this figure. On December 26th Gen. Nugent with the XXIX TAC complained that he needed replacement P-47s; he had started December with 16 combat-ready planes per squadron, but was now down to only 12. The German equivalent was the *Geschwader*, generally with three *Gruppen* of three *Staffeln* of twelve aircraft each. The smallest tactical unit was the four plane *Schwarme*.

2 Genfldm. Karl Gerd von Rundstedt, the German commander in chief had this testimony: "Three factors defeated us in the West where I was in command. First, the unheard of superiority of your air force, which made all movement in daytime impossible. Second the lack of motor fuel— oil and gas— so that the panzers and even the remaining Luftwaffe were unable to move. Third, the systematic destruction of all railway communications so that it was impossible to bring one single railroad train across the Rhine." He described the later influence as *"Katastrophal."*

hindered most by the untrafficable shell-pocked landscape. Even the Desert Fox, Genfldm. Erwin Rommel was critically wounded by strafing British Spitfires from 602 Squadron on July 17th. The field marshal had been traveling back to headquarters in his staff car when he was ambushed near St. Foy de Montgomerie. "The Allies have total air supremacy," worried Gen. Heinrich von Lüttwitz of the *2nd Panzer Division*, "They bomb and shoot at anything that moves, even single vehicles and persons...The feeling of being powerless...has a paralyzing effect."

And all during the summer, the Luftwaffe was seldom seen. Even when German planes were spotted, they were often unwilling to risk combat. Things had reached such a point, that Gen. Walter Model, in charge of *Heeresgruppe B* explicitly warned his officers to protect themselves from the ever increasing losses due to Allied air power. The edict, which was later captured by Allied intelligence, provided a powerful indicator of the damage wrought by tactical air power:[3]

> "Enemy number one is the enemy air force, which because of its absolute superiority tries to destroy our spearheads of attacks and our artillery through fighter bomber attacks and bomb carpets and to render movements in rear areas impossible. The armament industry at home and the leadership are trying with all possible means to render ineffective for the time being, this air superiority at least for the purpose of supporting our actions. During this time of year our attacking troops profit from fog and the danger of icing of aircraft. *Everywhere the troops will employ camouflage, and at every halt they will dig in deeply, troops weapons and vehicles.*"

That Hitler recognized the problem is certain. Barely three days after the invasion a massive Allied bombing raid on Munich killed Heini Handschuh-macher, a close friend of Hitler's mistress, Eva Braun. Eva and her friends returned from the funeral still in tears describing to Hitler the awful Allied bombing. The German leader swore to Braun that he would seek revenge "a hundredfold with the Luftwaffe's new inventions." On June 20th Hitler ordered Milch and Saur to begin examining ways to increase the output of the Me-262 jets to a thousand per month. He also railed against the flawed bombers, particularly the crash-prone He-177, which was so fuel thirsty that it had little place in Germany's poor man's war anyway. On June 29th, he signed a decree ordering that henceforth only fighter aircraft would be produced. At the same time he issued a challenge to Göring to examine ways

---

3 Another captured order from Model from late January, 1945 called for individual German soldiers to fire back at the strafing fighter bombers with their side-arms. The leaflet, which was passed out to German ground troops described how "a non-com recently shot down a Thunderbolt with his machine pistol... special favors will be shown to successful gunners and units. Each soldier who knocks down an enemy strafer with his infantry weapon received ten days special furlough." The leaflet then went on to enunciate the important means to protect against the "Anglo-American highwaymen:" 1) Maintenance of a proper march interval between vehicles, 2) No rest stops on roads, 3) Use of woods for camouflage, 4) Preparation of foxholes— "Spade work provides the best highway furnace!" 5) Only combat vehicles or supply columns on roads 6) Importance of night marches 7) Danger of icy serpentine roads..."Therefore, seek cover first, Then fire away!"

of achieving at least local air superiority over the battlefield. "The Allies only like advancing when air power is on their side," he observed, "That is why everything now depends on our fighter production. We must keep it top-secret and start stockpiling in a big way. Then just watch the enemy gape when we turn the tables on them four months from now!" But all this was a tall order. On the last day of July, 1944 at his *Wolfschanze* headquarters Hitler discussed the sources of the summertime catastrophes with his right-hand man, Gen. Alfred Jodl. The air war was at the top of the list:

> "...One must be clear that there can be no turn for the better in France until we can regain air superiority, even temporarily. So it is in my opinion that, however, hard it may be at the moment, we must do everything to ensure that in the last resort we can hold the Luftwaffe formations in keeping at home as a last reserve in readiness to be employed at some point where we can turn the tables once more. I cannot say now when and where that point will be...there is no doubt that if we could suddenly pump an additional 800 fighters and at once bring our fighter strength up to 2,000— as we probably could— the whole crisis now would be overcome at once..."

The time to turn the tables never came that summer of 1944. But by the fall of that same year, a number of events conspired to threaten the Allied grip on the air. Although the great Allied air assault on German petroleum production was beginning to pay off, efforts to wreck German tank and aircraft production were notable failures. Weather further denigrated the ability of the tactical air commands to intervene in the grueling ground battles raging around Aachen and the Hürtgen Forest in the fall of 1944. This gave the Luftwaffe an important breathing spell. Although the Germans benefited from a smaller area to defend and interior lines of communication, they had also lost valuable ground, restricting the limits of their air defense radars. Hence the warning the Luftwaffe received of the approach of the heavy bombers was shortened, as was the length of their run where they could expect to run into enemy fighters.

But the most serious new threat to Allied air supremacy was emerging from the German air force itself. For years the Germans were constrained by their inability to keep aircraft production ahead of losses. By September of 1944 the Luftwaffe had written off some 81,844 aircraft and pilot losses tallied to a similar figure. As a result, German aircraft availability had slowly fallen from 1942 to 1944. In late February 1944, the Allied air commanders attempted a knock-out blow. In five days of intensive bombing they called "Big Week," some 75% of German aircraft production facilities were severely damaged or destroyed. However, through an astonishing production program, Albert Speer, Hitler's armaments minister, had boosted German fighter strength to its greatest operational levels of the war. Hitler and Göring had made summertime promises that 3,000 aircraft would be available in autumn. However, on December 2nd, *Luftwaffen Kommando West* would inform von Rundstedt that although its numbers were still increasing from transfers, its available strength was now about 1,700 aircraft with considerably fewer operational. Although still far from equalling the 10,000 aircraft the western Allied air forces put forth, the German numbers were double what they had been in recent times. The prospect of German jet aircraft suddenly appearing in great numbers was the worst Allied nightmare. The Allied air forces instituted measures to menace the few jet aircraft bases the Germans were now operating. Standing patrols were posted over the few air fields like Rheine-Main that flew them and Allied air operational researchers scurried about in top secret, studying the weaknesses of the feared jets that Allied planes might exploit.

The air war over Germany reached a parlous state. The British and American air forces were not only doing the impossible— bombing Germany night and day, but they were devastating Hitler's armies in the field. On September 16th, Kreipe attended the usual meeting of Hitler and his generals at *OKW*. Word from the fighting fronts reported a dizzying series of German reversals. Searching for something optimistic, Genobst. Jodl, standing before his glum audience, groped for anything positive to say about the fix in which the Germans found themselves. The one positive item he could relate was how a handful of audacious panzer troops had thrown back a much larger attack by American units attempting to punch their way out of the Ardennes and into the German Eifel region. But at the word "Ardennes" Hitler bolted to his feet as if receiving an electric shock. He then fired off a rapid discourse to his bewildered audience. "I will attack," he said sweeping his hand across an unrolled map, "from here out of the Ardennes!" The audience at *Wolfschanze* was dumbfounded. Everywhere the German army was retreating. The means to make a stand on the German border, much less launch a great offensive, seemed to be completely lacking.

Fiery and animated, Hitler ran on about his idea for a great offensive, which he said could reverse the course of the war. "Führer's decision, counter-attack out the Ardennes, objective Antwerp," Kreipe tersely jotted in his diary, "Slice between the British and the Americans— a new Dunkirk!" There was certainly dissension at the meeting, the steady and trusted Gen. Jodl for one, being concerned with the "enemy air superiority." In 1940 he said, the Luftwaffe had been instrumental in the German victory. The new offensive would be launched in the winter, Hitler opined. "In bad flying weather," Hitler argued, "the enemy air force won't be flying either." It was a thinly veiled reference to the impotence of Göring's air force.

But the very next day the battle for the bridge over the Rhine at Arnhem began. The indian summer sky over Holland was filled with Allied aircraft. The British and Americans landed thousands of paratroopers to seize an avenue for a quick thrust into Germany. The Luftwaffe was able to send up over 600 planes to contest the Allied landings, shooting down many transports, but Hitler only saw the reports of the enemy progress towards the critical Rhine bridge. As he saw it, it was further evidence of total Luftwaffe opprobrium:

> Führer rages about Luftwaffe's failure. Wants immediate information on which fighter forces were scrambled in Holland. Führer violently abuses me...Says air force is incompetent, cowardly, and letting him down. He has further reports of air force units streaming back across the Rhine. I ask for concrete details. The Führer replies, 'I refuse to talk with you further. I want to talk to the *Reichsmarschall* tomorrow.' No doubt you are capable of arranging that?

Hitler sent for Göring. When he arrived, Kreipe warned him that the German leader was after their heads. When he met with Hitler on September 19th, Hitler asked Kreipe to leave— he wanted only to see Göring. The mood at the meeting was icy. At stake was the Luftwaffe; Hitler wanted results. Göring blamed Galland for the increasing woes of the fighter force. Hitler had other scapegoats in mind. He told the *Reichsmarschall* to get rid of the "defeatist and unreliable" Kreipe. Later that night Kreipe received word that he was never to set foot in *Wolfschanze* again. His tenure had lasted only three months. So disgusted was Hitler with the entire German air force, that he did not even bother to replace Kreipe. Instead, Gen. Eckhard Christian, nominally Gen. Jodl's assistant, became the sole Luftwaffe representative at Hitler's war headquarters. Christian was hardly qualified, holding no post in the Luftwaffe itself and possessed little knowledge of the operations of the German air force. Certainly, Göring did not show himself unless specifically summoned. Only in November did Hitler finally appoint Gen. Karl Koller as Kreipe's successor and by that time his plan for a big offensive in the West had been fully developed with little input from the pusillanimous Luftwaffe generals.

With Hitler now planning the last great offensive in the West, Göring sought out his offensive-minded air commanders. Dietrich Peltz and Werner Baumbach were perhaps the most able of the bunch. He invited Peltz to take up residence at Karinhall as the offensive grew closer, an obvious affront to Galland and the fighter captains. Meanwhile, at mid-month Galland announced that a colossal force of nearly 3,000 German fighters were standing by with fuel and crews for a grand defensive operation the next time the Allied day bomber force tried to invade German air space. By deploying the planes in two huge waves, he reckoned on blasting down 500 heavy bombers in one go. Göring would be able to flaunt his medals again and the *Jagdwaffe* would regain its respectability. Galland had only to wait for suitable weather and hope his credibility held out. Amid the rains and mists of winter, the Führer was developing a "grand slam" of his own. On November 20th Hitler left *Wolfschanze* in East Prussia for the last time. He headed for Berlin.

The Reichsmarschall. Hermann Göring before the war. *(National Archives/NA)*

Albert Speer, Hitler's minister of armaments, discusses production with German generals. *(USAF Historical Research Center/HRC)*

Fw-190F-8s of *NSGr. 20* are readied for operations in the fall of 1944. The Luftwaffe's few ground attack aircraft were unable to make a difference in Normandy. *(Bundesarchiv)*

Enemy Number One...

"America's Bluff." Hermann Göring at first discounted the threat of expansive U.S. manufacture. Here, a long line of Boeing B-17s are shown on the assembly line in Long Beach. *(HRC)*

BELOW: Wesel. The aerial view of this German city bears mute evidence of the tremendous damage wrought by the Allied strategic air forces. *(HRC)*

Major Gen. Hoyt Sanford Vandenberg, the handsome commander of the U.S. Ninth Air Force, receives commendation from Gen. Dwight D. Eisenhower, the Allied Supreme Commander in Europe, January 25, 1945. *(NA)*

Lt. Gen. James H. "Jimmy" Doolittle, the hero of *Thirty Seconds over Tokyo*, and the later commander of the U.S. Eighth Air Force in 1944. *(HRC)*

Sgt. Hubert Hayes of Parkersville, West Virginia, was a waist gunner on the Boeing B-17 Flying Fortress "The Bad Penny." Chances for surviving the air war were the lowest for those flying the heavy bombers. *(National Air and Space Museum)*

Lt. Gen. Carl A. Spaatz, the steady and pragmatic commander of Allied strategic air forces in Europe. *(NA)*

The Allies enjoyed an advantage in the quality and quantity of their supply of gasoline. Here, Ninth Air Force soldiers transfer gasoline to jerricans for transport close to the front lines. *(NASM)*

Microwave Early Warning (MEW) radar station of the XIX Tactical Air Command in Luxembourg. MEW stations were typically located 10-30 miles from the front to guide tactical aircraft employment. Four truck-mounted SC-584 radar sets provided finer guidance for blind bombing or precise target positioning. *(NASM)*

These Republic P-47 Thunderbolts look peaceful enough, sharing a new airfield in Normandy on June 28th with their bovine neighbors. The tough bottle-nosed fighters proved to be the end of numerous German motorized columns in Normandy. *(NASM)*

From the mount of his P-47 "Jug," Lt. Col. Louis T. Houch of Todd, North Carolina, sprayed this line of German road traffic with .50 calibre incendiary bullets. The enemy column, carrying fuel and ammunition, was 90% destroyed. *(NASM)*

The P-51D fighter, with its powerful Merlin engine, was superior to most German types. "Lou IV" was the mount of Col. Thomas J.J. Christian, Jr. with the 361st Fighter Group. Christian was killed in combat on August 11, 1944. The only real weakness of the P-51 was the susceptibility to a strike on the radiator of their liquid-cooled engines. As with the Spitfire, they were more suited to a straight fighter role than as a ground attack aircraft. *(NASM)*

The exotic Dornier Do-335 Pfeil or "Arrow" was a high-performance piston German fighter that never saw significant production during the war. *(NASM)*

A pilot of *JG 400* mounts his Me-163 "Komet." The suit was supposed to give the pilot a modicum of protection against the rocket plane's intensely corrosive fuels. *(Bundesarchiv)*

"Like angels were pushing!" Adolf Galland's description of his first experience with the German jet propelled Me-262. The role of the aircraft—fighter or bomber—became a contentious issue between Hitler and his generals in 1944. "White13" was a Me-262A-1 fighter of *Kdo. Nowotny* which operated in the fall of 1944 from Achmer. *(HRC)*

"People's Fighter." The He-162 Volksjäger was a product of the final desperate months of the Luftwaffe. Hastily conceived and assembled, the aircraft went from drawing board to flight test in 37 days! Powered by a single jet engine and with a very short range, fanciful plans called for production of thousands per month with the cockpits filled with SS volunteers with only glider training! *(NASM)*

In spite of years of efforts on advanced aircraft, the machines the Germans were able to mass produce in 1944 concentrated on conventional types like these Me-109s with which the Luftwaffe had begun the war. *(NASM)*

Buzz bomb. A V1 robot bomb that was shot down over the Ninth Air Force's area of operations on November 8, 1944 *(HRC)*

V2. The German A-4 rocket is shown being field erected for launch. *(Bundesarchiv)*

47

ABOVE: Destruction from a V2 strike in the streets of Antwerp, November 27, 1944. Over a dozen individuals were killed in the blast. *(NA)*

LEFT: The Bachem Ba-349 "Natter" rocket is shown being prepared for launch. Theoretically, the interceptor would be vertically launched into the path of a bomber stream, close with the bombers at 600 mph, loose a volley of Hs-217 rockets at the formation from its nose, with the Natter pilot ejecting from the machine to return from the one-way mission by parachute! The first pilotless launch was successfully conducted on December 18, 1944. (*NASM*)

II

Spaatz and Allied Airborne Might

Before entering the war, American strategic air power advocates had opined that a cross-channel attack would never be necessary; the heavy bombers would smash Germany into surrender without the need for conventional ground forces and excessive bloodshed. The strategic bombing, as the purists envisioned it, would take place from large, heavily armed machines flying at high altitude during daytime operations. Precision bombing techniques would be used to obliterate the enemy means of industry and war production.

"The bomber will always get through," ran the pre-war wisdom. But there were at least two flaws in that thinking. The first was the idea that civilians could not hold up under strategic bombing. The second premise was equally specious: strategic bombing would destroy a country's ability to wage war by eliminating its industry. Ground combat might be altogether unnecessary. After the slaughter of World War I, this idea had a special appeal. But, if anything, the constant bombing increased German resolve to continue the war against their tormentors; the campaign against German industry did not provoke an industrial collapse until the last months of the war, and several years after the strategic bombing began. "Strategic bombing was designed to destroy the industrial base of the enemy and the morale of the people," summed up John Kenneth Galbraith in the U.S. Strategic Bombing Survey, "It did neither."

The upshot of all this was that the Americans started the war with a superb long-range bomber, the B-17, but with an obsolete first-line fighter, the Curtiss P-36. Fighters, the most important link in winning the sky, had been given the shortest shrift. But if a strategic bombing partisan, Gen. Arnold was not inflexible. Watching the achievements of the Luftwaffe's tactical air force in the spanish civil War and later against Poland, the importance of the fighter became obvious. So powerful had been the Luftwaffe's participation in the *Blitzkrieg* that even the heretical idea of a tactical air force had to be given some credence.

Lt. Gen. Carl Andrew Spaatz possessed little of the demeanor that would flag a four star general. Outwardly "Tooey" Spaatz was prosaic— an almost ordinary man who nonetheless held the reins of the most destructive weapons in the world. His appearance was distinguished— graying hair, a distinctive mustache, but his brusque manners and intemperate language put off most of the invitations from the social circles in London. The General was certainly not a glory hound; there were no orders of the day, few interviews and publicity agents. Spaatz conducted his goings on a personal level. "The General will talk to anybody," his driver related, "He's about the only general I know who can talk to a G.I. and it doesn't sound as it he was doing the soldier a favor." While not much of a speaker, Spaatz was almost evangelical in this enthusiasm for the air weapon for anyone who cared to listen. The General's idea of a good time was to invite friends over for cocktails (whisky and water) followed by dinner capped off by a good natured game of poker. The general particularly liked five-card draw and was well known for bluffing with abandon.

But if unassuming and hardly general-like, Spaatz had the credentials. A 1914 graduate of West Point, he became a student of the Army's budding aviation school in the days when flying was novel and even frowned upon. Certainly, it was dangerous. During Spaatz's tenure, the mortality rate at the North Island flying school in San Diego was 18 percent! Regardless, he determinedly won his wings and two years later got his first operational flying experience buzzing Pancho Villa during the U.S. expedition in Mexico. When the Great War opened, Spaatz trained pilots at Issoudun, France, but eventually wrangled some combat operations in which he lead a pursuit squadron at St. Mihiel and destroyed two German bi-planes. In between wars, the General's star rose quickly. Spaatz became a leading advocate for the expanded role of modern air power in future conflict. And when World War II opened he found himself aligned against old enemies in Europe and in a race with Milch and Göring on the other side of the fence to cast an effective air weapon. Spaatz came over to England to learn from the Battle of Britain in 1940 and took command of the nascent Eighth Air Force in 1942. By 1943, while Göring had foundered on the reef of the resilient RAF, Spaatz and his strategic air force were delivering shattering blows to Nazi Germany.

Spaatz had another attribute perhaps more vital to success than any other: flexibility. While Hitler and Göring insisted on pursuing failing strategic aims, Spaatz was open to change. When he learned at Schweinfurt in 1943 that neither his Liberators or Flying Fortresses could go it alone into Germany without heavy casualties, he responded by building up a vast long-range fighter escort to solve the problem. More than any other event, this decision broke the Luftwaffe's back in the opening months of 1944. And while Spaatz disagreed with the idea that area-bombing German civilians, as advocated by Sir Arthur "Bomber" Harris would ever break the enemy will, he had subscribed in 1944 to the idea that precision bombing on manufacturing targets and war production would finally bring them to their knees. "If the German leaders begin to realize that they cannot count on an aircraft factory at Gotha or a tank plant in Berlin for replacements, because of our bombing, then their morale will break." But this was early 1944 thinking. Later Spaatz had become a complete devotee of the oil campaign, threatening Eisenhower with resignation over diverting his bombers to the Normandy Campaign. Eisenhower relented to allow a constant pressure on German oil, but even with an unending rain of bombs on enemy petrol production the end of summer brought no knock-out blow.

By the dark autumn of 1944, with its lack of progress, both in the air and on the ground, it was clear to Spaatz that precision bombing alone was not going to bring the Germans to the surrender table. On top of the enemy's new-found fighter strength, losses in the fall due to anti-aircraft fire increased, so much so that Spaatz was moved to write to Gen. Henry H."Hap" Arnold with the Joint Chiefs of Staff:

> "You have, of course, noted the heavy increased losses we suffered during the last week's operations into Germany...I am very much concerned over the possibilities involved. There is every chance, I think, that the Germans may be using proximity fuses or an improved type of radar for their flak...We are also watching carefully the development of the jet-propelled boys which will be a constant potential threat...All this adds up to the fact that the Hun still has a lot of fight left in him..."

That Spaatz read the enemy intentions in an uncanny fashion is revealed by a later letter: "...I still feel that the build-up of the GAF defensive strength is a growing threat. Presently, the GAF is using every possible means to attain a strength extremely dangerous to our strategic forces." Faced with these threats Spaatz deeply desired a way of ending the war quickly. Again demonstrating his flexibility, he reached back into his experience in the Mediterranean when his bombers had nailed Rommel's *Afrika Korps* in the wake of their surprise offensive at Kasserine Pass. Strategic air power could be used to aid the ground armies in gaining a decisive upper hand— at least to the extent that it did not interfere with the oil campaign. Harris in particular saw this use of heavy bombers as a sop. But Spaatz, ever ready with the poker bluff, was willing to make changes. His experience with the carpet bombing of St. Lô and the resulting breakout of Patton's Third Army was already changing his thinking. Perhaps strategic air power had a larger role in defeating the enemy's ground armies. It was with these thoughts that

Gen. Carl Spaatz opened the curtain on debate during the winter war in the air in 1944.

The creation of the U.S. Ninth Air force as a tactical command began in the Western Desert of Libya and Egypt in 1942, as a high-stakes battle see-sawed between the British and Rommel for control of North Africa. In an act of desperation, a few bomber groups under the command of Maj. Gen. Louis H. Brereton were sent to give assistance to the overtaxed Allied forces. The bombers were committed to tactical air strikes and ground support attack—completely foreign to the prevalent thinking of American strategic air power doctrine. But the unconventional "Desert Air Force" made a difference. Not only could B-17s and B-25s hit strategic targets, they could flatten enemy transport and supply lines as well. Soon perceived as vital to the critical battles being fought, Brereton was sent more bombers and new P-40 Curtiss fighters to join what would latr be known as the U.S. Ninth Air Force.

By October 1943 the Ninth was relocated to England in anticipation of the build-up for the invasion of Europe. The experiences from Africa had clearly shown the value of a tactical air force and even the strategic bombing purists had to admit that the enemy seemed far from ready to quit the war despite the increasing rain of bombs on Germany. Meanwhile, the effectiveness of the Ninth Air force in North Africa had become widely acknowledged. To further increase its striking power it was reorganized, with the new IX Fighter command under Gen. Elwood R. Quesada and the new IX Bomber Command with four medium bomber groups under Gen. Samuel E. Anderson. In August, 1944, Hoyt Vandenberg took over command of the Ninth Air Force from the distinquished leadership of Gen. Brereton.

Maj. Gen. Hoyt S. Vandenberg knew his tactical air force could be decisive. He was further convinced that his Ninth Air Force could be the aerial key for the defeat of Germany. They had certainly been pivotal in Normandy. Vandenberg's command provided tactical air support to the armies under the U.S. 12th Army Group of Lt. Gen. Omar N. Bradley. Bradley reported directly to the commander in chief of the Supreme Headquarters Allied Expeditionary Forces (SHAEF), Gen. Dwight D. Eisenhower.[4] From the American point of view, Bradley's First and Third Armies were key to getting the Allies on into Germany and ending the war. Tall and gregarious, Vandenberg was typical of many of the top-ranked airmen in Europe. The six-foot 45-year old commander had been a stand-out athlete at West Point and, when graduation came in 1923, had been serious about flying and aviation, but congenial when it came to the usual stuff. The usual stuff being golf, gin rummy, Scotch highballs and a good panetella. Vandenberg came to London in 1942 and had been Gen. Jimmy Doolittle's chief of staff in North

---

4 To the south, the First Tactical Air Force supported the Sixth Army Group whose forces held the Alsace region along the Rhine River down to the Swiss Border.

Africa, only getting into trouble when he snuck out on combat missions as a waist gunner on a trip to Gibraltar. In all Vandenberg chalked up some 5,000 flying hours including 25 missions against the enemy with the Twelfth Air Force. As wingman to Gen. Doolittle, he also flew fighter planes including P-38s and British Spitfires.

Although not solely spit-and-polish, Vandenberg usually looked the part— he always presented an impeccable uniform with his cap set at a rakish angle. Vandenberg got along famously with his men, flew around in his own P-47 Thunderbolt and became a big advocate of air-ground cooperation. The General talked up the air "slanguage" with the best of them.[5] That fall, he drew admiration from his willingness to provide air support to the ground commanders. On one hand he was fending off the strategic bombing folks who were unconvinced of the effectiveness of the Ninth's tactical mission, while on the other the ground generals he was supporting were, by their very nature, inclined to plead for all the close air support they could get. Like his boss, Eisenhower, "Van" struck a popular balance. And although Eisenhower's critics such as Montgomery had accused him of being more of a "chairman of the board" than a military tactician, Eisenhower understood the potential of air power in World War II. It was Eisenhower, after all, who had overruled his subordinates who questioned the wisdom of switching the strategic air forces from their targets in Germany to the carpet bombing in Normandy. Although imperfect in execution, the latter operation nearly destroyed a German panzer division and prefaced Patton's breakout at St. Lô.

Eisenhower's other heavy hitter was the mighty Eighth Air Force under Lt. Gen. James H. "Jimmy" Doolittle. Born in Alameda, California, Doolittle joined the Army signal corps in 1917 and earned a degree in aeronautical engineering from MIT in 1925. Doolittle was a true aviation pioneer, contributing significantly to the development of modern flight instrumentation and completing early experiments in blind-flying techniques. It was on Doolittle's recommendation that the Army Air force developed an emphasis on poor weather flight training that would prove essential in the fighting in the inclement skies over Europe in 1944. although Doolittle had participated in Billy Mitchell's much publicized bombing demonstrations off the Virginia cape before the war, it was his performance in air racing contests in the 1920s that first brought him to public attention. A truly significant contribution to the war effort came from Doolittle's pre-war devotion to the development of high-octane fuels to enhance the performance of aircraft powerplants. Not only did this fuel give the RAF a significant advantage in the Battle of Britain, it also helped the Allies maintain an aircraft powerplant propulsion advantage throughout the war.

---

5 Examples: "clobber" to destroy an enemy plane; "beaver" to shoot holes in an enemy aircraft; "wet feet" flight over the English Channel; "happy valley"— a zone with heavy anti-aircraft fire.

The commander was the wartime hero of the daring one-way B-25 raid on Tokyo on April 18, 1942. Doolittle led the epic *"Thirty Seconds over Tokyo"* mission and bailed out with his crew over China to become an instant air legend. He immediately was promoted to brigadier general and on May 19th was presented by President Roosevelt with the coveted Congressional Medal of Honor. Doolittle had taken over the reins of the Eighth Air Force on January 6th 1944. He immediately made changes. The General had already informed Washington that long-range fighter escort, while desirable in the past" was "essential in the future." Not only did did he expect the fighters to to escort his bombers and protect them from the enemy, but he also instructed them to actively hunt down the Germans. With the longer range of the P-51 Mustangs, Doolittle increasingly turned the Luftwaffe from the hunter to the hunted.

Although neither Doolittle nor Spaatz realized it, while the strategic bombing campaign had not been decisive in itself, the way it was used to draw the German air force into a losing battle of attrition was decisive. The attrition of the Luftwaffe became the prime ingredient in winning the air war in Europe. The Eighth was the most powerful strategic offensive air power in the world. It contained nearly 3,000 bombers and over a thousand fast fighters to protect them. In the summer and fall of 1944 this massive juggernaut was laying waste to the heartland of Germany. The added strength of RAF Bomber Command only served to increase the potency of the heavy bombers.

As the end of 1944 approached, the disparity between the German and Allied air forces widened beyond the closer match on the ground. Against the Germans, the Allied command wielded a greatly superior air force: [6]

TABLE 1

Allied Air Strength: September 1944				
Unit	Heavy Bombers	Med. Bombers	Fighters	Reconnaissance
9th USAAF	———	1,111	1,502	217
8th USAAF	2,710	———	1,234	———
2nd Br TAF	———	293	999	194
RAF BC	1,871	———	———	———
Total	4,581	1,404	3,735	411
Total Aircraft: 9,720				

6 The U.S. 15th Air Force is not included in the tabulation since it did not operate in the area over the Western Front. Also note that this includes all available aircraft; serviceable aircraft with crews would serve to reduce the total by approximately 15%.

Tactical Air Support

The Allied air forces in the West represented a well balanced offensive organization with nearly 10,000 machines to draw on. The Germans, on the other hand, had barely 4,500 aircraft for use on *all fronts* in the fall of 1944. With approximately 1,000 serviceable aircraft in the West, the Germans were outnumbered by over ten to one. Operationally, in supporting the ground forces the U.S. Army Air Corps functioned in accordance with the air war doctrine which was established two years earlier at Casablanca. The doctrine, outlined in FM-100-20, was primarily based on British experiences in winning the campaign in North Africa and provided specific ranked objectives for the air arm:

1. *First priority*: Gain the necessary degree of air superiority. This will be accomplished by attacks against aircraft in the air and on the ground and against those installations that the enemy requires for the application of air power.

2. *Second priority*: Isolate the battlefield by clipping off the enemy's communications lines, destroy bridges and roads, strangle the enemy supply route (air interdiction).

3. *Third priority*: Provide the ground forces direct support by attacking enemy troops, tanks and strong points.

Generally, the fighter bombers would be used for close support while maintaining air superiority. The medium bombers addressed the second priority, blasting bridges, roads and rails to the enemy's rear. The use of the heavy bombers for isolating the battlefield was acknowledged as possible, but considered heretical in that it deviated from the strategic mission.

The Tactics of Survival

Many foot soldiers fighting on the ground in Europe looked on the Allied airmen flying above them as having it easy. However, in many ways their occupation was even more dangerous. The chances for USAAF flyers to get out of their occupation alive were grim indeed. One in four airmen flying over Europe became casualties. The total casualties in the European and Mediterranean theatres of operations were 94,565 including dead, wounded, missing and prisoners. And unlike the ground army, where a great many more were wounded than killed, the odds in the air went the other way. Over half of the above figure were fatalities.

A detailed study of 2,085 Eighth Air Force aircrew in the second half of 1944 showed that for each thousand men starting their first combat mission only 358 or 36% could be expected to survive a 25 mission tour of duty. Since the typical tour was extended from 25 to 35 missions in August, 1944 (a bitter pill for many), the chances of surviving unscathed became remote. Those who did survive were often called "Lucky Bastards." which indeed they were. The same rates extended over a year long period showed the dangers of various air mission types. For each 1,000 aircrew starting, the heavy bombers experienced a casualty rate actually exceeding the number partici- pating (1,662), while fighters suffered 894 casualties and medium bombers the least at 673. The loss rate also reflected the value of crew experience. On their first five missions of a 25 mission tour, a typical airman would face a 5.4% chance of not returning from each mission, whereas for the last five missions the rate dropped to only 1.2%. The vital point, however, was that the odds of becoming a "Lucky Bastard" were daunting. There was only a 50-50 chance of making it through 14 missions. And what of the fate of the "Unlucky Bastards?" For each 10,000 aircrew sent on missions in December, 1944, 78 were reported missing in action, 9.3 were killed, 9.9 were wounded 10.4 were injured by frostbite or accidents. The situation with the fighters was somewhat different, but grim nonetheless. Rotation back stateside was only available after a tour with 200 combat hurs of flying time. the number of missions would depend on the flying time. With a P-47 flying tactical missions, it might take 100 missions, while only 40 as a long-range P-51 escort with the Eighth Air Force.

The risks were higher for some plane types than others. Men in the heavy bombers of the U.S. Eighth Air Force had a 32% overall chance of ending up a casualty, and, surprisingly, the fighter pilots suffered a nearly identical loss rate. It was the light and medium bombers who suffered the lowest casual- ties at 22%. Identical fighter aircraft had differing abilities in thwarting the enemy. For example, a raw comparison of the number of enemy aircraft shot down in the IX Tactical Air Command in December of 1944 showed that the three P-47 fighter groups shot down 95 enemy planes for a loss of 21 of their own (4.5 - 1) whereas the less nimble P-38 groups destroyed 68 enemy planes for a loss of 39 (1.7 - 1). Meanwhile the single 352nd Fighter Group (Col. James D. Mayden), which flew P-51s on fighter sweeps under operational control of the IX TAC recorded 46 enemy aircraft shot down between Christmas Day and the end of the month at a cost of only two Mustangs (23 - 1). The sharp end for the Allied airman ran up against the capability of their machines and their wit and skill.

Establishment of air superiority centered on beating the enemy's fighters in the air. To the man in the cockpit this reduced to survival. After World War II, operations analysis of fighter combat had conclusively shown what the pilots already suspected: "Speed is life." Maneuverability, altitude ceiling, acceleration, range, and rate of climb were important, but generally over- shadowed by speed itself. Studies showed that 80% of kills were made when one plane made a single pass at another and shot down the enemy plane before their opponent knew what was happening. One fighter pilot de- scribed the brevity of air combat from sighting to decision as "the ten-second eternity of the dogfight."

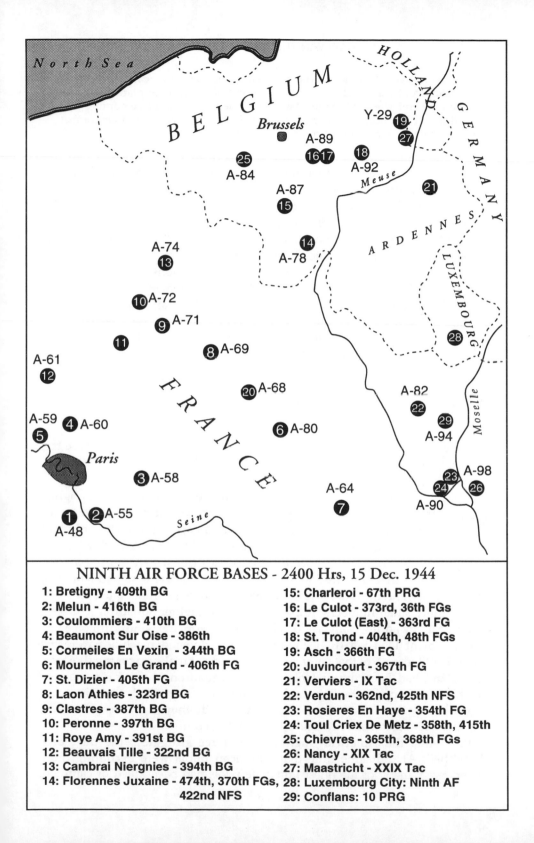

NINTH AIR FORCE BASES - 2400 Hrs, 15 Dec. 1944

1: Bretigny - 409th BG
2: Melun - 416th BG
3: Coulommiers - 410th BG
4: Beaumont Sur Oise - 386th
5: Cormeiles En Vexin - 344th BG
6: Mourmelon Le Grand - 406th FG
7: St. Dizier - 405th FG
8: Laon Athies - 323rd BG
9: Clastres - 387th BG
10: Peronne - 397th BG
11: Roye Amy - 391st BG
12: Beauvais Tille - 322nd BG
13: Cambrai Niergnies - 394th BG
14: Florennes Juxaine - 474th, 370th FGs,
                422nd NFS

15: Charleroi - 67th PRG
16: Le Culot - 373rd, 36th FGs
17: Le Culot (East) - 363rd FG
18: St. Trond - 404th, 48th FGs
19: Asch - 366th FG
20: Juvincourt - 367th FG
21: Verviers - IX Tac
22: Verdun - 362nd, 425th NFS
23: Rosieres En Haye - 354th FG
24: Toul Criex De Metz - 358th, 415th
25: Chievres - 365th, 368th FGs
26: Nancy - XIX Tac
27: Maastricht - XXIX Tac
28: Luxembourg City: Ninth AF
29: Conflans: 10 PRG

"When I recovered the sky was empty; as if by magic everyone had been made to disappear. I was all alone in the sky; I did not see another plane, friend or foe anywhere! The combat must have continued for at least five minutes, but I felt it had just been a matter of seconds. The funny thing about air combat was that everything seemed compressed in time."

With the introduction of the North American P-51 "Mustang" in the fighter arm, the Allied forces would enjoy a decided technological advantage over the most common German types. With a top speed of 437 mph, the P-51 was very fast. The mainstays of the Allied tactical air commands were the bottle-shaped Republic P-47D "Thunderbolt" with its air-cooled radial engine and the twin-engined Lockheed P-38 "Lightning." The primary British fighters in 1944 were the quick Supermarine "Spitfire" (which was in the process of going through countless souped-up versions) and the Hawker "Typhoon." The Typhoon became the British equivalent of the P-47— a tough air to ground fighter bomber. The Republic P-47, affectionately known as the "Jug," was the heaviest fighter-bomber of the war, yet exhibited several desirable characteristics not the least of which was its ability to take punishment. Don Clark of the 362nd Fighter Group:

"For the low-level job we had to do, where you couldn't keep out of the light flak and small arms fire, there wasn't a better plane than the P-47. It would keep going with damage with which other types would have fallen out of the sky. I was lucky and only got shot up once. We were strafing a patch of woods in which there was supposed to be some Jerry armor. I was flying the CO's plane which suddenly started to shake and smoke. When I landed at base I found a string of holes about two inches apart and stopped just behind the cockpit armor plate..."

The twin-engined P-38 was not as good in one-on-one fighter dogfights, but both the P-38 and P-47 could provide terrific close ground support with bombs or rockets as well as real fighter escort capabilities. The only real weakness in the Allied air forces were the tired P-61 "Black Widow" night fighter groups. So worn out were these planes (most had more than 300 combat hours), that often during the coming winter, fewer than half would be combat ready, and the radar sets in the majority no longer functioned properly. The pitifully small numbers in the 422nd Night Fighter Squadron had been propped up by adding some A-20 light bombers from the Ninth Air Force's IX Bombardment Division (BD). Predictably, the donated machines were the cast-off "old mares" of that command and could not make up for the shortage. The 422nd had been the first night fighter squadron in the ETO and was justifiably unhappy with their predicament which they called, "the disadvantage of being a bastard squadron." In the five months they had been operational, the 422nd had received only one replacement aircraft.

But while the American night fighter force struggled, the day force flourished. At the same time that American pilots were becoming more experienced, many of the finest Luftwaffe pilots had been killed or captured.

Aircrew skill was becoming ever more heavily weighted in the Allied favor.[7] The Allied air forces enjoyed a decided material superiority—more planes, more bombs and more gasoline. Like the reputation earned by the ground forces, in the U.S. Ninth Air Force "excellent results were achieved by brute force, wasted manpower and transportation rather than efficiency of operation."

Operationally, the 180,000-man Ninth Air Force seldom staged unified actions, but was divided into three Tactical Air Commands (TACs), with each assigned to a separate American army. The IX and XIX TACs were normally in support of the First and Third U.S. Armies, respectively. Each TAC was outfitted with either P-47 or P-38 fighter-bombers as well as a reconnaissance group with P-51 or P-38 aircraft to provide both visual and photographic information. The reconnaissance groups located targets for the fighter bombers, such as enemy troop concentrations, vehicle convoys and moving trains. Requests for air support were sent up channels from air liaison units with the divisions on the ground. Most of all, Vandenberg and his command prided themselves on the flexibility with which the combined air power of their organization could be concentrated for any purpose on short notice. The XXIX TAC had been added in September and was assigned to Gen. Simpson's Ninth Army.

Gen. Samuel Anderson's medium bombers of IX Bombardment Division (BD) were under Vandenberg's direct control. Selections of targets were made after a comprehensive review of the air and ground situation and consultation with the air liaison section which were stationed with the Advanced Headquarters of the Ninth Air Force in Chantilly, France. The IX BD's bomb groups were comprised of twin engined B-26 "Marauders," A-20 "Havocs," and a few of the new A-26 "Invaders."

The veteran British 2nd Tactical Air Force played a similar role with Montgomery's 21st Army Group. The Royal Air Force Bomber Command also provided a potent British strategic capability. Air Marshall Sir Arthur Harris' bomber command reached the zenith of its strength with some 1,609 Lancasters, 353 Halifaxes and 203 Mosquito fighter-bombers. However, Harris disagreed with the U.S. strategic bombing aim of destroying the enemy's means of production, believing that a terror campaign of area-bombing would induce the Germans to surrender. His bomber offensive would later be seen as inhumane and largely ineffective towards ending the war. In contrast, Air Marshall Arthur Coningham's 2nd Tactical Air Force provided very effective support over the battlefield and would serve as an important ingredient for Allied success in the coming battles.

---

7 However, stateside training was not perfect. At the end of December, 1944 Gen. Quesada of IX TAC complained that "many of our new replacement pilots never had the opportunity of firing their guns from an operational aircraft. It is felt that this training should have been done in the U.S., and the training burden should not be imposed on the operational fighter groups..."

TABLE 2

Organization of the Ninth U.S. Air Force: December 1944
Lt. Gen. Hoyt S. Vandenberg
IX TAC - Brig. Gen. Elwood R. Quesada
70th Fighter Wing
365, 366, 367, 368, 370, 474 Fighter Groups (FG)
67 Tactical Reconnaissance Group (TRG)
422 Night Fighter Squadron (NFS)
XIX TAC - Maj. Gen. Otto P. Weyland
100th Fighter Wing
354, 358, 362, 405, 406 FG
10 Photo Reconnaissance Group (PRG)
425 NFS
XXIX TAC - Brig. Gen. Richard E. Nugent
84th and 303rd Fighter Wings
36, 48, 373, 404, 363 FG
IX Bombardment Command - Brig. Gen. Samuel E. Anderson
97th Combat Bomb Wing (CB)
409, 410, 416 Bomb Group (BG)
98th CB
323, 387, 394, 397 BG
1 Pathfinder Squadron
99th CB
322, 344, 386, 391 BG
IX Troop Carrier Command - Brig. Gen. Benjamin F. Giles
52 Troop Carrier Command (TCC)
61, 313, 314, 315, 349 Troop Carrier Group (TCG)
53 TCC
434 - 438 TCG
50 TCC
439 - 422 TCG

Aircraft types in the fighter and bomber groups:

P-47: 36, 48, 50, 354, 358, 362, 365, 366, 368, 371, 373, 404, 405.

P- 38: 367, 370, 474.

P-47: 36,48,50,354, 358,362, 365, 366, 368, 371, 373, 404, 405.

P-38: 367, 370, 474.

P-51: 363.

B-26: 322, 323, 344, 387, 391, 394, 397, 1PF.

A-20: 410, 416.

A-26: 409.

Close-support

By December, 1944, most pilots of Vandenberg's TACs were well versed in offensive ground support. However, there were still problems with coordination between moving ground forces and the air commands. Air missions were generally assigned at least 24 hours in advance and with the movement of the front, close support became a dangerous proposition. The ever-present risk when attempting close combat support was of bombing your own troops. For this reason, really close coordination of air and ground forces would never be achieved during World War II. A notable exception was attacks against static enemy positions or those marked with smoke. The main function of the fighter-bomber, however, was to hit the enemy lines behind a "no-bomb" line. This disrupted enemy reinforcements moving up to the front and played havoc with supply of the forward troops.

The Allied air forces had a substantial advantage in their innovative use of a radar system to guide close support missions. This allowed American aircraft to provide close support to their ground forces with less risk of accidently bombing ones own positions. Forward air controllers were assigned to most of the U.S. divisions to assist in providing targets for friendly aircraft. Although the Germans were accustomed to the use of radar to coordinate defensive fighter operations, the Americans were learning to use ground radar to coordinate close support missions with greatly increased accuracy. General Elwood Quesada, in charge of the IX Tactical Air Command, used the Microwave Early Warning (MEW) radar and SCR-584 anti-aircraft radar in an unconventional way to coordinate the air battle. Generally, the MEW was too far away to use in the Ardennes, being located up around Aachen. Moreover, the MEW lacked the accuracy necessary for operations that required precise control, such as blind fighter-bomber sorties. However, the SCR-584 sets were portable. The SCR-584 was an anti-aircraft radar set with a very fine definition. Its very narrow beam was used to

TABLE 3

Organization of the Eighth U.S. Air Force: Fall 1944 Lt. Gen. James H. Doolittle
First Bomb Division, Maj. Gen. Robert B. Williams
1st Combat Bomb Wing
91, 381, 482 BGs
40th Combat Bomb Wing
92, 303, 305, 306 BGs
41st Combat Bomb Wing
379, 384 BGs
94th Combat Bomb Wing
351, 401, 457 BGs
67th Fighter Wing
20, 352, 356, 359, 364 FGs
Independent Units
Special Operations Group
495th Fighter Training Group
Radio Countermeasures Squadron
Night Leaflet Squadron
Second Bomb Division, Maj. Gen. William E. Kepner
2nd Combat Wing
389, 445, 453 BGs
14th Combat Bomb Wing
44, 392, 491 BGs
20th Combat Bomb Wing
93, 446, 448 BGs
96th Combat Bomb Wing
458, 466, 467, BGs
65th Fighter Wing
4, 56, 355, 361, 479 FGs
5th Emergency Rescue Squadron
Independent Units
496 Fighter Training Group

Third Bomb Division, Maj. Gen. Earle E. Partridge
4th Bomb Wing
94, 385, 447, 486, 487 BGs
13th Combat Bomb Wing
95, 100, 390 BGs
45th Combat Bomb Wing
96, 388, 452 BGs
66th Fighter Wing
55, 78, 339, 353, 357 FGs
93rd Combat Bomb Wing
34, 490, 493 BGs
Other Units
7th Photographic Group (R)

direct AA fire with incredible accuracy. However, Gen. Pete Quesada came up with the idea to use six of the SCR-584s to direct the fighters with precise control during poor weather conditions. Gen. Otto P. Weyland was the head of XIX Tactical Air Command who supported the demanding Gen. Patton of the U.S. Third Army:

"We were very mobile in Europe, and this caused a lot of communications problems. We always tried to stay as close to the action as possible to extend our range, increase our time over the target and run several missions a day. During the Battle of the Bulge, some of my units ran four or five missions a day. We had to be close to do that. I couldn't stay back in Brest or some Goddamned place 500 miles to the rear. We had some radio, but it was nothing like we have today. We depended heavily on spiral cable. One cable could handle 16 messages simultaneously. My intelligence people monopolized communications like hell, and the administrative boys also thought that the cable had been strung out for their exclusive use...Fighter control in the air was done through ground controllers using radar. Mission assignments came from my combat headquarters, and usually went out the night before the missions were to be flown. If an emergency situation came up the next day, my ground controllers could contact the fighter leaders and change their assignments on a moment's notice."

The ability to make such post-takeoff changes in assignment was important in the Ardennes, since the forward edge of the battle area (FEBA) was poorly defined. Even the bright identification panels were difficult to see in the low visibility of the Ardennes mists. Fighter group leaders were, therefore, understandably reluctant to attack unrecognized vehicles or positions

TABLE 4

Organization of the British 2nd Tactical Air Force Air Marshall Sir Arthur Coningham
34 (Photo Reconnaissance) Wing
16 Sqdn - Spitfire XI
69 Sqdn - Wellington XIII
140 Sqdn - Mosquito XVI
2nd Group Air Vice-Marshal Basil E. Embry
136 Wing
418, 605 Sqdns - Mosquito VI
137 Wing
88, 342 and 226 Sqdns - Boston III & IV; Mitchell II
138 Wing
107, 305, 613 Sqdns - Mosquito VI
139 Wing
98, 180 and 320 Sqdns - Mitchell II & III
140 Wing
21, 464 and 487 Sqdns - Mosquito VI
83rd Group Air Vice-Marshal Harry Broadhurst
39 (Recce) Wing
400 Sqdn - Spitfire XI
414 Sqdn - Spitfire IX
430 Sqdn - Spitfire XIV
121 Wing
174, 175, 184 and 245 Sqdns - Typhoon IB
122 Wing
3, 56, 80, 274 and 486 Sqdns - Tempest V
124 Wing
137, 181, 182 and 247 Sqdns - Typhoon IB
125 Wing
130, 350 and 610 Sqdns - Spitfire XIV

126 Wing
401, 411, 412, 442 Sqdns - Spitfire IX

402 Sqdn - Spitfire XIV

127 Wing
403, 416, 421 and 443 Sqdns - Spitfire XVI

143 Wing
168, 438, 439 and 440 Sqdns - Typhoon IB

A.O.P. Units - Auster IV & V

84th Group Air Vice-Marshal L.O. Brown

35 (Recce) Wing
2 Sqdn - Spitfire XIV

4 Sqdn - Spitfire XI

268 Sqdn - Mustang II

123 Wing
164, 183, 198 and 609 Sqdns - Typhoon IB

131 Wing
302, 308 and 317 Sqdns - Spitfire XVI

132 Wing
66, 127, 322, 331 and 332 Sqdns - Spitfire XVI

135 Wing
33 and 222 Sqdns - Tempest V

145 Wing
74, 329, 340 and 345 Sqdns - Spitfire XVI

146 Wing
193, 197, 257, 263 and 266 Sqdns - Typhoon IB

A.O.P. Units - Auster IV

85th Group

147 Wing
219, 410 and 488 Sqdns - Mosquito XXX

148 Wing
264, 409 and 604 Sqdns - Mosquito XIII

in the soupy weather. To remedy this situation MEW coordinators, with their wide-band radar, were stationed with radio intercept operators (the Y-service) to provide long-range navigation and control to Allied fighters. Close range coordination was performed by using the narrow beam of the SCR-584 sets to precisely vector planes to within 300 yards of their target from 30 miles away. The Y-service was listening in to all German frequencies, monitoring their non-encrypted instructions to their various fighter groups. This often yielded information as to the group involved, aircraft type, their bases, and even the fuel status of Luftwaffe flights. Along with radar, this information was used to catch the German pilots at their most vulnerable points. So guided, Allied planes were able to accurately blind-bomb targets such as St. Vith, through the otherwise overcast skies during the first week of the battle. Radar operators helped the fighters to reach their targets by triangulating known ground positions with tracked fighter locations. Similarly, if the fighters reported sighting vehicles below, the SC-584 radar could be used along with a map to determine their position and whether the vehicles were friendly or hostile. This system also worked equally well for the intercept of enemy aircraft.[8] Luckily for the Allies, the Germans never suspected the vulnerability of this important Allied advantage. Only six sets comprised the Allied air control system. Had they been knocked out or damaged, General Quesada reckoned that the Allied air power wou have been severely affected and air-ground coordination would have been "incredibly difficult and impossible under the weather conditions." As it was Quesada moved two of the SCR-584 sets right up to the front line during the winter fighting so that its range would be maximized.

---

8 During the battle, MEW intercepts were credited with the resulting destruction of 161 Luftwaffe aircraft.

III

The Luftwaffe: In Hitler's Dog House

The spectacular Allied failure to seize the bridges and cross the Rhine River at Arnhem in September had given the Luftwaffe a breathing spell to recover from the aerial fiascos of the previous nine months. Finally, Hitler had given fighter production precedence over bomber types; he could do little else after watching the vast armada of Allied planes pulverize the Reich throughout 1944. Then too, there was little in the way of fuel to keep any of the petrol-guzzling German bombers aloft.[9] Albert Speer warned the German leader, however, that if this desecration continued much longer, there would be no way of continuing the war.[10] In spite of increased production from other armament manufacture, the production of oil plummeted. By greatly expanding synthetic fuels production, German petrol stocks had reached an apex of some 574,000 tons by April of 1944. But then the Allied bombing campaign against German oil production began in earnest. Fuel stocks plummeted. By late June, production was down by 90%; only 52,000 tons were produced that month as opposed to 195,000 in May. With the

---

9 The ill-fated Heinkel 177 heavy bomber is a good case in point. A medium range mission for the eighty aircraft of *KG 1* needed nearly five hundred tons of gasoline to go forth. However, by fall, 1944 five hundred tons represented an entire **day's** output of the entire German oil industry! There was obviously not enough fuel to keep the heavy bombers in operation. So, after a long and painful development history, the He-177 units were immobilized and then disbanded for want of fuel, just after beginning successful offensive operations in Russia.

10 Speer would identify May 12th, 1944, the day the Americans began bombing German oil refineries, as the "day the technological war was decided...It meant the end of German armaments production...There is no doubt that the enemy's hopes for an end to the war in the winter of 1944-45 would have been accomplished if the chemical (fuel) industry had been knocked out...In general, transportation recovered much faster than we expected..."

refineries under a withering assault, the free fall continued. Only 35,000 tons dribbled out in July and barely 16,000 in August. Speer gave Hitler an honest appraisal:

> "The enemy has struck us at one of our weakest points. If they persist at it this time, we will soon no longer have any fuel production worth mentioning. Our hope is that the other side has an air force general staff as scatter-brained as ours!"

Although his genrals told him that things could be patched up, Hitler was too perceptive to believe the sycophants in his headquarters. The German leader was always calling for more tanks and planes from the German factories. Speer pointedly challenged him: what good would be these planes and tanks if there was no fuel for them? Hitler knew Speer was right. The German leader grudgingly approved the plan to re-build the fighter forces at the cost of the offensive air arm that summer. But was all this too late?

Under Hitler's direction, Speer forcefully addressed the fuel problem. The hydro-generation plants were repaired so that production could resume. A horde of army engineers were enlisted to harden the refineries. The engineers and repair crews were supervised by Himmler's SS, so that their "enthusiasm" would not flag. Thousands of the impressed laborers died. Where possible, facilities were moved underground. For those above, concrete ramparts were erected; and a thicket of heavy flak guns ringed the facilities. Along with smoke generators, this made bomb runs not only uncertain, but exceedingly deadly. The vital German facilities took on the air of fortresses; they were even called that— *Hydriesfestungen*. The *14th Flakdivision*, in charge of the defense of the important oil plants in the Leipzig area, possessed 374 heavy flak guns at the beginning of May, 1944. Over the following months, the dynamic Genmaj. Adolf Gerlach increased their strength six-fold and instituted effective fire control schemes to make future Allied blows nearly suicidal. On July 28th, Speer called for dramatic increase in the fighters allocated to defend German industry. One move designed to accommodate his desire was to post *JG 400*, flying the rocket-powered, but short-ranged, Me-163 *Komet*, at Brandis along the approach path to the oil facilities.[11] On August 24, eight of these fast rocket planes struck a surprised force of 185 B-17s moving to attack the refinery at Merseburg. Four B-17s were shot down with only superficial damage suffered by two of the *Komets*. Finally, the ultimate oil protection strategy was entrusted to Edmund Geilenberg, Speer's energetic head of the munitions organization. He proposed to

---

11 On September 24th, the rocket fighter unit had 19 Me-163s with 11 serviceable. The Luftwaffe had delivered over a hundred Me-163s at that point, but the lack of trained pilots was a constant limitation. Flying the volatile rocket plane was exceedingly dangerous— even to those fully trained in its nuances. The other difficulty was more insuperable. During Allied bombing attacks on Leverkusen and Ludwigshaven that month, the main production facilities for *C-Stoff* were seriously damaged, greatly reducing the supplies of the Komet's exotic fuel. The V1 Fi-103 also used *C-Stoff* and had a higher priority on its production.

dig in 41 small dispersed hydrogeneration plants in underground production facilities around Central Germany.

In spite of the far-reaching measures, oil production continued to flag. The experience of the sprawling synthetic oil plant at Leuna is illustrative. Between May 12th and September 28th, the facility was struck no less than twelve times by over 2,400 medium and heavy bombers. Although production resumed briefly with chaotic repairs during the summer, Leuna was bombed so often that at the end of the month repair work was again disrupted before operation could resume. Meanwhile, German fuel production had dropped to a war-relative drip: a mere 7,000 tons for September. The effects were not immediate— the Luftwaffe had accumulated a fuel reserve of over half a million tons before the disasters of summer— but soon the fat would be gone. With the total stocks down to only 180,000 tons at the end of September the promise of draconian conservation measures loomed. Gone would be profligate use by the Luftwaffe day-bombers. Even legitimate uses like reconnaissance and training operations would have to be sharply curtailed. Worst of all, the Luftwaffe, increasingly viewed as impotent, would be competing with Hitler's panzers for the trickle of fuel left.[12]

Fortunately for the Germans, there were so many pulls on the Allied air effort that it did not remain solely concentrated on oil. In the late summer the U.S. strategic air force was committed to the destruction of the rail system in France to hinder the ability of the Germans to respond to the invasion. Later, Air Chief Marshal Sir Arthur Tedder, the Deputy Supreme Commander at SHAEF, pushed for a greater portion of the strategic bombing effort to be devoted to wrecking the rail and water transport system in Germany on the basis of a controversial study by Professor Zuckerman. Zuckerman had become convinced from an analysis of the effect of bombing on the Italian campaign that destruction of enemy rail centers and rail marshalling yards was the way to speed the end of the war. Eventually, this plan would be translated into Operation Clarion— an all-out effort to wreck German rail capability in 1945. But an even larger factor was Air Marshal Harris' refusal to be drawn away from his area bombing of German cities to attack oil targets. Zuckerman, Tedder and Harris were frequently at odds with Spaatz who was the leading proponent of the oil campaign. But even Spaatz, frustrated with the refusal of Nazi Germany to roll over dead from his precision bombing, was now leaning toward using the heavy bombers to support the armies in massive carpet bombing attacks. A final German

12 To accumulate 17.5 thousand tons of fuel for the Ardennes Offensive, Gen. Jodl began withholding gasoline from other army groups on November 10th, more than a month before the offensive was to begin. Even before the rationing went into effect, Albert Speer had written Hitler at the end of September complaining that "A fighter group stationed at Krefeld with more than 37 planes must take two days of enforced rest in spite of excellent weather. It receives its fuel allotment on the third day and then only enough for brief sorties as far as Aachen with 20 of its planes." At a training center the commandant informed Speer that they only obtained enough fuel for their flying students to train one hour per week!

grace came from the poor flying weather. With the onset of autumn and the socked-in skies over Western Europe, constant bombing of the German oil facilities became impossible.[13]

Thus, through a combination of circumstances the Germans gained a breathing spell during the summer in which to reorganize. Speer would later write that "Had they continued the attacks of March and April with the same energy, we would quickly have been at our last gasp." But Speer shrewdly used his breathing room to repair the faltering industry. Synthetic fuel stocks wavered and then rose. Some 19,000 tons were produced in October, and 39,000 in November. This was still not nearly enough, but at least the likelihood of complete collapse was averted. Obviously, the fuel famine was not going to ever allow either the army or Luftwaffe to enjoy the surpluses of a year before. Even with spartan fuel conservation measures, the Luftwaffe would have to fight a poor man's war. Planes were horse-drawn to their take-off point; personal travel in motor vehicles was forbidden, and training flights were greatly abbreviated. Fuel depots were assiduously dispersed to prevent major losses to Allied air attacks. The gas-guzzling Luftwaffe bombers were relegated to deep mothball status. The list went on. But if Hitler was to have fuel for a major air and ground operation using a large reserve of new aircraft, even sortie rates that fall would have to be curtailed. It was not a good situation, but at least the poor flying weather helped.

Beyond the destruction of the facilities that distilled the German oil, there were limitations with the fuel itself. Although the ingenious distillation process certainly worked, it was inefficient and the produced cost of Hitler's "synfuels" were about four times the world market crude oil price. When the war began, the octane number of first-grade German aviation fuel was only about 89 and this was obtained only by fortifying the synthetic fuel with 16% aromatics containing tetraethyl lead. Meanwhile, the Americans had 100-octane gas courtesy the pre-war efforts of Jimmy Doolittle at upgrading refineries. The upshot of the difference in 1944 was that the P-51D's Rolls Royce Merlin engine produced 1,520 hp with 100-octane fuel, while the Me-109G's Daimler Benz 605 could only reach a similar level of performance with 25% more engine displacement and greater weight. In an effort to match the superior American fuels, the Germans in 1944 were adding 40% aromatics to their brew to pull the octane up to the 96-point range. This increase meant less fuel production overall at a time when the Germans were criti-

---

13 Having witnessed the fantastic destruction wrought by his enemies' mighty air forces and the German ability to cope with these exigencies, Hermann Goring firmly believed that while the air forces could render a decisive contribution towards winning the war, it could never be used to bring a great nation to its knees. "The air forces *cannot* occupy," he surmised, "they can only disrupt, interfere and destroy and thus prepare for the eventual last fight leading to final occupation and victory...The Allies owe the success of their invasion to their Air Forces. They prepared the invasion, they made it possible and they carried it through."

cally pressed for gasoline for pilot training. Then too, the increased fraction of the aromatics reduced performance in other ways: engines overheated more readily, richer-mixtures had to be run to prevent stalling (reducing aircraft endurance, fouling plugs and fuel efficiency) and the added compounds attacked rubber hoses and the seal-sealing bladders in German fuel tanks. And still the fuels were not equivalent. The Germans attempted to make up for the remaining gulf by using power boost, either methanol-water or nitrous oxide injection. This expedient did increase horsepower, but could only be used for short periods and had to be carefully turned on and off to maintain performance— a less than certain event in the heat of combat.

The prospect of increasing fighter output was brighter. With his usual efficiency, Speer set up the *Jägerstab*, or Fighter Committee, within his Ministry of Armaments to set things straight. Aircraft factories were scattered to prevent intervention by the omniscient Allied air forces: 27 main complexes were brought into being along with many other smaller factories dotted about the German countryside. Critical plants, such as the Junkers Aero-plant producing the Jumo 004 jet and 213 piston engines were sequestered to the safety of underground factories at Kohnstein in the Harz Mountains.[14] There they turned out their products in seven miles of tunnels offering the protection of 140 feet of solid rock. Except for the jet Ar-234 and the new Ju-388, all bomber production was halted; all resources would concentrate on increasing fighter output. Speer's programs were astonishingly successful. Single engine fighter *Gruppen* were able to build up to unprecedented operational strengths. German fighter production reached its highest point of the war in September of 1944 when 2,876 Messerschmitt Me-109s and Focke Wulf Fw-190s were produced. It was the final and most remarkable recovery for the Luftwaffe during the war in Europe. Allied intelligence learned of all this by ULTRA decrypts. On October 21, Gen. Spaatz warned that the cost of the air campaign would increase dramatically if the enemy was able to effectively field its new-found strength.

One problem, however, was that such levels of production had been attained by the *Jägerstab* by concentrating on existing fighter types. The important objective for the Germans was to contest the Allied air power through the use of a strong fighter force. But how would this be accomplished? Should more planes be produced, or fewer planes of higher quality? The most troublesome Allied fighters were the P-47D "Thunderbolt" (top speed: 429 mph), the P-51D "Mustang" (437 mph) and the British Spitfire XIV (448 mph). Production of promising high performance German aircraft

---

14 The Jumo 004 was also being produced at Muldwerke in Muldenstein under difficult conditions with much impressed foreign labor. Of the 3,000 working there, only 1,600 were Germans, the rest were Italians, Belgians, Dutchmen and French while the "Russian POWs did the dirty work in the yard." The two 12-hour shifts were producing 10 - 15 engines per day; each received two sixty-minute tests.

to counter these types proceeded at a much slower pace. These included such planes as the Ta-152H (top speed: 470 mph), the exotic Dornier 335 *Pfeil* or "Arrow" (477 mph) and the jet Me-262 (540 mph) and Arado Ar-234 (461 mph) models. But various problems, particularly the need for very high performance engines, prevented the exotic piston types from seeing service in any numbers. Only eleven of the push-pull propellered Do-335s were delivered by war's end and only 67 of Dr. Kurt Tank's beautiful Ta-152. Attempts to build a fighter based loosely on the Me-209, a racing version of the 109 petered out in 1944. With test pilot Fritz Wendel at the controls, this cleaned up piston-powered Me-209V-5 had shown it could reach 42,000 feet and reach speeds of nearly 500 mph. However, Speer did not dare suspend production of the standard Messerschmitt for re-tooling. Instead German production had concentrated on the Me-109G (390 mph), the high-altitude G-10 (426 mph) and the Fw-190A-8 (408 mph).[15] In late fall, production began concentrating on two improved versions, the Me-109K-4s with a nitrous oxide injected Daimler-Benz engine (452 mph) and the Fw-190D-9 "long nose" or *Dora* (440 mph).[16] Even so, these planes made up a minority of the Luftwaffe inventory. Alas, the Luftwaffe's new found numerical strength in the fall of 1944 had been achieved at the classic cost— quality. But what of the jets?

On May 22nd, 1943, Adolf Galland stopped by the flight testing center at Augsburg. He was to test perhaps the most revolutionary German technological aviation achievement of the war— the Messerschmitt 262 jet. Galland's flight made an indelible impression on the German officer. He was euphoric. "It was just like being pushed by an angel," he proclaimed. Without delay, Galland sent a teletype message to Genfldm. Erhard Milch. He suggested dropping the Me-209 and immediately transferring the production capacity to the Me-262. "The aircraft represents a great step forward," he cabled, "which assures us an unimaginable advantage in operations should the enemy adhere to the piston engine...The aircraft opens up completely new tactical possibilities."

Certainly the new jet aircraft were the most palpable of Hitler's promises of "wonder weapons" to turn the tide of the war. The Me-262 and the Ar-234, upon which so much hope was pinned, were coming off assembly lines in increasing quantities— nearly a hundred per month during the fall. But this was not enough. According to Hitler's grandiose plans, a new jet plane was

---

15 There were sub-types of the Me-109G. The G-14 featured a new DB 605 ASM engine with 1,800 horsepower giving the plane better speed at all altitudes. The G-10 has a supercharged DB 605DCM engine and was intended as a fast high altitude fighter (service ceiling was 41,000 feet; fastest speed at 24,000 feet was 426 mph).

16 The Me-109K-4s had a potent 30mm nose cannon in addition to 20mm guns in the under-wing tubs. Although potentially devastating to an enemy aircraft caught in a K-4's sights, the aerodynamics of the weapons led to lower maneuverability than the G-10s. Also, in the thin air at high altitudes above 28,000 feet the K-4s did not handle well and icing became a constant threat.

scheduled for mass-production, the *"Volksjäger"*— or "People's Fighter." The contract was awarded to Ernst Heinkel on September 8, 1944. The single-engined Heinkel-162 "Salamander" went from drawing board to test in the astonishing time of 37 days![17] In the first test flight made on December 6th, the tiny plane proved speedy, reaching 520 mph. The machine showed signs of it's abbreviated incubation period. The second test flight a few days later killed the pilot, Flugkapitän Gotthold Peter, when the plane shed its plywood wings due to defective wood-bonding adhesive. Other fliers filed varying reports on the futuristic-looking beast. Some indicated it was "pleasant to fly" while others related questionable flying characteristics. Almost all, however, agreed that any idea that glider trained recruits might fly the machine was mere fancy.

Clearly, however, Hitler would be unable to realize his summertime wish of "2,000 jet aircraft" to alter Allied air superiority overnight. On the desirability of the jet, Genlt. Adolf Galland, the *General der Jagdflieger,* was certain. "At the time I would rather have one Me-262 than five Me-109s," he had told Hitler. Galland fervently believed that only "technically superior planes" could make up for the wide gulf between German pilot experience and their Allied foes. But Hitler insisted that the twin-engined Me-262 be used as a *"Blitz* bomber."

Historians over the years have pointed to Hitler's decision on the Me-262 as an egregious error; another in a long series of meddlings which cost him the war. Most, however, have not been aware of the limitations under which the German jet was developed. There is little question that the aerodynamics and structural aspects of the plane were brilliant; it was far ahead of its time. A cruising speed of 525 mph with an endurance over an hour was a fantastic achievement for 1944 aviation technology. However, the big problem was the thing that made the propeller-less 262 such a potentially hot aircraft— the Jumo 004 turbo-jet engines. As with most new technologies, the revolutionary engine experienced many teething troubles.

The turbo-jet operated at much higher temperatures and rotational speeds that any piston power-plant. Moreover, the metals usually used for high-temperature strength, alloys of nickel and chromium, were in very short supply in the Nazi inventory. The engineers were forced to rely on less-reliable substitutes. As a result, even as late as fall, 1944 the mean serviceable life of the jet engines was only eight hours for the early models! Metal fatigue created engine failures and fires were frequent. All through the summer and fall of 1944, there was always a heavily guarded convoy with replacement jet engines somewhere in Germany looking for *Special Detachment E 51.* Oblt. Werner Muffey remembers being happy that the Ar-234s had *two* turbojets:

---

17 So frenetic was the working schedule for the Heinkel developers that they slept at their offices at Rostock to save time.

"...it was rare for a single engine to survive the 25 hours scheduled between overhauls. It was much more likely for only 5 to 10 hours to pass before something went wrong. In fact I once jealously preserved a unit for almost 30 hours which was considered a record. Then another turbojet threw several blades before I returned from my first sortie with it. After putting out a small fire in the Riedel gas tank, I returned directly to Oranienburg to change the engine."

Even worse, German pilots flying the new aircraft learned to their horror that the turbojet was prone to suddenly quit or even catch fire when throttled too quickly. Due to the raw materials shortages, the composition of the turbine blades was not up to the loads which could be imposed upon it. The flight born discovery of "flame-out" would prove fatal to a number of pilots putting the 262 through its paces. The solution to this was to only throttle the engines slowly, a luxury that only a bomber or reconnaissance application could afford. Fighter dogfights demanded sudden acceleration and hence the first use of the Me-262 was most appropriately restricted to less taxing reconnaissance and level bombing missions.

In spite of German engineering genius, the vexing problems with the jet engine were never completely solved during the war. Then there were other mechanical problems, such as roughness in the fuel metering system, which in a piston powered plane might only mean a momentary reduction in power. In an Me-262, such mundane troubles could overheat the engine which would promptly disintegrate as it shed turbine blades. Flying a jet Me-262 was significantly less forgiving than jockeying around in a piston powered plane. Most of the pilots converting to the elite units flying this plane were very experienced, but jets represented new territory. For instance, a common— even subconscious— habit in piston aircraft, was to push the throttle forward to rev up the engine before easing it back. In a 262, this could drop an engine— a potentially fatal mistake. There were even bizarre problems with the J2 fuel. In November and December of 1944 *KG 51* experienced mysterious symptoms of poisoning in some of its pilots who had received minor burns. Sr. Warrant Officer Kohler, died after receiving only minor burns to his hands. After the cause was established as the fuel, the jet pilots were provided with leather clothing including protective gloves.

The unparalleled power of the turbojets led to other dangers never encountered in conventional piston aircraft. It was easy to exceed the airframe limits even in a steep climb— full throttle would see speeds only encountered in the most daring dives in other planes. Also, unlike the howl of a piston plane under full throttle, the jet was deceptively quiet in the cockpit and a wary pilot had to be attentive to the airspeed indicator. There were high speed limits as well. Up to 570 mph the 262 operated faultlessly. However, as test pilots reached 585 mph, they found that control surfaces responded poorly. Beyond that things quickly became uncontrollable. Today, surviving Me-262 veterans reckon that a number of their compatriots succumbed to compressibility at the aerodynamic limits. Flying a V-2 chase sortie, Werner Muffey, the Technical Officer of an Ar-234 reconnaissance unit, learned that his jet powered craft could exceed the aircraft's "envelope":

> "This...was the only time I got into trouble with 'Dr. Mach.' Oblivious of my pilot's duties and staring constantly down to detect the exploding V-2, I inadvertently pushed the stick forward. The vibration going through the airplane was quite dramatic, and I had some problems recovering control."

In spite of early recognition of these problems, conversion training was not always satisfactory. Since there was no two-seater version of the 262, training flights were begun after cursory technical instruction. Usually the instructor, who often had little experience with the aircraft himself, would provide a pre-takeoff briefing, supervise the tricky start-up procedure for the engines and then talk the pilot through a flight over the radio. Often too much reliance was made of a pilot's experience with conventional aircraft. Lt. Walther Hagenah was an experienced Fw-190 pilot from *JG 3*:

> "Our ground school lasted one afternoon. We were told of the peculiarities of the jet engine, the dangers of flaming out at high altitude and their poor acceleration at low speeds. The vital importance of handling the throttles carefully was impressed upon us, lest the engines catch fire. But we were not permitted to look inside the cowling of the jet engine — we were told that it was very secret and we did not need to know about it! By the time I reached III/JG 7 there was insufficient spare parts and insufficient spare engines; there were even occasional shortages of J-2 [jet fuel]. I am sure all of these things existed and that production was sufficient, but by that stage of the war the transport system was so chaotic that things often failed to arrive at the front-line units. In our unit, flying the Me-262, we had some pilots with only about a hundred hours' total flying time. They were able to take off and land the aircraft, but I had the definite impression that they were of little use in combat. It was almost a crime to send them into action with so little training. Those young men did their best, but they had to pay a heavy price for their lack of experience."

Aside from all of this, Hitler had already decided that the He-162 would be the new jet fighter and the Me-262 must carry bombs. Knowing of the coming invasion of France, he was fixated on the idea of German jets dropping bombs on the heads of the Americans on the beaches. In May, 1944 when Hitler insisted that the 262 be modified to carry bombs, less than fifty had been assembled and all were in use in test programs. Due to the poor reliability (the Jumo 004s were lasting less than 10 hours before failure) none of the jet-powered aircraft would be suitable for *any* combat role for some time— even reconnaissance. The many critics of the decision to use the Me-262 as a fighter-bomber must remember that in 1944 the plane stood as the last chance for an effective offensive air weapon for the Luftwaffe. Any blame for lack of impact of the German jets must rest squarely on the technology itself, rather than on the manner in which the handful of planes were utilized. It was a matter of too little, too late.

However, the engineering problems loomed large; the Me-262 had been designed as a fighter. Change-over to a "hit and run" *Blitz* bomber required many modifications. The original plane had two fuel tanks, each holding about 200 gallons of J2 fuel. Armament consisted of four 30mm cannon. That the *Blitz* was to carry two 550 lb. bombs required more fuel to give it an acceptable range. Two additional fuel tanks were fitted— one 55 gallon vessel under the pilot's seat and another 130 gallons in the fuselage to the rear of the main tank. This additional weight not only decreased the plane's performance, it also resulted in troubles with the plane's center of gravity. The added weight in the tail of the *Blitz* was balanced by the two center mounted bombs and two of the four cannon were taken away. The rear fuel tank was never to be filled unless the plane had a bomb load. When flying, the pilot had to be careful that the rear tank was emptied first. Mishandling of the fuel cocks, draining the forward tank first, and dropping bombs would cause the aircraft to rear up violently. Elevator control could not restore such an ill-weighted 262 and pilots who forgot these procedures in the heat of battle could easily lose their aircraft.

The conversion of *KG 51* to the 262 was carried out at Lechfeld beginning on September 4th under command of Oberstleutnant Wolfgang Schenck. By late November, Schenk's command possessed some thirty jets with 26 operational and 48 pilots in training. As a bomber, the 262 reflected its bastardized upbringing. Unlike conventional types, such as the Ju-88, the *Blitz* was not fitted with a downward facing bomb sight. It had a simple reflector reticle suitable for aiming cannon fire. With practice, pilots found they could reasonably hit sizeable targets, but precision bombing was out of the question. Dive bombing was also *Verboten* since a personal edict from Hitler himself forbade it along with any flying over enemy territory at less than 13,000 feet lest a 262 fall into enemy hands from AA fire. All this made for some very inaccurate bombing; members of *KG 51* began to coyly refer to themselves as the "crop damage *Geschwader*." If that was not depressing enough, an "Edelweiss" pilot had to worry about his back, since there was no armor behind the pilot's head. This design flaw was found responsible for the death of a number of 262 bomber pilots who were killed before design changes went into effect in March, 1945. Some of the experienced Ju-88 and Me-410 pilots of the group had little confidence in the turbine engines and a perpetual fuel shortage made extensive training impossible. Some 65 tons of scarce petrol were needed to provide rudimentary training for a replacement pilot.[18]

---

18 The American training program provided quite a contrast. Pilots had already received extensive training stateside. Robert Stroball: "The base was equipped with P-47s and experienced instructors who had some combat experience. To me, the most impressive part of this training was the fact that the P-47 had far more capabilities than we were led to believe during our Stateside training...In the States we were taught not to exceed the redline on the instruments. In England we were taught to use much higher redlines and to ask the airplane to perform under maximum stress as a means of saving the airplane and ourselves if the need arose..."

Then finally in September, Hitler relented on the employment of the 262 as a fighter, at least in a limited sense. During a *Führer Konferenz* on September 22nd, on the further reconsideration of this thorny matter, Hitler spelled out a convoluted policy that would allow for some jet fighter versions of the 262 so long as a commensurate number of jet bombers were provided:

> "The Ar-234 will, with all possible dispatch continue to be turned out as a bomber in the greatest possible numbers. As it is possible to use this aircraft for the short range targets with three 1,100 pound bombs, and for long-range targets with one 1,100 pound bomb, under considerably more favorable general conditions than the Me-262 when used as a bomber, the Führer confirms his earlier promise that, for every single-battle worthy 234 accepted as a bomber, the General in charge of the fighters [Galland] will be allocated one battle-worthy 262 fighter."

The direct result was that some forty Me-262s became available for the formation of the first combat jet fighter unit. The incipient command was organized under the legendary Austrian fighter ace, Maj. Walter Nowotny. When he took over the command, "Nowi" had some 250 combat victories and was perhaps the most famous of the Luftwaffe aces. The distinguished title for his unit would take its leader's name— *Versuchskommando Nowotny*. With tremendous expectation, his unit became operational as a 262 fighter training unit in October with some 23 jets, flying from airfields at Achmer and Hesepe. Not surprisingly, the new jet fighter pilots experienced a rash of technical problems, which led to a very low serviceability rate; on November 1st the unit had only nine of its jets serviceable. There were also questions regarding effective methods of attack. So fast were the machines that the 262 would close on enemy aircraft very rapidly with the target in range for only a fraction of a second. The obvious conclusion, to slow to strike their quarry, was no good. This would only sacrifice their speed advantage.

> "Our strength lay in our enormous speed. The reaction propulsion system made us something like twice as fast as the enemy's airscrew driven fighters. Moreover, the armament of the 262— with 43mm cannon— was not only sensational; it was ideally suited to destroying the solid thick-skinned bombers. But the technology of this revolutionary machine also had its weakness that made high-level aerial combat and attacks on bomber formations problematical. Swinging into the target's wake from above was out because of the danger of exceeding the maximum safe [airframe] speed, the aircraft having no brakes with which to check the rapid acceleration involved in such a maneuver. Frontal attack on collision course with the bombers— a favorite method with the experts because the target was virtually defenseless and the crews of the Flying Fortresses were exposed to the hail of bullets— was also out because the combined approach speeds made such an attack impossible. In practice we went back to the old, conventional attack from behind, approaching the bomber formation— with of course a tremendous speed plus— through the defensive fire of the rear gunners and letting off our cannon at short range. The Me-262 was a pretty sensitive and vulnerable piece of machinery, however, and our losses turned out to be higher than we had feared."

Encountering the enemy jets for the first time was quite a shock for the P-51 pilots of the Eighth Air Force. So accustomed to being top dog, the Mustang jockeys were forced to admit that the jets were at least 75 mph faster in level flight. However, they reckoned that the 262 were much less maneuverable than the P-51 or even P-47, they accelerated more slowly and the engines appeared to be the target to shoot for when training guns on the enemy. Twenty-two year old Capt. Charles "Chuck" Yeager of the famed 357th Fighter Group (Col. Irwin H. Dregne) found that his P-51 steed, "Glamorous Glennis III," could not keep up with *Kommando Nowotny* on November 6th:

> "...north of Osnabrück we spotted three Me-262s going 180 degrees to us at two o'clock low. We were at 10,000 feet. I and my flight turned to the right and headed the last man off. I got a hit or two on him before he pulled away. They were flying a loose V-formation and they did not take any evasive action, but seemed to depend on their superior speed. They pulled out of range in the haze."

The Germans at Achmer were quite aware of these shortcomings. Even given all the difficulties, technical and tactical, Nowotny's advanced fighters claimed 19 victories in their first month of operations for a loss of six Me-262s in combat and another nine lost to accidents. The attrition on the highly prized German jet pilots was severe; more pilots were lost to accidents with the fickle jet engines than in dogfights. After all, the average experience level of the German pilots flying the jets was less than ten hours on the type. On November 8th *Kommando Nowotny* picked up its activity, flying several sorties against a bomber raid. Lt. Franz Schall felled three escorting Mustangs in a single outing, although was himself shot down (he bailed out after being hit by Lt. James W. Kenny of 357th FG) and Nowotny reported his third kill in the Me-262. However, even with the jets' superior speed, the P-51s got the better of the action and two of the Me-262s were shot down. Tragically, one of these was Nowotny himself. The holder of the Knight's Cross with Diamonds was killed as he tried to bring his machine back to Achmer with his left engine out. Picked off by Mustangs of the 20th and 357th FGs while at slow speed, his Me-262 plunged out of the clouds to auger into a meadow near Bramshe. So ragged had become the loss rate of the unit, that it was temporarily withdrawn from action for reorganization. It was to become operational within a few weeks as *Jagdgeschwader 7* at Lechfeld. The new detachment was to be commanded by Obst. Johannes Steinhoff.

In was decided in May of 1944 that the experienced Maj. Robert Kowalewski's *KG 76* would be the first Luftwaffe unit to receive the jet-powered Ar-234 bomber now starting to come out of the Arado factory. The only operation of the 234 in the summer of 1944 was as a high-performance camera carrying reconnaissance aircraft. Flying as *Kommando Sperling* the *Staffel*-sized unit demonstrated the dramatic capabilities of the B-series aircraft in several spectacular reconnaissance missions over the Allied invaders in August and later in the fall. After months of complete inability to gather aerial reconnaissance *Kommando Sperling* gave the Luftwaffe ability to scout Allied rear positions freely at will. The plane was a tremendous success.

But the *III/KG 76* under Hptm. Dieter Lukesch would be the first unit to be equipped with the revolutionary bomber. Lukesch first flew the plane in July; it was love at first sight. It was very fast, easy to control and with the bubble glass nose possessed excellent visibility. On August 26th the first two bombers were delivered to the unit. Conversion training from their Ju-88-A4s beginning almost immediately near Magdeburg. All the pilots chosen had extensive experience and Lukesch found that training went smoothly, although some had trouble with horizontal stability since the pilot was so far forward that there were no engines or wings to look at to help keep one's bearings.

Helmut Rast was one of the chosen pilots. Rast had been a 19-year old student at Munich Technical School when the war broke out and soon became a flight instructor. However, he was bored with student flying and in 1943 obtained a transfer to the Luftwaffe's major proving center at Rechlin as a test pilot. There he tested the very latest products of German genius, many of which were extremely dangerous in the test phase. But his personal favorite was the new Arado 234B— the "*Blitz*"— then in preparation for its assignment to the Luftwaffe as a reconnaissance aircraft. Rast found the jet a thing of beauty. The bubble-nosed bird handled smoothly and was exceptionally fast. Rast's reputation flying the 234 rose quickly, being enlisted to conduct a mock combat with a Fw-190A, at the time one of the leading German piston powered aircraft. Rast's 234 easily outpaced the Focke Wulf in level flight and was faster in climb and descent. One performance limitation was the 234's turning radius which was very wide relative to the piston-powered fighter. But the major weakness was acceleration; the throttles of the Junkers Jumo 004Bs could not be changed rapidly during takeoff and landings. Vulnerable to attack, the low speed on approach or takeoff could not be changed quickly enough to execute defensive maneuver. Regardless, Rast's superiors were greatly impressed by his mock combat. He was promoted to *Unterfeldwebel* and was eagerly assigned to the post of the first combat unit to use the 234, *III Gruppe* of *KG 76*. At Burg the pilots trained in earnest with their new craft.

There were problems with the bird, however, which had not really completed flight testing. "Hardly any aircraft arrived without defects," and Lukesch remembered they "were caused by hasty completion and shortage of skilled labor at the factories." Training continued throughout the fall, hampered by the slowly accumulating number of aircraft and a variety of accidents associated with the new type.

Two methods of aiming the 3,000 lb bomb load were developed. The first was to drop the bombs during a shallow dive with special periscope sight and a trajectory calculator; the second involved putting the jet on automatic pilot at high altitude and then using the *Lotke 7K* bombsight to release the bombs automatically after the target was centered in the crosshairs. This advanced technique had considerable safety advantages since high-speed, high-altitude flight could be maintained where the Ar-234 was nearly invulnerable to slower Allied fighters. However, Lukesch felt the method impractical since the Allies quickly learned to attempt attacks on the speedy jets from above with the faster piston types— particularly the Tempests, and having one's hands on the control and able to see behind the aircraft was vital to survive such assaults. Installation of the technically advanced autopilot also slowed the delivery of the aircraft to the unit and it was the end of October before *III/KG 76* had 44 Ar-234s available.

Training conversion continued in earnest for the fledgling jet unit in November, although plagued by accidents. Some problems, such as getting used to the tricycle landing gear, were due to differences with the Ju-88, but a variety of troubles arose from the machines themselves. One unexpected problem was that the two Jumo 004 engines were too powerful for their own good and an unladen Ar-234 could easily approach the speed of sound where Chuck Yeager's demon lived. A good example is the experience of Uffz. Ludwig Rieffel who was hurt when he mysteriously lost control of his Ar-234 near Burg on November 19th:

> "The effects of nearing the sound barrier were virtually unknown to us at this time, the high speed of the aircraft sometimes surprising its victims. Rieffel was practicing a gliding attack when he experienced a reversal of the controls at Mach 1. He bailed out successfully, but the shock of the parachute opening at that speed ripped three of its sections from top to bottom. A freshly plowed field prevented him from being seriously injured. This happened later to Oblt. Heinke...but he was unable to escape from the aircraft which crashed into the ground in a vertical dive..."

At the end of November *KG 76* was reaching its operational strength with 68 Ar-234s on hand. On December 1st, the famous bomber ace and veteran of some 620 operational sorties, Maj. Hans-Georg Bätcher, took command of *III/KG 76* to take the jet bombers into action. With so many bomber units now disbanded, Bätcher had the pick of the German bomber pilots. Pilots with the unit included Hptm. Diether Lukesch, holder of the Ritterkreuz with Oak Leaves and veteran of some 372 missions, as well as Hptm. Josef Regler, a veteran with 279 operational sorties under his belt. Unlike the fighter pilots, where the attrition and demand for pilots often meant low skill levels, the pilots with the *Gruppe* all had extensive flying experience.

Regardless of the minor danger posed by these small groups of German planes, the Allies had a phobia about them and kept their bases at Achmer, Hesepe and Rheine under constant surveillance. Only the profusion of

20mm flak around the bases and a standing guard of German piston-powered planes allowed the jets to get off the ground or land without being shot down during the vulnerable portion of their flight. Still the German bases harboring the jets received much unwelcome attention. A carpet bombing raid on the Rheine base on November 13th killed many members of *KG 51*.

Similar to the teething troubles of the Me-262 jet, Dr. Heinkel's entry, the He-162, was designed to use another problem-plagued turbo-jet (BMW-003E-1). And perhaps more significantly, with only one engine, the reliability of the turbojet powerplant would be critical. Operationally, the short-ranged fighter was intended for employment against the enemy escort fighters as soon as they crossed into German territory to cause them to drop their drop-tanks and leave the bombers open for attack from the conventional German fighters. Galland, however, was totally opposed to this aircraft. Not only did he believe it to be of "dubious airworthiness," but he also questioned whether the plane would ever come into production soon enough to alter the outcome of the war.[19] Certainly it's production would detract from assembly of great numbers of a proven design such as the Me-262. Even more fanciful was the plan to use Hitler Youth hastily trained in gliders to fly the *Volksjäger*. Regardless of such assessments, outlandish schemes called for production to be expanded from 500 to over 4,000 per month in salt mines and underground factories in Germany. But all this took on the special air of delusion typical of the last six months of the Third Reich. Neither the *Volksjäger* nor the Me-262 would be ready for the Ardennes in quantity; the main fighter available would be the Me-109 with which Germany had begun the war in 1939.

Regardless of their type, German aircraft numbers rose in a spectacular fashion that fall: from the end of the summer debacle on the ground in August of 1944 to the middle of November, German single engine fighter strength increased from 1,900 to 3,300 planes— a nearly twofold increase. The new aircraft were added to the day fighter force in the form of six new fighter *Gruppen* and by increasing the established strength of lower echelon units. This improvement resulted in an increase from three to four *Staffeln* per fighter group and each *Staffel* was increased from 12 to 16 aircraft. In December alone, a total of 2,953 new aircraft were delivered from the factories to the Luftwaffe. Indeed, so plentiful were the planes that the main problem was finding capable, warm bodies with which to fly the machines and aviation-grade fuel for the intended missions. Piston fighter aircraft

---

19 For all its shortcomings, the He-162 was remarkable in many ways. It was a cheap, lightweight machine which was designed to be built from readily available materials and in large numbers. It's take-off weight was just over 6,000 lbs.— less than half that of the Me-262. The "Salamander" was intended solely as a short-range day fighter with a range of only 385 miles with its sole armament provided by two 20mm cannons. Later trials of a captured He-162 by Allied pilots revealed that it was aerodynamically unsound and could have never been a satisfactory combat aircraft. The most innovative feature was its ejection seat, which would have likely become important to its pilots' survival had the plane become operational in large numbers.

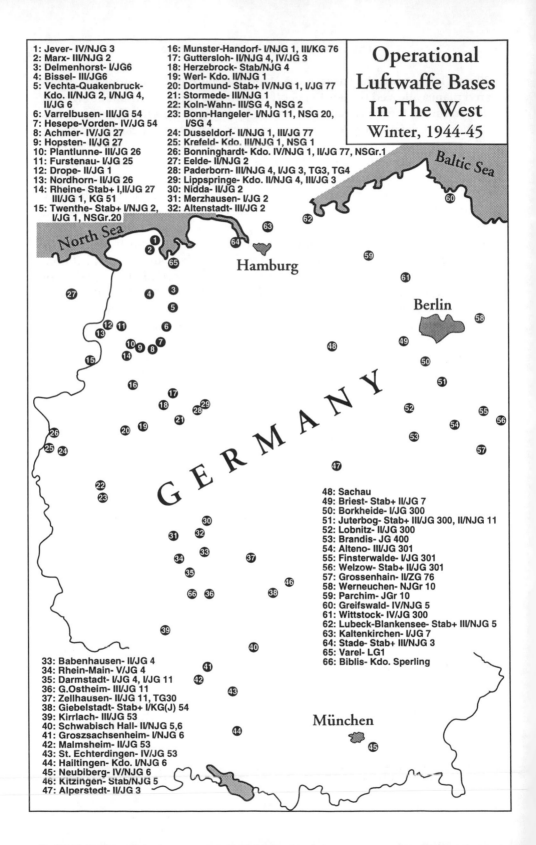

1: Jever- IV/NJG 3
2: Marx- III/NJG 2
3: Delmenhorst- I/JG6
4: Bissel- III/JG6
5: Vechta-Quakenbruck-
   Kdo. II/NJG 2, I/NJG 4,
   II/JG 6
6: Varrelbusen- III/JG 54
7: Hesepe-Vorden- IV/JG 54
8: Achmer- IV/JG 27
9: Hopsten- II/JG 27
10: Plantlunne- III/JG 26
11: Furstenau- I/JG 25
12: Drope- II/JG 1
13: Nordhorn- II/JG 26
14: Rheine- Stab+ I,II/JG 27
    III/JG 1, KG 51
15: Twenthe- Stab+ I/NJG 2,
    I/JG 1, NSGr.20

16: Munster-Handorf- I/NJG 1, III/KG 76
17: Guttersloh- II/NJG 4, IV/JG 3
18: Herzebrock- Stab/NJG 4
19: Werl- Kdo. II/NJG 1
20: Dortmund- Stab+ IV/NJG 1, I/JG 77
21: Stormede- III/NJG 1
22: Koln-Wahn- III/SG 4, NSG 2
23: Bonn-Hangeler- I/NJG 11, NSG 20,
    I/SG 4
24: Dusseldorf- II/NJG 1, III/JG 77
25: Krefeld- Kdo. III/NJG 1, NSG 1
26: Bonninghardt- Kdo. IV/NJG 1, II/JG 77, NSGr.1
27: Eelde- II/NJG 2
28: Paderborn- III/NJG 4, I/JG 3, TG3, TG4
29: Lippspringe- Kdo. II/NJG 4, III/JG 3
30: Nidda- II/JG 2
31: Merzhausen- I/JG 2
32: Altenstadt- III/JG 2

Operational Luftwaffe Bases In The West
Winter, 1944-45

48: Sachau
49: Briest- Stab+ II/JG 7
50: Borkheide- I/JG 300
51: Juterbog- Stab+ III/JG 300, II/NJG 11
52: Lobnitz- II/JG 300
53: Brandis- JG 400
54: Alteno- III/JG 301
55: Finsterwalde- I/JG 301
56: Welzow- Stab+ II/JG 301
57: Grossenhain- II/ZG 76
58: Werneuchen- NJGr 10
59: Parchim- JGr 10
60: Greifswald- IV/NJG 5
61: Wittstock- IV/JG 300
62: Lubeck-Blankensee- Stab+ III/NJG 5
63: Kaltenkirchen- I/JG 7
64: Stade- Stab+ III/NJG 3
65: Varel- LG1
66: Biblis- Kdo. Sperling

33: Babenhausen- II/JG 4
34: Rhein-Main- V/JG 4
35: Darmstadt- I/JG 4, I/JG 11
36: G.Ostheim- III/JG 11
37: Zellhausen- II/JG 11, TG30
38: Giebelstadt- Stab+ I/KG(J) 54
39: Kirrlach- III/JG 53
40: Schwabisch Hall- II/NJG 5,6
41: Groszsachsenheim- I/NJG 6
42: Malmsheim- II/JG 53
43: St. Echterdingen- IV/JG 53
44: Hailtingen- Kdo. I/NJG 6
45: Neubiberg- IV/NJG 6
46: Kitzingen- Stab/NJG 5
47: Alperstedt- II/JG 3

were abundant and pilots often found it more expedient to take a new plane than repair a damaged one:

> "We simply went to the depot nearby, where they had hundreds of brand new 109s — G-10s, G-14s and even the very latest K models. There was no proper organization anymore: the depot staff just said, 'There are the aircraft, take what you want and go away.' But getting fuel— that was more difficult..."

Even the jets were not exempt from the petrol shortage. An *OKL* circular commanded that J2 jet fuel must be carefully conserved. The German jet bases were hauling the world's most advanced aircraft to the end of the runway with oxen:

> "...the monthly production, compared with possibilities of consumption, is very small. As the jet engines have a relatively high consumption rate, it is absolutely forbidden for these particular aircraft to taxi under their own power prior to taking off and after landing...Remember that the Me-262 consumes 200 liters of J2 while taxiing for five minutes under its own power."

In spite of strenuous efforts Hitler's hope of "2,000 jet fighters by fall" never materialized. As it had been for the last five years of war, the Me-109 and Fw-190 would carry any German hopes of contesting Allied air power. As for filling the cockpits of the new aircraft, the German plans were sublime; it was anticipated that many of the needed personnel would come from the now moribund heavy bomber command or superfluous reconnaissance units now disbanded. Whether there would be fuel for any of this remained a major question.

IV

Secret Weapons, False Hopes

For those who fervently wanted to believe there was still some hope for Hitler's Reich, there were the "wonder weapons." "You were extremely lucky that the war did not last another year or that we were unable to start to use our weapons one year earlier," Göring told his captors after the war. His adjutant, Obst. Bernd von Brauchitsch, elaborated:

> "On the air and in the press there was more and more talk of new secret weapons and things of that kind. No one could believe that all this was merely invented by propaganda, for it was unthinkable that in such a matter of life and death any government could deceive its own people...It was only in that firm conviction that the civil population faced up to the ghastly sufferings of the bombing war."

The Nazi propaganda minister certainly did his best to increase Allied worry. For instance, after the catastrophic bombing of Hamburg in 1943, Josef Goebbels took to the airwaves telling of a recent visit to a Reich factory, where he had seen "weapons that froze him to the marrow." Certainly not all was hoax. The German genius of Professors Kurt Tank, Willi Messerschmitt and Werner von Braun had repeatedly shown that. There was even alarm earlier in the war that the Germans might be on the verge of realizing atomic weapons. And since summer, 1944 the Germans had been regular bombarding London with one of its secret weapons. This was the pilotless Fieseler Fi-103 V1 (short for *Vergeltungswaffe* or Vengeance Weapon). This was a pulse-jet powered robot bomb, carrying 1,870 pounds of explosives to a range of 150 miles. Long perceived as a threat, beginning in late June, 1944, the Germans were launching over a hundred V1s at London each day. However, British and American pilots had quickly learned that these low flying buzz-bombs could be easily sighted and then shot down by intervening anti-aircraft units or intercepted by speedy piston-powered fighters. Still the V1 campaign was imminently successful in tieing down British and American aircraft sorely needed elsewhere.

On October 21st, a new phase of the robot bombardment began when the targets were changed to Belgium, particularly the port of Antwerp and the Allied controlled rail center at Liège.[20] As the Germans planned their last great offensive in the West, they schemed to use the weapons to hit Allied targets to the rear of the front. Installed as the *155 Flak Regiment (W)* under Obst. Max Wachtel, the V1s were to be used in mass at night when interception was difficult. Between mid-December and the end of the year some 740 flying bombs and 924 V2s were launched from German sites in Holland. East of the Ardennes, several launching sites were located just east of Blankenheim. The robot bombs growled over Tondorf over the crossroads village of Losheim and on towards Liège. One participant in the V1 crews firing the bombs remarked how the German population in the line of fire lived in fear for their lives nightly as about one third of the bombs fell immediately after they had been fired. Many homes in Tondorf had been destroyed and a number of civilians killed. But conditions on the other line of the flight path were even more dangerous. The IX TAC combat operations headquarters relocated to Liège on December 19th and found the city under a frightening attack:

"Living there was not the same peaceful existence it was in Charleroi. Liège continued to be the main Continental target of the flying bombs. In Vervicro we used to anxiously listen as the V-1s sped overhead. But when the men moved to Liège they learned to appreciate the feeling of having the bombs land all around for 24 hours a day...One day during lunch a flying bomb fell near a chow line that was approximately 150 yards from the Headquarters building. Fortunately, that particular bomb had a delayed action fuse. One-half hour later the bomb exploded, but there had been sufficient time to permit the personnel and equipment to be evacuated...Another buzz bomb fell near the officer's quarters at the Hotel Moderne. Several windows were broken by the blast. The enlisted men lived in an orphanage, but after a flying bomb killed six men of the 926th Signal Bn, almost half of them moved in the cellar..."

The terrifying German V2 rocket could not be intercepted. This was the advanced 12-ton liquid-fuel A-4 rocket, which after being vertically launched into the stratosphere in a huge arc, approached its target without warning at hypersonic speed. Although inaccurate, and a military flop, the rocket was without a doubt the European war's most spectacular weapon.

---

20 This was not strictly true, since a Heinkel 111 unit, *KG 53*, was set up to launch the V1s while airborne from under their starboard wing. Already obsolete and lumbering under the heavy load, the modified He-111s could only operate a night. The accuracy and reliability of the V1 was also reduced. An example is enlightening: On the night of December 24, 1944 *KG 53* launched some fifty V1s at Manchester from off the east coast of England near Bridlington. Only thirty of the Fi-103s survived to cross the beaches; just 11 dropped within 15 miles and only a single bomb fell in Manchester proper. To add to the insult, an RAF night fighter shot down one of the He-111 intruders.

The thoughts of Obst. Johannes Steinhoff probably reflected those of many in the German army during this bleak time:

> "Only once, as I was climbing one of those winding pass roads in the Wester-wald and one of the new rockets (my retribution!) shot up with a flash and a roar and disappeared into a low cloud, did I feel something akin to pride at the fact that, on our knees as we were, and with the enemy long fighting on German soil, we were still capable of this kind of technological achievement."

One trouble with the rocket was its limited load of explosives. While Hitler called for 900 V2s to be manufactured each month and fired off, the 1000-plane Allied bomber fleets were dropping an average of 3,000 tons of bombs on Germany each day. The 24-ton load of the explosives of the thirty V2s fired off each day would only amount to the bomb load of twelve American B-17s— and twelve inaccurate heavy bombers at that. It was an absurdly disproportionate effort to manufacture the V2s compared to their limited military effect. Albert Speer, who had approved the V2 effort, called the project "one of my most serious mistakes."

However, by the end of November, 1944, the Germans were regularly delivering on their promise to bring these secret weapons to bear. There was no defense against the ton of high explosives carried by each missile and between October, 1944 and the end of hostilities the Germans hurled 1,115 against England and 2,050 against Brussels, Antwerp and Liège. But what of the further promises for miracle weapons?

In fact, these developments were a large reason for any remaining German optimism in the fall of 1944: Increasingly bizarre— and desperate— "secret weapons" were coming to German runways to oppose the Allied bomber fleets. These included the manned Me-163 Komet rocket interceptor, which although possessing fantastic speed, acceleration and rate of climb was hindered by its woefully short 25-mile range and seven minute flight duration.[21]

One of the more outrageous projects included the Bachem Ba-349 *Natter*. This was a human piloted rocket interceptor, which blasted off vertically, propelled both by solid fuel and liquid rockets. It was to be fired directly into the path of a bomber stream. Theoretically the pilot would take control

---

21 The futuristic *Komet* exhibited fantastic performance: on May 10th, 1941 German test pilot Heini Dittman had reached the terrific speed of 601 mph in the bullet-shaped rocket plane. The Germans at Lippisch/Messerschmitt were also working on a much longer duration version of the interceptor, the Me-263, which had a longer, better shaped body to house more propellants and was to use the more powerful (and somewhat less dangerous— more *Komet* pilots were lost to accidents than combat) BMW 708 nitric acid rocket motor. The rocket plane was fitted with two motors, one for cruising and the other for performance. A prototype (163D V1) completed in the spring of 1944 showed a flying time of nearly one hour with the fantastic top speed of 620 mph, reaching maximum altitude (49,000 feet) in just over three minutes! Fortunately, the tooling for the Me-263 was never completed amid the chaos created by the Allied bombing effort. In order to make the rocket interceptor useful at all, it had to be posted by tantalizing targets for the Allied bomber force. Later in the war, the *Komet* was often grounded due to shortages of its caustic fuels, a devilish hypergolic brew of *C-Stoff* (methyl alcohol, water and hydrazine hydrate) and *T-Stoff* (highly concentrated hydrogen peroxide).

after the solid boosters dropped off. Still under rocket power, he would close with the enemy at nearly 600 mph while loosing a shot-gun blast of cluster rockets from its nose as it sped through the bomber formation. In theory the pilot would push a button after his firing pass and the rocket would break into three sections which would come down by parachute! The disposition of prospective *Natter* pilots, who were to be given only cursory training in gliders, must have been exceedingly grim. The first human piloted test of the futuristic rocket on February 28, 1945 ended in the death of Lt. Lothar Siebert when the cockpit canopy tore off during its rapid acceleration from the launch stand. Amazingly, seven manned launches would be successfully completed by the time of the German surrender and although an operational unit was set up, it was never used. The German effort to bring such weapons to fruition illustrated in great detail the pitfalls of developing unproven advanced technologies on a crash schedule.

The development of high-speed aircraft had clearly demonstrated the need for "stand-off" weapons. For this, there were advanced anti-aircraft missiles in development. This included two unmanned anti-aircraft guided surface-to-air rockets, the Henschel Hs-117 *Schmetterling* (Butterfly) for hitting bombers at medium altitudes and the pint-sized V-2, the EMW *Wasserfall* (Waterfall) for use against Allied planes at high altitude. A plane launched air-to-air wire-guided missile, the X-4 *Ruhrstahl* was even nearing trial use.[22] Albert Speer believed that these projects could have made a crucial difference in the outcome of the air war had the proper decisions been made and the unproductive V2 project abandoned. The promise was especially great since Dr. Alexander Lippisch, the genius behind the revolutionary Me-163, was working on mating such a missile system with an infrared sensing system that would seek out enemy aircraft by the heat from their engines— the heat seeking missile:

"We would have done much better to focus our efforts on manufacturing a ground to air defensive rocket. It had already been developed in 1942, under the codename Waterfall, to such a point that mass production would soon have been possible, had we utilized those technicians and scientists busy with rocket development at Peenemünde under Werner von Braun...the Waterfall rocket was capable of carrying approximately 660 pounds of explosives along a directional beam up to an altitude of 50,000 feet and hit enemy bombers with great accuracy. It was not affected by day or night, by clouds, cold or fog...we could surely have produced several thousand of these smaller less expensive rockets monthly...To this day I think that this rocket, in conjunction with the jet fighters, would have beaten the Western Allies' air offensive against our industry in the spring of 1944..."

In a private memo dated June 29, 1943, Professor Carl Krauch had informed Speer of "the necessity of concentrating heavily on antiaircraft

---

22 Other significant German secret weapons systems were in development. One potentially revolutionary development consisted of infrared sensing equipment for German night fighters that its developers claimed would allow a deadly advantage over the British and American night fighters.

weaponry, on the C-2 device or Waterfall. We must be able to deploy it at once and on a large scale...every man-hour devoted to speeding this program will yield results proportionately far more effective for winning the war than the same resources invested in any other program. Delaying the program can mean the difference between victory and defeat." But the decisions advocated by Dr. Krauch were not made. With the V2 effort, according to Speer, "our most expensive project was also our most foolish one."

And if these scientific-weapon developments were not bizarre enough, the Germans were developing an ungainly piggy-back missile system called the *Mistel* (Mistletoe)— a pet project of Dietrich Peltz, the Luftwaffe bomber commander. Intended for use against hardened enemy targets, this was based on a Me-109 fighter rigidly mounted atop a pilotless Ju-88 bomber with the crew compartment replaced by a four-ton warhead. The idea was that the pilot in the Me-109 would control both planes and pilot the combination to within a half-mile of the target, then break free of the robot bomb, which would then fly straight line to the target before detonating. More than a dozen of these strange beasts were produced, operating under the providence of *KG 66* and the enigmatic *KG 200*. A big drawback with the Mistel system was the need for visual guidance by a ground or air-based operator to control the missiles to the target. Automatic homing systems, which would have made them much more deadly both in day and night use, were not yet available.

In spite of the signs otherwise, many in the Luftwaffe were still convinced that a new German miracle weapon would redress the military balance at this late juncture and ultimately give Hitler victory. When Speer visited various field commanders in the fall of 1944 he was embarrassed to be asked in hushed whispers "when the secret weapons would be coming along?" Even though Speer told them that there were none, most of those inquiring smiled knowingly. They didn't believe him. The armaments minister wrote Hitler of his misgivings on the issue:

> "Belief in the imminent commitment of new, decisive weapons is widespread among the troops. They are expecting such a commitment within a few days or weeks. This opinion is also seriously shared by high-ranking officers. It is questionable whether it is right, in such difficult times, to arouse hopes that cannot be fulfilled..."

Certainly not all Germans held out hope for miracle weapons at this stage. A *Kanonier* with the *401st Volkartillerie Korps* was witness to the field demotion of a highly decorated soldier. Although, the man was a veteran of WWI and a holder of the *Ritterkreuz*, his superiors busted him to buck private before sending him off to a penal battalion. And all this punishment came from the simple retelling of a joke that was making the rounds:

> Allied bombers are dropping hay on Germany.
> Why is that?
> For those asses who still believe in the *Vergeltungswaffen* (vengeance weapons)!

V

Adolf Galland and the "Big Blow"

Adolf Galland was a living legend in the German air force of 1944. Galland's credentials as head of the German fighter forces stood imposing. His distinguished career spanned the entire war. He had been a part of the close support Condor Legion in Spain and flew Hs-123 ground attack aircraft in the assault on Poland. He transferred to *JG 27* in 1939 and later moved to *III/JG 26*. He managed several victories in France and was heavily engaged in the fighting against Britain in 1940 and 1941. There his star rose quickly; on May 1, 1941 he shot down his 70th victim only to be shot down himself twice in the same day! During his career, Galland shot down 104 enemy aircraft. He was only thirty years old when he was made head of the Fighter Forces in November of 1941. So promoted, he was the youngest general in the Wehrmacht at the time.

Galland looked the part of the experienced veteran pilot: he was a masculine and well-built man with angular features and a professional polish. His shaft of slicked-down thick, black hair looked very non-German, which was true. His mother was French. Galland sported a well-groomed moustache and his dress was impeccable. Both handsome and famous, Galland was an incurable ladies' man. He forbade the men in his command to marry, which he believed dulled their fighting spirit. But he himself lived with two women, saying that he must set a proper example for his men. There is little doubt that Galland affronted many: he was brash and outspoken with a professed fondness for big Brazilian cigars.

In the fall of 1944, Adolf Galland, as *General der Jagdflieger*, faced a daunting prospect— the Luftwaffe was nearly absent from the skies over

Europe. However, in observing the continuous decline of the Luftwaffe during 1944, one lesson emerged from fighting the Mustang escorted Fortresses: individual or small group attacks against the bomber formations proved fruitless. Only on those occasions when a significant number of German fighters could be brought to bear to establish anything like numerical parity, were there any reasonable results. Digesting this kernel of truth, Galland devised an ingenious, if desperate plan he called *"Der Grosse Schlag."* The "Great Blow" was designed to cripple the U.S. Eighth Air Force in a single one-day massive retaliation to the day bomber force.

> "This was going to be the largest and most decisive air battle of the war. On November 12, 1944 the entire fighter arm was ready for action: eighteen fighter groups with 3,700 aircraft and pilots, a fighting force such as the Luftwaffe had never possessed before. More than 3,000 of these were waiting for the "Big Blow." Now it was a question of waiting for favorable weather, as good weather was one of the essentials for mass action. It was a difficult decision to hold back the defensive fighters, which were standing by in the face of the air armadas dropping gigantic bomb loads daily, but contrary to my previous experience, the leaders (ie. the High Command) kept calm and did not insist on vain and costly forced action..."

As Galland envisioned in his bold blueprint, no less then eleven battle units— at least a thousand of the new fighters— would storm the bombers of a single heavy bomber mission of the U.S. Eighth Air Force headed into Germany on a clear day. Four hundred of the fighters would then take off in second sorties that would eliminate damaged bombers. In addition, some hundred night fighters were to take to the air to intercept and kill off crippled Allied bombers attempting to reach refuge in Switzerland or Sweden. With wave after wave of attacking German fighters, Galland reckoned that at least 300 B-17 and B-24 bombers would be destroyed. Speer and Galland estimated that even with an exchange rate of one German fighter for each bomber— and they were prepared to lose up to 400— the aerial attrition would be advantageous to the Reich. Galland hoped that a success might even call a temporary halt to the Allied daylight bombing offensive against Germany. Even Göring supported the plan:

> "I must have 2,000 fighters in the shortest possible time, even if the battle fronts get nothing at all...The schools will have to make do with repaired aircraft. And then I shall want the 2,000 to be increased to 2,500. I must be in a position to meet any incursion into the Reich with 2,000 fighters. Then heaven help you if you don't send the enemy to the blazes!"

Whether Galland's spectacular plan for a massed counteroffensive against the day bombers would have inflicted significant damage to the Allied air effort is still a subject of considerable speculation. Some historians see it as another lost German opportunity. Others suggest that the results would have been much less favorable than Galland had estimated. All this hindsight is now academic, however, since *'Der Grosse Schlag"* did not take place. On one issue, there is general agreement: Galland's plan stood a much greater chance for success than did the eventual aerial Armageddon in which the German piston-powered fighter force was sacrificed. How, then, had Galland's influence fallen so that he could no longer influence air operations? To Hitler, the answer was simple. The Luftwaffe had failed him, and Galland like Göring was guilty by association.

Increasingly, Göring and his changing chiefs of staff were able to exert little influence in matters concerning the Luftwaffe, which more often than not fell under Hitler's own hand. The poor weather in the fall made impossible the planned massive employment of the German air force in Galland's "Great Blow." And more and more as autumn gave way to winter, Hitler's plan for his massive counterstroke in the West and its need for air support served to put Galland's plan for *Der Grosse Schlag* onto the back shelf.

In mid November Göring called a two-day conference at Gatow airfield near Berlin. All the high ranking air commanders of the Luftwaffe attended. The meeting was convened in a simply furnished "Third Reich style" conference room. A massive table stood at the room's center with simple chairs organized about it. A huge portrait of Hermann Göring hung on the wall with a bronze bust of Hitler juxtaposed against engravings of the other Teutonic military standards: von Moltke and, the eternal Third Reich favorite, Frederick the Great. German fighter *experten* Johannes "Macki" Steinhoff, Gunther Lützow and Adolf Galland waited for the meeting to commence. Steinhoff was struck by the extremely youthful appearance of the Luftwaffe's front line commanders. Presently Hermann Göring himself passed through the door. General Dietrich Peltz, the General of the Bombers, trumpeted his entrance as everyone stood up rigidly. "Gentlemen," Peltz called bolting to his feet, "The *Reichsmarschall!*"

The requisite pleasantries were dispensed. Göring took his seat at the head of the table. "Gentlemen," he began, "...I expect you to discuss in a critical manner anything in your service that may not— in your opinion— be satisfactory and that ought to be improved...I want you to help me give the Luftwaffe back its reputation. The German people expects that, because we have failed disgracefully. This is the Luftwaffe's darkest hour. The nation cannot understand why it is that the Allied bombers can come waltzing over the Reich as they did on the very day of our party congress and the fighters do not take off— because of fog, or because they are not ready or because they are indisposed..." Those around the table fidgeted nervously. They had heard all this before, the natural progression would ultimately move to a tedious diatribe of insults and ridicule. The blame came as expected: the faltering Luftwaffe morale, the cowardly conduct of the fighter pilots who do not close with the enemy, the endless meddling with changing the Me-262 to a fighter... But then Göring suddenly changed gears. "We are on the threshold of the battle that will win us this war!"

91

Few of the experienced Luftwaffe hands were stirred by Göring's obvious bromide. Then the expected letdown. He regretted that he had more pressing matters and could not personally conduct the meeting. He was turning over the "frank" discussion of Luftwaffe weaknesses to Gen. Dietrich Peltz, the General of the Bombers! And this while the German bomber forces had now lapsed into fuel-less ignominy. As if to assuage the ruffled feathers there was a sop to the fighter generals: "I should like to break the news that the General of the Fighter Pilots has been promoted to the rank of Generalleutnant. My dear Galland, I share your delight." Everyone clapped in perfunctory obedience. Galland shook hands and made a few polite remarks. When Steinhoff stepped forward to offer his congratulations, Galland whispered in his ear "Bad sign," he confided, "that means it won't be long now before they sling me out." Galland lit a big cigar and the discussion began. Predictably, the opening discourse was a litany of complaints: The night fighters were being asked to do too much and needed new aircraft; the day fighter situation was hopeless. Göring's restriction on even speaking of the Me-262 as a fighter lent an extra dose of pessimism to the discussion.[23] Only Gen. Peltz looked at the situation as one of opportunity. The generals of the *Jagdwaffe* could hardly believe their ears. Dietrich Peltz was advocating still another round of offensive bomber attacks on England. The last ones had failed miserably! Even a bombing retribution with a single squadron of Junkers bombers would meet the notion of "an eye for an eye." To Steinhoff, Peltz sounded like Hitler and Göring or the new SS men who were warily hanging around such meetings. The *Reichsmarschall*'s new right-hand man was concerned with flicking off a few token bombs over England, while the Allies were launching *thousand* plane raids over Germany *every day*. It was absolutely preposterous.

Mounting pressure to halt the Allied day bomber fleets threatened the very existence of the *Jagdwaffe*. In a meeting on October 26th in Berlin, Göring met with the various *Kommodore* and *Gruppen* leaders at a high-level conference. "Mustangs are practically doing training flights over Bavaria," Göring accused shrilly. He railed against his commanders, in particular eyeing Galland. He complained of cowardice, turning back from missions with minor defects and a loathing to close with the enemy. At one point the *Reichsmarschall* ripped the many medals off his chest and slammed them down in disgust. He would put them back on, he said, when his fighter pilots started shooting down planes again. According to Göring, both pilots and aircraft would shortly be coming out "on a conveyor belt" and that the despicable state of affairs must change. In regards to Galland's "Big Blow"

---

23 Peltz insisted that the Me-262 could be used to carry out bomb runs in bad weather by working out the approach and bomb trajectory mathematically in advance. Johannes Steinhoff and other dubious fighter pilots had witnessed his "pathetic" attempt at this during the fall. "...[It] just goes to show that he's never been in a dogfight and has no idea what aerial combat is like at 8,000 meters."

Göring issued a stern challenge. "Unless you bring down 500 Fortresses in the next big raid, you *will* go to the trenches!" The *Jagdwaffe* leaders would be henceforth accountable for the heavy bomber penetrations and even the *Geschwaderkommodore* would fly. So challenged, Galland would test the waters almost immediately.

Allied air supremacy over Germany remained crushing. With the Luftwaffe increasingly absent, the British now joined the Americans in the daylight bombing. On October 14th, in broad daylight, over a thousand heavy bombers thrashed Cologne and a similar number returned to hammer at Duisberg later that night. But German capabilities to respond were increasing. On November 2nd, a vast armada of 1,174 heavy bombers of the Eighth Air Force penetrated into Central Germany hunting for the notorious German fuel facilities at Gelsenkirchen, Castrop-Rauxel and Leuna. Because missions against German oil production usually brought out the Luftwaffe, the fighter accompaniment for the bombers was exceptionally heavy— some 968 P-51s, P-47s and P-38s flew along including a contingent from the Ninth Air Force.

The Allied air planners were more right than they knew. In the German camp the Luftwaffe was ready to try its massed fighter tactics— at least on a limited scale. It was to be a "Mini Blow" version of Galland's *Der Gross Schlag*. Four hundred and ninety German fighters scrambled to meet the American raid although only three hundred made contact due to the weather. For the most part there was 90% cloud cover down to 1,500 to 3,000 feet and only about two miles visibility. In the wild aerial fight that followed, the Germans lost 120 fighters (and 70 aircrew) while only shooting down 50 of the bombers. Three *Staffel* leaders were killed. The P-51 escort could verify that the Luftwaffe took a beating. The 352nd, 20th and 55th Fighter Groups (Col. George T. Crowell) claimed 38, 28 and 17 German aircraft destroyed respectively, for the loss of only eight of their own. In all the Americans claimed 134 German aircraft. According to German records 98 aircraft were lost with 24 of these in the *Sturmstaffeln*.

The ranks of the German fighter units were decimated. Hardest hit was *JG 27* which suffered 26 killed or missing and 12 wounded. Against this blow, the Luftwaffe was only able to knock out seven of the enemy's Mustangs. To place this catastrophe in perspective, it is useful to note that the losses suffered by Obst. Rödel's *JG 27* on this day was greater than its total losses in the twenty months of the North African campaign!

The German anti-aircraft units reported they had outdone the *Jagdwaffe*— claiming 32 more Flying Fortresses shot down.[24] The murderous fire came

---

24 U.S. sources would indicate that only 14 of the bombers were shot down by flak. It is possible and even likely that the claims by the fighters and anti-aircraft involved considerable double-counting. The losses acknowledged by the USAF amounted to only 40 heavy bombers with some 26 of these taken down by the German fighters. The American accounts also recognized that the *Sturmböck* had been the primary killers— a quarter of the losses were attributed to *JG 4*. The 91st Bomb Group lost 13 B-17s to the

from the *14th Flak Division* which ringed the Leuna plant. Still, in spite of the heaviest flak and the greatest sacrifice on the part of the fighters, the B-17s of the 3rd Division flattened their target with 2,648 tons of high explosives. Leuna would produce no more.

Hitler closely scrutinized the available numbers. They revealed that 30 of the downed bombers had been shot down by only 61 armored Fw-190A-8/R2 and R6 planes of two *Sturmstaffeln* units (*IV Gruppe, JG 3* and *II Gruppe, JG 4*). Two of the bombers were brought down by ramming, but at tremendous cost, when *IV/JG 3* completed its mission Hptm. Wilhelm Moritz at Schafstädt counted 15 missing; *II/JG 4* lost nine. Four had been wounded and came back by parachute; the other eleven were killed including Obst. Werner Gerth who rammed a B-17 and was unable to bail out of the falling mass of wreckage.[25] The Me-163 rocket planes at Brandis, charged with protection of Leuna, scrambled three *Komets* into oblivion. Ofw. Rolly was killed when his craft crashed on take-off and Ofw. Bollenrath and Starznicky made several unsuccessful passes at the bombers only to be dispatched by patrolling P-51s as they glided back to Brandis. When Hitler learned of all this at *Wolfschanze* four days later he launched his own personal inquisition. The Luftwaffe pilots claimed to have shot down 82 American aircraft although the actual figure was 56 (40 bombers and 16 fighters). With Werner Kreipe expelled from Hitler's headquarters it was left up to Gen. Christian and his junior, Maj. Herbert Büchs, to explain the failure. Both were pensive, they could see a Hitlerian rage coming on:

> Hitler:...I've taken another fresh look at the whole thing and my conclusion is that eighty machines have been recently shot down...Of those 80, 50 were shot down by fighters and thirty by flak. We'll discount the 30 for the moment. The Luftwaffe had 490 machines...
> Büchs:No, 305. The whole fighter wing at Frankfurt failed to make contact and of Jagdeschwader 4...
> Hitler:All right then, 305— it comes to the same thing. And among those, he said an assault *Staffel* with 42 machines was committed. This assault *Staffel* shot down 30 machines on its own.
> Büchs:There were two *Sturmgruppen*
> Hitler:With altogether...
> Büchs:With altogether 63 aircraft of which 61 made contact.
> Hitler:Right 61.
> Büchs:They shot down 30 heavy bombers.
> Hitler:That leaves 20 over. If you take away these 60 machines from the

---

concentrated attack of one of the assault units.

25 The volunteer pilots of the *Sturmstaffel* were required to sign a promissory note of almost suicidal effect: "I herewith promise to destroy, either by shooting or, failing this, by ramming, at least one enemy bomber on every mission on which I encounter enemy aircraft." The slow, heavily armored Fw-190s of the *Sturmgruppe* had to strongly rely on fighter cover for protection. Without such a protective umbrella, the casualties in the *Gruppen* were almost always large— a fact quickly discerned by the Allied air commanders seeking to disarm the potentially deadly tactics.

305 that leaves 240. So 240 machines made 20 kills in all, and themselves lost...30 in the *Sturmgruppen*.

Büchs:Yes, 30 in the *Sturmgruppen*.

Hitler:And the rest lost 90. Then we have 240 sorties with 90 lost and 20 kills altogether.

Christian: One point, the *Sturmgruppen* has another *Gruppe* with it to provide cover.

Hitler:I don't give a damn about that. The covering *Gruppe* must shoot [down bombers] too. It wasn't just bombers that were shot down—some fighters too.

Büchs:Yes, that's clear.

Hitler:Then the result is thoroughly unsatisfactory.

Hitler mused on these disturbing statistics with an eye to how a much larger expansion of the operation might fare. The operation he was thinking of was Galland's "Big Blow." The preamble on November 2nd had produced the greatest Luftwaffe losses of the entire war. To Hitler there appeared a very real chance of losing his entire air force in one day.

"That's a miserable result. I put in 260 fighters and get 20 kills. So if I put in 2,600 I get 200 kills. That means I just can't count on these machines producing any...and they're pouring out of the factories at the devil's own pace. They're just eating up labor and materials."

Finally, Gen. Christian stepped forward. "The real reason, mein Führer" he began, "is that the boys hadn't flown for ten days." Hitler would have none of it. "Reasons, reasons! We're always hearing about reasons." Christian was clearly exasperated, "Well that's the way things are."

Once more the German leader threatened to disband the *Jagdwaffe* altogether and solely concentrate on the flak arm. At least they were still knocking out Allied planes on a regular basis. Hitler struggled to comprehend the result and its implications for any future German success in the air war:

"This proves once and for all that either the pilots or the machines are no good. We can't argue that it's the pilots because it is they who get shot down! So it must be the machines. But, I have quite the opposite view of the Luftwaffe—their aircraft are good. The whole thing is ridiculous. If I try and work it out, I can't make the answer add up."

On November 21st, the Luftwaffe rose once again to challenge the Eighth Air Force. The objective of the 1,149 bombers and 858 escorting fighters was familiar— the Merseburg oil yards. The weather on the 21st was foreboding. A low-pressure front promised poor flying conditions over Central Germany, but visibility was still clear to the west. In recent months the Luftwaffe had established the fact that its fighters could not operate in sub-standard conditions without excessive loss. Other than the all-weather *JG 300* and *JG 301*, the other fighter groups lacked the radio, landing aids and, most of all, the training to effectively operate in less than ideal conditions. Committing them to fly in masse in the murk on that Tuesday would entail unwarranted sacrifice of the many green pilots— the *Nachwuchs*. But the desire to test the waters for *Der Gross Schlag* persisted at the Luftwaffe High Command; a victory would give the "Big Blow" the green light. Not only were *JG 300* and *JG 301* committed, but elements of five other fighter wings were cast into the fire: *JG 1, JG 2, JG 4, JG 27* and *JG 54*.

The German fighter command counted on the Americans to turn back before reaching the bad weather over the target. In this way they could mete out their punishment as the bombers turned back into the clear air. However, the flock of B-17s pressed on into the overcast, running into German fighters after they had planted nearly 500 tons of bombs on the target. The German *Gruppen* were still gathering in the overcast when they were surprised by P-51 Mustangs of the 352nd and 359th Fighter Groups. Many of the German fighters scarcely had time to jettison their drop tanks before they were shot down! Scores of Me-109s and Fw-190s tangled with the Mustangs in confused fighting in the clouds and rain. The Germans lost at least 61 aircraft while downing some 25 B-17s and 15 fighters. One *Gruppenkommandeur*, Hptm. Burggraf, and two *Staffel* leaders were killed. *I Gruppe, JG 1* with 20 aircraft destroyed was nearly wiped out. Even the assault *Staffel* of *III/JG 4* could not make it through the screen of buzzing Mustangs. And when the bombers retired from pulverizing the oil at Merseburg the fighters of *JG 27* and *IV Gruppe/JG 54* hove in to take their share of the wrath of the U.S. fighter escort. This time it was the P-47s of the Ninth Air Force's 366th Fighter Group. Fifteen German aircraft bit the dust. The operation was a total failure.[26]

The reason for the discouraging performance was fairly obvious to the front-line Luftwaffe commanders. Many of the participating pilots lacked even elementary operational experience. A number of those lost were on their first combat mission, having barely learned to fly circuits and bumps in the cantankerous Me-109Gs. Young students from flying schools were being posted to first line units before they had even mastered flying an Me-109, much less fighting with one. Such pilots were pitifully prepared to take on navigating themselves back to base and landing, much less taking on a seasoned and well equipped enemy in a dogfight.

Even after these disasters the Luftwaffe persisted in its attempt to stage a successful version of the "Big Blow." This time they would wait for blue skies. On November 26th, the weather was clear with unrestricted visibility when the U.S. Eighth Air Force struck once more with a thousand plane fleet bound for Hanover. But no sooner did the German fighters rise to contest the American moves, than the Mustangs pounced on them. In particular, the

---

26 An ULTRA intercept on the evening of November 21st recorded the losses to *I Jagdkorps*: 6 pilots killed, 33 missing and 20 wounded. Sixty-five aircraft did not return from the operation. This compared remarkably well with Allied claims of 71 aircraft destroyed.

home defense fighter group, *JG 301*, suffered its darkest day, losing 26 pilots killed or missing in a single engagement. *JG 27* suffered four pilots killed or missing and *IV/JG 54* lost Oblt. Heinz Sterr, a Knight's Cross holder with 130 victories under his belt. But most importantly, the unfavorable loss ratios of November 2nd and 21st were repeated. The Luftwaffe lost 98 aircraft (the Americans claimed to have destroyed 114) to shoot down 34 bombers and nine fighters— the most disastrous exchange yet. The U.S. 339th Fighter Group (Lt. Harry W. Scruggs) alone accounted for 29 of the kills. The next day, the 500 bombers of Doolittle's Eighth set a course to hit German marshalling yards in the Rheine-Main area. Even with the weather beginning to sour the Germans rose once more to oppose the swarm of American bombers. Minutes later many of the pilots were either swinging under their parachutes or plunging to a fiery death over Germany. The Luftwaffe lost over 50 planes (the Americans claimed 98 although German records reveal that 37 were killed or missing and 14 were wounded). While the *Jagdwaffe* managed to fell 15 American fighters, but they were unable to drop even a single bomber. The U.S. 357th FG claimed 30 German aircraft and the 353rd (Col. Ben Rimmermann) another 18.

The final insult came on the last day of the month, November 30th. The usual thousand-bomber group headed into Central Germany to pound German oil again. However, the weather was very bad and most of the sensible Luftwaffe commanders considered attempts at an interception out of the question. Unable to fly solely on instruments, most of the green pilots would be killed, if not by the wasp-like Mustangs, then by their inability to find their way back home. But as fate would have it Hermann Göring was visiting Jüterbog airfield on an inspection that day and demanded that *JG 300* put aircraft up to contest the intrusion. The *Geschwaderkommodore*, Oblt. Walther Dahl, refused to commit his *III Gruppe*. Less than half of its thirty pilots could fly on instruments. As the two argued, the other two *Gruppen* blundered into the bomber stream. Four of the German planes making contact were picked off as they emerged from the clouds. As *1 Jagddivsion* had feared, many of the other scrambled planes were unable to find their way back, forcing the green flyers to abandon their aircraft and take to their parachutes. The Americans had lost 29 bombers in the actions that day, mostly due to flak. Not a single one of the losses was due to damage from enemy fighters.

Although the GAF was at last operating on a large scale (some 400 and 750 sorties on the 26th and 27th), clearly working up to *"Der Gross Schlag"* proportions, the results were disheartening. The returning P-51 pilots of the Mustang groups attested to the apparent inexperience of their German adversaries. An example was the experience of Lt. J.S. Daniell of the 339th Fighter Group who shot down five Fw-190s in the actions on November 26th in his first combat of the war. Simple arithmetic showed a horrific Luftwaffe situation at the close of November. Regardless of the figures chosen, the German air force was losing at least five aircraft for every one of the enemy it destroyed.

For the month of November, *I Jagdkorps* reported the loss of 404 aircraft and 244 pilots against 155 enemy planes shot down. The disparity with respect to enemy effectiveness was not lost on Hitler. The experience of November 2nd had already eroded any remaining confidence he had in his air force. "I don't want to say anything against the pilots," the German leader declared, but "any hope of achieving decimation by mass tactics can be dismissed out of hand. So it's nonsense to keep on producing machines just for the Luftwaffe to play numbers games with..."

Hitler had, in fact, dismissed Galland's strategy. His assessment, however, had missed a central fact: courage and bravery in the air was no substitute for experience and skill. The declining quality of Luftwaffe pilots was the main reason for the poor results from the November operations. A quick examination of the planes flown by the leading German aces in the War showed that most were flying lower performance aircraft— Me-109s. Although the technical characteristics of the planes was undeniably important, training was often the supreme deciding factor in aerial combat. As the Red Baron is reputed to have said, "It's not the crate, but the man who is sitting in it." Indeed, Hitler would have found it enlightening to hear the opinion of Luftwaffe pilot skill from the leading American ace in the ETO, Maj. George E. Preddy, Jr. Preddy had made his twenty-fourth confirmed kill during the great aerial battles that raged over Central Germany on November 2nd. His after action report gave a telling assessment of his enemy:

> "The boys we are facing today aren't as good as the ones we battled a year ago. The current crop is not experienced. They were aggressive when we raided Merseburg the other day, but they probably had orders to stop those bombers from hitting the target regardless of cost. Well, they paid plenty. It looks to me like they are conserving their air power all the time, but on important targets they go to it."

Anticipating a short war, the Luftwaffe was never able to amass a reserve of trained pilots. Coupled with a ridiculously small aircraft production effort in the early years of the war, this handicap of too few pilots and machines allowed the Allies to steadily increase their numerical superiority over the skies of Europe. Later, as the sheer numbers took their toll, the quality of German pilots faltered, unable to keep up with the demands to keep thoroughly trained aircrew in their planes. In the fall of 1944 Johannes Steinhoff was the *Kommodore* of *JG 77*, stationed on the outskirts of Berlin to shield the German capital. Privy to Galland's plan for the "Big Blow," Steinhoff found himself deeply skeptical:

> "...We were given large numbers of new Messerschmitts. We were assigned young pilots who were timid, inexperienced and scared. We flew little (fuel

was in short supply), but were able to practice some formation flying and formation attacks on mock bomber flights. The young pilots were not yet ready for combat. It was hard enough leading and keeping together a large combat formation of experienced fighter pilots; with youngsters it was hopeless. They were just windy. They were expected to fly in precise formation, stuck in the middle of an enormous unit made up of more than a hundred fighters, keeping distance, height and spacing constant. They were supposed to watch their airspace and not let themselves be lured into dogfights with enemy fighters (they had absolutely no experience in aerial combat), and when the formation attacked the bomber armada they were told they must keep in position— come what may. It could never work..."

On December 6th Allied intelligence overheard Luftwaffe commanders worrying about the "state of training" of JG 4 and how it would influence their ability to provide close support to friendly forces; an inquest was ordered into the poor performance of II/JG 53. Indeed, training of German pilots had fallen to a sad state by the fall of 1944. After losing 31,000 aircrew between January, 1941 and June, 1944, the Luftwaffe had lost nearly 13,000 from D-Day to October. Appalling losses in the first half of the year had set the tone for the problem; the Luftwaffe suffered 2,262 pilots killed or missing from January through May of 1944— close to 100% of the front line air-crew strength of the day fighter force. This incredible attrition rate had far reaching effects on the Luftwaffe's ability to continue the struggle in the air.

While it was true that the Germans had instituted a program of "mass production" of Luftwaffe pilots in April of 1944, the basis of the program depended on a series of questionable assumptions and of the expediency of cutting the flying time of pilots in training. For instance, Allied intelligence officers interrogating captured Luftwaffe pilots in 1942 noted that the average pilot joined his operational unit with 210 hours of flying experience. But by 1943, this figure had fallen to 136 hours and when the "mass production" program was inaugurated, pilots were passed out into combat formations with only 112 average hours to their credit and only 34 hours when the experience in the operational aircraft type is considered. A single one-time expediency existed to vastly increase the fighter training output, which was conversion of volunteers from the bomber and reconnaissance forces. These were placed in a short conversion course— called *"Windhund"*— to introduce them to the cockpit of single-engined fighters in the shortest possible time.

The training for German pilots was conducted in three stages. The "A" schools where elementary flying skills were taught were quickly over-filled in spite of an edict to cut the number of hours of flying instruction from 72 to 52 and the overall time spent in the school from seven months to only eighteen weeks. The secondary fighter schools made similar concessions, with instruction reduced to a minimum of three months and training time to only forty hours. The final operational training course at the four *Ergänzungs Jagdgruppen* had already been cut in 1943 to a bare minimum of 14 days and 20 hours of flying in the operational type to be taken into combat. Meanwhile, the Ninth Air Force's IX Tactical Air Command mentioned in its fall report that its average pilot now had over 100 combat hours of flying experience above and beyond the extensive basic training received stateside.

Pressure to get German pilots out of training school and into combat units was so great that graduating pilots had half the training hours of their Allied counterparts. When the hours of training with operational aircraft are considered, the disparity was even greater. The typical German fighter pilot in late 1944 received 30-50 hours of training in the aircraft in which he would have to do battle; the Allied pilots averaged 225 hours. Obfhr. Hans-Ulrich Flade, who took part in the Me 109G conversion course in Rechenbach in 1944, described the frightening countenance of the few available veteran instructors:

> "I had almost completed my training as a reconnaissance pilot before I was posted to the fighter force, so my level of flying experience was well above average for students. In general the standard of instruction at the school was low: the front-line units were desperately short of experienced and capable fighter pilots, so the training schools had to make do with what was left. Many of the instructors had been 'flown-out' in action, and they were nervous, twitched and tired men who in many cases had spent up to three years in action and had crashed or bailed out many times."

Many of the newer planes, such as the 109 "Gustav," were less tolerant of mishandling. Should the pilot attempt to open the throttle too quickly in climb, the beast might suddenly flip over on its back and crash to the ground. The toll at the training schools from accidents was severe. Of the hundred pilots who trained with Flade, nearly one third were killed or seriously injured over the course of the 30-hour training program.

Even with these limitations, in the fall of 1944 the German fighter program as still capable of maintaining a steady supply of pilots to the operational units in spite of the increase in *Gruppen* strength from three to four *Staffeln*. However, this sufficiency was misleading. Theoretically the German schools could churn out 960 capable pilots per month. But this ideal proved unattainable. There was a chronic shortage of a suitable supply of petrol for training, long stretches of unreasonable weather for flight training and the disruptions to the schools in Eastern Prussia from the Soviet ground advance. Only about 300 pilots were turned out each month, and many of these can hardly be classified, with their abbreviated training, as more than fledgling flying enthusiasts to fill the brand-new cockpits turned out by Speer. The supply of capable unit leaders was also suffering from the increased losses and a new "Unit Leader's School" was opened by Maj. Johannes Wiese at Königsburg/Neumark. Here the pilots might learn important skills beyond the rudimentary such as gunnery practice, advanced dogfighting tactics and blind flying in weather. Many German pilots were not able to navigate by instruments, a fact blamed by many *Gruppen* leaders for the excessive losses during the poor flying weather of the fall of 1944. And as if these limitations were not damning enough, the extension of the Allied fighter range into the Reich posed another hardship. Luftwaffe training flights, both beginning and advanced, could now expect to frequently come under attack from roving American fighter squadrons.

Practical flying skills and an intimate knowledge of one's aircraft were crucial to survival in the skies over Western Europe at the close of 1944. Meeting the experienced and well-equipped Allied foe in combat would demand that the German pilot push his often obsolete aircraft to the very edge of its performance envelope. So sketchy was the training of many of the novice German recruits, that if the pilots pushed their planes to escape the Allied guns in the heat of dogfight, they might not be able to regain control of their planes before the limits were exceeded. Many nervous young German pilots reported forgetting to push the safety-catch off on the control column while grinding their thumbs on the firing button until they resigned themselves to being unable to fire back at the enemy. Either way, the odds were heavily stacked against the new German pilots in their unfamiliar planes. A properly packed parachute and a good working knowledge of popping the canopy and egress were probably high on the list of check-out items for new Luftwaffe pilots who expected to live past their first mission.

And although German fighter aircraft were numerous, they were not without defects— lots of defects. In order to rapidly expand aircraft production, Speer had greatly increased the use of impressed foreign workers in his underground factories. With this less than willing work-force came installed defects in many of the aircraft. The punishment for such sabotage— a swift summary execution— was not always a sure deterrent and many airplanes came off the assembly line with mechanical faults that made the job of the production test pilot hazardous indeed.

All these troubles greatly shortened the life expectancy of fledgling German flyers. New Luftwaffe pilots, with ever less skill, were lost at a steadily increasing rate. Of course, the pressure for new pilots was exacerbated by this trend; training schedules were further shortened to place warm bodies in the cockpit. Experienced Luftwaffe pilots called the green recruits "*Nachwuchs*"— new growth. Recalled Leutnant Flade of *II/JG 27*:

> "Each morning we pilots had breakfast together, and the replacements would come in. The older pilots regarded the newcomers as though they only had days to live— and with reason, for the standard of fighter conversion training was now so low that most of the new pilots flew only two or three missions before they were shot down. I remember many conversations along these lines— not exactly a cheerful subject for a young man who had just joined his first operational unit."

Field Marshal Hugo Sperrle, commander of *Luftflotte 3* in the summer of 1944 estimated that the average German pilot in late 1944 had only 8 - 30 days of active service under his belt— a telling indicator of the mortality rate of German flyers. Only about 10% of German pilots serving in the Luftwaffe in the war would survive unscathed. Most of these were the famous aces, such as Adolf Galland, Erich Hartmann, Heinz Bär and Josef Priller. An assessment shows that only eight of Germany's 107 aces with more than 100 kills joined the Luftwaffe after summer 1942. Thus, the Luftwaffe was now made up of two distinct classes of pilots, the few great aces who were killing machines, and the vast majority who were ill-trained and could scarcely navigate their way back to base. In fact, over 32% of German aircraft losses in the first half of 1944 came from non-combat related causes.

As it was, the Allies had a very good idea of the calamitous losses taking place on the other side. Based on interrogations and recovery of sortie information from dead German aircrew, Allied air intelligence could statistically discern that in late November, 1944 the average German pilot stood a 17% chance of not returning from his first mission and only a 29% probability of emerging unscathed from more than ten sorties. Whereas the monthly attrition rate for aircrews had been from 5 - 10% from 1942 to 1943, 1944 saw the loss rate soar beyond 20%. Meanwhile, Göring continued to lamely suggest that bold actions could make up for the greater experience of the average Allied flyer: "Our pilots must attempt to counterbalance this obvious advantage by greater enthusiasm and courage." The stage was set for a sacrifice of the Luftwaffe on an unprecedented scale.[27]

Even with German attempts at intervention, the Eighth and Fifteenth Air Forces renewed their massive campaign against German oil production— a campaign that was virtually guaranteed to starve out the Germans in a matter of months.[28] In October 12.5% and 5.9% of the American and RAF bomb weight was essayed again German oil. However, November saw the tempo of the oil campaign race, the fractional tonnage rising to 33% for the Americans and 25% for the British. In spite of Speer's best efforts, the Allied pounding paid off. Oil production started to fall once more; the armaments minister quickly rallied a virtual army of 72,000 workers, located in tent cities near the refineries, whose sole mission was to repair the blasted oil facilities. But even Speer's magic would not be able to raise production again. The Luftwaffe was now limited by more than the weather. Listening in late November, Allied intelligence overheard a telling message from Göring:

1) By reason of the strained fuel situation the following orders have been issued. Operations are to be ruthlessly cut, i.e. operations must only take place when the weather situation and other prerequisites promise success.

---

27 In contrast, the average aircrew loss rate per sortie of the IX Tactical Air Command ranged from 0.4 - 1.1% during the fall and winter of 1944-45 with the highest rate in December.

28 The oil plants hit included Gelsenkirchen, Merseburg-Leuna, Castrop, Sterkrade, Hanover, Harburg, Bottrop, Misburg, Bohlen, Zeitz, Leutzkendorf, Floridsdorf, Korneuberg, Vienna and Linz.

2) The following operations will be discontinued forthwith, and will be
   resumed only by special order:
   a. Night ground attack operations.
   b. Transport flights.
   c. Bombing and special operations (composite aircraft and mine
      detecting flights).
   d. Operations by *KG 53* are to be restricted to one *Gruppe* at a time
      (20 aircraft at most).

Even though diminished, the robot bomb carrying Heinkel bombers of
KG 53 were allowed to continue launching the pointless flying bomb attacks
against London. Days after the failed defense of the oil refineries at Merseburg, Göring was back with thinly veiled threats and exhortations to his
Jagdwaffe. In spite of this abuse and the dreary prospects of getting out of the
fighter service alive, morale among the *Jagdwaffe* pilots remained remarkably
high during the fall of 1944. Some of the newer pilots— the "freshmen" —
professed a near mystic belief in German invincibility even when captured
and exposed to the Allies' great numerical superiority. Part of this was due
to the oft heard propaganda refrain: "Life will not be worth living after the
war." Josef Goebbels had carefully depicted a horrific Germany if Nazism
should fail. Although the average Luftwaffe pilot was not particularly
political— especially when compared to the SS ground forces— the Allied
insistence on unconditional surrender struck a troubling chord. The dread
of the Soviets was severe: "*Sieg oder Siberian*"— literally "Victory or Siberia."
   Other circumstances inspired hope. Many young pilots believed that the
new jet-propelled aircraft would enable the Luftwaffe to make a startling
comeback. "In the autumn we were promised 2,000 fighters," one captured
German pilot optimistically insisted, "They have turned up and this makes
me prepared to believe that other new weapons will also turn up." Allied
interrogators studying their captured subjects in the fall of 1944 noted a
greatly increased fighting spirit in the Luftwaffe— some 62% of the average
23-year old pilots possessed what was termed "high morale," with this
reaching some 70% in the day fighter forces. But regardless of the unshakable
faith and courage of the German pilots, a new chapter was about to unfold
for the Luftwaffe. November had merely been a preamble for the final
journey down a sacrificial path. [29]

---

29 Interestingly, the Allied interrogators, during the Ardennes operations interviewing the "largest
batch of aircrew prisoners since the Battle of Britain," noted the most consistently high morale in *JG 4*
and *JG 2* with the worst fighting spirit in the down-trodden night fighters pilots.

VI

The War Below

On the ground in the West, at the beginning of December, the Allies were still struggling to force the enemy's hand along the Siegfried Line and the German border. The First, Third and Ninth Armies continued an unrelenting attack starting in mid-November to broach the Rhine River. The terrain was difficult; hilly thickly forested expanses with swollen rivers and roads made untrafficable by the mud producing rains. Early December was marked by a monotonous string of days with miserable weather: fog and haze sharply reduced air force operations, while the ground forces edged forward wallowing in the mud. But worst of all was the German resistance itself. Over the past weeks, the Germans had grown stronger with more artillery, and more determined troops; a resolute stand that required every ounce of Allied strength to extricate them from their Westwall bunkers.

Montgomery and the British were forcing the Germans from Holland; Patton was attempting to kick the enemy from the Saar and Gen. Bradley with the First and Third Armies was booting the Germans from in front of the Rhine River. Bitter fighting centered in the Aachen area where the enemy stubbornly resisted Gen. Courtney Hodges and his First Army's strenuous effort to reach the Roer River and its dams. To the south, the Germans were pouring troops into the Saar region to stop Patton's Third Army. During November von Rundstedt reinforced the western front with 16 divisions. Despite the crisis which appeared to be developing for the Germans— they were losing 10,000 soldiers a month— they had not yet committed the *Sixth Panzer Armee* which loomed as a counter-attack threat to the Allied forces.

In its sector, VIII Corps of the U.S. First Army cleared the approaches to the Roer during the first week of December and then hunkered down in the Ardennes in the cold snow and rain, harassing the enemy with artillery and patrols. Throughout the first two weeks of the month, stiff enemy resistance continued on the VII Corps front to the north which after finally breaking out of the deadly Hurtgen Forest, was faced with a hedgehog of defenses in the villages to the east. Bergstein, Gey, Brandenburg: each notorious hamlet was the scene of a desperate German defense. Fighter bombers torched most of the villages with incendiaries, but enemy counterattacks were launched against every American penetration. Then on December 13th the V Corps in the northern reaches of the Ardennes launched an attack on a narrow front towards the Roer dams. There was initial success, although some villages like gloomy Kesternich changed hands repeatedly. The Allies looked to be in reach of the dams at last. But the fanatic German defense did not bode well. Everyone expected a major counterattack when they finally reached the floodgates. Bradley craved to use the Ninth Air Force to pave the way for V Corps to the Roer— he asked SHAEF to approve a week-long continuous blitz on "every town, village, supply installation or facility between the Roer and the Rhine," but the soup-like weather made this impossible. To the fighter pilots of Pete Quesada's IX TAC, early December was one of the least interesting times in the war. Thickly overcast skies made conventional "what you see is what you destroyed" fighter missions impossible. Most of the response to Bradley's desire for persecution of the enemy before the Roer took the form of blind bombing. There was little glamour in this; the fighter pilot was little more than a truck driver who was steered to the target by an SCR 584 controller. He dropped his bombs at the controller's command, the bombs quickly sinking into the murk below. The bomb damage was rarely seen; "no results observed" became monotonously repetitive on the mission reports. Later everyone would also find out how poor the results were from such missions.

But no one in Europe was more frustrated by the weather that fall than Gen. George S. Patton, Jr. In charge of the U.S. Third Army, Patton was one of the most demanding and flamboyant of the Allied leaders. The commander of the Third Army had already been plenty frustrated by the weather all through his fall campaign in the Saar. The Germans seemed resolutely determined to hold onto Saarburg, his forces were short on fuel and his boss, Gen. Omar Bradley had even taken the key 83rd Infantry Division away from him. But worse than meddling and reneging from above was "the goddamned weather." Patton remembered the frustration of the static hedgerow fighting in Normandy in June and July of 1944. He also recalled how the air-bombing blitz had gotten things moving in his Cobra offensive, which eventually resulted in the sudden collapse of German resistance in Normandy and his own glorious advance to the German border. But the unending rains clearly made this type of operation impossible.

Working with Gen. Vandenberg, Patton had arranged some air support for the first day of December. Code-named "Hi-Sug," the affair was a concentrated 210 aircraft blind bombing blitz of the Germans stubbornly holding out in Saarlautern by the mediums of the IX BD. To assist the pistol-packing General's advance, and prevent the Germans from reestablishing their defenses, the XIX TAC flew some 281 sorties on December 2nd, paving the way for Patton's troops to finally enter the town. Even so, their progress was slowed by mines, booby traps and the usual tenacious German resistance. Two days later all of the town and the west bank of the Saar River were firmly in Third Army hands. Capture of a bridgehead over the river by the 95th Infantry Division overjoyed Patton. Maj. Gen. Louis A. Craig, in charge of the XX Corps there, directly attributed the span's capture to pounding by the medium bombers. That the Germans launched an immediate series of desperate attacks to erase the bridgehead— resorting even to explosive laden robot tanks— was proof to Patton of the prize at hand. What he needed now, the Third Army commander decided, was the ability to exploit his advantage. If this amount of air power had wrought a bridgehead, a St. Lô-style bombardment might catapult his command across the Rhine. He sought the advice of Gen. Weyland and his XIX TAC. Wrangling enough supply from Eisenhower along with massive air support, he believed he could breach the thorny German defenses and punch toward Berlin.

Gen. Otto P. "Opie" Weyland was in charge of the XIX Tactical Air Command that supported the Third Army. With pride, his men called themselves, "Patton's Air Force," only a slight exaggeration. Weyland, a native of Riverside, California, was a hard-boiled air commander— a style that distinctly suited his boss. Weyland was bitten by the flying bug while an engineering student at Texas A&M; he slipped out to fly on the weekends at Brooks Field. He soon found himself with a commission and signed up with Army air command graduating first in his class at the Air Corps tactical school in 1938. The 42-year old Weyland was a natural air leader: "I wrangled a combat command to take to Europe, which was the 84th Fighter Wing, but I was quickly reassigned as commander of the XIX Tactical Air Force," he later recalled, "We thought we were pretty good, we won the war!" Like Patton, Weyland was proud of his organization and wanted a really big mission to prove it.

On December 5th he got his chance. That Tuesday Lt. Gen. Spaatz called a meeting of all the senior air commanders at his headquarters near Paris. Attending were the kingpins of strategic bombing, Britain's Sir Arthur "Bomber" Harris and Jimmy Doolittle of the Eighth Air Force. The tactical people had been invited as well. Air Marshal Coningham represented the British 2nd Tactical Air Force and Vandenberg was there from the Ninth. Also in tow from Vandenberg's camp were Pete Quesada of the IX TAC, Weyland from the XIX, and Dick Nugent of the XXIX TAC. The Supreme Commander, Gen. Eisenhower, was the only ground forces commander invited. The meeting led off with the strategic air commanders describing their chief concern. Although progressing according to plan the strategic bombing effort was not taking the enemy to the precipice of economic collapse or surrender. A year before, Harris and Spaatz had optimistically ventured that their heavy bombers would defeat Germany without a land campaign, or even an invasion for that matter. But here they were facing another Christmas in Europe and their enemy showed no signs of quitting. Nothing, with the possible exception of the oil offensive, looked like it would bring the enemy to their knees. None of the Americans were interested in following the moral low-road of Harris' RAF Bomber Command in its terroristic area-bombing campaign— at least not yet. Spaatz and the leadership of the Eighth Air Force were morally opposed to proposals "throwing the strategic bomber at the man in the street."

Acutely aware of Eisenhower's distress with the slow going against the Germans' stubborn fall defense, Spaatz and Doolittle wanted to know if they might use their heavy bombers to do a tactical number on the enemy to get the war rolling again. Coningham demurred; this was not, he said, a proper job for strategic air power. When Pete Quesada's turn came, he ventured that he'd like to have the bombers knock out the Roer River dams which the Germans could use to flood the U.S. First Army when they tried to cross that river. After some discussion, it was decided that this would be too risky. Then came Weyland's chance:

> "I said I have a plan which would get our armies moving again and terminate the war much more quickly. I further said that I was associated with an Army which would really fight and that I had General George Patton's authority to commit his army. I did. I outlined the plan: First, Third Army given the go ahead and priority on supplies would advance to a secret line on the front. Second, on D-Day...all bomber forces would hit individual targets along the secret line in front of the army...Third, the Third Army would breach the secret line, advance rapidly to the Rhine River, cross it and go down the Rhine river behind the forward German armies...Eisenhower kind of grinned and said he'd buy the idea. General Spaatz agreed. I called General Patton and said I've just committed your army to an operation which will end the war in a hurry...I told him he would get top priority for everything he needed and that all strategic bombers and all necessary tactical air support would be put in front of him. Uncle Georgie said 'Hot Damn!' He was jubilant. The next day Generals Spaatz, Vandenberg and Doolittle arrived and confirmed the deal. Strategic air planners were sent to my headquarters. We worked up Operation Tink in detail. I wrote my wife Tink (Kathryn) and told her that she was going to get a rather unique Christmas gift..."

The detailed preparation continued while Patton's forces moved up to the "secret line" from whence they would jump off into Germany. On December 13th Weyland met with Patton and Vandenberg. With some 3,000 bombers escorted by another 1,000 fighter-bombers it would be "the biggest operation of its kind in history," he explained. "The ground forces must realize that this provides the surest way to a quick and decisive breakthrough." Operation Tink was to blow a hole in the German Westwall on December 19th. Patton was optimistic; his army would pour through— a terrific role for a reincarnated warrior.

Although Vandenberg and Doolittle assured their unlimited cooperation for such a strike, they pointed to the gloom outside and reminded Patton and Weyland that the weather was immutable: for best results it had to be good. It seemed as if it had rained for the entire month of November. Keenly frustrated, Patton summoned the Third Army chaplain, James H. O'Neill to his headquarters in Nancy on December 12th. Patton explained that he wanted to "get God on our side for a change." Patton informed O'Neill he wanted a spiritual appeal for better weather. A proper catholic, O'Neill resisted. He would be praying to God for conditions with which to kill. It made a mockery of the sixth commandment. "Sir," the chaplin politely replied, "it's going to take a pretty thick rug for that kind of praying." "I don't care if it takes the flying carpet," Patton boomed, "I want you to get up a prayer for good weather." So, there it was. O'Neill wrote the prayer.

> "Almighty and merciful Father, we humbly beseech Thee, of Thy great goodness, to restrain these immoderate rains with which we have to contend. Grant us fair weather for battle. Graciously harken to us as soldiers who call upon Thee that, armed with Thy power, we may advance from victory to victory, and crush the oppression and wickedness of our enemies, and establish Thy justice among men and nations. Amen."

The problem of losing his forces to the Supreme Command's desire for reserves was more troubling. To be sure, he ordered those divisions under his command not directly fighting to "get involved." Patton had a heartfelt contempt for idle front-line troops and made no secret of his disapproval of the relative inactivity of the U.S. First Army to the north. "The First Army's making a terrible mistake by leaving Middleton's VIII Corps static where it is," he wrote in his diary, "It's highly probable that the Germans are building up east for a terrific blow." On December 12th, the Third Army commander instructed his staff to begin studying counterattack plans should the Germans break through in the First Army sector. "If they attack us, I'm ready for them," Patton sighed, "but I'm inclined to think the party will be up north. VIII Corps has been sitting still— a sure invitation of trouble."

Eisenhower and Bradley carefully weighed the suggestions for use of their potent air weapon. With a combined move on the Roer dams to the north, and Patton slamming into the Germans in the Saar the enemy would be almost certainly stretched to the breaking point. One or the other tank team would surely get a bridge over the Rhine. Long coveted, a bridge over the Rhine was widely recognized as the surest key to the capture of inner Germany and the final dissolution of the German army. At least this was the theory. Adolf Hitler had other ideas.

General der Jagdflieger Adolf Galland. *(NA)*

Gen. Omar Bradley, in charge of the U.S. 12th Army Group and Gen. Dwight D. Eisenhower, the Supreme Commander of the Allied Expeditionary Forces (SHAEF) pose by a captured section of the "dragon's teeth" along the German Westwall. By late 1944, both men had warmed to the idea of tactical air power. *(NA)*

Hitler and the Iron Man. The two top leaders of the National Socialist Party enjoy the fanfare of the German crowds in happier days. *(NA)*

Gen. George S. Patton, Jr., commander of the U.S. Third Army, and Gen. Otto P. Weyland of the XIX Tactical Air Command. *(HRC)*

Kill over Merseberg. "Blue Streak" of the 486th Bomb Group goes down in flames on November 2nd. 2nd Lt. David Paris and the rest of the crew perished. Navigator 1st Lt. William Beeson was on his 32nd and last scheduled mission. The B-17 was struck by an 88mm shell which detonated the left main fuel tank. *(HRC)*

20mm Flak. These guns have been assigned to protect panzers unloading at a train station. The smaller anti-aircraft gun was commonly used against the low-roving Allied fighter-bombers. *(HRC)*

This B-26 Marauder has just received a direct hit by 88mm flak that has completely sheared off its right engine. The plane crashed minutes later. *(NASM)*

Arado 234. This two-engined German jet was a tremendous success. The Ar-234 gave the hard-pressed Germans both the capability for reconnaissance during late 1944, and an offensive bombing capability, albeit minuscule relative to Allied capabilities. The Ar-234 provided important reconnaissance of Allied dispositions in the Ardennes and available bridges over the Meuse River prior to the attack. *(NASM)*

Genmaj. Dietrich Peltz, commander of *II Jagdkorps* during the Ardennes operations. *(HRC)*

Genlt. Fritz Bayerlein, the commander of the elite *Panzer Lehr Division,* and his adjutant Maj. Wrede in the fall of 1944. *(H. Ritgen)*

An 88mm flak gun is fired against a ground target. Deadly against both aircraft and tanks, the "88" was a much feared weapon. The guns of *III Flakkorps* participated in the opening barrage of Hitler's Ardennes offensive. *(Bundesarchiv)*

Ground crewmen bomb-up a P-47 Thunderbolt of the 365th Fighter Group, the "Hell Hawks." *(NASM)*

Uffz. Alfred Nitsch had previously been a flight instructor when he was assigned to *III/JG77*. The Austrian officer trained in Neuruppin in the autumn of 1944 to learn to fly the new high performance Me-109K-4. *(Nitsch via Roba)*

Ju-52 "Auntie Ju" of *Transportgeschwader 3* which was brought down by AA fire in the Ardennes 1 km southwest of the village of Asselborn. *(NA)*

VII

Hitler Schemes; the Allies Unaware

The idea for the Ardennes Offensive had been born in the disasters of the summer of 1944. In Russia an entire army group was swallowed up and in the West the Allies landed at Normandy and liberated France by the end of summer. As it became apparent in early September that the German army might be able to hold onto a defensive line roughly on the German border, Hitler looked for some bold counterattack that could change his fortunes on the Western Front. In worrying about the effect of the Allied capture of the great port of Antwerp, the German leader found an inviting objective for a final offensive venture. For a German capture of Antwerp would certainly set back the Allied war effort in the West by months. Hitler affixed the location for the great offensive in the Ardennes, correctly believing that the Allies would only hold it lightly so that attacks into Germany could spring forth to the north and south of the notoriously difficult terrain. He quickly fleshed out the plan with his staff: an attack by two panzer and one regular army out from the Ardennes between Monschau and Echternach, sweeping across the Meuse River on the second to fourth day, bypassing Brussels and reaching the prize of Antwerp within a week.

So confident was the Führer in his brain wave, that he ordered the records drawn for the Blitzkrieg which had swept through this region in 1940. "A single breakthrough on the Western Front! You'll see! It will lead to collapse and panic among the Americans. We'll drive right through their middle and take Antwerp. Then they will have lost their supply port. And a tremendous pocket will encircle the entire English army, with hundreds of thousands of prisoners, as we used to do in Russia!"

The timing of the attack, slated for late November, was based on the earliest time that the German leader expected to be able to form his reserves. He also needed time to accumulate 17,500 cubic meters of fuel— a difficult task given the Allied aerial torment of that industry.[30] But one large exception to 1940 glared at the Führer and his generals as they ran their map exercises. More than anything else, Hitler required either Luftwaffe air superiority or bad weather. Without air cover, the Allied air forces would strafe their troops, bomb their tanks and destroy their supply lines. This certainly turned the tables on 1940, when the *Blitzkrieg* had been scheduled based on good flying weather for the Stukas. It was a telling indicator on the state of the German air force in the fall of 1944, that Hitler was more trusting of bad weather to shield his ground forces, than of promises of air support from Hermann Göring. Code named *Wacht Am Rhein* ("Watch on the Rhine"), the operation was not to begin without at least a five day forecast of poor flying weather from Hitler's chief meteorologist, Dr. Werner Schwerdtfeger.

> "...The only thing which is not in our favor this time is the air situation. That is why we are now forced to take advantage of the bad winter weather. The air situation forces us to do so. I cannot wait until the weather gets better. I would be happier if we could somehow hold off until the spring...I do not know whether the air situation will be any better in the spring than it is now. If it is not, the weather in the spring will give the enemy a decisive advantage, whereas now there are at least some weeks before there can be carpet bombing of troop concentrations. That means a lot..."

Days later the official record keeper at the *Wehrmachführungsstab* echoed this assessment in describing a discussion between Hitler and Gen. Jodl regarding prospects for the big offensive in the West. "The attack can only be carried out," Dr. Percy Schramm wrote, "at a time when the prevailing weather conditions will be a considerable handicap for enemy air forces."

Since surprise and secrecy was of the utmost importance, *Wacht Am Rhein* included an elaborate cover plan: the Germans would leak information that a large armored reserve was being accumulated to protect the southern entrance to the industrial Ruhr region. On October 21st the following message was sent from Maj. Gen. Eckhardt Christian at the *OKL Luftwaffenführungsstab*:

---

30 By mid-December the required accumulation for the offensive had been built up, albeit with only 7,500 cubic meters of petrol immediately on hand in the Eifel mountains. The original petrol allocation to the *Fifth Panzer Armee*, for example, was reduced from 3 to 2.5 consumption units (sufficient in the hilly Ardennes for only perhaps 125 km). Similarly, each tank of Hitler's namesake panzer division, the *1SS "Leibstandarte Adolf Hitler,"* had only 700 liters in their fuel tanks (2.5 consumption units). Resupply without an active truck convoy behind the moving panzers would be almost impossible. The rest was on the other side of the Rhine river and would require trucks or trains to bring it up— an egregious error on the part of the German logistical planners, for in transit it would be vulnerable to Allied air attack. The other problem was the actual available stores since the Germans reckoned on a 2,000 cubic meters per day consumption for the operation. Ideas of bolstering the available nine day supply with captured Allied fuel turned out to be quixotic fantasy.

Hitler Schemes; the Allies Unaware

"Basic Idea of the cover plan
Large scale attack to be expected against line Cologne-Bonn. To attack this from the flanks, two counterattack forces are to be formed, one northwest of Cologne, the other in the Eifel. Later to be concealed as far as possible, former to be made to appear more important. This is to be given as the reason for deployment of the Luftwaffe."

A lengthy series of instructions followed, all to give the impression that the phoney operation was for real. Movements were to be at night only in the Eifel area opposite the Ardennes whereas daylight unloading of troops was to be done in the Cologne area. The troop assembly areas were carefully staged a distance north and south of the breakthrough zone so as not to disclose the true intent of the far-reaching preparations. Special camouflage officers were designated and reconnaissance or artillery registration was expressly forbidden. All the more obvious moves, such as those of headquarters and armor units, were to be done only at the last minute. Of the greatest importance, the orders stressed, was that no wireless transmissions were to be made. All new arrivals would observe wireless silence, and without radio transmissions evidence of the build up from Eisenhower's "most secret source" vanished.

For the most part the Allies fell for the German ruse, mainly because it was what they expected. But at least as significant was that their top-secret intelligence weapon, ULTRA, provided few clues as to the German intentions. ULTRA had always forewarned the Allies of major impending enemy operations; no one suspected that the Germans might have caught onto this. As it was, the Allied top commanders were often aware of impending enemy moves with the subordinate commanders unwarned so as not to disclose Allied omniscience in intelligence matters. Gen. Pete Quesada of the U.S. IX TAC was one of the few lower level air commanders who were let in on the secret.

"On many occasions we were prevented from taking action that we would have taken had the information been obtained from another source. It was always felt that the retention of the source was more important than using it. Often using it would reveal its existence and it was very important to maintain the integrity of the system."

But used or not, so heavily had the Allies come to rely on ULTRA, that the G-2s, particularly Brig. Gen. Edwin L. Sibert, with the U.S. 12th Army Group, took the absence of direct evidence of a German attack as proof that one was not in the offing. And there was no overt sign of an impending German offensive from ULTRA. Or was there?

The fact was that the Germans had come to suspect that they had a security problem. Rather than the fallibility of their coding machine, a typewriter-like apparatus called Enigma, Hitler suspected that it was one or more internal leaks from his untrustworthy generals. Certainly the far reaching conspiracy associated with the attempt on his life on July 20th, 1944 did little to alter this perception. But the crowning moment, that showed the Germans that Enigma had been penetrated, may have come through the indiscretion of a member of the staff of Prince Bernhard of the Netherlands. The American intelligence service, the OSS, had long been concerned with the ability of the C-in-C of Dutch Forces to choose trustworthy associates. Their concern was warranted, for the Prince selected a certain Mr. Lindemans as his confidential agent. What Bernhard did not know was that 27-year old Christiaan Antoniius Lindemans was a very dangerous and shrewd double-agent who had been working for the German *Abwehr* since 1943. By November, SHAEF intelligence had found him out, but not before he had infiltrated the British sector of the Normandy beachhead the previous summer. In September he was able to get back to German intelligence at Driebergen where he was able to report the rather astounding fact that the Allies had broken Enigma. What is more, his other intelligence, that the British were about to stage a major airborne operation to seize a bridge across the Rhine was verified when the British began parachuting into Arnhem only a week later.

The German signals security chiefs had already begun to suspect that the integruty of their radio transmissions might be in question. In spite of some internal disbelief that Enigma could be broken all this seems to have filtered up to *OKW*. While it was true that use of radio would have to go on for simple military expediency, ULTRA or not, the Germans endeavored to make greater use of their field telephones as they retired to the natural safety behind their border.

So, it was perhaps with this in mind, that Hitler, when setting the ground rules for the planning of his surprise offensive, dictated that none of the orders related to the operation be sent over wireless. Instead a phoney defensive operation with the name *Abwehrschlacht Im Westen* (Defensive Battle in the West) was floated onto the airwaves. The hoax stated that the German armored reserves were to be used as the Allies threatened the Rhine crossings. For the most part, the Allied intelligence chiefs took the bait. This was precisely what their intelligence officers suspected, and their own prejudice aided the German delusion. Meanwhile, the security surrounding the true meaning of *Wacht Am Rhein* was extraordinary. Each of those brought into Hitler's confidence was sworn to secrecy through the signing of a declaration. And there was plenty of reason to obey their oath; if word leaked out they and their families would be shot! Hitler let only a few in on the plan. He did not even bother to inform his field marshals, Gen. Gerd von Rundstedt and Gen. Walther Model until October 22nd. There would be no mention or even acknowledgement of any of the operations associated with the attack by radio or telephone. All messages were to be delivered in person or by guarded courier.

The closest the Allies came to the secret was in a message decrypted from the Japanese. On November 15, 1944 the Japanese ambassador Baron Hiroshi Oshima met over lunch with Foreign Minister Joachim von Ribbentrop in Berlin. Oshima cabled the Japanese emperor the following day that "Hitler had promised him a German attack in the West" not realizing that the messages were straight away moving onto the ULTRA decrypt list. But Oshima clouded the intelligence with his own doubts as to the German Foreign Minister's trustworthiness: "In view of Ribbentrop's record...this can be recorded as one of the instances in which truth from the mouth of a liar reaches the highest pinnacle of deceptiveness." However, recently declassified documents show that the "COMINT (communications intelligence) gave clear warning of the German counteroffensive in the west...The timing of the attack was revealed only on very short notice...There were no clear indications of where on the front the attack was likely to take place, nor how big an effort it was to be." Most of the telling indications described in the declassified material came from the Luftwaffe preparations to support *Wacht Am Rhein*:

— From the last week in October ULTRA told the Allies that preparations were being made to bring the bulk of the Luftwaffe airfields to the West— a change in disposition that could only be interpreted as offensive in nature.
— By November 25 Allied observers noted a striking change in the organization of the High Command of the Luftwaffe and from 1 December, all measures were obviously being coordinated for fighter-close support operations to aid the attack.[31]
— Evidence that an attack was imminent appeared about 4 December with possible timing available from a message stating that pilots and aircraft were coming in "about 14 days," and imposition of radio silence on SS formations on 10 December.

That the various clues were not put together to form a cohesive picture of German intentions must be attributed to German deception and camouflage measures. American intelligence officers summarized the lapse in a secret study after the war: "The Germans had developed an extreme respect for Allied intelligence and distrust of their own countrymen...In this operation they gave false names, not only to their intentions, but to Army Groups and Armies. The deception proved highly successful". Germany's planning on the other hand, was greatly helped by the insecurity of certain Allied communications. Despite that fact that Gen. Bradley discerned a possible German attack in the West, he did not know where it would come (they expected to provoke a German response as they attempted to cross the Roer River) or in what violence (a limited spoiling attack). This was not worri-

31 An ULTRA decoded message intercepted on November 21st clearly portended imminent offensive operations: "According to the final decision of the *Reichsmarschall*, the fighter aircraft envisaged for the operations in the West are not to be equipped with bomb racks. These are to be stored...in such a way that they can be installed at any time..."

some enough to stop Allied plans. "At that moment," as Bradley himself wrote after the war, " nothing less than an unequivocal indication of impending attack in the Ardennes could have induced me to quit the winter offensive." Unlike the popular myth that Eisenhower and Bradley learned nothing from ULTRA of German intentions, they actually received numerous warnings of a coming blow. "It was," Bradley surmised, "a calculated risk." The Germans he believed, would have to be crazy to launch a full scale attack through the Ardennes. Allied intelligence was confident that cold, calculating von Rundstedt was in charge. Germany no longer possessed the troops or means to launch a large scale offensive; if they did their lack of fuel must surely doom the offensive from the start. "No damn fool would do it." But what the Allied oracle did not know that it was Hitler, and not von Rundstedt, who was in personal charge of the operation.

Even the German generals directly informed of the operation found it difficult to believe. Both von Rundstedt and Model objected to the plan's far-reaching goals when they learned of *Wacht Am Rhein*. Antwerp, they warned, was far too remote a military objective on which to stake Germany's last strategic reserve. Both field marshals were cold and calculating; futilely, they tried to get the German leader to settle for a more modest strike, such as recapturing Aachen, but Hitler would have none of it. He moved to his headquarters at Bad Nauheim on December 10th to await the start of the great attack. Nothing, he informed his subordinates, was to be changed. "This will be the great blow that must succeed...If it does not succeed I no longer see any possibility for ending the war well." It would be the *Ganzer Entschluss*— the "total decision." "There will be absolutely no change in the present intentions," Hitler declared. On December 2nd the Luftwaffe chief of staff, Gen. Karl Koller, cabled an optimistic assessment of the German capabilities for the coming blow:

> "Allied losses high, reserves largely committed, supply difficult, front thinly occupied at point of attack. In spite of German difficulties, full plan to be put into operation on Hitler's orders. Hitler agrees with C. in C. West [von Rundstedt] that it should be possible to seize Meuse crossings on first day... O-tag to be December 10, 44."

Genfldm. Model, who would be charged with carrying out the attack was deeply worried about Allied air power. For his part, he taciturnly informed Hitler and his aides that "We must have bad weather, otherwise the operation cannot succeed." Meanwhile, although the German army was strictly obeying Hitler's orders regarding the offensive plan, the Luftwaffe continued its lax policy of unrestrained radio transmissions. ULTRA listened in and discerned increasing signs of the coming German blow. Contrary to some post-war assessments, ULTRA was anything but quiet during this period. Some 40-50 decrypt messages were received from the European Theatre each day. The decrypts faithfully recorded the quadrupling of German fighter forces in the West, with enemy specifically called the assemblage a *Jägeraugmarsch*— a concentration of fighter-aircraft in a terminology that was almost always associated previously with an offensive operation. This was particularly odd, since a policy only two months before had concentrated the Luftwaffe fighters in Germany's heartland to fend off the bomber streams clobbering the Reich's industry. Now this was being reversed, even as the bomber forces stepped up their assault on German factories. Also, ULTRA decrypts began to fill with communiques regarding extensive rail and road movements to the Eifel region. On November 10th the Director General of Transport complained that the *2 SS Panzer Division* had fallen 36 hours behind schedule in its rail movement. The communique urgently requested that punctuality be ensured in the future. But for the Allied intelligence observers pondered this tidbit: why was it so important for an enemy armored unit to adhere to a strict schedule?

On December 2nd, *Heeresgruppe B* urgently called for the Luftwaffe to shield the unloading of its troop transports in the Moselle River Valley. These commands were not new, similar messages had been going back and forth for the last month. Within a week these requests would be asking for fighter cover over rail detraining points like Bitburg and Kall less than fifteen miles from the Ardennes front. Beginning in the last week of November, a series of orders were urgently issued each day. They called for top-priority aerial reconnaissance by the swift Ar-234B jet aircraft of *Detachment Sperling* (Sparrow). By the end of the month, daily reconnaissance mission requests were being filed for photographic snapshots of the bridge crossings over the Meuse River from Liège to Givet. They spelled out what they were looking for: the status of the bridges, the location of Allied supply and troop concentrations etc. The urgency of these requests increased almost daily.[32] ULTRA also announced that a big meeting was being held on December 5th of all the main fighter formations in the West: *II Jagdkorps, Jagddivisionen 1,3* and *5* and *Jafue Mittelrhein*. Why all this attention on this idle sector on the Western front? Then on December 10th came an ominous development: An intercept related the observation by *II Jagdkorps* that "SS units are maintaining radio silence." When this ULTRA was relayed to Gen. Patton, he immediately suspected trouble; his own army usually took to quiet on the airwaves just before a big attack.

---

32 On the receiving end were Oblt. Horst Götz (*Kommando Sperling*) and Lt. Erich Sommer (*Kommando Hecht*). The later made the first jet reconnaissance mission of the war on August 2, 1944 snapping a panoramic display of the American and British landings at Normandy from 35,000 feet, without the Allies even being aware of their existence! In late November the job of photographing the Meuse crossing became an unavoidable priority: "Constant bad weather in the target area as well as over our airfields prevent the execution of the job for over a week," remembered Sommer, "Finally, in the early morning hours of December 3, a radio message arrived directly from *Luftwaffen Kommando West* ordering the reconnoitering of the Maas river crossings between Dinant and Liege at whatever the cost." Sommer then proceeded to pursue a harrowing low altitude and ultimately unsuccessful mission. Later in the afternoon, however, Oblt. Werner Muffey from *Kommando Sperling* was able to take some suitable photographs in spite of a 3,300 ft cloud base.

On December 14th ULTRA listened in as the Luftwaffe ordered about its units with great urgency for undisclosed operations. Particularly noticeable, were orders to quickly move to Holland all three *Gruppen* of *JG 1*. The arrival of *JG 11* was a subject of constant inquiry while *II/JG 26* was ordered on the 13th to make ready to operate from Nordhorn without delay, regardless of its ability to fully re-equipment with methyl-alcohol boost. The same day the Allied code-breakers had learned that *JG 2* and *JG 4* were now fully equipped with bomb release gear as were *IV/JG 3* and *I/JG 27*. On December 9th ULTRA provided very strange news: evidently a German paratroop operation with some 100 Ju-52 aircraft was in the offing from Bielefeld-Paderborn. But the commentators decided that its intent "is probably to bring up paratroop reinforcements without delay to the Aachen sector, dropping being necessary due to lack of airfield facilities west of the Rhine...no suggestion that troops will be dropped in Allied territory." The intelligence pooh-bahs would regret their interpretation of this one. Meanwhile, transfer of *III/SG 4* from Kirrlach to Kirtorf was assigned special importance. This was a well known Luftwaffe anti-tank ground support unit. The ULTRA commentators added that this event:

> "supports other evidence indicating main German effort in the Cologne area. Further indication of imminent offensive intentions is transfer on 15/12 of 5./KG 51 (hitherto non-operational) to Achmer, thus building up Me-262 ground-attack force probably to maximum at present stage of training..."

The warning was very short, but the Luftwaffe's radio improprieties had all but foretold a German ground offensive. The ULTRA message on December 15th ended with a sternly worded warning:

> "...situation is now becoming such that Germans may decide to commit air forces on a major scale...the G.A.F. may entertain hopes, by striking a series of surprise blows, of securing the initiative for a sufficient period to enable it to exercise appreciable influence on the course of the campaign in the West..."

Conventional battlefield intelligence mushroomed as well. The aerial reconnaissance for Hodges' First Army was the responsibility of Col. George W. Peck's 67th Tactical Reconnaissance Group (TRG) with Quesada's IX TAC and the 10th Photo Reconnaissance Group (PRG) who flew for Weyland to the south. The 363rd TRG of Nugent's XXIX TAC provided the eyes in the extreme north. But the practical worth of the assigned units was greatly diminished due to the weather. In the month from mid-November to December 16th, there were ten totally non-operational days for all the groups and many missions were unsuccessful due to excessive overcast and troublesome navigational equipment. Only 242 of the 361 missions flown during the period by the 67th TRG were even partially successful. During the weeks leading up to the big offensive, much of the staged German movement was under the cover of darkness. It was thus unlucky for the Americans that the

Allied ability to see at night over the Ardennes was greatly hampered by the few worn out P-61s available.

In spite of dreadful weather, the sightings by "Peck's Bad Boys" of the 67th TRG increased each time they were able to take a look. On the last day of November, the pilots observed heavy rail traffic along the Euskirchen-Münstereifel railroad with twenty flat cars loaded with uncovered Tiger tanks. A sharp increase in rail traffic in the Cologne area was seen on December 3rd-5th with speculation from the pilots that the camouflaged cars were covering armor or other motor vehicles. Additional heavy motor traffic was observed in the northern reaches of the Ardennes around Nideggen. Closer to the Ardennes front, many dug-in gun positions were seen in the area between Dreiborn and Hollerath. Poor weather made observation impossible on December 6th and 7th, but pilots of the 422nd Night Fighter Squadron (NFS) reported seeing hooded lights along the banks of the Rhine River during the evening hours. Two days before, the 425th NFS reported "exceptionally heavy motor vehicle traffic" between Saarbrucken and Kaiserlautern. Missions flown on the days with passable weather— 8, 10, 11, 14 and 15 December all showed pulsing rail traffic west of the Rhine with many reports of "canvas-covered flat cars loaded with tanks or trucks." Even so, the full extent of the German activity was concealed as the enemy moved their tanks and troops up in stages by night. As the German attack approached, few of the 67th's "airspionage" missions were in the zone opposite VIII Corps and all of the executed missions were over Trier. The reason was the weather.

But so vast was the German concentration, that not all movement could be carried out solely at night. The 366th Fighter Group, flying a day mission on December 10th in the Zulpich-Euskirchen area, sighted German rail cars carrying 50 tanks which were then attacked for claims of four. On the same day the 368th FG discovered a train of 25-30 flat cars carrying covered tanks or trucks near Prüm. The bombing Thunderbolts claimed at least eight of the tank-carrying rail cars. And on December 14th a long serpentine column of German infantry was sighted marching south from Heimbach with more than 120 trucks seen west of the woods around Dahlem. On the same day, Lt. Chester H. Frahm of Peck's command, flying over the northern Ardennes, reported a long convoy of tanks and infantry passing through Schleiden.

The evidence from the XIX TAC's 10th PRG to the south was also persuasive. On the second day of December, a large volume of rail traffic was noted east and west of the Rhine in a triangle from Trier to Limburg and Ludwigshafen. A large number of trucks were sighted not far from Echternach. On December 5th "flats loaded with what appeared to be armor" were seen on the heavy rail traffic between Frankfurt and Bingen. On the following evening the 425th Night Fighter Squadron reported seeing numerous road bound convoys between Kaiserlautern-Homburg and Traben-Trarbach.

Daylight observations by the 10th PRG saw intense road traffic in the same area on December 12th and 14th including searchlights and stacks of boxes along the roads in the Moselle River valley.

On the ground American soldiers heard the sounds of tank treads, and civilians reported large collections of German equipment and weapons just across the Our River. But all of this seems to have made no real impression. On the day before the German offensive, Eisenhower's G-3, Maj. J.F.M. Whitely, in a briefing to the air commanders on the ground situation, had dismissed the Ardennes with a simple "nothing to report." The real question after the war became how the Allied intelligence community did not suspect an enemy operation in the Ardennes.[33]

Maj. Gen. Kenneth Strong, the head of Allied intelligence for the Supreme Command, even went so far as to warn Gen. Dwight D. Eisenhower and Gen. Omar Bradley, 12th Army Group, of the possibility of an enemy spoiling attack in the Ardennes. "The enemy's hand is dealt for a showdown before Christmas," he warned. Eisenhower, who had experienced the cunning of his cornered enemy in North Africa, was mindful of the possibility of a "nasty little Kasserine" and asked Strong to have a word with Bradley. Strong ventured down to Luxembourg City to visit with Bradley and Maj. Gen. Edwin Sibert, his G-2.

A graduate of the same 1915 West Point class that had produced Eisenhower, Gen. Omar Bradley was known as the "infantryman's general." The 12th Army Group commander had a reputation for being stubborn, informal and clearheaded. No monkey business. Those in his headquarters reflected their boss; his intelligence people were immediately inclined to dismiss the possibility of a major German attack, pointing to the continuing dirge of ULTRA decrypted reports describing the poverty of enemy troops, weapons, and most of all fuel. They argued that even if the enemy did try something big, they hardly had petrol to sustain a drive of more than 120-150 miles. What they didn't say was that both considered Strong something of a doomsayer, which of course, was part and parcel to the pessimism expected from a British G-2. In spite of such incredulity, Strong drafted a top-secret memo to all Army Groups on December 14th. In the message he warned of the possibility of a "German relieving attack" through the Ardennes. Montgomery even thought Strong was becoming alarmist and denounced his counsel.

But others in the Allied camp needed less convincing. Col. Benjamin A. "Monk" Dickson, in Lt. Gen. Courtney Hodges' First Army headquarters,

---

33 The same question puzzled the authors of the official U.S. Air Force History: "Just why, in the light of the mounting information regarding the enemy's preparations and noticeable shift of his activity into the area opposite the Ardennes, the Allies should have been surprised by the German offensive of mid-December remains something of a mystery. It is clear enough that the failure was one primarily of interpretation." The answer to the mystery was that Craven and Cate in 1951 did not know of the influence of ULTRA. This magnificent oracle blinded its creators to the conventional intelligence.

was a well-known pessimist. On December 9th, he puzzled over evidence of the relocation of the mysterious missing enemy armored reserve:

> "G-2 reports keep putting emphasis on the fact that the *Sixth Panzer Army* is drawing up... with at least six of its armored divisions facing the First Army Front. Reports from prisoners indicate that morale is high and that the Boche will soon be ready to stage an all-out counteroffensive."

For the blinded Allied intelligence officers, the *Sixth Panzer Army* was the tail of the donkey; find it and you knew the enemy's intentions. Of that they could be certain. On November 6th a reliable German prisoner from the *81 Machine Gun Battalion* was interrogated; he had seen elements of the *Sixth Panzer Army* north of Senne. Although obviously exaggerating, the POW claimed to have seen "thousands of Tiger tanks with new trainloads arriving every two or three days with sixty tanks at a time from Sennelager." But just where would the enemy strike? Then on December 14th, Dickson was informed of a Luxembourg woman, Elise Delé, who had observed "many vehicles, pontoons and boats and other river crossing equipment coming from the direction of Bitburg!" This set off a ferment in Dickson's head "It's the Ardennes!" he blurted out to Hodges' staff. But Monk Dickson had a bad reputation for this sort of thing. Crying wolf on this one earned him a "don't-come-back-until-you-stop-seeing-Germans" leave to Paris. In a wink, Dickson was gone. Meanwhile, Bradley and his optimist G-2, Gen. Sibert, were inclined to dismiss the whole thing. The German army was like a staggering wounded man, ready to collapse at any moment, "With continuing Allied pressure in the south and in the north," recited Sibert's estimate of December 12th, "the [enemy] breaking point may develop suddenly and without warning." Rather than an enemy counteroffensive, the Germans could fall apart at any time with the Allies only required to march to Berlin to pick up the pieces. The admonitions of Kenneth Strong and Monk Dickson were judged preposterous. The British 21st Army Group agreed. "The enemy," read a mid-December assessment, "is in a bad way and is incapable of launching major offensive operations." But it was Edwin Sibert and the other nay-saying intelligence pundits who would soon be in a bad way.

VIII

Enter Dietrich Peltz

To take charge of air cover for his great offensive, Hitler demanded someone from the Luftwaffe with a blinding offensive ambition to match his own. He didn't want defensively oriented "defeatists" like Galland. The man chosen had the right qualifications. Perhaps more than anyone in the German air force, Genmaj. Dietrich Peltz was a bombing expert. He had carried out many of the pyrrhic operations against England in the West and in spite of their hopelessness, had carried out his orders with the efficient obedience that Hitler admired. As reward, he was handed the responsibility for providing air support to *Wacht Am Rhein*. In deference to Hitler's wishes, Peltz scrapped Galland's *Der Grosse Schlag*. The plan clearly did not fit within the framework of Hitler's offensive bombast. Plus, after the experiences in early November, Hitler had lost faith that such an operation would work anyway. As a Luftwaffe leader of *II Jagdkorps*, Peltz stood in stark contrast to the strapping profile of Galland. Dietrich Peltz was a young and proper soldier with slim, fine features and was diminutive in stature. Although certainly not so fanatic as many of the SS men, Peltz was dedicated to the Hitler's cause. Having established his career in leading Luftwaffe bombers over England, the 30-year old air commander preferred to create an Ardennes operation tailored around ground support and "offensive operations." Unfortunately, almost none of the German aircrew that would be available to him had any training in flying ground support missions, long having adapted to defensive fighter tactics to simply survive in the hostile skies over Europe.

Peltz's assignment to the task was vehemently denounced by most of the fighter commanders since he was clearly not qualified to handle a large collection of fighters. Whereas Galland was intimately familiar with fighter operations, Peltz was a bomber man. On the other hand, Peltz was an extremely intelligent and capable officer with a fine mind for offensive air operations. Moreover, he was aggressive and enthusiastic and more apt to follow the expressed wishes of Hitler for *Wacht Am Rhein* than the obstreperous Galland.

Peltz had joined the Luftwaffe in 1935 and had started the war as a Stuka *Staffel* commander in the glory days of Poland and the West in 1940. Later he transferred to heavy bombers and taught dive bombing courses in Foggia, Italy. During the Battle of Britain he took Ju-88s into the skies over England with *KG 77* and in September 1942 he was given command of *I Gruppe, KG 66*, a bomber group which supported Rommel in air operations in North Africa and the Mediterranean. Later, in 1942, he commanded *KG 60* to support Mediterranean operations during the Allied invasion of North Africa. In December he was made the *Inspekteur der Kampflieger*— chief inspector for bomber aircraft and later in March of 1943 was designated *Angriffsführer England* to coordinate the bombing attacks on Great Britain. For three months, he conducted the ever-shrinking *Mini-Blitz* on the island. While it was true that with imaginative tactics his limited forces tied down many squadrons of RAF fighters and a large collection of British anti-aircraft weapons, his legions suffered debilitating losses. But with the Normandy invasion and the relentless Allied bombing of Germany, such operations became irrelevant. So outnumbered were Peltz's forces that he could only direct his *IX Fliegerkorps* to strike the shipping of the invasion force at night. This proved almost totally ineffective, as did attempts to mine the shallow waters off the invasion coast. His bombers moved to storage hangars. There was no fuel anyway. Accosted by the disasters that summer, even the aggressive Peltz agreed that all Luftwaffe energies should now be devoted to fighter defense to stop the Allies from pulverizing all means of German war manufacture.

So when it came time to support Hitler's last great panzer offensive, the aircraft Peltz found available for his command were almost exclusively fighter aircraft. Their usefulness for ground attack operations was even questioned by Peltz— many had simply been moved over from defending the skies over the Reich to interdiction and ground support! But with typical Germanic zeal, Peltz improvised as best he could.

As he envisioned it, the German air operation to support *Wacht Am Rhein* was to consist of two important tasks. First, a concentrated surprise air strike by all fighters on Allied air bases would first knock out the Allied fighter force on the ground in France. That done, the close-range danger from the troublesome U.S. Ninth Air Force and British 2nd Tactical Air Force would be averted. The Luftwaffe would then be free to establish a protective umbrella of German fighters to seal off the battlefield while fast German bombers of the *3 Flieger Division* worked over the American columns in the rear areas. Night fighter-bombers were to attack enemy ground targets and shield the movement of the German armies. Model's order on December 11th was clear on what was expected:

> *Support through air units*: *Luftwaffen-Kommando West* will support the attack of *Heeresgruppe B* with all available flying units. For this purpose, strong fighter and fighter-bomber units have been made ready.
> Reconnaissance: During the operation, this will consist above all in watching the movements of enemy reserves, and especially their motorized units, directed against the vanguards and flanks of the attacking armies.
> *Commitment of Combat Elements*: The key point is the commitment of the fighter units, whose main responsibility will be to protect the panzer spearheads, the roads along the axis of advance, and the preparation areas. Next to this comes the question of a surprise attack against the airfields of the enemy close to the front. Considering the limited number of our available flying units, the use of air units for immediate support of ground units will only be possible at key points. Under favorable weather conditions, air attacks against important crossroads will be the main targets for night operations.

Regardless of the change in plans, this large collection of pilots and planes, so carefully hoarded, had been trained single-mindedly to shoot down Allied bombers in Galland's "Great Blow" over Germany. The limited training of the German pilots had concentrated on the tactics of air to air combat, and not on the even more difficult and dangerous activity of ground air support. Munitions and equipment were also oriented towards air-air combat. That the woefully under-trained Luftwaffe pilots could be effective in the rough and tumble arena of the front-line air bases while attempting to interdict in a ground battle stood as a great conundrum.

Regardless of all questions, the scope of the German air operation began to take shape. For the duration of the offensive all of the fighter units (12 fighter *Geschwader* with 40 *Gruppen*) would be moved closer to the area of the offensive coming, under the control of *Luftflotte West* in Limburg. On November 14th Göring sent out an operational order detailing the expected conduct of the Luftwaffe contribution:

> *Aim of operation*: To destroy allied forces north of line Antwerp-Brussels-Luxembourg.

> C. in Chief West to break through on X-day with *Heeresgruppe B*: (15th, 6th Panzer, 5th Panzer, 7th Armies) the weak front of the 1st American Army between Monschau and Wasserbillig after about one hour's artillery preparation using bad weather. First objective Meuse crossings between Liège and Dinant. Thence to thrust through to Antwerp and west bank of the Scheldt estuary to cut off all British forces and the northern wing of the 1st American Army from their lines of communications area and to destroy them in co-operation with *Heeresgruppe B*... Luftflotte Reich, with subordinated *Luftwaffen Kommando West* (II *Jagdkorps*, 3 *Fliegerdivision*, III *Flakkorps*) to put in all-out effort to protect army against air attack and to give direct support at decisive points, especially the Meuse crossings.

Conduct of Battle.
A) *II. Jagdkorps* with subordinated *3 Jagddiv.*
  a)A single concentrated stroke against all airfields near front to knock out close support forces.
  b)Main task fighter protection to assure freedom of movement of troops. Units in rear to be available for protection of industry in Central Germany under *Jagdkorps I.*
  c)*S.G. 4* to be used at *Schwerpunkte*, particularly Meuse crossings. Rocket units to be used against tanks. In addition, under favorable circumstance, fighters to be used for low level attacks. Special care to establish position of front line and to establish liaison with the army...

B) *3. Fliegerdivision.*
  a)The fast bomber (*Schnellkampf*) units to take part in attacks on airfields. Then against airfields and towns.
  b)Bomber and night ground attack against reinforcements and reserves, particularly at nodal points of communications. *III. KG 66* (Mistel) and Einhorn staffel against important objectives such as bridges on flanks. Night fighters (*NJG 2*) also perform night strafing.
  c) Main task of night fighters protection of German deployment.

C) *III Flakkorps*
  Main task protection against expected strong air attacks. Operation against tanks and other ground targets only in critical situations. *Flaksturm* regiments under *2 Flak Division* to keep close contact with spearheads and seize and defend bridges, particularly Meuse crossings. As advance continues, these units to be relieved by bringing up forces of the *19th* or *1st Flak Brigades.* Searchlights to be used to defend bridges and road nodal points...

D) *Recce*
  a)Thorough reconnaissance of battle zone before attack, as far as rear of artillery zone and of Meuse crossings. Cover plan reasons to be given [to subordinates].
  b)After attack begins, watch flanks and lines of advance, Meuse crossings and area north of Maas-Albert canal...

Uninterrupted patrols would be made over the zone of the offensive's operations through use of the relay principle, one formation being relieved as another retired. The key objective would be to prevent the Allied fighters from achieving air superiority. To keep pace with the superior enemy numbers, during the critical phase of the offensive, pilots would be expected to fly at least two sorties per day.

According to Göring's final orders the preparations for the implementation of the above was to be complete by November 27th. The *Reichsmarschall* indicated that he would personally participate in the execution of the offensive, an unusual event given his long absence from the day-to-day matters of the war.

At the end of the month, Göring again toured "Macki" Steinhoff's *JG 77* at Schönwalde near Berlin. Driving up in a luxurious Mercedes, Göring stepped out to inspect the men of the "Red Hearts." It was raining and the young German pilots stood at attention in an open hangar. Göring moved up and down the line, shaking hands with the senior officers and saluting approvingly. Suddenly he eyed a young Lieutenant and fired off a mysterious question. "Could you today, in this weather, fly deep into enemy territory— say France or Belgium— attack aircraft with your cannon, and fly back here again." The Lieutenant was dumbfounded; he said he could do it, but navigation would likely be a problem— and he was one of the more experienced pilots!" Göring seemed satisfied with the answer. As for the navigation problem, didn't their new planes have "those new gadgets?" Göring was ignorant of the electronic homing gear in some of the newer aircraft, and knew even less of how such instruments were little substitute for pilot experience. Steinhoff wondered at the reason for this strange question. He would soon find out.

Consisting of a ground attack followed by fighter cover, *Operation 'Boden-platte'* (Base plate) was quite different in tactical complexion from Galland's original proposal to strike the Allied bomber forces in the air over Germany.[34] He later recalled:

> "In the middle of November I received an alarming order, the whole impact of which I could not foresee. The fighter reserves were to be prepared for action on the front where a great land battle was expected in the West. This was incredible!"

Although none of the German ground crews knew it, the need for ground support of the great tank offensive was behind Göring's order of November 14th requiring that all fighter aircraft be capable of arming for fighter-bomber missions with a 24-hour notice. Meanwhile, the preparations went on. Only two fighter groups (the *Reichsverteidigung*) were to be left to defend Germany itself— *Jagdgeschwader (JG) 300* and *JG 301*. All the others would be enlisted for support of the ground forces. The re-deployment of the *Jagdwaffe* was complete in November with the 33-odd squadrons of the fighter units in the west placed under *Luftwaffen Kommando West* and Genlt. Josef "Beppo" Schmidt.

---

34 Over the years, the translation of 'Bodenplatte' has been often misinterpreted to be "Ground Slam." The actual code word likely means "Base plate" since a German military dictionary clearly shows that this is the standard term for a mortar baseplate. The name of the operation was likely chosen for its deception potential.

TABLE 5

Organization of Luftwaffenkommando West: December 1944	
Genlt. Josef Schmidt	
II Jagdkorps - Genmaj. Dietrich Peltz	
3rd Jagddivision - Genmaj. Walter Grabmann	
Geschwader	**Gruppen**
JG 1	(3)
JG 3	(3)
JG 6	(3)
JG 26	(3)
JG 27	(4)
JG 77	(3)
JG 54/IV	(1)
Jagdabshnitt Mittelrhein - Oberst. Hannes Trübenbach	
JG 2	(3)
JG 4	(3)
JG 11	(3)
JG 53	(3)
JG 54/IV	(1)
SG 4	(3)
3rd Flieger Division	
LG 1	
KG 51, 66, 76	
NSGr. 1, 2, 20	
NJG 3	
Aircraft Types :	
Me-109: JG 77, 53	
Fw-190: SG 4, NSGr. 20	
Me-109/Fw-190: JG 1, 2, 4, 6, 11, 26, 27	
Ar-234: KG 76	
Me-262: KG 51	
Ju-87: NSGr. 1, 2	
Ju88/Ju188: KG 66	
Ju-88: NJG 3, LG 1	

TABLE 6

| German Aircraft Availability to *Luftwaffenkommando West* December 20, 1944 ||
Aircraft Type	Strength
Single-Engined Fighters	1,770
Ground Attack Aircraft	155
Night Ground Attack Aircraft	135
Twin-Engined Fighters	140
Reconnaissance Aircraft	65
Level Bombers	55
Jet Aircraft	40
Total Available	2,360

Approximately 2,300 Luftwaffe aircraft would be available for the operation, although perhaps only 65-75% of these were serviceable.[35] Another encouraging note for the planners were the 42 jet Me-262A-2 bombers available in two *Gruppen* from Maj. Wolfgang Schenck's *KG(J) 51 "Edelweiss"* and the 16 serviceable Arado-234s of Maj. Hans-Georg Bätcher's *III/KG 76*.

The German reconnaissance forces included *Nahaufklarungsgeschwader (NAG) 1, NAG 13* with Me-109s. *Einsatz Kdo. Braunegg* had five Me-262A-1 jets; *Kommando Sperling* had another four Ar-234Bs earmarked for reconnaissance for the attack. Their main assignment would be to obtain a photographic record of the Meuse crossings before the approach of the German armor and then spy on enemy movements on the flanks of the offensive. So fast (470 mph) and high (33,000 ft) did these advanced reconnaissance jets fly that although they had been operating in a reconnaissance role since August, it was not until November 21st that the Allied fighters even sighted one.

Specialist ground attack units were brought forward. These included the Fw-190F-8s of Obstlt. Janssen's *SG-4* and Maj. Kurt Dahlmann's *NSGr-20* and the Ju-87Ds of *NSGr 1* and 2. Due to the latter plane's well known vulnerability, these groups would only operate at night against enemy rear areas. Bomber support would be provided by Peltz's old unit, *I/KG 66*, now under the leadership of Maj. Helmut Schmidt. Considered a specialist pathfinder unit for night bombing raids, the command had a strength of approximately 22 Ju-88s and Ju-188s in three *Staffeln* and was based at Dedelsdorf.

---

35 In contrast to the German aircraft readiness, the average autumn serviceability of aircraft in the IX TAC of the U.S. Ninth Air Force stood at 80.4%.

Also available would be the *I & II Gruppen* of Obst. Hellwig's *Lehrgeschwader (LG) 1* flying out of Varel and Ahlhorn with a total strength of some 45 Ju-88s. Each unit had recently been reorganized for their special ground attack role in the upcoming offensive. In particular *JG 4* was to provide dedicated daytime fighter cover for the German armored columns as they sped to the Meuse River. Part of the wing was armed with armor-piercing rockets.

Other than aircraft, the Luftwaffe would provide other vital support to the German offensive. By 1944 Göring's anti-aircraft flak guns were destroying as many or more Allied planes than the German fighters— a fact that Hitler was only too ready to point out to Galland and the *Jägerstab*.[36] At its height the Flak (*Fliegerabwehrkanonen*) arm of the Luftwaffe included nearly a million men and women, over 14,000 heavy guns, some 35,000 medium and light pieces and thousands of barrage balloons and search-lights. The flak units were assigned to the various defense districts in Germany. Each battery had four to eight guns, with the famous "88" being the most numerous of the heavy type. Defensive rings of flak batteries were erected approximately two miles around prominent targets so that the bomber streams would be most pounded in the last minute of their bomb run. The hope was that this would disrupt the bombing formation and reduce aiming effectiveness. The guns could either be radar or visually aimed with the shells time-delay fused and taking roughly twenty seconds to reach a bomber formation at 20,000 feet. The firing prediction system to determine azimuth, slant range, elevation, etc. was largely automated. Even so, flak was inaccurate and German wartime studies estimated that upwards of 4,000 shells were needed to bring down a single bomber. It was for this reason that the Allied development of the radar-controlled proximity fuse was such a closely guarded secret. All involved knew that should the Germans acquire this technology that the lethality of the flak arm could increase dramatically. Luckily for the Allies, the Germans never learned of it. Regardless, German flak was effective enough. At least half of U.S. air combat losses were attributable to flak, and the AA fire reduced the effectiveness of the bombing campaign and often crippled or threw Allied bombers out of formation where they could be picked off by opportunistic German fighters.

On November 4th the German leader provided his endorsement, "In his reports on his terror attacks on the German Reich the enemy is always speaking of the 'hell' of the German anti-aircraft fire...we must step up the firepower of the flak in every conceivable way." The flak included many guns from 20mm up; the most notorious was the "88." As Rommel had so effectively demonstrated in the desert, these 88mm anti-aircraft guns that

---

36 Fldm. Milch did not agree: "Flak is not magic," he said, "and can never make the enemy cease his air attacks. It can force him to high altitudes and cause him losses but cannot keep him away. Only the fighter component can do that."

were so capable of shooting down planes at altitude could provide a lethal fire when turned against tanks on the ground. Increasingly as the war progressed, the use of the flak arm became central both to protecting the German troop columns from the scornful attention of Allied air, as well as bolstering the defense and attack of its ground forces. More and more, the larger calibre 128mm guns were installed to protect Germany, which unlike the 88mm, did not have to get a direct hit on an enemy bomber to bring it down. The 20mm - 40mm guns were increasingly fundamental to operations of the German army to protect against low-flying fighter-bombers. That the big flak guns were deadly was beyond doubt:

> "I didn't suspect for a moment that I was about to see one of our ships disintegrate before my eyes, then it happened; there was a brilliant flash and the entire plane was enveloped in flame. The flaming mass slowly fell from the formation and began to disintegrate into bits of flaming wreckage that twisted and turned dizzily toward the earth. I strained my eyes towards the ghastly sight in the hope of seeing parachutes of survivors, but there were none. It was hard to believe that the men I sat with only a few hours before were riding that blazing inferno to the ground. It's difficult to express my exact feelings at witnessing that sight."

For *Wacht Am Rhein* the Luftwaffe assembled 47 heavy and 51 medium and light batteries of flak. The heavy guns included 120 heavy pieces of 88mm or greater under the leadership of Genlt. Wolfgang Pickert, an old hand at anti-aircraft warfare in the Russian Campaign. Not only would his guns provide a potent anti-aircraft umbrella over the German forces, and improvised anti-tank capability, but Pickert was able to promise his big flak guns to bolster the German artillery that would bombard the unknowing American line on the first morning of the great attack.

Preparations for the Luftwaffe's support of *Wacht Am Rhein* were essentially complete by December 15th; 23 *Gruppen* had been assembled in Germany and a further three *Gruppen* of Fw-190s had been transferred from Russia. All designated fighter units had been redeployed to the Western Front leaving only *JG 300* and *JG 301* to protect the homeland. Operationally, the dispersion of the fighter forces would make it difficult to coordinate the coming operations, since the various *Gruppen* were spread out over an area of some 250 miles from Oldenberg to Rheine-Main.

As Saturday, December 16th drew near, the Allied air forces were still completely unaware of German intentions. But the Allied high command might have taken solace in the fact that even as late as December 12th, top German generals who would carry out the operation were just learning of the plan. One of these was Genlt. Fritz Bayerlein.

Bayerlein was a soldier's soldier. He had entered the service in 1917 and served out World War I as an infantry non-com, becoming an officer between the wars. He served with the panzer divisions in the campaigns in Poland and France in 1939 and 1940. He became Rommel's trusted chief of staff in the *Afrika Korps,* serving there until the Germans were ejected from North Africa in 1943. He returned to Germany to find himself briefly on the Russian front when he was recalled to train and command the elite *Panzer Lehr Division*. His mission, he learned, would be to throw back the expected Allied invasion of France. That mission had proven disastrous for the young members of the unit. Although stoutly defending for weeks, Bayerlein's men were continually harassed by Allied air power throughout the month of June, creating constant delays and losses. On July 25th, his command had been almost completely destroyed by a fantastic pounding from a carpet bombing around St. Lô which opened the floodgates to France for Gen. Patton's Third Army. *Panzer Lehr* arrived on the German border at the end of August at barely battalion strength.

During the fall, Bayerlein's command had been in almost constant fighting with Patton's armor in Lorraine. Even though battered, Bayerlein's battle-hardened command held together; he stood as a seasoned front line soldier and a tough tanker. But in stopping Patton at the end of November, the elite panzer division cutting edge had been blunted; losses had been severe. In early December his depleted division had suddenly been recalled to Westphalia for emergency refitting. For this point in the war replenishment went amazingly fast— new tanks, guns and a copious allocation of automatic weapons came in by train every day. Only gasoline was insufficiently supplied; only five liters were allocated to each panzer to get from the tank parks to the entraining station— and this was to be the break-in period for the new engines! The reason behind the haste of all this was unclear. But on December 12th, Gen. Bayerlein received curious orders to report to *OB West* at 4 PM, taking only one vehicle with no accompanying officers. When he arrived at the old castle at Ziegenberg he found all the various army, corps and division commanders all assembled. No one knew why. Even more mysteriously, they were ordered to leave pistols and briefcases in a cloakroom and were then herded out to a bus. The bus left the castle at about 5 PM in a pouring rain. Presently, they arrived at Hitler's *Adlerhorst*.

The generals were discharged from the bus between two grim lines of SS men and were soon ushered into the dreary gray walls of an earthen concrete bunker. The first action was hardly an inspiring one. All were forced to sign a declaration of their willingness to maintain the secrecy of what they were about to hear. If word leaked out of the operation, they would be shot! The contract signed, they were escorted to a briefing room lined with taciturn SS guards. The generals were seated in front of these SS at a rectangular table with their chairs carefully arranged to be at least three feet apart. Presently, Hitler walked in with his entourage including Gen. Jodl and Gen. Keitel. To Bayerlein, Hitler lookd old and broken. He put on a pair of wire-framed glasses, his hands visibly shaking as he held the notes for his speech. A two-hour-long harangue began. The first hour was a lesson in history for the generals— how Frederick the Great had triumphed over adversity in the Seven Years War. This new operation, he told them, would be his Rossbach and Leuthen! Everyone had heard all this before and some were visibly bored. Meanwhile the SS guards looked on so menacingly that Bayerlein was afraid to reach for his handkerchief.

The second hour got down to the details of the operation. As befitted all of the grandiose ventures of late, Hitler's final outing would be a desperate all-out attack through the Ardennes designed to capture Antwerp and bring the Western Allies to the negotiating table. The German leader described how everything had been scraped together for this last supreme effort, how it would decide the fate of Germany; the monologue went on as Hitler became more visibly excited. Hitler closed in asking all of the generals present to do their utmost to see that *Wacht Am Rhein* would succeed. Everyone had questions, but Hitler seemed to sense them. There was no need to worry about Allied fighters he told his audience; large Luftwaffe units would achieve air superiority. No one dared roll their eyes. The generals were dismissed and loaded back into the bus. Hitler withdrew to attend a party celebrating Genfldm. von Rundstedt's 70th birthday. Gen. Bayerlein hurried off to spend some time with his family. After hearing of the upcoming operation, he feared that it might be the last opportunity of his life.

Frenzied preparations continued. On December 14th a conference of the commanding officers of *II Jagdkorps* convened at an inn east of Bonn near Altenkirchen to discuss Luftwaffe plans to support the attack. Security measures for the meeting were extensive. Most of the various *Geschwadern* and *Gruppen* commanders were present. Obst. Walter Grabmann, the head *3rd Jagddivision*, was there, as well as Obst. Hannes Trübenbach and Obst. Gotthardt Handrick of *Jafü Mittelrhein*. Among them was Obstlt. Johann Kogler, the *Kommodore* of *JG 6*. Kogler was surprised by the scope of the ambitious plan and even more to find that Peltz, the General of the Bombers, would be in charge of a fighter operation. Code words would be used to announce when the great air attack against Allied airfields would take place along with authority to brief the pilots and arm the planes with special bombs and ammunition. The specific timing of the ground attack on Allied air bases would be announced by the codeword 'HERMANN' followed by a date and time on which the operation was to begin. The Luftwaffe planners acknowledged the lack of experience of German pilots in preparing for the operation. They would make up for this deficiency with numbers. Peltz told his audience that at least 1,100 German planes would take part. For the envisioned ground support operations an air liaison unit was assigned to each panzer division to promote smooth communication with the Luftwaffe. To maintain security, the division staffs were only to be briefed on the air operations the night before the attack. By the end of the session most of the commanders were more hopeful of German success than they had been in months. Obstlt. Johann Kogler hurried back to his headquarters and briefed the *Gruppenkommandeure* and *Staffelkapitäne* of JG 6 on the plans. He had detailed maps prepared for his pilots, marking their routes for the operation. Thoughtfully, he had someone on the staff prepare a detailed sand-table model of the Dutch airfield at Volkel which his unit would attack.

In spite of assurances from on high, the senior German wing commanders were gravely doubtful. They also knew that even though this 2,300 aircraft order of battle represented the largest concentration of German airpower massed on a single front up to that point in the war, they also knew that it would still be greatly outnumbered by the Allied air forces. Although German fighter aircraft were plentiful they were painfully aware that the Luftwaffe pilots of fall, 1944 had little in common with the experienced veterans of the previous German campaigns in the West. They knew their pilots were not well enough trained for a complex ground support operation such as 'Bodenplatte.'

The beginning of December saw that Hitler's holy grail of "hundreds of jets" had gone the way of the other wonder weapons dreams. Old pragmatic Genfldm. von Rundstedt was dubious: "After our previous experiences we no longer believed in the delivery promised by *OKW* and *OKL* of complete, modernly equipped air formations... Of course we asked for every bit of support we could get." In a memo on the air battle plane for the Ardennes operation, even *General der Flieger* Werner Kreipe, confessed, "I fear that all remains pure theory." Even Hitler wondered. As the day for launching the attack drew near, he compared the current situation with that in 1940, attempting to divine his potential by looking to the past. Calculating the number of the divisions, he found them similar. He then turned to the other factors:

> "The objection may be made that there is a major difference between 1940 and the present situation: at that time the enemy's army had no battle experience, and now we are facing an enemy we have learned to know in war. That is true, gentlemen. But as regards relative strength, there is little difference, apart from the Luftwaffe— that is of course a most important factor..."

And although German fighter strength was greater than it had been at any time in the war, it remained to be seen if the Luftwaffe was still capable of making satisfactory use of its strength. They would soon find out. 'O-Tag' was fast approaching. On the very eve of the great attack, Gen. Jodl dispatched Hitler's last-moment instructions to Genfldm. Model with *Heeresgruppe B*. They brimmed with hope and confidence:

> "The final decisions have been made;... everything points to victory. The magnitude and scope of which...depends entirely on the handling of the operation; ...if...these basic principles for the conduct of operations are adhered to...a major victory is assured."

139

At his *Adlerhorst* headquarters, Hitler had his usual nightly war conference. The mood on the evening of December 15th was decidedly upbeat in anticipation of the opening of *Wacht Am Rhein*. For dinner, he ate his simple vegetarian meal in the company of his secretaries. Later he moved back to the situation room to nervously go over last minute preparations with Martin Bormann and his adjutant, Maj. Johann Meyer. He retired to his dreary quarters to fall asleep only a half hour before his 2,000 artillery guns were to open up on the unsuspecting U.S. troops in the Ardennes.

IX

"Support the Attack..." December 16th

G renadier Otto Bauer found himself in an unexpected predicament on the morning of December 16th, 1944. A native of Doenitz, Germany, Bauer had worked with the Luftwaffe since before the war in 1937. At Kühlungsborn, on the Baltic Sea, Otto had been a technical researcher on anti-aircraft explosives for the flak arm. Göring's ubiquitous anti-aircraft command made up nearly a million of the Luftwaffe personnel before D-Day. During the course of the war, the flak repeatedly proved its worth, in later years claiming more Allied aircraft destroyed than did the German fighters. Although Hitler had ordered in November that "All current experimentation and developments designed to increase the efficiency of the guns and their ammunition...must be pursued relentlessly," the Führer's edict did not translate into job security for Bauer.

For years, Otto had labored with his colleagues to produce improved shells and explosive formulations to shoot down enemy aircraft. The relative importance of the 88mm, both in contesting total Allied air superiority and serving as a superb anti-tank weapon, had provided years of complacent job security for Bauer and the others at Kühlungsborn. But the summer disasters in Russian and France in 1944 had begun talk at the research center of a new round of conscription to find able bodies to carry German rifles at the front. Rumor became reality in October when Bauer, along with 600,000 others in the Luftwaffe "excess staff," found themselves conscripted by Heinrich Himmler's draft.

What followed was nightmarish enough— a few weeks of threadbare training by convalescing wounded veterans or frighteningly young commissioned officers. What cannon fodder unit was he to be thrown into? Otto was then surprised to find a totally unskilled old conscript like himself suddenly ending up as part of a supposedly elite tank division, the *Panzer Lehr*. In the pre-dawn of December 16th as the German guns along the Western Front fired off in unison to herald the opening of Hitler's great *Wacht Am Rhein* offensive, Bauer found himself a lowly replacement grenadier surrounded by other apprehensive very young or very old faces. Soon the orders came, the 1 *Kompanie*, 1 *Battalion* of the 901 *Panzer Grenadier Regiment* was to move down to the Our River and into the attack. This was to be Bauer's first and last battle. He would be captured on January 26th, 1945.

All along the eighty mile front, hundreds of squads of gray-clad German soldiers, many inexperienced like Bauer, surged forward to assault the American outposts in the Ardennes. But the opening day of Hitler's last offensive in the West began rather inconspicuously for those still with the flying Luftwaffe. The German *Gruppe* commanders waiting for the order to attack the Allied airfields found thick, soupy ground fog had grounded most aircraft. Similarly, the Ninth Air Force bases reported dense fog and light rain. Genmaj. Peltz informed his subordinates that *Operation 'Bodenplatte'* was postponed for better flying weather. Allied ULTRA intercepts of German communications traffic would later reveal that the Luftwaffe had suspended operations until the following day to help preserve the element of surprise in the ground assault. Even so, at 10:40 PM that evening Peltz ordered *II Jagdkorps* to "support the attack of the 5th and 6th Armies the following morning." If the operation to neutralize Allied airfields could not be struck just yet, then the Luftwaffe would bolster the German ground forces.

That night, Hptm. Armin Köhler drew his fledgling pilots of *III/JG 77* together. "Thousands of tanks are on the move in the West," he told his audience, "the Luftwaffe must support the army. All the German eyes are fixed on you, the pilots." Their were many new faces, having only trained together at Neuruppin, North of Berlin, since October. The *III Gruppe* was designated as the *"Höhenjagdgruppe"*— the high altitude cover— in Me-109K-4s for *JG 77*. A number had been killed in learning formation flying. Soon they would be asked to fly in combat. On Sunday morning the K-4s of *III Gruppe* joined the G-14s of *I* and *II Gruppe* and flew West to Düsseldorf-Unterrath. On their way to the new airfield the German civilians scurried for cover, unaccustomed as they were to German planes flying in such a large formation. Moving to an old school for billets, the pilots ate in the mess and went to sleep to the sound of gunfire from the front. They would fly the next day.

Like their commanders, the Allied air forces, for the most part, spent December 16th in a state of unknowing. That 250,000 German troops and some 717 tanks and assault guns with over 2,600 artillery pieces could be launching the largest offensive in the West since 1940 seemed absolutely impossible. Rather than worry about a comeback of the Luftwaffe, that night more Allied aviators were talking about the fate of band leader Glenn Miller.

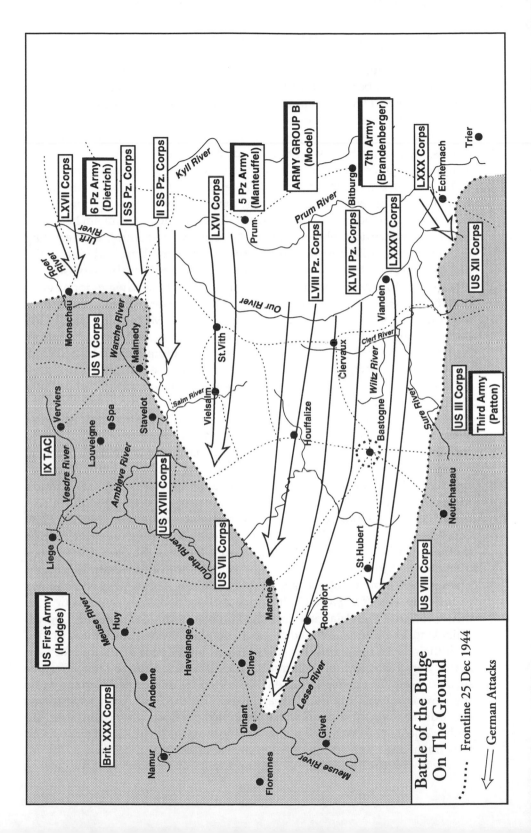

Battle of the Bulge
On The Ground

.... Frontline 25 Dec 1944

⇨ German Attacks

Miller's AAF band had given a hotly anticipated performance in England on Thursday, December 14th at the Bedford Corn Exchange. There were other big names present— David Niven and Humphrey Bogart— and the place had been jammed with American airmen. The band ran through the whole gamut of swing tunes, with Miller bringing the crowd to its feet. But on Friday, Miller left in a light plane for Paris where the band was already waiting. Mysteriously disappearing over the English Channel he was never heard from again.

There were only nine shopping days left before Christmas and the attention of many turned back to the States. Bing Crosby and his "White Christmas" were unavoidable on the air waves. The infectious optimism had risen all the way up to the intelligence staffs. After all, were not the Allies decoding secret German radio transmissions as they sent them? Time and time again, this greatest Allied secret of the war had told the top SHAEF brass of German intentions. Moreover, it had *never* been wrong. *Never!* So when reports began flooding into the S-2 catacombs of German attacks everywhere in the Ardennes, the facts were met with astonished disbelief. Meantime, the ULTRA code-breakers were busy decoding a sudden tirade of German radio traffic. As always, it would be some hours or even days before it could be decoded, translated and enciphered for transmission to the select few Allied commanders "in the know." What they would learn was unwelcome. Their faithful oracle had deceived them.

So convinced were the Allies that their enemy was beaten, that the senior commanders in late fall 1944 were obsessed with their own operations to end the tiresome war. The terrible ground battles of autumn— Aachen, Hurtgen Forest, Lorraine— had all been grinding attritional battles reminiscent of the First World War. The conventional wisdom was that the Germans were now sapped and ripe for destruction. In mid-December Bradley's 12th Army Group was poised for two powerful assaults on the Siegfried Line. One was an attack by the U.S. First Army, already beginning to push out of the northern reaches of the Ardennes to thrust towards the Roer River dams ultimately to thrust to the lower Rhine river, the gateway to Central Germany. The southern blow would be landed by the dashing Third Army commander, Gen. Patton. His effort would be to breach the Siegfried Line near Saarburg and thrust towards the Palatinate and the southwestern corner of the German Rhineland. The Germans would be caught between the two pincers and pinned with their backs up against the Rhine. Allied intelligence knew that the Germans were building up a reserve. A counterattack against their offensive seemed likely. The general opinion, supported by intercepted German radio transmissions, was that the Germans would hit the First Army as it moved towards the Roer River dams which controlled the flood stage of the river. But with adequate planning for that eventuality, some luck and a lot of air support, they might bag a substantial chunk of the German army.

It was with the knowledge of the importance of air support to the coming offensives that the top Allied tactical air commanders met on December 16th. They attended the meeting hosted by Pete Quesada and his IX TAC in Verviers to determine how they would support upcoming ground offensive operations. The First Army had been attacking slowly east past the German Westwall and would soon prepare for a major offensive operation to cross the Roer River along with Gen. Simpson's Ninth Army. General Vandenberg in charge of the Ninth Air Force was there along with Gen. Sam Anderson with the IX Bombardment Division and Gen. Richard "Dick" Nugent of the XXIX TAC. Nugent's command was providing air assistance to Simpson's Ninth Army to the north and would also be involved.

The plan called for massive air support along the seam of the two armies and that meant heavy bombers. Two representatives from the Eighth Air Force were also included as well as Air Commodore Dickens from the RAF. Almost immediately the men got down to studying the details of the air operation. The only consensus was the weather. Everyone agreed that it couldn't be counted upon; "blind bombing" would be required. Beyond that almost no one agreed on how the air operation should be staged. Ninth Army would not attempt a crossing without fighter-bomber support, whereas First Army wanted bombers for their attempt. Gen. Anderson rightfully pointed out that the weather conditions affected fighter bombers and medium bombers differently. The mediums could not operate if the overcast was below 10,000 feet while the fighters could. There were other complications: the RAF would not blind bomb less than five miles from friendly troops, whereas the Eighth Air Force would. Bomber Command and the Eighth Air Force also disagreed on the minimum ceiling at which they would perform visual bombing. The whole plan was devolving into a morass of complication. Vandenberg suggested they meet again the next day, including the army commanders, to resolve the mess. As they left the meeting, none suspected that the greatest German ground offensive in the West since 1940 was under way less than thirty miles to the east. Returning to their headquarters, the air commanders found the Luftwaffe was out in force. "Heavy German night air action in this vicinity," Gen. Nugent recorded in his diary back at headquarters in Maastricht, Holland, "Flare dropping, bombing and strafing at various hours throughout the night."

Not divining the enemy intention, Allied air operations on the 16th had little to do with the Ardennes. Bad weather limited the IX TAC to only 90 sorties; XIX TAC managed another 237. The experience of the 367th Fighter Group is illustrative. Completely unaware of the chaos in the Ardennes, Capt. Chester A. Slingerland led a swarm of P-38s to escort the Lancaster bombers of the Royal Air Force (RAF) to a blitz on the town of Siegen, Germany. Some 26 enemy fighters attempted to run the bombers off, but the twin-engined fighters drove them away. A replacement pilot, Lt. Jack H. Hallett, vividly remembered his only encounter with the enemy:

"...I picked up the heading we had been flying, but within a few seconds spotted four more 109s below me. I figured that if Dick Bong could do it, so could I, and went after them. They were flying over the top of an under cast and disappeared into the clouds when they saw me coming, so I picked up the heading again. After a few more minutes on course I saw a single Me-109 coming at me from behind. I waited until the last second, then hit my throttles and combat flaps, and racked the ship around. He sailed by me and when he turned, I got on his tail after a few Lufberrys. I fired a few bursts, but missed the hell out of him. I was a lousy air-to air shot. The Me rolled over and split-essed. Without rolling, I followed him down, still firing and still missing. We both went screaming through the under cast, and when we broke out I realized how low we were and yanked back on the column with all the strength I had. The '109 didn't have a chance because he was partly inverted when we dived out of the clouds. I saw him hit the ground and explode just before I blacked out...Coming to, I couldn't find the horizon and realized that I was going almost straight up...I finally found the rest of our planes after the flight and returned to base. This was the only time I saw enemy aircraft in the air."

The IX TAC's 67 Tactical Reconnaissance Group was active over the Ardennes and reported sighting 75 German trucks and seven tanks in the U.S. 28th Division's vicinity. Likewise, XIX TAC reported heavy enemy traffic on the Koblenz and Trier railroads and highways.

By the early hours of December 17th, the intelligence pundits at Eisenhower's headquarters recognized that they had been had. Just before midnight on the first day of the offensive, an ULTRA decrypt arrived that electrified the staff. Word was that *II Jagdkorps* had received orders to "support the attack of 5 and 6 Armies" the next morning. The "5 and 6 Armies" could be none other than the *Fifth Panzer Armee* and the missing elite SS army, the *Sixth Panzer*. A de-coded order of the day from the venerable head of the German forces in the West, Gen. Gerd von Rundstedt further fanned the flames:

> "The hour of destiny has struck. Mighty offensive armies face the Allies. Everything is at stake. More than mortal deeds are required as a holy duty to the Fatherland."

Unless it was a ruse, a major enemy operation was underway. The worst nightmare of all was discussed in hushed tones behind blackout curtains. The dreaded logic went like this: if the Germans had pulled over the wool then they must now know about the code breaking and they were now using it to move the Allies into a trap. Could they rely on ULTRA anymore? Were there other nasty surprises just around the corner? Intelligence officers were beside themselves with apprehension. Lions and tigers and bears were now jets and rockets and secret weapons. There was a terrible paranoia. Doubters turned to the conventional means of intelligence. That augury was none too reassuring. The troubled region, the Ardennes, was under a murky cloud cover, seemingly as impenetrable as the enemy intentions. The few POWs who had fallen into Allied hands had warned of something particularly devilish to come. This had all been discounted as mere hysteria before. With a seemingly defeated enemy, suddenly possessed of a maniacal strength, who could tell? For all the uncertainty on December 16th, one thing was sure: Allied intelligence was in the dark. It was an unfamiliar state.

That evening any lingering doubts of an enemy feint faded. At 9 PM some 50 - 60 German night ground support aircraft appeared in five waves over the U.S. V Corps, dropping flares and indiscriminately strafing the Monschau area.[37] Over the next two hours individual German aircraft droned over the dark sky. A number of night ground attack bombers dropped a few bombs pell mell about the city of Eupen. Eupen was the U.S. V Corps headquarters of Gen. Leonard T. Gerow, along with the billets of the U.S. 1st Division's 18th Regiment. This did little to reduce the developing confusion. No one was hurt by this ineffectual pyrotechnic display, but it did raise questions. What was the German air force doing carrying out these seemingly pointless raids against a rear-echelon American outpost in the Ardennes?

The U.S. First Army made its headquarters in the High Belgian Ardennes in the town of Spa. Long known for the curative powers of its mineral waters, Spa was the watering hole from which all such places took their name. A 58-year-old Georgia native, Lt. Gen. Courtney Hodges was an aging and serious commander. His major fault, according to Eisenhower was that "God gave him a face that always looked pessimistic." Unlike most senior American commanders, Hodges had considerable combat experience as a machine gunner in Meuse-Argonne battles of the Great War. Perhaps his knowledge of this grim business gave him his melancholy demeanor. But in the Ardennes, Hodges saw a gift horse. The region was a resort area and his staff settled into comfortable accommodations at the famous Hôtel Brittannique. Steeped in history, it was here in 1918 that von Hindenburg was forced to inform the Kaiser that the Great War was lost. The autumn there had been comfortable; the accommodations were good and army life had settled into a routine. The First Army band pumped out marching tunes for the townspeople on Sundays. It was all very civil.

The situation at Spa on the morning of Saturday, December 16th hardly seemed a momentous occasion. Hodges was just sitting down to breakfast when word arrived of an enemy attack in the Losheim Gap and "the heaviest artillery fire ever received in the 28th Division area." Curious. Presently, Hodges was joined for breakfast by Gen. Bradley and Gen. Elwood "Pete" Quesada in charge of the IX Tactical Air Command. After their meal, the men were met by Monsieur Francotte who was to fit the avid shooters with brand-new shotguns that he had brought from Liège. No one suspected that the Germans were loosing a colossal artillery barrage and tank-led infantry attack on the thinly manned U.S. line not even thirty miles away. As the

---

37 These were identified by Allied observers as Fw-190s and obsolete Ju-87 "Stukas" pressed into night ground attack aircraft. The Stukas were from *NSGr 1* and 2 with approximately 70 serviceable Ju-87s; the Fw-190s were from *NSGr 20* with approximately 25 aircraft. They would make an almost nightly appearance over the Allied front.

generals were measured for the stock and drop of the guns, aides kept intruding with messages. Each note told the stodgy American commander that there were more attacks at the front, some as far south as the Luxembourg village of Echternach. Hodges, for one, was nonplussed; he had been attacking for the Wahlerscheid crossroads and had expected some sort of counterattack response from the Germans. That's what they always did. Even so, Bradley hustled off to meet with Eisenhower at Versailles. Quesada and the other men finished their fitting for the shotguns; they had a big meeting of the air minds slated for later that day. Later messages from the front had assuaged some of the alarm brought out from the earlier reports; at 4:15 PM the 28th Division, which previously had reported intense shelling, announced that the situation was "well at hand." But just as Hodges was getting to bed, disturbing news arrived from Gen. Nugent's XXIX TAC in the Ninth Army. German transports, the notice said, were in flight to their vicinity from German airfields near Paderborn. The guards were doubled at the gatehouse with the unusual warning to be on the alert for enemy commandos. No one got much sleep at the Hôtel Brittanique that night.

Guards at air bases were promptly doubled, leaves were cancelled and restrictions on civilian and other "unknowns" around the bases were restricted. Sergeant Gilbert Perass was an assistant crew chief with the 509th Fighter Squadron at the home of the "Thunder Monsters" at St. Dizier, France, 120 miles east of Paris:

> "...we got rousted out of the sack about 2:00 AM because a report had come through the Germans had dropped paratroopers near Nancy and we were to defend the airfield. Our Flight Chief, R.L. Smith, from Louisiana, led us down to the gasoline dump. We lay in the snow for about five hours. The gasoline tanks were in open pits. Some idiots across the field started firing and bullets were cracking over our heads so we slid down the sides of the pits for cover. Someone suggested that maybe this wasn't the best idea should a bullet hit one of the gasoline tanks, so we scrambled out en masse, and lay on the flat ground again. Our brave Flight Chief said we would make our stand here should the Germans appear. We told him he could make a stand and we would be right behind him— as far away as possible..."

The Supreme Headquarters of the Allied Expeditionary Forces (SHAEF) had its headquarters in at Versailles on the outskirts of Paris. The Trianon palace, with its timeless buildings, ornate decor and sculptured courtyards, made for a distinctly fashionable setting for the Allied Supreme headquarters. December 16th was bitterly cold and the Parisian skies were gray and overcast. But regardless of the weather, the 16th was a big day on the social calendar at Trianon palace. The Supreme Commander, Gen. Eisenhower, was receiving a promotion to five-star general— the U.S. Army's highest rank. As usual, Eisenhower was up at 6 AM for a breakfast of sausage topped with hominy grits. At the end of his meal he received a note from Montgomery requesting holiday leave and reminding Ike that he owed him five pounds on a bet fourteen months before that the war would be over by Christmas.

"I'll pay," Eisenhower quipped to an aide, "but not before Christmas." Later Eisenhower and Gen. Walter Bedell Smith, his SHAEF "manager," followed along to the Louis XIV chapel at Versailles. They both attended the wedding of Eisenhower's personal aide, Sgt. Michael J. "Mickey" McKeogh to a petite bespectacled lady from the Women's Army Corps (WAC), Sgt. Pearlie Hargrave. After the ceremony, all moved over to Eisenhower's quarters at Saint-Germain for champagne. Everyone was in high spirits.

But while Eisenhower celebrated the festivities, his chief intelligence officer learned of a troubling development. While still at his English breakfast, Gen. Kenneth Strong had received a message reporting an enemy attack during the pre-dawn hours on the First U.S. Army front. Strong kept his composure, although somewhat alarmed that several participating enemy divisions had been identified there. Allied air intelligence was still blind because of the icy fog and low clouds that covered the enemy front. That afternoon he met with Ike in his map room at 2 PM, to discuss the latest information. Present were Generals Bradley, Bedell Smith and Maj. Gen. Harold R. Bull. The air commanders included Air Marshal Sir Arthur Tedder, Eisenhower's deputy commander at SHAEF, and General Carl Spaatz, the senior American airman in Europe. Montgomery, in charge of the 21st Army Group, was not present, being off on the golf course at Eindhoven with the Welsh professional Dai Rees.[38] Ostensibly, Eisenhower's generals had gathered to discuss the critical shortage of infantry replacements in Europe.

The six generals listened attentively around a large table as Eisenhower discussed his continued intention to remain relatively idle in certain sectors like the Ardennes, so that he could gather the forces to smite the enemy and capture the Roer River dams. Bedell Smith inquired of Bradley as to what he thought their chances were of capturing the dams before the Germans flooded the surrounding countryside. At that moment, Brig. Gen. Thomas J. Betts interrupted and called Strong away. He had an urgent message. Gen. Strong knew Betts as an otherwise steady and calm subject. At this moment, the man at the door looked nervous and rattled. The news from the Ardennes was serious, he began. There had been a continuing series of very violent attacks with a massive artillery barrage. The news from the battlefront was sparse and the content was worrisome. "Situation obscure," read one report, "regimental command posts under attack." More enemy divisions had been identified including some panzer units. Strong returned to the meeting with the bad news. After hearing of the row, Bedell Smith turned to Bradley admonishing him that Strong had given him a warning of something like this a week ago.

The men crowded around a map that Betts had marked up identifying

38 On that very day Montgomery had signed an intelligence appraisal by his 21st Army Group which would later prove embarrassing: "The enemy is at present fighting a defensive campaign on all fronts; his situation is such that he cannot stage major offensive operations. Furthermore, at all costs he has to prevent the war from entering a mobile phase; he has not the transport or petrol that would be necessary for mobile operations...

the attacking enemy. It was apparent to everyone that the U.S. front in the Ardennes was very thinly defended. Bradley retorted that he had two divisions in reserve to respond to the development. "Sensing that this was something more than a mere local attack" Eisenhower urged Bradley to move the 10th Armored up from the South and the 7th Armored down from the North. Bradley excused himself to make telephone calls to set them in motion. While he was away, the generals noted that the Germans identified already outnumbered the tired or green U.S. forces along the "ghost front" in the Ardennes. Strong ventured that the Germans might try to thrust west across the Meuse to reach Brussels, cutting off much of the U.S. First Army from its supply base. Eisenhower nodded, but Bradley, who returned to an agitated group was skeptical of the whole thing. He again stated his doubt that this was anything more than a spoiling attack designed to draw Allied attention away from the Roer River offensive or Patton's coming attack into Germany from the Saar. But Gen. Strong disagreed. It was not prudent, he told those getting up from the table, to underrate their enemy. Strong was concerned that those around the table had only known the *Boche* in retreat—Africa, Italy, France. They did not know the terror of 1940 and the ferocity of their opponent on the attack. "He who has not fought the Germans," went the British adage, "does not know war."

After the meeting Lt. Gen. Everett S. Hughes and other generals joined Eisenhower for celebratory dinner. Ike enjoyed his favorite food, a big plate of oysters, and Hughes pulled out a bottle of Highland Piper Scotch. There was no more highly prized gift in Eisenhower's entourage. Everyone quaffed some of the spirits and a few lit cigars. All enjoyed basking in the afterglow in the promotion of the new General of the Army.

But their reverie was interrupted once more with news from the Ardennes. Fragmentary reports identified an increasing number of German divisions involved in the operation. Bradley, who had elected to stay with Eisenhower to await developments, spoke with Sibert in Luxembourg City. His G-2 seemed strangely unperturbed; the attacks would soon peter out for want of supply, he ventured. At one hour till midnight Sibert entered an appraisal into his G-2 journal that would long haunt him: "The sudden attacks and seemingly overwhelming array of six enemy divisions...should not be misinterpreted," he opined believing these actions a spoiling attack designed to forestall the planned upcoming Allied offensives, "The quality of the divisions involved ... and the apparent lack of long-range objectives would seem to limit the enemy threat." He discounted rumors that German tanks had been sighted "miles behind the Allied lines" and took solace in the fact that no SS divisions from the *Sixth Panzer Armee* had been sighted. But Bradley, on hearing of the enemy numbers, decided to leave for Luxembourg City immediately. He would have to drive, with this God-forsaken weather it was impossible to fly.

Schönberg. The German village as seen by a Ninth Air Force reconnaissance pilot. *(NASM)*

The SS *Kriegsberichter* caught the attack of several P-47s of the 366th Fighter Group aganist the armor of *Kampfgruppe Peiper* on December 17th near Büllingen. The attack ended at 10:20 AM when a group of German fighters broke up the aerial assault. Two Thunderbolts were shot down and seven German fighters fell. *(NA)*

While attacking German columns in the Ardennes on December 17th, Maj. Buckingham Dalglish of the 354th Fighter Group destroyed this Me-110. The twin-engined fighter has been hit in its right wing fuel tank. *(NASM)*

Blind bombing. B-26 medium bombers often found the weather in the Ardennes as difficult an obstacle as the enemy. *(NASM)*

Gen. Elwood R. "Pete" Quesada, commander of the IX Tactical Air Command on the phone in the fall of 1944. *(HRC)*

Nugent and friend. Maj. Gen. Richard E. "Dick" Nugent at the headquarters of the XXIX Tactical Air Command in October of 1944. *(HRC)*

Col. Ray J. Stecker, the distinguished commander of the 365th Fighter Group. Stecker had been an All-American backfield football star at West Point in 1932. *(NASM)*

The burning remains of a German fighter shot down near the town of Eupen, north of Monschau. *(NA)*

This Mk V Panther tank of *Kampfgruppe Peiper* was knocked out by air attack just outside Stoumont on the way to the bridge over Lienne Creek at Neufmoulin. *(P. Gossot)*

Lt. Col. Ed Chickering, the youthful commander of the 367th Fighter Group, with his P-38, "Gung Ho." *(Roba)*

The poor flying weather from December 19th-22nd meant that scenes like this one were common. Crew chief S/Sgt. Sirous Benoit sweeps snow off the wing of a Republic P-47. The wings were treated with alcohol so that snow would not stick and could be brushed away. *(HRC)*

Field Marshal Bernard L. Montgomery (left) in charge of the 21st Army Group and Gen. Matthew B. Ridgway in charge of the XVIII Airborne Corps in the Ardennes. *(NA)*

BELOW: Capt. Kenneth H. Dahlberg, 354th Fighter Group was one of the leading aces with the Ninth Air Force. Here, Dahlberg supervises the loading of machine gun rounds into his Republic P-47. Assisting are Sgt. Harry D. Phillips, his crew chief (center), and Pfc. George Spikos. *(NASM)*

Mosquito of No. 2 Group, RAF, probably from 305 (Polish) Squadron. This fast plywood aircraft was one of the most successful night fighters of the war. *(Imperial War Museum)*

Rocket-firing Typhoon of 164 Squadron, RAF. *(Roba)*

C-47s of the IX Troop Carrier Command parachute supplies to the surrounded Bastogne garrison, December 23rd, 1944. *(HRC)*

Cpl. Kenneth Pendergast and Sgt. Sebastian P. Interrante take a weather observation with the aid of a balloon at the Ninth Air Force Headquarters. *(HRC)*

X

The Contested Sky: December 17th

On the morning after the beginning of the offensive, Hitler's *Adlerhorst* headquarters bustled with excitement: noisily tapping teletype machines, messengers coming and going with messages and jangling phones. Hitler was not there. The great Führer was still asleep, having typically stayed up the night before till 5 AM to ring up his various commanders and remind them of their duty and to challenge them to make *Wacht Am Rhein* a success. When he was awakened at 11:30 AM the news was good. Complete surprise had been achieved in the attack. The weather was overcast as Hitler was relieved to learn; the Allied air forces could not intervene.

When the great German attack opened, Göring would be close to the 2,000 planes Hitler desired to support the operation— at least on paper. Many were not serviceable and the skill of the new German pilots remained a question. The weather was inclement, but not poor enough to keep the Luftwaffe from fielding its new-found strength. On December 17th, when the Germans would support the attack with the greatest number of air sorties since D-Day, Göring strutted into Hitler's Eagle's Nest headquarters near Bad Nauheim. The mood at the cloister-like compound was upbeat. Hitler and his aides took a quick stroll above ground at the compound. The roar of gunfire from the Ardennes front could be clearly heard. One of Hitler's staff stenographers recorded the euphoria: "When [Ewald] Reynitz and I went over at 3 PM for the war conference, an imposing number of German fighter planes swept low overhead, and Maj. Büchs...turned to all of us as we excitedly watched our fighters roaring past after so many months of German air inferiority, and said challengingly, 'Who dares say anything against the Luftwaffe now!'"

It was still very dark at 2 AM on December 17th when 15 pathfinders of Maj. Dahlmann's *NJG 20* and 106 aging Ju-52s of the *Transportgeschwader 3* and 4 took to the air. Leading *II/TG3* was Obstlt. Otto Baumann of the famous 'Stalingrad Squadron.' The Ju-52s droned through the night skies flying from Paderborn to Belgium. Their mission was to drop a battle group of 870 parachutists on the Baraque Michel crossroads. The commander of the improvised German battlegroup was Obst. Baron Friedrich-August von der Heydte of Crete fame. The plans had called for the operation to take place right at the beginning of the offensive. But this idea had fizzled when fuel could not be obtained to transport the paratroopers from their billets to the airfield at Paderborn! But much to von der Heydte's dismay, the requisite transport was rounded up for December 17th. They would jump before dawn that Sunday; it would be the first German night parachute operation and their last of any kind in the war!

Uffz. Josef Heinkelbein was a crew member on one of the twenty Ju-52s of *III/TG 4* that took off from Paderborn that cold and misty night. Each plane was loaded with eleven parachutists and four crew members. Heinkelbein recalled that the operation represented a "maximum effort" by *10 Gruppe* even though only half of their Junkers were serviceable. All the crew and parachutists boarded in the pre-dawn darkness. Soon their three engines coughed to life and they waited their turn on the runway. Once aloft, conditions were very turbulent at 3,000 meters and Uffz. Seconemeyer, the pilot, found it frighteningly difficult to maintain formation in the windy night. German searchlights on the ground turned on along their path to help guide their way and the transports sported their red and green running lights. But all this served to nicely pinpoint the targets for U.S. gunners on the ground. Just east of Aachen intense anti-aircraft fire commenced to burst around the slow flying "Auntie-Jus." Suddenly their aircraft took a direct hit. There was a flash of light, a deafening explosion and Heinkelbein had a sensation of tumbling. Their Ju-52/3m, "G6+DU," had broken in half after being struck by an enemy shell. But somehow Heinkelbein was somehow thrown clear of the falling wreckage at low altitude and opened his parachute. Taken prisoner upon landing, he turned out to be the only survivor of his ill-fated crew. The rest of the crew and the *Fallschirmjäger* were all killed, the wreckage slamming into the frozen ground nearby. By any accounting Uffz. Heinkelbein's escape was miraculous.

The airborne operation proved a disaster. Heavy winds and intense anti-aircraft fire scattered the slow planes and fewer than a dozen machines actually reached the flare-marked drop zone. Packing away his parachute and moving to the drop zone Von der Heydte was dismayed to find no more than 25 men had assembled there; by 8 AM the next morning he had only

150 in hand. In all, less than 300 of the original 900 would reach the rendezvous point over the next several days. Some parachutists had been unloaded by their inexperienced pilots as far east as Bonn! One of the transports crashed shortly after take-off and ten others dropped their paratroopers far away from the jump zone or returned with them still on board. "With the pitifully small number of men...I had only the slightest chance of success." Von der Heydte could take small solace in the fact that before his paratroop unit flew, Genfldm. Model told him that even if he believed *Operation Stösser* stood even a 10% chance of success it should go ahead. The *Heeresgruppe B* commander explained that was better than odds he perceived for the entire *Wacht Am Rhein* offensive. But the frustration from *Operation Stösser* knew no boundaries; just after 4 AM, General Elwood Quesada, commanding the IX TAC, received unwelcome news:

> "...our unhappy Officer of the Day was notified that German paratroopers had been dropped at Eupen less than 20 miles away. Similar scare reports had been received earlier, but this time we were also told to arm and put all enlisted men on alert. Instructions like this had never been received before, so we believed that the Jerries had started a little diversionary attack. The plotting table in the Fighter Control Center show 10-12 different enemy formations and the controller estimated that there were 150 German aircraft operating in the First Army area. That night a Combat Command of the 7th Armored Division was passing through Verviers and one of the Officers in the advanced detachment stopped to inquire from the O.D. if the parachutes seen dropping were actually German paratroopers. When told they were Germans he said, 'Paratroopers don't bother us, just tell us what their strength is.' We could not tell him... but the Combat Command moved ahead anyway."

The ULTRA intelligence community was embarrassed by their lack of warning about this; they had seen the planned airborne operation as merely an expedient to transfer German paratroop reinforcements to the Aachen front. Sunday evening, they estimated that 90 Ju-52s had taking part in "dropping 1,500 men in the area South East of Aachen," and now hedged their bets warning that "repetition of this undertaking and/or re-supply operations are to be anticipated during coming nights."

The 365th Fighter Group, the "Hell Hawks," were assigned that Sunday to fly support missions for the 8th and 78th Infantry Divisions in the area between Monschau and Düren. They knew nothing of the enemy operation underway. The first flight with 13 P-47s flew off at 10:41 AM under Capt. John H. Slinde. Each plane had two 500-lb. bombs slung underneath. However, arriving over the front, the controller for the 78th Division, "Foundation," announced that he had no specific targets and asked the pilots to take a look around since German counterattacks had been reported to the south. Maj. John W. Motzenbecker, the Blue Leader, descended down for a low-level search. What he saw shocked him: the roads to the south of Monschau were clogged with trucks, infantry and tanks. At least 150 vehicles, including many tanks, were bunched up in a single convoy.

Motzenbecker had spied *Kampfgruppe Peiper* of the *1SS Panzer Division* and the chief spearhead of Hitler's great attack. All the side roads were similarly infested with the enemy; Motzenbecker hadn't seen anything like this since the massive German retreat across the Seine the previous August. Presently, though, the German column began firing at him and a chunk of flak tore through one of his wings. The surprised pilot called "Sweepstakes." "There's a hell of a big convoy heading into out lines just south of Monschau," he told the controller, "They fired at me. Could that be us, or is it the enemy?" "That," the controller called back excitedly, "is the enemy!"

Motzenbecker called for reinforcements and took his squadron in for a strafing run. By the time they got there the enemy column had dispersed into the woods and put up light flak. The P-47s strafed the column, dropping their bombs on the densely packed roads. The German fire found its mark, however, and hit the mount of 2nd Lt. John D. McCarthy. McCarthy was so low that he never had a chance to get out, slamming into the Ardennes hills. Soon the 388th Squadron under Capt. Robert M. Fry showed up to relieve Capt. Slinde's pilots. Fry's P-47s continued to bomb and strafe the bumper-to-bumper traffic; they claimed 15 destroyed vehicles before they departed. A third mission of 12 planes took off at 12:59 PM under Maj. George R. Brooking. This group located some 150 motor- and horse-drawn vehicles between Monschau and Simmerath (*326 and 272nd Volksgrenadier Divisions*). This enemy convoy was strafed as well, with sixty claimed destroyed by the time the mission was over. Another pilot was lost to flak. Lt. Herbert A. Sting, Jr. was hit by automatic weapons fire, his machine exploding as it slammed into the ground near Monschau. All told, the 365th claimed 107 enemy vehicles destroyed in the action.

Morning of the second day of the offensive saw the soupy weather improve a little, the temperature was 45°F with a clinging mist over the Ardennes. Rain and overcast dominated the picture at the German airfields. Regardless, the orders from *Luftflotte West* would not go unheeded. A group of Fw-190s of *JG 26* scrambled at 9:30 AM in bad weather to intercept the 404th Fighter Group (Lt. Col. Leo C. Moon) moving towards the Bonn - Hangelar airfield, the home of the German night ground attack unit, *NSGr 20* and elements of *KG 55*. So poor was visibility that morning that 26 of the Fw-190s completely missed the U.S. P-47s. However, *I Gruppe* under Oblt. Alfred Heckman had better luck. For all the inexperience in the German air force in the fall of 1944, the *"Schlageter Geschwader"* maintained a sizeable cadre of experienced pilots and perhaps enjoyed a higher morale than some other Luftwaffe units.[39] Call it unit pride; *JG 26* considered themselves elite. And it was with the usual fighting spirit that *JG 26* scrambled from Fürstenau airfield in the midst of scattered snow flurries. Soon they reached the

---

39 Their name came from a German martyr, Alfred Leo Schlageter, an officer turned national hero when he was executed in 1923 by the French for his resistance to occupation of the Ruhr Valley.

Eifel area just east of the front line. Off in the distance they spied a group of eight twin-engined P-38s strafing German columns. The Focke Wulfs pushed their throttles forward to bounce their enemy.

The German prey was the 428th Squadron of the 474th Fighter Group. The 474th was operating in the Moselle area and had already destroyed seven German fighters around Trier during the morning hours. Their P-38s had been strafing German trains in the Bitburg area when the ground controller vectored them to the area northeast of St. Vith. There they found an abundance of enemy transport and other targets. The 500 lb bombs were dropped and the twin-engined aircraft had soon pasted seven German trucks. Then it happened. A gaggle of some two dozen German Fw-190s dove out of the sky on the fork-tailed planes. Soon four of the eight P-38s fell out of the sky at no cost to *JG 26*.[40] The fighter group claimed four Fw-190s destroyed, although they were likely from *I Gruppe* of *JG 2* since *JG 26* reported no losses. Only one pilot of the strafing Yellow Flight came back. This was Lt. Alexander "Greek" Zeece, whose plane was the most shot up aircraft ever to return to the base at Florennes. Lt. Oliver Berg brought back another aircraft in similar straits. Lt. John W. "Jack" Mahoney's P-38 was badly damaged and the Lieutenant was wounded. Mahoney had no choice but to bail out over enemy territory; he spent the rest of the war in captivity at *Stalag Luft I*. The squadron commander, Maj. Ernest B. Nuckols, Jr., was also seriously shot up and forced to play a game of cat and mouse with the German fighters in low hanging clouds to escape back to base. After those still flying had returned, the 428th FG saw itself as nearly out of the fight. Four pilots were lost and only four serviceable aircraft remained.

Their sister squadron, the 430th, successfully engaged 16 Me-109s during a morning bombing mission north of Trier. Seven German fighters were claimed without loss. The squadron returned later in the afternoon, bombing two bridges and a train in the same vicinity. Presently, however, a number of Fw-190s showed up. A battle raged over the Moselle valley with four more enemy fighters claimed against the loss of two P-38s. Another Lightning was forced to make a belly landing in Luxembourg and two more were badly shot up and had to limp back to base on a single engine. Their stalkers had likely been Uffz. Delor and Lt. Günther of *JG 26* who had claimed three P-38s in the swirling air battle that afternoon. By the end of the day, the 474th would tally 13 victories for six losses.

The good German fortune against the P-38s proved to be an exception. A group of Me-109Gs of *JG 27* tangled with the 404th Fighter Group that *JG 26* had missed over Euskirchen. The action cost *JG 27* six pilots in the wild dogfight including *Staffelkapitän* Herbert Rehfeld who perished near Aachen. Another four German pilots were wounded. While this was going

---

40 Killed in action were 2nd Lts. George J. Gildow, George W. Holland, Jr., and Hershel L. Hopper.

on, *I/JG 27* met Hawker Tempests of 56 Squadron, RAF south of Nijmegen. The Me-109s and Fw-190s were providing top cover for the jets of *KG 51* at Rheine airfield since the Me-262 bombers were vulnerable during takeoff and landing. This action, too, did not go well for *JG 27* and four pilots were killed or captured. The British got away without a scratch, landing safely at Volkel. Fhr. Rudolf Achilles was one of the German pilots scrambled from Rheine airfield. He and approximately 30 others took off at 10 AM under Leutnant Winkler, the acting leader of *I/JG 27*, to intercept fighter bombers reported near Nijmegen. The group flew at a height of only 1,000 feet until it ran into the formation of British aircraft that Achilles took to be Typhoons. As he closed to attack, he suddenly recognized that these were the much faster Tempests. Achilles and his comrades were of the firm opinion that the "Gustav" was a reasonable match for the Typhoons, but under no circumstances should its pilots mix it up with Spitfires or Tempests. In a flash, four of the fighters were on the tail of his "Yellow 4" chasing him to tree-top level. His Me-109G-14 took several bursts of fire with the fuel tank bursting into flame. Achilles pulled up quickly and bailed out into captivity after only his fourth combat mission.

The 404th kept up a strong effort, returning in the afternoon to tangle again with the German fighters. Ten miles east of Bonn the 508th Squadron was jumped by several dozen Me-109s and Fw-190s. Two Messerschmitts were destroyed and another two damaged before the 507th Squadron intervened. Soon four more 109s had fallen out of the sky. Nearby, the 506th Squadron tangled with nine enemy fighters and claimed two. Later in the afternoon, the 404th ran into a web of aggressive Fw-190s. One German pilot abandoned his ship after taking hits, the tail of a second was shot off, another was chased into the ground and a fourth exploded when fired on. In all, the 404th would claim some 15 enemy fighters shot down for a loss of two pilots. Even so, *JG 27* would have 16 kills to it's credit by day's end— a total which exactly matched the reported loss by the US Ninth Air Force. *IV/JG 54*, which fought with *JG 27* during the Ardennes operations, lost three pilots killed at the controls of their Fw-190s in the swirling combat over Bonn and Düren (Obfhr. Werner Timpes, Uffz. Heinz Winkler and Fhr. Otto Schelnest).

The *Richthofen Geschwader*, *JG 2*, reported that eight pilots failed to return on December 17th: the losses in *I Gruppe* included Lt. Elser, Gefr. Eube, Fhr. Selpin and Lt. Snobeck. *II* and *III Gruppe* were given direct orders to support the attack of the *Sixth Panzer Armee*. In particular they were to erase a collection of American artillery west of Monschau that was causing a lot of trouble for the ground forces. Hptm. Georg Schröder provided the briefing at Nidda airfield. The contribution from *II/JG 2* would consist of some two dozen Me-109 G-14s with the mission to provide fighter escort for ten Fw-190s of *III Gruppe* from Ettingshausen. These carried 21 cm rockets under each wing to blast American artillery positions around Monschau. The force took off at 10:30 AM; the Messerschmitts joined the Fw-190s over Nidda and headed west at 13,000 feet. Near Monschau the group was assailed by a group of fifteen P-47s near Krinkelt, Belgium. The German fighters attempted to escape in the clouds. Obfhr. Hans Kowalski, a 20-year old veteran with some sixty missions was one of these. His "White 11" was hit in the engine and cockpit by one of the P-47s and Kowalski bailed out and became a prisoner near Eschweiler. Others lost from *II Gruppe* included Ofw. Nowack, Fw. Fester and Gefr. Rebmann who all managed to bail out of their stricken machines. Gefr. Frischer was not as lucky. He plunged to his death in his Fw-190A-8 after a dogfight with a group of P-47s near Bitburg. *JG 2* was unable to claim a single American aircraft shot down in these engagements.

Most of the other German fighter groups were also out in force. All took severe losses. *JG 4* suffered most. According to the previously drawn up plan of air operations, *Kommodore* Michalski's *Geschwader* was assigned to intervene directly in the ground battle. Maj. Michalski's command was a veteran unit with air-ground cooperation, having fought with distinction in the operations in Italy against the Anzio beachhead. Brought to the Western Front to support the big German offensive, *JG 4* was cast into a killing sky over the Ardennes. Most of the German fighters never made it beyond the border. *JG 4* reported ten killed, another missing and three more wounded in a bitter air battle just east of St. Vith. One of the predators could have possibly been the 362nd Fighter Group, whose Maj. Loren W. "Ace" Herway shot down a Fw-190 after "scaring the hell out of the pilot with four 5-inch rockets." Prior to the operation, morale in the *Geschwader* had been good as evidenced by the un-mailed letter taken from a captured pilot of 6 *Staffel*:

"Dear Parents, especially Dear Dad,

I almost forgot your birthday. We are very busy here. They almost got me on my last operational flight. You must realize that we are now the first unit in the West to meet the enemy. As you know 800 fighters accompany the bombers as escort. Our unit is praised again and again. All heavy fighters ask for us as high altitude cover. So you can imagine how busy we are with only 30 planes. Losses are high. Two of my best friends did not return last Sunday, and never will. In our *Staffel* with ten pilots you feel that sort of thing. But now I am finding just how useful experience is. Aachen is our sector for ground strafing missions. That is a terrific sight. When one sees the front for the first time. You hear nothing, but below you see clouds of smoke and guns flash. The flak fires like mad. In this madhouse you force yourself to be calm, seek your target and shoot. I have four operational flights now, among them two against enemy bombers over Reich territory...I have not had any mail for a very long time on account of my transfers....
Yours ever,
Kurt"

Needless to say, Kurt was shot down. Even before the German fighters could reach the battlefront, they were set upon near Hunsrück by a covey of

P-47s. The air battle eddied over the sullen skies to Trier with the Americans enjoying a numerical advantage. Lt. Heinz Krause spun to his death over Cochem and Lt. Brindlinger and Uffz. Heyne fell near Zemmern. In the *II Gruppe*, Lt. Lehmann and Fw. Eippold were killed. Uffz. Weichmann was wounded, bailing out from his falling Fw-190 to swing down under parachute to the nearby German headquarters of the *LXVI Armeekorps* near Pronsfeld. The fortunes of *IV Gruppe* and *III Gruppe* were nearly as bad. Over the Eifel, they found themselves facing twenty angry P-47s. Uffz. Heinrichs was blasted by a number of Thunderbolts spinning in near Mürlenbach. Uffz. Gras and Walther were killed and Uffz. Ziegler was listed as missing.

After being hit, near Bonner, over the Ahr Mountains, *JG 3 "Udet"* fought a tough battle with the enemy. Uffz. Werner Thiel jumped from his aircraft over Nierendorf and Gefr. Gustav Neiszl did the same over Krinkelt, Belguim. Lt. Rolf Lahne was last seen over Bonn in "Red 5" his Fw-190A-8. Also operating in the same battle zone was *I Gruppe* of *JG 11*. The Me-109G-14s were hotly engaged, first by Thunderbolts over Münstereifel, and later by a number of P-38s. Four of the German pilots were wounded with Uffz. Liebeck taking to his parachute. Similarly, Uffz. Heyer was able to knock out a P-38, but was then himself seriously wounded and forced to bail out from "Black 1." Meanwhile, another confused dogfight raged near Wittlich with three Fw-190 pilots killed: Uffz. Dalecki, Grätzer and Schäfer.

Over the Ardennes battlefield, the German air action appeared as several waves of German fighters buzzed noisily overhead in the early morning with at least two dozen fighters. These planes strafed American positions in Losheimergraben and north of Monschau before departing the area. These were rocket-carrying Fw-190s of *JG 2*, with their escort. Overall these attacks were of little tactical value, but for the GIs on the receiving end, the idea of being strafed— even if ineffective— was troubling. At his headquarters in Eupen, Maj. Gen. Leonard T. "Gee" Gerow, shook his head as he witnessed the indiscriminate bombing that the Germans parceled out that night. "What are those bastards of huns up to?" he wondered out loud. Gen. Gerow's thoughts echoed those of many on the Allied side. All hell was breaking loose.

But if bewildered, the Americans were not to be outdone. They matched the German flurry of activity with a mad morning of their own. The U.S. IX TAC moved to support the teetering Allied defense in the north and counter the sudden upsurge in German night fighter activity. The social plans of the 422nd Night Fighter Squadron were interrupted:

> "Doc Whitner had big-dealed a lot of eggs and by scouring the countryside, found enough rum and Cognac to provide the wherewithal for an egg-nog Christmas and New Years...Things were proceeding along a very even tenor of existence with everyone's minds on Christmas, crews going on combat leaves to England and Paris, the usual bitching about the mail situation, the chow and the weather. All of a sudden things began to pop..."

Things "a poppin'" meant that the 422nd Night Fighter Squadron with P-61 "Black Widows" was up in the night sky claiming a mixed bag of five enemy planes (one each Fw-190, Me-110, He-111, Ju-87 and Ju-88). "By the next day we realized that this was it. Leaves were cancelled and everyone worked like mad to get our aircraft serviceable." But the P-61s were too few in number to halt the German intruders.[41]

Scrambling to serve a rebuttal to the German intruders of the previous night, the Ninth Air Force assigned 12 of its 14 fighter groups to the IX TAC by 10 AM, including two groups from Nugent's Command. The weather hampered daytime operations, however, and the IX Bomb Division was unable to operate at all. Nugent's XXIX TAC put up 105 sorties on the 17th, but none of these were over the Ardennes. Their claims totalled four enemy aircraft for the loss of a like number of their own. Out of the total 647 fighter-bomber sorties flown by the Ninth Air Force, only about ninety operated over the battlefield. Many other sorties were vectored to the Ardennes, but were forced to engage the aggressive German fighters operating west of the Rhine. And although the Ninth Air Force claimed 68 enemy aircraft destroyed that day, they were forced to admit the loss of 27 of their own. In its report to High Command that night, Model and *Heeresgruppe B* announced that "Over the entire front there has been only limited enemy bomber and recon activity. Considerable relief was achieved by the commitment of German fighter units over the attack area." For the first time in late 1944, the Luftwaffe was successfully contesting Allied air superiority.

It was the evening of December 16th at 10 rue Auxerre in Nancy, France. After dinner, Bradley's chief of staff Maj. Gen. Leven C. Allen, called the Third Army headquarters. Col. Harkins took the call; he quickly relayed the message to Patton. He had orders that would take Morris's 10th Armored Division away from Third Army and send it off to Maj. Gen. Troy H. Middleton and his VIII Corps. "What!" Patton said, biting his after-dinner cigar. The Third Army commander promptly rang up Bradley. Regardless of his prior premonitions, Patton protested vehemently. "Don't spoil my show," Patton pleaded, "Third Army has sweated and bled to bring this damned thing to a head. Without 10th Armored we won't be able to exploit to Saarlautern." But Bradley would not even discuss the matter; the orders were from Eisenhower. The 10th went to Middleton in the Ardennes and that was final. Patton wearily resigned himself to the decision, "I guess they're having trouble up there," he sighed, "I thought they would." His G-3, Col.

---

41 The maintenance troubles for the few P-61s of the 422nd and 425th Night Fighter Squadrons were so severe that the night fighter squadrons were only able to average 12 to 20 sorties per night. The 422nd operated for a time during the Ardennes operations with only four operational P-61s available— each being flown two or three times in a single evening. This shortage was underscored during the campaign, for the Germans emphasized their night operations during the period and completely overwhelmed the few night fighter sorties that the Americans could mount. During December the 422nd destroyed 16 enemy aircraft against the five claimed by the 425th.

Halley G. Maddox thought the bleak development might have a silver lining. Without reserves, after Operation Tink blasted through the Saar, the Germans would have little to stop them. It would be a race between Patton and Hitler in opposite directions! "You're right," Patton agreed, "that would be the way to do it. But that isn't the way the gentlemen up north fight. My guess is that our offensive will be called off and we'll have to go up there and save their hides."

With the situation degenerating, Patton and the commander of his XIX Tactical Air Command, Gen. Otto Weyland, yearned to know the situation on their north flank. "German attacks have materialized in VIII Corps front," Weyland entered in his diary, "First Army very surprised!!...ground attack by sixteen German divisions supported by GAF (German Air Force) in some strength." Early on the morning of December 17th, Weyland sent the 12th Squadron from the 10th PRG to the north to scan the enemy zone to the east of the Ardennes. Unfortunately, upon arriving near their appointed "look-see" targets, they discovered that the Luftwaffe was lurking about in great numbers. Capt. William Winberry and Lt. Karl Brandt had been assigned to make passes over Lambstein, Cochem, Bingen and Sobernheim. However, both men counted themselves lucky to escape with their lives; they were set upon by twenty enemy fighters intent on shooting them down. Only the superior speed of their Mustangs enabled them to evade the enemy. They were pursued for more than fifty miles.

The experiences of Lt. Goodermote and Lt. Merlin Reed were identical; they were able to evade the surprisingly strong enemy, but could not complete their assigned missions. In spite of the less than optimal weather, the 31st Photo Reconnaissance Squadron flew 19 missions on the 17th. However, they also found the Luftwaffe's new presence a daunting prospect in their unarmed F-5A Lightnings. Lt. James Butler had a harrowing experience. Having received an exceedingly warm reception by flak over his assigned photo runs over Merhausen and Bad Nauheim airfields, he was soon set upon by angry hornets— a quartet of irate Fw-190s. Completion of the mission was out of the question; Butler pushed the throttle and headed west. Even so, shaking the enemy was another matter. One of the 190s chased Butler all the way back over Allied lines. Upon landing, he found he had been fortunate to make it back: part of his Lightning's stabilizer had been shot away and the fuselage looked like swiss cheese.

The American tactical-recon group had the better of it in the afternoon, however. The Germans were still out in force, but the 10th's 15th Squadron managed to shoot down seven German aircraft in the Giessen-Wiesbaden area— the biggest day in the group's history. The action began when Lt. Clyde East spied an Me-109 with gaudy white and orange paint, zipping along 200 feet above the Autobahn east of Giessen. Two machine gun bursts on the surprised German fighter saw it drop to the ground and explode.

While this was happening, Lt. Ronald Ricci and Lt. Lawrence Leonard come upon two Heinkel 111s flying near Wiesbaden. The slow bombers were no match for the nimble P-51s and the two enemy aircraft were sent earthward.

But the top scoring pilot for the 10th PRG on December 17th was Capt. John H. Hoefker. Covering enemy highways near Frankfurt, Hoefker came upon two Me-109s which passed under him near Giessen. He put his F-6D Mustang into a hard diving turn, closing to within 150 yards of the enemy plane before he opened fire. Almost instantly, Hoefker saw a cloud of hits all over the plane and the German pilot popped his canopy and prepared to bail out. So damaged was the Me-109, however, that the crippled machine went into an uncontrolled wing-over and the German pilot was unable to escape. As the first Me-109 slammed into the ground, Hoefker found himself under attack by the other enemy fighter. But the captain quickly turned into his enemy and managed to get off a wild shot at a hundred yard range. The German pilot took evasive action, climbing to 1,500 feet and then began winging-over and diving to tree top level. Hoefker stayed right with the German closing to within 100 feet at low altitude before firing a burst that sent the plane crashing into the ground. After the second victory, Hoefker met a Fw-190 as he flew along the *Autobahn* towards Kirch. Again surprising the enemy, he closed to within 50 yards before pumping bullets into the plane. After a wild series of acrobatics in which the German plane received three more doses of machine gun fire, the Luftwaffe pilot jettisoned his canopy and bailed out. But even with three victories, the day was not over for Hoefker. After completing their reconnaissance at about 3:40 PM, he and his wingman, Lt. Charles White, were amazed to see an enemy Ju-188 bomber ambling across their return path. Avoiding defensive fire from the enemy bomber, Hoefker slipped behind the bomber and hosed the plane with gunfire. White joined in and soon the bomber flipped over on its back. The enemy crew jumped out and the plane exploded as it fell into the suburbs of Wiesbaden.

But if the 10th PRG was overmatching their enemy, the reports they brought back to Patton struck an ominous chord. Capt. Edward L. Bishop of the 12th Tactical Recon Squadron had been detailed to the Third Army headquarters in Nancy since early December. With much of the morning attempts at reconnaissance turned back, Patton asked Bishop to personally fly over the Luxembourg sector and let him know of the situation. Bishop promptly sped aloft in his old P-51B Mustang. Peering through the mist over the battle zone, Bishop observed a wholesale enemy advance in the northern part of Luxembourg. Many American units, now greatly outnumbered, were being forced to pull back; others were surrounded in the villages he passed over. It was a calamitous scene quite unlike any Bishop had never witnessed. He later remembered that it "scared me quite a bit and I turned my Mustang around and headed back to report the sad situation to General Patton."

Bishop landed and gave his commander the less than reassuring news. Patton knew Bishop as a steady man not prone to exaggeration. He called Gen. Omar Bradley, in charge of the 12th Army Group, and asked for an urgent meeting the very next morning. Gen. Weyland was despondent. "If this goes through," he said of Patton's prediction of an imminent move north, "Operation Tink will be off since 3rd Army will not have the punch to exploit the Air Force's effort."

While Patton and Weyland were scouring the cloud-ridden skies to find out what was going on, the 368th Fighter Group (Col. Richard C. Sanders) attempted to sweep the enemy fighters away from the northern zone of the battlefield. His squadrons concentrated on helping the beleaguered 106th Division, now in danger of encirclement in the mountainous Schnee Eifel. The 396th and 397th Squadrons plunked bombs on a German attack column of the *18 Volksgrenadier Division* near Schönberg with 28 P-47s at 1:40 PM. Meanwhile, the 395th Squadron waged a fierce dogfight with twenty Me-109s of Obstlt. Kurt Bühligen's famous *JG 2* "Richthofen," that dropped out of overcast skies near Prüm. Bühligen was then one of the few German aces to have amassed over a hundred kills against Allied fighters in the West. Maj. Leary, in charge of the 397th Fighter Squadron, asked the controller for the most urgent target. The controller replied that "Our troops are holding St. Vith, but there is a very strong enemy column about a mile and half away. If you can knock out the leading tank and slow them, we may be able to hold the town tonight." Although radio interference prevented communication with the rest of the squadron, the Major sighted a group of vehicles assembling in front of St. Vith and repeatedly strafed the column destroying many trucks. In a freak occurrence, enemy flak guns firing at the U.S. planes managed to hit their own column effectively halting any advance. A second mission returned to the scene and hit Schönberg once more claiming 30 trucks and several tanks knocked out. Five Thunderbolts were damaged by flak. Also mixing it up in the same area were the "Hun Hunters" of the 366th Fighter Group, whose pilots bombed the village of Auw in the face of intense flak from the Germans who were moving through the Losheim Gap.

The 405th Fighter Group (Lt. Col. J. Garrett Jackson) also scrambled from St. Dizier, putting up 80 sorties in support of the U.S. 106th Infantry Division. The 510th Squadron reportedly bombed German vehicles observed headed west at Brandscheid while the 509th Fighter squadron blasted a marshalling yard at Hillesheim. Other "Thunder Monster" planes hit Wahlen, near Trier, and Ruhrburg leaving the latter town in flames. But these actions were uncontested. In another mission, the 405th reported 14 direct 500 lb. bomb hits on an ammunition dump near Koblenz. However, in this action the 510th Squadron ran into a bevy of Me-109s with Lts. Orange and Schaeffer shooting down three. After the enemy planes fled, the group ran into another dogfight in progress between several German Fw-190s and some P-38s.

Captain Harry G. Sanders shot down one of the enemy planes and Lt. C.A. Black seriously damaged another. One P-47, that of Lt. Edwin A. "Mac" McGachan was forced to belly land after flak damage.[42] Further south, the 509th Squadron led by Capt. Chester L. Van Etten was escorting Lancasters from RAF Bomber Command, when they were jumped by Me-109s. Van Etten's group managed to shoot down one before the scrap ended.

The 367th Group (Col. Edwin S. Chickering) took off at 1:05 PM to attack a German held pontoon bridge near Bollendorf. The P-38s braved four enemy fighters to strike at the span. Later, the group was vectored to attack an enemy column northeast of St. Vith at Born with 75 trucks and an estimated 50 tanks— possibly the *1SS Panzer Grenadier Regiment* which was passing through the area that afternoon. During the mission, Lt. Elson Rodewall had his Lightning's right engine shot out by enemy flak. Soon, his Lightning caught fire and the cockpit filled with smoke "It's time to get out of here," he called over the radio to his squadron leader, "I gotta go." Quite unexpectedly another pilot broke in, "Well, when ya gotta go, ya gotta go." Rodewall bailed successfully, but never learned his jester's identity. But on the ground, the soldiers were more respectful. Describing the action the U.S. 112th Infantry Regiment reported "air tremendously effective."

The "Raiders" of the 406th Fighter Group registered a major portion of the day's claims for Weyland's command. Flying west of Zulpich, the 513th Squadron joined three P-38s in chasing down four Me-109s. But the enemy had friends; an encounter followed with nearly 40 Me-109s. Regardless, seven of the enemy were claimed without loss. 1st Lt. Elton V. Kern accounted for three and Lt. Eldon Dunkleberger, Myron A. Stone and Paul C. Davenport each accounted for one each. Meanwhile, the 513th on a heading given by "Ripsaw" (XIX Air Controller) found eight P-38s northeast of Prüm near Steffeln, Germany in a dogfight with six Fw-190s. The P-47s jettisoned their bombs and closed on the enemy, claiming three. One of the P-47s collided with a P-38 in the engagement, but the pilot, Lt. Richard Moulton, was seen to bail out, albeit over enemy territory. Further south, 1st Lt. Don Dorman, Jr. flew a morning mission with the 514th Squadron which was changed to a secondary target, Strasbourg, because of weather. After returning to base he was approached by the Operations Section Chief who was looking for someone to fill in for a pilot who was sick. But Dorman had failed to learn one of the fundamental tenets of basic training, that is, *not to volunteer*. The 514th took off for Patton's front line; when reaching 6,000 feet the No. 3 pilot indicated that his engine was running rough and he had to turn back. Dorman moved into his position. In about 20 minutes they

---

42 McGachan managed to make his way back to the 405th Fighter Group after a series of misadventures behind friendly lines in which he was suspected of being an undercover German commando. This was only resolved by correctly identifying "Blondie" and "Dagwood."

zoomed over a German panzer unit, hastily scurrying about to camouflage their exposed tanks:

> "We dropped our napalm bombs on them and went down to strafe. 20mm flak opened up on us and we had to break away. I located the gun emplacement and dove down to strafe its location, but did not see another gun to my side. He made several hits. My engine quit and a fire started near the left side of my feet in the cockpit. I pulled the stick back, flipped open the canopy, unfastened the seat belt, stood up and dove for the trailing edge of the wing, and pulled the rip cord. My leg hit the tail of the plane, my chute opened, I swung once and hit the ground, rolling into the ack-ack position I had been strafing seconds before. The German gunner very carefully removed my 45 automatic, and with his knife cut the chute cords from around me and said 'For you the Var isst over!'"

The pilot became a self-described graduate, "Magna Cum Laude, of *Stalag Luft 1*, Class of '45." But American POWs were of small consolation to the Germans under the watchful eyes of the fighter-bombers. That day, the *79 Volksgrenadier Division* reported its *212 Regiment* held up because the railroad tracks between Mosel-Kern and Mueden had been slashed by Allied *Jabos* who blasted the town from "front to rear" between 1 and 2 PM. Four soldiers were wounded and two killed with six railroad cars demolished. At about the same time, near the town of Duisdorf, the *Führer Grenadier Brigade* was subjected to an attack by three fighter bombers as they unloaded their tanks from the train. No equipment was lost, but three soldiers were killed and another ten wounded.

Near Trier, the 474th Fighter Group (Col. Clinton C. Wasem) ran into a dozen fighters of Obstlt. Josef "Pips" Priller's *JG 26*. Eleven German planes were shot down at a cost of three of the P-38s. The 354th Group attacked a German command post near Merzig, starting several fires, and one of its squadrons caved in a railway tunnel. Meanwhile the 362nd FG hit German artillery positions northeast of Saarguemines. Near Dahlen some 40 single engine German fighters challenged the 377th Squadron in a furious engagement. One Fw-190 was destroyed and one damaged at no cost to "Mogin's Maulers." In all the XIX TAC put up some 153 sorties on December 17th, claiming 15 German aircraft shot down for the loss of five of their own.

To the north, the Thunderbolts of the 366th Fighter Group (Col. H. Norman Holt) hit the *1st SS Panzer Division*'s armored spearhead in the vicinity of Büllingen destroying several vehicles including a Wirbelwind flak panzer and scattering the accompanying grenadiers into the surrounding woods. As usual, U.S. claims for the destroyed German vehicles far outweighed the actual count. The 366th claimed thirty tanks and vehicles destroyed! This foray ended, however, when a dozen Me-109s and four Fw-190s moved to break up the attack at about 10:20 AM. This forced the American pilots to jettison their bombs, although they claimed seven German fighters in the melee, losing only two of their fighters to enemy flak.

"The enemy attack brought out a great many vehicles, troops and equipment out into the open," the IX TAC recorded. Total ground claims for Quesada's command included 107 vehicles of all types destroyed. Close by all this commotion in Ambléve was Corporal Albert C. Schommer of the 291st Engineer Combat Battalion who was on the radio in the town. Strangely, a sudden flow of traffic appeared in streets headed west. Then, he saw Thunderbolts north of the town obviously bombing and strafing something. Puffs of flak peppered the air and Schommer saw one of the plane burst into flame and crash. German flak, Schommer thought; what was German flak doing out here? Soon Sgt. William H. Smith showed up in Ambléve out of breath and white as a sheet. The Germans were coming: they were right up the road. Schommer and the 291st bugged out with the rest.

The German view of the action was reported by Fw. Karl Laun, an Austrian flak officer with the *Flaksturm Battalion 84* assigned to the *1 SS Panzer Division*:

> "Another halt is called before Losheim. We advance 300 meters and then stop again no doubt an order to await noon or rather the Jabos. There they are already those Thunderbolts and Lightnings. Their flying order is perfect with only two Mustangs [SIC], those *Katzenjammer* kids, diving in and out of formation and generally indulging in gymnastic horseplay. They are always where there is something interesting to dive on. Now the first wave of Thunderbolts starts diving at us. Our quadruple flak platoon opens up and succeeds in setting the last plane on fire. However, our positions there along the highway are so unfortunate that a series of prematurely bursting flak shells makes seven men of our Battery candidates for the *Verwundeten* medal. Instead of the advertised 1000 planes, approximately 50 Messerschmitts and Focke Wulfs arrive, who are evidently very reluctant to enter into dogfights. One can easily sense it from down here; how they wriggle and turn to get out of the *Jabos'* field of vision...the proportion of airplanes shot down is 3:1 in favor of the U.S...In the late afternoon we continue the advance..."

Not all the American pilots were as gung-ho as the enemy assessment might suggest. Allen V. Mundt was a new replacement pilot with the 387th Fighter Squadron of the "Hell Hawks"— the 365th Fighter Group:

> It was morning 17 December 44, the day I thought I must die. The early mission had discovered the break-through and returned somehow. There was one loss, a "new boy" named McCarthy. It was his first or second mission. The base was a former Luftwaffe field with good cement runways near a Belgian village named Chievres. And now it was socked in. Really socked in! You couldn't see out the window to the next building. 0900 was briefing time for the second mission. I was scheduled. It would be my second and I was thinking about McCarthy. We had both joined the squadron on Thanksgiving Day— six of us. We'd been more or less enroute for three months and hadn't flown. We were *not* hot. Our total time each couldn't have been over 300 hours, and about 85 in the T-bolt. My first training flight was really hairy. We didn't get many more. Anyway, my first mission on the 14th was a milk-run. It was obvious that the second would be the other side of the coin. We filed into the briefing room, took our seats and waited. It wasn't until the Group CO came in that I really

began to sweat. Colonel Ray. J. Stecker, former all-American halfback at West Point with grey hair still looked like he could play. His look and manner now made it obvious that this was for real. The fog seemed thicker than ever. My thoughts: They don't send good young, all-American boys on suicide missions— do they? I resigned myself that this was going to be a one way trip for me. Even if I got the airplane off the ground in one piece, a bailout was the best I could hope for. We were given a start-engine time and a take-off time. The rest I don't remember. We had about an hour to suit up and get ready. There wasn't time to write a last letter. I'm not sure I thought about it. Next scene: the parachute tent. Sid Rabinowitz was the rigger. We had scarcely met. The tent was crowded with pilots— all old-heads. Old boys from when the group formed at Richmond. I was the only "new boy," the untried pledge in the fraternity. They had my respect. Some even had a victory or two. We all sat on the floor. I have never been so afraid. It must have been obvious to Bob Robinson. He alone made an attempt at reassurance. He sat by me and said a few quiet things; I'll be forever grateful. Then it was time to go the aircraft...The phone rang...Stand down for an hour...waiting for a break...But the mission's still on...More waiting...waiting...more sweat. Maybe another hour. The phone again! Mission scrubbed...Wow! They put it together again for the afternoon. But there had been time enough to reschedule. This new boy was not on it. In fact all of the new guys were grounded until the big scare was over. We got to pull guard duty around out remote BOQ that night and on a few more. Skorzeny was rumored to have dropped his saboteurs in American uniforms in the area. One was picked up on a street car in Mons. Spookey duty for the new boys. We had .45s and carbines, and the cold fog. Lucky we didn't shoot each other.

Mundt ended the war with 58 missions, but solemnly noted that five of the twelve "new boys" who joined the "Hell Hawks" along with him did not survive.

All told, a total of Allied 1,020 non-battlefield fighter sorties were carried out on the 17th, many to engage the large number of German aircraft moving west from their airfields. The weather remained poor, however, and the IX Bomber Command and the U.S. Eighth Air Force were grounded. Pete Quesada's IX TAC saw more of the enemy on December 17th than they had encountered in a long time. An early mission by Col. Peck's 67th TRG verified the obvious. Once they were up, the P-51 pilots saw German traffic everywhere. Capt. Max C. Spencer snapped pictures of a long enemy column near Düren while Lt. Robert D. Wesley reported a "bumper to bumper" column of enemy vehicles with armor headed for St. Vith. But few pilots could look long. German "bandits" were all over the place. Lt. Lewis P. Johnson was jumped by a Fw-190 west of Koblenz and Lt. Arthur A. Degenhardt was bounced by four Me-109s northwest of Düren. Although Degenhardt's plane was riddled, Lt. Turner managed to shoot down one of the marauders. Of the 31 missions flown by Quesada's command, most were intended to provide close support to the pressured American GIs below. In all, IX TAC put up 398 sorties on December 17th. However, in many instances German fighters caused the American pilots to jettison their bombs to meet the enemy. IX TAC claimed 49 enemy aircraft shot down, while losing 18 of their own.

The Luftwaffe was very active with 500-600 aircraft over the battle zone, more than twice the number which ordinarily operated over the Western Front. Quesada's IX TAC alone reported 543 encounters with enemy aircraft in its sector. The IX summary of operations reflected German intentions: "The enemy aircraft were aggressive and although the enemy intention of attacking our troops was generally forestalled, in several instances the GAF succeeded in breaking up attacks by our fighters on his ground troops." Perhaps more telling than the numbers of German aircraft observed was where they were encountered. Whereas, the Ninth had usually found the enemy over Germany in recent days, most of the 15 engagements reported on the 17th were further west in Belgium. According to Luftwaffe records, *II Jagdkorps* launched some 650 planes from 16 fighter wings to intervene in the Ardennes battle on the 17th. The Allied intelligence community counted at least 350 sorties in the morning alone, "mainly ground-strafing immediately in the area in which paratroops were dropped." Most of these operated between Monschau, Malmédy and St. Vith. Evening plans were also overheard by ULTRA:[43]

> "*II Jagdkorps* orders night 17-18 December were to support 6 SS Pz Army's attack by covering right flank by continuous harassing attacks on roads, railways and localities area Sittard - Aachen - Eupen - Liège - Maastricht. Objective: materially delay Allied movements."

True to the intelligence, later that night the Luftwaffe sallied forth with another 250 sorties flown by the night fighter and night ground attack aircraft Allied rear areas. The Allies estimated that 100 Ju-88 sorties were flown in two missions. That night the Luftwaffe again took to the skies. Fifteen Ju-88s of *I/LG 1* took off from Varel to pelt Verviers with fragmentation bombs while two dozen bombers of *II Gruppe* left to attack Allied troop positions in the Ardennes S.W. of Aachen. Also joining in were nine Ju-88s of *I/KG 66* who took off singly at ten minute intervals beginning at 3 AM on Monday with orders to disrupt American troop movements over roads in the Aachen area. The idea was to slow Allied traffic trying to reinforce the Ardennes attack zone. At least three of the nighttime phantoms were shot down by anti-aircraft fire. The Junkers dropped fragmentation bombs and flares on Allied motor columns, but one captured participant meekly described the missions as "not overly successful." Although the Luftwaffe's evening shenanigans were dutifully reported by the American motor columns headed for the Ardennes, the German sorties were of no more than harassment value. The Ju-87s released flares and dropped a few poorly

---

43 ULTRA also warned of the arrival of "*Staffel Einhorn*" from Italy, an air ground-attack unit which was "known to employ special Fw-190 aircraft carrying 4,000 lb. bombs and specializing in attacking Allied headquarters."

aimed bombs.[44] But none of this did anything to retard the massive flow of American reinforcements to the threatened Ardennes. In the following week, the First Army moved nearly 200 convoys from the north with 48,711 vehicles and some 248,000 personnel.

The British, too, were up that Sunday evening. RAF Bomber Command launched a massive nighttime heavy bombing raid that dwarfed the German nightly effort. The German cities of Ulm, Duisberg and Munich, each important to the German lines of communication, were flattened by a rain of bombs. Some 5,000 tons of high explosives were dropped on the cities from 1,200 sorties. An additional 44 Mosquitos attacked the rail center at Hanau with another 50 tons of bombs. Another 16 Mosquitos of No. 2 Group, RAF strafed ten enemy convoys seen east of VIII Corps in the Eifel that night with "strikes seen in all cases."

But during the day the Luftwaffe had at last frustrated the total Allied domination of the air space over the Western Front. However, the achievement was at grave cost. The balance sheet for the day showed 68 German planes shot down at a cost of 16 American machines, all of the latter being claimed by *JG 26* and *27*. Although likely inflated, the Allied AA units claimed a further 54 knocked down that Sunday. The Luftwaffe, by it's own estimates, wrote off 55 pilots killed or missing and another 24 wounded in its attempt "to support the army." These included irreplaceable flight leaders such as Hptm. Herbert Rehfeld to *JG 27* who fell near Aachen.

Far away from the air and ground war, the Allied intelligence officers hurriedly distributed their ULTRA material to anxious Allied commanders. The news was disquieting. A nearly complete order of battle showed over twenty German divisions taking part in the operation. The enemy attack pointed to Liège as its objective. The Luftwaffe commitment also looked significant; *Jagdkorps II* announced that it would put up 100 - 200 aircraft the next day to support the advance of *Sixth Panzer Armee*. The orders for the Luftwaffe reconnaissance forces were explicit: "protection of advance of 5 and 6 Panzer Armies and 7 Army." There was more, nearly disclosing the immediate German objectives:

Establish-
  a) Conditions of Meuse crossings near Huy as well as from Namur to Givet.
  b) Whether Allies are bringing up forces from North via Hohes Venn.
  c) Whether Allies are bringing up forces from area on both sides of Luxembourg.

In addition to this ambitious agenda, Genfldm. Model nervously requested the reconnaissance services of the Luftwaffe to locate his prime armored spearhead. *Kampfgruppe Peiper* was advancing so rapidly that it was out of radio contact. Model hoped to find that his spearhead was near the

---

44 One of these created momentary alarm at the headquarters of the U.S. First Army in Spa, Belgium. On the night of December 17th, a lone German bomb suddenly exploded in the night only a mile away.

Meuse River, for there was little time to lose if they were to get to the prize at Antwerp.

The atmosphere at the Hôtel Britannique had reached something of a tumult. The staff at Hodges' converted suite had stayed up the previous night trying to make sense of the rapidly developing situation. His nearby V Corps commander, Gen. Gerow, was excited. This was troubling since Hodges knew Gerow to be a cool character. Communications had been shot out by a big artillery barrage just before daybreak and the Germans were playing marches on the available radio frequencies. From what Hodges could tell, there were reports of German attacks all up and down the line. Worst of all were the 7,000 surrounded American soldiers of the U.S. 106th Infantry Division, now cut off by the Germans east of St. Vith in the Schnee Eifel. Without resupply they could not hold out for long. The First Army commander set about arranging an air drop of 127 C-47 plane loads to the besieged division. Unable to reach Bradley, who was on the road from Versailles to Luxembourg City, Gen. Hodges knew he needed help. He rang up Lt. Gen. William H. "Big Bill" Simpson, the commander of the U.S. Ninth Army to the north. He asked Simpson to meet him the first thing in the morning. Finally, at 7 PM Bradley, having just walked in, returned Hodges' call. The First Army commander implored him to release the two airborne divisions he was holding in reserve. Bradley who could hear the strain in his voice, acceded. The theatre reserves were urgently needed; the 101st Airborne would go to Bastogne; he could use the 82nd to help protect his zone. In spite of an increasingly frantic tone, Hodges' record keeper, Maj. William C. Sylvan, strove to preserve soldierly restraint in the First Army combat diary: "The situation developed badly during the day and may be considered to be serious if not critical."

Punctually at 5:30 AM on the 17th, Gen. Simpson arrived at Spa, his jeep prudently escorted by some armored cars. With Simpson was Dick Nugent who was to meet again with Pete Quesada and the others to resolve the question of air support for the coming Roer River offensive. The group of the day before was there. Nugent was bleary-eyed, having been woken at three in the morning by word that "a tremendous German air action was evident on the board including troop carriers and night fighters." What Nugent did not know was that the Germans were unloading 800 parachutists not fifteen miles from First Army headquarters where he was to attend another air operations meeting. What he did know was that the spectral German night fighters had the audacity to bomb and strafe in the vicinity of his headquarters in Maastricht. The XXIX TAC plotters had traced the bandits from the Bonn area. He quickly cancelled the scheduled support missions for the Ninth Army and ordered a flight of his 404th FG to slam the German airfields at Bonn and Wahn air field at first light. While Nugent was at First Army headquarters for the meeting, Nugent's retribution mission headed for the German air fields. They never made it. Crossing into Germany they were set upon by a large pack of Fw-190s and Me-109s and were forced to jettison their "frags" and dogfight the enemy. Even so 23 German aircraft were claimed for a loss of eight. Later in the day another effort was made to reach the enemy airfields, but again this was intercepted by the enemy. In spite of the opposition, however, the field at Wahn was attacked and large fires reportedly started near its hangars.

The repeat meeting the next day was all business; everyone was less inclined to bicker over the details. All knew of the German counterattack. Hodges looked nervous, there were constantly messages interrupting their meeting and the scene at First Army headquarters was chaotic. The final resolution was that Ninth Army would have its preparation for the Roer River crossings softened up by RAF Bomber Command; the First Army would use the Eighth Air Force. But by the end of the meeting, it was obvious that these plans might soon be completely impertinent. The discussion changed to the developing storm. Hodges, everyone agreed, could use some immediate help. "Today the first appearances of a large scale German counterattack on the First Army front," Nugent entered in his diary, "Tomorrow I am furnishing two [fighter] groups to the support of First Army."

When Simpson arrived at Spa, he found the Hôtel Britannique bristling with guards and Hodges in low spirits. First Army had a captured German staff officer with a map with the entire enemy attack plan. One of the main panzer advance routes went right by his headquarters! Hodges told Simpson of the reported breakthrough in the Losheim Gap and the enemy armored column that had been sighted just twelve miles away. All he had available to defend his headquarters were some towed anti-tank guns, a few half tracks and the "palace guard," the 99th Infantry Battalion. With the continued bad weather, his information was poor. If only they could hit the Germans from the air. "Well, from what I see here, I don't feel too much alarmed," Simpson tried to reassure him, "...I think eventually we'll stop this thing." First Army needed help, he told Simpson, "I've been trying to get in touch with Bradley or Eisenhower and I can't reach either one of them." He needed to ask them for the loan of a division. "Hell, you don't have to!" Simpson retorted, "I've got the 30th Infantry Division in reserve...I'll turn it over to you right now!" Hodges quickly accepted. Soon word came that the German armor was at Stavelot, very near a depot with over two million gallons of gasoline— one of the largest American fuel dumps on the continent. Simpson and the others hurried off.

XI

Achtung Jabos!: December 18th

As leader of the IX Tactical Air Command of the U.S. Ninth Air Force, General Elwood R. Quesada was not known for his modesty. Of course, the name Elwood did not fit the scarf and flying jacket image of the dashing pilot— and "Pete" Quesada looked the part. Angular features under a dapper flying cap and an "aw shucks" grin from ear to ear and commander looked like Hollywood's version of a World War II Errol Flynn flying ace.

Pete was proud of his command in the fall of 1944, and for good reason. Quesada's career reflected his ambition. Hailing from the District of Columbia, Quesada had been obsessed with leadership from an early age. In high school he was the football team captain; he chose the Wyoming Seminary and University of Maryland based on their athletic possibilities for a budding college football quarterback. But while at the latter school he had been lured to Brooks Field to try his hand at flying; the Air Service was looking for football stars that it could use to embarrass Navy. Most of the recruits washed out; of 150 that started in Quesada's class only about 15 finished. But the competitive atmosphere of the military was attractive to Pete's disposition.

Quesada's star rose quickly in the new Army Air Corps. He had won his wings and commission in 1927, and logged 3,000 hours in three years to lead all air corps pilots in flying time. Quesada's father was Spanish and it was natural that he use his language skills. He served as the air attache to Cuba, Gen. MacArthur's chief of staff and flight commander at a bombardment school at Mitchell Field. Quesada then became a technical advisor to the Argentine Air Force and later, in 1940, the chief foreign liaison in the

Intelligence Section for the Chief of the Air Corps. When the war opened, Quesada was commanding a fighter group at Mitchell field, expanded to an air defense wing by the time he took his planes over to Africa in 1943. There he assumed the duties of the XIIth Fighter Command, flying many operational missions himself over Tunis, Sicily and Italy. Returning to Britain, Quesada was promoted to Maj. Gen. in May, 1944 at a time when his IX Tactical Air Command was being fleshed out for the invasion of France.

Having thoroughly trounced the fleeing German army in France that summer, Pete liked the honorific of his group. *"Achtung Jabos!"* referred to the oft-heard German cry to duck and run for cover when American fighter-bombers were sighted. Quesada relished the thought that Germans would be quaking in their jackboots whenever his fighter-bombers were around. His constant prodding was to keep all the pilots and machines in readiness so that he could maximize their impact. "I am confident that every man will give that extra ten percent of his energies," he exhorted them, "which puts more planes in the air." There was even a hint of friendly competition between his command supporting First Army and that of Weyland's XIX TAC which supported Patton's Third Army to the south.

Some thought that Eisenhower played favorites with Quesada. Indeed, had not the Supreme Commander actually asked Pete for a personal tour of the Normandy battlefield on July 4th? Ike accompanied Quesada on a visit to a rough and tumble new Mustang base. Eisenhower hammed it up with the men and Pete announced he was taking a brief flight over France to have a look at the war. Eisenhower asked to go along. "What the hell," the IX TAC commander thought to himself. Quesada took the controls of GRB, a two-seater P-51 Mustang of the 354th Fighter Group. He and the Supreme Commander took to the skies over France, heading to a "little sweep over Paris." Eisenhower was exhilarated by the nimble machine, Quesada's gung-ho attitude and his Independence Day eyewitness view of the developing American victory. That Quesada was one cool cookie; he buzzed Ike along the front line and even into German territory until artillery flashes turned them back. Eisenhower was enthralled with the 45-minute ride, but both men returned to an irritated Gen. Omar Bradley who had disapproved of the whole thing. "I'll probably catch hell for this," Eisenhower mentioned to Bradley. He did; hell came in the form of a reprimand from Gen. George C. Marshall with the Combined Chiefs of staff in Washington D.C. The joy ride was no big deal, said Quesada— a scenic milk run. But Hoyt Vandenberg let Quesada know that the adventure was not to be repeated.

That Pete believed in the omniscience of the air arm had become evident during the slugging war along the German border that fall. Although only a precocious Major General, on November 18th Quesada submitted a detailed plan to Eisenhower expressing his frustration with the inability to fully use his collection of fighter bombers in tactical support due to the weather. He requested his fighters be moved into the arena of strategic inter-diction, now the domain of the Eighth Air Force. Noting that the Ninth Air Force now had "the largest collection of fighter-bombers the world has ever seen," Quesada opined that the Luftwaffe could hardly keep up with the strategic bombers, much less his "*Jabos*" if let run amok. He suggested each plane freely bomb one or two targets and then strafe three more while able to "roam the length and breath of Germany on every day that weather permitted contact flying," Quesada told Eisenhower that these seek and destroy missions could crush the Germans' will to resist. Although unwilling to take the air support away from Bradley, the Supreme Commander did acknowledge that "the policy of wide spread fighter sweeps...will be continued."

But the situation a month later did little to end Quesada's frustration. On December 18th Quesada was still assigned to provide direct support for the U.S. First Army. Although Hoyt Vandenberg was nominally his superior, Lt. Gen. Courtney Hodges, the commander of the First Army, was the guy he didn't want to let down. At First Army headquarters in Spa, Belgium, December 17th witnessed alarming developments. A powerful SS armored column had plowed through the Losheim Gap and rolled up the Amblève River valley. There were now reports of the Germans having brutally killed unarmed American soldiers in a massacre near Malmédy that afternoon. "There is absolutely no question of its proof," the First Army diary ventured of the grisly event, "immediate publicity is to be given to the story. General Quesada has told every one of his pilots about it during their briefing." And that was not all. Enemy parachutists had landed scarcely twelve miles away from Quesada's chateau in Spa. Now word arrived that German commandos dressed as American soldiers were operating behind friendly lines.

At 3 PM came disastrous tidings. The SS tank column had bowled through Stavelot and was headed west towards Spa. Hodges was shaken by the news. At 4 PM he ordered his entire staff out of the Hôtel Brittanique and sent them with a few half tracks and some anti-aircraft guns to defend the road leading into town. "Monk" Dickson, who had come back from his leave to Paris, met Hodges and urged the First Army commander to escape in a waiting Piper Cub while there was still time. But Hodges waited for news from the roadblock. Miraculously, he learned, the enemy tanks had turned due west and not only had missed his headquarters, but a huge fuel dump as well. To hedge his bets, however, he ordered his bedraggled headquarters to pack everything and head for their rear headquarters at Chaudfontaine near Liège. No sooner were the Americans gone than the town of Spa fell into a panic. The mayor ran to the jail and hurriedly released a group of suspected Belgian collaborators; American flags were quickly pulled down and pictures of Roosevelt and other signs of Americana suddenly disap-peared. The Germans were coming! At Quesada's headquarters in Verviers:

"Up to 1130 hours on 18 December we continued to work as usual, and only occasionally we thought of the heavy fighting going on at nearby Monschau and Malmédy. But our complacency was shaken at 1145 when we were told that all administrative personnel would IMMEDIATELY go to Charleroi. By noon a tremendous change had taken place in the Palais de Justice and all the staff sections were hastily packing up their equipment....The townspeople had been a little apprehensive of the German break-through, but when they saw us leaving they became terrified because they thought the hated Boche would return to the city at any moment... They hated to see us go, and some girl friends of our GIs cried as the trucks pulled out. However, none of our old friends were angry with us for running out on them...On the trip from Verviers to Charleroi we saw marker flares dropped on Liège by the GAF, and the flying bombs continued to land in that unhappy city with annoying regularity. That night Liège was bombed and so was Verviers...Many men would have preferred to remain in the city and defend it, but individuals have no choices in war..."

Quesada was mindful that there was nothing between the German armored column and the English Channel and by road the Germans at Stavelot were only 22 miles from the huge Allied supply stores at Liège. Pete also knew that normal operations in this pea soup would be impossible, but he was determined get to the enemy somehow. Dense fog covered the ground and hugged the valleys of the Amblève River. The murk was hardly reasonable for flying under any conditions— the ceiling was barely 200 feet. Any attempt to fly underneath the overcast risked the steep forested Ardennes hills. But desperate situations demanded desperate solutions. Hodges had used a serious tone that day to describe the developments to Quesada that Monday. The First Army commander told Quesada that the 15-mile panzer column had been sighted less than ten miles from his headquarters. If the German panzer column turned north, much of V Corps might be trapped by the enemy armor.

Determined to somehow serve a riposte, Quesada phoned Col. George W. Peck of the veteran 67th Tactical Reconnaissance Group, and asked if any of his fliers might be willing to brave the 10/10 fog and locate the enemy spearhead. Two Mustang jockeys volunteered: Capt. Richard H. Cassady of Nashville, Arkansas and 2nd Lt. Abraham Jaffe, a native of the Bronx in New York. Gen. Quesada spoke to both personally over a field phone and briefed them on the last known location of the enemy, somewhere near Stavelot, Belgium. Meanwhile, Quesada's 27-year old combat operations chief, Col. Gilbert L. Meyers began to organize the fighter-bomber mission that would follow up, should Cassady and Jaffe find anything. He called on Col. Ray J. Stecker and his 365th Fighter Group. Meanwhile the two recon men set off just after noon, guided by MEW and SC-584 radar. Four of Stecker's P-47s took off a little later and took a direct approach to the target. But after an hour-long immersion in the fog the flight leader radioed back "Deadbeat," airman slanguage for impossible.

So low was the impenetrable overcast that the men had to drop to tree top level— dangerously close to the undulating 450-foot hills. "It was so foggy," Jaffe said later, "we had to fly in the valleys, sometimes at less than a hundred feet, in order to miss the hills and still be able to see the ground." The two flew on for nearly half an hour without seeing anything. Then, suddenly, they spotted a serpentine formation of sixty enemy tanks and armored vehicles "We made three runs over that column, and the Germans were so surprised to see us they didn't fire until the last run," remembered Capt. Cassady, "We could see the Germans' faces as they fired rifles at us. There were machine guns, 20mm flak and pistols too— everything they had." The two pilots soon spoke with Col. Meyers. Meyers quickly organized a fighter bomber mission to hit the Germans, sending off four-plane flights in waves towards the spotted enemy. They were guided to the target by every direction finding radar facility that Pete Quesada's IX possessed. Meanwhile Cassady and Jaffe remained over the target to guide the fighter-bombers in for the kill. Each of Stecker's "Jugs" carried two 500 lb. bombs, twisting and threading through the fog-laden Ambléve Valley to strike at the Germans. In all Meyers sent out seven four-plane flights up until it became dark at 5 PM.

The German column was *Kampfgruppe Peiper*, under the hell-for-leather leadership of SS Obersturmbannführer Joachim Peiper. Peiper was driving ruthlessly west of La Gleize. In fact, Peiper, having to cross the troublesome Ambléve River, was aiming at the bridge across Lienne Creek at the tiny village of Neufmoulin. If it could be captured intact, it would open a clear road for the *1st SS Panzer Division* to the major immediate German objective of the crossings over the Meuse. From there the way to Antwerp over the flat undulating Belgian plains would be laid open.

At Chievres, Belgium, December 18th was invisible, the entire base cloaked in an impenetrable white mist. They could only land, the crew chief ventured, with flares bracketing each side of the runway. In spite of this, the first mission of 17 planes took off under Capt. Fry at 9:12 AM headed south to aid the U.S. 4th Infantry Division in Luxembourg, which was also reportedly under enemy assault. But the pea soup was thick and the mission was recalled— a harrowing experience of blind landing for the crews. There were several close calls, but all were safely back by 10:33 AM. Everyone thought that was the end of the flying for the day.

At noon the phone rang in Col. Stecker's office. On the horn was Col. Gil Meyers. The operations officer told Stecker he had an important favor to ask. The request came to Stecker because of the reputation the "Hell Hawks" commander had developed with the Desert Air Force years earlier. During that campaign British intelligence officers came to Stecker and challenged him: "The Germans move at night. During the day, they camouflage their vehicles and hide in the dense olive groves. It's up to you to find them and shoot them up." Stecker had personally taken a P-40 and come up with a tactic to accomplish the feat without getting plastered by flak. Now he was known as a sort of specialist in hide-and-seek aerial warfare.

Meyers got to the point: "That Jerry column that you hit the other day," he said, "has been reinforced and has broken through our lines at Stavelot. In fact, there is now nothing between it and the English Channel but service troops, cooks and bakers!" Stecker mentioned the ice-fog outside. "I know," nodded Meyers, "the weather is down on the deck, and it probably will be suicide, but God-damn it, the Army says we've got to get something in there or the bastards will be in Liège." Stecker said he would try and hung up. Soon he had briefed a few hand-picked men for the mission. "This is going to be rough," he told them, "but the Krauts have just given us a hell of a kick in the pants at the front."

Just after 1 PM Maj. Brooking took off with Lt. Robert C. Thoman, Lt. Roy W. Price and Capt. James G. Wells, Jr. into a solid fog bank. Other flights would follow at 20 minute intervals. Presently, Brooking arrived over the zone where they expected to find the enemy; nothing could be seen but clouds. The other flights soon turned back. Frustrated as they orbited over the region, Brooking dropped down lower. "You're crazy," insisted Lt. Thoman, his wingman. But Brooking set out anyway. Following the Amblève River valley and narrowly avoiding ridges and tree tops the Major suddenly popped out the fog scarcely 20 feet above a line of German tanks. Both the enemy and Maj. Brooking were equally surprised to see each other. Brooking left to get help. Soon he brought other P-47s back to the fogged-in valley. They roared over the German convoy, and Capt. Wells placed a bomb squarely in the middle of eight tanks.

That shook the hornet's nest; then the flak came up. There was no place to hide and they were in pistol range. Lt. Price called on the radio, "I've been hit badly Brook," he said, "I'll try to belly land somewhere." Price congratulated himself on successfully putting his plane down without killing himself in this fog and forest. But he was behind German lines. For two days he evaded the Germans, always heading to the west. On December 20th, he was captured by the U.S. 30th Infantry Division who had some questions regarding his origins (he was carrying a German Luger rather than the standard Colt .45). He spent that Wednesday in Malmédy until the Sunnyvale, California native could convince his captors that he was American.

Meanwhile, the strafing went on. Shortly after Price was forced to ditch, Wells came on the com announcing that he too was hit, but thought he could make it home. Lt. Thoman escorted Capt. Wells back to base while Brooking stayed on to use up his ammunition on the Germans. But Chievres was so socked in that both pilots headed elsewhere to put down. Maj. Brooking continued to orbit above the German column, hiding in the clouds, all the while asking "Sweepstakes" to send more fighter-bombers to the scene. Soon squadrons from the 368th Fighter Group showed up. Brooking introduced them to the location of the Germans and a new tactic: scoot out of the clouds at tree-top level to bomb and strafe the column and then dash back into the clouds before the flak gunners could draw a bead. The German column would be under attack for the rest of the afternoon. At 3:35 PM Brooking returned home to Chievres and put down in a blind landing, coasting in on fumes. At 2:20 PM, another flight from the 365th took off under 1st Lt. Howard R. Dentz, Jr., arriving over Stavelot just before 3 PM and bombing and strafing the tanks, troops and vehicles moving through the town. Other flights under Maj. Arlo C. Henry, Jr., Capt. Neal E. Worley, Capt. Robert E. Robinson and Capt. Samuel E. Saunders kept up the strafing of *Kampfgruppe Peiper* until dusk. Col Stecker himself led the last flight of the day which was vectored to drop its bombs on the supply lines of the *1SS Panzer Division* near Blankenheim. The Hell Hawks claimed 56 vehicles, 15 tanks or half-tracks. The group lost one plane shot down, one bellied in at base and seven were severely damaged by flak. Maj. Brooking received the Silver Star.

By 4 PM, the German panzer column had been strafed along its length from Lodometz through Stavelot all the way to Cheneux. The 365th FG provided the lion's share of the fighter-bombers with additional missions coming from the 390th Squadron of the 366th FG and the 506th Squadron of the 404th. At Cheneux, the German commander had just found a bridge over which to pass his spearhead after having one blown in his face at Trois Ponts. Just as the German advance guard crossed over the bridge, the Allied fighter bombers struck. The German flak fought back, sending a Thunderbolt blazing into the ground near Francorchamps. Two Panther tanks and ten other vehicles were destroyed before Peiper was able to disperse his battle group into the cover of the woods. As usual, American air force claims bore little resemblance to reality: 32 tanks and 56 other vehicles. But nonetheless, great damage was done the German forces, as the two hours lost in hiding from the American planes alerted the engineers guarding the bridge. At 4 PM the engineers of the 291st Engineer Combat Battalion blasted the span just as the enemy armor approached the crossing. Rather than racing for the Meuse bridges that afternoon, Peiper was forced to turn back to La Gleize. Witnesses recall that the German commander had cursed those "Damned engineers!" that had denied his advance, but it had been Quesada's airmen who had tipped them off. "*Achtung Jabos!*"

But the bid to turn back the main German armored spearhead was but part of the action of the third day of the German counteroffensive. As the might of Hitler's great blow began to gather momentum on the ground, the weather worsened. The forecast was forbidding for even the most deter-mined pilots— thick nearly impenetrable mist punctuated by treacherous squalls with freezing rain. In spite of the danger of mid-air collisions and very poor visibility, the sheer desperation of both sides led each to commit sorties to a situation that otherwise would have cancelled all operations.

Regardless, Allied sorties were half of that mounted on the previous day—500 missions. The IX TAC, under orders to use rockets against ground targets to the maximum extent possible, flew some 337 sorties claiming a total of 34 enemy aircraft shot down for a loss of four planes of its own.

The 368th Fighter Group (Col. Frank S. Perego) was assigned to provide assistance to the surrounded 106th Infantry Division in the Schnee Eifel. Unfortunately, weather over the target area made it impossible for the P-47s to provide much assistance. Battlefield support by the 368th was moved to the 28th Division, also in dire straits. Meanwhile, the 396th Squadron moved on to bomb trains in the Aachen area while 12 other aircraft of the 395th attacked the town of Houffalize through which the *116th Panzer Division* was moving.

In an ominous development for any Luftwaffe hopes of air superiority, the British committed their fighters alongside the already numerous American aircraft.[45] Spitfires of 610 Squadron ran afoul of fifteen Fw-190s in low visibility conditions, but could make no claim and lost two of their own due to mechanical troubles. Meantime, Spitfires of the British 2nd Tactical Air Force's 66 Squadron tangled with 15 Fw-190A-8s of *IV/JG 54* over Cologne who were seeking to halt the medium bombers of the Ninth Air Force. Plt. Off. Silver claimed one probable victory. Three more German fighters were damaged for the loss of one Spitfire.

In spite of losing much their of escort to deal with the German fighters, the A-26 Havocs and B-26 Marauders continued on in their bomb run to hit the villages of Harperscheid, Hellenthal and Dreiborn with 274 tons of bombs. The bombing assault was designed to interrupt supply routes to the northern wing of the *Sixth Panzer Armee*. Unfortunately, the cloud cover was unbroken and the mediums were forced to use blind bombing. Gen. Anderson had just obtained the blind-bombing equipment from Jimmy Doolittle's Eighth Air Force that fall. However, they had little experience with the technique which had a reputation of being haphazard and inaccurate. Even so, one of these runs flattened Gen. Otto Hitzfeld's *LXVII Armeekorps* headquarters in Dalbenden east of Monschau. So paralyzed was the German command there, that the *IISS Panzerkorps* had to take over temporarily.

The Luftwaffe pilots of *JG 27* were engaged in very heavy action in the skies over Cologne. Typical of problems suffered by both sides, Uffz. Fink of *I Gruppe* was shot down by German flak near Burgsteinfurt. *III/JG 27* suffered severe losses in swirling combat over the Rhine. Hptm. Richard Hasenclever crashed in "Chevron Bar," his Me-109K-4 near Rondorf and Uffz. Fritzsche did not return to base. Gefr. Heinz Merkel was also reported missing. In fact,

---

45 On December 17th and 18th the British 2nd Tactical Air Force operated north of the German breakthrough area, making 327 sorties, encountering approximately 100 enemy aircraft and shooting down 11 of these. By way of comparison the Ninth Air Force put up more than 1,150 sorties, claiming 96 aircraft destroyed.

his Me-109 K-4 had been shot down, crashing into the Rhine River. His body would not be found until the following spring. Uffz. Wolf Korn was also among those who did not return. To this day, his fate remains a mystery. Two other pilots were at first listed as missing, but later returned. Obgefr. Herberg and Uffz. Scheiber had bailed out over Cologne after having had their machines shot out from under them.

On the morning of the 18th, Hptm. Langer of the *JG 3* reluctantly readied the men of his *III Gruppe* to take to the air. Although the orders came directly from *Luftflotte West* and *II Jagdkorps*, he protested the commitment of his green pilots under the poor weather conditions on December 18th. In spite of his misgivings, all four *Staffeln* of the *Gruppe* took to the air and headed for the Ruhr. On the way, they received notice from their ground controller that the enemy bombers were converging on Cologne. Setting course for an interception, Langer's Me-109G-14s and K-4s were never able to reach the bombers. Southwest of Bonn they ran into a ring of P-51 fighters. In minutes *III/JG 3* had eight fewer pilots. Three were killed, a similar number were missing and the other two were wounded. One of these, Uffz. Horst Witzler, was lucky to get out of his stricken plane and parachute to safety.

North of the battle zone over Holland, the Luftwaffe also appeared in force. Opposing them were the RAF's Tempest V squadrons. Five planes from 56 Squadron scrambled to respond to enemy incursions over Rheine. Upon reaching altitude, the Tempests sighted four Me-109s over Grave. They attacked and one of the enemy was sent spiraling to the ground. Minutes later, four more "bogeys" appeared and a further two of the enemy were destroyed at no cost to the pilots of 56. Eight aircraft from 274 Squadron also found more of the Me-109s. Flt. Lt. D.C. Fairbanks claimed a further two, these showing poor flying skill when the enemy pilot crashed after losing control of his plane while trying to evade his pursuer. Later in the afternoon, 56 was again airborne over Münster. They sighted two He-219s near the ground. Again one crashed during the pursuit and the other was damaged and made a forced landing. Meanwhile, the rest of the squadron was stalking a nearby train when they spied a pack of 25 Me-109s. The Tempest pilots attacked and felled two of the enemy. The 3rd New Zealand Squadron was also involved in dogfights with the German fighters in the area. The wing commander of 122 Squadron, J.B. Wray, shot down an enemy Me-262; it was his second German jet claimed in the last five weeks. Another Me-109 was downed near Scahle. During a heated low-level pursuit over Nijmegen, Flt. Sgt. M.J.A. Rose hit a tree, but was able to coax his crippled machine back to base.

To the north, Nugent's XXIX operated in a limited fashion over the Malmédy-Düren area, dropping some 53 tons of bombs on enemy targets to claim some 40 vehicles. The operations were largely changed to favor the interdiction area. So although the 84th Infantry Division was requesting air support over Horst, the requested mission for the 404th FG was cancelled with the P-38s sent to support the troubled First Army. The 404th was assigned to perform an armed recce of the area between Gemünd and Trier and "attack any road, rail traffic or troop or armor concentrations in the area." The 373rd FG was assigned to support the 78th Infantry Division with additional operations in the Northern Ardennes by the 36th FG and the 48th FG flying escort. Eight German aircraft were claimed in the day's actions for no loss. However, the weather had really begun to close in and XXIX would only manage 58 aircraft dispatched during the bad weather period from December 19th - 22nd.

In spite of the beating the 428th Squadron had taken the previous day, the 474th Fighter Group sent three aircraft aloft just before noon out on an armed reconnaissance. The ground controller, "Marmite," sent the P-38s into a dogfight between numerous P-47s and Me-109s east of Düren. The aerial battle was a confused ordeal in the developing cloud cover. By the end of the melee the 474th FG claimed two Me-109s destroyed. Only one aircraft that day was lost, and that to mechanical troubles.

The weather to the south was worse in Gen. Weyland's operational area. Operations of Patton's XIX TAC amounted to only 66 sorties. The 362nd FG flew four effective missions although all of these were in support of XII Corps which was south of the zone where the German offensive was under way. The 354th FG (Lt. Col. Jack T. Bradley) flew one mission in cooperation with the First Army east of Düren sighting a dozen Fw-190s dive bombing Allied troops. The P-47s attacked, destroying four of the enemy planes at a cost of two of their own.

By December 18th von Rundstedt's *OB West* had recorded a total of 849 sorties, dispatched to aid *Wacht Am Rhein*. The Ninth Air Force claimed to have shot down 61 of these for a loss of 14 of their own. The lion's share went to Quesada's command, who reported shooting down 34 of the enemy for the loss of four. "For the second day running," went the IX Tactical Summary, "the GAF flew 400 plus sorties over the First U.S. Army effort. In general, enemy pilots were not so aggressive as the previous day, and were less engaged in support of their own troops..." The Allied air command also estimated that there were some 30-40 German night bomber sorties active that night with second line Ju-87s also active. During the morning and early afternoon the Luftwaffe launched approximately 150 aircraft each hour in formations with five to sixty aircraft each. The intruders operated mainly in the München-Gladbach-Köln and Düren areas. There were two reasons: the cordon of the Allied fighters was tightening and few German aircraft were able to operate over the battle zone after 12:30 PM. Another reason was the operations of the Eighth Air Force which drew away much of the German strength and precluded the numerical parity the Luftwaffe had enjoyed on the 17th. In his evening report Genfldm. Model reported, "Strong enemy fighter bomber activity was evident on the front," but then added, "Also, on 18 December the German Luftwaffe supported the efforts of the attack forces with strong fighter and fighter-bomber support."

By the time the weather closed back in on December 19th, the Ninth Air Force could reflect that it had withstood the strongest attacks the German Air Force had ever mounted on the Western Front. Between December 17th and 22nd the Ninth Air Force chalked up 136 destroyed German aircraft as well as 572 enemy motor vehicles and 34 tanks against only 43 fighter-bomber losses. Never again did the Luftwaffe attempt the large-scale ground support missions that it tried to achieve during these two crucial days in December.

The usual task for the Eighth Air Force was to strike deeply into Germany, destroying its oil factories and rails. But with the great German offensive, Gen. Doolittle showed his command's flexibility. With the blessing of Eisenhower and Spaatz, he changed their mission almost overnight. The Eighth Air Force would neglect its customary targets to hammer the German logistical support and communications systems just east of the Ardennes. It was a change that almost instantly changed the numerical equation over the battlefield. With this additional 3,500-plane force, any chances the Germans had for air superiority in the zone between the Rhine and the Ardennes evaporated. Not only would they face the Ninth Air Force and the British 2nd Tactical Air Command, but now the offensive juggernaut of the Eighth Air Force as well.

Only worsening weather could change the immediate balance. That afternoon the weather soured, reducing the overall effort of both air forces; the Americans were able to accomplish only about 300 successful sorties throughout the day. However, the German numbers committed to support the German attack had little to do with the air missions actually appearing over the Ardennes. Only a fraction of the 400-500 sorties actually reached the battle zone. Most of these consisted of Obstlt. Herbert Ihlefeld's *JG 1* operating in the Monschau-Malmédy area with some 28 Fw-190A-8s of *I Gruppe*. These planes were some of the 200 fighters *II Jagdkorps* dispatched on the morning of the 18th to the aid of *Sixth Panzer Armee* including reconnaissance of the Meuse bridges performed by the jets of *Kommando Sperling*.

Typical of the German experience was the episode of *JG 77* under Maj. Johannes Wiese. At daybreak, their pilots were ordered to fly from Dortmund to the Ardennes to "provide cover for the panzer spearheads at the line of contact." They never got that far. Just south of Cologne, they, along with fighters of *JG 3, JG 27* and *JG 54*, were drawn into a swirling dogfight with the U.S. 365th and 368th Fighter Groups. *III Gruppe* suffered the loss of three Me-109K-4s, including the mount of Lt. Hubertus Rogal who led the *Schwarm*. Uffz. Schulze was also shot down and wounded; Uffz. Albin

Micheliak was listed as missing. *II* and *III Gruppen* of *JG 2* were also swept into the conflict. Fw. Pfeiffer died at the hands of an American fighter and Obgefr. Melda was last seen in his Me-109K-4 trying to evade a gang of fifteen P-47s near Aachen.

At 8:50 AM six Fw-190F-8s ground attack aircraft of *SG 4* took off from Kirtorf with orders to attack American troop concentrations near St. Vith. The attack group had been hastily moved from the Eastern Front to the west to support the attacking panzer units. Its 45 heavily armed planes carried both two MG 131 machine guns and two MK 151 cannon and were also equipped to carry a 550 lb. bomb. Four aircraft from the *7 Staffel* carried a dozen 9cm *Gartenzaun* or *"Panzerblitz"* rockets under their wings. However, the planned support mission was foiled by bad weather over the target. On the return trip four P-47s jumped the laden F-8s. At least one was lost, the mount of Lt. Schlegel. The pilot bailed out into captivity over the battle zone. In his captured diary the Leutnant waxed optimistic on the new German attempt to seize the initiative. "The all-out decisive offensive began today," his entry for December 16th read, "and once again we were in the thick of it. We were alerted today without anything special happening." Schlegel could hardly suspect that two days later his diary would serve as a source of information for his interrogators. His little black book proved of particular interest for the Ninth Air Force interrogators who were perhaps thinking of future romantic possibilities in occupied Germany: "...apparently somewhat of a Lothario, maintained an enviable address list, he has provided us with information the value of which may very well improve with time."

The evening report on December 18th at *II Jagdkorps* could hardly have been less sanguine: of the 14 fighter *Gruppen* committed, the tally of results from the day's air battle saw 34 German fighters shot down against only 4 Allied planes claimed. Another twenty-one Luftwaffe pilots perished in the skies over the Western Front with another 12 wounded. But perhaps worst of all for the German hopes, was the failure on the third day of the great offensive to halt ground support by the Allied air forces. In all, the Americans and British claimed 497 German vehicles destroyed. Although doubtless an exaggeration of the actual damage, the *Jabos* were hitting the German attack force in spite of the Luftwaffe's increasing sacrifice of men and machines.

In spite of some success the previous day, the 18th would be remembered by the Luftwaffe ground crews as the day the bombs fell. The prospect for German supply was further dimmed by the Luftwaffe's inability to still the U.S. Eighth Air Force. An imposing armada of 985 bombers, escorted by some 773 fighters, moved to pulverize German rail supply centers along the Rhine, feeding logistical support into Hitler's offensive. Rail marshalling yards in Cologne, Koblenz, Kaiserlauten, Ehrang, Mainz and Mayen were slammed in an effort to create choke points in the German rear. Passing through the city of Ehrang, Ofw. Kistier, a parachute soldier with the 15th

Fallschirmjäger Regiment noted "heavy damage" and that "streets were only partly cleared and repaired." And *Luftgau VII*, on December 18th, ordered that "in view of the continuously rising scale of the attacks on traffic installations...railway flak units are to be brought up to prevent further severe damage to the German southern railway network."

The entirety of the 2nd Bomb Division (324 B-24 Liberators) was recalled due to poor weather, but the B-17s of the 1st and 3rd Division droned on to plant 1,087 tons of bombs on the *Reichsbahn*. Not only that, but the fighter escort alongside the bombers did damage of their own, shooting down seven enemy aircraft for the loss of four of their own. The 4th Fighter Group (Lt. Col. Harry J. Dayhuff) bounced seven German fighters near Dortmund and sent three of them spiraling to the ground. Other credits went to the 356th FG (Lt. Col. Donald A. Baccus) and the 359th (Lt. Col. John P. Randolf). Only two of the American bombers were lost.

Included in contesting the bombing was *JG 1* who reported losing one machine during the fighting with the B-17s near Bonn. Lt. Klaus Holz was lucky to be able to safely bail out from "White 5," his stricken Me-109G-14. Some of the fighters of *JG 1* did get to the battle zone, but this contested air space was exceedingly dangerous: Uffz. Lothar Mietling perished in a dogfight near Malmédy in "Red 14," his Fw-190A-8.

On the 19th, the Eighth Air Force heavies struck again, returning with 328 B-17 and B-24 bombers escorted by the 78th Fighter Group (Col. Fredrich C. Gray) to blast the Ehrang and Koblenz marshalling yards as well as the nexus of roads west of the latter city with some 932 tons of ordnance. Further, the 78th Fighter Group managed to shoot down another seven German planes over the Moselle Valley at a cost of three P-47 pilots who managed to crash land after taking damage.

The medium bombers of the IX Bombardment Division were also up in force, 165 of these dropping 274 tons of high explosive on Harperscheid, Hellenthal, Blumenthal and Dreiborn. Even though the skies were overcast, the bombs were on target, as evidenced by the testimony of four German POWs from the *246 Volksgrenadier Division* who were passing through Blumenthal and Hellenthal when scores of bombs suddenly dropped out of the low hanging clouds. Their tormentors were the B-26s of Col. Thomas G. Corbin's 386th Bomb Group. The road to Schleiden was temporarily blocked and the railroad station was hit. At least eight German soldiers were killed and traffic was reduced to one-way movement. The nearby town of Schleiden was hit on the following day and twice more on December 24th and 27th. All traffic halted until the piles of rubble could be cleared.

Allied ground observers again reported 30 - 40 night sorties by the aging German Ju-87s on the night of the 18th. Some of these along with Ju-88Gs of *NJG2* warily trailed the columns of the U.S. 82nd and 101st Airborne Divisions, dropping flares, as the airborne troops motored in freezing rain from

France to Belgium. Some of the captured aircrew from the German night fighters, such as Fw. Rudolf Haupt, told of flying two or even three sorties that evening.

Having enjoyed the lull in operations brought on by the poor weather in early December, the British night-fighter squadrons noted a great increase in activity on the night of December 18th associated with the "Von Rundstedt Offensive." The Canadian Mosquito Squadrons (409 and 410) claimed three Ju-88s knocked out that night along with an Me-110. The intense enemy nighttime activity would be mirrored by a similar RAF effort over the last week of the month.[46]

At 7 PM that night, Pete Quesada called Col. Ed Chickering, the boyish-looking 32-year old commander of the 367th Fighter Group at his headquarters in Juvincourt, France. Chickering had known Quesada since they had worked together in Normandy. A product of Kelly Field in Texas, Chickering was dismayed to find himself out of the flying war. His reputation had taken him out of the pilot's seat and into that of a staff officer. Chickering worked as an operations chief for the IX TAC during the summer of 1944. It was prestigious, even if not a pilot's dream. Realistically, it looked as if he would finish out the war that way. But in early November, Quesada had offered Chickering a fighting command with the 367th— an offer he readily accepted. By December, Chickering was well acquainted with his P-38 fighter group. But from his previous days he knew it was odd for Pete Quesada to be calling this late in the day.

"I want you to pick a top notch flight commander to act as a forward air controller," Quesada began, "Give him a jeep with a radio, a radio maintenance man, and a driver and get them into Bastogne." "Yes, sir," Chickering acknowledged, "I'll get them going first thing in the morning." Chickering missed his superior's urgency. "First thing in the morning?" Quesada replied, "Colonel, why do you think I'm calling you? I want a forward air controller up there just as fast as you can get them on the road!" It was less than an hour later when Capt. James E. Parker of the 393rd Squadron was headed for the market town. He worried whether he had brought the right crystals for air-ground communication. Then too, in Quesada's great rush, he was unable to locate a working jeep radio. Early on December 19th Parker arrived in Bastogne, now the headquarters of the 101st Airborne Division that was defending the town. "Glad you're here, Parker," the airborne staff said introducing themselves. He began the imposing job of finding an operating radio and getting a communications link set up. He would have plenty of time, however; less than three hours after Parker entered Bastogne,

---

46 From the evenings of December 22nd, 1944 through January 1st, 1945, the Mosquito night-fighters of the 2nd TAF (219, 409, 410, 488 Squadrons) would tally significant damage to the German night-fighters: 15 Ju 88s, 8 Ju 188s, 3 Ju-87s, 4 Me-110s, one He-219 and one Me-410. There was only one loss, a 219 Squadron Mosquito that did not return on the night of December 26-27.

the Germans cut the last road into the town. They were surrounded. The enemy attacks on the perimeter had already begun. Some of the opening assaults were particularly vicious and the Americans were forced back. "This is our last withdrawal." a battalion commander grimly informed his men, "Live or die this is it."

The Americans were not the only ones garnering support for the seemingly inevitable battle for the road net at Bastogne. On the afternoon of December 19th, the monocled leader of *XLVII Panzerkorps*, Gen. d. Pztrp. Heinrich von Lüttwitz, had two tank divisions bearing down on the town just to his west. Protected from air attack by the sullen skies, over the past two days he had methodically crushed the resistance of the American defenders west of the Our River and was now intent on snatching Bastogne and getting on to the Meuse. Unfortunately, there was little information as to what American forces lay before him. He had pushed his tanks ahead to try to win the race to get to the road hub first. He also knew from his own radio intelligence that Patton was just to the south and the 82nd and 101st Airborne Divisions were on their way. At 1:30 PM he urgently requested an aerial reconnaissance of the "Bastogne area and approach roads South." But this request went nowhere. The weather made it impossible for the Luftwaffe to comply and Lüttwitz was forced to throw his panzer spearheads forward blindly. He quickly found the enemy. His 2 *Panzer* was rebuffed at Noville just to the north of Bastogne, while *Panzer Lehr* was turned back as it attempted the straight-ahead approach through the villages of Neffe and Magaret. His opponents were the elite troops of the 101st Airborne Division. He decided to make an end-run around the flanks of the "Screaming Eagles." Lüttwitz inquired if he should use 2 *Panzer* to grab Bastogne. "Forget Bastogne," his superiors snarled at his request, "and head for the Meuse!"

At Eisenhower's headquarters in Versailles, the situation was worrisome. Keenly aware of the sparse road network in the Ardennes, Bedell Smith, Strong and Eisenhower had seen to it that the strategic road hub of Bastogne was defended. However, the number of identified German divisions seemed to grow hourly: the count had reach 25 by mid-day on the 18th. Many of these were armored including the elite SS tank divisions. Some of these had made deep armored penetrations behind American lines and the air situation, in spite of heroic efforts, could not stop the German wedge in the murky weather. Later that day, Gen. Juin brought in a delegation of French officers to discuss the developments. Bedell Smith, who conducted them to the briefing at the War Room, noticed that the visitors seemed to take a keen interest in the SHAEF offices. Eventually, one of the French generals turned to Gen. Strong. "Why are you not packing?" he asked. They were thinking of their experience in 1940 with the Germans in the Ardennes, "Aren't you making any preparation to leave?"

At the 12th Army Group headquarters in the Hotel Alpha in Luxembourg

City, Bradley showed Patton the latest intelligence map. It was covered with angry red German symbols. The planned air drop to the beleaguered 106th Division had been cancelled due to the weather in England. Some 21 C-47s had actually taken off from the United Kingdom, but so thick was the pea soup over England, that they were called back. The First Army's downhill ride continued. Bradley knew he needed help from Patton. "I feel you won't like what we are going to do," Bradley sighed, "but I fear it is necessary." Patton knew his big attack on the Siegfried Line had just gone out the window. Regardless, Patton told Bradley that he would have the 4th Armored Division on the road north by midnight.

Patton drove back to his headquarters at Nancy. When he arrived he received a message to call Bradley immediately. He reached his commanding general at 8 PM. "The situation is much worse than when I talked to you," Bradley informed him. The 101st Airborne Division was under strenuous attack in Bastogne and the Germans were surging across the Clerf River. It looked like the paratroopers would be enveloped at any time. "Tomorrow isn't good enough anymore— the movements must begin at once." Meanwhile Eisenhower called as well and told Patton to attend an emergency meeting at Verdun the next day at 11 AM. They were to plot out their move to counter the German offensive.

Patton was already relishing the prospect— an old Southern cavalry general to the rescue of the stodgy army-types. "We pride ourselves on our ability to move quickly," he briefed his staff, "but we're going to have to do it faster than we ever have before. I have no doubt that we will meet all demands made on us, and whatever happens, we will keep right on doing what we always have— killing Germans wherever we find the sons of bitches." Mindful of the German strength his G-2 had so colorfully pinned-up on the Third Army situation map, Patton called up his headquarters. About that weather... where was that prayer from O'Neill. For a true cavalry style rescue, he needed Weyland's XIX TAC and their air support to help pull this off. Operation Tink would have to wait.

XII

Stormy Weather: December 19th

By Tuesday, December 19th, every American flyer in the ETO was cursing the weather. The people of Luxembourg told Americans who would listen that St. Peter was God's weatherman. The trouble, the Luxembourg villagers insisted, was that St. Peter was a German. The Allied air commanders were beginning to think they were right. On December 19th, the gloom in the Allied command mirrored the weather. The overcast and patchy precipitation that had restricted operations on the preceding days became an impenetrable thick mist. Aware of the ominous ULTRA decrypts, the German parachutists and the commandos dressed as GIs masquerading behind American lines, Maj. Gen. Kenneth Strong added to the gloom with his latest intelligence summary:

> The Führer himself launched his Western Armies on a gamble, massive, long premeditated, and final. Into one counteroffensive were to be thrown all panzer forces in the West worthy of the name, all the fresh infantry made available by the culmination of the Volksgrenadier programme and all the last dregs of thuggery still fermenting in the Fatherland."

Events had taken a wicked turn. The weather remained a constant worry. Maj. Stuart J. Fuller, the weatherman for Hoyt Vandenberg could only tell it as it was— more mist, fog and overcast.

> "Each morning our gloom had deepened as the Ninth U.S. Air Force's youthful meteorologist opened the daily briefing with his dismally repetitious report. And each morning Gen. Vandenberg, in the chair next to me, pulled his head a little tighter into his leather flying jacket. On more than 100 socked-in air fields from Scotland to Brussels, an Allied air force of more than 4,000 planes waited for the end of Von Rundstedt's conspiracy with the weather."

Meanwhile at his headquarters in Nancy, Gen. Weyland held onto a thin hope that Operation Tink might still go forward. Patton had left for Verdun to meet with Eisenhower and promised to let Weyland know as soon as he learned anything. The head of the U.S. strategic air forces, Gen. Carl Spaatz, a Pennsylvania dutchman, had a reputation as a hard-bluffing poker player who was unafraid of risks if the payoff was high. Spaatz and Vandenberg were betting their chips on Operation Tink.[47] At 2 PM that afternoon Weyland received an upbeat note from his two bosses stating that they were still favoring the carpet bombing of the Westwall in the Saar. Weyland quickly wired back urging "that Air Force opinion back continuation of current [plan for] Operation Tink and that no ground forces be diverted." But at ten minutes after 4 the bad news came; Gen. Gay had called, Patton had informed him that Operation Tink was off. "I pleaded that this [the German attack] was made to order for our operation," Weyland recalled, "It would enhance the success of Operation Tink and its encirclement. But we were ordered to immediately intervene directly in the Bulge." At 6 PM the official word came from SHAEF: "Because of changes in the ground situation Operation Tink is cancelled." That was that.

Verdun decided the matter. Gen. Eisenhower convened the conference at the 12th Army Group's rear headquarters at 11 AM on the 19th. Included were his closest generals: Patton, Tedder, Bedell Smith, Devers and Bradley. Verdun was a sullen place, the location of a mass slaughter in the Great War that had devoured the flower of European youth. As if to underscore the grim seriousness of the meeting, the countryside was covered with cemeteries. The weather was still bitterly cold. The men met on the second floor of a musty old French army casern and crouched around a pot-bellied stove. The meeting was crowded and the atmosphere tense. Still without supply, and under attack, men of the U.S. 106th Division were now laying down their arms in the Schnee Eifel. It was the largest mass surrender of U.S. forces since Bataan. Mindful of all this, Eisenhower called for "only cheerful faces round this table." Gen. Hodges was noticeably absent, now in the process of hurriedly relocating his First Army headquarters after being almost ambushed by the Germans on the preceding day. But if the air force couldn't help, at least ULTRA could provide information. When Ike met with his subordinates at Verdun, he already knew much of the importance the enemy attached to the counteroffensive, much of the order of battle on the other side of the fence, and most importantly, the immediate enemy objectives.

Gen. Strong gave the briefing. This was, he said, "an all-out German attack directed at Brussels and aimed at splitting our armies." Foremost of the German objectives appeared to be establishment of bridgeheads over the

---

47 Nominally, Sir Arthur Tedder was the immediate superior in charge of the Allied tactical air forces, although during the Ardennes Campaign, Spaatz assumed an unofficial lead role and the two commanders communicated with each other on a frequent basis.

Meuse River. This, he told those present, must not be allowed. To counter the enemy aims Eisenhower sought a cohesive response from his commanders. From the south he would prevail on the Third Army. "When can you attack?" Eisenhower asked, turning to Patton. The Third Army commander did not even hesitate. "December 22!" he blurted, "with three divisions." It was Patton's supreme moment. Others were aghast and some unbelieving. "Don't be fatuous George," Eisenhower implored him. He only wanted a move when Third Army could deliver a full-blooded blow. But Eisenhower was mindful not to pull the reins on Patton, "Every time I get a new star," he declared, "I get attacked." The Supreme Commander was referring to his promotion before Kasserine Pass. "And every time you get attacked," Patton offered, "I bail you out." It was true.[48]

But the proper elixir for the troubles in the north was more elusive. There was no George Patton there. Hodges seemed shaken; while he was moving his HQ back to Chaudfontaine a V1 flying bomb had fallen right on one of the staff trucks killing all aboard and causing further chaos. The Germans had driven a deep wedge into the American line and Bradley in Luxembourg City was nearly cut off from Hodges to the north. In one of the most controversial decisions of the war, Eisenhower took command of the split US First Army from Bradley and gave it Field Marshal Montgomery, who was nominally in charge of the 21st Army Group— made up of mostly British forces. There was no love lost among the generals, but Eisenhower saw a need to involve the British to gain their participation in stopping the enemy incursion that had erupted through the American lines. Eisenhower picked up the phone and called Bradley. Eisenhower informed the 12th Army Group commander of his decision. As might be expected, the 12th Army Group commander protested vehemently. "Well Brad," Ike said before putting down the phone, "those are my orders."

A prompt reorganization of the air effort was also in the offing. To aid Montgomery, Air Marshal Sir Arthur Coningham was given temporary assistance from both Quesada's IX TAC as well as Nugent's XXIX Tactical Air Commands. Both headquarters were also to relocate from the front to avoid the danger of being overrun: the IX TAC went to Charleroi and Nugent's XXIX went from Maastricht to St. Trond. Gen. Weyland requested three additional fighter groups "in view of changes in ground situation. Changed situation now gives the Third Army a 90 mile front while combined frontage of 1st and 9th Armies aggregates 45 miles..." Meanwhile, Gen. Nugent, with a nightly procession of German night fighters buzzing over his sector, urgently asked that three night reconnaissance aircraft with crews be attached to his command at the Le Culot airstrip. The squeaky wheels got

---

48 The next morning Gen. Weyland's diary reflected a touch of sarcasm: "0845 Conference at 3rd Army HQ. Per SHAEF decisions yesterday, Third Army pulls the First Army chestnuts out of the fire by taking over VIII Corps and shifting weight to north to counter German thrust toward Liege."

the grease. Vandenberg transferred three fighter groups to Weyland's XIX TAC and also brought over two P-51 fighter groups from the Eighth Air Force in England. These would conduct fighter sweeps and free Vandenberg's fighter-bombers from air defense commitments so that the full strength of the Thunderbolts and Lightnings could be flung at the enemy on the ground. The next day too, the orders came from the Ninth Air Force granting Dick Nugent the night reconnaissance aircraft he desired.

Eisenhower's air strategy would be to destroy the power base of the enemy counteroffensive. This would be accomplished by heavy interdiction from the air while containing the attacking elements on the ground within a pre-defined area. "Full priority is given to the area and plan for interdiction and destruction of enemy movement supporting their counteroffensive," went the 12th Army Group directive, "with special emphasis on close-support by fighter-bombers to our own counterattacks." The heavy bombers of the Eighth Air Force and RAF Bomber Command would be used against communications targets to the enemy's rear whose destruction would have an effect on enemy combat effectiveness within 24 hours. The medium bombers of the Ninth Air Force would interdict German movement into the battle zone by destruction of the bridges at Euskirchen, Ahrweiler, Mayen, Eller. Selected marshalling yards and road centers were to be assailed in the following priority: Pronsfeld, Prüm, Gerolstein, Junkerath, Hillesheim, Bitburg, Erdorf, Wittlich, Wengenrohr, Gemünd, Schleiden, Kall, Daun, Vianden, Neuerburg, Waxweiler and Lunebach. The roads crossing the Our and Sauer Rivers were natural choke points feeding the logistical tail of the German monster. Accordingly Echternach, Wallendorf, Vianden, Dasburg, Burg Reuland, Winterspelt and Seltz were added to the list to get the treatment.

The interdiction bombing capability would be greatly expanded. The strength of the IX BD would be supplemented by the addition of the B-24s of Maj. William E. Kempner's 2nd Bombardment Division of the Eighth Air Force which would make its heavy bombers available without resorting to the usual channels. The role of the bombers of the Eighth and Ninth Air Forces would be destruction of enemy railway yards, communications centers and bridges along two concentric lines of interdiction east of the salient. On the hit list were the marshalling yards at Homburg, Kaiserlautern, Hanau and Aschaffenburg. The role of the fighter-bombers would be to first establish overall air superiority over the battle zone and then to provide close support to the armies as well as interdiction along the forward roads and railheads at the front lines.

But if the Ninth Air Force was severely curtailed by the weather on the 19th, the Eighth Air Force in England was still out in limited strength. Foggy conditions improved throughout the day to a visibility of 1-2,000 yards in places. The 1st BD put up some 172 B-17s to hit tactical targets in Luxembourg as well as the rail marshalling yards at Koblenz. At the same time, 156 B-24s of the 2nd BD struck other tactical targets as well as the rail centers at Ehrang. The tactical targets pummeled included road choke points at Glaadt, Schleiden, Bitburg, Blankenheim, Hillesheim and rail junctions at Kall, Gemünd, Kyllburg and Ehrang. Some 932 tons of bombs were dropped in the first attempt by the Eighth during the counteroffensive at isolating the Germans from their supply heads. The 78th Fighter Group (Col. Frederick C. Gray) provided the P-47 escort for the 2nd BD missions with some 41 fighters dispatched. The Eighth had planned a massive fighter escort, but the weather was so poor that the escort for the 1st BD was unable to take off. Luckily opposition from the Luftwaffe was light. "Fifteen fighter groups were available...and it was decided to use them all in support of the operation. It was at first believed that the enemy would make an all out effort to protect and assist the counterattack being made by his ground forces, but later weather forecasts made it seem impossible that the enemy would be able to take off at all." The Fighter Command was right. The 78th strafed a German airdrome with hardly a rise out of the enemy. Later they did meet some 75 German fighters over Koblenz and managed to shoot down seven. Bad weather in the later afternoon over England caused trouble, however, and many of the returning bombers were diverted to West England.

On the ground, Patton was animated. The general announced that his Third Army would attack to relieve the surrounded 101st Airborne Division in Bastogne within 48 hours. Regardless of those who doubted, Patton made good his promise. By December 20th he was on the move with three divisions from the south after having "primed Bradley" for more fighter groups to be assigned to Weyland's XIX TAC. The additions included the 365th, 367th and 368th FGs and the Mustangs of 361st which transferred to Asch from the Eighth Air Force. Two tactical reconnaissance squadrons (the 160th and 161st) came from Dick Nugent. The switch-over began on Christmas Day. Now, more than ever, he needed airpower, but the flying conditions over the battle zone remained abominable. Of some 400 Allied sorties, few were over the cloud-hidden Ardennes. Those venturing there reported "unobserved results." The fighter-bombers of the XIX TAC flew some 214 sorties in support of RAF heavy bombers that day, but that was all. The 405th FG's 509th Squadron attacked approximately 20 tanks about 25 miles northwest of Trier and the 510th hit German troop concentrations seen along the Sauer River south of Echternach. All of the returning pilots able to see below the murk reported massive German traffic between Trier and Merzig. The 354th FG did work with VIII Corps and bombed a marshalling yard at Kall. After the mission the P-47s were attacked by a flock of Me-109s at 4,000 feet. The 354th claimed nine destroyed for the loss of three of their own. Quesada's IX TAC was able to field only 79 sorties and many of the flights of the

370th, 474th and 366th FGs dropped their bombs unobserved through overcast on Dahlem, Prüm, Rohren, Bollendorf and Marmagen.

The experience of the 428th Squadron of the 474th FG was typical of the few missions the Ninth Air Force fighter-bombers were able to fly. Capt. William Siegel took off with seven P-38s just before noon, although one was forced to return to Florennes with engine trouble. Two of the remaining six lost the formation in the soupy clouds, although sighting and attacking a German truck convoy on the roads in the northern battle zone. The rest of Red Flight was vectored to hit the enemy troops just east of Höfen where a fleeting glimpse showed at least a hundred enemy vehicles (probably the transport for the *326th Volksgrenadier Division*). By the time Siegel and his group got around to attacking through the murk, the bomb drops were "not too productive." Just before 2 PM the Lightnings returned to base with little to show other than no losses of their own. Another group from the 474th did locate the enemy column and claimed 30 vehicles destroyed.

The bombing by the 474th was better than they knew. Grenadier Ernst Wagner, a 17-year old antitank company member of the *752nd Grenadier Regiment*, later told his captors that the village of Imgenbroich over which the Lightnings operated, was dubbed the *Todesstrasse*— "Death road." Five other fighter-bombers attacked a radio car of the headquarters of the *326th* at Olef that day at 11 AM killing a civilian, destroying the car and wounding several soldiers. In coming days the U.S. fighter-bombers dominated the air over Imgenbroich completely and neither vehicles nor soldiers dared use the path during daylight hours. According to the petrified German prisoner the town was in ruins with many bombed out houses, burned out vehicles and dead horses. Two German soldiers were killed and many others wounded. Similarly, Obgefr. Theodor Bohner of the *12 Volksgrenadier Division* was passing through the town of Kall on December 19th when six "twin-boom Allied fighters" attacked at 9 AM. Everyone ran for shelter, but when the smoke cleared one of the group had been killed and another two wounded. A good part of Bohner's train was flattened.

The Germans were less willing to fly in the bad weather than their enemy, with the U.S. Air Force estimating their total sorties at perhaps only 200-250 on December 19th. The lack of activity is reflected in the total claims, the U.S. recorded only 2 enemy aircraft destroyed in the air with the ground anti-aircraft crews claiming another 9. By December 20th and 21st the Luftwaffe contribution had dropped to some 100 sorties per day with many of these coming as night fighter raids. On the 19th the Luftwaffe ordered that its nightly operations would consist of harassing attacks in the area around the Meuse crossings and in the area Maastricht-Vise-Liège and Huy. Typical of these were the eight Me-110s of *NJG 6* launched from Kitzingen during the late evening of December 20th with the objective of attacking American forces behind their lines. The night fighters flew at 4,000 feet below the clouds looking for targets over Luxembourg. However, the pilot of "2Z+EV" lost his nerve after being fired at and pulled into a cloud bank where he became totally disoriented and lost control of his aircraft. Uffz. Edwin Schnös and Obgefr. Fritz Lägel were able to bail out from the spinning craft, but Lt. Brand, the pilot, went down with his ship. The two survivors were picked up near Esch, Luxembourg.

During the night of December 18th - 19th some 73 Mosquitos of the 138th and 140th Wings of the British 2nd Group were ordered to blast any evening enemy movement seen on the Ardennes in the Trier-Koblenz area. Three Ju-88s and one Me-110 were reported destroyed in the Aachen area by No. 85 Group. Bomber Command reported some 32 sorties dispatched. However, once there they reported the Ardennes cloaked in an impenetrable nighttime mist; in some places the overcast did not break in places until aircraft dropped below 300 feet! The British night-fighters had to be content with blindly dropping their 136 tons of munitions on a few scattered road junctions and villages in the enemy zone. It would be December 23rd before they tried to operate again.

Southwest of Prüm one of the leading U.S. aces with the Ninth Air Force, Capt. Kenneth H. Dahlberg of the 354th Fighter Group, had a particularly revealing encounter on the 19th. Assigned to attack the headquarters of the *116th Panzer Division* which was in the vicinity, the Minnesota native led his Thunderbolts below the mist hugging the hills of the Schnee Eifel.[49] To his amazement, he and his cohorts were confronted with bumper-to-bumper German traffic on the roads behind the enemy front. But before Dahlberg and the other 12 P-47s could attack, the enemy showed up with some 70 Me-109s:

> "Twelve of us started out, but we got jumped by more than forty Messerschmitts and had to drop our bombs in order to fight. I'd like to say right now that the Luftwaffe was successful, because it prevented us from carrying out our bombing mission. You can't maneuver a fighter if your carrying bombs, so we had to dump them or get shot down. Four of our fighters never got into the scrap because our formation was broken up by the intense German flak. Eight of us who did get into the fight knocked down nine Germans."

Dahlberg accounted for four of the German planes, bringing his total to 15 1/2. He added that the German pilots, unlike his previous experience in

---

49 The 354th "Pioneer Mustang" Fighter Group had a curious history. Under the Ninth Air Force, when it was brought over to England, the group was armed with some of the first P-51B Mustangs. Gen. Ira C. Eaker, then commander with the Eighth Air Force, immediately asked that the group be assigned to them since they had the first long-range fighters on the continent and they were urgently needed for escort of the heavy bombers. The Ninth Air Force did not wish to lose their P-51s. As a result they ended up operationally assigned to the Eighth Air Force, but administratively attached to the Ninth. "We found this set-up made us much like distant cousins of both commands, but child of neither," remembered ace Richard E. Turner. And worst of all, at the end of November they were stripped of the Mustangs and forced to take on P-47 Thunderbolts.

earlier months, were aggressive and continued to bear in, even after taking losses. The results of the engagement amounted to nine German fighters destroyed for the loss of three fighter bombers. Four P-47s of the group also managed to attack a German fuel dump near Speicher, north of Trier, through a hole in the overcast.

Even amid the fog and mists, Patton sought to keep his "eyes" in the air. The 10th PRG had only limited success with its photo missions due to the cloud cover and the missions of the 12th TAC R were aborted due to the obfuscation. However, the 15th TAC R was able to fly seven missions, sometimes providing artillery fire information to the ground forces below. Every time the pilots got a good view through the murk, they saw the roads crawling with enemy movement. But even in the bad weather, the threat of the Luftwaffe could not be discounted. Lt. Clyde East and his wingman Lt. Henry Lacey spied four concentrations of enemy trucks including a number of transport convoys. East had just flown over to observe a V2 launching site, when a Me-109 slipped behind his tail, totally missed by East who was intent on photographing his quarry. Luckily, Lt. Lacey saw all of this happening. He quickly swooped in on the enemy plane which was getting ready to open fire. The first burst from Lacey's guns scored hits on the planes fuselage; the second volley set the engine aflame. This was enough for the surprised German pilot who bailed from his stricken machine.

The Luftwaffe effort that salted the tail of Lt. East consisted of some 290 planes essayed to "fighter-bomber hunt" although many of these were ordered to engage the Allied air activity south of the battle zone in the domain of *Heeresgruppe G*. Even so, General Peltz wired *OB West* that he was pleased with the performance of his fliers on the first two days in spite of losing some 65 pilots. That evening, ULTRA listened in as *II Jagdkorps* announced its intention that night to harass Allied movements across the Meuse River and to "supply Battle Group Heydte." The truth was, that Gnfldm. Model had lost all contact with the 800-man team of German parachutists strewn about the hills between Monschau and Malmédy. They had simply vanished.[50]

At midday on December 20th when the *Sixth Panzer Armee* signaled that its main armored spearhead, *Kampfgruppe Peiper*, was marooned without gasoline near Stoumont, the decoded message provided a clear direction for the Allied air interdiction effort. The Germans were desperately short of fuel. An ULTRA communique several days later from Göring himself cinched it. The *Reichsmarschall* decreed that all motor transport not required for the conduct of operations be immediately immobilized. By the new year, Obst. Polack from the quartermaster's department at *OKH* was reporting that the

---

50 *Kampfgruppe von der Heydte* would show up several days later in dribs and drabs, infiltrating back to the German lines near Monschau. Baron von der Heydte himself, suffering from frostbite, was made prisoner. The last German parachute operation of the war came to an ignominious end.

petrol situation had reached such a state that "it may be necessary to de-motorize the army, even the panzer grenadiers moving on foot or by bicycle with only the panzer brigades remaining fully motorized."

If the Allies were having any doubts regarding their current read on German intentions, this must surely have been dispelled by ULTRA which overheard the Luftwaffe announce that attacks on any Allied crossings over the Meuse River were still forbidden. Obviously, they were being preserved for the German advance. And on the following day, an intercept recorded orders that the *Sixth Panzer Armee* was to proceed to the Meuse while passing through Elsenborn, while the *Fifth Panzer* was to advance to Marche on its way to that river. The *Seventh Armee* would continue its mission to establish a cordon of defense facing south above Arlon.

As if the stupefying weather and terrible ground fighting was not enough, a new threat appeared for the Allied generals. On Wednesday, the 20th, Eisenhower received an urgent warning. German commandos in American uniforms had been seen near Epernay.[51] They were part of Otto Skorzeny's commando organization: *Panzer Brigade 150* which had the mission to send a tank unit in American uniforms and vehicles to drive through Allied lines and seize the Meuse bridges. One captured German commando revealed what he said was their ultimate goal: rendezvous at the *Café de Paris* and make their way to Versailles to assassinate the Supreme Commander. Eisenhower unwillingly became a prisoner in his own headquarters. Meanwhile, Lt. Col. Baldwin B. Smith of Chicago, a reasonable Ike look-alike, was driven about in a staff car around Paris hoping to lure out Skorzeny and his crew. To Eisenhower, it was all preposterous.

Even with the treasure trove of intelligence, frustrated commanders could do little to actually fight the German foe. The weather remained the biggest enemy. Conditions on December 20th were even worse than the day before; a heavy ground fog cloaked the battlefield and visibility was often less than 500 yards. Air operations for both antagonists all but ceased. The only Allied air sorties were the actions of two P-61s of the 425th NFS who strafed German traffic in the Traben-Trarbach area. The rest of the day consisted of orders without missions. Ninth Air Force informed the 474th FG that on the first good weather it was to attack the village of Osweiler and two pontoon bridges across the Sauer River. The bridges were just south of Echternach, where the German *Seventh Armee* was giving the 4th Division a hell of a time. Moreover, Hoyt Vandenberg sent an urgent message to SHAEF imploring Spaatz and the others to support his request for help from the Eighth Air Force to smash German communications centers east of the Our River:

---

51 The previous day Eisenhower's security colonel had insisted that the General take a bullet proof vehicle to his historic meeting at Verdun. "I have positive knowledge," he told the Supreme Commander, "that Otto Skorzeny has sent special teams of American dressed commandos to assassinate you." Of course, the whole story was a hoax, having spread as a rumor within the ranks at the commando training center for the *Panzer Brigade 150* at Grafenwöhr.

"Most of these targets would never be requested for attack by heavies under normal conditions. However, they are designed to stop enemy movement and hit troop and supply concentrations immediately in front of our most seriously threatened area. All weather forecasts indicate mediums certainly cannot and fighter bombers probably cannot operate tomorrow which intensifies importance of their attack. General Hodges and Ninth Air Force consider them vital air objectives. In addition it is requested all available Eighth Air Force fighters conduct armed reconnaissance west of Rhine south to Mannheim."

To all these requests, Spaatz gave his blessing. Heavy bombers would be diverted from their strategic missions to augment the IX BD in the interdiction program. Spaatz cut through the usual protocol and red tape through which the tactical participation by the heavies was typically secured. Ninth Air Force operations was authorized to pass requests directly to the Eighth where they were laid on without further ado. Everyone knew that the clearing of the weather would be a signal to the Luftwaffe to put up an unusually fanatic resistance. At the same time, German night air activity— dropping of parachutists, ground attacks and resupply missions— had increased alarmingly. The heavies would be directed to put in several missions to shut down the Luftwaffe airdromes from when the enemy effort was originating. The two Mustang fighter groups would provide fighter support to the fighter-bombers and prevent their distraction to dogfights as had occurred on December 17th and 18th. The job would be to cast the German fighters out of the battle zone, pound the panzer spearheads and slam the railheads, roads, bridges and rolling stock feeding the German counteroffensive. One job of paramount importance was planned without regard to diminution of the effort: the isolated forces at Bastogne had to be resupplied by air if they were to continue to defend that key road center. Special emphasis would be given to cover the Bastogne area with fighter-bomber support to make enemy moves against the garrison an expensive proposition.

The weather seemed unwilling to cooperate with any of Vandenberg's plans. The Eighth Air Force was unable to fly a single combat mission from Wednesday, December 20th until the following Saturday. On Thursday, the 21st, the bad weather continued along with snow and freezing rain. German air operations were suspended. The only potentially effective Allied air operation consisted of a British daytime dispatch of heavy bombers on Trier, a vital rail center for the *Seventh Armee*. The 354th FG (Col. James H. Howard) and the 362nd (Col. Joseph L. Laughlin), escorted the 94 RAF Lancaster bombers with some 100 P-47s that afternoon. The British bombers dropped their wares through the total overcast. After the escort, the fighter bombers added their napalm and white phosphorous contributions, but so opaque were the cloud conditions near the ground, that the pilots were unable to vouch for their results.

Storm clouds were also brewing within the Allied command.

Montgomery, having just gotten the command of the U.S. First Army, strode into Hodges' headquarters on the second floor of the Palace Hotel at 1:30 PM "like Christ come to cleanse the temple." "The situation in the American area is *not* good." he would later report, "There is a definite lack of grip and control and no one has a clear idea as to the situation..." It was true that the hotel was disheveled; another V1 buzz bomb had just exploded in the street a few hours before and blown all the windows out. Hodges was tired, having gotten little sleep in the past few days. Being awakened at 2:30 AM the previous evening by one of Montgomery's inquisitive staffers didn't help matters. "The weather was foul all day," the First Army diary recorded, "Buzz bombs in countless numbers passed over the C.P. ... the planes and the continual traffic moving up and down the main road make it difficult for the General to obtain the quiet which is necessary in making of these vast decisions." Meanwhile, Montgomery affronted nearly everyone present. "Morale was very low," he told his superiors that evening, "They seemed to be delighted to have someone to give them firm orders." But Montgomery did have one bit of news that Eisenhower and the others were looking for. He informed Hodges that his XXX Corps had taken charge of the Meuse bridges and had orders to blow them should the Germans approach.

So abysmal was the weather on December 21st, that even the air bases were now shrouded in fog. The Allied tactical effort claimed 191 sorties flown, although target acquisition was next to impossible and claims were small. A good example of the conditions was the experience of the 405th Fighter Group which was sent to aid the counterattack of the U.S. XII Corps along the south wing of the Bulge, only to turn back when the weather became impossible. The British Bomber Command did strike Cologne and Bonn with 234 sorties on the night of December 21st. Unknown to the Allies, the air campaign was beginning to pay dividends. To the south of the Battle of the Bulge, Gen. d. Inf. Baptist Kneiss of *LXXXV Armeekorps* was forced to acknowledge the effect of the bombing on the rail system which was so vital to the German supply system:

> "...already by 20 December all railways between the Luxembourg front and the Rhine were out of commission, and thus a great deal of motor and horse transport was missing from the start. In the face of the shortage of gasoline already being strongly felt, the added necessity of using precious fuel to transport all supplies for the offensive was an important factor in limiting the striking force..."

The German advance continued. St. Vith was captured and the Americans were surrounded in Bastogne and the panzer spearheads were advancing on the Meuse River. Unfortunately, the prime German battlegroup *Kampfgruppe Peiper* was out of gas, surrounded and bottled up in the Amblève River valley. At 8 PM on December 22nd the *ISS Panzerkorps* requested a supply drop of fuel for the marooned panzer group. Later that evening twenty Ju-52s of *Transportgeschwader 3* attempted to parachute gasoline supplies to the German garrison. Somehow the Luftwaffe got word that Peiper was in Stoumont. In fact, Peiper's panzer group had been so battered in Stoumont that they had pulled back to La Gleize. Most of the fuel drums floated down into the hands of the 30th Infantry Division, which was now in Stoumont. Peiper estimated he received less than 10% of the supplies that were dropped. It was just enough fuel to operate the radio and inform headquarters that the supply attempt had failed and to move a few tanks into better firing positions. The Luftwaffe refused any future attempt at resupply of the German *Kessel*. Peiper's contempt for the German air force reached new heights. Could the Luftwaffe do nothing?

Meanwhile, the American Air Force showed that they could get it done. Although Patton's "eyes" had been grounded on the 20th, on the next day the need for reconnaissance was such that an effort had to be made. Patton needed to know of the location of the American and German lines in the Bastogne salient. Although thwarted on a similar mission on December 19th, Capt. E. B. "Blacky" Travis took off in his F-6 Mustang "Mazie, Me and Monk" without an escort to locate the American lines. It was a desperate attempt. The weather conditions were ridiculous for flying: ceiling 50 feet! visibility 100 yards! He located the target area by instruments, but could see nothing in his first pass over. Another pass at higher altitude in search of a "hole" in the overcast convinced him that this was useless. He rechecked his position with his radar controller. With a silent prayer, Travis dropped his Mustang down to tree-top level. This was hilly country, he thought to himself. A single mistake— a missed ridgeline, a small down-draft— and it would all be over. But as he leveled out, the mist below melted. The blur of pine trees was right below his feet! There was little doubt that he was in the right vicinity as his Mustang streaked over a collection of vehicles. The machines were obviously German, for everyone in them was shooting at him! But presently, he located the American side of the fence. In all, Capt. Travis made four passes before calling it a day. Both enemy and friendly dispositions in the Bastogne pocket had been successfully charted when he set for home. Blacky Travis would earn the Silver Star.

German eyes were also aloft. One Luftwaffe mission proved impervious to the Allied fighter screen and poor weather. The unarmed, but speedy Ar-234 B jet reconnaissance plane of Oblt. Erich Sommer of *Kommando Sperling*, took off from Biblis airfield and raced upward, depending on shear speed to take its pilot through the swarm of Allied fighters. After finishing his high-altitude photographic run over the front, Sommer was set upon by several P-51 Mustangs at 3,300 feet as he scooted back for the German border. These probably included "Little One," the P-51D of Capt. Donald S. Bryan of the 352nd Fighter Group who chased and fired on an Ar-234 south of

Verviers, Belgium during his group's transfer to its new base at Asch, Belgium:

> I commenced my attack much sooner than I would have against a conventional airplane. When I squared up behind him, I was only about 1,000 yards away. He was pulling away from me, but I put a little Kentucky windage into my sight picture and opened fired at him. I saw one strike, on a wing, but that didn't even show up on my film...

So pursued, Sommer quickly re-opened the throttles and dove, only being able to lose the Mustangs when his craft exceeded its critical design Mach number at 606 mph. The jet began to buck violently and Sommer was lucky to be able to use his trimmers to pull his plummeting machine out of its dive and land safely at Biblis. Regardless of the Bryan's claim, his craft sustained no damage. But the same could not be said for his adventure three days later. After an uneventful reconnaissance of the southern part of the battle zone, Sommer returned to Biblis to find the airfield had just been trans-formed into a cratered wasteland courtesy of Eighth Air Force bombs. He made an emergency landing on a grassy field at Wiesbaden-Erbenheim on his last bit of petrol only to be fired on by nervous German flak gunners. His "T9+IH" was struck and caught fire. A furious Oblt. Sommer was able to escape the flaming jet to curse out the higher ranks at the airfield. His first greeting upon eluding death consisted of a German party who raced to-wards him on the field brandishing a Luger. They had mistaken him for a hell-bent American!

On the evening of December 23-24 the Germans launched 88 night fight-ers: 32 to hit Liège, 36 to harass the Allied rear area between Sedan and Metz and the rest to Bastogne. The Bastogne operation materialized, as the town was bombed for the first time by approximately two dozen Ju-88s from *LG 1*. Bastogne would be assailed nightly by the German fighter-bombers over the following week.

The increasingly nocturnal habits of the Luftwaffe were completely frus-trating to the Allied air command. On December 17th Me-110A-4s of *8./NJG 1* shot up nighttime road traffic near Maastricht while *6./NJG 2* carried out similar missions of aggravation against rail movement near Charleville. On the evening of December 22nd *II Jagdkorps* was overheard by ULTRA intend-ing that night to launch "continuous attacks on town of Liège (not on bridges)" Ju-88 night-fighter units were also be employed on ground attack missions to punish the American positions in Luxembourg. The reality was something less. On December 23rd a Ju-88G-1 was shot down near Epernay. The captured crew revealed they had orders to shoot up Allied road traffic behind the lines. During the same evening Fw. Albert Johänntges was captured near Hannut after his Ju-88S-3 from *4./LG 1* was shot down. Just before midnight on Christmas Eve the Ju-88F-1 of *4./NJG 2* flown by Lt. Wolfram Möckel was brought down near Hasselt, Belgium.

On December 26th the nightly operations of *LG 1* extended its reach to include attacks with anti-personnel bombs on suitable military targets "between Huy and Namur within 10 km of the Meuse." One of the three phantoms were shot down some six miles southwest of Liège at 10 PM. One Ju-88G-1 of *III/NJG 4* was shot down over Bastogne on the evening of the 26th with the pilot, Oblt. Walter Riederberger taken prisoner.

NJG 5 was added to the list on December 27th when four Me-110s of *II Gruppe* flying from Schwäbisch Hall strafed railroad traffic near Neufchateau. During the same night *11./NJG 3* flew seven Ju-88G-1s from Varel with orders to attack Allied rail traffic in Belgium. Some were unable to find target, however, and at least three were brought down, one near Weyler, Belgium. Another Me-110G-4 from *III/NJG 1* was shot down near Grandhan, northeast of Marche, on the night of December 26th. *NJG 2* was also very active during the evening losing four Ju-88s over the front, one brought down by a P-61 of the 422nd NFS near Verviers and another which crashed into tall conifers near Grandrieu, Belgium while strafing an American motor column. Aging Ju-87D-5s of *NSGr 1* also began flying nightly missions against the Allied positions in the Aachen-Eupen area beginning on December 24th. Each Stuka carried one 1,100 lb. bomb and two 500 lb. fragmentation canisters and reported it easy to find Allied motor transport on the roads below. The night ground attack aircraft would fly additional missions in dozen-plane strength on the nights of December 30th and 31st.

Although the daylight hours up through 23 December were marked by fog and clouds, the nights were clear and the inadequacy of the night striking force of the Ninth Air Force starkly revealed. On the ground, the attacking Germans were practically free to make any movements they wished, under cover of the overcast during the day and by darkness at night. Certainly, the attacks had little military value, but they proved a source of constant bother, and of casualties in the case of the night raids over Bastogne.

The short-handed Americans did get some help from their Allies. The British night fighters stalked the darkness with orders to assault any enemy they could discern on the ground. The 2 Group flew some 37 sorties hitting enemy troop concentrations near Darscheid and Schmidtheim although the participating 342 Squadron noted that "the Ardennes are white with snow, the rivers are frozen and target identification is very difficult." The RAF heavies also assailed the German heartland on the night of the 22nd-23rd with a massive attack. A total of 512 bombers dropped more than 2,000 tons of bombs on Koblenz (attacked twice), Bingen, Trier and Cologne. Another 26 RAF Mosquitos operated in front of the U.S. VIII Corps, destroying an ammunition train; "the subsequent fire could be seen for twenty miles."

The 2nd TAF did manage other missions between Aachen and Trier; the British also flew some 36 medium bomber sorties against troop and supply concentrations south of Düren and some 220 fighter-bomber sorties against enemy transport in the Münster area. But virtually all other operations were cancelled. Indicative of the degree of the German advantage from the weather was the fact that over the first week of the enemy offensive, Vandenberg's Ninth Air Force was only able to fly some 2,818 sorties of which only about 1,800 were over the battlefield. And this from an air command which reported a daily average operational strength of 1,550 planes during mid-December.

On the ground Patton concentrated three of his divisions south of Arlon to attack north to relieve the surrounded garrison at Bastogne. True to his word, his Third Army jumped off to advance along a twenty mile front at 6:30 AM on December 22nd. However, without air support German resistance was terrific and Patton was only able to advance seven miles by nightfall. Similarly, Gen. Collins was concentrating his armored and infantry divisions southwest of Liège. According to Eisenhower's plan, he was to lop off the German panzer spearhead near the Meuse. Together, Patton's and Collins' attacks were designed to wrest the initiative from the enemy and perhaps to even cut off and surround the German forces in the salient, now clearly resembling a "Bulge" in the Allied line. Still the overall Allied mood was jittery. Eisenhower, who had had his fill of the cloak-and-dagger routine with the German infiltrators, was losing patience with the whole matter. Nothing could go right that Thursday. Gen. Strong brought Eisenhower more unwelcome news. The Germans, he said, were pulling divisions from the Eastern Front. There was the unspoken possibility that they would be used in the West. If only Vandenberg's planes could take to the air and hit the enemy in their darkest hour! "This is the shortest day," Eisenhower wrote home on the 21st, "how I pray that it may, by some miracle, mark the beginning of improved weather!"

Meanwhile, Montgomery visited Hodges at his headquarters at the Hôtel des Bains. Once more he found the General preparing to move, to Tongres 15 miles further west. The official reason was to "obtain peace and quiet." The reality was that the other side of the Meuse would be safer. V1 robot bombs roared over Chaudfontaine almost constantly and many were falling with deadly effect in Liège. Montgomery reported back to Eisenhower that Hodges was "a bit shaken early on and needed moral support and was very tired." But he said that the First Army commander was coming around. Eisenhower informed the British commander that he knew he would: "...Hodges is the quiet reticent type and does not appear as aggressive as he really is." Meanwhile, Joe Collins and his powerful VII Corps prepared to deal a mortal blow to the German spearhead. "This is our big chance," Gen. Nugent wrote in his diary, "Several days of good weather for air action followed by a heavy, well-placed counteroffensive should end the war."

The wish was not fulfilled. The morning of December 22nd began with a snowstorm. The daily weather briefing had reached something akin to a painful tradition. First Maj. S. S. Tomlin, the Air G-3, gave the ground picture— gloomy enough of its own accord. Col. George F. McGuire, the Director of Operations, outlined the proposed air activities on the next day. But with "no ops" conditions, even McGuire's most enthusiastic plans to take the pants off Hitler's new offensive faded in the cold and gloom. Then it was Maj. Stuart J. Fuller's turn to do his magic. The audience was sober and quiet, but listened attentively, hoping to see some glimmer of improvement. Most steeled themselves for another dose of bad news. The briefing laconically described the obvious: wretched fog and mist and now snow. As if to underscore the Air Force's impotence, all through the disheartening diatribe, Patton's tanks rumbled slowly through the Luxembourg streets outside. Soldiers bundled up against the snow trudged along outside the windows. Meanwhile 10,000 Allied planes— the world's most powerful air force- stood impotent before the weather. It was galling. Vandenberg tried hard to make light of it, "Do you think that Hitler *makes* this stuff?" he cracked. But as news of the German advance spread that day, the humor wore thin. Later he called in his weatherman, Maj. Fuller, for a one-on-one at the end of the day. "How much longer is this going to last?" Vandenberg queried. His patience was growing thin. Fuller looked away as if to gaze into a meteorological crystal ball. Stagnant high pressure regions existed both to the east and west of the Ardennes; it seemed unlikely that anything would start them moving. He took a weatherman's guess. It should improve around December 26th, he ventured. "Suppose its clear tomorrow," Vandenberg posed rhetorically, "what are you going to do?" Fuller turned away "Shoot myself," he muttered under his breath.

On the 22nd, the American 101st Airborne Division had been surrounded in Bastogne for three days. A team of German emissaries from a frustrated Gen. Lüttwitz approached the garrison on that day asking for surrender, aware of the capitulation of the 106th Infantry Division encircled on the Schnee Eifel only a couple of days before. The defiant reply of Brig. Gen. Anthony C. McAuliffe of the 101st Airborne, "Nuts!," would forever be associated with the Battle of the Bulge. But that the air commanders were worried about the situation was understatement. By late that Friday, Quesada's IX TAC was issuing its air plan for resumption of operations once the weather permitted. The plan contained a dark contingency. If the Germans were held behind the Meuse, designated U.S. combat formations in the Ardennes would get the majority of the direct support. However, if the Germans advanced across that river "Plan A" went into effect. In this scenario, a majority of the discretionary fighter-bomber sorties would be used to "cover every road movement" west of Givet to Namur.

The night of December 22nd and the early morning hours of December 23rd were long ones for the 430th Squadron of the 474th Fighter Group. At their base in Florennes, the P-38s and their pilots and ground crew were less than thirty miles from the German armor advancing towards the Meuse. At 8 PM that night word came from headquarters that the enemy was approaching and that "the field would be defended at all costs." More guards were posted and some dug foxholes. "Everyone went around armed to the teeth," wrote a member of the 422nd NFS posted there, "it was a wonder no one was shot." The situation was made even more tense when a single night fighter flying at dusk incorrectly located the enemy even closer to Florennes. Something of a panic ensued. The entire base was alerted to move at a moment's notice and trucks were made ready. Pilots were pulled from their chateaus where they normally slept and put in the day room to be ready to take off as soon as signaled. In the barracks, the enlisted men were talking about "infantry tactics" and other stuff that an airman wasn't supposed to know. One of the anti-aircraft guns from the field was even hauled out to the road leading into the base from the east. Finally, word came that the whole thing was a false alarm; the Germans weren't that close. The problem was that the enemy tanks *were* still moving unchecked in their direction. Everyone was frustrated at not being able to fly. Would their air fields be overrun by the Germans before the weather cleared?[52] Lt. John C. Calhoun wrote home just after the tumult had passed, first writing his mother and informing her that he had made out his full allotment of his GI insurance to the family. "I have done my best to provide for you in case I do not come home," Calhoun wrote, "a possibility we must all face together the way the fighting is going over here for us airmen."

At the advanced weather center for the Ninth Air Force the gloom was nearly as impenetrable as the unbroken gray smothering the Ardennes Front. Maj. Fuller was again on duty. He wearily looked over the teletype data coming in from the remote weather stations. Then a little after midnight a report came in with roused one of the weary group to closer attention. "Look at this," he called to the others. It seemed that the barometric pressure was rising to the east. They waited anxiously for the next bulletin.

Gen. Sam Anderson of the IX Bombardment Division was sleeping soundly in his quarters in Rheims, France. Just after midnight his bedside phone rang. "General, you won't believe this," Anderson's weather officer began, "but it is going to be clear tomorrow." Anderson wondered if he was dreaming. "Wait a minute," he told the lieutenant. He walked over to this bedroom window. There was nothing but fog. "I can't see across the street," Anderson said returning to the phone. The lieutenant explained the high pressure moving in from the East. Anderson was finally convinced and rang

---

52 Gen. Pete Quesada considered it fortunate that the German ground advance "woke up" the lethargic AA defenses at the American air bases: "...I was of the firm conviction that if the Germans...made sorties against our forward strips, that it would result in a lot of planes being shot down...Our airdromes had almost been confronted with an air attack, and they were not exercised. Any military force that is not exercised becomes very lazy and complacent... I was terribly anxious to get rid of the complacency...and make them aware of the fact that the Germans were around."

up Vandenberg's headquarters. The phone call came through just about the time the weather personnel in Luxembourg were getting other encouraging readings from remote instruments. It is axiomatic that weathermen everywhere become animated when a big front pushes through. But this was different. The eagerness of the Ninth Air Force meteorologists for good weather bordered on obsession. Spirits rose in the huddle in the teletype room with the barometric pressure. Suddenly one of the meteorologists leapt to his feet. "I think its breaking!" he cried. The officer in charge was incredulous. He too studied the data long and hard. Finally, he gestured to his subordinates with gathering confidence. "Notify the general," he told them with a rising voice, "Tell everybody that it's almost certain we'll fly tomorrow."

While combat crews snoozed in their frigid tents and ramshackle buildings, Hoyt Vandenberg and the operations officers of the Ninth Air Force were burning the midnight oil behind black-out curtains. Within minutes word went out to the far flung bases around England, Belgium, Holland and France. They would fly tomorrow. Hitler's conspiracy with the weather was over.[53]

---

53 The weather had cleared over Eastern Germany even before it changed over the Allied weather stations. An ULTRA decrypted message from *II Jagdkorps* on the evening of December 22nd was distinctly upbeat, noting that the weather would be clear over German airfields first: "The weather will, in the morning, probably bring relief to us and difficulties to the enemy. In the afternoon the enemy will be able to fly. All forces are to be made ready, so as to be able to successfully engage in an air battle on a grand scale. Four-engined bombers are the Army's greatest danger. All formations will therefore direct their ruthless attacks against them."

P-38 Lightning pilots of the 367th Fighter Group are seen with a contrived sleigh train for transportation from the briefing hut to the dispersal area. *(NASM)*

Buddies. Pilots of Lockheed P-38 Lightnings discuss their latest mission, Floronnoo, 1016. The P-38s proved unexceptional In encounters with German fighters, but their very heavy armament and dual engines made them a formidable ground attack aircraft. *(NASM)*

Pfc. H. Mark Connell, armorer for the 406th Fighter Group at Mourmelon, France, December, 1944. *(Connell)*

Capt. John H. Hoefker. Hoefker was part of "Patton's eyes," the 10th Photo Reconnaissance Group of the XIX Tactical Air Command. *(Ivie)*

Legend's end. Ofw. Heinrich Bartels of *IV/JG 27*. The 26-year-old German pilot had just claimed his 99th victory when a P-47 sent Bartels crashing to his death just outside of Bonn in "Marga," his Me-109G. Auguring into the ground, his remains would not be located until 1968. *(Bundesarchiv)*

Lt. Hans Oppl was the pilot of the Ju-88G-6 night fighter "4R+NU" of *IV/NJG 2*. Oppl lost his life when he crashed into the high conifers near Grandrieu while strafing a U.S. motor column on the evening of December 27th. The evening of December 27th was a costly one for the Luftwaffe night fighters over the Ardennes. Most were brought down by anti-aircraft fire. *(Oppl family via Roba)*

Martin B-26 Marauders attacking the railway town of Euskirchen just east of the Ardennes. Euskirchen served as an important communications link from Cologne to
the front. *(NASM)*

This P-47 suffered severe damage over the battle zone, yet managed to return to base to make a crash landing. The pilot escaped before the aircraft exploded. The P-47 was a tough aircraft, its resilience partly due to its air-cooled radial piston engine and ability to sustain severe punishment and keep flying. *(NASM)*

Fred Castle gets another star at Bury, England, to mark his promotion to Brigadier General. December 4, 1944. *(HRC)*

As AA gunners look on, the largest air battle in Europe is etched out in the December sky on Christmas Eve. *(HRC)*

"Furniture Vans." Unflattering though the German moniker may have been, the squarish Consolidated B-24s were powerful bombers. Here, Liberators of the 458th Bomb Group queue up to take off for their Christmas Eve mission over Germany. *(NASM)*

The bridge over the Moselle River at Trier gets the treatment from the Marauders of the 394th Bomb Group, December 24, 1944. *(NASM)*

Angriffswaffen. Heavily laden Fw-190F-8s, like this aircraft in operation in Russia, were ideally suited for taking on enemy tanks from the air. Most of the aircraft were fitted with a belly rack to hold a 1,102 lb. bomb plus wing racks for two 551 lb. bombs. Unfortunately, the air cover that made the *Schlachtgruppen* so successful in the East was lacking over the Ardennes. *(Bundesarchiv)*

Adolf Hitler commends Maj. Anton Hackl, one of the leading Luftwaffe pilots. Hackl, a member of *JG 26* in 1944, fought on all fronts and was shot down no less than eight times during the war. Hackl survived the war with 192 victories to his credit. *(Hackl)*

Maj. Hans-Georg Bätcher, the commander of the world's first jet bomber unit, *III/KG 76*, (left) and Dieter Lukesch (center), the leader of its *Einsatzstaffel* in January of 1945. Bätcher, who flew missions with the Ar-234, was the most experienced bomber pilot of the war (658 missions). *(Creek)*

A Junkers Ju-188 lies peacefully in a field in the spring after the winter war. *(NASM)*

XIII

War's Most Beautiful Sunrise: December 23rd

Morning December 23rd. The mists and ground fog slowly faded to show a clear, steely blue winter sky. A pale December sun hesitantly rose above the horizon to at last reveal itself. Within hours the sun was like a blazing arc illuminating the snow dusted forests over the embattled hills of the Ardennes. It was, according to one beleaguered GI on the ground, "the war's most beautiful sunrise." During the previous night, a "Russian High"— a seldom seen eastern European high pressure system— had moved westward finally drawing the veil of clouds and fog from the Ardennes. So long frustrated, the Allied air bases all over Europe teemed with activity and relieved optimism. At last they could fly! George S. Patton had a predictable sobriquet for the blue skies. "What a glorious day," he remarked, "for killing Germans!"

The Eighth Air Force was taking off to pound German communication targets east of the battlefield. RAF Bomber Command was planning a big strike on Cologne and the Ninth Air Force would be intervening directly in the Ardennes fighting. And at air bases in Germany, the Luftwaffe was also hurriedly readying its fighters to respond. Although it was not able to signal the news until a day later, ULTRA overheard the Germans planning to cover their offensive with 150 aircraft launched hourly to provide an "umbrella over the spearhead of advance."

At daybreak the mighty Allied air forces rose in strength to lay a mortal blow on the German enemy. The skies over Luxembourg and Belgium were filled with Allied planes; it was as if a dense flock of metallic starlings had choked the skies. Everywhere there were P-47s and B-26s roaring about. The streets of Luxembourg filled with people, craning their necks to see the vast aerial display. The Ninth Air Force produced a massive effort: 696 fighter-bomber sorties. The great preponderance of the flights came from the XIX TAC who put up 451 that day with all seven groups active. Weyland's staff expounded heavy use of fragmentation bombs and napalm to check the Germans over the southern part of the battlefield.

Nugent's XXIX TAC put up 105 sorties, although the 48th and 404th FGs were unable to participate because of poor weather, but the other two were out, albeit in missions that were outside the arena of the fighting. The 36th and 373rd FGs concentrated their efforts on shutting down the German airfields at Bonn-Hangelar and Wahn, which radio intelligence revealed were once more active. At Wahn the U.S. pilots bombed numerous hangars and buildings, destroying nine enemy aircraft on the ground. However, immediately after the strafing, 60-plus bandits engaged the U.S. pilots. Three of the German fighters were shot down. At Bonn-Hangelar thirty Fw-190s and Me-109s challenged the U.S. fighters in the process of attacking, making any assessment of damage impossible. Fourteen of the German fighters were shot down and seven P-47s were lost in the two engagements. "Y" service intercepts after the attacks revealed that many German aircraft were in trouble. Unable to land on the two unserviceable fields at least one was overheard to crash and others put down where they could with empty fuel. Meanwhile P-38s of the XXIX TAC hit Höfen, Prüm and Rocherath. And true to their word, the rocket-firing Typhoons of the British 83 Group were also out interceding in the ground battle.[54]

The IX TAC flew some 19 missions comprising 211 sorties and dropped 64 tons of ordnance. The 366th FG was unable to operate due to weather conditions, but the 370th and 474th FG were up in force. Forty-two German aircraft were claimed for the loss of five. In addition, a recce aircraft of the 67th TAC R Group was lost in an encounter with an Fw-190; during its missions the 109th Squadron spotted thirty tanks, jeeps and several vans motoring south east of Monschau. Another flight observed heavy German traffic north of Trier.

The P-38s of the 367th FG flew escort for Marauders striking the rail bridge at Ahrweiler. Four of these missions were uneventful. However, two others ran into the enemy while watching bombs from the IX mediums slam into Euskirchen. Southeast of the city the 392nd squadron was bounced by two dozen Me-109s at 17,000 feet. A furious and sprawling air battle ensued with the P-38s getting the best of it; they shot down 11 of the enemy for a loss of one. In an afternoon mission another squadron missed its rendezvous with the bombers, but found four Fw-190s with three shot down for no

---

54 The British were not the only ones impressed by their rocket-firing Typhoons. An ULTRA intercept on January 1st detailed the observation by an officer of the *1st SS Panzer Division* who ruefully noted that a single direct hit by one of the rockets on a Panther tank meant a total loss.

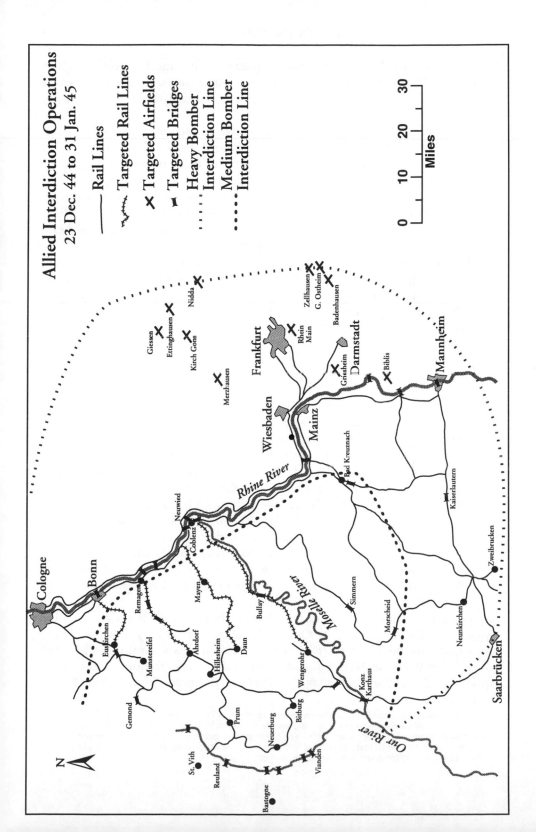

Allied Interdiction Operations
23 Dec. 44 to 31 Jan. 45

— Rail Lines
〰 Targeted Rail Lines
✕ Targeted Airfields
▮ Targeted Bridges
•••• Heavy Bomber
      Interdiction Line
•••• Medium Bomber
      Interdiction Line

Miles
0   10   20   30

N

Cologne
Bonn
Remagen
Euskirchen
Gemond
Munstereifel
Ahrdorf
Hillesheim
Daun
Mayen
St. Vith
Reuland
Prum
Neuerburg
Bitburg
Vianden
Bullay
Wengerohr
Moselle River
Our River
Konz Karthaus
Coblenz
Neuwied
Morscheid
Simmern
Bad Kreuznach
Bastogne
Saarbrücken
Zweibrücken
Neunkirchen
Kaiserlautern
Mannheim
Biblis
Darmstadt
Griesheim
Badenhausen
G. Ostheim
Zellhausen
Nidda
Kirch Gons
Ettinghausen
Giessen
Merzhausen
Frankfurt
Rhein Main
Wiesbaden
Mainz
Rhine River

losses. Later in the day the same squadron saw another four Fw-190s preparing to join in a raging fight between other German planes and some P-47s. The P-38s intervened, however, and claimed three of the enemy without loss.

The 368th FG ran into enemy aircraft on two armed recces. On one mission 30 Fw-190s and Me-109s were seen attacking B-26s— the Germans called them *Halbstarke*— about ten miles southwest of Koblenz. In a swirling half-hour engagement the 396th Squadron claimed 13 enemy fighters. Another air battle took place to the northwest of the city where 15 German planes were destroyed for the loss of one P-47 pilot. Elsewhere, the 394th Squadron bombed train and marshalling yards at Oberstein while the 395th hit rail targets near Mayenne and Cochem.

The Germans in the St. Vith and Recht area were repeatedly strafed and bombed by 370th FG (Lt. Col. Seth J. McKee). The fighter group was unable to make contact with its assigned controller with the 82nd Airborne Division, but its pilots on free lance made life dangerous for Germans nearby. The 402nd Squadron hit a German convoy just southeast of St. Vith, the 485th attacked ten other German vehicles at Crombach and the 401st assisted the 3rd Armored Division in attacking several tanks of the *116 Panzer Division* near Soy, Belgium.

For the two P-38 Lightning Groups at Florennes, their mission on the 23rd had special import. The German armored spearhead, the *2nd Panzer Division* was near Dinant and headed straight in their direction. The ground crews at the base could even hear the distant thunder of gunfire from the east; the night before eerie orange flashes to the east were a constant reminder that the battle was not far away. At dawn it was cold, but at last clear. Nervous mechanics had used the time to get all the P-38s ready. One of the last Lightning groups in the Ninth Air Force, the 474th had many tired hand-me-downs from groups converting to the Mustang or P-47. The old war horses required constant attention to keep them serviceable. Now, they were to put up a maximum effort. The pilots walked out to their waiting P-38s in the pre-dawn; the engines coughed to life. The ground crews pulled the wheel chocks. As the dim winter sun etched over the horizon, the twin-tailed fighters took to the air.

Once aloft, the 474th FG bombed and machine gunned the enemy in nine separate missions that day. One flight struck an enemy column, likely belonging to the *89 Infanterie Division* just west of Rocherath.[55] A flight of four P-38s from the 428th Squadron bombed a concentration of many German vehicles of the *9SS Panzer Division* observed near Vielsalm. Maj. Nuck-

---

[55] Uffz. Heinrich Engelhardt was on the receiving end of one of these attacks. His *1055 Grenadier Regiment* had just been relieved at the line and was on its way to Heimbach for refitting. Engelhardt marched along with a rag-tag group of fifty men of a depleted company on the road in dispersed marching order. Suddenly, just before 5 PM half a dozen P-38s attacked the march column. Eight of the fifty soldiers were killed and another twelve wounded.

ols reported sighting the "juicy convoy of possibly 200 vehicles" only to have his 500 lb. bomb refuse to drop. Flak became very thick after the failed run and the rest of the flight had to return with little to show for the effort. A later attempt in the afternoon met a wall of enemy flak in the woods north of St. Vith. Lt. Knox was hit by fire from a German gun with his aircraft bursting into flames. Knox was seen to bail out of his stricken plane in enemy territory near Stavelot; only after the war did his friends learn that he had been killed. The heavy flak also made for poor bombing accuracy against the numerous sighted ground targets. A number of the ten remaining planes in the flight were damaged.

But the big target for the 474th that day was the German spearhead just east of Dinant on the Meuse. The American effort from Florennes was all-out; even a tired P-61 of the 422nd NFS was sent out during an unusual day mission. Just after 2 PM they reached the roads between St. Hubert and Marche. The Germans were everywhere; they dropped their single bomb load on a dozen enemy vehicles southeast of Rochefort.

The little hamlet of Foy Notre Dame lies less than five miles from the German objective of the Meuse River. Intent on reaching the Meuse at Dinant, the *3 Battalion* of the *766 Volksartillerie Korps* was following in the general advance of the *2 Panzer Division* as the spearhead of *Fifth Panzer Armee*. Just before noon the supply column of the artillery moved into the village along with elements of the reconnaissance battalion of the *2 Panzer*. Just then, Obgefr. Edmund Linkiewicz looked up to see an angry swarm of fighter-bombers swooping down upon the German column. Before anyone could take cover six trucks went up in flames along with three halftracks damaged or destroyed. Worst of all, the battalion's only fuel truck exploded in a blaze consuming 3,400 precious liters of the stuff. The advance of the *2 Panzer* sputtered out of gas.

Mourmelon, France was home to Col. Anthony V. Grosetta's 406th Fighter Group with the XIX Tactical Air Command. As the Thunderbolt flew, from the shack city of Mourmelon-le-Grand to Bastogne in the Ardennes was not more than 80 miles. Mourmelon did have some pluses. The field was an old French military base dating back to the Franco-Prussian war and had been used in turn by the various armies that had swept back and forth across Western France. The camp was close to Rheims with its famous towering cathedral and although restaurants there were off limits to American soldiers, there was no shortage of champagne with the source at Epernay. In the late fall, part of the 101st Airborne Division moved to Mourmelon at the other end of the airfield. The airmen quickly made friends with the rowdy "Screaming Eagles." Booze was common currency at Mourmelon and some of the 406th guys bartered the whisky-loving paratroopers a bottle of bourbon for souvenirs. It seems that after each flight was debriefed, a shot of whisky or scotch was issued by the Flight Surgeon, Doc Grace. A good flight surgeon, but a poor bartender, Grace started to issue full bottles after so many missions. These vessels might have well have contained bottled gold to the "Screaming Eagles." A treasured bottle of blended bourbon could be traded for a captured Walther P-38 pistol or even a German flag. And during the extended bad weather period where no one was flying, everybody at the base got together for raucous USO shows or put away a couple of drinks while the "Stardusters" plied everyone with a few swing tunes. Although liberty runs didn't go to nearby Chalons, many of the men hitch-hiked there or to Epernay to return with a few magnums of champagne. At first the men lived in tents on the far side of the airfield, but eventually a number of concrete barracks and homes were made available for use. After the tents, four walls felt good, but the rain and snow and lack of operations were frustrating. Then the 101st Airborne guys had been whisked off in flatbed trucks before dawn on December 18th. Rumor had it that they were headed for the front where "all hell had broken loose." As they left they irreverently taunted the 406th guard on duty. "Air Force soft jobs!" one called as the trucks roared off into the fog.

Somehow the 406th learned that their former GI friends were at a Belgian town called Bastogne. The Germans had them surrounded and under a big attack. The rumor mills at the base were working overtime. Soldiers passing through told them that in Belgium and Luxembourg it had really hit the fan. Extra guards were posted and security, which was usually almost casual, became heavy-handed. Everyone was cleaning their guns. Pvt. Henry Mark Connell was one of the many ground crew that maintained the U.S. air forces in Europe. Although few realized it, there were about ten ground personnel working to keep each pilot in the skies over Europe. Mark's occupation was straightforward— he was an armorer. He lashed bombs, napalm and "frags" under the wings of the 513th Squadron Thunderbolts at Mourmelon. The officers that flew the "Jugs" dropped them on the heads of the Krauts. It was that simple.

The lot of the ground crews in Europe was particularly unappetizing that winter. Most of those with the 406th thought the Germans were finished after the conquest of summer; many were surprised to find themselves still fighting that Christmas. Connell's bunk-mate was no exception. "This war's got to be over soon," he would complain each night giving a litany of reasons why he assumed the Germans were on the verge of quitting. Why bust their butts? "Because," as Mark was fond of reminding everyone, "assuming makes an ass of you and me."

Connell and the rest worked on the P-47s, usually not in a hangar, but on the exposed expanse of the runway in the slush, wind and snow. There was little in the way of spit-and-polish for the 406th ground crew. Most of the ground crews looked like hell, particularly Mark who sprouted a midnight shadow within hours of infrequent shaving. But more than this, the weather really made it miserable. The aircrew were quartered in wood huts, equipped with small coal stoves that were hard to start. Some ingenious service personnel had learned that adding a little napalm to the ash pans made all the difference for a quick fire.

Like almost everywhere else, there was a lot of complaining at Mourmelon. But then word came later that month that the army was getting itchy for rifle replacements and was eying any excess at the air bases. Suddenly, the bitching ended and everyone kept busy. Pvt. Connell liked it like that anyway. Then word came that the Germans had opened a big attack in Luxembourg and Belgium; the news coming from the battlefield was bad. The Germans were coming this way! The airfield was alerted to be on the lookout for enemy paratroopers, there were rumors of German commandos afoot and somebody in the 514th Squadron found two Germans hiding in a farmer's haystack. Paranoia. "It was colder 'n hell," remembered the native of Bushnell, Florida, "Everyone was talking about how the Germans were coming. So, we worked their tails off to keep bombs on those P-47s." When the weather suddenly cleared on the morning of December 23rd, the pregnant-looking 406th Thunderbolts were all lined up on the airfield. They were armed to the teeth.

First light. Without delay, the 406th launched one flight after another of the weighted down P-47s before the sun rose over the frosty landscape. In less than half an hour the fighter-bombers were over the battlefield. Lt. Howard W. Park, a veteran of panzer busting in Normandy, was among the first up that morning heading for Bastogne in his famous red-nosed "Big Ass Bird II."[56]

"On the morning of the 23rd, the first lifting of the weather, we took off two abreast under a 200 foot ceiling. Flying at a fixed rate of climb for one minute, then a 180 turn, continue until we broke into the clear which was up at 12-15,000 feet. We would contact ground controller (Capt. James Parker), and given as much altitude as possible in the clear, up to a couple of thousand feet weather permitting, we began a high speed dive toward designated targets— tanks, troops and guns— then jinxing violently away from the target...I had flown continuously sine early May 44 and had never before experienced such intense light flak. Intelligence informed us that about 700 four-barrel, coaxial mount 20mm flak guns were about Bastogne...The flak tracers were like garden hoses with projectiles arcing lazily though the air towards me. I remember so vividly my slipping and skidding as streams of flak fire reached for me, sometimes within three feet of my wing surfaces. Despite skill, a lot of luck was needed to escape unscathed. The flak took a toll. It seemed as if the 513th

56 Park began flying "Big Ass Bird" on July 7, 1944. Later that month, on July 25th he made combat history when he destroyed a Panther tank near St. Lo with the new HVAR air-to-ground rockets. In August he shot down a German fighter, but on the last day of that month was badly wounded by ground fire while attacking a German position. On September 29th, Park's colorful P-47 was peppered in a dogfight with several Me-109s, and although again severely wounded, managed to land just over front lines. Returning to duty, he found his crew chief, S/Sgt. Thomas Menning, had thoughtfully painted "Big Ass Bird II" onto his new ship.

was always first out and it seemed we lost one of four in lead flight every time. Actually, we lost five of the 513th in three days, and seven in a week during which the group lost a total of 10 pilots. Most of those who didn't return were recently transferred to us from the States and had no feel for the flak as those of us who dealt with it regularly."[57]

During the course of the morning, the P-47s flushed out twenty German tanks disguised as haystacks. Several German tanks were attacked between Houffalize and Noville and the 513th Squadron blasted German flak positions in the woods northeast of Bastogne. Another flight ranged further north and fired on German convoys of the *2 SS Panzer Division* southeast of Manhay. Other American fighters joined the fracas and the German division commander cancelled his attack on the stubborn defenders at the Baraque de Fraiture crossroads until the *Jabos* had gone home for the day. P-47s of the 514th Squadron under Capt. Bedford R. Underwood ran into twenty Me-109s east of Trier and in engagements at 12,000 feet claimed six of these for the loss of two of the own. Capt. Bernard J. Sledzick was among these:

"I was in a flight of six aircraft that took off in the early morning hours to support the embattled 101st at Bastogne. We arrived over the town in 20 minutes and received instructions from the Ground Controller ("Ripsaw", XIX TAC). Four of the planes led by Lt. Miles Jones went down on the target with 500-lb bombs and left me and my wingman, Lt. Fuller to provide top cover. Twelve Me-109s appeared in the skies above us, approaching from the direction of Trier, Germany. We alerted the flight that "Bandits" were coming down on us, jettisoned our bombs and turned into them in a steep climbing turn. Ten of the enemy fighters went down on the four that were attacking the target, leaving two Me-109s to attack Fuller and me. I maneuvered my plane onto the tail of one of them, fired and saw strikes on him which caused a fire, but the fire went out although the plane was smoking badly. I gave him another burst and the pilot turned the plane over on its back and bailed out. In the meantime, the second Me-109 had gotten on my tail and Lt. Fuller promptly disposed of it. I saw two tracers hit the Me-109 and it exploded in the air...Below us the aerial battle was raging. Every time we saw an Me-109 on the tail of a P-47 we dove down on it causing it to break away. Lt. Jones received a hit in the cockpit and three of his toes were blown off by a 20mm burst. Lt. McLane and Lt. Price were shot down and both bailed out. Lt. Sickling shot down three Me-109s before the aerial battle ended. Lt. Jones made it back to Mourmelon and crashed on landing due to his injuries...Lt. McLane bailed out over enemy territory and became a prisoner of war...It seemed like the battle only lasted a few minutes and parachutes of downed pilots filled the sky."

German troops assembling in the village of Noville, to the northeast of Bastogne, were struck. Other planes hammered the village of Chaumont which lay in Patton's path to relieve the U.S. garrison at Bastogne.

Capt. James Parker, the emissary Quesada had sent to the encircled

57 There were other dangers for the young pilots. Lt. Donald J. Crevier with the 512th Squadron became lost while returning from a ground support mission on Christmas Day when his compass failed. He died attempting to crash land his plane ten miles north of Rouen, France.

enclave was constantly radioing instructions from within Bastogne. Presently he sent some of the planes to the west where German soldiers were reported concentrating in the woods for an all-out assault on the town. Without sufficient ammunition, the Bastogne garrison had been powerless to do anything about it till now. As the P-47s swarmed in, they could see the tracks of the German tanks leading into the woods. Napalm set the trees on fire and sent the Germans running. After the bombs were loosed, most of the pilots moved down to strafe the enemy. By the end of the day, almost every German occupied village around the Bastogne perimeter was smoking. The 406th claimed destruction or damage to 97 vehicles, 11 tanks, 20 horse drawn vehicles and 24 gun positions at the end of the day. If the count was perhaps exaggerated, the damage was not; the Germans postponed their attacks until night. With the "*Jabos*" operating, Obst. Otto Remer commanding the *Führer Begleit Panzer Brigade*, emphasized how the oft repeated wisdom was never more true than during the Ardennes fighting: "Lord, let the evening come, then is the battle won."

Inside Bastogne, Capt. Parker was amused to find himself now the darling of the 101st Airborne. Whereas during the days of poor flying weather, he had all but been ignored, now praise for the air controller was quick in coming. Col. William L. Roberts, whose Combat Command B of the 10th Armored Division was stuck in the American pocket waxed enthusiastic: the fighter-bombers were worth "two or three infantry divisions." Capt. Parker earned a Bronze Star.

Gen. Patton had his long-desired good flying weather and with it came a medal for Chaplain O'Neill. As soon as the ground fog burned away, the 10th PRG was out in force. Not only were the Germans in the Ardennes under the gun, but they were also under the camera. In all, the 10th, 67th and 363rd TRGs flew some 113 visual and photo sorties that day.

The 363rd TRG flew aerial surveillance in the Ansbach-Koblenz area where the planes of Lts. Norman and Mahler were attacked by a determined Fw-190. The plane made two firing passes, before Lt. Norman managed to turn inside to fire two quick bursts into the enemy aircraft. The second hail of gunfire evidently killed the German pilot, for although not critically damaged the Fw-190 went into a lazy spiral before smashing into the ground. The 15th Tactical Recon Squadron was also aloft and looking for targets for the medium bombers. The enemy fire along the front was intense. Two pilots of the 15th were shot down, although one managed to bail out. Capt. Hoefker and Lt. White were out again, snooping on the German positions. However, the great danger was not always the enemy. While the two pilots buzzed along inspecting the ground situation, so touchy were the American pilots providing air cover in the area that they mistook the 10th PRG recon for a German attempt to hit ground targets. Seven red-tailed P-47s bounced the two Mustangs and only the superior aerobatics of Lts. White and Hoefker allowed them to escape.[58] Presently, after a lot of complaining over the radio, the SNAFU was resolved, but not before the two pilots had become separated. Now, off course and low, Capt. Hoefker flew through a wall of flak damaging his Mustang when the glycol tank was holed. Within minutes his Merlin engine seized and Hoefker had no choice but to jump. If the ordeal had not been enough already, after hitting the frozen ground and working to stow his chute the Captain was horrified to see soldiers shooting at him. After all this, he thought, to end up shot behind German lines. But as his stalkers drew closer, he could see that these guys blazing away were Americans with M-1 rifles! He quickly hid behind some rocks from his assailants. He screamed that he was an American. The bullets still flew. The GIs from the 4th Infantry were understandably jumpy. Word had it that German infiltrators, dressed as soldiers were all about and rumor had it that some where parachuting into the area. Then too, Hoefker's F-6 had nearly crashed into their mess hall! Enough was enough, Hoefker thought, he loosed a blistering trail of obscenities until the shooting stopped. "No German," the Captain recalled, "could have known some of those 'colloquialisms.'"

The big news, however, was the resupply of the men at Bastogne. On word of clear weather, the 490th Quartermaster Unit in England had spent a frantic morning packing parachutes and resupply canisters. Soon over 200 loaded C-47s were ready to attempt Operation Repulse— the resupply of the 101st Airborne Division. The first 21 parachute resupply aircraft were those flying from the continent that had been unable to assist the 106th Division on December 18th. Approaching from the west they floated down sorely needed supplies. One of the bulbous planes went down from enemy flak. Next, 82 P-47s drawn from the 354th, 362nd, 405th and 406th Fighter Groups escorted the 241 C-47 transports of the IX Troop Carrier Command over the garrison to drop some 192 tons of ammunition, 12 tons of gasoline, and 35 tons of provisions and medical supplies. Red smoke marked the drop zone. Even through the planes approached from the south, seven more C-47s were lost to enemy flak guns ringing the town.

Another resupply effort was made to a group of American tankers of the 3rd Armored Division surrounded behind enemy lines north of La Roche along the Ourthe River. This was Task Force Hogan, a hapless outfit under Lt. Col. Sam Hogan, that had driven into the enemy's flank only to find itself surrounded by the *116 Panzer Division*. At 4 AM SHAEF received their

---

58 Strangely, there was a rash of such incidents. Earlier on December 11th, 247 Squadron of 124 Wing of the British 2nd TAF was abruptly attacked by four P-47s while hitting German ground positions. Luckily none of the Typhoons were damaged, but "All pilots were greatly disappointed when their formation leader refused to let them shoot down the Thunderbolts." The general opinion among the more experienced chaps of the Fighter Wing was that the American pilots were rather inept, shooting wildly at the Brits, hitting nothing and then pulling away directly across their line of fire. They recorded in their diary that day that they hoped the Germans were learning similar tactics!

request for 4,000 gallons of gasoline, rations and ammo for the 1,000-man garrison. Thirty C-47s took off for the mission, but somehow had been briefed that Hogan and his crew were in the village of Marcourt. They were actually in Marcouray over a half a mile away. Meanwhile the C-47s faithfully followed their coordinates dropping the loads onto Marcourt. Needless to say, Hogan's men were dismayed to see the packages floating into German hands just out of arm's reach! The next evening Hogan and his battalion abandoned their equipment to escape German encirclement in the dark.

After completing their escort of the C-47s, the fighter-bombers turned on the Germans ringing Bastogne with bombs, machine gun fire and napalm. Now coordinating the aerial fighters around Bastogne from a hastily improvised radio net, Capt. James Parker directed the throng of fighter-bombers with great precision. It was not unusual for a report of enemy armor from an outpost to be followed within minutes by a covey of P-47s to hit the German tanks. "This is better hunting than the Falaise Pocket," one fighter pilot radioed, "and that was the best I ever expected to see."

After their resupply escort, the P-47s of the 362nd Fighter Group attacked the Germans around Bastogne with some 107 sorties. "Mogin's Maulers" were all over the battlefield. The 377th Squadron attacked the bridge of the German *Seventh Armee* at Echternach with rockets and napalm. Another mission put in near misses on the bridge further north at Bollendorf. Another narrowly missed the German span at Vianden, but napalm set five nearby enemy vehicles afire. Meantime, over the battlefield, the 379th Squadron hit some 45 troop-laden vehicles headed north on the road between Recogne and St. Hubert. The pilots reported the German troops piled out when the P-47s hove in for the strafing run. The same squadron also struck a tank-truck convoy between Houffalize and Bourcy. The 378th Squadron dropped napalm and bombs on Bourcy itself which was discovered to harbor 15 trucks and five tanks. In all, the group claimed 84 motor vehicles and 12 tanks. One P-47, that of Lt. Albert C. Bruce was lost over enemy territory with engine trouble. But so punishing was this aerial bombardment that the commander of the *26th Volksgrenadier Division* was forced to call off a planned German attack on the town until after dark when the *Jabos* had gone home. Later that evening, Genmaj. Ludwig Heilmann, in charge of the *5th Fallschirmjager Division*, entrusted with defense of the German encirclement reported a grim sight. "At night," his report began, "one could see from Bastogne back to the Westwall, a single torchlight procession of burning vehicles."

Thunderbolts of the 354th Fighter Group ranged far enough west to send tanks of the *Panzer Lehr Division* scurrying for cover. The pilots could see that Rochefort was surrounded on the south, southwest and north sides of the town and intended to give the hard pressed soldiers of the 84th Infantry Division a helping hand. Tanks and trucks were hit with napalm and fragmentation bombs near Forrieres; the 356th Squadron bombed and strafed another group of ten tanks and twenty trucks near Nassogne.

Roving armed reconnaissance by 15 aircraft of the 405th Fighter Group ran into a passel of German fighters near Trier-Nonnweiler including at least one jet. 1st Lt. R.W. Yothers managed to shoot down one Me-109 of the German flock. The 406th's 514th Squadron bombed a train southeast of Trier, gun positions at Bigelbach, Prüm and the German held rail station at Ettelbruck. The 509th Squadron attacked a German pontoon bridge near Echternach and silenced eight light flak positions near the bridge and sent two staff cars running.

The Mustangs of the "Yellowjackets," the 361st Fighter Group, were in the process of moving their command to St. Dizier. They would be flying for Weyland's XIX TAC. They chalked up numerous fighter sweeps east of the battle zone on the 23rd. At 2:30 PM several P-51s of the 375th Squadron sighted two "bogeys on the deck and going east" near Bonn. Lt. Caleb J. Layton and Lt. William H. Street dove on the enemy, with Layton sending one Fw-190 spinning into the woods. Layton then closed on a second 190 and observed many strikes about the wing roots and cockpit; it too fell away in flames. Lt. Street then sighted an Me-109 down below:

> I got on the tail of the 109 and followed him around the hills and gullies, firing short bursts at 200 yards and observing some strikes. After turning around one of the hills, the 109 pulled up. I fired a ten second burst at 100 yards, 0 degrees deflection, and saw strikes all over his fuselage and wings. The 109 caught fire and went into a sharp turn to the right and crashed into the top of one of the hills.

December 23rd marked the beginning of a carefully planned campaign of rail and road interdiction east of the salient. Over 1,000 medium bombers of the IX and RAF Bomber Commands pounded rail centers, roads, bridges and other choke points to the east of the Ardennes with 900 tons of bombs during the evening of December 22/23. Some 485 Lancaster bombers blasted transportation centers near Trier while the medium bombers of the 2nd TAF hit road targets in the area between Malmédy and St. Vith and rail targets at Kall and Gemünd.

During the day 423 heavy bombers of the Eighth Air Force were dispatched to smash the marshalling yards to the enemy rear. Although some of these had been damaged in earlier raids, Doolittle's air force aimed to totally shatter enemy rail capabilities feeding Hitler's monster offensive. A total of 1,131 tons of explosives were released over towns that would continue to attract fearful devastation over the coming days: Ehrang, Junkerath, Ahrweiler, Dahlem, Kaiserlautern and Homburg. German fighters attempting to stop the conflagration would face a daunting prospect; some 632 fighters soared alongside the heavy bombers to ensure that they made their target. In spite of strong enemy opposition, the fighters protected their charges (only one bomber was lost), while shooting down an impressive total of 69 German fighters for the loss of seven of their own. In particular, the scoring of Schilling's 56th Fighter Group was phenomenal with 32 enemy aircraft taken out.

Simultaneously, with the pounding from England, the IX Bombardment Division sent off some 624 medium bombers in a massive morning raid to smash railroads and communications targets just behind the enemy front line. Gen. Anderson personally visited Vandenberg at his headquarters to obtain targets. There weren't enough fighters to go around and some of the missions could not be provided with fighter escort. Of the total dispatched, 465 were able to hit their primary or secondary targets with a total of 899 tons of bombs. Targets included the railroad bridges at Mayen, Euskirchen, Eller, the railhead at Kyllburg and the Prüm marshalling yards. Communications centers to the rear of the *Fifth Panzer Armee* were blasted: Waxweiler, Neuerburg and Lunebach. That the attacks were effective is certain: a German POW passing through the village of Kyllburg, bombed both on December 19th and 23rd by the 410th BG reported that it took two hours on Christmas Day to get through the devastated hamlet due to the damage.

"In the entire army area, heavy enemy air activity," submitted the *LXVI Armeekorps* in position near St. Vith that evening, "Fighter bomber attacks on German attack spearheads as well as bomb drops from four-engined bombers on roads and traffic targets in the area." Most of the evening reports of the other German units in the Ardennes told the same thing. Genfld. Model, reporting directly to Hitler, tried to put the best possible varnish on the situation:

> "The enemy was able to employ its air force fully again on 23 December due to the favorable weather conditions. The focus of its attacks was the roads and traffic targets, as well as the march routes of the German panzer formations. The German flak and heavy use of the Luftwaffe brought relief."

To Gren. Franz Thauer of the *62 Feldersatz Battalion*, the air attacks were "terrifying." His replacement unit was passing through Daun by train on the way to Prüm. However, as the train emerged from Mayen the bombs fell. Everyone ran for cover just before the train was derailed and overturned by the bomb blasts. Eighty were killed and the rail station and the greater part of the town was destroyed. When Thauer's battalion gathered itself out from the shelters a hundred fewer grenadiers were available.

In an assault on the railroad viaduct at Ahrweiler, the 391st Bombardment Group was unable to meet up with its assigned fighter escort. Knowing of the critical importance of their mission, they went on ahead without their "little friends." The result was a disaster. The weather was so poor over the target area that the B-26s of the second box were forced to make two runs through a terrific wall of flak. But a red colored flare suddenly burst in the air and the flak stopped. The bomber formation had lingered over Arhweiler long enough for the Luftwaffe to call out the dogs. The bombers were bounced by sixty German fighters from *JG 2, 3* and *11*. The vicious attacks began at 11:55 AM and went on for a terrible 23 minutes in which no friendly fighter assistance was available. The German fighters attacked the box formations of the bombers in waves four deep and 16 abreast. Bandits were everywhere; the Group's gunners reported 69 different engagements. The medium bomber group was shattered. Sixteen of the thirty B-26s were shot down, including the pathfinder aircraft. Of small consolation was the fact that they managed to claim seven of the enemy. Many crews had wounded and nearly every plane was shot up.[59]

In one of these actions, Capt. Edward M. Jennsen of Beaverton, Oregon led a box of Marauders behind their pathfinder. German flak was heavy and their crippled pathfinder was forced to turn back. Undaunted, Jennsen headed for his rendezvous with fighter escort. None met him. He then doggedly led his formation to the target at Ahrweiler running into severe flak and a swarm of enemy fighters. Flying through this rain of shrapnel and bullets the B-26s loosed their bombs over the target. Jennsen's Marauder was now on fire and five of his other planes had already careened out of the sky leaving ugly looking swaths of black smoke. It was 25 terrible minutes before they could limp back to friendly air space. Their gunners had shot down at least three German fighters.

Many of the other groups were snared by the German fighter net. The 322nd BG was attacked near Euskirchen by 50 enemy fighters and lost two bombers. The 397th was assailed by two dozen German Me-109s and Fw-190s after hitting the Eller bridges. Eight bombers did not return. The 387th Group lost four bombers and a pathfinder to some twenty German fighters that blasted away at the B-26s between Bastogne and their target at Daun. Others were more fortunate; the 344th BG was attacked after assaulting the Mayen bridge, but suffered no losses. Similarly, the 386th BG also participated in the bombing of the viaduct in a morning operation, and later returned in the afternoon to bomb Nideggen. But unlike the other groups, the 386th suffered no casualties at all.

In the hit on Mayen, the 387th suffered the loss of four Marauders to enemy fighters and another two to flak after failing to find their escort from the 367th Fighter Group. The B-26s did, however, claim four German fighters downed. The 397th struck a railroad bridge at Eller. The "Bridge Busters," too, missed their fighter escort, and met a wall of intense flak as they approached the bridge. Three B-26s were damaged and fell out of the sky. Then just as they completed their bomb run, they were jumped by two dozen Me-109s. Seven more bombers fell to earth and only five planes of the group

---

59 Included in the Luftwaffe casualty list were Uffz. Kleybrink, Fw. Land, Obgefr. Maas and Uffz. Pfeifer, all shot down from *JG 2*. All told the losses of *JG 2* would total 10 pilots killed or missing from the widespread actions that day.

remained undamaged. Sgt. Neil McGinnis watched the B-26s in the first box of bombers from his position within the second. Suddenly, McGinnis watched in horror as a German fighter appeared out of nowhere, pulled behind one B-26 in the first box and pumped bullets into it as the tail gunner stubbornly fired back at point blank range. Both pilots hit their mark and the German fighter and the Marauder burst into flame and plunging to the ground carrying both to their deaths. Three German fighters were shot down for the loss of seven of the medium bombers. The 397th received a Unit Citation for their bravery under the enemy fire and the bridge at Eller was gone, but many lost friends in the action. McGinnis wondered if he would live to see 1945. On Christmas Day he flew his 65th mission over Luxembourg. Two of the Marauders in his group "bought the farm" and when landing back at base, another exploded on the icy runway. They learned that another had blown up on take off. McGinnis was relieved that his tour was over. Many of his companions who had flown fewer missions over the last year with the 397th were either dead or in German POW camps. He was one of the lucky ones; he was going home.

As the 322nd Bomb Group approached the target bridge at Euskirchen, a tremendous air battle erupted. A score of Me-109s bounced the B-26 Marauders of "Nye's Annihilators" and several penetrated the P-38 screen from the 392nd Fighter Squadron. Eight mad minutes ensued. Two aircraft fell from the sky, and some 22 others were damaged. The lead pathfinder plane was knocked out and the wing of another B-26 suddenly caught fire and it spun down in flames. One B-26, trying to limp back home, was so damaged by flak and German fighters that its crew had to jump ship near Sedan. The Lightning pilots exacted a significant retribution; four enemy fighters were downed for a loss of one P-38.[60] And the mission had certainly succeeded; captured German prisoners would later pronounce the city of Euskirchen "one field of bomb craters."

The 416th BG was assigned to attack a highway bridge south of Trier. The weather conditions were poor and as the A-26 Invaders came up on the target, eight of the flights failed to recognize the bridge and held their bombs. The remaining flights, however, hit the span squarely. The only loss was an A-20K pathfinder in the attack which was damaged by flak, but managed to limp to a crash landing near Rheims.

Although given a bloody nose in the morning raid, the IXth BD was made of stern stuff. During the afternoon they came back for more. The 391st BG returned to blast the German road center of Neuerburg, to the rear of the *Fifth Panzer Armee*, with some 37 tons of bombs. The 21 Marauders completed the mission without loss. The firm discipline of the 391st earned it a Presidential Unit Citation. Similarly, the 387th and 394th BGs hit the village

---

60 The ill-fated pilot was Capt. James F. Fishburn who was on his first and last mission of the war. Fishburn was captured after successfully jumping from his crippled P-38.

of Prüm east of St. Vith. The 387th lost only one plane due to flak damage. The crippled bomber was hit just before the bomb run and suddenly arched over on its back. The pilot somehow managed to roll over and straighten out in time to drop its bombs before the B-26 fell off to the side and spun to the ground. The 410th BG, an A-20 unit with a reputation for bombing accuracy (over 40% of bombs within 500 feet of the target over a 12-month period), managed two successful bombing missions during the day with their light A-20 bombers "putting them in the pickle barrel" over Kyllburg.

Having plastered Mayen in the morning, the 392nd Squadron of the 367th flew a second mission in the afternoon, this time to escort the 322nd Bomb Group. They were to attack the German town of Zulpich. Unfortunately, as was typical of the day, the bombers did not show due to weather conditions. What no one knew at the time, was that six B-26s of the 322rd dropped sixty 250 pound bombs on the American held town of Malmédy, mistaking it for Zuplich.[61]

Once set afire on the 23rd, however, the town attracted errant American bombers like a magnet. Malmédy was mistakenly bombed on three successive days. Losses to the U.S. 30th Infantry Division and the townspeople were severe; some 125 civilians and 37 American soldiers were killed. Soldiers of "Old Hickory" the 30th Infantry Division, had been bombed by their own bombers in Normandy; and had taken to calling the U.S. Air Force, the "American Luftwaffe." And that wasn't the only SNAFU. Another wayward group of five bombers, searching for an enemy target, blasted the U.S. marshalling yards at Arlon. Five tanks cars of precious gasoline for Patton's Third Army went up in an ugly boil of flame. Still another incident of fratricide occurred when the town of Verviers was hit east of Spa, even though it was in American hands. These mistakes were damning, and the next day the commander of the IX BD, Gen. Anderson, issued a stern warning that secondary targets were to be positively identified.

In all, the IX BD lost 35 medium bombers, three pathfinder aircraft and one light bomber destroyed. Moreover, four others crashed, two crash landed and a total of 182 of the participating aircraft were damaged. Many would never fly again. At least part of the blame could be attributed to several missions missing their fighter escort. Anderson was dismayed by this incompetence. To end future confusion, the commander of the 367th Fighter Group, Col. Ed Chickering, ordered that a direct telephone line be

---

61 While circling the vicinity, Lt. Bob Dillion, of the 367th FG, spotted four Thunderbolt fighters engaged in a dogfight with a quartet of German Fw-190s. Another four enemy fighters circled this action at 18,000 feet. Taking advantage of their situation, Dillion maneuvered his fighters into a position to suddenly fall on the enemy planes without being detected. The tactic was successful and three more enemy fighters were added to the tally of the 367th Fighter Group for that day. After the action, Dillion returned to his rendezvous point, but the bombers never showed up. It turned out that they had been held up by degenerating weather.

established between "Bombay," the IX BD Headquarters at Rheims, and his command at Juvincourt, some twelve miles away.

Even given their terrible punishment, the IX Bombardment Division (motto: "Smash the Enemy Until He Quits") recorded more medium bomber sorties in the air than anytime since Normandy. And the bridges had been pounded. "The consequences were disastrous," von Rundstedt would later say of the bridge interdiction, "it meant that we could not get supplies or troops forward. The further we advanced the further the troops had to march...the deep penetration of heavy bombers east of the Rhine against our communications...were painful for moving our troops, our supplies and our gas...On the roads our convoys or single motor transport could not move during the day. We could never count on when a certain division would arrive at its destination." All five bomb groups of the IX BD would receive Distinguished Unit Citations for their courage that day.

Gen. Anderson was shocked by the losses— approaching 8% of those who reached the target area. Taking in the devastation, he sent off a tersely worded message to Vandenberg: "...we urge a program of attacks on enemy fighter airdromes by 8th AF and RAF Bomber Command." Vandenberg understood that a loss rate of this magnitude would quickly take IX BD out of the fight. He contacted Gen. Spaatz at SHAEF and requested that the German airfields be given a thrashing right away. Spaatz agreed; the mission plan was laid on for the next day.

But on the 23rd the Eighth Air Force was still on its program of derailing the *Reichsbahn*. Doolittle's operations staff assigned 417 heavy bombers to the marshalling yards west of the Rhine from which the German offensive was being fed. The bombers hit rail heads to the southeast of the enemy salient at Homburg, Kaiserlautern and Ehrang along with road and rail junctions at Junkerath, Dahlem and Ahrweiler.[62] A total of 1,150 tons of bombs were dropped. The 433 escorting fighters encountered determined German fighter attacks from an estimated 78 planes. The Americans claimed 29 of these shot down for a loss of two bombers and six fighter aircraft. Another 183 fighters from the Eighth Air Force were sent on broad fighter sweeps and encountered a numerous and determined enemy. Fifty-six Thunderbolts of Col. David C. Schilling's 56th Fighter Group flew from Boxted that morning hunting for the enemy west of Bonn. The MEW controller sent the group looking for several large packs of enemy fighters only to come up with nothing in three frustrating attempts. Heading again in the direction recommended by the MEW, Schilling at once spied a big swarm of the enemy orbiting over Euskirchen airfield. He cleverly maneuvered his group behind the enemy and came up on them from the east as if he and his planes were

---

62 The latter town was terribly damaged; when the *167th Volksgrenadier Division* passed through the town five days later, the cratered roads had only been partially repaired, one-way traffic was in effect and the route was passable only by foot or horse.

another *Staffel* of German fighters. The ruse worked and Schilling's fighters were almost on top of the enemy before they were recognized. The out-foxed formation was at least 90 German fighters of JG 4, 11, 27 and 54 which passed over Cologne just after 10 AM. The German contingent included a number of experienced pilots including Heinrich Bartels, with JG 27. A wild 45-minute dogfight raged from 28,000 feet to the deck, but when it was over the result was greatly in the Americans' favor. When they returned to Boxted, Schilling and his group counted some 37 Me-109s and Fw-190s knocked out for a loss of four of their own (and one of these had managed to nurse his crippled Thunderbolt over Belgium before bailing out). All told, the fighter sweep shot down 46 enemy aircraft at a loss of only nine U.S. fighters. It was one of the largest dogfights and most successful American air battles of the war in Europe. The commander at the time of "Zemke's Wolfpack," Lt. Col. David Schilling, remembered:

"As the group reached a location approximately 30 miles west of Bonn at an altitude of 27,000 feet, MEW Control changed our previous vector of 103 degrees to 90 degrees magnetic, telling us that a large number of enemy aircraft was ahead to the east. In about two minutes a gaggle was sighted about ten miles to the north flying west. We turned to a vector of 330 degrees in an effort to cut them off, but they managed to get away in a large patch of cirrus clouds. We then returned to a vector of 90 degrees and in one or two minutes sighted another large gaggle about ten miles to the south with a heading of west. We turned south, but lost them the same as the first. I then called MEW and asked them why they had not picked the enemy aircraft up and to give us some help. Their reply was: 'Don't worry. There is plenty straight east at 22 to 23,000 feet.' About two or three minutes later the 63rd Squadron leader (Maj. Harold Comstock) called and said a large formation of FW 190s was directly below me. At the same time I sighted a large number of enemy aircraft, approximately forty, flying south in a wide turn to the left about 1,500 feet below me and several miles ahead. I told the 63rd to attack and the 61st to aid, as I was going to hit the enemy aircraft ahead, since we had altitude and speed on both formations. I flew straight ahead, pulled up, applied full power, and made a slow diving turn to the left to position my flight on the outside and allow the other three to cross over inside so that we might bring as many planes into position to fire as possible. In so doing I managed to hit the rear right Me-109 with about a 20-degree deflection shot at a range of about 700 yards. There was a large concentration of strikes all over the left side of the fuselage, and he fell off to the left. I then picked out another more of less ahead of the first and fired from about the same range as the first, causing him to smoke and catch fire immediately. By this time the first Me-109 was slightly ahead, below and to the left, at whih point he started to smoke and caught fire. I then picked another and fired at about 1,000 yards and missed as he broke right and started to dive for the deck. At about 17,000 feet I had closed to about 500 yards and fired , resulting in a heavy concentration of strikes, and the pilot bailed out. At this point I had become separated from the other three flights and had only my own with me. I heard Maj. Comstock of the 63rd Squadron in a hell of a fight and called to get his position. As I was attempting to locate him, I sighted another gaggle of 35-40 Fw-190s 1,000 feet below circling to the left. I repeated the same tactics as before and attacked one from 500 yards' range and slightly above and to the left. The plane immediately began to burn spinning off to the left. I then fired at a second and got two or three strikes. He immediately took violent evasive action, and it took me several minutes of maneuvering until I managed to get into a position to fire. I fired from about 300 yards above and to the left, forced me to pull through him and fire as he went out of sight over the cowling. I gave about a five second burst and began getting strikes all over him. The pilot immediately bailed out and the ship spun down to the left, smoking and burning , until it blew up at about 15,000 feet. By this time I was alone and saw a lone 63rd plane. I called, and he joined up just as a 35-40 plane formation of Fw-190s flew by heading west about 1,000 feet above. I had hoped to sneak by and turn upon their tails, but they saw me just as I started my climbing turn. I knew I would have to hit the deck sooner or later, but I thought I could get their tail-end man before I had to. My wingman lagged back, and just as I was getting set, he called and said two were on his tail. I thought I saw him get hit and told him to do vertical aileron rolls and hit the deck. At that time two got behind me and were getting set, so I did several rolls as I started down, hit the switch and outran them by a mile as I got to the deck. I lost themand zoomed back up to 8,000 feet."

While Lt. Col. Schilling was clobbering five German planes in a single day, others of the 61st and 62nd Squadron were having similar fortune. Capt. Felix Williamson and his wingman quickly KO'ed two Me-109s. Lt. Robert E. Winters of the 62nd pounced on one Me-109 and set it afire with a stream of bullets. However, as Winters closed on his quarry, the German pilot cut his throttle and Winters shot ahead to ram into the wing of the enemy plane. Amazingly, Winters recovered, but never knew what happened to his opponent.

Above this chaotic shoot-out Capt. Joseph H. Perry with the 61st Squadron circled overhead as Schilling and his partners tore into the swarm of German fighters. However, as the fighting broke up, Perry dived down to provide assistance. Sighting a friendly P-47 with two Fw-190s on its tail, Perry gave pursuit, but the enemy refused combat and fled. Suddenly, Perry and his wingman found themselves in the midst of an angry "beehive" of German fighters. However, as several crossed his path, Perry fired bursts at the enemy and hit one which whipped up in a sharp left-hand turn before the German pilot bailed out. Still, Perry knew that he and his wingman would not last long in this outnumbered arena. They both hit the throttle and pulled up sharply into the sun, hoping the angry swarm would not follow. The tactic worked, and soon another lone Thunderbolt joined them. However, Perry presently sighted another Fw-190 dropping down to intervene in the dogfight. Perry pursued the German plane down to ground level until the enemy plane ran into light flak at 500 feet.

Lt. Lewis R. Brown was not as lucky. Brown pursued several Fw-190s into a cloud bank and quickly scored hits on two of them. Leaving the clouds, he pursued another 190 using the balance of his ammunition. Suddenly, Brown's canopy was shattered as bullets blasted into his instrument panel. Swinging his head back, Brown saw the 190 right on his tail pumping bullets into his stricken machine. Almost immediately, his plane became unresponsive and fell away. Brown bailed out to become a prisoner of war. Brown would later emerge from a POW camp at the end of the war to claim three of the Fw-190s shot down that day.

Maj. Comstock and his 63rd Squadron did nearly as well as Schilling's group. Comstock lit into a gaggle of enemy planes immediately hitting one of the enemy in the wing. By the time the damaged enemy plane pulled away Comstock was facing an enemy 190 coming at him head on. Like medieval jousters, both planes opened fire at a range of about 1,000 yards. The Fw-190s shots were low, but Comstock's fire ripped up the enemy plane's engine with the first burst. The German pilot jettisoned his canopy and bailed out. Pulling up, he then snuck up on another 190 from underneath, firing at the enemy from nearly point blank range. The enemy plane was shattered and immediately began to come apart and fall out of the sky. With the same group, Lt. Randel L. Murphy, Jr. experienced firsthand the power of the new "long-nosed" Fw-190 when he gave chase in "The Brat", but found himself unable to catch up with the faster German plane. In the meantime, however, Murphy spied a friendly T-bolt in trouble and fell on the enemy plane attempting to shoot down the Wolfpack member. In a head-on pass Murphy recorded hits all along the body of the German plane which fell straight to the ground and exploded. But as Murphy climbed back up, a German plane immediately passed by him firing as he went. Desperate to shake the faster Fw-190, Murphy dived for speed and made a tight diving bank to the right 500 feet off the ground. However, as the German plane attempted to follow the violent maneuver, the enemy aircraft shuttered and stalled, falling to the ground. Nearby, Capt. Cameron Hart also experienced the "hunter and the hunted" when he at first shot down a Fw-190 only to get into trouble almost immediately thereafter:

> Slightly above them were four more coming in on my tail as I started to fire. This encounter is sort of hazy in my mind, but I do remember seeing hits on one and possibly two enemy aircraft before I had to barrel-roll down to shake my 'friends' in the rear. I came back up trying to find someone to join, but they were all in a big Lufbery at about 18,000 feet. I found several more targets, but each time I was about to fire, several 190s would come in from the rear and force me to go down again. This happened four or five times. Those Jerries were really aggressive and good, hot pilots. I got too close to a formation of fifty-plus 190s coming in from the southeast, and four of them came after me, chasing me over past Aachen, where I shook them in the clouds.

Hart had been very fortunate to live through this chase. But several others of the Wolfpack were not as fortunate. Lt. John E. Lewis was bounced by a Fw-190 into a cloud-bank and shot down and the 62nd Squadron lost Lt. Charles E. Carlson, who was last seen in the vicinity of the Euskirchen airdrome. But, by any accounting, it was a resounding American victory with the "Wolfpack" claiming 34 enemy aircraft.

Included in the German losses was a leading Luftwaffe ace, Ofw. Heinrich Bartels. Bartels was a veritable mentor for the younger German pilots of *JG 27*. A native of Linz on the Danube, Bartels had been flying with *IV/JG 27* since May, 1943. Holder of the prestigious Knight's Cross, the 26-year old pilot had just finished shooting down his 99th kill when another Thunderbolt caught him unaware. The P-47 blasted Bartel's Me-109G-10 "Marga" which plunged to earth just outside of Bonn with Bartels at the controls. Bartel's remains and that of his aircraft were not discovered until 1968, his plane having augered deeply into the frozen ground near Gudenau Castle. Many of the German pilots fortunate enough to return from this disaster told sad tales: friends of Uffz. Willi Bach of *16/JG 54* saw his Fw-190A-8 take numerous hits about the cockpit which either killed or wounded the German pilot for he made no attempt to escape before his mount smashed into the ground near Rottingen. Another Fw-190 of the same *Gruppe* tragically fell near Villip. Friends of Uffz. Klaus Gehring watched in horror as the German pilot bailed out of his stricken Fw-190 only to get his parachute snagged on the plane's tail which took him to his death.

Fighters of *JG 4* and *I/JG 11* attempted to head off the American bombers before they reached the crucial region around Trier. However, this plan was largely foiled by U.S. fighters from the Eighth Air Force flying sweeps through the region. Maj. Arthur F. Jeffrey of the 479th Fighter Group (Col. Kyle K. Riddle) personally shot down three of the dozen Fw-190s destroyed by the formation and lost only a single Mustang. Fhr. Ernst Amman of the *11th Staffel* was killed over Roth near the southern battlefront along with Uffz. Karlheinz Witt. Uffz. Herdtle also did not return. *II/JG 4* launched some twenty Fw-190s from Babenhausen to attack ground targets in the Bastogne area. The operation was disastrous, with six aircraft lost from *8 Staffel*. Of these Oblt. Markoff managed to get back over Germany before he bailed out and eventually returned to *JG 4* by train. Uffz. Haug, Nefzger, Dehr and Walter of *8./JG 4* were listed as missing and three others, Lt. Dietman Bischoff, Lt. Edward Schmidt and Fw. Höflich were taken prisoner.

But the worst losses trying to stop the bombers came in the ranks of *JG 11*. A total of 12 pilots were killed with four missing and another 11 wounded. The three *Gruppen* of *JG 11* fought all over the area of operations. *I/JG 11* and *IV/JG 4* attacked the heavy bombers over the twisting Moselle while the other two *Gruppen* operated under the control of *JG 2*, doing battle with fighter escorts both with the Eighth and Ninth U.S. Air Forces. Fhr. Kaluza and Oblt. Georg Ulrici of *I/JG 11* did not return from the operations over Daun and Cochem that day and Uffz. Ehrke and Gefr. Eiden were killed in dogfights near Gillenfeld. Ofhr. Hansjoachim Wesener was shot down south of Kaisesch.

JG 3 suffered four pilots killed or missing on December 23rd along with another four who bailed out. It was this unit which attacked the 322nd Bomb

Group while it parceled out a deluge of bombs on the rail bridges at Euskirchen. As the Marauders neared the bridge they were set upon by some twenty enemy fighters of which they claimed six shot down. Fhr. Adolf Tham managed a miraculous escape when he rammed a B-26 with his Me-109K-4 and was able to parachute away from the falling wreckage. Ofw. Gerhard Wilhelm and Uffz. Wichmann of *IV/JG 3* were killed and Uffz. Kröber later died of wounds received from the hail of return fire from the medium bombers.

William Breuer of Company B of the 87th Mortar Battalion near Sadzot, Belgium witnessed this action, most likely mistaking the pack of German fighters for jets:

> "As the miles-long stream of bombers was nearly overhead, bright and twinkling specks high in the sky, the initial elation the mortar men felt on the ground quickly was replaced by a chilling surge of concern. From out of the bright sun, a swarm of Me-262 jet fighters [sic] pounced on the American bombers and the ultra-high speed Luftwaffe planes promptly began knocking Flying Fortresses and Liberators out of the sky. Several bombers, burning brightly, plunged to the earth with their crews... There were no parachutes. The P-47 Thunderbolt and P-51 Mustang fighters that were accompanying the four engined craft sought in vain to protect the bombers from their tormentors, but the speedy new jet fighters simply flew faster...The sky was filled with pieces of destroyed American bombers which were tumbling and spinning downward in a crazy-quilt pattern— part of a wing here, a portion of a fuselage there, a tail assembly twisting and turning in grotesque movements...Crisscrossing the winter skies were countless vapor trails..."

The Mustangs of the Eighth Air Force also got a piece of the action. The MEW controller was able to vector the 479th Fighter Group to still another group of Fw-190s. The P-51s were able to shoot down 12 of these for the loss of one Mustang. One of the group's top aces, Maj. Arthur F. Jeffrey took three by himself. The 364th Fighter Group (Col. Roy W. Osborn) added another twenty claims during the day's actions in the process of escorting a group of Flying Fortresses to their target. Maj. George Ceuleers accounted for four of the Me-109s shot down, including one that he blasted away from the tail of a fellow P-51. One of the Luftwaffe pilots leaped from his Focke Wulf as soon as Ceuleers pulled in behind his tail; he didn't even have to fire a shot.

JG 1 was again in the thick of it as they tried to evict the Allied bombers from German aerial turf. Hptm. Hans Ehlers and Lt. Emil Demuth both knocked out a Thunderbolt each. Oblt. Jochen Janke managed to bring down one of the Flying Fortresses before he himself was shot down and forced to jump from his plane. Ironically, Lt. Herbert Neuner's Fw-190A-8 was shot out from under him by German flak near Bucholt. Uffz. Karl Fürstenau and Alfred Thienert went down over Wesel and Dortmund and Uffz. Kurt Malkwitz was forced to bail out of his stricken craft over Frankfurt-Main.

The prospects for the Luftwaffe on the 23rd are well illustrated by the experience of Hptm. Armin Köhler's *III Gruppe, JG 77*. The weather in the morning was poor with low clouds. At Unterrath the young pilots of the group played cards, wrote letters and listened to music. After lunch they expected to be soon called back to their quarters. But then the phone rang. They were being urgently scrambled to stop a group of enemy medium bombers headed into Germany. Taking off quickly at 1:45 PM, the Luftwaffe pilots found that after they crawled through the low-hanging mist, there was a blue sky above. The 11 and 12 *Staffel* flew as high altitude cover in their Me-109K-4s. However, the German pilots were only able to reach the Ahr Valley before being set upon by a pack of P-47s of the 373rd Fighter Group.

The 12 *Staffel* was nearly wiped out over Münstereifel before 11 *Staffel* could intercede. Two pilots, Fw. Rössner and Uffz. Walter Silwester were killed, and five others were wounded before they turned back to their base at Düsseldorf. Lt. "Sepp" Unverzagt was one of the few who were able to bail out and escape his crate without injuries. The 11 *Staffel* also suffered in a furious dogfight; Leutnant Walter Wildenauer was forced to jump from his plane and was machine gunned while hanging under his parachute. Amazingly, Wildenauer survived the experience and returned to his unit. Also wounded, Uffz. Hasso Fröhlich was forced to belly-land his wounded K-14 near Walsum. The Messerschmitts were forced to drop their belly tanks in the scrap and soon the red "low fuel" lamps began to glow in their cockpits. The pilots headed for the closest spot to put down, many keying on the visible landmark of the spires of the Cologne cathedral. The airfields around Cologne were scarred by craters and abatis, but the Germans had no choice but to put down. A complete *Schwarm* was destroyed landing at Köln-Ostheim although the pilots were safe. Hptm. Kohler himself was forced to land at Ostheim. The planes landed in dribs at airfields all over; it would take days to reorganize the scattered command. III/JG 77 had lost twenty planes for the probable claim of two Thunderbolts!

Those that did reach the battlefield, such as JG 11, found the skies around Prüm - St. Vith teeming with American fighters. Among these was Maj. Erich Putzka of the *Gruppenstab* whose remains have never been found. Ofw. Holland was last seen under chase by a gang of thirty P-47s; Ofw. Titscher was felled by a Spitfire over Cologne. Two other pilots were wounded in desperate aerial fighting over Münstereifel. Other *Staffeln* of JG 11 opposed the seventy B-26 Marauders of the 387th and 394th Bomb Groups bearing down on the marshalling yards at Mayen. Oblt. Herbert Planer, the leader of 9 *Staffel* was shot down along with Uffz. Pfaffinger. 10 and 11/JG 11 were drawn into dogfights over the Steinbach Dam. Obfhr. Bühmann was shot down, although able to jump from his stricken plane. Lt. Küke was killed near Rheinbach. In all, sixteen pilots were killed or missing. Later the 394th BG, Col. Thomas B. Hall's "Bridge Busters," returned with 32 bombers in the afternoon to put the Prüm marshalling yards out of commission. The bomb run was successful, but the Marauder of Lt. Fred Riegner, Jr. was hit by flak during the approach and ended up in a flat spin. Two of the crew of six, 2nd Lt. Lester Fowell and Sgt. Wilson Voorhis, Jr., escaped by parachute to become prisoners of war.

JG 53 "Pik As"— the "Ace of Spades" *Geschwader* took off with a dozen Me-109Gs from Germersheim at 10 AM to intercept fighter bombers reported to the west. Near Wissembourg the German fighters ran into a pack of P-47s at 10,000 feet. Uffz. Zimmermann was lost in the vicinity of Rastatt. Lt. Wilhelm Westhoff had his Me-109G-14 shot away by P-47s fighters as he tried vainly to climb to a favorable position. Hit in his cockpit and fuselage, the adjutant of *IV/JG 53* parachuted into captivity. The 24-year old Luftwaffe veteran had been with *"Pik As"* since joining in Africa in March, 1943. Two others were lost in the engagement: Uffz. Desaga and Krüger also were forced to take to their silks.

JG 26 had orders to defend the panzers of *Heeresgruppe B*, now advancing on the Meuse River. Some 23 FW 190A of *I Gruppe* launched from Fürstenau at 11:14 AM. Their first task, that of evading American fighters swarming over the airfield, set the tone for the day. Six of the German fighters were so entangled with the Thunderbolts it was all they could do to protect the take-off of the rest of the German fighters. The remainder proceeded to the battle zone, diving on a group of B-26 bombers. Two of the Marauders were claimed before the P-47 escorts showed up and shot down four of the German fighters at no cost to themselves. Five German planes crash landed just east of the Ardennes.

That night, the British No. 2 Group took to the air in mass. One hundred and six Mosquitos of the 138th and 140th Wings lurked over the Cologne-Düren-Stadtkyll area to the rear of the German *Sixth Panzer Armee*. Stalking German vehicles on the roads, they fired off nearly 80,000 machine gun and cannon rounds at ground targets near Blankenheim, Mayen, Bitersborn and Prüm. "Many large fires," were seen after 56 bombs were dropped on the latter town. The German night fighters countered with raids by 88 aircraft sent on harassing patrols in the Metz-Sedan area. Some of these included the bombers of *II/LG 1* who took off from Ahlhorn just after dark with orders to plant incendiary bombs on any troops or vehicles that they sighted between Aachen and Metz. Fw. Albert Johänntges completely lost his bearing in his Ju-88S-3 when over the battle zone— both the PeGe 6 radio and the compass going on the fritz. Their fuel supply running low, he and his crew of four sighted a railway station west of Liège on which to drop their fire bombs. They just pulled out when they were struck by machine gun fire from a night fighter. The pilot, observer and wireless operator bailed out, but the bombardier went down with "L1+KM." The others were rounded up east of Hannut, Belgium.

The two night fighter squadrons of the Ninth Air Force were only able to fly 13 sorties, strafing the German held area around St. Vith and bombing towns near Nohfelden. One P-61 was lost. The three active reconnaissance groups flew another 113 sorties. The P-61s of the 425th NFS, XIX TAC had a wild and wooly night. One flight was uneventful, save for the spectacular evening sight of the German city of Trier in flames. Lt. William A. Andrews shot down a Ju-88 over Oberstein and Lt. Slayton blasted an ammunition train near Bitburg, but considerably more strange was the experience of Lt. Carl H. Byars and Lt. Emil J. Brolick, his radar observer. In the dark night over Verdun, the two picked up radar of two aircraft nearby. On closing the distance, one was found to be a British Stirling. However, as they neared the second at 18,000 feet, the unidentified aircraft opened fire with twin guns in its tail. Lt. Byars was slightly wounded in the shoulder, but the right engine of the Black Widow was hammered and burst into flame. Byars quickly broke off the engagement and high tailed it for their base at Verdun. Approaching their base they found the hydraulics were out as well and were lucky to crash-land the plane on the dark airstrip. Just after the men pulled themselves out of the wreckage, the P-61 exploded in a boil of flame.

The German air force had put up its greatest effort so far. The Luftwaffe reported to *OKW* that it launched some 800 sorties on the 23rd, although hard pressed by the superior Allied weight of both the Eighth and Ninth U.S. Air Forces and the RAF. The Allies estimated that slightly less than half of the German fighter sorties were in the battle area, with a further 150 night fighter sorties plotted. The massive reappearance of the Allied air forces prompted the Luftwaffe to divide its effort between ground support and interception of the Allied bombers. Obviously, the Luftwaffe had planned an air strike against Bastogne during the day, but this had to be shelved. ULTRA overheard *II Jagdkorps* complaining that, "Because of [enemy] bombing, ground attack operation Bastogne impossible."

In all, some 500 German pilots took part in the operations on December 23rd and records show that of these, 63 were killed or missing with another 35 wounded. The actual number of German air missions reaching the battlefield is uncertain, but appears to have been in the neighborhood of 200 - 300. The Allied air force reported encountering some 60 - 70 German fighters over the southern sector of the battlefield including several engagements with a pair of Me-262 jets. In all, the Ninth Air Force reported flying 696 sorties while shooting down 91 enemy aircraft at a cost of 19 of their own. The Ninth Air Force admitted the loss of some 35 medium bombers. Quesada's IX TAC summarized the enemy disposition:

"It appears that the enemy during the morning was able to enter the battle area, whereas during the late afternoon he was prevented from doing so either by the nature of his mission or by Allied aircraft. His effort for the day is best described as an aggressive defensive effort. Fighter bomber attacks were intended...Possibly his highest priority may now be on protecting [troop] concentrations that are assembling to enter his offensive salient."

Meanwhile, the Eighth Air Force claimed 75 enemy aircraft destroyed while losing one bomber and seven fighters. Ground claims by the fighter bombers totalled to some 230 vehicles of all types. The first day of good flying weather had clearly not gone the Luftwaffe's way. "In the entire army area," reported Model's headquarters at *Heeresgruppe B*, "there was heavy enemy flying activity with fighter bomber attacks on German spearheads as well as bomb drops from four-engined bombers on roads and traffic targets in the attack zone."

To compound their problems, the petrol situation in the Luftwaffe was reaching the same state of abject poverty as that of the ground forces. On the 23rd, Göring ordered his air force to "immobilize all transport not needed for immediate combat support in order to conserve fuel." Meantime, the *Kommodore* of JG 27, Obst. Gustav Rödel, expressed exasperation with the day's performance from his fighters. In an ULTRA intercept, he accused 20% of his pilots of breaking off attacks early and flying back to base. Perhaps it was the survivalist instinct of those who had flown in the clear skies of early autumn and knew the consequences of a protracted tangle with the Allied fighters. Court martial was threatened for others who avoided their duty in the future. Another problem overheard was the lack of air cover over the panzer spearheads. It seems that most of the fighters were being drawn off to stop the bombers of the Eighth and Ninth Air Forces. The orders for the 24th "insisted that, even in the event of such Allied air activity, a proportion of the fighters must avoid air combat and penetrate without fail into the area above the foremost panzer spearheads." Easier said than done.[63]

It was Christmastide at *Adlerhorst*. Göring was still in Hitler's company, but the day had worn his welcome a bit thin. The massive Luftwaffe commitment was certainly not German air superiority, but at least the skies were in contention. For the first time in nearly a year, Göring had been welcome at Hitler's abode. He was even invited to tea with Hitler for nearly a week. But on December 23rd the good news stopped. The Allied strategic air forces were back in operation over Germany drawing Göring's fighters into the melee and overwhelming the Luftwaffe's ability to counter. As the situation soured, Göring hurried off once more to Karinhall for his last Christmas of the war. The Luftwaffe leader returned once to see how things were going on Christmas Day, but the calamitous events, particularly the beating the air forces were giving the German tank columns in the Ardennes cut Göring's stay short.

Sequestered with her father at Karinhall, Little Edda Göring was something of a princess in a glass menagerie. Her parents adored their "Sunshine," and her godfather was none other than the Führer himself. The

---

63 Intelligence revealed that the German High Command was apprehensive about fighter-bomber attacks to its armor, although they are "more prepared during the present phase to take the chance over the maintenance of supply."

Luftwaffe had taken up a collection which had been used to build the child an elaborate doll house in the orchard at Karinhall. The fantastical mansion was replete with Karinhall-sized rooms, kitchens and baths— all exquisitely detailed and to scale. Edda lived a life protected from the war, taking piano lessons in 1944 while the war ranged around her. But by Christmas, 1944 even her mother, Emmy, could no longer protect her six year old daughter from the conflict. That Christmas she would find less interesting the six pink silk night dresses that she received than the frosty scene outside the latticed windows. Edda saw something of the war from which she had been sheltered. It was disquieting: grim refugees from the East fleeing on the road past Karinhall. Where were these people going?

Meanwhile, at Allied headquarters the air commanders reveled in at last being able to get their planes into action. Although jubilant over the weather, Eisenhower was still quarantined at Versailles for worry of an assassination attempt. They had not caught the non-existent German commando squad. The town was crawling with MPs trying to track down rumors of sightings of the German hit men; the curfew in Paris started at 9 PM. Meanwhile, for the apprehended Germans dressed as Americans in the Ardennes, justice was swift. That day, the first of those condemned were put to death by firing squad at Eupen. "The prisoners' last request," Hodges' diary described, "was to hear Christmas carols, sung by a group of German women prisoners."

XIV

The Greatest Air Battle: December 24th

Brig. Gen. Frederick Walker Castle was one of the best liked and most experienced pilots in the Eighth Air Force. A veteran of some 29 missions, Castle was recognized as a commander who did not fit the common mold. Unlike the many hard-talking and brusque personalities in the Eighth Air Force, Fred Castle was a thoughtful and considerate man. And this, in spite of an insatiable appetite for work. In 1943 he left the comparative safety of a desk job to take over the command of a down-trodden B-17 Group. Friends knew Fred Castle as a steady character.

Christmas Eve dawned clear and cold over the Ardennes with visibility of 3-5 miles. In the predawn hours that Sunday, the teletype in the headquarters of the Eighth Air Force in England chattered noisily with a curious message. The message read that every serviceable B-17 and B-24 bomber was to participate in a "total effort" against the German airfields that had produced the vexing effort by the Luftwaffe the day before. An aerial showdown was at hand.

To comply with the field order for Mission 760, most groups of the Eighth put every serviceable aircraft they possessed into the air. Some war-weary battlewagons were launched with hastily fitted waist machine guns. In all some 2,034 heavy bombers of the Eighth took to the frosty morning skies escorted by 803 fighters. The Eighth's effort was accompanied by 502 RAF heavy bomber sorties and also a massive display by the U.S. Ninth Air Force. It was the largest single bomber strike of the entire Second World War! The display of Allied air power muscle was massive— over 5,000 total sorties were committed to combat the German offensive. The Eighth Air Force alone dropped some 5,052 tons of bombs designed to rob the Luftwaffe airfields of the ability to put aircraft aloft. All of the fighter groups of the Eighth Air Force, with the exception of the 78th and 339th which were socked in, accompanied the vast flotilla of heavy bombers into Germany.[64]

Brig. Gen. Castle quickly recognized the importance of the mission that day; he elected to fly personally as commander of the 4th Wing. In the crisp morning air Castle took off from Lavenham in a B-17 of the 487th Group. However, a ground hugging haze prevented the escorting fighter cover from taking off on time and his group proceeded across the Channel fully expecting the fighters to soon catch up. Undaunted, a tremendous procession of heavy bombers, led by the 3rd Division, with the 1st Division to the rear was to hit eleven enemy airfields and take them out of the fight. The B-24 Liberators of the 2nd Division were to assist the bombers of the Ninth Air Force in blasting the German lines of communications. The bombers rode from Clacton in the UK to Ostend and then turned to cross Luxembourg and head into enemy territory.

At the Luftwaffe bases around Germany, there was a similar hub-bub of activity. Somehow, even after suffering many damaged aircraft and mechanical troubles the day before, *Jagdwaffe* mechanics had made ready between 700 and 800 fighters. Most of the "men in black" had not slept on Saturday night, working non-stop until morning to prepare the Luftwaffe's machines. Everyone knew, that with crystal clear weather forecast for the following day the Allied air force would be out to deal a knock-out blow to Hitler's carefully nurtured winter offensive. In the early morning hours observant Luftwaffe radar controllers sighted the gargantuan American bomber stream. Never before had they seen so many blips on the screen! They quickly vectored a contingent of fighters to meet the intruders in the Liège vicinity. Scores of German fighter roared into the cold air to smite the American phalanx.

For once the Luftwaffe managed to get the drop on the Americans. German fighters suddenly pounced on the unprotected box of bombers as they crossed the Meuse River. Included in the bombers was the Fortress carrying Lt. Gen. Castle. Castle's Boeing had engine trouble and had fallen out of formation when a gaggle of Me-109s suddenly appeared. His adversary was one of the most experienced of the *Sturmgruppen, IV/JG 3*. The German fighters spotted the flock of bombers while they were passing Liège. Their fighter escort was not yet in evidence— a fleeting event that invited a frontal attack. The German pilots pushed their throttles forward and readied their cannon. Ripping into the box of bombers, they blasted away at the

---

64 Visibility in England was still poor, however, and there were many weather-related accidents. At Podington, Lt. Robert K. Seeber's B-17 crashed into a forest, hidden in the fog, barely 200 yards from the runway. Six of the crew were killed when the Fortress exploded. In another incident, the seventh B-17 sent aloft from the 457th BG crashed at the end of the runway, temporarily rendering Glatton unserviceable.

Fortresses. Almost immediately four of the Boeings burst into flame and plunged to their doom. Five others were so damaged that they had to struggle to make crash landings.

Fw. Wilhelm Hopfensitz was in on this attack at the controls of "Yellow 19" his Fw-190A-8. He and the other thirty aircraft of *IV/JG 3* had been in readiness at Gütersloh since 7 AM. They took off to intercept the bombers at 9:30 AM. Hptm. Weydenhammer led the formation to the west under "Y" control at 22,000 feet. They had been airborne for almost an hour when they sighted three boxes of B-17s. Hopfensitz attacked the middle box from the rear, picking out the outer Boeing on the starboard side. Diving from above, the *Feldwebel* peppered his target with his two MG 151 machine guns and MK 108 cannon. The blast sent the B-17 spiraling out of control. Recovering from their surprise, however, the B-17 gunners showed why their mount was called a "Flying Fortress." On a second attack Hopfensitz approached a second B-17 only to miss another that was only 70 feet underneath him. The gunner in this bomber caught him with a jolting stream of machine gun fire. His engine burst into flame as he fell away. Hopfensitz's wingman, Obgefr. Hubert Hirschfelder suffered a similar fate, being nailed by the tail gunner of a B-17 he was stalking. Both pilots bailed out to become POWs near Liège. Hirschfelder's interrogators found his morale "exceedingly high... a typical example of the familiar bone-headed Nazi youth." Uffz. Kurt Klose and Fw. Josef Sommer were shot down by the fierce return fire of the B-17s. Sommer was on his first sortie with *IV/JG 3*; Klose, who had finished fighter school at Liegnitz between October and December, was on his third mission. Sommer's oil feed to his Fw-190 was severed and the former brick-layer made a belly landing at 11 AM near Liège. Klose bailed out after his aircraft was drilled by an aft gunner.

Soon, however, the American Mustangs showed up and began pressing the Germans away from the bombers. A desperate aerial battle ensued as the *Staffeln* of JG 3 flew on to the area over the battlefield where they were joined in the high altitude air battles by *I/JG 27* and all of *JG 6*. Swirls of wispy white contrails were etched across the steely blue sky— evidence of the desperate attempt by the Luftwaffe to contest Allied air superiority. Hptm. Wolfgang Kosse and Ofw. Egon Schulz from JG 3 were shot down; neither have ever been traced. Another five had their machines hammered by the Mustangs and took to their parachutes. One, Uffz. Franz Mörl, evaded the Mustangs only to be chopped up by American AA fire as he dove for the deck. Mörl crash landed into captivity West of Aachen. All were taken prisoner as soon as they floated down. One of the downed aircraft was "Green 14," the Me-109G-6 of Uffz. Kurt Möllerke. The 20-year old German pilot was a veteran of 55 missions. He had returned to *I/JG 3* after an extended stay in a Quedlinburg hospital after being shot down by a P-47 while taking off at Evreux airfield the previous August. In this engagement he was closing with bombers only to be suddenly jumped by a Mustang. He sharply pulled away, but his engine was hit and stuttered to a stop. Möllerke was forced to jump. Taken prisoner, his interrogators found him "arrogant and confident that von Rundstedt's offensive would succeed and force the Allies to accept a compromise peace." A number of other *JG 3* pilots were missing including Lt. Franz Ruhl, who wore the Knight's Cross, and the commander of the *4th Staffel*. In all, twenty pilots of the *Geschwader* were reported killed or missing.

The peril was great for *I/JG 27* and *JG 6* as well. Obfhr. Max-Heinrich Klick was seen by his wingman to take to his parachute after a fighter crippled his plane. Three other pilots of *I Gruppe* were listed that night as killed or missing. *JG 6*, "*Horst Wessel*," reported the loss of 13 pilots, including the commander of its *10 Staffel*, Oblt. Weyl. At the time, Weyl had 27 victories, most of them accumulated in Norway. The story of Uffz. Paul Borth is also illustrative. Borth had been posted to *JG 6* after only 25 hours training in the Focke Wulf 190. He took off with the rest of *5 Staffel* on his fifth mission at 11:20 AM from the bombed-out airfield at Quakenbrück. They were headed on a free lance fighter patrol between Aachen and Malmédy. Their 12 Fw-190s were joined by another twenty aircraft of *II/JG 6*. The combined formation proceeded to 23,000 feet where they were jumped by a group of P-47s coming out of the sun. Borth's "White 5" was immediately hit; he jumped from his ship east of Aachen and was taken captive upon reaching the ground. *III/JG 6* also took losses, some arising from the frigid weather. Fhr. Jürgen Thieck, a 19-year old with *10 Staffel* took off at 11:30 AM to intercept the bomber stream, climbing over the course of an hour to 26,000 feet. In that rarified sub-zero atmosphere, Thieck's "Black 5" began to develop severe icing. The pilot lost all vision through his Me-109 G-14's iced-over canopy and shortly thereafter received a burst of gunfire from an unseen source. Thieck immediately bailed out becoming a POW upon reaching the ground near Liège. Less fortunate was Ofw. Heinz Schmidt, of *4./JG 6*, who fell to his death near Alleur.

But the Americans suffered greatly too. Castle's B-17 was struck broadside by the first hail of gunfire as the General struggled to bring his stricken plane back to the rear of the box. Although the lumbering bomber was still under close attack, Castle refused to jettison the bombs for fear of killing innocent Allied troops or civilians below. As the situation deteriorated, Castle took over the controls so that the crew could parachute to safety, holding the crippled bomber steady so that they could make an escape. But finally a German fighter moved in to deliver the *coup de grace* to the slowing craft. A burst of cannon fire from a Fw-190 struck the B-17's wing, severing it at the root. The doomed bomber promptly went into a high speed spin with centrifugal forces from which there was no escape.[65] The B-17 struck the ground near Rotheux-Rimières, Belgium. Six of the crew did bail out to safety, however, knowing that they owed their lives to Castle. Five other B-17s in the group were so beaten by the German fire that they were forced to crash land in Belgium rather than continue or head back to England. Castle, the "gentle hero," was awarded the Medal of Honor posthumously. Those who knew Castle eulogized him with great respect. "A man of high intelligence," remembered Gordon Thorup, his Air Executive at the 94th Bomb Group, "...He was quick to sense weakness, steadfast in his determination to improve the operational capability of his command, and was indefatigable..."

Though small consolation for the tragedy, the mission on which Castle was embarked was a noteworthy success. Over 4,300 tons of bombs were dropped on 11 German airfields and numerous other tactical targets. The story on the receiving end is quickly told. Since November, Uffz. Horst Tharann in *II/JG 4* had been located at the airfield of Babenhausen. At about 2 PM Tharann spied a group of some 120 heavy bombers headed directly for the airfield. Everyone ran for cover. Most jumped into slit trenches. A devastating rain of bombs rendered the strip "one hundred percent useless," but with only a few aircraft damaged. Still it took an all-out effort from a team of laborers and *Gruppe* personnel to bring the cratered airfield back to operation. It was only pronounced serviceable on the last day of the year.

German fighter interception and interference was too scattered and under attack by U.S. fighter sweeps to prevent the armada of bombers from smashing their objectives. Visibility for the bomb run was acceptable over Western Germany, but on attempting to return home the bombers found the haze closing in England. A number of bomber groups were diverted from home to other bases where visibility was more reasonable. The crowding at the few operational bases put a severe strain on the maintenance and service facilities at the bases, to say nothing of the griping about wayward Christmas plans. Only two landing accidents were reported. A B-17 lost power on a second approach and crashed into the runway killing seven of the crew in a terrible fire. In another incident, "The Floose," a 100-mission B-17 of the 303rd BG, had a jammed landing gear and was forced to put down on its belly.

Over the battlefield, the Allied air presence was undeniable. Gen. Richard Nugent's diary:

"Today is clear. Uncle Henry [intelligence] indicated that the Germans on the

---

65 One of the most widely feared horrors in the Eighth Air Force was to end up pinned in a spinning crippled machine where centrifugal force made it impossible either to get to one's parachute or to make it out of the door. A great many aircrew lost their lives to this terrifying phenomenon which was the unspoken explanation for many B-17s that spun down to their death with seeming opportunity for escape, but no parachutes seen.

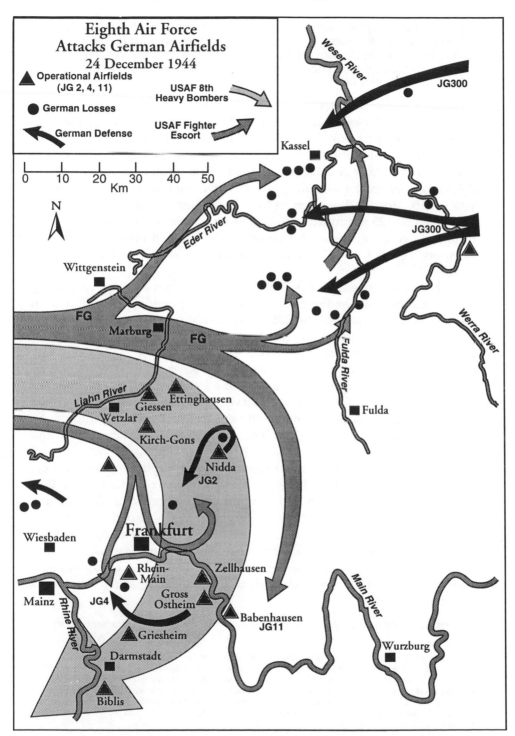

Eighth Air Force
Attacks German Airfields
24 December 1944

▲ Operational Airfields
(JG 2, 4, 11)

● German Losses

← German Defense

⇨ USAF 8th
Heavy Bombers

⇨ USAF Fighter
Escort

0 10 20 30 40 50
Km

N

Weser River

JG300

Kassel

Eder River

JG300

Werra River

Wittgenstein

FG

Marburg

FG

Fulda River

Fulda

Liahn River

Giessen

Ettinghausen

Wetzlar

Kirch-Gons

Nidda
JG2

Frankfurt

Wiesbaden

Rhein-Main

Zellhausen

Gross
Ostheim

Main River

Mainz

JG4

Babenhausen
JG11

Wurzburg

Rhine River

Griesheim

Darmstadt

Biblis

ground had been promised air coverage. Shortly before noon, Eighth Air Force heavies came on the board and all German fighters were rallied to attack them. This uncovered the German columns on the road as completely as though they had their clothes stripped from them. As a result my fighter bomber squadrons have been having a field day."

The air effort represented the greatest number of planes employed against the enemy counter-offensive and one of the most awesome displays of concentrated air power in the entire war in Europe. The Ninth U.S. Air Force flew 1,138 tactical sorties with about 700 of these over the battlefield. A further 2,442 bomber and 161 reconnaissance missions were flown. A total of 4,300 tons of bombs were dropped on 31 tactical targets in the Ardennes with over 500 tons of these coming from the fighter-bombers. The Ninth Air Force claimed 125 enemy aircraft. Claims on the ground in the battle zone, if inflated, were nonetheless tremendous: 156 armored vehicles, 786 motor transport, 167 rail cars, 5 ammunition dumps, 31 rail cuts and 85 gun positions.[66]

To the north, Nugent's XXIX TAC put up 299 sorties with approximately 148 of these over the battlefield. The 36th Fighter Group's 22nd Squadron assailed German armor of the *2SS Panzer Division* at Grandmenil and the *9SS Panzer Division* at Poteau. The 22nd and 53rd Squadrons attacked other German troop concentrations observed in Noville. A dozen P-47s of the latter squadron were forced to jettison their bombs when they were jumped by German fighters over Lierneux. East of the battle zone the 36th attacked German positions at Kall and Lunebach while the 48th FG attacked German foxhole positions south of Stavelot and enemy trucks passing through St. Vith. Other missions attacked German positions near Pronsfeld and Blankenheimerdorf.

The IX BD put up 376 medium bomber sorties dropping some 691 tons of bombs. The targets included the rail bridges at Konz-Karthaus (386 BG), Trier (394 BG), Grevenmach and communications centers at Zulpich and Nideggen. So effective were the countermeasures of a dedicated fighter escort and a pounding of German airfields, that not a single medium bomber was lost in spite of heavy flak. The damage of the bombing missions was ruefully noted by German ground forces. The *IISS Panzerkorps*, was now standing in for *LXVII Armeekorps* which had been incapacitated by an air attack on the 18th:

"Strikingly heavy employment of Marauder aircraft against rearward corps

---

66 Air attacks on enemy tanks were often less effective than American fighter bombers would have suspected. For instance, Lt. Josef Heindel of the *8 Kompanie, 33 Panzer Regiment* witnessed the frequent strafing of German tanks moving along the Clerf-Noville road on the afternoon of December 24th with virtually no effect, while serious damage was done to the truck transport following behind. The fighters, Heindel observed, would usually attack in groups of four, first dropping their bombs and then strafing. The panzers, impervious to machine gun fire, would pull out from cover as soon as the *Jabos* had dropped their bombs.

area. At 1315 hours bombs dropped on Schmidtheim. *LXVII Armeekorps* bombed out again. No casualties...[2SS] Division urgently requests fighter protection...for own attacking spearheads. Own attacks were hampered today by massed fighter bomber attacks. Losses of personnel and equipment. Flak protection weak."

Of equal importance to the Allied tactical air mission, was the aerial support of the Americans still surrounded in Bastogne. In all, some 161 C-47 transports, escorted by the 367th Fighter Group, dropped 1,446 bundles to the surrounded U.S. garrison within four hours. The drop totalled 319,412 pounds of supplies.

The British 2nd Tactical Air Force managed an additional 1,243 sorties with its medium bombers making a rare attack on enemy ground positions. Most of the fighter and fighter-bomber sorties were flown in the Malmédy-St. Vith-Düren-Euskirchen areas. Although stymied earlier during the offensive, the glorious weather on the 24th brought out the full strength of the 2nd Group's medium bombers. RAF medium bomber sorties totalled some 144, dropping 56 tons of bombs on their targets. The RAF squadrons pounded the crossroad towns of Kall, Gemünd, Trier and Recht. 226 Squadron's fighter escort managed to fight off an attack by German Me-109s, but the enemy anti-aircraft guns remained a deadly foe. In a swirling fight with a pack of Me-109s above Gemünd, the 84th Group could not completely protect their escorted ships and one of the Boston bombers of 88 Squadron was seen descending in a trail of smoke. Worse still, their target was cloaked in ground fog and the bombers hit rail sidings north of Gemünd rather than at the target. Flying along one of the British aircrew spied a lone German jet against the frozen Ardennes backdrop. Although they watched in rapt fascination, the lumbering bombers were pleased that the nimble German jet did not attempt to close.

Rocket-firing Typhoons poured into the skies, on the look-out for enemy armor, which was reported closing in on the Meuse River. In the air, the RAF found "numbers not met since Caen the previous summer." 193 Squadron sighted three Me-109s while on a sweep and diving on them suddenly found themselves in a wild melee with more than fifty German fighters. One of the Typhoons was shot down and another was badly damaged. 197 Squadron, patrolling the Lingen-Osnabrück area, listened in on the air battle over their radios. Hastening to the scene they were hit by twelve Me-109s and Fw-190s who dove out of the sun. Two more Typhoons were lost. The 143rd Wing suffered perhaps the hardest luck of all. Two aircraft of 438 Squadron were lost on a strafing mission while German flak destroyed a Typhoon of 440 Squadron on reconnaissance in the Malmédy area.

British air reconnaissance had mixed fortunes. 4 Squadron of the 35th Recce Wing put up 29 sorties, although losing Flg. Off. T.A. Priddle who was shot down in his Spitfire XI. In another case of mistaken identity, one of 400 Squadron's Spitfires came under a sustained attack by an American P-47, but was unharmed. 414 Squadron with the 39th Recce Wing had the best of the day, however. With some 36 sorties aloft, one mission ran afoul of 15 Me-109s at 11:55 that morning. Flt. Lt. D.I. Hall shot down two of these some 6,000 feet over Cologne. Later in the afternoon a dozen more German fighters were encountered near Neuss. In the action that followed, Flt. Lt. W. Sawyers managed to shoot down three Me-109s.

412 Squadron ran a morning fighter sweep with its Spitfires in the Düren area and met up with 45 Fw-190s south of Julich. In the action, Sqn. Ldr D.H. Dover and Flt/Lt C.W. Fox each claimed one of the enemy. Sqn. Ldr. E.D. Mackie had already earned the Distinguished Flying Cross and as a Spitfire pilot had shot down 16 German planes when he was posted to 274 Squadron. On Christmas Eve, the veteran pilot led his Tempest Vs on a patrol in the Julich-Malmédy sector. At 12:45 PM Mackie spied a Fw-190 shooting up two Typhoons of 440 Squadron. He dove on the enemy and fired; the German fighter spun into the ground and exploded. The 3rd Squadron of the New Zealanders was also in action; Flt. Lt. K.F. Thiele shot down one Me-109 and Flg. Off. Dryland destroyed another although one Tempest was lost.

The British foe was a mixed bag, including elements of *I* and *III/JG 1* and two *Gruppen* of *JG 6*, three from *JG 27* and *IV/JG 54*. 193 Squadron spotted a cloud of fifty German fighters shooting down a Typhoon and on the tail of another near West Münsterland. Ten of the British fighters raced in to save the assailed Hawkers only to be themselves bounced by another group of German fighters diving on them from out of the sun. The air battle swirled in confusion from Malmédy to Eindhoven. *III/JG 1* sighted a group of British bombers between Maastricht and Cologne and put in an attack. The escorting fighter group, Spitfires of 421 Squadron, RCAF, shot down two of the assailants including the celebrated *Gruppenkommandeur*, Hptm. Erich Woitke who fell near Aachen in "Grey 20," his Me-109G-14. At the time of his death, the 33-year old Woitke had 28 credited victories. Lt. Heinz Schöne was the other unfortunate, falling to his death over München-Gladbach. Lt. Hans Halbey remembered the action:

"Shortly after take-off, Woitke called to us to release supplementary fuel tanks as enemy aircraft were in the area and to be able to escape them we had to lighten our load. The action was not long in coming. Woitke's aircraft was hit by a full burst and was transformed into a ball of fire. Shortly after the explosion, I shot down a Spitfire in a circling combat; one of my comrades confirmed the victory over the radio. I was the only pilot of our formation to regain Rheine safe and sound. In accordance with instructions, I made out a combat report which was sent, as usual, to the *Kommodore* [Obstlt. Herbert Ihlefeld]. In the evening I was called to the telephone; 'The *Kommodore* wants to speak to you!' I waited for his congratulations on my victory...On the contrary, he told me off, which made me angry. In effect, I was the only pilot of the *Gruppe* to release the fuel tank after take-off. Because of this, it being impossible to become involved in a long combat, I returned to base far earlier than my comrades. He announced his intention to place me before a court martial for cowardice in the face of the enemy. I argued vehemently against these accusations, gave him a piece of my mind...and slammed the phone down...My fellow officers intervened on my behalf, and later, the *Kommodore* appeared to have completely forgotten about our telephone conversation. On the following day, 25th December, the day was sunny, but cold. I was shot down (my fifth time) by a Spitfire and had to bail out."

The IX Tactical Air Command put up 457 sorties on Christmas Eve.[67] Of these some 162 were over the battlefield. One hundred and forty-eight tons of bombs were dropped on targets. A total of 158 enemy planes were sighted by Quesada's command during the day and 12 enemy aircraft were claimed shot down against 13 losses. The 366th and 474th Groups made some 141 claims on concentrations of enemy vehicles near St. Vith.

Christmas Eve found little holiday spirit at Chievres, Belgium. The day before, the 365th Fighter Group had been alerted to move at a moment's notice, now that they were transferring to the XIX TAC. The prospects of leaving their familiar surroundings, their winterized tent-city and all the hard-won local friendships and romances was heartbreaking. But at 6:30 AM on Christmas Eve the move to Metz, France began with the men riding in the back of open trucks. It was freezing cold and many suffered frostbite. Christmas Eve dinner was frozen K-rations and icy Spam chunks, that crunched between your teeth. Such was the holiday gastronomic on the road to Verdun. It was Christmas Day before the majority of the command reached Metz; some incautious member of the group neglected to black-out their headlights on the road and were shot up by a German night fighter. Two were wounded. Unlike other French towns, the men were immediately struck by the coolness of the civilians in Metz. The place had a distinctly Teutonic feel to it; the 365th later learned that Metz, although in France, was so close to the German border that the people's allegiance was confused. Like much of the rest of Alsace-Lorraine, many of the inhabitants sympathized with the Germans. There were even buildings in town where the large black outline of a man was painted with a white question mark below— the sign of the rumored German *Werewolf*— the dark Ninja-like Hitler Youth organization that eventually turned out to be a Nazi propaganda ploy. Still, such stuff around town did little to increase the friendliness of the atmosphere. As the men grimly pitched their tents that night a German Ju-88 strafed the vicinity to warm their welcome.

Meanwhile, back at Chievres the flying part of the group still managed to put up several sorties. One flight took off that morning strafing and bombing enemy columns eight miles west of Stavelot— their old nemesis the *1SS*

---

67 The numbers from various sources for IX TAC sorties on December 24th reflect the changing command situation. Three of the command's six groups (365, 367 and 368) were in the process of being transferred to XIX TAC. Not counting the sorties of these three groups the remaining IX TAC sorties for the day total 201. Not surprisingly, in the records, both commands claimed the sorties for the three transferred groups. Officially they came under Weyland's command after the 21st.

Panzer Division. The 386th Squadron, directed by the 7th Armored Division, attacked eight German vehicles just south of Stavelot. Another flight hit the enemy north of St. Vith and a third strafed the enemy along the Our River between Schönberg and St. Vith. Other afternoon missions struck the Germans again near St. Vith and then two other flights flew missions south over Bitburg and Echternach where "Ripsaw" had asked them to bomb 300 gas trucks north of Echternach. They could not locate the trucks, so instead, loosed their bombs on Bitburg.

Matters were reaching a climax at A-78, Florennes, Belgium. When Lt. Robert L. Freeman took off in the early morning with an infantry officer in an L-5 observation plane to look over the tip of the German advance it only took him three minutes to reach the enemy controlled area. A week before it had taken half an hour! They saw what had been feared— the Germans were pushing west around Celles, not four miles from the Meuse River and not even thirty miles from Florennes. At 1 PM the 428th Squadron sent a mission to rendezvous and escort B-26s to hit a bridge near Trier. This went smoothly with the group strafing the enemy in the area between Houffalize and Malmédy on their way back. The pilots saw many enemy transport and tanks and claimed thirty destroyed. But the real worry at the base was the enemy ground advance. Just after 4 PM that afternoon, Maj. Nuckols took a flight of seven P-38s to hunt for the dangerously close enemy. They had no trouble finding them, and although without bombs, the first group repeatedly strafed the Germans, claiming a knocked out self-propelled gun, a quartet of armored vehicles and another four trucks. P-38s of the 370th and 474th Fighter Groups concentrated on the German spearhead panzer column, inflicting fearsome punishment on the *2 Panzer Division.* One flight after another attacked the Germans. Enemy fuel trucks went up in flames, tanks were set afire and trucks and staff cars were mercilessly gunned down. So complete was the devastation that the sixth flight from the 370th Group returned with all bombs from Celles because all sighted vehicles were burning and more P-38s of the 428th Squadron, 474th FG were observed laying waste to the surrounding woods. Other P-38s of the 429th Squadron were vectored to nearby Bourdon where the 84th Infantry Division requested a pounding of the *116 Panzer Division* in the vicinity. The 430th Squadron attacked St. Vith, strafing the hapless enemy threading through the town. Although the enemy shot back with small arms, the planes sustained no damage and all returned in the gathering darkness of Christmas Eve with the knowledge that they had punched the enemy in the face.

Christmas Eve at Florennes was a relief for the men of the 474th Fighter Group. Word had finally come that the Germans were not almost on the doorstep. It was not peace on earth, but it sure beat being drafted into the Air Force infantry. Besides, their Lightnings had dealt a savage blow to the German tank force just east of Dinant. The enemy was out of gas and ravaged by air strikes and Allied armor. Everyone loosened up a notch. Isham G. Keller remembers:

> Like children anxiously awaiting the long expected Santa, officers and men reached deep into their gear to produce highly touted liquor and multi-blended whiskeys...In many minds, thoughts of home were foremost, and nostalgia presided. Others turned to comradeship and spent the evening joking and singing, united and warmed by rich mellow drinks...Witty remarks and raucous conversations were constantly punctuated by the ever present rumbling of the distant bellowing guns. Occasionally, their eyes were lifted in alcoholic uncertainty at the sound of closer shelling, while the stars looked coldly down on the progress of the not too distant Germans.

While it was true that the Germans were not "right at the edge of the airfield," they were nearly within artillery range of the base. And while the frost-bitten tents and snow bound shacks at Florennes were not much, they were home.

Weyland's XIX TAC had a tremendous day with 424 battlefield sorties, chalking up a massive string of impressive if inflated ground claims (588 vehicles, 117 tanks, 68 guns and 115 rail cars).[68] Against the 24 enemy aircraft shot down, Weyland's command lost only 11. All fifteen fighter groups in the Ninth Air Force were active as well. "A tremendous concentration of enemy artillery, armor and trucks at P-7570 (Trois Vierges) with tanks parked under the eaves of houses," radioed a reconnaissance aircraft. The *2SS Panzer Division* had been sighted as it struggled to get its armor into place for a full blooded attack towards the Meuse.

P-47s also struck the German *Seventh Armee* area from Echternach to Ettelbruck, bombing truck columns, dropping napalm on flak positions and even strafing German staff cars. Bridges near Bollendorf were priority targets for the XIX planes. And on the other side of the fence, the chief of staff of the *Seventh Armee* would bitterly report not sighting a single German plane among the Allied armada which was so harassing his ground troops.

The 367th Fighter Group flew an armed reconnaissance of the Krauznach and Trier areas. The 393rd Squadron had uneventfully attacked German trains near Wolfstein and the 392nd put in a glide bombing attack on Trier. However, the 394th Squadron, which also was to assault the old Roman city, was not as lucky. Over Trier, "Ripsaw," the ground controller, informed the group that twenty enemy fighters were approaching. In only a few minutes, the German fighters emerged and a violent acrobatic dogfight began. Caught flat-footed, the P-38s were forced to jettison their bombs. At first the Germans got the best of it. Lts. Owen and Curtis banked hard away from B flight's second formation, with Lts. George Croker and James Baxter. As he banked hard to lose

---

68 Elsewhere, the XIX TAC tally is posted as 638 sorties, adding operations from the three fighter groups being transferred to Weyland's command.

the German pursuit, Curtis looked down to see hits all over both Lightnings. Croker called out that his plane was critical. He had lost an engine and could not maintain altitude. Baxter was not heard from again; he was last seen spiralling down in his smoking craft. Moving away from this scene, Lt. Curtis spied a Fw-190 climbing behind him; he turned his P-38 around to close with the enemy fighter from a 45-degree angle. "I got a little too close," Curtis remembered, "but when I finally fired I saw hits all along his fuselage as he passed directly in front to me. I got a little shook, as I had nearly rammed him. I guess he was scared too, because he broke for the deck." Lt. Donald L. Mygatt's P-38 had been hit early in the going over Trier. He felt hits on his aircraft and looking back saw an ominous vapor trail billowing from his left boom radiator. He pulled back on the throttle and slowed down.

> "In looking back on it, it was this speed disadvantage that probably saved me. Everyone else was going flat out, and here was this steaming and burning P-38 lollygagging in the middle of the scrap. A Fw-190 appeared ahead of me, so I turned a bit and fired. Some of his cowling flew off before he passed out of sight under the '38's nose. I looked back to see three more Fw-190s pursuing me in a left turn 100 to 200 yards behind. All were at different angles of bank, indicating that they were having trouble slowing down enough to stay with me. Two of them were firing and I thought I could feel their bullets hitting. Taking evasive action, I pushed and pulled the yoke violently forward and backward, simultaneously kicking left and right rudder. Then a quick roll to the right, and I started down, hanging on the belt a bit to be sure to get maximum diving speed...By now there was no more steam, but black smoke was coming out of the left cowl vent. I opened it wide, and the inrushing air from the dive blew the fire out. Passing 6,000 feet and still diving, I decided to level out at 3,000 so I'd have a better chance of jumping if the other engine was knocked out. As the '38 leveled, I huddled behind the armor plate waiting for the 190s to finish me off, but nothing happened. I looked back and found them gone...I flew this way [on one engine] for an hour or so, maintaining radio silence so enemy aircraft could not home in on my transmissions...Finally, the airfield appeared. Snow covered the ground, but I was determined to make a good landing after coming that far. A wide right turn into the good engine, careful speed control and the P-38 settled on the runway as easy as you please. Later examination showed that the ship sustained about fifty cannon and machine gun hits. If I had been flying a single-engined fighter, I would have either had to jump or go down with the plane..."

Fuel and ammunition almost gone, the remaining seven pilots headed for home. In the 45-minute air battle the Germans had killed Baxter and forced Lt. Jesse E. DeFrance to parachute out of his smoking twin-engined fighter.[69] Croker and Mygatt straggled home in their wounded craft. Against these losses, the 367th claimed eight German fighters shot down.

---

69 Lt. DeFrance bailed out behind German lines, and was almost blind when he landed, his eyes having been burned from a cockpit fire. Disoriented and in shock, DeFrance stumbled down the road until he ran into a huge obstacle. Groping his way around it, he learned that he had walked into a German Panther tank. The surprised German crew made the burned pilot a prisoner and sent for medical treatment. It was mid-morning on Christmas eve.

Motor transport continued to be the most frequent tactical mission however with over 700 missions assigned this target on the 24th. Heavy fighter bomber attacks by the 365th, 404th, and 406th Fighter Groups were made on the villages of Marnach, Clervaux, Diekirch, Vianden, Noville, Chenogne, Tintange and Harlange. The 406th Fighter Group continued its dedication to VIII Corps, blasting any Germans who were indiscreet enough to show themselves in daylight. The 406th FG was shifted all over the Bastogne battlefield by "Maestro" (101st Airborne Division) and "Blendwell" (VIII Corps). The 512th Squadron report: firebombs were dropped on German vehicles in Vaux and ten tanks seen in Noville. Napalm destroyed German staff cars in Bourcy. The 513th Squadron blasted Wardin and Marvie to the southeast of the town where part of the *Panzer Lehr Division* was attempting to form up to put in an assault. Other targets included, Cobru, just northeast of Bastogne as well as Houffalize through which German troops were moving west. The planes flew till darkness made it impossible to find Maestro's targets any longer. The 514th Squadron fire-bombed Morhet and Chenogne. They also attacked the 2 *Panzer*'s bridge at Ortheville and the enemy sally point north of the town at Noville. The daily tally of ground claims that Saturday included a dozen 40mm German flak guns incinerated by napalm near Tavigny and 92 other vehicles and 15 tanks claimed destroyed. The villages around Bastogne were left smoking.

The 405th Fighter Group put up 92 sorties in eight missions from St. Vith to Trier dropping anti-personnel bombs, napalm and strafing any Germans they could find on the roads. Capt. Van Etten in "Look No Hands" lead the 509th Squadron against German rail transport, blasting several trains and boxcars and even closing the end of a rail tunnel. The 509th Squadron hit German tanks observed in the Noville vicinity. Capt. Wayne Stout, leading the squadron, hit the jackpot in an afternoon mission sighting a road jammed with an estimated 200 enemy vehicles north of Echternach at Wallendorf. Several gasoline bearing German trucks were hit as the flight worked the road from one end to the other. At least 70 vehicles were flamed up including one German fuel depot— an increasingly precious commodity to the enemy. The 511th Squadron joined in by attacking enemy transport in the Bollendorf vicinity. So significant did the Ninth Air Force view this victory, that the Christmas Eve broadcast by the BBC told of their deed. However, on the way home an Me-109 suddenly dropped out of the sky, firing right at Capt. Daniel A. McKinnon, who was luckily helped out when his wingman, Lt. "Moe" Morgan, picked off the bandit with a 900 deflection shot. Three other enemy planes were shot down in engagements with enemy fighters. The group also did well in close support: members plastered the Germans in front of the 5th Infantry Division with fragmentation bombs and napalm, greatly aiding their attack this day. But tragedy struck as well; a morning sortie against the *Seventh Armee* bridge at Bollendorf took the bridge out, but cost the life of a popular officer. Lt. Charles R. Grubert was last seen flying through a wall of German flak in his dive towards the Sauer River crossing.

The 354th FG, on an armed recce in the Trier-Merzig area, hit a petrol dump at Siegburg. Other sorties hit German marshalling yards at Hoxel, and an enemy convoy southeast of the battle zone. While on one of these missions the 353rd Squadron was bounced by 16 Fw-190s northeast of Trier at 1,500 feet and claimed two shot down with no losses of its own.

Meanwhile, the 362nd FG flew nine missions claiming 84 vehicles destroyed in the day's actions. The 379th Squadron alone counted 45 trucks wiped out near St. Hubert and also reported destroying a tank-truck convoy near Houffalize and Bourcy damaging more enemy transport. Observing vehicle tracks leading into the woods at Tintange, the P-47s of the 377th Squadron laced the woods near the village with napalm and flung rockets at camouflaged vehicles near Bavigne, Luxembourg. A second mission struck Bourscheid and the *79 Volksgrenadier Division* courtesy of directions from the U.S. 80th Infantry Division. A final mission again blasted the Germans near Tintange with 16 bombs, 18 rockets and 8 incendiaries. The 4th Armored recorded "excellent results" and pilots observed Combat Command A's tanks moving in after the mission. The 378th Squadron flew missions against German rolling stock in Marnach, Clerf and Diekirch. Another attack was directed by III Corps to Eschdorf, but on the way the unit was attacked by 12 Fw-190s ten miles northeast of Arlon. One P-47 was damaged in the engagement which forced most of the Jugs to jettison their loads. Those remaining were dropped on Ettelbruck and on the bridge at Fouhren. The German-held town of Ettelbruck was doused with napalm, followed by the strafing of the *352nd Volksgrenadier Division*. Two more missions were flown by the squadron that day. One hit Cobru just northeast of Bastogne, while another blasted Sainlez and Chaumont south of the town.

The 379th Squadron added to the troubles for the Germans around Bastogne, hitting Bourcy where 14 trucks and three tanks were claimed. An ammunition dump in the nearby woods was bombed creating a tremendous explosion. A mission at dusk provided important support for the U.S. 26th Infantry Division, then in a scrambling battle with Hitler's bodyguard, now transformed into an elite panzer formation. Maj. Kent C. Geyer led the P-47s low to bomb and strafe the advance column of the *Führer Grenadier Brigade* between Bourscheid-Eschdorf. In a bizarre episode the fighter group was repeatedly fired on by a P-47 with an orange tail supposedly escorting other German planes. This episode began a persistent rumor in the U.S. Third Army that the Germans were flying captured P-47 Thunderbolts. Just west of this encounter, Lt. Donald Stoddard definitely ran afoul of the enemy, one of which he damaged:

"We were circling Arlon, Belgium at approximately 4,000 feet. Twelve Fw-190s approached from about 12 o'clock about 200 feet above us. I called in on the

R/T saying there were Fw-190s overhead...I dropped my belly tank and wing bombs, turning to the left with a Fw-190. I got strikes. He straightened out and then hit the deck. I followed him down firing short bursts. My guns went wild, but I followed him on the deck to about Diekirch, Belgium where they opened up on me with light flak. I got two hits in the canopy. One hit in the left wing and a 20mm in the right wing...I pulled up taking evasive action..."

The 362nd lost two aircraft; Capt. Robert A. Doty's machine was crippled by flak, but he was able to bail out and return to the unit. Less fortunate was Lt. Richard K. Grant, who was killed when his motor quit and his Thunderbolt flipped over during an attempted crash landing southwest of Harlange. The 362nd claimed three enemy aircraft destroyed.

The 368th FG's 396th Squadron observed over two dozen Fw-190s attacking westbound B-26s near Mayen at 20,000 feet. The P-47s closed with the German fighters who tried to run. Even so, the 396th claimed 11 enemy aircraft destroyed for the loss of three of their own. In ground action the 395th Squadron hit a German tank park near Dochamps while the 396th Squadron bombed a dozen armored vehicles near Losheim and a 150 vehicle motor convoy just east of St. Vith. One aircraft of the 395th was hit by flak during the strafing over St. Vith. The 397th Squadron bombed and strafed the Germans in and around Freyneux, southwest of Manhay, claiming 11 tanks and 12 trucks.

The XIX TAC summarized a very successful day: "Movement of all kinds was very heavy today," recorded Weyland's record keepers, "Intense activity was observed in grid-square L-04 (Echternach) consisting of a probable gasoline dump, m/t parks and possible headquarters. The road from Neuerburg to Vianden was very active along with those from St. Vith to Hallschlag and from Büllingen to St. Vith. The furious battle going on for the road center of Bastogne was reflected in the large amount of movement and concentrations near the town..."

Fighter groups with XXIX TAC also had a decisive impact on the ground battle that day. The 36th FG (Col. William L. Curry) and 48th FG hit German lines of communication in the Prüm-Pronsfeld area. While the 36th was over St. Vith the 53rd Squadron was jumped by ten Fw-190s and Me-109s; four German fighters were shot down against two of the P-47s. The 48th lost two aircraft to flak although both pilots, Lt. Charles W. Riffle and Lt. John P. Crow, were able to safely parachute out from their aircraft. Riffle was credited with shooting down one Fw-190 that day as was Lt. Bernard L. Kupersmith.

The air attacks on Prüm had been devastating. Uffz. Martin Petrowske, passing through the town, observed that nearly all its buildings were ablaze and the dead were carried out of "practically every other house." Most of the vehicles in the town were wrecked and the winding streets were nearly impassable with rubble. The scene in Recht was even more horrifying. At 4 PM four waves of five twin-engined bombers struck the town with incendiary bombs which exploded with "a blinding white flash." These were 32 ary bombs which exploded with "a blinding white flash." These were 32 Mitchells and 23 Bostons of 2 Group, RAF who dropped some 70 tons of bombs on the town. Units of the *9SS Panzer Division* were billeted in the village which was soon ravaged by fire at least partly due to the 900 gallons of fuel of the division struck by the bombing raid. SS Sturmann Kurt Krell with the *20 SS Panzergrenadier Regiment* witnessed the conflagration. Several of his company were killed and some 25 were wounded. The attack came so suddenly that the vehicles in the town square could not be dispersed. The ration trucks were destroyed and the unit was short on food for the next week. In all, nearly forty vehicles were lost between Recht and Poteau, the sudden and intense fires sparking momentary panic among the SS troops.

In the air space to the north, over a thousand fighter sorties were executed in the Malmédy, St. Vith-Düren and Julich areas. Most targets were tactical consisting of guns, trucks and tanks. The medium bombers of the Ninth Air Force were escorted by the 373rd and 474th fighter groups. After the escort the 373rd FG swooped down to harass and destroy German tanks and troop positions between Stavelot and Losheim. Enemy transport in the Hotton-Rochefort and Malmédy-St. Vith areas were heavily damaged.

The strategic impact of Allied air power was dramatic on the day before Christmas. The strong German air opposition of the previous day demanded an effective Allied response. On the 24th the Eighth Air Force executed a crushing bomb attack on 11 German airfields west of the Rhine. *Reichsmarschall* Hermann Göring would later recount that these attacks were immediately effective in stifling their response. However, he claimed it was also easy to make quick repairs— what he called the "race between the shovel and the bomb." But this was only part of the damage. A total of 1,400 heavy bombers of the Eighth Air Force escorted by 726 fighters led the assault dropping 3,506 tons of explosives. A further 634 bombers of the air force attacked 14 communications centers in the area with 1,530 tons of bombs to interdict the flow of supply to the German spearheads. A total of 13 bombers and 10 fighters were lost in the Eighth Air Force.

However, the pilots of the fighter groups flying with the Eighth had a field day, shooting down some 70 fighters. The 357th Fighter Group led the others in claiming 31 of the enemy. The group flew as two separate units, the "A" group under Maj. Richard A. Peterson went to Fulda and the "B" Group led by Col. Irwin Dregne flew over Koblenz. Both groups ran into stiff opposition. With the "A Group" Lt. Otto "Dittie" Jenkins shot down four Fw-190s that day making him an ace and running his tally up to 8 1/2. Jenkins pulled into the rear of a group of unsuspecting Fw-190s and quickly blasted three before being fired on himself by a 190 that got in on his tail. Jenkin's wingman, Lt. Edward Hyman managed to fire two bursts of gunfire into the German aircraft which promptly fell away with the German pilot jumping ship. Saved by his wingman, Jenkins then quickly destroyed another Fw-190 before heading back home with a sieve-like left wing. Meanwhile, Lt. John Kirla shot down three German fighters and Lt. William T. Gilbert and Paul Pelon knocked out doubles. Unfortunately, Gilbert was later shot down and killed. Four P-51s were lost in the melee.

The 361st Fighter Group, under a new commander, Lt. Col. Junius W. Dennison, Jr., had just come to the continent to provide fighter support for the Ninth Air Force. As the group prepared a party for 200 orphans (Pvt. Jack Levy would be the rotund Santa), the rest of the P-51s were out to provide support to the heavies over Koblenz. There they ran into "very aggressive" enemy fighter activity. The group claimed four Me-109s shot down in a wild dogfight in the vicinity of Wengenrohr. Unfortunately, the one loss of the day was Lt. William J. Sykes, the leading ace with the 361st. Lt. George R. Vanden Heuvel describes the action that led to Sykes being taken prisoner:

"We were in the vicinity of Wengenrohr when White Leader called out 'bogies below.' Lt. Sullivan followed White Flight down. White Leader, Lt. William J. Sykes, called out that they were Me-109s when I saw an Me-109 approaching Lt. Sullivan from the right. I started towards the Me-109 and he turned into me. I got my pipper on him and began firing at extreme range, but the rate of closing was so great only a short burst was possible. There were a few hits in his canopy. He made no effort to dodge so I broke under him and turned to the left to get after him. He made no turn, but continued straight ahead in a gradually increasing dive and dove into the ground and exploded and burned. I believe the pilot was killed by one of my strikes. I then turned to rejoin Lt. Sullivan and heard Lt. Sykes call for 'someone to get this guy off my tail.' Down at ten o'clock I saw an Me-109 firing at Lt. Sykes plane from which pieces started flying off. Lt. Sykes called out that they got him, then jettisoned his canopy and bailed out the left side. His chute opened almost immediately. Meanwhile, Lt. Sullivan was closing on the Me-109 and registered numerous hits on his first burst. Lt. Sullivan pulled up right off the trees and the Me-109 went into a steep dive and crashed into the ground. As I made a turn I flew past Lt. Sykes in his chute and he seemed to be alive and kicking..."

Meanwhile, in the air battles over Koblenz, the 55th Fighter Group destroyed fifteen enemy aircraft and the 359th claimed a further ten. Lt. Col. Elwyn Righetti with the 55th Fighter Group, had developed quite a reputation for ground strafing missions. He was returning from an escort mission as well as hitting some German locomotives when his flight came across some twenty Fw-190s southeast of Münster in close formation with belly tanks. Righetti and his five Mustangs surprised the German contingent by allowing them to cross in front before pulling in behind them.

"By this time the E/A were starting to turn and take evasive action. I closed on the nearest 190 which was in a tight left turn, and fired a one second burst securing hits on the left wing tip and believe I saw pieces fly off. I turned with the E/A and as I did so, I saw two Fw-190s directly ahead belly in, one heading due west and the other northwest. Both raised large dust clouds as they hit, but they did not explode...The E/A I was pursuing continued to tighten his turn to the left and when he reached a bank of 70-80 degrees, he snapped under and went straight into the ground at 800 feet. I completed my turn and observed my wingman, Lt. Griffith, in trouble with a 190 on his tail. I turned to engage this E/A and as I did so took short bursts at two other E/A which crossed my path and secured scattered strikes on both. Lt. Griffith was in a tight left turn and as I approached the 190 on his tail, I secured a good group of hits on the E/A. He apparently saw me and broke off into a climbing turn to the right. I followed, firing from about 300 yards and closing rapidly. I secured a scattered set of strikes all along the E/A and when he reached 1,000 feet he rolled over on his back and went straight into the ground, crashing and exploding...Lt. Griffith called that he was hit in the arm and that his engine was out. Due to the haze I could not locate him so I advised him to bail out. He stated that he was too low, but was very calm as he wished me a Merry Christmas. I feel sure Lt. Griffith was able to belly-in as the terrain was suitable."

Just after dark, the British came back for more. Another 442 RAF Halifaxes and Lancasters of the bomber command pounded German airfields at Düsseldorf, Essen and Bonn-Hangelar with some 1,830 tons of explosives. Another 94 British bombers struck the rail yards at Cologne-Nippes in the early evening hours. Nearly all the rail tracks were hit, much of the rolling stock was destroyed and the yard was 100% unusable. Decrypts from ULTRA verified the damage:

> Air attack on Cologne 1725-1837 hours 24 December. Four traffic installations and one ammunition train hit. Stretch of line Cologne-Neuss closed. Nippes marshalling yard hit...entire superstructure destroyed...Repairs will take 5-6 days...

Even the massive attack on German airfields could not still the Luftwaffe. Over 650 sorties were earmarked for the Ardennes battle in what the IX TAC characterized as the "greatest German air effort since D-Day." The Luftwaffe recorded a total of 1,088 sorties sent aloft and the twisted white contrails of dogfights were a common sight over the battlefield. "The enemy's strength was up on offensive missions, but was forced over to the defense to intercept bombers." About 9:00 AM numerous formations of German fighters entered the air space in the Stavelot area. More German planes appeared in the afternoon roaming from Trier to Aywaille, although these planes could offer scant assistance to the German ground forces, having their hands full with the Allied fighters. Later, the Allied air forces erected steel-curtain fighter defense: "The fighter bombers of the XIX TAC set so close a screen in front of the German Air Force that only one squadron was observed in the immediate Third Army battle area, and Bombay (IX BD) carried out 365 successful sorties without sighting an enemy aircraft." For their part, however, the American air commanders were pleased that the Luftwaffe was finally coming out in the open. "We've been trying for months to make them come up," Hoyt Vandenberg announced, "Now we've got them where we want them."

The Luftwaffe vigorously opposed the Eighth Air Force with 200-250 sorties of its own. *JG 3 "Udet,"* commanded by Obstlt. Heinz Bär, hit the armada of bombers as they passed Liège, later to be joined over the Hohes Venn by *JG 27* and *JG 6* (Obstlt. Johann Kogler). In minutes four B-17s were in flames crashing to the Ardennes. Among these was the Flying Fortress flown by Brigadier General Castle.

The bomber groups split into two masses, one aiming for the airfields of *JG 4* and *JG 11* and the other targeted at the bases for *JG 2*. Three *Gruppen* of *JG 4* raced into the air from Frankfurt-Darmstadt to challenge the B-17 armada south of Koblenz. Two pilots, Fw. Erler and Oblt. Ullmann were almost immediately shot down and killed by the aggressive fighter escort. Uffz. Ferchland of *III Gruppe* was killed near Erbenheim and Oblt. Stark was gunned down over Mörfelden. Luckily for Stark, he was able to jump from his Me-109G-14. On his way down, he could see his base at Rhein-Main under a torrent of bombs as he hung under his parachute. Meanwhile, the Liberators pressed home their attack, planting tons of bombs on Biblis, Gross-Ostheim and Zellhausen. Although *JG 11* endeavored to protect their home turf, they were unable to stop the B-24s and in doing so lost three pilots. Uffz. Stöhr was killed over Gross-Ostheim, while Fw. Horlacher lost his plane over Gross-Karben. Lt. Richter and Fw. Schulirsch did not return from their mission along the Moselle near Trier. Neither have ever been found.

The second arm of the bomber fleet moved on five airfields of *JG 2*: Ettingshausen, Giessen, Merzhausen, Nidda and Kirch-Göns. The bombing plowed up the runways without significant opposition, the fighter sweeps already having taken on Bühligen's *Richthofen Jagdgeschwader* in the bid to intervene in the Ardennes west of the Rhine. The few that struggled into the air found the skies deadly. *JG 2* suffered the loss of Uffz. Maier who was killed in action over Nidda airfield with a pack of P-51s and Uffz. Löbering was killed as he sought to defend Merzhausen airfield. Uffz. Kühn and Patzelt also did not return.

Maj. Anton "Tony" Hackl of *II Gruppe, JG 26* was one of those scrambled to halt the armada of American bombers. The 30-year old Hackl was one of the legendary aces in the Luftwaffe. Having served on all fronts and survived being shot down eight times, he had amassed 165 victories through his aggressive style of air combat and was awarded the Swords to the Knight's Cross on July 13th the previous summer. Having just converted over the new Fw-190D-9s, the *"Doras"* were thrown into battle on the 24th. Hackl's pilots were unable to reach the bombers, but did inflict damage on their escort, dropping five P-47s near Liège. The success was not without cost, however. Hackl's group lost three pilots and four planes, one evidently shot down by an over-enthusiastic cohort from *JG 27*. The attempt of *I Gruppe* using their new D-9s was a disaster. Eighteen planes took off from Fürstenau at 11 AM led again by Oblt. Heckmann. Eight planes aborted with various troubles and another set off after an artillery spotter plane. The remaining nine aircraft formed up against at least sixty B-17s with a heavy escort northwest of Liège. The result was distinctly in the American favor: only one P-38 destroyed at a loss of four of the long-nosed 190s. Two developed engine trouble forcing their pilots to crash land.[70] *II Gruppe/JG 26* counted another four losses. And one pilot, Lt. Siegfried Benz, was shot down by a German fighter who mistook his D-9 for a Tempest. At mid-day Maj. Rudolf Klemm's *IV Gruppe/JG 54*, flying from Varrelbusch, set upon several British fighters of the 2nd Tactical Air Force. Two Typhoons were shot down, but this episode ended when the assailing planes were themselves attacked by Tempests of No. 274 Squadron. One Fw-190, likely that of Lt. Paul Brandt, was immediately shot down and another two *Grünherz* pilots did not return.

Once the heavy bomber fleets had breasted the fighters over Belgium and attacked the airfields, they came up against their familiar foes, *JG 300*, on the way back to England. As usual, a desperate air battle broke out. Lt. Bretschneider, decorated with the Knight's Cross after some 31 aerial victories in twenty missions, fell prey to a skilled P-51 pilot over the Knüll Mountains. Another five pilots of *II Gruppe* were killed and five more of *III* and *IV Gruppe* suffered a similar fate. One horror presented itself to the members of the *12 Staffel*. They watched as Lt. Günter Rudolph bailed from his smoking Me-109 G-10 only to see him plummet to his death as his parachute would not open.

Other desperate air battles over the northern Eifel were fought by *JG 77*. So short was the *Geschwader* of pilots that Lt. Armin Fitzner, who had been wounded the day before, was cajoled to fly again. However, December 24th saw the fighter group lose some 13 aircraft along with eight pilots killed and one missing. Tragically, the wounded Fitzner was among these. The aircraft of the *Kommodore*, Maj. Johannes Wiese, was blasted by a British Spitfire. Wiese managed to get clear of his damaged machine, but his parachute did not open properly and he was seriously injured after a hard landing near Euskirchen. However, Wiese was luckier than Hptm. Lothar Baumann, the commander of *I Gruppe*, who crashed to his death in his Me-109G-14 near the little village of Hoscheid, Luxembourg. Also, the head of *2 Staffel*, Oblt. Iring Englisch, plunged to his death near Euskirchen. Two others of his unit, Uffz. Köberlein and Morgerauer were killed at Münstereifel not far away. December 24th was the 21st birthday of Lt. Rolf von Kampen who flew "Blue 2," his Me-109 G-14. He and two dozen others had scrambled from Dortmund at 9 AM to run a *"Freie Jagd"*— a free lance fighter sweep— over the southern battle zone. However, his most valued present on that Sunday was his parachute. Encountering a group of American P-38s, von Kampen had trouble jettisoning his drop tank and fell to 11,500 feet. By that time his

---

70 Kurt Tank, the developer of the FW 190 did not like the liquid-cooled Jumo 213A engine and teething problems still plagued the use of this powerful new powerplant

aircraft was under hot pursuit and he was hit numerous times by machine gun fire in his engine. Von Kampen celebrated his birthday in American captivity near Bissen, Luxembourg. Meanwhile, *III Gruppe*, returning to base, ran into a real inferno. Some 338 bombers of the 4th, 5th and 8th Groups of RAF Bomber Command were in the process of bombing their airfield at Düsseldorf. The Me-109K-4s, nearly out of fuel, were forced to land amid a rain of bombs. Amazingly not a single pilot was wounded although several aircraft were damaged.

The ground attack aircraft of Oblt. Jannsen's *SG 4* had a mission on Christmas Eve to attack the Americans in and around Bastogne. The Fw-190F-8s were loaded up to bomb and strafe with a briefing given by Oblt. Bleckl. Some of the aircraft carried rockets, while most hoisted a 500 lb. bomb and their formidable cannon. The flock of F-8s headed off from Köln/Wahn for the battle zone at 8:55 AM with about 40 aircraft. During the course of the flight, the mission was changed for a location some 35 miles south of Bastogne. Unfortunately, the fighter escort ran low on fuel and was forced to turned back to base. However, no sooner did *SG 4*'s F-8s reach that vicinity than they were set upon by American fighters. Three aircraft and pilots were promptly shot away by P-47s in the area. Oblt. Eissele was killed and Obfhr. Heinrich Zotlöterrer was listed as missing. Zotlöterrer had, in fact, completed his mission, dropping his bomb in the prescribed manner from a glide from 3,000 feet. However, flak was thick near the target and the German pilot's "Black 10" was struck while pulling away. Zotlöterrer made an emergency crash landing and was captured 8 miles southeast of Longuyon. Given the circumstances, the ground-attack group counted itself lucky to escape with no greater losses given the deadly atmosphere over *Kampfraum Bastogne*.

The farmers in the small villages in the Ardennes and Eifel were agog on Christmas Eve. It was as if the sky was falling. Never had they seen so many airplanes come crashing out of the skies, now eerily painted with knotted contrails. Here and there parachutes were seen for those lucky enough to escape their crippled machines. Others less fortunate were found in smoking sites in plowed up fields or a in splintered copse of trees. At the bottom would be the twisted, charred and shattered remains of what had been an airplane. Somewhere about, often unrecognizable would be the pitiful remains of the pilot. It was a sad and terrible way to usher in the holiday season.

In all a total of 44 Allied bombers and 12 fighters were lost in these operations against 125 German fighters claimed shot down. The Luftwaffe would morosely record that 85 German pilots were killed or captured in the great air battle on Christmas Eve including two *Gruppe* and five *Staffel* commanders. Another 21 were wounded. Attempts to cover the armored wedge the Germans had driven into the Ardennes posed an additional hazard for German pilots. Flying over Allied territory, any pilot who bailed out of a stricken plane had a greater chance of being captured. Also, unlike the more range-limited operations associated with defending the Reich, the attempts to cover the offensive further west found Luftwaffe fighters often far from their bases. Damaged or low on fuel from increasingly dangerous encounters with the numerous Allied fighters, Luftwaffe pilots returning from sorties often had no choice but to set down at the nearest available airfield. Even this was fraught with danger, as the more local fields were closer to the front and frequently under attack by Allied fighters. Obtaining fuel and ammunition was almost always less than certain and even the flight back to the home base was exceedingly dangerous as any lone German fighter could easily find itself under assault by the far ranging Allied fighters.

The Allied air forces had set up a layered defense that made German attempts to reach the battlefield difficult indeed. The first line of defense came from the Eighth Air Force which was bombing and strafing the forward Luftwaffe air bases. Next, the Luftwaffe fighters had to negotiate the fighters of the RAF 2nd Tactical Air Force and the XXIX TAC which buzzed over the Eifel region. Finally, the German pilots could expect to run into the XIX and IX TACs over the Bulge. And if that was not enough to make a survival-minded pilot turn back, the entire gauntlet had to be run again to get back to base. There, the Allied fighters would often be waiting, alerted to the return of the German sorties by ground radar or "Y-service" radio intercepts.

The one German bright spot was that their jet bombers at last went into action. Hptm. Diether Lukesch had received orders in early December to make his jet bomber *Einsatzstaffel* of *KG 76* combat ready to support the big German offensive. He moved his Arado 234s to Münster-Handorf on December 18th. However, on arriving, Lukesch, like the Allies, found the weather impossible for operations. But, with the clear sunrise on Christmas Eve, this all changed. At 10:14 AM nine of the single-man jet bombers took off to bomb rail complexes at Liège and Namur. Each bomber carried a single SC-500 1,108 lb. bomb loaded with the Trialen high explosive. Unlike the German piston-powered planes, Lukesch had no difficulty penetrating the Allied fighter screen and reaching his target. The jet bombers of *9 Staffel, KG 76* buzzed along at 560 mph:

> "I attacked a factory complex at Liège in a shallow dive from 13,000 feet releasing my bomb at 6,500 feet. Our airplanes flew individually in loose trail. Since they were fast enough to avoid fighters in a dive and carried no defensive armament, there was little point in wasting fuel getting into formation. On the way back I flew past the tail of a Spitfire engaged on a standing patrol. The British pilot, who had no way of knowing that the only weapon I carried was my pistol, banked away to throw the 'attacker' off his tail."

Uffz. Helmut Rast was third in line in the attack formation, witnessing the violent explosion of Lukesch's bomb drop barely 35 minutes after leaving Burg. As Rast closed in on a long line of freight cars he could see puffs of flak rising ahead of him. Releasing the bomb, his Ar-234 jerked upward gaining speed and altitude. Uffz. Winguth, behind Rast, saw his companion's bomb scatter the parked rail cars in a blazing explosion. The AA fire had missed all of the 234s, and the bombing had left the railyard crippled. The 9 *Staffel* made its way uneventfully back to Münster-Handorf, flying at 6,000 feet at a speed of nearly 500 mph.

The jet sorties were completely successful with the only loss the Arado of Uffz. Winguth which collapsed on its undercarriage during landing. The pilot was not hurt although it would be several days before the 234 was repaired. Undaunted, Lukesch led another mission with eight Ar-234s back to Liège in the afternoon to complete another bomb run. On Christmas Day the attacks continued against Liège, with a further two missions of eight sorties each. However, the Allies were getting wise to the jets and one of the 234s was hit by a British Tempest flown by R. Verran of No. 80 Squadron, RAF. The German pilot, Lt. Alfred Frank, was forced to crash land his jet in Holland, but escaped unscathed nonetheless. Although the few missions run by 9 *Staffel* were mere pin-pricks to the Allies, they clearly showed the promise and superiority of such aircraft; the morale of the tiny jet-bomber unit soared.

Darkness provided a non-technological answer to the daytime Allied fighter patrols. Some of the German phantoms struck Bastogne while others stalked the roads over the battle zone. At 10 PM the available pilots with II/LG 1 were briefed at Ahlhorn to fly over the Luxembourg-Metz area at 30-minute intervals to hit American road traffic. Each plane was to fly over the target area at 1,500 - 4,500 feet for at least half an hour so that the area would be under constant surveillance. The crews were told that the purpose of the nuisance raids was to force American motor columns to black out and cause delays and create other damage if any columns disclosed their presence. Uffz. Hans Fischer took off with his crew of four at 11:30 PM, dutifully located Allied traffic and dropped their fragmentation and anti-personnel bombs on the target. However, on the way back to base their aircraft was hit by a night fighter and the crew was forced to bail out over Holland.

But other raids by the German bombers had more than nuisance value. Bastogne provided an easily located target. Twice during Christmas Eve, beginning at 8:30 PM, the Ju-88 bombers of I/KG 66 and LG 1 struck the town after marking its center with magnesium flares and then strafing after the work was done. The two tons of bombs killed a Belgian nurse, four officers and two dozen wounded paratroopers. The town center was obliterated, but the headquarters of the 101st Airborne was untouched.

Eyeing the improved weather, the British night-fighter command was also determined to strike. That evening, the British put up the 138th and 140th Wings, pumping some 139 Mosquito sorties into the air. Hitting known enemy communications points at Neuerburg, Vianden, Prüm, St. Vith and

271

Euskirchen, the fighter-bombers loosed some 351 500 lb. bombs and thousands of machine gun and cannon rounds on the Germans. A collection of enemy armor was hit in the Forêt de Bullange, the enemy rail center at Gerolstein was left in flames and a ammunition dump at Meurenbruch "disappeared in a gigantic explosion."

That night at his headquarters near Münstereifel, Genfldm. Model, in charge of carrying out *Wacht Am Rhein*, submitted an assessment of the day's aerial carnage. Over the last week, he had attempted to put his best foot forward in describing the situation, but the debacle that Sunday defied optimism. He bluntly informed Hitler and *OKW* that:

> "The enemy air force employment on 24 December reached its former zenith (Normandy). While the focus of the four-engine formations was the rail installations and traffic targets in the Eifel and the area of Cologne-Bonn, the enemy fighter bomber attacks went on almost incessantly over the attack points, as well as the German march and supply routes. On the other hand, flak and German fighters shot down countless enemy planes, but were not able to bring the necessary relief in the front battle area. Because of the attacks on roads, railroad stations and rail installations, which then lead to countless blockages on roads, we can expect considerable disruption of transport. Accelerated repair of areas and roads which have been incapacitated must be taken care of immediately, using all forces and even summoning up the population for assistance."

In the small hours of Christmas morning in Juvincourt, France, the men of Col. Ed Chickering's 367th Fighter Group were huddled under blankets inside their frigid tents. Drained by the day's exhausting schedule, most slept soundly in their barracks. If anything, visions of leave danced in their heads. Off in the distance came the drone of aircraft engines. Slowly the sound got closer suddenly punctuated by the staccato ripping sound of machine guns. The dark shape of a German night fighter swept low over the officer's quarters spraying the area with bullets. "...We did not have time to get to our air raid shelters," Chickering remembered, "All we could do was roll out of bed against the solid brick wall and hope we wouldn't be hit." The "Wheelhouse" where the Colonel and his officers made their quarters was the former home of the Luftwaffe. The night raiders saw to it that Chateau Cormicy received special attention. Each evening for the next week "Pee-Call Charlie" made a nightly appearance. "A persistent son of a gun," observed Lt. Dick Brennan. One man, Lt. Charles B. Hux, was even rudely chased out of the sheet metal outhouse by flying bullets from "Charlie." But with frightful stories of desperate fighting from the Ardennes, the pleasant holiday laxity at the base became a thing of the past: sentries were doubled, everyone carried firearms and some unfortunates were singled out to try to dig foxholes in the frozen ground. Several inebriated pilots in a drunken stupor weaved outside their barracks boasting that they would shoot down "Charlie" with their holstered .45-calibre pistols. None did.

Aftermath. The market square of Bastogne after repeated nighttime bombings by the Luftwaffe. *(NA)*

BELOW: A medium bomber crew goes over their mission plan just before take off. *(HRC)*

273

56.

Douglas A-26 Invader of 416th Bomb Group plunks down bombs on German rail center at Gerolstein, December 25th. *(NASM)*

Jet bomber. An Me-262A2a in action with *KG(J) 51* in December of 1944. It is carrying two SC-250, 551 lb. bombs. *(NASM)*

The Greatest Air Battle: December 24th

German fuel train hit near Satvey, Germany. First sighted by the 67th Tactical Reconnaissance Squadron, other P-47s closed in for the kill. *(NASM)*

BELOW: Tempest V in flight. *(NASM)*

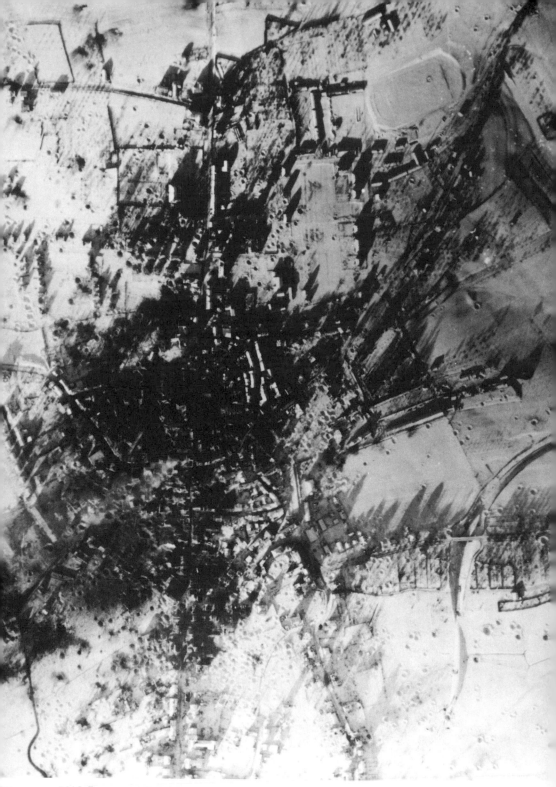

"110 Percent Job." German POW's description of the bombing of the German city of Bitburg, just east of the Ardennes. *(HRC)*

"Black 7." Uffz. Franz Mörl of *2./JG 3* was hit by AA fire from the 413th AA Battalion on Christmas Day and forced to make a crash landing near Eupen. The injured German pilot was taken into captivity. Curious soldiers and civilians look over the shot-up Me-109G-10. *(NA)*

The Luftwaffe pilot of this Me-109 was less fortunate. The German fighter was hit by 40mm anti-aircraft fire and plowed into the ground near Eupen. The pilot was decapitated. *(NA)*

"The one who gets you is the one that you'll never see." This truism was constantly drummed into training fighter pilots, given vivid illustration in this gun camera shot snapped by Lt. George Bauer, a P-47 pilot with XIX TAC. High over the Ardennes, Bauer's gun camera caught the moment when his strikes blasted away a piece of the Me-109's engine cowling. The fact that the German fighter still carries its belly tank indicates that Lt. Bauer probably caught the German fighter by surprise. *(NASM)*

The Right Stuff. Capt. Charles "Chuck" Yeager of the 357th Fighter Group. Yeager flew P-51 Mustang "Glamorous Glennis III" during late 1944. A natural pilot with keen eyesight, Yeager became an ace in a day on October 12, 1944, when he shot down five German fighters in a single engagement over Bremen, Germany. *(HRC)*

Maj. George E. Preddy. The leading U.S. ace in Europe, Preddy shot down six enemy aircraft in a single mission. Ironically, Preddy was killed by U.S. AA fire on December 25, 1944. *(NASM)*

"Mission Maid." This B-17 Flying Fortress of the 457th Bombardment Group is shown after completing its 75th consecutive mission. *(NASM)*

This Martin B-26 had other "marks" added to its prominent notches from its most recent mission. *(HRC)*

2nd Lt. Forrest R. Fegan of Kankakee, IL, 379th Fighter Squadron, 362nd Fighter Group, destroys an Me-109 over the Ardennes on December 26th, 1944. *(NASM)*

BELOW: Any German daylight traffic on the roads around Bastogne became a hunting ground for fighter bombers of the 362nd and 406th Fighter Groups. *(HRC)*

XV

The Saddest Christmas: December 25th

On Christmas Day 1944 the air war over the Ardennes was reaching a climax. The weather over Western Europe featured early morning fog that burned off to "visibility unlimited" by afternoon. The bid for total control of the winter sky witnessed another massive Allied air effort over the Ardennes. The battlefront and the rear areas of *Heeresgruppe B* were hit by almost 1,700 fighters and some 820 medium and heavy bombers. "The enemy carried on with its heavy air attacks on the same focal points," Model's staff reported. "Because of bomb attack on St. Vith, traffic through the town not possible."

The resolute stand of the Luftwaffe on the 23rd had prompted a loan of two of the Eighth Air Forces's P-51 fighter groups. The high-scoring 352nd FG (600 enemy aircraft destroyed) went to Asch and the 361st flew to St. Dizier airfield. The P-51 fighters were to help the Ninth Air Force sweep the German invaders from the battle zone. The 352nd found themselves housed in shabby tents, like the rest of the Ninth Air Force groups housed there. The environment was quite primitive relative to their digs in England and it was freezing cold. There was also the matter of "Bedcheck Charlie" at Asch airfield— a German night fighter similar to that haunting the 367th FG that seemingly visited the base like clockwork each evening.

The lot of the other transferred fighter group was a little better. The yellow-nosed Mustangs of the 361st were housed at St. Dizier, France along with the P-47s of the 405th FG. The Eighth Air Force pilots were housed in an old German barracks and mess hall. It wasn't much, but at least the accommodations were warmer than tents.

Although limited by less favorable weather conditions in England, the Eighth Air Force continued its pounding of German communications centers on Christmas Day. Some 422 bombers were dispatched. A total of 1,091 tons of bombs were dropped. Near the German border, the B-24s hit numerous villages: Wahlen, Pelm, Prüm, Hallschlag, Murenbach, Pronsfeld, Hilleshiem, Marmagen, Nettersheim, Budesheim and Mechernich. A number of targets were hit just to the rear of the German front lines. One of these was an attack on Prüm by the Liberators of the 466th Bomb Group. The tail gunner, Melvin Robinson, had a terrifying experience:

"After bombing troop and supply concentrations near Prüm on Christmas Day 1944, we were about two minutes from the Belgian border when I noticed a few bursts of red flak at 6 o'clock level. I had forgotten what this meant but a few seconds later was quickly reminded when I noticed a series of small bursts in a horizontal line coming directly at my turret. Following this line back I saw a Fw-190 at the end, cannon blinking...There was just enough time to warn the crew, throw the main power switch to my turret, take my guns off safety and start firing as the Fw-190 came into range. I gave him one long burst as he closed from about 800 to under 100 yards. He broke away to my left and repositioned on the tail of a lower B-24. As the Fw-190 rolled he briefly gave me a full side view and I opened fire again, observing several pieces of metal fly off his plane...I swung the turret back to the 6 o'clock position. I was just in time to catch a second Fw-190 coming in at our ship. I leveled the guns down on him and started firing. His bullets were hitting all around me, knocking out the turret Plexiglas. The fighter broke away at about 75 yards and went to my right, coming into firing position on another B-24. Again, I had a good view of his side and in opening fire once more observed pieces of metal come away as the 190 faded out of sight. Instinctively, I brought the turret back to the 6 o'clock position and was confronted with a third Fw 190 coming in at me. I started firing and immediately saw strikes on his cowling. A line of 20mm burst were coming straight at me and I prayed I would get the 190 before he got me. The next thing a 20mm hit the armor plate at the base of my turret and another exploded against the armored glass. The blast shattered the heavy glass and lifted me off my seat and clear out the back of the turret, temporarily stunning me..."

Robinson was blinded by glass splinters and although the B-24 was lucky to make it through the pack of German fighters, the pilot set the plane down in Brussels to get the wounded man to a doctor. Hospitalized, Robinson eventually regained his sight, but his combat days were over.

At Hallschlag the Allied planes dropped flares during the night observing heavy traffic of the *Sixth Panzer Armee* on the roads. Later, at 10 AM on Christmas morning Gren. Lucien Vanarx saw four waves of 12 B-17s drop their bombs on the town. Some thirty men were killed in the first wave as everyone sought cover. At least a dozen trucks went up in flames. The road was cratered and efforts by the *Organization Todt* to repair it were hampered during the day by harassing Allied fighter-bombers. One of these caught a column of 30 vehicles on the Krewinkel-Ormont road and destroyed at least four.

The Saddest Christmas: December 25th

The B-17s struck Kaiserlautern and a multitude of other rail bridges at Bad Münster, Hermeskeil, Ahrweiler, Bad Kreuznach and Eller. The 44 plane strike on the bridge at Ahrweiler inaugurated a series of daily attacks on strategic rail bridges over the following nine days. The aim was to eliminate German rail traffic crossing the Ahr, Rhine and Moselle Rivers to strangle the German logistical capability and force them to truck supplies all the way from the Rhine— a vulnerable and costly process. The participation of Doolittle's fleet was not so extensive as the previous day due to ground fog at the bases in England. Still, a group of 2nd and 3rd Division bombers set off to assail German communications centers. The groups again met stiff Luftwaffe resistance in the air over St. Vith, with the 389th and 467th BGs taking a number of losses. A total of five bombers did not return, including one whose entire crew bailed out over Belgium after their craft was badly damaged. Amazingly, the B-24 continued to limp along unpiloted to crash land at Vowchurch, England.

Some 460 P-51 fighters escorted the huge force. The Germans made a desperate attempt to stop the bomber juggernaut as evidenced by their losses. The fighter groups of the Eighth Air Force claimed 46 enemy aircraft shot down at a cost of only nine Mustangs. Most of the Eighth Air Force fighter groups operated, including the following fighter groups: 4th, 55th, 56th, 352nd, 353rd, 355th, 356th and 479th. The top-scorer of the day was the 479th FG with 14 enemy fighters to its credit. The continuing problem of aircraft identification is illustrated by the losses due to friendly AA fire on this day: one each in the 4th, 352nd and 479th FGs. At Polebrook, England S/Sgt Edgar Matlock of the 351st Fighter Squadron wrote in his diary:

> "It was cold this morning, the ground was frozen and the fog which moved to our vicinity in the morning of the 19th continued throughout the day in undiminished intensity— aside from Christmas services conducted by the chaplains there was little activity at our base. During the afternoon some combat personnel came back to the base in trucks from the bases at which they landed yesterday, skeleton crews were left with the airplanes to return to the base if this infernal fog ever lifts— Christmas dinner was served in all the mess halls at the evening meal. There was turkey, dressing, cranberry sauce, and most of the usual fixings. Our second Xmas in England— low temperatures today 17 degrees F."

The Ninth Air Force tally for Christmas Day reveals a remarkable effort: 1,920 sorties with 1,100 from fighter-bombers, 629 by the mediums, and 177 reconnaissance and 14 night fighter missions. Of these, 1,095 were fighter-bomber sorties who claimed the destruction of 99 armored vehicles, 813 trucks and 24 enemy aircraft shot down for the loss of 24 of their own, mostly lost to enemy flak.

The weather was less advantageous to the north. As a result, the XXIX TAC's 48th and 404th FGs were weatherbound, but the 36th and 373rd FGs flew some 170 sorties in an armed reconnaissance in the northern battle zone in the area Euskirchen-Stavelot-St. Vith. Also, in spite of a "gauntlet of flak," the two groups again harassed the enemy at its airfields in the Bonn-Hangelar area. The 373rd attacked battlefield targets: three tanks north of Weiswampach and motor transport near Steinbruck and St. Vith. The 36th FG attacked well-camouflaged German transport near Euskirchen and Büllingen and flew an armed reconnaissance over the Marche area. The other two TACs put in one of the most concentrated displays of air power in the war— running wide ranged fighter sweeps as far east as the Rhine River, while constantly attacking the enemy on the ground and amassing an astonishing score on enemy motor transport on the roads below. The total count amounted to 813 motor transport, 99 armored vehicles as well as a litany of destroyed gun positions, rail cuts and ammunition dumps.

Pete Quesada's IX TAC put some 482 sorties into the air, delivering a total of 159 tons of bombs onto the heads of the Germans in the salient. Within Quesada's command, sightings of the enemy were numerous: 113 German aircraft were counted in the actions on Christmas Day. At least 229 of the sorties were over the battle zone. The 352nd Fighter Group with some 79 sorties was vectored on a gaggle of forty Me-109s sighted around Koblenz at 11:30 AM; in the ensuing action six of the fighters were sent spiraling to the ground. Capt. William J. Stangel shot down two of the Messerschmitts. On the way back to Asch, one flight of the group ran into four Fw-190s north of Maastricht shooting down all. The victor was Capt. Charles J. Cesky who went on a rampage in his P51 Mustang, "Diann":

> "We were in the vicinity of Maastricht when I sighted four Fw-190s crossing our path at about 500 feet above us. I led my wingman in climbing up and to the rear of them. When we got into position, I opened fire on the third in the enemy formation, observing strikes in the cockpit, motor and wings. The Nazi pilot bailed out. While still in a turn, I fired on the German in the number two position, and landed hits in the wings and cockpit. Parts of the plane came flying off and then the 190 went into an uncontrollable spin, with smoke pouring from the fuselage. Proceeding on to the leader, I followed him around in a tight spiral until at 4,000 feet the pilot bailed out. I saw the plane crash. Meanwhile, my wingman accounted for the fourth 190, causing the pilot to bail out without firing a single shot."

Only one of the P-51s did not return from the mission. The 390th squadron of the 366th Fighter Group contacted the 30th Infantry Division for targets, but at 11,000 feet they met 15 Fw-190s south of Stavelot. In another aerial battle east of Liège four Me-109s were engaged, with one shot down. Against ground targets, the 389th Squadron attacked 20 plus German tanks near Manhay at the behest of the 7th Armored Division. After the attack the panzers were seen to turn tail and head south for cover. Another eight P-47s attacked German vehicles moving through Winterspelt and the 391st Squadron hit some 25 German vehicles moving on the road to St. Vith. Eight were claimed destroyed and some of the trucks exploded as if they carried

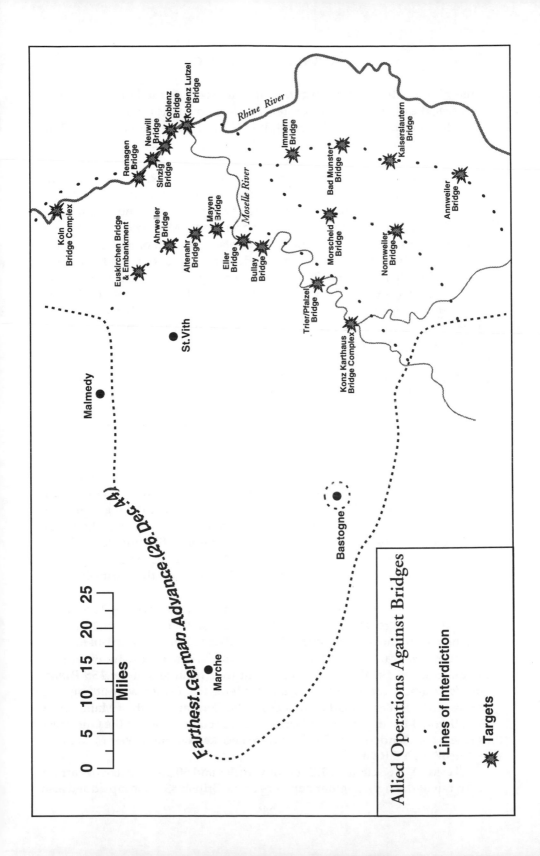

Koln
Bridge Complex

Remagen
Bridge

Neuwill
Bridge

Koblenz
Bridge

Koblenz Lutzel
Bridge

Sinzig
Bridge

Euskirchen Bridge
& Embankment

Ahrweiler
Bridge

Mayen
Bridge

Immern
Bridge

Bad Munster
Bridge

Kaiserslautern
Bridge

Altenahr
Bridge

Eller
Bridge

Bullay
Bridge

Morscheld
Bridge

Nonnweiler
Bridge

Annweiler
Bridge

Trier/Pfalzel
Bridge

Konz Karthaus
Bridge Complex

Rhine River

Moselle River

St. Vith

Malmedy

Earthest German Advance (26 Dec '44)

Bastogne

Marche

Miles

0 5 10 15 20 25

Allied Operations Against Bridges

• • • Lines of Interdiction

✳ Targets

ammunition. All scattered into the trees as soon as the bombing began. However, the light flak was accurate and intense over the target and one P-47 went down near Andler after being hit. The 391st also contacted the 30th Division which vectored the P-47s to attack German positions just west of Trois Ponts.

The 365th Fighter Group continue to operate its P-47s from Chievres, Belgium while its ground crews transferred to Metz. Maj. George R. Brooking attacked enemy transport scurrying through Bitburg and south of St. Vith. In a bizarre episode, the 387th Squadron under Maj. Arlo C. Henry was attacked over Charleroi by a lone P-51 Mustang with an orange nose and a silver rudder. In spite of this strange incident, the P-47s continued with their mission dispatching some five enemy vehicles and several motorcycles moving eastward from Bastogne to Trois Vierges. Just then, a second silver P-51 made three hostile passes at the Squadron. The "Hell Hawks" claimed to have identified it as belonging to the enemy. Other missions struck German transport near Bitburg and Ettelbruck. The final mission on Christmas Day consisted of an attack on a 200-vehicle enemy convoy sighted passing through the town of Beho. As they strafed and bombed the enemy traffic, the pilots watched the Germans abandoning their vehicles and running for cover. "Achtung Jabos!" indeed. While the squadron was in the process of the mission, a box of B-17s passed overhead. Ten enemy Fw-190s were seen closing on the bombers, aiming to take them out. 1st Lt. Roswell D. Roberts saw the German planes diving to attack and headed to intercept them. Then all of a sudden there were two Fw-190s on his tail; his wingman was able to pull both off. Roberts then caught two of the Fw-190s with a long deflection shot at 4 o'clock high. The two were claimed as damaged and the last of the "Hell Hawks" fighters landed back at Chievres. On their way home, the pilots reported that all the villages around Bitburg were aflame. Meanwhile, Christmas at the new base at Metz was ushered in by seven Luftwaffe bombs which dropped without warning on the unfinished airstrip.

At 3 PM the P-38s of the 370th Fighter Group were bounced by 11 Fw-190s southwest of Liège. The P-38s turned the tables on their assailants, however, and three were shot down without loss. The 370th Fighter Group put in some 70 sorties and was all over the battlefield on Christmas day. Two flights of the P-38s struck St. Vith and another sent the grenadiers of the *1SS Panzer Division* running for cover near Grand Halleux, where they were attempting to cross the Salm River. Other attacks hit the Germans south of Malmédy. A final flight of the day caught a German motor column east of the Our River northeast of Vianden. Two Fw-190s were knocked out northwest of Koblenz by the 67th TAC R Group.

All told, IX TAC claimed 275 motor vehicles and 50 pieces of enemy armor taken out of the fight. Fighter bombers of the British 83rd Group added also to the German torment, hitting enemy motor transport and armor near St. Vith. One squadron of the 366th FG was vectored west of this road center where it discovered at least twenty tanks and fifty other vehicles attacking to the north (likely the *9 SS Panzer Division*). Ten tanks and trucks were claimed and the enemy was seen to halt its thrust to the north after the air strike. P-47s from the 368th FG spied a large concentration of the enemy northeast of Prüm with claims of 101 motor transport and another six armored vehicles. Near the Meuse, Combat Command B of the U.S. 2nd Armored Division was involved in flushing out the enemy near the town of Celles. In an admirable display of air-ground support, the tankers marked a wooded area near Foy-Notre-Dame with smoke with one squadron of P-38s bombing and strafing the copse of trees until ground control told the fighters to stop because the Shermans were moving in.

That night the tired 422nd Night Fighter Squadron flew 23 defensive patrol sorties in the St. Vith-Kall - Dahlem area. Although a Ju-88 and Me-110 were destroyed without loss, the effort could not still the more numerous German night missions.

The IX BD also put in another big effort with some 629 medium bombers dropping 1,237 tons of bombs on road and road targets at Konz-Karthaus (386 BG escorted by 361 FG), Nonnweiler (394 BG) and road bridges at Taben, Keuchingen. Road centers near the enemy offensive front were also struck: St. Vith, Bitburg, Wegenrohr, Irrel, Vianden, Ahrdorf, Ahutte, Hilleshiem and Münstereifel. Over the battlefield St. Vith was on the receiving end of 160 tons of high explosives; Vianden was hit by 23 tons. The 416th BG plunked down its bombs on Gerolstein with the *167 Volksgrenadier Division* passing through the town the following day reporting traffic able to move through the town only at walking speed. Escort was provided by the Mustangs of the 352nd Fighter Group. Lively enemy opposition was encountered over Koblenz, although only three bombers were lost. The challenge to the Allied bombers came from *III/JG 6, III/JG 11, JG 27, IV/JG 54* and *I/JG 77*, all of which were ordered by *Luftflotte West* to intervene. A total of 223 of the bombers were damaged, primarily by enemy flak.

The Allied pounding east of the battle zone continued; the Germans were gradually being forced to shift their rail heads supporting the offensive back to the Rhine and to try and make fuller use of the road net. However, the fighter-bombers relentlessly stalked the highways for German motor transport; so debilitating was their attack, that supply movement was all but halted during daylight hours. In spite of the Luftwaffe opposition, the bombs rained down and some of the German occupied targets, like Bitburg became *Mondlandschaft*— lunar landscapes. The town had been hit on the 19th, 24th and 25th. One prisoner threading his way through the ruins observed that, "Bombs were dropped in bomb craters of the day before...Bitburg is done for; your Air Force did a 110 per cent job." It would be the end of the month before the laborers of *Organization Todt* had cleared away the rubble. Genfldm. Model's assessment of the air situation had become more pessimistic:

> "The enemy carried on with its heavy air attacks on the same focal points given the favorable weather conditions of 25 December. The employment of the German air force, however, prevented them from repeated accurate bomb drops. The numerous area of destruction of rail lines is bringing the transport situation into question. The rapid repair of damaged areas is being urgently pursued by appealing to the population."

What Model did not say was that much of the German formations, including reinforcements, were virtually unable to move in daylight. That morning, the *11 Panzer Division* was attempting to come to the aid of the sorely pressed *Seventh Armee*. Leaving after breakfast at 7:30 AM, they found that when they tried to move forward from Rittersdorf to Obersgeggen, the division attracted the ire of roving fighter-bombers. They were forced to cancel the move until after dark. The *IISS Panzerkorps* reported that "because of bomb attacks on St. Vith, traffic through that town is not possible." Similarly, 200 replacements for the *48 Volksgrenadier Regiment* were attacked as their dozen trucks moved from Münstereifel to Losheimergraben. Uffz. Ernst Walter saw three fighter-bombers destroy five of the trucks they were riding in, killing two men and wounding eight. The *Jabos* had struck so suddenly that no one had time to disperse.

The greatest effort on Christmas Day came from the XIX TAC which recorded 596 sorties and mercilessly pounded the German forces around Bastogne.[71] Targets over the battle zone were lucrative. The recorded ground claims of Weyland's command were astronomic: 766 vehicles, 74 tanks and armored vehicles and 71 gun positions. Press correspondent Demaree Bess was present in the salient to the south of Bastogne as the American fighter-bombers mercilessly battered the German held towns in front of Patton's impatient armor:

> "I traveled in a jeep to the battle zone between Arlon and Bastogne in Belgium. The 101st Airborne Division was making its celebrated stand at Bastogne, and we soon caught up with the advanced outposts of the 4th Armored Division which was pushing through to relieve them...The destination of our jeep was an observation post on a hill near the surfaced highway where we had been told we could get the best view of the day's battle. We reached it early in the afternoon, just in time to see the panorama of ground and aerial warfare staged

---

71 The XIX TAC was concerned, however, that its pilots might be getting a little too carried away. Instructions for Christmas Day read: "Pilots will be reminded that road bridges will not be attacked unless specifically requested by ground units. If the targets are found on the roads, other enemy installations close to the battle area should be attacked...The amount of road traffic on the roads leading towards Echternach may indicate a build up in this area for the purpose of launching an attack against the shoulder of XII Corps." Meanwhile, Maj. Gen. William B. Kean of IX TAC, provided the emphasis for operations that day: the junction of XVIII Airborne and VII Corps near Manhay "where the enemy is attempting penetration."

with all the perfection of a Hollywood pageant. From our hill, the rolling plains of Belgium stretched out for several miles, dotted with frequent patches of evergreen woods. On this Christmas Day, the countryside was idyllic in its beauty— the ground white with fine snow, contrasted with the dark green of pine and cedar clumps. For the moment everything was so quiet that we instinctively lowered our voices...Then, behind us, came the roar of planes. They passed almost over our heads— a flight of fighter bombers— and then turned in a diving attack upon the silent village. One after another, they dropped their bombs and were far up in the air again, soon out of sight. Great clouds of smoke and bursts of flame rose from the picturesque little houses, and at the same time the whole countryside below us sprang into activity...we saw a column of tanks advancing upon the village...We could imagine how the Germans must have felt, with no German planes taking part in that battle."

A major feature of the Allied air operations on Christmas Day was the concentrated bombing attack on the town of St. Vith. The IX Bomber Division with the 323rd and 387th Groups struck the town with 70 B-26 bombers dropping 135 tons of high explosives. The assault caused the Germans to immediately evacuate the town. The following day the aircraft of RAF Bomber Command struck St. Vith as well with 1,146 sorties and over a thousand tons of bombs. The 370th, 366th and 362nd Fighter Groups also joined in on the conflagration, bombing, strafing and firing rockets at the roads in the vicinity of the communications center. The 362nd FG claimed one Me-109 destroyed over the town after its 379th Squadron had bombed twenty enemy vehicles moving south of St. Vith towards Grüfflingen. As a result of the sustained bombardment, German traffic was completely halted through St. Vith for a period of two days while workers' removed the rubble and bomb craters.

At ground zero, St. Vith was hell. Many houses were on fire and the vital highway to the west was blocked by expansive bomb craters and debris. Vehicles of the *18 Volksgrenadier Division* vanished in the torrent of bombs along with half a dozen men of the division. Following the attack, the nervous traffic moving through the town had to make their way across the frozen fields to the west which were under American artillery fire. Three German engineer battalions were called in to begin road repairs immediately. They toiled throughout Christmas night. But everyone was evacuated the following morning; an intercepted Allied radio message had called on another massive air attack on St. Vith the following day. The hour-long bombing came as predicted. When he came back to St. Vith, Uffz. Walter Schwarz found it a ghost town. The marketplace was a mass of rubble and bomb craters. Passage was completely blocked. Word had it that 47 men of the *3 Engineer Battalion* had been buried alive in a shelter and more were missing and wounded from the *755 GHQ Engineer Battalion*. Traffic had to be totally detoured around St. Vith, but by 9 PM all the major craters had been filled and small convoys carrying critical supplies attempted to move through, only to come under attack by the ubiquitous Allied fighter bombers. After this experience, German motor columns attempted to negotiate the blasted streets of St. Vith only at night. Work began on the 27th to repair the nearby rail lines. However, completion of this task was problematic given the frequent interruptions by Allied strafing. In the early morning hours of December 27th a mission by the 155th Night Photo Squadron over the town showed all roads blocked by a series of massive craters and huge piles of debris.

In the air, the 405th Fighter Group was again active, claiming 147 destroyed German motor transport and engaged in numerous encounters with an aggressive enemy. During one of these missions, Lt. W.A. "The Brow" Barrow chased an Me-109 into the ground and Lt. Francis "Buzz" Norr mixed it up with six Fw-190s. The German swarm seemed experienced and aggressive, but in less than five minutes four of the German planes were shot down. Norr bagged his second Fw-190 in as many days. However, these operations were not without cost; one American pilot, Lt. John A. McNeely, Jr. struggled to shake two Fw-190s on his tail and called for help. Lt. Larry Gaughran responded. His first burst of gunfire convinced the first German pursuer to break off; a second burst at the second sent the Fw-190 spiraling into the ground. McNeely limped away in his smoking craft only to go down before he reached friendly lines. Other 405th pilots claimed three more German planes in the melee. Ground claims were also substantial. The 510th Squadron claimed many vehicles and a number of tanks at Vianden, Sinspelt, Neuerburg. The 511th Squadron dropped napalm on Bollendorf and attacked troop convoys on the roads near Vianden. East of the battle zone, the 510th Squadron attacked "bumper to bumper" German columns near Oberkall and Binsfeld while the 509th bombed German positions to the rear of the *Seventh Armee* near Meckel and Wissmansdorf. The 511th attacked a dozen enemy tanks seen south of Prüm and a railway tunnel near Neuerburg.

The 474th FG's 428th Squadron fired at six dug in German tanks near Manhay and strafed a number of well-camouflaged motor vehicles. Later the 429th Squadron struck 12 German tanks observed in the same vicinity; two were claimed destroyed. Another attack by the 429th was led by the P-51s of the 67th TAC R to Rochefort where a courtyard was pointed out with six German tanks from the *Panzer Lehr* division. Fourteen 500 lb. bombs were dropped. Other attacks were made on German troop and vehicle concentrations in Dochamps, Humain and Bourdon-Marche and Champlon. However, the 474th and its 428th Squadron would long remember Christmas, 1944 as a particularly sad one. That morning in an armed reconnaissance near Pronsfeld the group lost Capt. Leland W. "Smitty" Smith, one of its better officers when he was hit by small arms fire while leading a diving attack on German vehicles seen there. Smith never pulled out of the dive and crashed in a field one mile south of the town in a tremendous explosion.

Other tragedy struck the squadron later in the day when Lt. Bobbie R. Rankin was killed at 1:55 PM while leading an attack on a number of dug-in enemy tanks seen near Manhay. The third and final mission that Christmas was flown over St. Vith where a group of a dozen enemy tanks were attacked heading northeast out of the town. However, as it was nearly dark with a gathering ground haze, the results of the strike were masked.

An armored drive by the *2nd SS Panzer Division* towards the Meuse was halted by attacks from the 368th Fighter Group. "The Germans seem to be moving their equipment off the roads," one of its fighters observed, "at times leaving a few worthless cars sitting on side roads with the hope that our fighter-bombers will expend their ammunition on them instead of more lucrative targets." But errors of identification still plagued attempts at close support. A Christmas Day attack by P-47s of the 366th Fighter Group in support of the battle to finish off *Kampfgruppe Peiper* near Petit-Coo resulted in losses on both sides. In one of the verified cases of "tank-busting" the fighter-bombers scared a German tank crew out of their *Königstiger* with near misses, but then turned on the nearby 740th Tank Battalion. The mistaken bombing and strafing damaged one Sherman and wounded three men.

Bad weather in England had precluded another air resupply mission to Bastogne on Christmas, although this did not stop the Ninth Air Force fighter-bombers. Around the town, the 406th and 354th Fighter Groups continued to punish the *26th Volksgrenadier* and *15th Panzer Grenadier Divisions*, flying 115 and 24 sorties respectively. It was the busiest day of the month for the 354th who flew ten missions, many pilots flying twice in between gulping down turkey dinner at Rosieres-en-Hay between sorties. The enemy took note of the effort. The motorized *33 Artillery Regiment* reported that two well-placed bombs from fighter bombers had destroyed four of its 150mm guns and then machine gunned most of the crews as they ran for cover. Close by, the *901 Panzergrenadier Regiment* in the village of Lutrebois was ravaged by combined air and artillery action. The regimental command post there was blown apart.

Both the 362nd (377th Squadron) and 406th (513th Squadron) FGs shared in the conflagration of Tintange, south of Bastogne, watching from the air as 4th Armored troops surged forward following the strikes. The 362nd flew nine missions which ranged widely over the front: the 378th Squadron struck German troops and transport moving through Clerf and nearby Marnach and *Volksgrenadiers* forming for an attack in Sibret, just west of Bastogne. Bourscheid and Diekirch were also hit, foiling an attempt by the Germans to assemble a counterattack force to blunt Patton's advance.

The 406th was all over the Bastogne vicinity. Its targets Christmas Day read like a manifest of the surrounding place names: Lutrebois, Assenois, Sainlez, Bourcy, Lutremange, Noville. "Maestro," the 101st Airborne air controller requested special attention be paid to troop concentrations northwest of the town who had recently put in a desperate attack on the American defenders. The 406th obliged; enemy troop concentrations in the streets of Bertogne, Morhet, Remagne, Flamierge, Salle and Givry all were sprayed with napalm, bombs, rockets and bullet fire. Although two aircraft were lost to the increasing flak concentration, the intrepid 406th submitted claims of 156 German vehicles torched that day along with 16 tanks and 21 half-tracks destroyed. Later a German order to ground units in the vicinity was intercepted: "Due to the very favorable weather conditions for enemy operations, we have suffered unreasonably high losses in vehicles through hostile fighter-bombers. It is therefore ordered that all ration supply trips be made at night or when the weather does not permit air operations."

The 367th Fighter Group hit German motor and rail targets near Trier. Lt. Claude M. Cely led a squadron to bomb railroad yards in the town that afternoon. Returning from the mission after leaving the yard a twisted tangle of rails, the group of Lightnings looked for targets of opportunity. Lt. Harry Curtis spied a group of halftracks and swooped down to strafe them in "Pattie Ann" the last of the 394th Squadron's original 25 P-38s. But as Curtis closed in on the enemy vehicles, his aircraft was hit and the pilot fell to his death.

The 56th Fighter Group was again in action in support of the Eighth Air Force. The group flew a fighter sweep in the Bonn-Koblenz area vectored by MEW. Capt. Mike Jackson sighted a group of about 30 Me-109s and shot down one of the enemy planes in a firing pass at nearly point blank range. Capt. Cameron Hart, leading the 62nd Squadron, chased down an Me-109 using water injection and blew the plane apart with an attack from 600 yards. So quickly did it all take place that Hart had to sharply barrel-roll to avoid the flaming debris. Altogether, the "Wolfpack" was credited on Christmas Day with downing eight enemy planes for no losses.

While the weather was excellent, the British decided to mount a supreme effort. The 2nd TAF again contributed in a large fashion. With some 371 aircraft, 83 Group carried out an extensive aerial reconnaissance between Düren and Prüm with claims of 170 motor transport and six armored vehicles destroyed. 193 and 266 Squadrons flew ground attacks against German rail movement to the east north of the Ruhr. After just having destroyed an enemy train, the Typhoons were set upon by a large gaggle of Me-109s and Fw-190s. 226 Squadron suffered a loss of two aircraft, but Flg. Off. Bulleid of 193 Squadron shot down one Fw-190 and Flt. Lt. Smith damaged another, although himself being shot up as well. Thirteen Spitfires of 401 Squadron hunted down two Me-109s in the mid-morning near Duisberg. Flt. Lt. MacKay knocked out one and Flt. Lt. Connell and Flt. Sgt. Woodill shared the victory over the other. Unfortunately another British flyer was hit by debris from the second destroyed Messerschmitt. Squadron Leader Everards was forced to bail out over German territory.

But later, just after noon, Flt. Lt. Boyle of 411 Squadron shot down a German Me-262 moving over his own airfield! The machine was the mount of Oblt. Lamel of *KG(J) 51* who had been returning from a bombing mission near Liège. Lamle saw the fighters closing on his tail as he approached Rheine airfield, but he had already throttled back on the turbojets and was a sitting duck for Flt. Lt. Boyle. The Canadian squadron then encountered three more jets over Eupen while patrolling the airspace between Malmédy and Houffalize at 14,000 feet. Sqdn. Ldr. Collier of 403 Squadron managed to destroy one of the jets. Again, the victim was from *KG(J) 51*, this time being Fw. Hans Meyer. However, this victory was marred by the news that a Spitfire from 416 Squadron had been mistakenly shot down by an American P-47. The Tempests of 486 Squadron also scored a victory over an Me-262 which was intercepted south of Arnhem. Flg. Off. R.D. Bremner observed the German pilot to bail out of his stricken jet, but no parachute was seen. Flt. Lt. Sherk of 402 Squadron, RCAF sighted a lone Fw-190 from the mount of his Spitfire southeast of Düren. He shot down the plane, which may have been Uffz. Wolfgang Rosenow of *11./JG 11*. That evening Rosenow's Fw-190A-8 did not return from its mission to Euskirchen.

The British bombers were out once more for a daytime bombing of the Ardennes. Some 36 bombers of 2 Group attacked Junkerath and environs just to the rear of the *Sixth Panzer Armee*. The mediums had orders to hit the towns of Tondorf and Stadtkyll. No. 98 Squadron managed to paste scores of enemy trucks snaking through Stadtkyll, although encountering heavy flak. A number of planes could not take off due to wing icing and the men of 226 Squadron had the frustration of being only minutes away from their targets when they were called back since the poor weather had prevented their fighter escort from coming along. Most of them couldn't see the logic since American fighters were so numerous that it hardly seemed a reason to cancel the mission. "We never saw so many Allied fighters in the air!" complained one. Late that afternoon, the mists closed in on the British airfields as the pilots hove back to their bases. Landings were precarious. But once that was done, the men relaxed. The 2 Group began with the traditional Christmas dinner, the officers having waited on the enlisted men. The men of 226 Squadron remembered that their French cook did his best to help capture the Christmas spirit. For a short time, the cares and worries of the war were forgotten with "much dining, wining and inebriation."

At the tip of the German advance, the *2nd Panzer Division* was surrounded, out of gas and under a very heavy air attack, Typhoons of the British 83rd Group firing rockets into the panzer troops hiding in the Bois de Geavelant. The reconnaissance battalion of the division was trapped in a pocket near Foy Notre Dame where it was assailed by the twin-tailed P-38s of the 370th Fighter Group. Some miles southeast of this scene, Gen. Fritz Bayerlein of the *Panzer Lehr Division* was attempting to effect a rescue of his cohorts in the pocket. He had set his forward command post up at Humain ushering his panzers and grenadiers forward. The sky was clear and full of gnat-like Allied fighter bombers. Evidence of what was happening to 2 *Panzer* was seen in Havrenne as Bayerlein's troops passed through the village. The surrounding roads were littered with destroyed artillery, trucks and even tanks which appeared to have been set afire by Allied fighter bombers. As Bayerlein attempted to move his tanks up to punch through to the pocket, he could see that the fighter bombers up ahead pummeling the surrounded pocket. Over his right shoulder the previous day, he had seen the long procession of the American transport planes bound to resupply Bastogne. Other word from his division's rear revealed that his supply lines, extending back beyond the American hold-out at Bastogne, were suffering severe losses. A whole flak battery had been caught on the road and wiped out, his tank repair workshop at Birresborn was bombed into uselessness and the road to Champlon was reportedly littered with blackened and burned out supply vehicles. As it was, petrol was very short and every drop had to be brought up the treacherous roads from Troisdorf; his men were now reduced to draining gasoline from destroyed Allied or German vehicles. Another relief force of the *2nd Panzer* reported itself under a "hellish fire" from air-directed artillery and fighter-bombers around Hargimont and was forced to pull back. As Bayerlein made his bid, the pesky artillery spotter planes sighted his armored column near Buissonville and brought it under a withering bombardment. He too was turned back, losing half a dozen vehicles in the process. Bitterly, not a single German fighter was to be seen.

Later that afternoon Bayerlein returned to his rear headquarters at the marketplace in St. Hubert. There, his staff had hastily decorated the hotel to make things at least a little festive to capture the Christmas spirit. But Bayerlein was greatly annoyed by word that his troubled supply units were being ejected from their billets in Hives, south of La Roche. With the Allied command of the air, they could not hope to move until nightfall. It seems that a Belgian fascist, Leon Degrelle, had taken over the town with a train-load of lesser quislings with the intent of setting up a stooge government for the reconquered territory. The panzer commander thought of all the troubles with the fighter-bombers and the resulting delays and supply troubles. If only the German military preparation could have been so thorough! But Bayerlein's sarcastic assessment on this ridiculous situation was suddenly drowned out by the buzzing sound of rapidly approaching low-altitude aircraft. Several fighter-bombers roared overhead as bombs exploded in unison. Others zoomed low over the town and let go a machine gun blast that went right through the front windows of the hotel. Everyone dove for cover. No great harm had been done, but any pretense of Christmas gaiety was shattered with the windows. During the night, with the P-38 Lightnings off his back, Bayerlein moved up his Panther battalion to Custinne ready to break through to the pocket at first light on the 26th. But that morning brought attacks against his flank by the 2nd Armored Division and word from fugitives of the *2 Panzer* that their comrades in the pocket had been liquidated and further attacks would be useless. It was just as well, Bayerlein thought, for with the clear sky the fighter bomber would soon be darting about. He ordered his tanks to hide in the woods until nightfall.

Bayerlein's tormentors were the P-38 Lightnings of the 370th Fighter Group and the rocket firing Typhoons of the British 83 Group. All through the day the 370th had harassed the Germans advance westward. The first flight out had bombed and strafed German troops near the crossroads at Champlon. A second flight struck the *2SS Panzer* in and around Manhay. The P-38s of the 3rd flight coordinated their attack with Combat Command B of the 2nd Armored Division who marked the targets with smoke. 402 Squadron "bombed and strafed a wooded area bounded by P-0784 to P-0782 (just east of Celles) until the controller requested they stop firing as infantry was moving in." Ninth Air force claims (again to be taken with a generous grain of salt) amounted to 813 motor vehicles and 99 tanks.[72] However, combined with the grinding assault of the 2nd Armored Division on the ground, the coordinated attack had decimated the *2 Panzer*. The losses amounted to some 3,700 men, 81 armored vehicles, 405 trucks and some 81 guns. When the elite panzer unit crossed back to the German border a month later, it counted only 1,500 frost-bitten grenadiers and a few Panther tanks.

The Luftwaffe continued to make a bid for air space over the battlefield and fighters assigned to support *Wacht Am Rhein* totalled some 600 sorties. However, German presence in the southern half of the battlefield was reduced by a close screen of XIX TAC fighters. They reported that "the enemy seems to be taking a greater interest in the Luxembourg area. He is aggressive and sometimes enthusiastic in combat." German losses were considerable; the Eighth Air Force recorded 46 enemy aircraft destroyed in its daily operations; the Ninth added another 34 claims. Although the decrypts could only be signaled days later, ULTRA listened in as the Luftwaffe demanded greater attention to protecting the German ground forces, many of which had complained the previous day of insufficient air cover against the damaging Allied fighter-bombers:

"...main task is protection of spearheads and flanks...avoid engaging four-engined aircraft, and concentrate on freeing attacking forces by preventing Allied low-level tactical bombing strikes...revision of tactics, avoiding large unwieldy battle formations, splitting up instead into formations of 12-15 aircraft for

---

72 Examination of the records of ground claims versus actual damages for various incidents in the Ardennes battle suggests that the ratio of claims to actual losses against enemy motor transport was typically high by a factor of 5:1 and 10:1 for enemy armor. USAAF claims against enemy aircraft were generally good, although submitted claims and inclusion of "probables" invariably inflated the actual enemy losses as recorded by the Luftwaffe. These results are also born out by a methodical study of ground claims by the 2nd Tactical Air force's Operational Research Section.

combing the front area...attempt to extract last ounce from pilots, appeal to honor, denunciation of lack of zest, injunctions to continue even with misfiring engines and faulty drop tanks on pain of court martial...further mobilization of night-fighters for ground-strafing..."

JG 26, Priller's *"Schlugeter" Geschwader*, reported two kills at the cost of three of their planes east of the battle zone. Fw. Meindl's parachute failed to open and Fw. Hoppe was killed in his "Brown 13" near Dortmund. However, *JG 27* lost 13 pilots in these actions without a single claim of their own. The *Geschwader* had its fighters spread all along the battlefield.

The Me-109G-14s of *JG 3* from Paderborn were assigned to provide air cover for the German spearhead near Dinant. This proved an elusive objective. Just west of St. Vith the German pilots were jumped by a pack of P-51 Mustangs quickly losing ten pilots. Two of the Mustangs pulled in behind the aircraft of Uffz. Markl and pumped bullets into his engine. Markl was able to jump from his craft, but was hurt when he slammed into the frozen ground near the V-1 launching sites at Tondorf. Two other pilots were lost. Gefr. Orth died near Merten and Fw. Kühn did not return to base. That afternoon, the U.S. Liberator bombers of the 467th Bomb Group were streaming over the Hohes Venn north of Malmédy, when *IV/JG 3* under Hptm. Hubert Weydenhammer struck. The Fw-190s closed in for the kill, sending a whole string of the Liberators crashing into the dense forests between St. Vith and Liège. One of the attackers, Lt. Werner Mebesius was hit by AA fire as he himself pumped bullets into a Liberator. His "White 19" lost power and the pilot jumped from his stricken A-8 to be taken captive near Eupen.[73] Soon, however, the P-51s of the 479th Fighter Group showed up at the scene. Hptm. Weydenhammer was last seen maneuvering into position behind a Liberator. He along with Fw. Clässen, Uffz. Gaspers and Obfhr. Vaitl failed to return from the encounter. The 479th reported engaging some 15 Fw-190s and chased one of these into the ground. Two others from *JG 3* took to their parachutes becoming prisoners upon reaching the ground. However, one Fw-190, that of Fw. Hoffmann managed to out dive his pursers, although running into American flak. Somehow, however, he managed to return to tell of the debacle at Köln-Wahn. His Focke Wulf was peppered like swiss cheese.

The attempt to stop the medium bombers of the Ninth U.S. Air Force involved the Me-109G-14s of *III/JG 6*. Emerging from Oldenburg, the German fighters ran afoul of the Allied fighters between Cologne and Düren. Uffz. Scherf was killed over Bergheim as his *12 Staffel* attempted to flee from

---

73 The career of 22-year old Lt. Mebesius is a telling indicator of Luftwaffe fortunes in 1944. He was transferred from twin-engined training to fighters in June of 1944, joining *13./JG 3* later that month. However, in July he was injured in an attack on Memmingen airfield and remained hospitalized until the end of October at which point he rejoined his *Staffel* at Schafstädt. On November 27th he was shot down by four Mustangs while making an emergency landing at an airfield in northeastern Germany after having trouble with this Fw-190A-8.

the actions over the Erft River. Other Messerschmitts ran into Allied resistance near Cologne; Lt. Siegfried Dönch and Obgefr. Werner did not return from their sorties. The *Gruppe* ran into the Typhoons of 193 Squadron near Quackenbrück. The British claimed one downed German fighter which was almost certainly the mount of Oblt. Paris of the *Gruppenstab*. Paris was seriously wounded and died a few weeks later. Just before noon, another Me-109 slammed into the ground at high speed near Bergisch-Gladbach. Little of the pilot's body or the aircraft could be recovered. Even today, the identity of the pilot is unknown.

South of Cologne *IV/JG 54* fought a desperate battle. Lt. Franke died over Heckenbach and Obfhr. Ernst Hoffmann was unable to escape from his Fw-190A-8 before it augured into the frozen ground near Walberberg. Ofw. Eugen Lude fell into a forest near Duisburg and Fhr. Erwin Schommert died in Jammelshofen where he was later buried. Eight pilots perished in the actions that day; only a small fraction of the scattered "Green Hearts" pilots returned to Vörden.

In the notorious region between Bonn and Cologne two pilots of *I/JG 77*, including Uffz. Helmut Forrell, were lost and *III/JG 11* reported four pilots missing from actions in the same vicinity. Further south, over the Eifel, *I/JG 11* ran into Allied fighters and Uffz. Holzinger and Weismüller were lost in their Fw-190A-8.

The jets of *KG 51* were committed to battle in speedy strafing runs on Liège. These were the three Me-262-A2s encountered by the Canadian pilots near the German border. Cover for landing the returning jets was being flown by *III/JG 54* of Hptm Robert Weiss in its first combat with its new Fw-190D-9s. Unfortunately, no sooner had the group gotten airborne over Rheine base than a swarm of Allied fighters scattered the formation. The result was that one of the Me-262s was shot down. Similarly, *KG 76* with its jet bombers twice successfully struck two railway stations in Liège with 16 sorties, but lost one plane to a Tempest of No. 80 Squadron, RAF.

The fighter escort for the Eighth Air Force bombers was heavily engaged on the 25th. The 4th Fighter Group wiped out a dozen enemy fighters in combat over Bonn, but lost two Mustangs. Lt. Poage became a POW, and one of the group's aces, Lt. Donald Emerson, was killed when his aircraft was hit by German ground fire over Belgium. The 355th Fighter Group (Lt. Col. Everett W. Stewart) also ran into a huge group of at least 75 German fighters attacking a group of bombers over Hamburg and shot down several of these as well as breaking up the attack on the "big friends."

But the real news on Christmas Day for the Eighth Air Force was the fate of its greatest ace. Maj. George Earl Preddy, Jr. hardly looked the part of the most celebrated air force war hero in the fall of 1944. "If anyone looked like a non-fighter," remembered his commanding officer, Lt. Col. John C. Meyer, "it was George." A native of Greensboro, North Carolina, Preddy was slight of build with angular features and a closely cropped mustache. His voice and tone were subdued and unremarkable, save his Southern twang. But Preddy was first and foremost an intensely patriotic competitor with a Southern sentimental soul. Preddy's personality was something of a contradiction. He, like his family, professed a belief in religion and "clean living." Yet George Preddy was not above whiskey, gambling or women. He enjoyed life. But the thing that made George Preddy most unique, however, was not his complex personality, but his ability to fly piston-powered fighter aircraft in World War II and shoot down the enemy with a steely resolve and deadly efficiency.

George had been struck by "stick-and-rudder-fever" when he was introduced to flying on a Waco at a small dirt airstrip south of Greensboro. Soon, Preddy was flying a summer barnstorming tour with his friend, Bill Teague. But Preddy wanted more than the challenge of the Waco in 1939, so he began applying to the Navy to get into combat aircraft. Small for a pilot, with curvature of the spine and high blood pressure, the Navy washed Preddy out of three separate attempts to get in as an aviator. Finally, George decided to put in with the new Army Air Corps and was accepted almost immediately. By September, 1940 when he was accepted, the war was bubbling in Europe and the Far East. In 1942 Preddy found himself flying Curtis P-40s against the Japanese from Darwin, Australia. Preddy survived several close calls and was nearly killed in a flying accident in the summer of 1942. Transferring back to the States for recuperation, Preddy was assigned to the 352nd Fighter Group in the winter of 1943. That summer, George and the rest of the 352nd shipped out to Bodney, England with their new P-47s. On December 1st, 1943, Preddy scored his first victory ten miles south of Rhedt while on escort for 300 bombers attacking industrial targets deep in Germany. George Preddy was known for his good luck with dice, and had taken to naming his planes "Cripes A'Mighty," after his favorite good luck call when throwing in crap games. Preddy obviously needed luck in other departments too, for on January 29, 1944, he had just finished shooting down his third German kill, a Fw-190 over the French beaches at the Pas de Calais, when his P-47 was hit by flak. Preddy was forced to bail out into the frigid English Channel, and survived for an hour before being plucked by the Air Rescue Service from his inflatable dingy. In the spring of 1944 the 352nd converted to the much faster Mustang and Preddy's kills rose rapidly. When D-Day came on June 6th, Preddy was up in multiple flights, totalling 17 hours in the air during the first 48 hours of the invasion.

But George Preddy's most famous mission came on Sunday, August 6th over Berlin. After a long night of craps (Preddy won over $1,000 which he sent home as a war bond) and the revelry of excessive drinking with his buddies, Preddy had stoked himself up with coffee and pure oxygen to clear out the cobwebs so he could fly his next mission. Preddy was so tipsy the following morning that he managed to fall off the platform while giving the mission briefing. Later he professed that he hoped for a milk run; his head hurt. But if hung-over, Preddy put in a stunning performance. In a freewheeling dogfight between Berlin and Hamburg the 25-year old pilot shot down six enemy Me-109s in as many minutes. With that done, he immediately became the leading American fighter ace (he and his pipe-smoking commander, John Meyer, were in a friendly competition). The event created a media sensation. An instant war hero, Preddy toured the states and returned to Greensboro for a short rest. In October, George returned from North Carolina to resume his tenure with the 352nd. Flying resumed almost immediately in a fourth generation P-51D named "Cripes A'Mighty" and more kills were made as Preddy escorted the Eighth Air Force bombers into Germany. By the time the 352nd Fighter Group had transferred from Bodney to Asch, Belgium to help stop the German offensive, it was December 23rd. On Christmas Eve, 1944 George Preddy's score stood at 26 enemy aircraft destroyed with more probables and ground kills. "I sure as hell am not a killer," Preddy said reflecting thoughtfully on his avocation, "but combat flying is like a game and a guy likes to come out on top."

High over the Ardennes, the German fighters of *JG 1* and *JG 3* sighted the Liberators of the 467th Bombardment Group over the Belgian Hohes Venn. Before help could arrive, the Germans sent a string of the machines plummeting to earth. Presently, however, their protection, the silver-nosed P-51s of the 479th Fighter Group, arrived on the scene. Soon six German planes were lost to the fast Mustangs. The 479th split into two groups in the engagement, the "A" group engaged a gaggle of enemy aircraft approaching from Bonn while "B" group hit a dozen Me-109s near Limburg, Germany. The leading scorer was Lt. George Gleason, who shot down three of the enemy. However, the 479th lost four pilots of their own, including Lt. James Bouchier who would be involved in the incident that cost the 352nd Fighter Group its greatest ace. The P-51s ran into severe resistance from the Luftwaffe, but the 479th was able to shoot down 17— its biggest claim of the war. A total of 14 of these actually verified— a count that agrees precisely with the German records.

JG 1, with all three *Gruppen* in action, suffered eight casualties in the day's fighting. Oblt. Fritz Bilfinger, the leader of *10 Staffel*, crashed to his death over Meckenheim after having attempted to close with the Flying Fortresses. Bilfinger, Fw. Joachim Sperling and Uffz. Heinz Zinnen were shot down by the fighter escort, likely the Mustangs of the 352nd Fighter Group who recorded victories in the Bonn area where the German pilots were lost. These were likely the adversaries of Maj. George Preddy. Oblt. Jakob Schneider and Ofw. Otto Soetbeer were wounded in combat with the "*Viermots*" and bailed from their planes over Liège. Schneider died of his wounds the following day. Other pilots of *10./JG 1* penetrated the Allied fighter sweeps to reach the airspace over the battlefield and never came back: Ofw. Friedrich Zander who led the *Schwarm* was killed over Bastogne and Uffz. Harri Kühn went down over Marche in "Black 9." Lt. Rudolf Schnappauf of *I Gruppe* died at the controls of "Green 21" over Bastogne. Reported as missing, the experienced pilot was found in the shattered wreckage of his Fw-190A-8 a week later. Fw. Rudolf Lehmann was killed in combat with the bombers over Münster and Fw. Günther Gensch was wounded. Lt. Hans Halbey, who the day before had downed a Spitfire, was himself shot down over Nettersheim although able to escape his stricken Me-109G-10.

George Preddy's Mustangs had the mission of wiping out any German fighters who were able to penetrate to the battle zone. Ground control vectored the P-51s to the hot spots. Presently, the 328th Squadron received orders to intercept a group of bandits spotted near Koblenz, Germany that were on their way to intercept U.S. bombers. Preddy's Mustangs arrived in the vicinity at 24,000 feet and soon spotted the enemy in two gaggles. Capt. Bill Stangel dove on one of the groups and quickly shot down two Me-109s. Blue Flight was frustrated to lose the enemy in the clouds near Koblenz, although they did find four Fw-190s near Maastricht on the way back to Asch. Capt. Charles Cesky quickly shot down three of the aircraft with his wingman, Lt. Al Chesser, knocking out the fourth. Preddy's group also did well; the commander destroyed his 26th and 27th German planes over Koblenz. Lt. James Lambright and Ray Mitchell, also managed to shoot down others of their own. With these victories, the daily total claims of the 328th Fighter Squadron stood at eleven German aircraft.

However, after these victories, Preddy's White Flight was sent to Liège, Belgium where they were to bounce some low flying German aircraft reported in the area. Flying along with Preddy, was Lt. James T. Cartee, his wingman, and Lt. Bouchier, who had joined up after having gotten separated from the 479th FG. As the three Mustangs flew over the dense forests at the northeastern reaches of the Ardennes, Preddy spotted a Fw-190 flying at very low level. He gave chase at treetop level.

Flying after the plane at low altitude, Bouchier saw Preddy's Mustang suddenly pull up trailing an ugly plume of coolant. Bouchier realized that they were under anti-aircraft fire when his craft shuddered from the blast of a 40mm shell. Damn! Just then he saw the lead Mustang crash into a field, but there was little time to look. He was in big trouble, his cockpit quickly filling with smoke. Although only 1,000 feet in the air over the hilly Hürtgen Forest, Bouchier thought fast and flipped his P-51 over. Shedding the plexiglas canopy, he dropped out of his stricken machine. His parachute blossomed with a sudden jolt, barely having time to break his fall. He landed very hard on the frozen ground, rising to release his chute and lucky to be in one piece. Above, Lt. Cartee was also hit by the ground fire, but managed to get away in one piece.

"As we went over the woods, I was hit by ground fire. Maj. Preddy apparently noticed the intense ground fire and light flak and broke off the attack with a chandelle to the left. About halfway through the maneuver and about 700 feet altitude his canopy came off and he nosed down, still in his turn. I saw no chute and watched his ship hit."

On the ground Jim Bouchier was quickly approached by soldiers. Much to his relief, he saw that they were Americans. As he was escorted to an artillery command post at Langweiler it slowly dawned on him that the guns that had shot him down were *friendly*. He had almost been killed by his own people! But the Mustang he had seen collapse into the field below had not been so lucky. This was "Cripes A'Mighty," the mount of Maj. George E. Preddy. Preddy was dead.[74] When the flyers from the 352nd returned to their frozen tents at Asch, they were told of the terrible news. There was an air of disbelief. For friends like Lt. Ray Mitchell, it was a cruel day. A fellow P-51 pilot asked that he join him to a least celebrate the holiday. "Christmas dinner, " Mitchell answered morosely, "Is it really Christmas?" It was the saddest day that anyone with the 352nd could remember.

At Bastogne, a few German bombers indiscriminately dropped bombs around the 502nd Parachute Infantry Regiment, doing little damage. So much for the promised Luftwaffe support for the big attack by the *15 Panzergrenadier Division* on Christmas morning. Further south, General Patton was attacking towards the surrounded U.S. garrison providing personal ginger to Combat Command A of the 4th Armored on the road to Chaumont. Two German aircraft suddenly swooped down to a low level, strafing and dropping bombs all around the general. Luckily the Third Army commander was unharmed. "This was the only time in the fighting in France or Germany," remembered Patton, "that I was actually picked out on the road and attacked by German air."

At mid-day Hitler ventured out from the dark gloomy catacombs of his *Adlerhorst* headquarters. The concrete bunker from which he directed the Ardennes offensive was situated in the woods at one end of a grassy valley near Bad Nauheim. Only a mile north was Ziegenberg Castle where the haughty and aging von Rundstedt maintained his *OB West* headquarters. Outside *Adlerhorst*, it was a cold frosty day with a low sun and not a cloud

---

74 Preddy was mortally wounded by two 50mm slugs from a Quad-50 of the 12th Anti-aircraft Group. Capt. William S. Cross described the tragedy: "...On Christmas morning, planes had been flying overhead all day long trying to attack ground targets behind our units. There was very little enemy activity in our unit on that morning. We could hear the planes, but we couldn't see them because they were above the overcast...We were told there were two Me-109s flying in strafing ground targets— a typical attack. Suddenly, over the trees, two planes appeared. The gunner on the quadruple .50 caliber machine guns fired a very short burst at these planes. He had only an instant to fire because the planes were flying so fast and low...he simply touched those trigger and recognized that he had fired on a friendly plane. The plane was hit and crashed nearby. It was not a terrible crash, it didn't go in head first, and the pilot could possibly have survived the impact...The gun crew ran to it as fast as they could...Unfortunately, the pilot had been hit by one of the .50 caliber rounds. It was then—when they got the dog-tags off— that we found it was the leading ace in the ETO, Maj. Preddy. You can imagine our sorrow..."

in the sky. As Hitler and his entourage strode about, over a thousand enemy bombers glittered in the steel blue sky, streaming long white contrails. The droning could still be heard even after they had passed. The procession was the Eighth Air Force headed to blast out the heart of Germany. Returning from the walk, Hitler ate his vegetarian lunch with his personal secretary Fräulein Christa Schröder. In time, the conversation carried over to the sight of the vast armada of shimmering silver B-17 bombers. Hitler's secretary looked pained. "Mein Führer," she confessed, "we have lost the war—haven't we?" Hitler calmly reassured her. Things would be different soon he said. Later he would confide in his assistant, Fräulein Traudl Junge. She who had just returned from Munich the morning after British bombers had razed the city with 4 million pounds of explosives. In a very few weeks this nightmare would stop, Hitler declared, "Our new jet aircraft are now in mass production. Soon the Allies will think twice about flying over Reich territory."

The official German description of the Christmas Day battle reflected little of Hitler's hopes. *OB West* recorded that, "Yesterday, German fighter units again intercepted strong enemy formations and prevented them from bombing their intended targets." But *Heeresgruppe B* was overheard with a less rosy assessment: "Throughout the day heavy losses inflicted by fighter-bombers. Own fighters completely absent."

What was not apparent to the German field commanders was that the Luftwaffe had made a valiant effort on Christmas Day. They had lost some 60 planes and 49 pilots including a *Gruppe* and *Staffel* leader; a further 13 were wounded. Christmas, 1944 had been a distinctly unhappy time for the Luftwaffe. Increasingly, each German pilot wondered secretly how much longer he could beat the odds— the odds against staying alive.

The night skies of Christmas 1944 were a bit more peaceful than the preceding evening. The main reason was the fouling weather. Just after getting airborne from Cambrai, a group of Mosquito bombers of the British 2 Group, sent to harass the enemy over the battle zone had to be recalled as the fog closed in on their base. They would not operate for several days. But somehow, the enemy still managed to keep up his nighttime harassment. At the home base of the 10th Photo Recon Group in Giraumont, France, all was not calm on Christmas night. In the early evening observers spied a lone German Ju-88 who buzzed the field at slow speed and "gave the impression of being lost." The plane then made a wide lazy turn and headed for the runway as if to land. This time the base anti-aircraft gunners were alert and a wall of tracers met the Ju-88. After many hits, the bomber staggered and stalled before exploding on the runway.

The crisis in Allied command continued. On Christmas Day Bradley visited Montgomery at Zonhoven. The Field Marshal used the opportunity to gloat over the change in command: "I said the Germans had given us a

The Saddest Christmas: December 25th

real 'bloody nose;' it was useless to pretend that we were going to turn this quickly into a great victory...The enemy saw his chance and took it. Now we're in a proper muddle." After returning to Luxembourg City, Generals Bradley and Patton shared Christmas dinner. Bradley told Patton that Montgomery had informed him that the First Army could not launch an offensive for three months. Both men were disgusted. Eisenhower was counting on him to start a general attack in the next few days. Patton went on a tirade to his staff: "If Ike put Bradley back in command...we could bag the whole German army. I wish Ike was more of gambler, but he is certainly a lion compared to Montgomery...Montgomery is a tired little fart. War requires the taking of risks and he won't take them." Weyland was also disgusted at the described prospect of a massive retreat of Allied forces in the Ardennes, "Saw Gen. Patton and Gen. Maddox— plan of Gen. Montgomery presented," he entered in his diary, "From an air standpoint relinquishing ground now is no good. We cannot abandon airfields now developed." At the headquarters of the IX TAC in war-torn Liège, the mood was somber: "Christmas 1944 was the saddest we had spent in along time," the record keeper sighed.

But Liège seemed a far better place to spend the holidays than as an Allied air POW in war-torn Germany. Carl O. Flagstad had been a navigator with Col. George Y. Jumper's 385th Bomb Group of the Eighth Air Force. On January 4th, 1944 Flagstadt's B-17 flew a mission to bomb the Kiel Canal Ports. His Fortress was the only one of the 385th that did not return. The Me-109s and Fw-190s suddenly struck just as the P-38 escort turned back. The crew jumped at 2,000 feet and became prisoners of *Stalag Luft I*, an infamous holding ground for other U.S. flyers such as Francis Gabreski and Hubert Zemke of the 56th Fighter Group. Flagstad describes a grim holiday, far removed from the Hollywood levity of *Hogan's Heroes*:

...The setting was *Stalag Luft I*, a Luftwaffe prison camp for American flying officers near the medieval town of Barth on the bleak and barren Baltic Sea coast, an area now part of East Germany. Crowded together in Room 9 of Block 2, the 24 men were among the most veteran of the American *kriegies*, some spending their second Christmas behind the barbed wire...

Hunger stalked this barren land, especially *Stalag Luft I* as Red Cross food packages became less and less frequent while the German transportation system crumbled. Horse meat, would, in fact, become the staff of life within two or three months.

Still, we Americans had one friendly voice that sustained morale, that of a BBC announcer heard each night on a homemade, clandestine and well hidden radio receiver. From him we knew the war was being won and, maybe, we thought, it might be all over in about a year.

One overriding worry we all thought about but rarely mentioned was what might happen in those final days. Would Hitler in a maddening frenzy order the extermination of all the prisoners?...

For the low ranking, low paid guards, life at Barth was far from pleasant though safe, at least for the present, from the combat zone. They had long since

303

started to ignore reports of vaunted German superiority and new weapons that would turn the tide. For them, the question now was survival when the curtain came down on this war— for themselves and their families.

And they, too, worried about those final days, fearing orders would arrive sending them to join the depleted ground forces on the eastern front facing the dreaded Russians.

Bruno Bediger, a short, stocky and wily interpreter who visited Room 9 daily relaying messages from the commandant, freely acknowledged it appeared to him that Germany had lost yet another war. He had seen it before, this little man, who at the age of 13 when WWI ended was an orphan roaming the streets of Hamburg, living by his wits; often, he admitted, illegally.

He later became a merchant seaman, eventually jumped ship at New York and obtained a job as a short order cook in a small, greasy New Jersey cafe where he learned the English he commanded. But, he said ruefully, like a lot of other displaced Germans, he became intoxicated by Hitler's early successes, returned to the Fatherland in 1938, was conscripted into the Luftwaffe and here he was, an interpreter and a corporal, fighting the war in a God-forsaken place like Barth and trying to support a wife and a two-year old daughter.

His duties varied. Too often, he would announce that the commandant, Maj. Von Müller, had ordered all barracks emptied, even in freezing weather, while day long searches were made, especially for that radio receiver which the Germans knew existed.

Or he might, with some sadistic pleasure, chide the Americans for thinking of escaping, especially through the futile method of digging tunnels. Nobody, Bediger said, had ever escaped from Barth and nobody ever would, certainly not through a tunnel, since the Major knew about each one started and kept a map of its progress.

He was right on that. Nobody did escape by tunnel. Those that were not abandoned were always dug up. Quite often a sign was erected, again by the order of the major, stating: "The Weasel Strikes Again." Von Müller, Bediger pointed out, considered it sort of a game.

Christmas, 1944 was now only about three days away and Bediger grew increasingly morose, talking at length, not about the war, but of his wife and daughter, usually the latter. Life was hard, he lamented. He and his wife wanted desperately to make the child happy on Christmas Day, but there was little, if anything, to buy even if one had money. And he had no money.

But, he hesitatingly pointed out, he had noticed Red Cross packages usually contained a bar of soap with a swan on the wrapper and he had an idea.

Maybe, Bediger proposed, if he could smuggle in some thin wood and hand tools, maybe the Americans might do him a favor — not him exactly, but his daughter. What he had in mind, he blurted out, was a two-sided swan rocker with a seat in between. Of course, he admitted, there would be risks to all, including himself; and, naturally, he would have to pick up the tools each evening. But it could be done, of that he was positive.

That was how it all began on this strange Christmas of 1944 in that dismal camp, an enemy asking his enemies of help, asking, if only for a moment in a war torn world, that a tiny flicker of good will and the age-old message of love for children be kept alive. Smiles were his reply, smiles from the 24. No words were needed.

In the short days that followed, as the rocking swan took shape, life appeared happier at Barth, even the weak winter sun seemed to spread more warmth. On the night before Christmas Bediger picked up the finished swan which was gleaming in a coat of paint smuggled in under his great coat, nodded briefly, and departed.

He was back the next day as usual— Christmas. This time he took out from under the coat a small bottle of schnapps and some pumpernickel.

From my wife, he said brusquely, she wanted to thank you Americans. From me, too, he added defensively. My little daughter was very pleased.

Bediger's worst fears came to pass in March when he was ordered to the eastern front. Many years later an occupant of Room 9 tried to find out his fate through diplomatic channels. Nobody knew, and no one would waste the effort to find out. Bediger, after all, was a very small statistic in a very big war. Those of the twenty-four still surviving wonder each Christmas about that child they never saw. She would be a woman of about forty now. They wonder, too, about that rocking swan. Did it survive and gladden the hearts of another generation of children?

Yet it does survive each Christmas as we remember the strange one we had in 1944 in that hopeless, worried place on the Baltic. For that brief moment, something reached out and touched all those involved; Bediger, the twenty-four, and yes, most likely, the camp officials who looked the other way while he smuggled in his material. Something that showed love and concern for the happiness of a child can transcend any barrier — even the barbed wire of a prison camp.

XVI

The War is Lost:
December 26th

Boxing Day, the holiday observed in Britain on the day after Christmas, was distinctly unfestive in the skies over Europe. In England, the conditions were particularly bad with a freezing fog that promised deadly wing icing for the unwary. Rime ice covered the trees, planes and anything else exposed. So poor were the conditions, with visibility less than 100 yards, that the Eighth Air Force flew only about 150 bomber sorties. The day's victims were the marshalling yards at Andernach, the rail lines and bridges at Neuwied, Sinzig and Niederlahnstein. Some 336 fighters were dispatched to fly escort, with many groups not operating due to the inclement conditions. In spite of all, however, the Eighth Air Force fighters downed 11 of the enemy at a cost of two of their own while plunking down 348 tons of bombs on their targets.

One of these few heavy bomber sorties included a B-17 flown by Capt. Dick Grace. Dick Grace was one of the most outrageous characters in the Eighth Air Force— and the Eighth was full of them. At 46, the oldest combat pilot in the organization, Grace had flown a Spad in dogfights during World War I, nearly being shot down on one occasion. Although a small man, Grace was absolutely fearless. Between wars, the hell-bent pilot had worked as a daring stunt flyer, providing daring crash scenes for Howard Hughes' Hollywood cameras in the movies *Wings* and *Hell's Angels*. In spite of a broken neck and other near-fatal injuries, flying remained his first love. When the Second World War came along, Grace wanted to fly in combat in the worst way. Understandably the U.S. Army Air Force had qualms about hiring an aging war-horse like Grace, and he was accepted on a condition of limited service. Maybe a rear echelon instructor— that was all. But Grace was not to be denied. He was soon meddling his way into a test pilot job. All the while, he worked everyone he knew to get himself into the cockpit of a combat aircraft. Somehow, he wrangled his way into a ferry position, flying B-24 Liberators over to England. On one of these deliveries, he arranged to see an old friend, Jimmy Doolittle. Doolittle managed to get Grace a job with the Eighth Air Force, albeit supposedly for instructional duties. But soon Grace was flying as an observer and continued his campaign to get a combat position.

The one really endearing thing about Grace, as everyone soon learned, was that this little son-of-a-bitch could really fly. Finally, he was where he wanted— a Squadron Operations Officer with the 486th Bomb Group. For Grace, this amounted to *carte blanche*; he could fly whatever he wanted. On December 26th, Grace was flying the lead B-17 for the 486th as they made there way into Germany to hit rail bridges. However, passing Koblenz, his Fortress was drilled with flak. The ship shuddered and bucked from the impact of no less than 167 shell fragments. A three quarter inch splinter had ripped into Grace's side just above the waist. A quick check showed two engines severely damaged with the hydraulics out. He was hurting, but that wasn't the serious thing. He was worried about keeping his machine in the air. With the plane badly damaged and the pilot wounded, the crew on board was shaken. Grace assured them that everything was okay. Although their B-17 lost altitude and fell out of formation he believed they could make it back on two engines. He turned west towards England. Luckily none of the German fighters sighted the lone bomber limping over Belgium. As he nursed his crippled Fortress back to Sudbury, his crew remained calm with the realization that crash landings were nothing new for Dick Grace! Reaching England with two engines and manual controls, Grace gingerly put the bomber down on the runway. He was promptly taken to the hospital, although he was back flying in combat on January 10th. It was his 47th birthday!

The icy weather during the last part of December, 1944 was the most severe experienced by the Eighth Air Force in 1944. Weather related take-off accidents were common. On the 27th a B-17 from the 390th BG at the Suffolk hamlet of Parham rose some 50 feet only to stagger to gain altitude and ultimately fall back onto the runway killing its crew. Two days later, an attempt to take off through the fog by instruments ended in a horrible accident with two B-24s hurtling into each other at the end of the runway.

The conditions for the Ninth Air Force were better if not optimal; clear with visibility 1-3 miles except for morning fog patches. However, the 365th and 368th Fighter Groups were grounded due to fog. The thermometer was also very low and pilots reported problems with high altitude icing. Regardless, the intense Allied air effort was beginning to show dividends. Cratered roads, severe losses to transport and knocked out rail passes and bridges had thrown German logistical support into a tailspin. Flagging fuel deliveries had immobilized much of the panzer forces and German prisoners were reported shortages of ammunition and food. "Heavy damage is accumulating," reported Reichsminister Speer, "and the transport situation is becoming extremely grave." The artillery commander of the *Fifth Panzer Armee*, Richard Metz, had an even more evocative memory of Boxing Day, 1944: "The attacks from the air...were so powerful that even single vehicles for the transport of personnel and motorcycles could only get through by going from cover to cover."

On the northern side of the enemy salient, the IX TAC flew 306 sorties with some 214 over the battlefield. A total of 88 tons of bombs were dropped and Quesada's pilots claimed to shoot down 19 enemy aircraft of 62 sighted at a cost of four losses. The 487th Squadron of the 352nd Group, while on a morning patrol under Lt. Col. John C. Meyer, engaged a dozen Me-109s west of Bonn that were attempting to bounce a group of P-47s that were dive bombing German targets. Meyer claimed one German plane and shared in the destruction of another; the squadron claimed a total of seven for one P-51 missing. Returning west, the same group clashed with a score of Me-109s, shooting down six of these without loss.

In the St. Vith area some 150 vehicles were sighted during the morning hours, but these were well dispersed and camouflaged. Even so, the American fighter bombers worked over these targets for most of the day making claims of 75 vehicles destroyed including 8 enemy tanks. The majority of the claims were made by the 366th FG which put in 81 sorties operating over the most advanced German ground targets. The 389th Squadron attacked the *9 Panzer Division* in Humain and tanks of the *2SS Panzer* near Erezee. The 390th blasted several "Tigers" seen to the northeast of St. Vith and other enemy trucks along the forest roads north of Amblève. The 391st Squadron worked over a dozen tanks at Poteau (*9SS Panzer Division*) and bombed "woods full of equipment" near the Baraque Fraiture crossroads.

The P-38s of the 370th Group attacked the town of Houffalize twice with good results and smashed an enemy convoy moving through the defile across the Ourthe River. Most the sorties Quesada's command flew were armed reconnaissance as well as added missions against the enemy-held village of Houffalize and La Roche. The first raid on the latter town rendered the bridge there impassable, a fact which the *LVIII Panzerkorps* acknowledged in its evening report. Other German positions were bombed near Bleialf. The 474th FG attacked targets in the St. Vith area. A number of enemy halftracks and trucks were brewed-up on the road to Schönberg with napalm. The 474th also continued to bomb and strafe the *Panzer Lehr Division* near Rochefort. An interrogated tank man from the German division described how during the clear weather he had been attacked by Allied

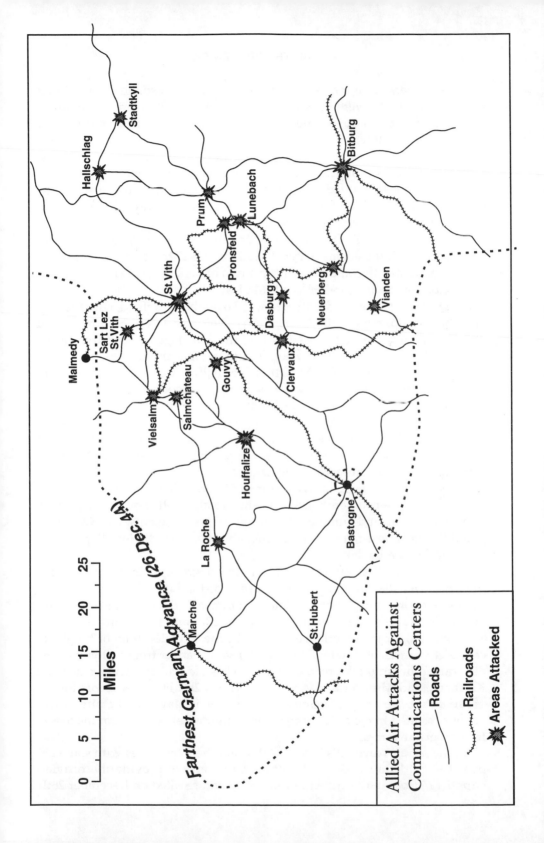

Allied Air Attacks Against Communications Centers

Roads
Railroads
Areas Attacked

Farthest German Advance (26 Dec 44)

Miles
0 5 10 15 20 25

Stadtkyll
Hallschlag
Bitburg
Prum
Pronsfeld
Lunebach
St. Vith
Dasburg
Neuerberg
Vianden
Sart Lez St. Vith
Malmedy
Clervaux
Vielsalm
Salmchateau
Gouvy
Houffalize
La Roche
Bastogne
Marche
St. Hubert

fighter-bombers "as often as three times a day." Even so, he reported that none of their tanks were disabled by these actions. The roads were not so tough, however, and the German *62 Engineer Battalion* busied itself the day after Christmas filling bomb craters in the cratered roads from Houffalize to La Roche. Near the scene of desperate fighting at the tip of the Bulge, the town of Humain was attacked twice by the twin-engined fighter bombers of the 428th and 430th Squadron. Returning P-38 pilots from the enemy zone saw few German vehicles moving on roads during the daylight and others saw signs that the Germans were digging in.

Pilots of the 67th TAC R destroyed one Fw-190 on the 26th during two encounters with the enemy. Later that night, the 422nd NFS conducted its nightly patrols with some 17 P-61s and two old A-20s. Five enemy aircraft were shot down with another two P-61s lost.

The XXIX TAC managed 202 sorties, 157 over the battlefield, with the 36th and 48th Groups striking the *116th Panzer Division* between Houffalize and Hotton. Flying from Le Culot, Belgium, the 23rd Fighter Squadron of the 36th tangled with 15 Me-109s, shooting down nine and losing only one of their own. At the same time, the 404th FG provided support for the U.S. 78th Division. Air-ground cooperation was unusually good with fighters hitting many targets marked by smoke including bombing runs by the 373rd FG on the *1 SS Panzer Division*. Fighters of Nugent's command had been assigned specifically to harass and destroy rail and motor transport in the *Sixth Panzer Armee* area from Düren to just north of Clerf. On the 26th and 27th Nugent's command attacked numerous towns and villages with some 364 tons of bombs during the course of flying some 651 sorties in support of the Allied effort against the counteroffensive. Claims totalled 191 motor transport, 49 armored vehicles and numerous buildings and railroad cuts. The XXIX TAC noted that GAF resistance was slacking, although they did lose 11 planes to the ever-dangerous flak.

All of the tactical air commands noted a greatly diminished enemy presence over the battle zone, preoccupied as the Luftwaffe was, with the Eighth Air Force and IX Bombardment Command which had resumed their heavy blows east of the Ardennes with some 330 sorties. Two missions, with 86 mediums, struck Houffalize and La Roche with 136 tons of bombs to constrict German ability to supply its forward panzer troops. Bombs were also rained down on the road center at Pronsfeld and rail bridges at Konz Karthaus, Bad Münster and Ahrweiler. The 352nd FG, flew escort for the medium bombers in the vicinity of Euskirchen, Mayen and Prüm. These actions resulted in the claim of 45 German fighters shot down for the loss of five American aircraft.

To the south, Weyland's XIX TAC flew another 558 sorties with some 233 over the battlefield. "General Patton requested we provide the heaviest support in front of the 4th Armored," Weyland recalled on December 26th, "clear skies and another big day." Two of the fighter groups being transferred to XIX TAC, the 365th and 368th FG, were grounded by fog and haze, but the rest of Weyland's command had a big day. The 362nd, 405th and 406th Fighter Groups were assigned to provide direct ground support to the U.S. VIII and XII Corps in the Bastogne to Echternach zone. Weyland's fighter bombers claimed 22 enemy aircraft in six separate encounters. Ground claims totaled 412 enemy motor transport.

Bastogne clearly got the most attention. The German front line south of that town was pummeled incessantly by the 406th, 354th and 362nd FGs. Bourscheid was fire-bombed and a powerful strike at dawn by the 362nd FG blasted the stubborn *14 Fallschirmjäger Regiment* loose in Remichampagne. The 377th Squadron bombed Sainlez, and Harlange; the 4th Armored Division reported many enemy prisoners captured at Tintange after the strike the previous day. The 378th Squadron attacked German vehicles in Donnange with napalm and assailed German tanks and troops in the villages of Wardin and Sibret. Another flight attacked the village of Dahl near the Sure River, where the Germans were reportedly forming for an attack. In two engagements, the group also tangled with some 30 Fw-190s who were attempting to stave off their attacks. The 362nd claimed eight enemy fighters for the loss of three of their own. But there was a cost; the Group's acting commanding officer, Maj. Berry Chandler was killed, as well as Lt. Fred C. Ford. Lt. Howard Sloan was hit by flak, but managed to crash land and return to his unit. The P-47 of Lt. E.M. Meyers was also damaged while strafing, but Meyers managed to bail out northwest of Luxembourg City. It was the "biggest mission in quite a while;" the group hit six German occupied villages and claimed 98 destroyed motor vehicles.

The supply line of the enemy *Panzer Lehr* division was cauterized when fighter-bomber attacks by the ubiquitous 406th FG left every building in St. Hubert destroyed except the church. A total of 112 sorties were mounted with attacks on most German held-villages near Bastogne: Noville, Bourcy, Longvilly, Senonchamps, Mande-St. Etienne, Remoifosse, Arloncourt, Givry, Bertogne, Sprimont and Wardin. On the 26th, the ground controller at Bastogne, Capt. Parker, called a flight led by Capt. Warren T. Lenhart to "fly down the bores of German 88mm guns" and attack a bridge near Bertogne which the Germans were using to bring up troops for an attack. "I really didn't expect them to try that," Parker later said, "and neither did Gen. McAuliffe, but they took it against all the flak the Germans could throw up at them." Lenhart attacked the bridge and called for another target. Total claims for the intrepid group that Tuesday amounted to 32 armored and 75 thin-skinned motor vehicles.

The last village before Bastogne in the path of the 4th Armored Division was the tiny hamlet of Assenois. Using napalm, Grossetta's 406th Fighter Group turned the town into a funeral pyre for the German defenders there.

With this terrific close support, Patton's 4th Armored Division finally managed to blast through the German defenders encircling Bastogne. The siege was over. At 6 PM Maj. Gen. John Milliken, Patton's III Corps commander, phoned up Weyland to extend his thanks for the air support which had sprung 4th Armored loose. The fighter bombers and Patton's tanks were inflicting a terrific punishment on the German *5th Fallschirmjäger Division.* "The damn Jerries have stuck their heads in the meat grinder," Patton morbidly joked, "and I've got hold of the handle."[75]

The 354th and 367th FG were sent on armed reconnaissance in the Saarbrücken, Merzig, Trier and St. Vith areas to disrupt the German communications and supply lines immediately behind the front line troops. The 354th, still adapting to its new Thunderbolts, provided escort for the C-47 transports which were again flying resupply to the Bastogne garrison. After the escort mission, the Thunderbolts bombed a German motor column hauling bridging equipment just east of Clervaux and another ten fighter-bombers hit the village of Bourscheid held by *79 Volksgrenadier Division.* Other flights bombed Echternach, Bitburg, Stahl and attacked a rail bridge north of Prüm. During these missions pilots of the 353rd Squadron sighted ten Fw-190s strafing a friendly village; the P-47s attacked and shot down one for the loss of one of their own. Although the fighter group performed well, the pilots complained that the short-ranged P-47s could not "wander far enough afield to find the Jerries and, when they did find a stray formation, they couldn't catch them."[76] The 361st FG, on loan from the Eighth Air Force, also helped to escort the medium bombers and performed fighter sweeps from Bonn to Trier to prevent the German fighters from reaching the battle zone. In a dogfight southwest of Trier the Mustangs fought a dozen Fw-190s at 10,000 feet. The 376th Fighter Squadron claimed six of the German fighters.

A hundred sorties in seven missions from the 405th Group were vectored to hit German supply columns near Prüm and in the Echternach-Bitburg area in support of the U.S. XII Corps. Twelve miles north of Bitburg the 510th Squadron encountered 30 enemy Fw-190s in a scrambling melee. For almost five minutes, the two opposing groups of aircraft warily circled each other, refusing to lock horns. Lt. Larry Gaughran cut across the cautious string of

---

75 Over the two-day period from December 26th - 27th the XIX TAC flew some 1,102 sorties dropping 450 tons of bombs and claiming 690 motor transport, 90 armored vehicles and 25 enemy aircraft for the loss of 17 fighter bombers. All but four of the losses were due to enemy anti-aircraft fire.

76 1st Lt. Donald F. Snow of the 'Pugnacious Pups' of the 355th Fighter Squadron remembered that: "Nasty rumors made their way into camp...Our squadron was to fly P-47 Thunderbolts. Spirits of both crewmen and pilots dropped to a low. It was quite a come down at first to an outfit whose whole core had been formed around the P-51 Mustang...by the time we moved to our new tent city at A-98, Rosieres near Nancy, France our pilots were well on their way to becoming expert throttle-jockeys on our new 'Thunderbuckets'...Our pilots were right in the thick of the fight to throw the hated Krauts back into Germany during Rundstedt's Ardennes Offensive. Flying in poor visibility we pounded the attacking columns with all the bombs and 50-calibre shells we could muster. It was extremely cold at A-98, snow had fallen and the airfield was in the throes of winter...Dances for officers and men were plenty and popular. Many romances resulted from our association with the friendly French native folk..."

German planes blasting two out of the fight in a matter of seconds. Buzz Norr, shot down two more, making it four enemy planes destroyed in three days for the Lieutenant. Before the short air battle was concluded three more German planes were knocked out. The cost was two American planes, both of which were able to crash land behind friendly lines. Ten other 405th P-47s were lost to enemy flak. Ground claims for the fighter group amounted to 172 enemy motor transport.

The 10th PRG was up trying to deliver photographs of the enemy positions to the surrounded garrison in Bastogne. The photos were taken satisfactorily in some twenty missions, but trying to parachute the developed prints to the garrison was another matter. Attempts to fly through the gauntlet of enemy flak saw two pilots of the 31st Photo Squadron killed, Capt. Roger Wolcott and Lt. Al Lanker. Elsewhere, the 10th was still having trouble with the red-tailed P-47s. After sighting numerous trains in the Bingen area, Lt. Logothetis and John Rhoads had to shake consistent attacks by two of the traitor P-47s. It was spooky. Then Lt. Ricci brought back a report of sighting a very strangely adorned P-47. It was green with a bright yellow nose and black crosses on the fuselage. Were these red-tailed jugs, captured planes flown by the Luftwaffe and part of Hitler's subterfuge?[77] More attacks were reported the next day, and Lt. Don Lynch's P-51 was damaged while evading two of the red-tailed P-47s in the Bastogne area. What next? A paranoia about the "enemy" P-47s was simmering in the Third Army, while American pilots were increasingly being shot down by their own anti-aircraft units. On December 31st the Ninth Air Force could take no more.

"Prevalent reports of strafing of our ground troops by friendly aircraft have resulted in a conference of the 12th Army Group, 9th Air Force, Third Army and XIX TAC. In order to reduce to a minimum the possibility of friendly aircraft attacking our ground troops and friendly AA firing upon our aircraft, the following measures are being taken. No 50 calibre weapon will fire upon aircraft unless the aircraft has started to bomb or strafe friendly troops or installations. Instructions have been issued to the armies to initiate an intensive recognition of aircraft program. An intensive program is being initiated in the armies to stamp out the rumor that Germans are flying American aircraft...Effective immediately no fighter of this air force will be flown over the 12th or 20th Corps."

An armada of 278 British Lancaster and Halifax bombers blasted St. Vith with 1,140 tons of explosives. This pounding completely blocked roads entering the town which was now described as a "mass of flames."

Warrant Officer Reay MacKay was a pilot of a Lancaster I of 195 Squadron which was detailed on December 26th to bomb troop concentrations near St. Vith. As the Avro bomber droned over the target, MacKay observed that the

---

77 Allied air commanders were clearly worried about this possibility. On January 4th, Gen. Weyland noted that in spite of terrible weather an alert flight was scrambled at A-94. "because an unidentified P-47 which stooged around...we had no aircraft operating. Possibly GAF plane on recce."

town had been marked with green flares although relieved to see no enemy fighters in the area. A camera on board recorded the bomb drops with St. Vith disappearing in smoke and fire:

> This was the occasion of our 19th mission, just after my 21st birthday. Heavy snow lay on the ground and our bombs were released at 3:33 PM from an altitude of 11,500 feet— much lower than the usual altitude of 20,000 feet for main German targets. On our final bombing run, my Canadian bomb-aimer reported that all he could see through the smoke was what looked like a "church spire." As soon as he reported 'bombs away' he exclaimed that the spire seemed to have collapsed. I have often wondered what effects this raid on St. Vith had. I do hope that it did not affect too many innocent people as wars inevitably do.

Fw. Karl Laun of *Flaksturm Battalion 84*, had just escaped from the pocket at La Gleize on Christmas Day with the remnants of *Kampfgruppe Peiper*. He was searching for his unit north of St. Vith:

> "Looking for the rest area of my battery, I become from afar a witness to the U.S. (sic) bomber attack on St. Vith. The forest forms a sound-proof wall against the rumbling detonations of the bombs, but thick smoke indicates that six kilometers in front of me a town is dying by disembowelment. A never ceasing array of airplanes flies in loose formation over St. Vith. The thunder of the motors resounds in my body. How often I have witnessed such a modern Pompeii...I make my way through the kitchen of a neighboring battery. A limping bomber appears overhead, returning from the St. Vith show. All of a sudden, the damned thing starts diving towards the nearby kitchen...And now the bombs start dropping. I throw myself down. When I dare to rise again I look over for the field kitchen. It's gone; the cook and mess personnel are dead or severely wounded. Well, there went our supper..."

The British fighters were also busy. The Spitfires of 135 Wing, flying cover for the bombardment of St. Vith were buzzed by two Me-262s, managing to hit and damage one of them. A morning patrol of 421 Squadron ran afoul of two Me-109s attempting to ambush the squadron. Both were shot down by Spitfire pilots Sqd. Ldr. Browne and Flg. Off. T. DeCourcy.

The 56th Fighter Group was back in the Bonn-Cologne region where they noted that the enemy fighter presence appeared to have diminished from the preceding days. However, in a short, but intense dogfight, the P-47s shot down three German planes. Two were credited to Lt. Alfred O. Perry and another to the 62nd Squadron leader, Maj. Leslie Smith.

On the 26th, the German air effort continued on at great sacrifice. So severe were the losses sustained over the preceding two days that the Luftwaffe recorded only 404 sorties sent aloft. In a typical action, German fighters tried to intervene in the developing battle along the Sûre River only to be driven off by Allied fighters. The *II Jagdkorps* war diary for the 26th painted a dismal picture:

> "Very cold. Limited operations by the Americans and the British and our own operations were reduced according. *II/JG 1* had the heaviest losses of the day.

Eight pilots failed to return and are reported missing following dogfights in the Bastogne area. Fifteen "long-noses" [Fw-190Ds] of I/JG 26 led by Oblt. Hartigs were airborne at 10:58 and engaged Mustangs over Belgium.[78] Oblt. Hartigs and Fw. Schöndorf taken prisoner near Carlsbourg. Flieger Bergmeier and Feldwebeln Grad and Sattler were killed in action. Stabsfeldwebel Schwarz reported one victory. JG 27 also lost six pilots killed in action near Liège. In the southwest, II/JG 53 engaged an American incursion in the Stuttgart area. Hptm. Meimberg, the Gruppe commander was shot down and bailed out over Schaichof. Oblt. Ludolf was killed near Rutescheim; he was too low when he baled out and the parachute did not have time to open fully. Gefr. Rutland was wounded and made a wheels-up landing near Flacht. Gefr. Meermann was shot down and killed near Wimsheim. SG 4 lost four pilots, including two Staffel leaders. Hptm. Jungellausen and Hptm. Schürmer were killed in action in map reference LK. Ofw. Weinrich and Ofw. Zumkeller missing."[79]

The continuing attempts of JG 1 to provide air cover for the army was proving a costly prospect. II Gruppe, JG 1 lost a number of experienced pilots in the clear skies that Tuesday in the dreaded Bastogne sector. These included Lt. Horst Ertmann, Ofw. Georg Hutter and Ofw. Reinhard Flecks of 5 and 6 Staffel. Others lost in the same area included Uffz. Ferdinand Nüsse and Fw. Johann Ruberg with three pilots killed from the 8 Staffel: Lt. Heinz Fresia, Obfhr. Paul Brühl and Obfhr. Helmut Bullenkamp.

Hans Kukla, with JG 26 reported a dangerous encounter with the P-51 Mustangs in which half of the other members with his 4 Staffel including, Oblt. Hartigs, the Staffel leader, were killed or taken prisoner. The ten Fw-190D-9s had taken off at 10:30 AM with the mission of intercepting Allied fighter bombers— the Luftwaffe pilots called them "Indians" — over the Ardennes. Although they were to rendezvous with other German fighters, Hartigs' FuGe 16Z radio malfunctioned after takeoff and rather than entrust the leadership task to someone with less experience, he decided to lead the small formation on a free lance fighter sweep. Hartigs sighted the condensation trails of the Allied fighters while at a height of 21,000 feet and watched them turn to attack. I/JG 26 turned to meet the fighters which proved to be the dread P-51 Mustangs. In the scrap that followed, Hartigs saw at least three friendly planes plummet after being struck including the craft of Fw.

---

78 IV/JG 26 had its mission on the 26th to cover the German tank spearheads. Flying at low altitude, Oblt. Hartigs quickly lead his D-9s into Belgium without interference from Allied fighters. Much to his chagrin, however, Hartigs spotted the lead panzer units just east of the Meuse River only to find that they had been abandoned for lack of fuel! Under orders not to return from a mission without engaging the enemy, Hartigs turned his 12 aircraft to the south, climbing in altitude knowing that Allied fighters would be vectored by radar to meet his group. Over Trier, the group of German fighters was bounced by P-51 Mustangs from the 361st Fighter Group who were flying a sweep. Hartigs was forced to bail out after being hit by one of the P-51s and having his canopy oil over. Hartigs was captured upon reaching the ground although one of his other pilots was shot by Belgian resistance fighters after having parachuted to safety. In all, five FW 190D-9s were shot down at no loss to the P-51s.

79 SG 4 had scrambled seven Fw-190F-8s at 8:30 AM to bomb American troops near Bastogne. The losses to the unit occurred on the return flight to Kirtorf when the group was set upon by two P-47s and two Typhoons.

Hans Bergmeier. Another of those he saw falling was likely "White 15," the mount of Uffz. Otto Schöndorf who was taken prisoner at 11:30 AM ten miles west of Florenville. He himself shot down a Thunderbolt after which his own D-9 was hit, evidently by Capt. Jay Ruch and Lt. George Vanden Hucvel of the 361st Fighter Group. His engine caught fire so Hartigs took to his parachute becoming a prisoner when he floated down some ten miles east of Florenville, France. The superiority of the Mustang, even to the D-9, was evident in Kukla's description of the engagement.

> "...I engaged in a turning battle with Mustangs at a altitude of about 3,000 meters (10,000 feet). In order to not be shot down, I spun out. I came out of the spin at about 500 meters and saw a Mustang in front of me, in a right bank. I immediately positioned myself behind it and opened fire, but did not hit it. The Mustang pulled up, still in its right turn. I followed it, but it was much faster and escaped."

In all, the Allied Tactical Air Forces claimed 60 German planes shot down from their operations— most east of the battle zone. One bright spot for the Germans was the continued success of the Ar-234 jet bombers of *KG 76*. A morning strike by six Ar-234s including that of Uffz. Rast, hit the American-held town of Verviers, now vacated by Quesada's IX TAC, while another afternoon mission of eight bombers hit the rail station at Libramont not too far southwest of Bastogne. The pilots noted the much greater anti-aircraft fire in this zone (some of it may have been German!) although no losses were sustained. Enemy fighter opposition was also increasing: "Strong formations of enemy fighters (Mustangs and Spitfires)," went the unit diary, "flying standing patrols in the Monschau Düren area. On the roads in the Aachen area columns of trucks were moving south. No movement seen on roads in the Neufchateau and Libramont areas." The following day *KG 76* suffered its first jet combat casualty when Lt. Erich Dick's aircraft slammed into an airfield embankment when condensation on his bubble-like canopy blinded the pilot. The other five planes of the mission continued to drop their bombs on the American troops of the U.S. 28th Division defending Neufchateau. Another mission of an additional eight Ar-234s was successfully flown in the afternoon, although another jet bomber was lost to technical troubles.

At the front, German soldiers seldom saw a friendly plane while the American *'Jabos'* continued their unchecked destruction. This prompted some German commanders to denounce their air force's efforts. "All that comes from the Luftwaffe is crap!" charged the blunt commander of the *Sixth Panzer Armee*. Others would agree. They had no way of knowing of the great sacrifice of Luftwaffe planes and pilots just to the east.

The only sustained German air operations over the battle zone were the nightly nuisance sorties flown over the Ardennes. Typical of these were some nine Ju-88S 3s of *I/LG 1* sent aloft on the night of December 26th to bomb and strafe any Allied ground activity along the Meuse River. At least three of these were brought down by AA fire near Huy. Some aircrew of two of the German bombers were able to escape and Hptm. Rudiger Panneborg, the *Gruppenkommandeur* was posted as missing. A half dozen Ju-88s from *NJG 2* prowled the night skies near Chalons, France. Similar sized groups of *NJG 2* stalked the night skies over Belgium from Christmas Eve to December 27th, with at least one aircraft lost on each evening.[80] *NJG 4* flew a handful of ground-attack missions on Christmas Eve and Christmas Day over Belgium, losing at least two night fighters, one of which could not navigate itself back to Bad Lippringe and ran out of gas. Another crew of *2./NJG 4* were shot down over Neufchâteau just after midnight on December 30th. Six Me-110G-4s of *NJG 5* took off from Schwäbisch Hall during the evening of December 27th and struck the railway station at Neufchâteau in the Ardennes which the crew of "C9+FP" reported already in flames as they added their bombs. *NJG 3* also put in a big effort during New Year's evening, launching the entirety of *III Gruppe* (some 33 aircraft) with the objective of strafing Allied rail traffic in the Verviers-Huy area. At least four of these were brought down by a combination of AA fire and night fighters.

But by far, the most interesting German night-fighter incident occurred during the evening of December 27th. The Ju-88G-1 "D5+AM" of the 4 *Staffel* had orders to fly alone from Husum airfield and proceed to the Bastogne area. The wireless operator, Uffz. Otto Kraus was to report the sightings of any bomber formations to the HQ of *NJG 3* so that a night-fighter attack could be launched. The aircraft started out at about 9 PM and set a westerly course for Bastogne. However, after about 30 minutes the aircraft came under violent anti-aircraft fire while passing over Luxembourg. The pilot took evasive action ending in a steep dive. Uffz. Kraus was lifted from his seat and slammed into the cabin roof. When the pilot suddenly pulled out of the dive Kraus slammed back into the floor with such force that he flew through the escape hatch. Amazingly, Kraus had on his parachute and finding himself out in the night air he pulled the rip cord. He landed near Weyler, Belgium and was taken prisoner.

But the daytime situation had soured to the point that Genfldm. Model was forced to forbid major German daylight movements. In his war diary he recorded that:

> On the entire front there was the heaviest enemy low-flying attacks, with a focus on the *Fifth Panzer Armee* which made movement and supply on the battlefield nearly impossible for the entire day...For this reason the supply of fuel to the 2 *Panzer Division* still not sufficient...An officer sent by the *Gen. Inspector der Panzertruppen* has reported considerable destruction of vehicles

---

80 NJG 2 losses confirmed by interrogation of aircrew: December 24th: one Ju-88G-1 of 4 Staffel shot down over Hasselt, Belgium; 25th: one G-6 southwest of Roermond; 26th one near Chalons-sur-Marne; 27th one G-6 west of Roermond, one G-1 near Chaumont and one G-6 near Malmédy. All had orders to attack Allied rail and road traffic behind their lines and to otherwise conduct fighter patrols.

as a result of low-flying air attacks...The Luftwaffe could only offer localized and temporary relief in the face of massive employment of enemy aircraft over the battle zone.

Model was right; the total German commitment to the Ardennes battles on the 26th totalled only 400 aircraft which was totally dwarfed by the nearly 3,500 Allied machines that operated to repulse the German attack. "The presence of fighter bombers caused the enemy to take cover, when aircraft were seen or heard, and then to proceed mainly by night." surmised observers for the British 2nd Tactical Air Force, "The delay so induced must have been considerable."

So concerned was Adolf Hitler about these developments, that he asked Albert Speer, his Reich armaments minister, to make a personal assessment of the situation for him. Speer motored to the Ardennes after Christmas to make a personal reconnaissance. In addition to chaotic traffic conditions in the wake of the offensive, Speer would report on December 31st that:

> ...the flow of supplies ceased when the foggy weather changed in a few days and the cloudless sky by day filled with innumerable fighter planes and bombers. A drive by daylight became a problem even for a fast passenger car; we were often glad to seek the shelter of a small patch of woods. Now the supply services could only operate in the night, groping their way forward virtually without visibility, almost from tree to tree . . ." or "Vehicles must move at night without headlights. Since all daytime movement is unsafe and night-time travel is slow, our troop movements amount to only one half to one third of the enemy movements. The enemy can move in broad daylight and with lights on at night. An additional serious obstacle, especially to the bringing up of supplies, is the condition of the roads in the Eifel region and the Ardennes...

Late in the afternoon of December 26th, the situation at *Wacht am Rhein's Adlerhorst* headquarters had reached a state of morose tension. The day had witnessed a series of serious reverses for Wacht am Rhein. The German *Seventh Armee* had been nearly forced back to the German border, the haggard men of the prime spearhead of the *Sixth Panzer Armee, Kampfgruppe Peiper*, had escaped total encirclement in La Gleize, albeit only being able to bring back 800 of its original 3,000 troops and none of it heavy tanks. Worst of all, Patton's 4th Armored Division had broken through the siege around Bastogne and his attack from the south was increasing the threat of cutting off the entire German salient. Finally, although the *2 Panzer Division* had nearly reached the Meuse River, it was now out of fuel and under terrific attack by Allied *Jabos* and the U.S. 2nd Armored Division. Genobst. Jodl confronted Hitler with difficult news. "Mein Führer," he implored, "we must face the facts. We cannot force the Meuse!" Even Hitler the eternal optimist had to admit that things were not going well. "We have had unexpected setbacks because my plan was not followed to the letter, but all is not lost." He went into his usual "fight to the last cartridge" diatribe.

At the close of the day *Reichsmarschall* Göring quietly approached Hitler regarding the degenerating events. The two men began to argue ever more loudly as to whether the current situation could be salvaged. Finally, Göring lost his patience. "The war is lost!" he blurted. The *Reichsmarschall* meekly suggested that Hitler seek a truce. He recommended that Hitler contact Count Folke Bernadotte, whose father was the brother of Swedish King Gustavus V. Surely he would help with armistice negotiations. Hitler flew into a fantastic rage. "I forbid you to take any step in this matter," he screamed, "If you go against my orders I will have you shot!" Göring demurred. He knew Hitler did not bluff. The *Reichsmarschall* hurried off to Karinhall. When reaching its confines his wife, Emmy, could see that her husband was shaken. "This is the final break," he concluded, "There's no sense my attending any more daily meetings. He does not believe me anymore."

XVII

Sheer Hell: December 27th

By December 27th, Hitler's Ardennes offensive had been largely halted on the ground. No longer capable of reaching Antwerp, the German leader made Bastogne, the small market town of 4,500 the object of his revenge. Albert Speer, who was surveying the battle zone for Hitler met with Sepp Dietrich, the commander of the *Sixth Panzer Armee*. The SS-leader entrusted with the reduction of the American-held road center "at any cost," Dietrich grumbled about the toughness of their foe in Bastogne and of the crumbling logistical support. "We are receiving no ammunition," he bitterly complained to Speer, "The supply routes have been cut by air attacks." Eavesdropping, ULTRA overheard a similar complaint from *Heeresgruppe B*:

> "Air Force dominated the skies today and made full use of this by systematic destruction of all traffic centers. All-out employment of our own fighters resulted in only very limited relief. The progressive destruction of the railway lines, and stations and of multiple road junctions in the Eifel was making the supply situation tense and dangerous. Certain trains had to be unloaded along the Rhine, which were intended for the *7th Armee*, too far from troops and given the lack of fuel and tonnage space needed for quick transport.."

Another communique came from the Director General of Transport West. Rail traffic east of the battle zone had nearly slowed to a standstill:

> ...many tracks out of operation. The lines Ettlingen-Karlsruhe interrupted by bomb craters...attack on Cologne/Gremberg marshalling yard. All traffic blocked. Traffic will be resumed in about 14 days...enemy fighter bombers have, during the last few days, destroyed the traffic installations on an extensive scale and brought the laborious repair work to nothing in a few hours.

Telephone facilities hardly exist and it is impossible to re-route trains. Fighter protection requested...

The German advance route for the *Fifth Panzer Armee* from the Belgian border to Foy-Notre-Dame on the Meuse River was dotted by the smoldering hulks of tanks and trucks, continually bombed and strafed by the Allied air forces. On the ground, the German armor before the Meuse was nearly paralyzed for lack of fuel. Those formations that did get gasoline were able to only move in starts and stops. But even facing failure on the ground, Hitler bade air operations to support the faltering offensive continue. The day dawned clear and cold with some 2,770 aircraft of the U.S. air forces aloft. Against this menacing total, the Luftwaffe was able to commit a paltry 415 aircraft, 337 on a "fighter-bomber hunt" and 78 in ground attack sorties.

Many of the heavy bombers of the Eighth Air Force were unavailable, socked-in as they were back in England with a freezing fog. Still, some 575 of the heavy bombers flew in operations over rail targets in Western Germany including Gerolstein, Euskirchen and Hillesheim rail-works just east of the Ardennes. The fighters of the Eighth also provided yeoman support to the Allied effort. The medium bombers were out to hit targets in the Rhineland, escorted by the 364th Fighter Group which had just converted from P-38s to the superior P-51 Mustang. The sweep ahead of the bombers ran headlong into several groups of German fighters and by day's end the Eighth Air Force tally would reach 29 victories. Capt. Ernest Bankey, Jr., leading the 383rd Fighter Squadron in "Lucky Lady III," ran into a large number of the enemy 15 miles southwest of Bonn. By the time the actions were over, Bankey was credited with 5 1/2 victories to become an "ace in a day."

For the third day in a row, the 352nd Fighter Group was also in the thick of the action east of the battle area and came out of the fighting with 22 1/2 victories. Southwest of Bonn, the group engaged a large contingent of enemy fighters. Lts. Dick Henderson and Bill Reese of the 486th FS each knocked out two German fighters and Maj. William Halton KO'ed 3 1/2, Lt. Ray Littge managed three and Lt. Col. Meyer, the group commander, and Lt. Marion Nutter each scored doubles.

The Ninth Air Force effort consisted of 311 sorties from IX TAC, 544 from XIX and 383 from XXIX— a total of 1,294 of which about 700 were over the battlefield. In addition, 326 B-26 and A-20 Bomber sorties of the IX Bomber Division struck Houffalize (60 tons), La Roche (55 tons) and railway bridges at Ahrweiler, Kall, Eller and Nonnweiler. Over the following weeks the village of Houffalize was bombed no less than seven times, killing nearly 180 Belgian civilians there.[81] Even so, the 1,200 tons of explosives which had

---

81 December 26: 49 B-26s (85 tons of bombs); December 27: B-26s (60 tons); December 30/31: 90 Lancasters and six Mosquitos (507 tons); January 3: 36 Mitchell and 24 Boston (64 tons); January 5: 18 B-26s (33 tons); January 5/6: 95 Lancasters and 5 Mosquitos (425 tons); January 11: 26 B-26s (44 tons).

pounded the river valley village into ruins did not succeed in destroying the bridge through the town nor altogether halting German traffic there. A total of 1,277 tons of bombs were dropped on the rail bridges on the 26th and 27th although only the Nonnweiler and Konz-Karthaus spans were rendered unserviceable.[82] The span at Ahrweiler, the objective of the 386th BG on both the 26th and 27th, continued to defy destruction. Still, the tracks approaching the crossings were usually damaged and enormous piles of rubble from demolished buildings lay in the streets of many of the bombed towns. German prisoners passing through Pronsfeld reported that scarcely a house was still standing.

One problem made the job of the medium bombers more dangerous— a lack of fighters to accompany them into German airspace. Gen. Anderson was angry about the lack of escort promised from the British on the preceding day. The terrible losses on December 23rd had already shown how risky this could be. Vandenberg sent a terse message explaining:

> "Due to present situation on the ground it is necessary that every P-47 fighter bomber be employed against ground targets. This reduces availability of fighters to escort medium bombers. 2nd TAF has agreed to furnish escort for a great proportion of medium effort within their range. Poor visibility at 2nd TAF fighter airdromes have made this escort difficult. 2nd TAF admits errors in arranging escort and promises to improve..."

Pete Quesada's IX TAC reported an increase in enemy resistance in its area of operations with 150 German aircraft sighted. In numerous dogfights, some 33 enemy fighters were claimed for a loss of ten of its own. Of these, the intrepid 352nd FG accounted the lion's share with 22 claimed in swirling air battles between Euskirchen and Mayen. The group reported no losses.

One Squadron of the 366th Group engaged ten Fw-190s north of St. Vith, claiming one. The 366th also had a big day in the ground support effort. The Germans were out in the open, with an increased flow of traffic particularly in the St. Vith- Houffalize area. This was the early movement of the *Sixth Panzer Armee* towards Bastogne. The 391st Squadron bombed and strafed Geromont after it was marked with smoke so that the 30th Division could move in. The 389th Squadron attacked German troop concentrations in Amblève, while the 390th Squadron sighted nearly 400 vehicles on the road to Schönberg. This was likely the *3 Panzergrenadier Division*, which was threading through the area. The German unit was repeatedly attacked by

---

82 Not all these attacks were that effective. Grenadier Franz Wienecke, with the *326th Volksgrenadier Division*, had formerly been with the Luftwaffe and was witness to the attacks on Kall on December 24th and 27. On December 24th, approximately 30 P-38s attacked the town at 11 AM, destroying nearly twenty vehicles in the town, killing some 15 and destroying the local rail station. However, the POW had also witnessed the much heavier raid on December 27th and characterized this as the work of "beginners" who wasted bombs by simultaneously releasing them from a large formation. The railroad station, which was already destroyed from the raid on the 24th was hit again, but the road junction in the town was untouched. Losses in personnel and vehicles were much smaller since soldiers had much more time to get out of harm's way during a high level bombing.

bombs and rockets with 56 vehicles including 8 tanks claimed with "many soldiers killed." An ammunition and supply dump southwest of St. Vith near Trois Vierges was hit and large explosions and fires were observed. The 370th FG put in 87 sorties. These attacked fuel dumps, motor transport and troop concentrations in the Malmédy and Ligneuville area.

The 365th FG flew three missions on December 27th, including their last from Chievres, Belgium before transferring all aircraft to Y-84, Metz, France. The first flight, led by Capt. Herbert J. Rogers struck German transport making its way between Prüm and Schönberg; 1st Lt. Thomas Manjak led a second flight to blast German vehicles near Lunebach and a third under Maj. Motzenbecker attacked targets of opportunity near Adenau, Germany. In contrast to the gay surroundings at Chievres, the pilots landing at Metz found the base somber, and unappetizing. Most of the nominally French population spoke German and ugly rumors abounded that civilian *Werewolf* agents were using piano wire garrotes to do-in unsuspecting night owl GIs. The disposition of the local populace gave would-be Romeos pause. The people seemed as cold as the ugly frozen ground.[83]

The 474th FG hit German transport in the Prüm area with the 429th Squadron bombing German tanks near Verleumont. Another mission by the 428th Squadron was coordinated by the "Marmite" ground controller to support the U.S. 82nd Airborne Division west of Vielsalm. The Lightning pilots found the roads near Lierneux "crawling" with the enemy. The flights dropped their "blaze bombs" but suffered badly from vicious flak thrown at the twin-engined planes. Lt. Lew Blakeney's aircraft caught on fire, forcing him to bail out at 5,000 feet. Blakeney had flown 115 missions in the P-38s, but this would be his last in World War II. Floating below his parachute he sailed into enemy territory where he became stuck in a tree. The enemy waited below for him to disentangle himself and he spent the rest of the war as a POW. Capt. George G. Guyton's plane was also serious damaged, but he was able to limp back home. Another P-38, that of 2nd Lt. Carl W. Coale was not so lucky. His aircraft was hit by flak, possibly killing the pilot, for the plane went into a gentle dive streaming coolant. No parachute was seen and the plane crashed into the Ardennes hills about 15 miles east of Bastogne. The hard-luck 428th Squadron ended the day with but three flyable aircraft.

The Belgian village of Florennes was home to the 474th and 370th Fighter Groups. But the sights these days at Florennes hardly resembled the tourist post cards. A rabble of pathetic Belgian refugees streamed through the muddy streets headed west from the battle area. Meanwhile, British troops, their faces marked with apprehension, marched through the town the oppo-

---

83 The threat was not entirely fiction. On January 7th a civilian from Metz tossed a hand grenade into a gun emplacement of the 365th Fighter Group, killing two airmen. The same evening, a French civilian shot and killed an American soldier in a local cafe. Both civilians were apprehended.

site direction on their way to fight in the Bulge. Some of the sights were humorous, broad rear-ended Belgian madames improbably peddling small bicycles through the icy streets. But other sights were heart wrenching; worst of all were the hungry children who begged for anything to eat. Although against official policy; the quartermasters looked the other way when GIs provided food and chocolate. The German offensive had put an obvious damper on the plans for the Christmas holiday. Florennes had intended to host a large group of Belgian orphans on Christmas Eve, but the order to "defend the airfield" ended any thought of this. All leave was cancelled as well as visits to nearby Charleroi and Doc Whitner's egg-nog party. The only one who saw anything positive in these developments was the 474th's physician who reported that the "no passes" policy resulted in a much lower rate of venereal disease that month.

The evening hours of Wednesday, December 27th continued the 474th's ill fortune. The flyers and ground crew had enjoyed their first dinner in their recently constructed mess hall. The mess hall looked like a shack, and the food was leftover turkey, but the building was warm. After a satisfying meal, the men were praised by their commanding officer for their excellent performance during the past three days. It was a clear moonlit night, the stillness only interrupted by the sounds of fighting, still audible to the east near the Meuse River. Things were looking up when the 474th bedded down for the night. Just then, however, a dark shape roared overhead. It was a German Ju-188 night fighter. The enemy plane did not see the line of P-38s parked about the darkened airfield, but opened up with machine gun fire on a jeep with its lights on in the 422nd NFS area. Three men were wounded before the apparition swooped in for another strafing run. This time the German plane was brought down by AA, "a beautiful example of the preaching from the intelligence section, that there is no future in asses that make second passes." Predictably, however, blackout discipline at the base became an obsession. Ghostly German planes would return the following evening with more injuries from the 370th Fighter Group that also made the frozen base their home. Guns and helmets quickly became the fashionable accoutrements for the well-dressed airman at Florennes at the close of 1944.

That night the war against the German night raiders continued. Eleven Black Widows of the 422nd NFS along with two Mosquitos of 488 Squadron, RAF flew defensive patrols in the V and VII Corps area over the battle zone. Claims included two Ju-88s and one Me-110 destroyed for the loss of a further two P-61s.

On the 26th, the crews of the IX Troop Carrier Command accomplished one of their most outstanding missions. A flotilla of 289 C-47s took off on instruments over England and assembled on top of the fog. The C-47s were drop escorted by numerous P-38s (367 FG) and P-51 fighters (361 FG). Some

169 tons of supplies were floated down to the Bastogne garrison including 93 tons of ammunition and 7 tons of gasoline. The 440th Troop Carrier Group also brought in 46 gliders, laden with medical supplies and gasoline. Lt. Charlton W. Corwin, Jr. brought the lead glider containing a badly needed surgical team. Flak was very heavy; one of the aircraft had been pierced by 70 machine gun bullets. Amazingly, although many of the CG-4A gliders were spouting fuel from their holed containers, none were set afire.

However, the German flak gunners had the range of their tows. The 440th TCG, which was carrying ammunition, took particularly severe losses. One of the C-47s disappeared in a tremendous mid-air explosion when flak detonated the plane's TNT cargo. Seven other C-47s from the 440th were shot down and only four of the C-47s managed to return to Orleans. In spite of the loses—19 C-47s in all—138 C-47s dropped 127 tons of supplies over Bastogne on December 27th. By that time, the U.S. 4th Armored Division had opened a supply corridor from the south to nourish the airborne troops in and around Bastogne. All told, since December 23rd the IX Troop Carrier Command had dropped a total of some 850 tons of supplies over the town in some 962 sorties.

After their escort mission, the 85 fighter bombers swooped down to strafe the hapless Germans around the road center. Lt. Everett Barnes of the 367th Fighter Group took his 393rd Squadron to blast the German occupied village of Bourscheid. The town was in flames as the fighter-bombers departed. However, the operation was not without cost; the plane piloted by Lt. Paul Toups was shot down by flak.

Of the nearly 600 sorties in Weyland's XIX TAC, some 197 were over the Ardennes fighting. In the Bastogne area, the 406th Fighter Group under Col. Anthony V. Grosetta, had maintained a furious attack on the Germans laying siege to the town. Since at first light on December 23rd, when the fog and clouds suddenly lifted, the 406th had been constantly in action. 1st Lt. Howard W. Park flew "Big Ass Bird II" with the 513th Squadron and even though a veteran of extensive action in Normandy, never had his fate seemed so uncertain:

"Our group of three squadrons flew continuous cover over the city and environs in missions of eight— two four-ship flights— approximately four missions per day for each squadron. This occupied about ten daylight hours of target time per day. The missions were on a rotating basis, like a conveyor belt, with rotation of the entire roster of pilots (32) per day for each squadron. This is about 96 sorties per day; the record shows we flew 105 sorties per day. Each individual flight consumed about four hours of time with briefing, field preparation for takeoff, mission flight time of 2 and half hours, conferring with the crew chief on return, and debriefing...The whole five days— the critical days— seem almost a blur in my memory...It was the first time in the war where I felt I didn't have enough control over my own destiny! So much depended on luck in evading the flak. Usually, during the infrequent air-to-air and "normal" flak, I felt as if I could survive on the basis of my abilities, but not so the winter war over Bastogne. It seemed as if it came down to the luck of the draw... We went out on the mission determined to help our ground forces, especially as we had developed a relationship with the men of the 101st who were bivouacked with us at Mourmelon. I can recall our being on alert each day from the 18th to the 22nd, champing at the bit to go as unfavorable reports of the German advance kept coming in. Then as we began, we had a sort of rude awakening because none of us could believe the intensity of the flak. The enemy, without an effective air force, could only utilize the predicted weather and an ungodly number of flak guns to protect his ground movements. On each of those missions, I think back, and believe that I just took a fatalistic turn of mind, figuring I'd do my damnest to evade the flak, but know the odds were pretty tough in carrying out the requests from the ground. Capt. Parker suggested our targets and we never shirked regardless of flak or feelings. I do not believe I was consciously scared, just fatalistic..."

But survive Park did. The group had flown continuously in support of the 101st Airborne Division since December 23rd. Over the five day period of clear flying weather, the group flew some 81 missions with 529 sorties, most within a ten mile radius of Bastogne. The "Jugs" braved intense enemy flak from the Germans in the vicinity, and on several days arrived to intervene in the battle just as the Germans were drawing together assault forces to seize the town. The damage inflicted on the enemy ringing the surrounded U.S. enclave was tremendous. The 406th claimed the destruction of 13 German aircraft, 610 trucks, 194 armored vehicles, 226 gun positions and 13 fuel and ammunition dumps. On the 27th alone the group claimed 86 motor transport, 53 armored vehicles and 12 enemy guns in its ninety sorties. The enemy positions around Bastogne were reported by observers as an "eruption of smoke and flame." The 406th earned a Distinguished Unit Citation and praise all up and down the chain of command. Brig. Gen. Anthony C. McAuliffe, the hero of Bastogne, personally paid a visit to the 406th at Mourmelon on New Year's Day to express his appreciation to its new commander, Lt. Col. Leslie R. Bratton:

"I wish to express to you and the personnel of your command who supported us at Bastogne, the admiration of the 101st Airborne Division for the tremendous support received from the fighter bombers. Despite intense flak, these fighter pilots repeatedly attacked and disrupted German formations preparing to act against the town. Attacks were made on targets within 400 yards of our infantry lines...If it had not been for your splendid cooperation we should never have been able to hold out...I thought the flak in Holland was bad, but the stuff your boys flew through here was much worse."

The 405th FG flew 86 sorties in support of Patton's XII Corps in the Trier-Bitburg area. The 5th Infantry Division was preparing to cross the Sauer River north of Echternach. The group's actions left 64 enemy motor vehicles destroyed. Two enemy Fw-190s were also claimed near Trier, one Me-109 by Lt. R.W. Yothers and an FW-109 by Lt. W.H. Spencer. Other U.S.

sorties prowled the skies over the battlefield from Pronsfeld (365 FG) to Prüm (354 FG) and Diekirch (405 FG). The 368th FG attacked the village of Recht while in the process of moving from Asch, Belgium to Juvincourt, France. The 362nd and 406th FG continued the punishment of the Germans near Bastogne. The 362nd flew eight missions with 69 sorties over the area between Wiltz and Bastogne claiming a further 107 enemy vehicles detroyed. Returning pilots noted that the enemy was taking care to camouflage and disguise tank and gun positions as haystacks or even locate them in buildings.

An excellent performance was put in by the 354th FG which flew an armed recce of enemy railways south of Trier. In an attack on a 100-car train at Konzen, the train was missed, but the entire town was set ablaze by napalm. East of Prüm their P-47s ran into a group of Me-109s, one being damaged and another so shot up that the pilot was forced into a belly landing.

To the north, the XXIX TAC put in planes from the 36th FG (Lt. Col. Van H. Slayden would shortly take over from Col. Curry) which hit Vielsalm, Tondorf and Clerf. The 48th FG (Col. James K. Johnson) attacked the Recht-Poteau vicinity and ran into a gaggle of 21 Me-109s and 4 Fw-190s near St. Vith. The 494th Squadron lost three aircraft, but claimed five Me-109s destroyed. Lt. George M. Riegler bailed out over friendly territory and was taken to a hospital, Lt. Charles W. Looper took to his parachute and was made a POW near Bovigny and Lt. Nelson W. Koschenski was last seen in the dogfight over St. Vith. The 493rd also had two aircraft brought down by flak over St. Vith although both the mission leader, Maj. Stanley P. Latiolias, and Lt. William G. Dilley, were able to successfully bail out. In an all-too familiar episode the group was fired on by a pair of red-tailed P-47s with bubble canopies. Meanwhile the P-38s of the 404th which patrolled the St. Vith - Houffalize sector. To the north, Col. McKee's 370th FG decked the *9th Panzer Division* near Hargimont. "They gave them everything they had," a triumphant U.S. 4th Cavalry Group reported, "much flame and smoke observed." General von Mellenthin, who had been assigned to the panzer division described the scene from the German side:

"I set off for the *9th Panzer Division* which was in the hills northwest of Houffalize. The ice bound roads glittered in the sunshine and I witnessed the uninterrupted air attacks on our traffic routes and supply dumps. Not a single German plane was in the air, innumerable vehicles were shot up and their black wrecks littered the roads."

Similarly, while in transfer to the Bastogne area, the *3 Panzer Grenadier Division* was repeatedly attacked from the air. One captured officer from the division said his *103 Panzer Battalion* had been attacked 17 times in one day,

327

but that his vehicles had suffered only superficial damage. Many supply trucks had been destroyed, however.[84]

The Luftwaffe put in a strong showing on the 27th, although few of the German planes ever reached the Ardennes front. Luftwaffe records indicate that some 337 aircraft were assigned to a "fighter-bomber hunt" with a further 78 to support the German forces on the ground. But the Allies claimed 86 of these enemy fighters shot down, losing but few of their own.

The losses in *JG 1* resulted from attempts to satisfy the continuing demand for cover of the German spearhead. Responding to the call was *I Gruppe* which took to the air at 10:15 AM with 18 Fw-190s under the command of Hptm. Hans Ehlers. The German flight had orders to proceed to the west to provide cover for the panzers near Dinant. However, east of Mayen the German fighters ran afoul of the P-51 Mustangs of the 364th Fighter Group. Six German fighters went down in the aerial battle including Ehler's "White 20." It was a crippling blow to *I Gruppe*. At the time of Ehler's death, the Gruppenkommandeur had 55 victories including 23 against four-engined bombers. His Fw-190A-8 went down near Bereborn west of Mayen. There was a long casualty list. Lt. Gottfried Just (*Staffelkapitän* of *2 Staffel*), Uffz. Adolf Schiller, Lt. Johannes Birnbaum, Fw. Herbert Mehl, Oblt. Walter Pörsch were all killed. Lt. Richard Förster, the leader of *4 Staffel* was also killed. Two pilots, Uffz. Ernst Schaumberg and Uffz. Riehl were forced to make belly landings. In all, *JG 1* lost some 14 pilots killed, missing or wounded. Against this bloodletting, six P-51s were claimed by *I Gruppe* including one by Lt. Demuth and two by Lt. Lüpke. Obfhr. Gerhard Stiemer was badly injured in the combat over Euskirchen that killed Ehlers.

Although short on combat experience, 21-year old Gerhard Stiemer had developed an reputation as one of the most aggressive young pilots in *JG 1*. Stiemer was from an old Danzig Catholic family, so when Hitler came to power, joining the Hitler Youth was considered bad form. Consequently, Stiemer and his two brothers joined the Luftwaffe. Since joining the air force in December, 1941, Stiemer worked his way through the flying schools eventually ending up in 3./*JG 1* in September of 1944 out of Greifswald. He experienced his first air combat on November 21st in the last of Galland's massive air operations against the B-17 bomber armadas. In the dogfights over Erfurt-Weimar he brought down a Flying Fortress with his guns and cannon, but was himself was shot down by a Mustang. Stiemer counted himself lucky to escape with only minor wounds. Twenty planes were lost and some fifteen other pilots of *JG 1* did not return. Eight days before Christmas, Stiemer and the others in his unit received orders to move to

---

84 The British 2nd Tactical Air Force's Report 19 on the Ardennes air operations concludes that "the contribution of the air forces towards the stemming and final elimination of the enemy thrust into Belgium was very considerable, but that it was not by the direct destruction of armor, which appears to have been insignificant, but rather by the strafing and bombing of the supply routes which prevented essential supplies from reaching the front."

Enschede. But during the flight his Fw-190A-8 experienced engine troubles and he was forced to belly land near Celle.

On December 26th Stiemer flew from Twente airfield. *I/JG 1* had orders to patrol over Bastogne on a "fighter bomber hunt." But on their way back, the controller had told them not try to return to their base in the Netherlands— it was currently being bombed by the *Viermots*. Stiemer and his friends split up, proceeding to the airfields at Paderborn and Bad Lippspringe. The idea on Wednesday was that the group would reassemble and fly back home to Twente. The planes at Lippspringe were fitted with auxiliary fuel tanks to make the long haul, but not those at Paderborn. Nevertheless, Hptm. Hans Ehlers, in charge of the group, mapped out their course on the assumption that all would have drop tanks. All the planes headed for the Ardennes to support the German ground forces; the approach was made a very low altitude— only 400 feet! They were to receive an escort from *III/JG 3* at Lippspringe to help them reach altitude without being set upon by the Allied fighters. However, over Cologne the group lost their escorts who turned back before the low-hanging barrage balloons. Continuing on over St. Vith the German pilots were surprised by a group of P-47 fighters. At such low altitude, a diving escape was impossible; Stiemer watched in horror as the A-8 of Fw. Wolf Oswald burst into flame and fell away. Next, Stiemer witnessed Hptm. Ehlers' "White 20" being hit; out of the corner of his eye he saw it smash into the snowy landscape. Other friendly fighters were going down in smoke all around him. Suddenly, a P-47 pounced on his tail. Stiemer made a hard left turn to fire on his pursuer. The stream of gunfire from his A-8 hit the P-47 which began to smoke. No time to see more. Suddenly another fighter appeared, closing quickly on him from the right. Stiemer brought his craft into a head-on approach with the aircraft. As the two zoomed towards each other, he strained to identify the rapidly closing machine. "Friend or foe?" he thought, "If he shoots I'll shoot." Suddenly, the aircraft began firing at Stiemer. Bullets slammed into his machine and the engine stopped. As the aircraft roared by Stiemer was enraged to see its distinctive propeller spiral. It was another Luftwaffe ship! There was little time to think, however. Without power, his machine fell like a rock. He surveyed the surrounding terrain; the hilly Eifel was treacherous. Even so, he had no choice, looking for a reasonable place to put down. Stiemer plunged to the east into a snowy valley. He slammed his "Yellow 3" down onto the frozen ground at Tötenfeldt near Euskirchen. A surprised panzer crew helped the badly injured Luftwaffe pilot out of his shattered Fw-190. Stiemer counted himself lucky to be alive; soon he was on a train to Bonn to a hospital. Returning to recuperate in his home town at Danzig, he learned that only two of the 17 pilots on the mission that day returned to *JG 1*. He was a lucky one.

II/JG 2 took part in the same operation, but escaped with only two planes lost in a scrap with 20 Mustang fighters. Uffz. Trefzer was able to bail out over Wershofen and Fhj. Alfred Richter was able to plunk down his damaged Me-109G-14 in a crash landing about twenty miles away. JG 27 under Maj. Ludwig Franzisket also managed to penetrate to the Bastogne area and shoot down a P-38. However, immediately thereafter a pack of P-51s closed with the German group from two directions. Uffz. Karl-Heinz Klempau and Lt. Beckmann both had their Me-109G-14s shot out from under them over the Eifel and were soon hanging under their parachutes. Uffz. Sauter was killed when Flt. Lt. Fox of 412 Squadron, RCAF, destroyed the German machine. Fw. Bürger was more fortunate, having abandoned his flaming "White 4" west of Düren. JG 27 suffered other losses in the St. Vith area. 440 Squadron, RCAF, reportedly shot down three Me-109s, likely including that of the *Staffelkapitän* of 7./JG 27, Lt. Gernot Stein. Gefr. Leitner may have suffered a similar fate over the Lower Rhine from the Tempests of 274 Squadron. In all the *Geschwader* lost five pilots killed or missing and another three wounded. It is a telling statistic that JG 27 with eight losses enjoyed the day's greatest success; with ten kills they actually exceeded the claims of their enemy.

Others like JG 54 had a more discouraging performance. The "Green Hearts" lost eight pilots and a *Staffel* leader to only shoot down a single British Tempest fighter. After a long period retraining in Germany with the FW 190D-9s, the sixty aircraft of III/JG 54 were on a combat training flight, only to get bounced by eight Hawker Tempests of 486 (New Zealand) Squadron over Münster. The British machines shot down five German planes— mostly the new, less experienced members of the "Green Hearts." In spite of a protracted engagement, only one member of the group, Leutnant Peter Crump, even managed to get off shots at the enemy. Oblt. Breger and Fw. Dähn were killed over Telgte and Everswinkel with the other losses coming in the Münster-Handorf area. Fw. Hutz was killed by a P-47 in the engagement.

While *III Gruppe* was tangling with the Tempests over Münster, IV/JG 54 flew sorties with JG 26 and JG 27th to provide ground support over the Ardennes battlefield. High over St. Vith, the armored Fw-190 A-8s fought an unequal duel with a group of P-47s, losing four of their number without inflicting loss on their enemy. Lt. Alfred Budde, an experienced commander, did not come back to Vörden. Others did not return either: Uffz. Hervert Muller-Welt, Lt. Hans-Georg Baur-Bargehr and Oblt. Ludwig Drexler were all listed as missing. II/JG 77 also flew several sorties in the area around St. Vith-Olzheim, losing two pilots and their Me-109G-14s in the process.

Obstlt. Jannsen's SG 4 command produced a totally unsatisfactory performance that Wednesday. An excerpt from the unit's combat diary suggests pilot inexperience:

"Take-off of ten aircraft at 0755. Mission: Bombing of troop concentrations in Bastogne. Command of *Geschwader* in the air: Commander of I/SG 4; commander veers off course after engine trouble, *I* and *II Gruppen* follow and drop their bombs on friendly territory. *III Gruppe* either drops their bombs or brings them back. Radio transmission of formation leader is garbled and his orders to fly on were not heard. 2nd Take-off with the same mission. After 20 minutes the aircraft are recalled by radio: large bomber and fighter formations are inbound. 1230 hours strafing attack on the field by two Mustangs. 1245 hours, *Gruppe* commander drives to see the *Geschwader* commander. Court-martial investigation of the morning action."

The *"Udet" Geschwader, JG 3,* took heavy losses in the aerial battles on the 27th. The *I, III* and *IV Gruppen* flew over Cologne and the Ahr Mountains running afoul of numerous American and British fighters patrolling that vicinity. Chased by a swarm of P-47s, Lt. Glaubig fell out of the sky in his "Black 9" near Antweiler. *IV/JG 3* counted five pilots who did not return that afternoon, including Lt. Rennewanz and Obfhr. Büchsenmann who met their fate over St. Vith. *III Gruppe* fought it out with a numerically superior enemy over Cologne and Malmédy; Gefr. Stump, Uffz. Aigner and Obgefr. Hirschmann were all shot down. The latter two have never been found. In all, twelve pilots were reported killed or missing.

According to the IX TAC, "The GAF was much more active in and near the battle area today with total sightings being about 150 enemy aircraft...Again, the enemy seemed to be more interested in defensive air effort." This was echoed in greater frustration by Gen. Peltz, who was overheard by ULTRA complaining that "attacks are being broken off without good reason." Some survival-minded pilots were jettisoning their tanks and high-tailing it home. At the same time the commanders of the two panzer armies, Gen. von Manteuffel and Gen. Dietrich called for the heaviest possible German air strike against the Americans holding out in the woods north of Bastogne. Decryption of German radio transmissions also yielded a report of the German air order of battle assigned to support *Wacht Am Rhein*— a force on the 27th amounting to some 1,800 aircraft with 1,250 fighters.

The combined claims from all Allied operations on the 27th totalled 86 German aircraft shot down. But meanwhile the German soldiers at the front felt abandoned by the Luftwaffe. The *Sixth Panzer Armee* complained bitterly of "heavy enemy air activity while the German air force has not put in an appearance."

On both the 26th and 27th Allied heavy bombers pounded enemy communications centers. Simultaneously, some 274 RAF heavy bombers wrecked St. Vith in a massive raid. Although freezing fog in England again reduced their contribution, the 1st, 2nd and 3rd Divisions of the Eighth Air Force put in a respectable showing. In spite of the conditions, some 674 B-17 and B-24 bombers were sent to blast the German rail bridges and marshalling yards once more. A total of 1,578 tons of bombs were spread over familiar targets: Fulda, Andernach, Neuwied, Kaiserlautern, Homburg, Neunkirchnen, St. Wendel, Euskirchen, Gerolstein, Bullay, Altenahr and Hillesheim. Only two of the assaulting bombers did not return, the light damage courtesy the 390 P-51 and P-47 fighters who flew the escort. The Eighth fighter pilots continued to chip away at the Luftwaffe means of defense, claiming 29 of the enemy while suffering the loss of only five of their number. The worst bomber losses came now from the frigid weather: a B-17 of the 453rd BG collapsed to the ground during takeoff and another of the 384th killed its crew in a crash landing at Manston. Particularly bad was the fate of a B-17 of the 390th BG which plummeted into the center of Framingham, killing the crew and knocking out every window in the village. Miraculously, none of the inhabitants were harmed.

On the following day, the Eighth Air Force was again out over the same targets with a few new ones (Remagen, Zweibrücken, Bierbach, Irlich, Brühl) in a massive bombing raid: 1,275 medium and heavy bombers blasted German rail and railroad bridges with another 3,200 tons of bombs, with only two losses. The escort comprised some 600 Mustangs although no aerial claims were made as the enemy was "not in evidence." With no enemy opposition only a single P-51 of the 364th FG was lost, and this was due to an aircraft malfunction; the pilot bailed to safety.

The British contribution was growing in the air battle. RAF Bomber Command also put in a substantial showing hitting rail yards at München Gladbach in a 191-plane day raid, and Opaladen in a 313- bomber hit later that evening. On December 27th the Typhoons of 83 Group participated in the continuing destruction of St. Vith. After completing his bombing mission Flt. Lt. D. Jenvey suddenly sighted three German fighters below him. Closing to the enemy, the pursuer became the pursued. While avoiding two Me-109s on his tail, Jenvey blasted a third and turned on one of his pursuers only to have his guns jam. 440 Squadron found itself in a number of dogfights that day with Fw-190s. One was shot down. Continuing the inter-Allied identification problem 137 Squadron was bounced during the day by blue-nosed P-51s, but suffered no loss. Daring more problems of this type, the Spitfires of 411 Squadron joined in with a group of American P-51s and P-47s wheeling through the skies over the Julich-Durbuy area. The Canadians managed to shoot down three German fighters. Then minutes later 412 Squadron was surprised by enemy fighters over Rheine, but the wily pilots managed to evade their attackers and Flt. Lt. Fox managed to shoot down one. 274 Squadron ran into a group of Me-109s over Arnhem at 11 AM and Flt. Lt. J.A. Malloy shot one down. A short time later Tempests from 80 Squadron sighted four Fw-190s over Paderborn; all were shot down in the ensuing combat. Finally 486 Squadron bounced a group of 40 Fw-190s over Münster and lost one of their Tempests in the process of shooting down four German fighters. The final tally of the 2nd TAF from December 24th - 27th amounted to some 32 victories. The British added a 278-bomber raid on

Cologne-Gremburg and 338 night bombers to blast München-Gladbach and Bonn. The following day they would plant 1,516 tons of bombs on Koblenz (262 bombers) and Troisdorf (176 bombers).

The medium bomber missions of IX BD amounted to 663 aircraft dropping some 1,277 tons of bombs. During the same period, the IX TAC dispatched some 590 sorties, claiming 45 enemy aircraft destroyed while losing 11 of their own. The same tally for Weyland's XIX TAC counted 1,102 sorties claiming 25 German planes and 90 armored vehicles, 690 motor transport and 38 rail and road cuts for the loss of 17 aircraft. Nugent's XXIX TAC flew some 651 sorties losing 11 aircraft, but claiming the destruction of 49 enemy armored vehicles and 181 motor transports.

With orders to help stop the enemy's nightly attacks on Bastogne and environs, the 422nd Night Fighter Squadron was active that night. The few P-61 "Black Widows" that they had operational managed to shoot down five German intruders over the battle zone, but the number of night fighters was simply too small to still the German raids. Once again the German bombers hit the town of Bastogne in what was becoming a deadly nighttime occurrence.

Luckily for the hemorrhaging German pilot corps, the weather on December 28th offered time to regain their balance. Flying conditions ended, ushered in by heavy snowfall with low hanging stratus clouds. Most aircraft of the Ninth Air Force were grounded due to the visibility conditions on the continent which were less than 100 yards at many of the bases. The conditions were better in England with foggy conditions improving to 2-3,000 yards in the afternoon. Doolittle's unflagging contribution to the Allied effort to turn back the German onslaught consisted of a massive 1,232 sorties dropping 3,172 tons of bombs at Cologne, Irlich, Remagen, Bullay and Kaiserlautern in an attempt to halt German rail traffic supporting the attack. The Luftwaffe sorties were greatly reduced, reporting only 15 aircraft committed to the battle that day. Meanwhile, Genfldm. Model, while welcoming the respite from air attack brought on by the bad weather and snow complained that, "The essential improvement of the heavily burdened railway system is not yet evident."

The Allied air forces had operated on an immense scale in the preceding four days, flying nearly 10,000 sorties, claiming 2,323 motor vehicles, 207 armored vehicles, 45 trains and seven bridges.[85] The attack had taken a fearful toll on German transport capability: "The progressive destruction of

85 American losses of aircraft to reach this achievement were not inconsequential. Although claiming 390 Luftwaffe aircraft shot down between 17 and 27 December, the Ninth Air Force reported losing some 147 fighters and 45 medium bombers. On the 27th Gen. Vandenberg informed Spaatz that "Replacement fighter aircraft including P-47, P-38 and P-61 negligible during past ten days. Operational efficiency of each command will be seriously affected unless fighters of all types are furnished to the TACs immediately. This applies particularly to the 474 and 370 Ftr Gps. IX TAC estimates that 422 Night Ftr Sq will be non-operational within one week if replacements are not received..."

railway lines and train stations as well as road junction in the Eifel made the supply of goods very difficult," *Heeresgruppe B* recorded, "Therefore, certain trains had to be unloaded along the Rhine which were intended for the *Seventh Armee*. Because of the distances, the troops cannot be adequately supplied." Model further reported that "considerable tension arose due to the continuing heavy air attacks on the railway centers in the rear region." Another blunt report submitted to *OKW* on the 28th noted a "rapid increase of damage and losses" due to the assault from the air and "in the areas near the front, it is already similar to Normandy."

Shattered Neufchateau. German Ar-234s struck the Ardennes village on December 26th. This is the way *Rue Albert Clement* appeared four days later as Belgian villagers attempted to clear the rubble. *(NA)*

Euskirchen marshalling yards. The nexus of road and rail junctions has been transformed into a lunar landscape by bombs of the Eighth and Ninth Air forces. *(NASM)*

Members of the IX Troop Carrier Command load up parapacks for air drop to the surrounded Bastogne garrison. *(NASM)*

GIs of the U.S. 30th Division try their luck firing their rifles at low flying Luftwaffe aircraft over Franchorchamps. December 27, 1944 *(NA)*

Sheer Hell: December 27th

This dramatic photograph was taken of a Luftwaffe pilot jumping from his aircraft which was just damaged by .50 calibre fire from the P-47 of Maj. James Dalglish, 354th Fighter Group. Seconds later the German fighter exploded. *(NASM)*

BELOW: Symbol of air might. A striking photograph of a Republic P-47 of the 365th Fighter Group at Chievres, Belgium. In the foreground is a "quad 50" .50 calibre AA gun. *(NASM)*

Uffz. Otto Schöndorf of *1./JG 26* was shot down on the day after Christmas on only his third flight of the war. Hit by a P-51, Schöndorf was forced to take to his parachute at very low altitude, plunging hard into the thick woods at Botassart near Bouillon. Although the conifers broke his fall and saved his life, his leg was broken. Belgian locals tended his injury at a nearby hotel until a U.S. jeep arrived to take him prisoner to a French hospital in Sedan. *(Schöndorf via Roba)*

BELOW: Then and now. Otto Schöndorf points out the location of his Dora-9's crash at the "Tombeau du Géant" ("The Giant's Grave") to Cynrik DeDecker. *(DeDecker)*

Obfhr. Gerhard Stiemer with *I/JG 1*. *(Stiemer)*

Uffz. Hans Kukla with *4/JG 26* photo-graphed at Fürstenau in late 1944. Kukla received the abbreviated training course typical of *Nachwuchs* ("newgrowth") re-placements, but was atypical in that he survived the war. (*Kukla via Caldwell)*

Rare shot of Hptm. Robert "Bazi" Weiss, the youthful commander of *III/JG 54*. *(Robertson)*

Fw. Fritz Ungar of *III/JG 54*. (*Ungar via Caldwell)*

Allied fighter pilot's view of the 6th Armored Division in action northeast of Bastogne. January 13, 1945. *(NA)*

A Douglas C-47 of the 439th Troop Carrier Command burns after crashing into a building in France. December 30th, 1944. *(NASM)*

Lt. Helms and his crew of the 452nd Bomb Group posing before their Boeing Flying Fortress. *(NASM)*

The scouting force of the 364th Fighter Group are briefed before their mission at Honnington, England on December 31, 1944. *(NASM)*

St. Vith under a punishing bombardment by the RAF. Photograph taken from the Lancaster bomber piloted by Wt. Off. Reay MacKay. *(MacKay via DeDecker)*

XVIII

Black Friday: December 29th

Even at 24 years, Hptm. Robert Weiss looked distinctly youthful for one of Germany's leading aces. His wavy blonde hair and boyish features hardly fit the Ritterkreuz that dangled from his neck. "Bazi" to his many friends, Weiss was one of the *Wunderkind* of the Luftwaffe, having shot down 121 Allied fighters in his short career. And unlike many of the other German aces, Weiss's victories had been mainly earned against the more skillful British and American fliers. "Bazi" had greatly impressed his superiors in the disastrous summer of 1944, taking over command of the *III Gruppe* of JG 54 on August 10th, during the extremely chaotic Luftwaffe operations in Normandy. In spite of increasingly disadvantageous odds, his command had surprising success during the later summer and fall. As *Kommodore* of *III Gruppe*, the "Green Hearts", Weiss knew he needed to provide every advantage possible to the many inexperienced pilots under his command.

Weiss and *III Gruppe* were situated at the Varrelbusch aerodrome, nominally under the command of JG 26. During the Ardennes operation, his command had been given the multiple assignment of providing protection to the jets flying from Rheine base as well as ground support sorties to the Ardennes and even bomber interception. This was a very tall order for many of the pilots Weiss found under his command. Many had less than three weeks of operational experience. On Christmas Day, Weiss addressed *III Gruppe*, informing senior officers and the more experienced flyers, that they would be expected to help the fledgling pilots and not just leave them to fend for themselves. The youthful leader knew that although veteran German pilots naturally liked to fly together, this was a sure way to kill off new pilots.

"We have little to lose but our lives," he joked nervously with his attentive audience. "We will continue to fly in the sure knowledge that our NCO pilots are backing us up." Many of the younger pilots naturally looked up to Weiss. Here was a guy who looked to be their age— who still smiled and even bantered in the face of death— and yet he was one of the hottest aces in the German air force. But most of the fledgling German pilots kept their feelings to themselves. Even with the holidays, there was almost constant action for the Luftwaffe airmen. In spite of Weiss's plans, each passing day saw more pilots killed or wounded and more planes lost from his *III Gruppe*. December 29th was no different, but the tragedy of this day exceeded all others for the "Green Hearts."

The poor weather of the previous day had broken, but was certainly less than optimal. On the American side of the fence, the Ninth Air Force managed only 460 sorties. The IX and XXIX TACs were grounded so that almost all of these were flown by Weyland's XIX. Approximately half the flights were over the battle zone. All of the fighter groups of the XIX TAC were out, with some 456 sorties. Even with poor weather, some of these were very effective, but others were costly. One example was the 405th Fighter Group. The unit flew 74 sorties, but lost two pilots to enemy flak in the Bitburg-Habscheid area. The 362nd FG was also up with 46 sorties in four missions; the 378th Squadron hit a large collection of German tanks observed near Hamiville and Longvilly with good results. This was likely the *1SS Panzer Division* which was moving into the area northeast of Bastogne to deal a knock-out blow to the Americans defending the town. Pilots reported the enemy tanks were packed on the road, lined up two abreast and that the crews were seen boiling out of the turrets during the bombing runs. Group claims amounted to 41 vehicles and 52 pieces of enemy armor. The 406th FG was out again with 31 sorties, peppering a half-mile long cache of German ammunition boxes east of Houffalize which promptly exploded. Other claims for the day included 18 tanks and 4 heavy field guns seen massing in the vicinity.

On the morning of December 29th, the command post of the *79 Volksgrenadier Division* was located in a large restaurant next to the church at Bourscheid, Luxembourg. Obst. Alois Weber, the division commander was on the phone just before noon when the roar of the fighter-bombers filled the air. Eight P-38s, likely from the 367th FG, thundered overhead at only 150 feet, strafing and dropping bombs. Amid the din of the gunfire and explosions Weber ran for cover down dark cellar stairs, but tripped and suffered a concussion. The divisional command post, including all the radios, was completely wrecked leaving the German infantry division without effective control.

On December 30th 470 fighter-bomber sorties were flown, again by Wey-land's command. The sorties were divided between ground support in the Echternach-Bastogne region and armed reconnaissance in the less active front between Bastogne and the Our River, around St. Vith, and in the Koblenz-Mayen area. Only the dedicated 406th FG over Bastogne was flying exclusively over the battlefield. Twelve aircraft were lost during the two days to enemy flak; the Luftwaffe had disappeared from the zone of opera-tions. The claims tally continued to swell: another 234 motor transport, 101 tanks and armored vehicles and numerous other targets were accumulated. Maj. George I. Ruddell was on a hair-raising flight with the 514th Squadron over Bastogne that Saturday:

> "I was leading our squadron on one of its many missions against the Germans surrounding Bastogne. In my flight, Smith (Lt. John I.) was my wingman and Pittala (Lt. Vincent R.) was number four...It was an afternoon mission and it was our initial attack. Smith moved out to my right as I rolled in and com-menced strafing three German trucks moving in a trail up a slope. Two of the trucks had barely caught fire when suddenly, Smitty's plane was nothing but a huge ball of fire with only prop, engine cowling and wingtips showing. At almost the same instant, I saw over my shoulder Pittala's aircraft upside down, with landing gear extended, plunging to the ground. About then, I also encountered my own problem; a hit by what was later found to be a 40mm AA shell, rendering my elevator control linkage inoperative. I became extremely busy cranking my elevator trim tab as fast as I could, desperately trying to get the nose up to climb the slope. I knew I was dead, but somehow lucked out. After that, the landing back at Mourmelon was no big problem. But what a rough mission!...The day before the mission Smitty learned that his wife had just had a baby boy, their first child (he was just a kid himself). After dinner that evening, we had toasted his good fortune with a glass of our liberated champagne. By then, our squadron and group losses had made us pretty casual over losing buddies. Still, some of us could not hold back a few tears after that mission. Fatigue I guess. . ."

The 365th FG resumed its support with four missions from Metz airfield. One mission bombed the German town of Daun, another hit Trois Vierges and escorted B-26 bombers over the Ardennes. A third mission in the afternoon struck Bernkastel, Germany and a fourth stalked the Germans over the St. Vith area. A further six missions were flown the following day, mainly as armed recce runs against rail targets in the Saarbrucken-Ne-unkirchen area.

The only bombing attacks by Vandenberg's Ninth Air Force consisted of a 12-ton bombing strike by six Marauders on St. Vith. As usual, the U.S. Eighth Air Force was more active, dispatching over 800 heavy bomber sorties, escorted by 724 fighters bound for communications targets and rail bridges. Hundred-ton bombing missions included the Frankfurt marshal-ling yards and the Bingen, Bullay, Irlich and Remagen bridges. Several of the crossings were not damaged, however, and taking out these targets was becoming considerably more difficult than expected. Through ULTRA, the

Allied high command learned a few days later that Bingen had not been damaged, although at Remagen the "bridge was damaged by bombing and was probably closed for several weeks." Battlefield targets included St. Vith, Diekirch, Prüm, Lunebach, Stadkyll and Gerolstein. Five bombers and three fighters were lost in the operations, although the enemy was seldom seen. On the following day, some 1,315 bombers escorted by 572 fighters were sent against German rail and communications centers. Over 1,300 tons were dropped atop the Kassel and Mannheim marshalling yards with the rail bridges at Bullay, Kaiserlautern and Irlich continuing to attract attention.

While the punishment of German ground forces continued, the Luftwaffe support for *Wacht Am Rhein* was reduced to 130 machines committed to strafing attacks and a further 35 night fighters set aloft under cover of darkness. At least two Ju-88s of *NJG 4* were lost in these nuisance raids over Belgium, one coming down southwest of Bastogne and the other near the Lesse, River. Most of the German air activity was to the north in sorties against the British. Involved in these operation were elements of *JG 54*, *KG 51* (Me-262 jets), *JG 6* from Oldenburg and a *Staffel* of *IV/JG 27* from Achmer. Finally ready for large scale commitment in the West, *JG 54* had managed to assemble 70 Fw-190D-9s to support the operation. Their mission would be to shoot down any Allied aircraft that threatened the security of the guarded German jets taking off or landing from Rheine base.

The experience of the "Green Hearts" in their first large scale engagement in this region was tragic. On the morning of the 29th the *III Gruppe* was ordered by *3 Jagdivision* to proceed to the Osnabrück - Rheine area at low altitude in successive *Staffel*-strength waves to intercept British fighters reported to be operating there. They were to be guided to their targets by ground control at Wiedenbruck which was using VHF R/T in combination with the FuG 16 ZY radio on board each plane. In theory, slant range measurement would be used to vector the German fighters to the location of Allied fighters. Unfortunately, the system did not function properly on this day. The orders to split up the *Gruppe* at very low altitude ran against the established rules of fighter employment. Small groups would likely be sitting ducks for Allied fighters patrolling at higher altitude. Regardless of his misgivings, Hptm. Robert "Bazi" Weiss followed his orders and commanded that the squadrons take off one hour apart. Ominously, control spotted a heavy concentration of Allied fighters in the Tecklenburg region. The dozen fighters of each *Staffel* would likely meet up with a numerically superior enemy.

As Weiss had feared, the first in line, the *9 Staffel*, under Lt. Willi Heilmann, was savagely ambushed as it approached Rheine by Spitfire IXs of 411 Squadron of the Royal Canadian Air Force. Caught at an altitude of only 6,500 feet, the Canadians dove on the German planes as they crossed the Lingen-Rheine area. The German *Staffel* planes struggled for altitude, but were so many clay pigeons for the Spitfires. Six German pilots were almost immediately killed and a number of others were forced to bail out. Uffz. Busch and Reichardt were felled, their D-9s crashing to the earth near Lingen. "White 6" with Uffz. Fernau at the controls crashed near Messingen and Lt. Bartak fell to his death near the German border at Bentheim. Fhr. Schmauser and Uffz. Toepler were killed in the skies over the Ems River between Rheine and Lingen. On the ground, Hptm. Weiss watched in horror as lone survivors from the massacre straggled back to the base at Varrelsbusch, most of them showing signs of battle damage. Several struggled to make it to the air strip. Seeking to intervene, he ordered that his plane be made ready.

Weiss hastily took off with his staff at 10 AM. Following close behind was the *11 Staffel* under Lt. Hans Prager. Leading his group back to the scene of the destruction of *9 Staffel*, Weiss spied a large formation of Spitfires from 331 and 401 Squadrons. This time, having the advantage of altitude, his D-9s dove on the British planes. A wild dogfight ensued over Lingen in which the tables turned. Presently, Typhoons of 168 and 439 Squadrons arrived on the scene . 439 Squadron shot down one Fw-190 which was likely the A-8 of Uffz. Wolfgang Miebach of *III/JG 6* who fell in Holland near Oldenzaal. In spite of losing two Typhoon flight commanders in 168's first engagement, the British with superior numbers now had the upper hand. Fw. Gerhard Neerson and Oblt. Eugen Schreiner were shot down as the Allies pressed their numbers. Soon Weiss himself was fighting for his life in a wild aerial battle with several Spitfires. The *11 Staffel* was also drawn into the fray. The Dora-9 of Ofw. Wilhelm Philipp fell west of Nordhorn. Philipp was able to bail out of his burning "Yellow 4" although sustaining serious injuries. Two others were not so lucky: Fw. Kreisel and Uffz. Rupp were killed. Only a single plane of Weiss's small group would return. The rest, including Weiss and his wingman Oblt. Bellaire, were hunted down by Tempests of 56 Squadron west of Rheine in a repeat of the destruction of the previous wave. The sad fate of Hptm. Weiss is recounted by the testimony of Fw. Fritz Ungar, the only survivor:

"The *Staffel* and the *Stabsschwarm* flew in a combat formation led by the *Kommandeur*, Hptm. Weiss. At 10:45 while in quadrant HP (southwest of Rheine) at 1,500 meters, we made contact with enemy Typhoons and Thunderbolts. In several minutes of combat, several aircraft were shot down. I myself shot down a Typhoon. After this battle, at about 10:50 I saw two FW 190D-9s flying north at low altitude. I was alone, and attached myself to them. A fourth FW 190D-9 joined us, and we all flew on in a generally northerly direction. The *Schwarmführer* was Hptm. Weiss; I did not recognize the other two. I flew in the far right position. We were in quadrant GP-3 (west of Rheine), when three aircraft were observed approaching from directly behind us. I watched them closely. At about 200 meters distance, the left-most plane banked to the right in order to place itself behind me. At that point I made a positive identification of it as a Spitfire. Immediately, Hptm. Weiss and the other two broke sharply

347

to the right. I continued to fly straight ahead at minimum altitude, since if I had broken right I would have flown right through the core of fire of the turning Spitfire. I was followed briefly, but was soon able to shake it off."

Back at Varrelbusch airfield, Oblt. Dortenmann, who was scheduled to lead the third and final wave, listened in horror to the radio transmissions from the preceding two groups. Interviews with the few surviving returnees sealed his decision. He took off for Rheine with the 12 planes of his *12 Staffel*, climbing to an altitude of 20,000 feet. Ignoring orders to drop to 6,500 feet— orders that had killed numerous pilots from the previous German waves— Dortenmann's squadron managed to pounce on a group of 22 Spitfires of No. 56 and No. 3 (New Zealand) Squadrons of the RAF, sighted west of Osnabrück. Near Dummer Lake his group shot down two at a loss of only one of his own. Uffz. Adam Siebert was went down and Uffz. Gunther Zessin bailed out of "Red 12" after being wounded by enemy cannon fire. These were likely the Tempests of 56 Squadron who reported losing two of their pilots in a wild engagement with fifty Fw-190Ds and Me-109s in that vicinity in the early afternoon. The RAF victor was Fg/Off Turner, who filed one claimed destroyed and another probable. The RAF fortunes did not improve in later engagements. Four more Tempests from 3 (NZ) Squadron were surprised by an aggressive pack of 20-40 German fighters in the Rheine-Dummer lake area. The New Zealanders were lucky to lose only two further fighters and only managed to shoot down a lone Me-109.

The actions over the northern section of the air battle front were exceedingly confused. Differing aircraft of single units were often spread over a large area due to the scattering that took place with large scale air combat in limited weather. Involved in this scrap with the British was the *7 Staffel* of JG 6 and *13 Staffel*, JG 27. The RAF killed Uffz. Schneider's A-8 near Wallenhorst. Meanwhile, Fw. Steinkamp of 13./JG 27 claimed two British fighters shot down in this sector with another credited to *11 Staffel*. In all the British 3 and 56 Squadrons reported four Tempests which did not return to Volkel. Three Me-109s of *13 Staffel*, JG 27 were lost over Alsstätte. Two pilots, Fhr. Ferdinand Miebach and Fw. Patan, were killed.

However, in spite of the greater German success, upon returning to Varrelbusch Obstlt. Priller informed Dortenmann that *3 Jagdivision* had ordered his court martial. However, Priller knew that Dortenmann had almost certainly saved himself and the rest of his pilots from a suicidal mission. Priller advised Dortenmann to keep a low profile and although assigned to an administrative post, the orders for court martial were dropped. The demand for qualified pilots was great and Dortenmann would soon find himself in charge of *III Gruppe* which was still grieving over the loss of the popular Hptm. Weiss.

The surviving pilots of *III/JG 54* would henceforth call December 29th "*Schwarze Tag*"— Black Day. A total of 14 pilots were killed including Weiss.

At least 17 Fw-190D-9s were lost.[86] Including all participating units, the Luftwaffe lost 31 machines. For this they only managed to shoot down 11 British planes. The result was devastating; the "Green Hearts" never really recovered. Counting other casualties from *JG 6* and *JG 27*, the Germans lost a total of twenty pilots in the disastrous melee. British claims exceeded the enemy count by nine aircraft, but by any accounting, it had been a disastrous day for the Luftwaffe. Nearly 30% of the *Jagdwaffe* pilots taking to the air from the three fighter groups on the 29th did not return.

Including the action against *JG 54*, the Canadian fighters had a stellar day. The Allied side of the actions is quickly told: at 9:30 AM 411 Squadron ran into Fw-190s in the Rheine area. Flg. Off. Giberstad peppered one German fighter, but was then bounced by two more, whereupon he dove and then pulled up quickly. His pursuer smashed into the ground. In a mid-day mission, 401 lost one Spitfire when it was hit by twenty German fighters during a reconnaissance sweep, but managed to shoot down two Fw-190s in the melee. Later that afternoon, 411 Squadron was back up when a dozen German fighters were sighted near Osnabrück. Flt. Lt. R.J. Audet, an experienced pilot, but one who had never seen an enemy plane, managed to shoot down five German planes (three Fw-190s and two Me-109s). This was the first and only time in the war that a 2nd TAF pilot shot down five enemy aircraft in a single mission. Three other pilots in the squadron managed to down an enemy fighter each.

The Norwegian-flown Spitfires of 331 Squadron also enjoyed one of their most successful days during the war. West of Arnhem a group of 12 of the fighters sighted five Fw-190s while hunting for enemy motor transport west of Arnhem. Four German fighters were claimed, although Allied losses were high as well. Capt. Raeder's mortally wounded craft was seen to tumble to the ground after having the tail of his Spitfire shot away, Sgt. Nicolaysen was forced to bail out of his stricken machine and two others did not return from the swirling battle. However, later in the afternoon, a further ten Spitfires ran into about 25 Me-109s over Enschede. These planes proved easier hunting for the Norwegians with a dozen being shot down. One pilot, Capt. Grundt-Spang, claimed three himself. Unlike the engagement with the Fw-190s, there were no casualties.

Diminishing visibility retarded the contribution of Anderson's IX Bombardment Division. On the morning of the 29th 111 medium bombers were

---

86 The opinion of German pilots flying the long-nosed FW 190D-9s was mixed. The Jumo 213A engine gave the plane better high altitude performance, greater speed (426 mph at 21,650 feet) and dive capability. Acceleration in combat was improved by the use of a methanol/water injection system which boosted the powerplant output from 1,750 to 2,240 horsepower. However, the big engine had required increasing the length of the fuselage by four feet, and the resulting airframe lacked the incredible turn and roll rate of its predecessor. The armament was also less than the standard FW-190 with two 13mm machine guns above the engine and two 20mm cannons in the wings. And perhaps most important, the changeover from an old familiar aircraft to a new machine was a particularly dangerous juncture for a veteran pilot.

dispatched to attack the road bridges at Keuchingen and Salmchateau, but had to be recalled due to the weather. Some 37 aircraft were dispatched the following day to hit the Eller bridge, but were unable to see to attack; another planned mission that afternoon to the railroad bridges at Simmern, Bad Münster and Konz-Karthaus were also cancelled. The only contribution came from six medium bombers who added to the massive destruction at St. Vith with another 12 tons of bombs on the afternoon of December 29th. Although good results were being obtained in the interdiction program, many of the targets would have to be continually harassed to stay ahead of the German repair crews. [87]

Later that night, in spite of the awful weather, the British Mosquitos were able to fly a mission to blind bomb the German-held town of Vielsalm. Weather conditions were still horrid the next day, but the British were determined to hurt the target and repeated the attack on Vielsalm once more with 36 Mitchells dropping 60 tons of bombs at 2:44 PM. Another Bomber Command assault would attempt to hit the town by radar on December 31st with an additional 35 tons, but the bombs fell on the nearby village of Bech.

Mercifully for the German pilots of the beleaguered *Jagdwaffe*, the weather again closed in on December 30th. The Allied effort comprised only 470 sorties by XIX TAC with XXIX TAC managing another 36 missions. Of these, only 68 sorties were over the Ardennes, most being flown by the indefatigable 362nd and 406th Fighter Groups. The few missions were effective, however, and were gauged instrumental to the American victory in the fierce tank battle fought south of Bastogne. Claims for the 406th included 23 tanks and 32 motor transport.

The 405th FG again supported the XII Corps with 57 sorties only to lose another pilot, Lt. Charles W. Loesch, to friendly flak while giving chasing to two enemy Me-109s over Luxembourg City.[88] It was to be the last operation of the group in 1944. December had been a tough month: 15 pilots had been lost with 22 aircraft and 111 aircraft of the group had suffered flak damage. Against this the 405th claimed 44 enemy aircraft shot down with another five probables. Although the weather prevented direct intervention over the

---

87 Anderson's IX BD dispatched 2,196 bomber sorties between 23 and 27 December, concentrating on destruction of the rail bridges feeding trains to the marshalling yards to the east of the Ardennes. Reconnaissance on the latter date revealed the following results: Bridges out: Euskirchen, Altenburg, Mayen, Ehrang, Konz-Karthaus, Nonnweiler and that at Morscheid taken out by the Eighth Air Force; damaged or probably out: Ahrweiler, Eller; Not out: Bad Münster, Kaiserlautern, Bullay.

88 This incident was the last straw in a series of troubles with friendly anti-aircraft units. On December 27th American gunners had shot down a P-61. Other P-51s and P-47s were fired on in Luxembourg on the day that Loesch was killed. The issue went all the way up to the Ninth Air Force and to Bradley's headquarters. "Request restrictions of friendly AA on any except identified enemy aircraft which are actually strafing or bombing," requested Weyland, "We do not want bad feelings." But the ID problems went both ways. On December 31st, Vandenberg ordered an immediate investigation to begin on four P-47s which had strafed a group of American tanks on the road that day between Luxembourg and Thionville. The problem became so contentious that XIX TAC was ordered not to operate over the XII Corps in the Southern Ardennes.

battlefield, this did little to stop the interdiction of the German rail communications to the east. The 367th Fighter Group bombed the Siegfried marshalling yards, destroying rail lines, two trains and creating havoc at the enemy collection point.

The 362nd FG, with seven missions, flew against Bourcy and Derenbach on the 30th and the rail marshalling yards at Neunkirchen on the 31st giving them "the napalm treatment." They also kept up their torment on the Germans around Bastogne— a dedicated support alongside the 406th FG which would continue over the next few days as the Germans attempted to recapture the town in desperate ground fighting. West of that town, the village of Chenogne was effectively bombed by the 362nd FG after which U.S. troops were able to advance. To the southeast, the group sighted some 32 enemy tanks of which 15 were claimed knocked out in the ensuing action. The price of the actions were two pilots and Thunderbolts lost. Lt. Robert E. Daw clipped a tree while strafing south of Bastogne and Lt. Joseph J. Maucini, Jr. was hit by flak and bailed out only to have his chute fail to open. Meanwhile, in Chenogne, the *39 Regiment, 26 Volksgrenadier Division* reported the town a funeral pyre with its *2 Battalion* badly cut up.

Hitler's order to "displace enemy forces at Bastogne" had taken effect. In an effort to comply with the Führer's request, the Luftwaffe launched 52 German planes to strike the town just after dark on the 29th and before dawn on the 30th.[89] The Ju-88s and Ju-188s of Helmut Schmidt's *KG 66* struck in two waves; the bombing was severe, driving Combat Command B of the 10th Armored out of it's headquarters and sending the local civilian populace into headlong flight. This was the largest single ground attack mounted by the German Luftwaffe during the Ardennes Campaign.

The weather certainly did not still the Eighth Air Force, however, which dispatched 1,315 bombers and 572 fighter aircraft on escort to hit German rail communications. This time, however, the Luftwaffe did not even show and only four bombers and two fighters were lost in another massive operation. The 3rd Bomb Division planted explosives on targets at Kassel; the 1st BD hit Bullay, Kaiserlautern, Mainz and Bischoffsheim. Meanwhile the 2nd BD plunked a rain of bombs on bridges at Altenahr, Auskirchen, Irlich, Remagen and Mechernich. In all, nearly 3,500 tons of bombs were leveled at German communications.

The effect of this punishment on the German transport system was dramatic. *Heeresgruppe B* announced that Allied air power was dominating the air space over the battle zone and was destroying all traffic centers. The systematic destruction of the rail system in the Eifel meant that supplies and troops now had to be unloaded along the Rhine and trucked west, resulting in "double consumption" and great delay in getting the logistics to the

---

89 OB West reported some 73 sorties dispatched for Bastogne in the two attacks that evening.

fighting units at the front. Entire convoys ran out of gas; on January 4th the *Sixth Panzer Armee* reported that its two supply routes were now obstructed by stationary trucks.

Against the total 2,600 Allied aircraft aloft, the Germans sent a mere 130 fighters that day. Noting the extensive damage to the rail resupply stations at Euskirchen, Düsseldorf, Koblenz and Remagen, *OB West* reported a "further battering of all rearward communications," and "the attempt by the enemy to create a "traffic desert" in the entire rear area of *Heeresgruppe B* and G. A German POW from the *5th Fallschirmjäger Division* described Koblenz on December 30th: "...the city was still burning as result of the air raid on December 29th. Most of the streets were completely destroyed and all traffic in the city was stopped. Almost no stores were open and food and water was unattainable." Even the night was not safe. The previous evening 380 Allied medium bombers had attacked road centers under the cover of darkness. Only 35 German night fighters had been scrambled to oppose them. *OB West* gloomily recorded "a substantial strain on supply," adding that "the severity of the effects of the enemy air force could definitely be compared with that of Normandy."

XIX

Year's End: December 31st

On the last day of the year, the weather improved slightly and all three American TACs were aloft. A total of 703 sorties were flown. Most, however, were not over the Ardennes. Of the battle zone sorties, IX flew 140, XXIX flew 70 and XIX flew 296, but were unable to support friendly ground forces due to sky conditions over the southern part of the Ardennes. Anderson's medium bombers of the IX BD were totally grounded.

In the IX TAC, the 474th FG was very active, attacking the German- held towns of La Roche and Nadrin. The 366th FG put up sixty sorties with most over the Malmédy and Trier areas. The 370th FG put in numerous sorties in the Malmédy area. Nugent's XXIX TAC flew largely armed reconnaissance missions in the St. Vith-Hollerath-Euskirchen area, the 48th FG hitting Prüm with napalm.

Weyland's XIX TAC was frustrated in its attempts to assist Patton on the ground— the fog and mists were too low. Instead his fighters flew free-lance sweeps between the Saar and Koblenz areas. In all, XIX ground claims for the day totaled 501 motor transport and 23 armored vehicles. The 367th FG attacked three towns near Bastogne, but found the murk too thick to provide really close support. The 397th Squadron of the 368th FG did manage to strike the village of Bleialf east of St. Vith where the Germans, obviously desperate, were towing artillery pieces with ambulances. But most sorties were not over the Ardennes due to the conditions. A good example is the 362nd and 406th FGs, which, upon finding the weather too poor to allow them to intervene in the confused fighting around Bastogne, took their missions to expand on the accumulated damage to the old Roman city of

Trier. Other XIX missions were south of the battle zone. The 354th FG hit the rail bridge at Bingen and bombed the town of Ingleheim.

However, one group now flying for the XIX TAC, the 365th FG, had a big day with some six missions and a protracted encounter with the increasingly scarce Luftwaffe. The "Hell Hawks" continued their missions against rail targets in the Saar area. Targets included marshalling yards and rail bridges at Zweibrucken, Neunkirchen, Simmern, Kuzen, Bad Kreuznach, Bingen and Hetzerath. However, while chasing locomotives near Simmern, the 386th Squadron, under 1st Lt. Melvin Q. Carlson, ran into Me-109s and a tense dogfight developed in which four German fighters were destroyed by 2nd Lt. John H. Wallace, 1st Lt. John H. Mooney, Lt. Howard R. Dentz and 1st Lt. Thomas Manjak. The Thunderbolts returned to Metz to land in the midst of a snowstorm. The pilots went to sleep in their bunks in the knowledge that tomorrow would just bring more of the monotonous diving bombing missions against their hapless enemy. There was little partying that night. The inhospitable environs of Metz inspired little socializing. Most of the weary flyers pulled up the covers believing that the Luftwaffe was all but defeated.

RAF Bomber Command was in operation that night. Ninety-seven bombers dropped 530 tons of explosives on the town of Houffalize. The mediums of the IX BD added to the destruction by dumping 60 tons of bombs during a daylight raid on December 30th. The town, through which the Germans were attempting to escape from the region west of the Ourthe River, was devastated and a wide area around it was heavily cratered. Many civilians were killed in the bombing. The same night, another 457 bombers hit Cologne-Kalk Nord. The following morning Bomber Command launched a daytime strike to hit the rails at Vohwinkel with 763 tons of bombs.

The weather in the north in Quesada's IX TAC operations area was also poor and no direct ground support missions could be flown due to the weather. However, the 352nd Fighter Group was out once more and reported sighting three Arado 234s which it attacked. One Arado was claimed by Lt. Col. John C. Meyer, but the records of III/KG 76, while agreeing on the encounter and the fact that it was fired upon, shows that none of its jet bombers were harmed. All told, the IX TAC flew 147 sorties dropping 29 tons of bombs. Two enemy aircraft were claimed for the loss of three.

The intrepid Capt. Hoefker of Weyland's 10th PRG was again out in the Bastogne area looking to provide information on the enemy to aide the intense fighting there. While looking for a hole in the dense cloud cover, Hoefker's luck ran out. A lucky shot from enemy light flak guns hit his aircraft. Smoke filled the cockpit and the plane immediately caught on fire. He had no choice but to bail out. It was Hoefker's second plane in eight days!

However, after his last encounter with those on the ground, this was the least of his worries. But the soldiers who were searching for him weren't from the 4th Infantry Division. They were the enemy. He had came down over German lines. Hoefker hid in some nearby woods and used some of his parachute material to cover his freezing feet and the rest to try to stay warm in the frigid cold. For two days he hid in the forests while the Germans looked for him. He could hear their voices and played a cat and mouse game with his would-be captors. At one time they came within fifteen feet of his hiding place. But on the third day, Hoefker was hungry, freezing and increasingly desperate. The weather closed in on January 2nd with cold, thick ground fog. Although growing weaker, Hoefker used the night and fog to work his way towards American lines. On January 3rd, the Captain was back again with his unit, albeit with frost-bitten feet.

Ninth Air Force claims from December 23rd to the year's end were impressive, if obviously inflated. They amounted to the supposed destruction of 264 German aircraft, 2,323 motor vehicles, 207 tanks, 173 gun positions, 620 rail cars and 7 bridges.[90]

Although the poor weather since December 26th had limited the operations of the Ninth Air Force, Doolittle's Eighth was able to fill in. With the enemy obviously turned back in the Ardennes, the Allied air commanders moved to reestablish priority for the strategic bombing offensive. On the last day of the year a huge operation with some 1,327 bombers escorted by some 785 fighters moved to hit a number of oil facilities, particularly those in the Hamburg area. Unlike recent days, however, the Germans put up much greater air opposition. Most of this was due to a change in targets back to oil, which could always be expected to get a rise out of the enemy. They did little to stop the eventual conflagration— 3,500 tons of bombs were dropped.

The operation was a costly one for both sides. With the Allies estimating only 200 Luftwaffe sorties up against the Eighth Air Force, some 87 German fighters were claimed shot down at a cost of 27 bombers and ten P-51 and P-47 fighters. The enormous bomber fleet was met by the old, but deadly, adversaries of the Eighth Air Force, *JG 300* and *JG 301*. Flak defenses over Hamburg were severe and the 3rd Bomb Division lost ten bombers to anti-aircraft fire and fourteen to the defending enemy fighters. Half of the losses were concentrated in a single unit, Col. Thomas S. Jeffrey's 100th Bomb Group. The "Bloody 100th" was a hard luck outfit, having suffered intensely on six separate occasions starting in the Regensberg debacle in 1943. Even the 91st and 96th BGs, who had losses in excess of the 100th,

---

90 A tally of inspected German armored vehicles that *Heeresgruppe B* left on the Ardennes battlefield, destroyed from all causes, amounted to 413 vehicles. A good example of the ratio of air claims to kills is given by the inspection of 91 of those in January by the Allied Ordnance Evacuation Companies. Of the total, only seven were diagnosed as being disabled by air attack.

considered the unit a "jinxed group." Alone, the 100th BG accounted for 12 of the losses that day. William B. Sterret, flying as the navigator on Lt. Billy R. Blackman's crew with the 100th BG, poignantly captures the terrible drama:

> "December 31 1944 is one day in my life I will never forget. When the map was uncovered in the briefing room we all gave a sigh because we knew that Hamburg was a rough target. For some unknown reason I believe that all of the crew had a feeling that this was going to be our last one...When we finished all the last minute checks we gathered in the tent and waited by the fire until time came to start our engines. It was our usual procedure to kid one another and 'shoot the bull' but everyone was very quiet on this particular morning...We took off at 7:15 and went through the usual procedure of assembling over England. We left the English coast at 9:00 and went up to the North Sea...The wind was supposed to be about 150 knots at altitude, but it was actually much stronger. Consequently, we drifted about 30 miles which put us almost over Holland. The lead navigator began to correct our heading which made us fly directly into the wind. This reduced our ground speed to about 100 mph...We were all talking over the intercom and wondering what was going to happen next...We finally got to our IP, turned on our rack switch, opened the bomb bay doors and started down the bomb run. At this point we all usually cut off our heated suits because the nervous energy was enough to keep you warm even though it was 50 degrees below zero...The target could be seen from our IP even though it took us about ten minutes to actually get over it...We could also see the groups in front of us getting shot at and we knew that we would soon be in the middle of it. No-one was saying a word. We were all just hoping and praying that we would come through without any trouble. Finally, we got into the flak, which was really accurate. We could hear the shells as they burst, which is too close for comfort...I could hear the pieces of shrapnel beating on the side of the ship...At 11:33 the lead ship dropped his smoke bombs, which was a signal for all of the wing ships to drop their bombs. Andy hit the toggle switch and out went our bombs. You always fet better as soon as the bombs were gone because you felt like your job was done."

The B-17s on their bomb run flew in a very tight formation and the well-practiced flak gunners at Hamburg let loose one volley after another. As the Fortresses dropped their bombs, the B-17 led by Lt. F. Henderson was hit by flak and dropped off sharply, suddenly smashing into another Fortress flown by Lt. C. Williams. Both aircraft plunged to the ground in a flaming wreckage. Meanwhile, the flak had riddled Lt. Bill Blackman's B-17:

> "...We started for our rally point, but had only flown for two minutes when Carson, the ball turret gunner, called Bill and said oil was pouring out of number three engine...Bill feathered the engine. As soon as number three had stopped running Carson called again and said number four engine was also losing oil. Bill feathered this engine too. We were unable to keep up with the formation with only two engines, but we could hold our altitude. Bill Blackman called us all and said, 'Stick with it boys. We'll get this thing

home yet.'...Bill called for fighter escort, but he couldn't contact any because they had been unable to get off the ground in England due to bad weather. He turned back on the intercom and said, 'Bandits in the area!' At that instant Joe Pearl, the engineer, yelled, 'They're coming in at 6 o'clock!' I looked up through the astrodome and saw two Fw-190s coming in on our tail. I turned around and grabbed my gun hoping I could get a shot in. No such luck. We could see tracers as they passed us. 20mm shells were also flying around. We all realized that our chances of getting through were pretty slim. A 20mm shell exploded in the cockpit and knocked out all the insulation between the pilots' compartment and the nose section where I was. The ship was on fire and started spinning. I realized that it was time to leave. When we got to the escape hatch Bob Fortney, the radio operator, was lying on his back on the cat-walk. I thought he was hurt so I started to help him, but he got up and told me to get out so I put one foot on the door and pushed it out. Then I jumped. As soon as I cleared the ship I took off my helmut, pulled my ripcord and looked back to see the ship blow up. Bill said that he reached behind his head to fire the Very pistol to call for help and a 20mm shell exploded and knocked him out. When he came to he rang the bell and managed to get his chute on. When he got to the nose, the ship blew up. He came to falling through the air and pulled his ripcord. The next thing he knew he was on the round and Krauts were standing around him. They told him that another boy (Bob Freshour) had been found with his chute open, but he was dead. Basil Numack, one of the waist gunners and Joe Pearl were killed by the fighters. Carson was unable to get out of the ball turret and Fortney did not have his chute on. Andy Herbert, the tail gunner, and Tom Pace survived and were made POW...I landed in the middle of a field which was surrounded by woods, but Krauts were coming at me from all directions with rifles. This was enough to make me stop. There was about six inches of snow on the ground. They searched me and said, 'For you the war is over.'"

As usual, the German fighters had been prepared to sacrifice themselves to protect the refineries; numerous packs of Me-109s and Fw-190s were encountered in the vicinity. Capt. Julius Maxwell of the 78th Fighter Group shot down its last German fighter using the P-38 aircraft (the group's 400th claim). The 56th Fighter Group closed out the year in a combat with the enemy in the vicinity of Hanover. Capt. James Carter led the group to engage several Me-109s. They were in turn bounced by seven Fw-190s. In the ensuing melee, three of the Fw-190s were downed, but two "Wolfpack" members were also lost. Lt. Andrew Chasko had his plane shot out from under him and became a prisoner and Lt. William H. Stovall, Jr. was killed. In another action, the 355th Fighter Group escorted a group of B-17s to the area around Hanover. In these actions Maj. Gordon Graham knocked out two Fw-190s.

Meanwhile, the 364th Fighter Group had some of the toughest fighting of the day. The group fought off numerous packs of enemy planes and blasted 25 enemy fighters out the sky.[91] The aerial combat was nip and tuck and the German pilots were obviously skilled. Lt. William N. Hess flew into a collection of enemy fighters and managed to shoot down three German fighters, although running into an aggressive German pilot. In a jousting match, Hess and the Luftwaffe pilot traded half a dozen straight-on passes at each other with guns blazing. Hess felt certain this game of aerial "chicken" would soon end in collision, when the Fw-190 burst into flame on the final pass. Hess dived down, barely missing the flaming aircraft and watched the German pilot pop his canopy and bail out. Maj. Sam Wicker, of the 364th shot down four enemy fighters that day in combat that was even more hair-raising. His group was about 35 miles south of Hamburg when he spotted a massive collection of German fighters: three gaggles of 50-75 fighters each!

"I don't believe they had seen us until now, if so, they believed us to be Me-109s because we were able to close in to about 600 yards before firing. I closed on the first gaggle of six 190s with my squadron (6 P-51s) and fired from 600 yards on what I believed to be a wingman. At this time they still had drop tanks...I fired about a three second burst at this wingman and saw a concentration of strikes in the cockpit. There seemed to be an explosion and the canopy blew off. The pilot was wounded, the ship went out of control and spun in. The pilot tried to bail out, but could not make it. Next I slid in behind the leader of the flight and fired 4 to 6 bursts into his left wing and engine. It smoked, but did not catch fire until about five seconds later at which time the pilot bailed out. By this time the rest of the pilots in the gaggle realized what was going on and split-essed for the deck. This gaggle did not reach the bombers. As I rolled to follow them down I took a quick look around and noticed the other two gaggles were being engaged. I only had one ship with me, my wingman. The other flight of four had split up and were on their way down after the Fw-190s. My wingman and I singled out one 190 and went hell-for-leather to the deck after him. We pulled out at 1,000 feet and the 190 pulled back, straight up. Then we went into a Lufbery and he did things with that 190 that no ship was ever designed for. In my 10 months of combat I have never seen a better Jerry pilot. I hung on his tail, but it was impossible to use the K-14 sight as we were pulling 7 Gs. I was wearing my G-suit and did not black out but nevertheless I could not hit him. I fired on my back and in every position possible until I ran out of ammunition. Then I called my wingman and told him to take over and I would become his wingman. We changed positions and my wingman made one pass at him. He took evasive action by doing an Immelmann and two snap rolls at the top, to end up on my tail! From that point on I did not see my wingman as I tried to sake the Jerry off my tail. I was out of ammo and low on gas as I tried to run for it, but could not break off combat...I did a very tight loop, with flaps, on the deck and succeeded in getting on his tail. However, this was no good as I was out of

91 The 78th was in the process of converting to the Mustang, a change-over that the intensely dedicated "Jug" pilots opposed. Both the 78th and 56th Fighter Groups were part of the original P-47 groups with the Eighth Air Force and remained steadfastly loyal to their Thunderbolts. The conversion was being done based on recent performance data showing that the P-47D was inferior to the new Fw-190D in speed and climb. However, the 56th Fighter Group let it be known that they were not interested in the P-51 and preferred to entrust their fate to their ever-popular P-47D and the coming delivery of new souped up P-47Ms with a top speed of 473 mph.

ammo. As I was just about to break off and run for it again, I looked back and saw three more Fw-190s in position and firing at me. This was too damn much for me and I was sure I had had it. I used flaps at 120 mph and closed to about 25 yards on the lead 190 at which time he pulled up and tried to split-ess from six to 800 feet. He went in and exploded. At this time I saw tracers passing in front of my nose so I shoved the stick forward and kicked bottom rudder, doing what I think was an inverted vertical reversement. I redded out with a terrific headache and when I recovered I saw I had pulled negative 4 Gs. This threw the three 190s off. I tried to run for an overcast, but they caught me before I made it, so I turned with them a few more times and ended up on the tail of two of them. The wingman must have been a Junior Birdman because he was so scared he pulled up and bailed out. I did one more turn, all the time working nearer the overcast. Then I broke off and then pulled up into it and flew on instruments. I found that I had only 50 gallons of gas left and didn't know exactly where I was. I flew 245 degrees until I came out the overcast. At this point I could see the Zuider Zee so I turned south to our lines. I crossed lines with only a few minutes of fuel left and saw a small field with Spitfires on it. I made a straight approach, running out of fuel as I was taxiing to a parking area."

The Royal Air Force was also in action; 137 Squadron had just completed pasting a German train near Meppen-Menhaus when Plt. Off. R.A. Egley spotted two Fw-190s approaching from their side. Coming about, he shot down one with his Typhoon, although tragedy struck when Plt. Off. J.A.D. Shemeld, the longest-serving member of the squadron, was killed by enemy flak. During the day 182 and 247 Squadrons busied themselves flinging rockets at enemy motor transport. However, the squadrons paid for their kills with two losses from each Squadron. 411 Squadron was again airborne, shooting down a Ju-88 south-west of Rheine and another Fw-190D. On the return leg of their mission, 442 Squadron ran into a group of fifteen Me-109s near Münster and shot down four; 416 also downed a further Fw-190. But when everyone came back, the end of a terrible 1944 was there to celebrate. To think of the days gone by; "Auld Lang Syne" indeed. For the RAF pilots, just like everyone one else. There were many friends to remember and much to forget. That night back at the RAF airfield at Eindhoven, Corp. E.W.J. "Ted" Sadler, the guard on watch, listened as the drunken Canadians at the airfield celebrated midnight with an off-key rendition of Robert Burns old Scottish melody. It was a beautiful and sad moment. Another year, soon punctuated by the Canadians firing off their small arms into the dark New Year's sky. Everyone, Sadler thought, was happy to be alive in 1945. But his reverie was suddenly interrupted when a German nightfighter "spy plane" suddenly flew overhead at low altitude. By the time Sadler got his Sten gun it was gone. What was it doing here? He would find out the next morning.

The total German air effort of some 550 sorties on the last day of the year was not principally over the battlefield. Most of the Luftwaffe missions were essayed to stop the bomber fleets of the Eighth Air Force. The sharp end of the counter was the 175 Me-109s and Fw-190A-8s of the two "Reich" *Geschwader JG 300* and *JG 301*. The Germans took the usual excess of losses— some forty aircraft of the two units would fall out of the sky near Bremen over Rotenburg. Most of these were felled by the 78th and 364th Fighter Groups. However, the American also suffered; the 100th Bomb Group lost seven B-17s shot down by German fighters out of the 14 felled from the 3rd Bomb Division. In these actions, *I Jagdkorps* reported some 188 aircraft dispatched during the day to forestall the Allied bombers. The cost was heavy. In all, *JG 300* and *JG 301* would lose 24 pilots killed or missing and another eleven wounded in some of the fiercest air combat of the entire year.

Elsewhere the Luftwaffe effort was low-key; *II Jagdkorps* reported only 196 sorties— under orders to preserve their strength for an important upcoming mission. Thirteen planes did not return from the day's sorties. Elements of *JG 4* did fly close to the Ardennes only to be sharply repulsed by U.S. fighters. They had orders to intercept the American fighter-bombers over the Palatinate. The mission would cost four Luftwaffe pilots with not a single kill of their own. One of the casualties was Lt. Hans Schleef, the experienced leader of the *16 Staffel* with 98 kills to his credit. *JG 1* was also up in limited action. However, 1944 ended on a low note for *6 Staffel* which lost three pilots that day. Uffz. Gerhard Hartig and Rudolf Wezulek were killed over Mesum and Ofw. Werner Essinger bailed from his Fw-190A-8 over Burgsteinfurt. Meanwhile, Hptm. Hans-Georg Hackbarth a veteran of *JG 1* since only November 15th, now found himself the successor to Hans Ehlers, who had been killed the previous Wednesday. He would lead the shaken *I Gruppe* into its most difficult battle the following day.

On the last day of the year, *III/JG 77* launched an offensive patrol over the Ruhr Valley. However, Spitfires surprised six Me-109s, shooting down three of them. Two of the German pilots were killed. The third, Fw. Karl-Heinz Böttner of *11./JG 77* was forced to jump from his damaged K-4 to drift to the ground. Badly injured, the veteran was sent to a hospital. Böttner was one of the few veterans of the group, having come to *III Gruppe* at the end of 1942 and having fought in Africa, Italy and Rumania, gaining many victories. He would never fly again.

Meanwhile, the Germans attempted to gather intelligence for the upcoming venture. The close-reconnaissance Me-109s of *NAG 13* were called on to carry out four missions in the Rochefort, Kesternich, Malmédy and Arlon areas. Unfortunately all eight aircraft were called off due to weather or pursuit by the Allied fighter defense. Only a single Ar-234 of *Kdo. Sperling* was able to fly over the Antwerp-St. Trond-Venlo area during the late morning hours.

There were other offensive hiccups for the Germans on the last day of the year. In the early morning hours of that Sunday, 63 German night fighters droned over Allied rear areas dropping bombs indiscriminately. One of these, a Ju-88G-1 of *S./NJG2* was shot down over Palenberg, west of Aachen another fell over Venlo. *I Jagdkorps* reported 36 night-fighters out on a continuous mission from 6 PM to 4 AM on the 30th in the area of Sedan-Luxembourg-Metz-Verdun with the focal point of the operations over Bastogne. *Jafue Mittelrhein* assigned another 12 Ju-88s to night nuisance raids in the St. Quentin-Paris-Marne and St. Dizier areas. Three Fw-190s of *SG 4* were earmarked to attack American troop assemblies around Bastogne, while two others were sent on a weather reconnaissance. But these raids were scarcely more than a wake-up call for many of the Allied outposts, accustomed at they were to the antics of the German night fighters over the previous two weeks. More successful were the 31 speedy jet Me-262s of *KG(J) 51* which succeeded in penetrating Allied air space nearly undetected. They dropped their bomb loads on Liège, Hasselt and Neufchâteau without incident, but these missions were mere pin pricks compared to the devastation meted out by the Eighth Air Force.

A total of 137 German planes of *II Jagdkorps* were essayed to intervene in the Ardennes fighting, including the jets. As with many of these Luftwaffe sorties, most German flights were turned back long before they crossed the Rhine to reach the Ardennes. One of the German missions that was not intercepted was another operation by ten jet-bombers of *KG 76* under Hptm. Diether Lukesch who was ordered to hit Bastogne:

> "I took off at 10:30 hours in F1+BT carrying one SC-500 Tr bomb. As we reached our planned altitude of 20,000 feet enemy bombers approached head on at the same altitude, protected on both sides by fighter screens. Under the circumstances turning aside was too risky so I flew straight through the bomber formation without changing altitude. The other pilots did the same...After bombing the Bastogne pocket we were attacked by fighters on the right. I began a slow climb in order not to lose too much speed, keeping the fighters in sight. Since I was looking directly into his firing guns, the bullets were passing behind me. Suddenly he rolled over on the right wing apparently stalling his aircraft and I escaped. One Arado was, however, damaged by gunfire in the wings and stabilizer during the attack."

Lukesch's would-be assailants were the P-51 Mustangs of the 352nd Fighter Group, who that day reported sighting three Ar-234s near Euskirchen and shooting down one. To the contrary, the *Einsatzstaffel* had gotten out of the engagement with all its aircraft and pilots.

For their troubles on the last day of the year, the Germans would shoot down a total of 27 American bombers and 10 fighters at a very heavy cost. The USAAF claimed some 61 enemy aircraft destroyed; the German loses totalled 49 pilots when the wounded were included. Thirty-seven Luftwaffe pilots were killed. Later that night, *LG-1* struck the town of Bastogne in a 52-plane bombing raid, designed to pave the way for a coming German ground assault.[92] A smaller raid also blasted the road communications center a Neufchâteau some 25 miles away. Describing the mission, *II Jagdkorps* reported "good aiming of bombs at the middle of the town. Entire target covered." The report was accurate; the air raid killed many civilians. In the town of Bastogne, fires raged throughout the night.

Returning from their dangerous missions, the weary pilots of the Luftwaffe looked forward to some drink and merriment that night to cut the gloomy prospects of the New Year. From December 16th - 31st the Luftwaffe had lost some 464 pilots killed or missing in the effort to support Hitler's last offensive.[93] Another 150 had been wounded. The week of December 23rd - 31st was particularly deadly— 316 German pilots did not return during this time. On Christmas Day alone, *Luftflotte West* recorded 260 aircrew casualties. With one pilot in every four that had begun the operation dead, there was plenty to try and forget. Even the solace of home base could not be taken for granted, for some 80 Allied bombing raids had been conducted against the German airfields over the last two weeks. German aircraft were destroyed on the ground with a further 140 damaged. The situation for the protection of the Reich was at least as gloomy; since Boxing Day the Eighth Air Force had flown 5,516 heavy bomber sorties. An average daily full daylight mission strength comprised over 1,000 bombers dispatched (with 700 fighters on escort) to pulverize the German heartland. *I Jagdkorps* (*JG 300* and *JG 301*) was hardly able to ruffle this great force— only 63 bombers and 23 fighters were claimed during a period when the German home defense suffered the loss of 128 fighters.

New Year's eve did not witness any attack on the German aerodromes; all was quiet. However, upon returning to their quarters, the Luftwaffe crews were dismayed to learn that all evening passes had been cancelled and all alcohol was strictly forbidden. The orders for *KG 51* called for lights out at 19.00 hrs with very tight security. Every possible plane was to be made ready. No one knew what the mission would be, but clearly something was up. Lt. Moser, the technical officer for *I Gruppe* worked long into the night to make every possible Me-262 serviceable. When the "black men" at Rheine wearily headed for bed before sunrise, they could count 21 of the speedy jets ready for battle.

Meanwhile, back at Juvincourt, France, the men of the 367th Fighter Group asked their young commander if they could use their signal pistols

---

92 A good example of these operations was the odyssey of "L1+AH" of 2./*LG 1*. At 5 PM eight Ju-88A-4s of I/*LG 1* took off from Varrel with orders to continue the punishment of the troops in Bastogne. The aircraft, piloted by Lt. Rolf von Kampen, was flying at 3,500 feet in approach to the target when hit by light AA fire. The controls were severed and the crew of five all parachuted to safety north of Arlon. The crew had been on their 11th nighttime raid when captured. The pilot had been shot down on his fifth mission during an operation on Christmas Eve, but had returned to his unit soon thereafter. The American interviewers found von Kampen "a confirmed Nazi who built high hopes on the Rundstedt offensive."

93 Before the operation, from December 1-15, the Luftwaffe recorded 136 fighter pilots killed or missing.

to celebrate New Year's by firing off flares. Col. Ed Chickering was generally against such drunken festivities as some of his young men had been injured by accidents. But what the hell, it was New Year's. "That sounds like a great idea," he agreed, "We'll have a countdown, and everyone can fire them off at the same time. But as Capt. Lloyd Sellin, the Group Intelligence Officer, waited to give the signal, the men heard a growling drone off in the distance. It was "Pee-Call Charlie!" Sellin looked at Chickering. "Colonel, what'll I do?" "Hell," the commander shrugged, "go ahead and give them the count-down." Just as the German night-fighter appeared, the night sky around the tented compound erupted into a blinding cascade of flares and gunfire. The German plane turned tail and buzzed away. Still, Chickering had tired of these enemy intruders. Night after night his precious slumber had been interrupted by the machine gun firing apparitions. The next morning he called on a friend with an anti-aircraft battalion to obtain the loan of a .50 calibre quad-mount machine gun. He set up the "meatchopper" in a field near the chateau to wait out Charlie. It was a long vigil in the bitter cold. "I sat up all night," Chickering remembered, "but the Germans never came back. I darn near froze to death waiting."

Precisely at midnight, Adolf Hitler took to the airwaves. His shrill mono-logue could be clearly heard throughout Europe:

> Only the turn of the year causes me to speak to you today, my German men and women...Although our enemies have predicted our collapse during every one of our past years, they set special hopes on 1944...But once again, we have turned fate away...That this fight itself is an incredibly hard one is due to the enemy's aims...to exterminate our people. When destroying our towns they do not only hope to kill German women and children, but also to eliminate our 1,000 year old civilization...Our people are resolved to fight the war to victory under any and all circumstances...the world must know that this State will, therefore, never capitulate...Germany will rise like a phoenix from its ruined cities and go down in history as the miracle of the 20th Century!...We shall fulfill our duty faithfully and unshakably in the new year too, in the firm belief that the hour will strike when victory ultimately will come to him most worthy of it, the Greater German Reich.

Two hours after midnight, Albert Speer arrived by automobile at *Adler-horst*. It had taken him and his liaison officer, Manfred von Poser, some 24 hours to drive the 200 miles from the Ardennes to Bad Nauheim. Both men were mentally exhausted, depressed by the destruction they had witnessed at the front. On the way back, they were hard-pressed to evade the hornet-like swarm of Allied fighter-bombers overhead. In a game of cat and mouse, there had been several close calls. Presently, they arrived. After passing a maze of checkpoints, Speer entered the cloister-like blockhouse that was Hitler's headquarters. Inside he was surprised to find everyone but the Führer toasting the New Year with champagne. All of the secretaries, party officials and generals seemed strangely cheerful. The German leader made wistful prophecies. This was the low point, he said; in 1945 things would be better. Ultimately the Third Reich would be victorious. The gathering around Hitler took his forecasts in an uneasy silence until Martin Bormann stepped in to second them. The German leader's self-serving optimism continued for nearly two hours, his charisma sweeping most of those around him into a pleasant state of unwarranted credulity and hopefulness. "Hitler seemed to be the only one in the company who was drunk without having taken any stimulating beverage," Speer recalled, "He was in the grip of permanent euphoria."

This P-51 Mustang skidded off the icy runway on return to England. (NASM)

The Flying Fortress "This is It" is in the foreground and other B-17s of the 381st Bomb Group encounter flak as they approach their target of Mainz, Germany, on December 30, 1944. *(NASM)*

Fw. Karl-Heinz Böttner of *11./JG 77* is shown in his K-4 at Neuruppin. Böttner was shot down on the last day of the year by Spitfires, and although wounded, managed to parachute to friendly lines. *(Böttner via Roba)*

Adlerhorst. A bespectacled Hitler and his top generals discuss *Operation Bodenplatte* on January 1st, 1945. To Hitler's right, Reichsmarschall Hermann Göring leans over the table. Behind Göring is Gen. Karl Koller, the Luftwaffe chief of staff. To Hitler's immediate left is Genmaj. Dietrich Peltz. Gen. Heinz Guderian, visiting from the endangered Russian front, points to the map. *(Böttner via Roba)*

Year's End: December 31st

Obst. Josef. "Pips" Priller, the long-time *Kommodore* of *JG 26*. (Cranston via Caldwell)

BELOW: Men in black. German ground crew service a Fw-190A-8 with a generator used to ensure sufficient electrical power to start its BMW 801D engine. *(Bundesarchiv)*

RIGHT: Lt. Col. John C. Meyer. The high-scoring ace of the 352nd Fighter Group was deputy commander of the unit when the Germans struck on New Year's Day. (HRC)

BELOW: Lt. Melvin Paisley (left) and Lt. Jack Kennedy pose with part of a wing of a German aircraft shot down over Asch airfield on January 1st, 1945. (HRC)

Spitfire IXs of 412 (Canadian) Squadron at Heesch. *(IWM)*

Missed quarry. A P-47 of the 36th Fighter Group comes in for a landing at A-89, Le Culot, Belgium. In the distance are B-17s which have made emergency landings at the field. *JG4* completely missed its assignment to attack the base. *(HRC)*

Werner Molge, a 19-year-old pilot of *II/JG 26*, was one of the few late-war replacement pilots of the *Gruppe* to survive the war. *(Molge via Caldwell)*

Uffz. Jürgen Killian with his chief mechanic. Killian, with *3./JG 1* was shot down and killed on January 1st by friendly anti-aircraft fire. *(Stiemer)*

Youthful sacrifice. Uffz. Gerhard Behrens of *8./JG 1*, killed during *Operation Bodenplatte. (Roba)*

Obst. Alfred Druschel, the ill-fated commander of *SG 4*. Druschel was killed on his first mission with his new command by German flak over Aachen. His remains have never been located. *(Bundesarchiv)*

Obstlt. Heinz Bär, the leader of *JG 3* during the Ardennes operations, was one of the Luftwaffe's greatest aces. Bär would finish the war with 220 claims, including the largest number of jet victories (16), during his operations with *Jagdverbände 44* during the final days of the conflict. *(unknown)*

Long-nose. A Fw-190D-9 takes to the air. *(Bundesarchiv)*

XX

Operation Bodenplatte: January 1st, 1945

L ate on the afternoon of December 31st the *3rd Jagddivision* signaled four of it's *Geschwader* with a mysterious message. It was quickly picked up by ULTRA:

"Varus 1.1.45 Teutonicus"

The first code word indicated that all flying was to immediately end. "Teutonicus" indicated that the pilots were to be informed of the secret upcoming mission and all aircraft were to be made serviceable for a maximum strength operation the very next day. Just after midnight the second part of the orders:

"Orders for HERMANN Time: 0920 Hours"

The messages were the signals for *Unternehmen 'Bodenplatte.'* The great German blow against the Allied air forces was to take place the following morning. A simultaneous attack on Allied air bases by all fighter groups would take place at 9:20 AM. Every serviceable aircraft would be flown; over 900 aircraft were to take part.[94] And not only were all of the normally operational pilots to participate, but also the experienced *Gruppen* and *Geschwader* leaders who often directed operations, but did not fly. There would be brass in the German cockpits as well as green pilots.

---

94 The OKW war diary indicated that 1,035 sorties were flown in the operation. As for the code names, "Hermann" did not allude to Göring, but to the ancient German leader Arminius who destroyed three Roman legions. "Varus" and "Teutonicus" also allude to this period. Most of these battles took place in what later became North Germany and the Netherlands, the area of operations for *Bodenplatte.*

Obst. "Pips" Priller of *JG 26* was one such staff officer. The experienced *Kommodore* was astonished by the orders. Priller was one of the more colorful and enthusiastic pilots in the German air force. Although a small, jolly looking man, the avuncular *Kommodore* of *"Schlageter"* pilots was also one of the Luftwaffe's more outspoken commanders. He was one of only a few who dared speak his mind to Göring. The "Base plate" operation had been planned for early in the Ardennes Offensive by Genlt. Peltz and the fighter commanders at Altenkirchen on December 14th. When the weather proved unsatisfactory, Priller, along with most others, assumed that the operation was cancelled. To execute the operation now seemed futile, for the panzers had been stopped in their tracks in the snowy forests of the Ardennes. Why had it not been carried out on the first day of good weather, December 23rd or 24th, when the German were still advancing on the Meuse? There was no good answer to this question, other than the a common speculation: hit the enemy while he has a hangover. While it was true that many Allied flyers were suffering from an overindulgence that "bordered on total paralysis" the timing seemed to have little to do with catching the Allies nursing their livers.[95] It seemed altogether fantastic that the plan would be seriously considered at all in light of the terrific punishment endured by the *Jagdwaffe* in recent days.

But orders were orders. The airstrip near Fürstenau buzzed with activity as the ground crews endeavored to bring every last machine to airworthiness. On Sunday afternoon, a score of Dora-9s from *III/JG 54* flew in from Varrelbusch. This unit was to come under the command of *JG 26* during the operation. The pilots had just come into the hangar when Maj. Karl Borris, in charge of *I Gruppe*, started the mission briefings in Kloster Handrup, a monastery some two miles from Fürstenau airfield. This was the unorthodox location of the pilots' quarters at the end of 1944. They had been moved closer to the base to save on precious gasoline. Maj. Borris passed along Priller's orders. The operation, he told his pilots would be "a maximum effort." The operational orders from *II Jagdkorps*:

> Maintaining complete radio silence up to the moment of attack, all Geschwader will fly low over the frontier simultaneously in the early hours of the morning, to take the enemy air forces by surprise and catch them on the ground...The *Geschwader* will receive air photos of the targets allotted them and will use their briefings to take every pilot through the operation in detail.

Sixty pilots were present for the briefing; their objective would be Grimbergen airfield just north of Brussels. They were to take off at 8:15 AM. Over

---

95 Although referred to as the "Hangover Raid," there is no historical basis for speculations after the war that the timing of the German air attack was aimed at taking advantage of red-eyed Allied pilots suffering from the previous night's excesses. The real reason for the delay was the requirement of unrestricted visibility. So inexperienced were the young German pilots, that they would have been hard pressed to find their targets under any other circumstances. Only on the last day of the year did the Luftwaffe meteorological services feel confident in forecasting clear skies for the following 24 hours.

the target, three waves of German planes were to slash across the airfield with each wave consisting of sections of four aircraft attacking abreast simultaneously. The first thing to do was to call off the traditional New Year's celebration. Not a popular thing to do, even for Priller.

Fighter pilots everywhere have always been known for their fondness of spirits— what Tom Wolfe in *The Right Stuff* called "the traditional essentials for the blissful hot young pilot: "Flying and Drinking and Driving and Drinking." To take away this basic tenant of pilots— even obedient German ones— was a thing of blasphemy. Not that anyone would take this momentous event away from the Allied fliers, who would tell anyone who cared to listen that what they can remember (pitifully little) of the evening of December 31st was one of alcoholic revelry.[96]

Soon hundreds of Allied air crew would be able to see if they had the "right stuff" or not, awakening as they would to challenge the enemy from their bunks, many still in shorts, jumping into their aircraft which they would taxi across the runway under the muzzle of strafing enemy guns. But for now, they were sleeping, snugly in their bunks in France or Belgium, many with splitting headaches from which only unconsciousness could protect them.

The German pilots on the other side of the fence knew little more than their enemy, but what seemed obvious: something big was up, and worst of all, the big party had been cancelled. Indeed the Fw-190D-9s of *III/JG 54* had been attacking a group of Liberators on the 31st, ordered to patrol in the vicinity of Bastogne, when they were suddenly recalled to Varrelbusch. Bad visibility had forced most to land at Achmer. By 6 PM they had transferred by lorries to Handrup from the base of *I/JG 26* at Fürstenau. For the "black men" of the ground crews the situation was even worse. The orders to make all the planes ready was a sentence to an insomniac 24-hour work day. Still, by 8 AM all the aircraft stood ready on the snowy runways sporting 65 gallon drop-tanks slung underneath for the long journey. Uffz. August Michalski was a ground crew member with 1 *Staffel* of *JG 1*:

"On 31st December, just before nightfall, our chief came into our quarters, situated six or seven km from the airfield, and told us to get to work. All the aircraft had to be in flying state by 0:500 hours in the morning. The Fw-190 which I was working on had serious damage in the oil sump. We worked

96 "We did a lot of drinking," remembered Lt. Albert C. Martin. Al and his brother, Clarence, flew B-26s out of Roye Amy, France with the 575th Bomb Squadron, 391st Bomb Group. Anyone not posted to fly the next day could be admitted to the "Club" where beer, wine, champagne and cognac could be purchased for a quarter a drink. Since Clarence had a master's degree in economics and was a good pilot, he was made the "Club Treasurer." As required, Clarence would fly an empty B-26 to Cognac, France (entered in the logbook as a "training mission") and return with the bomb bay filled with the best ("Hennesey's Five Star being a favorite). So lucrative was Club business that later that spring Clarence discerned that their profits could likely fund inebriation through the rest of the war. Over the base loudspeaker he proudly announced, "Free drinks until further notice." No one remembered paying after that, "just a lot of hangovers."

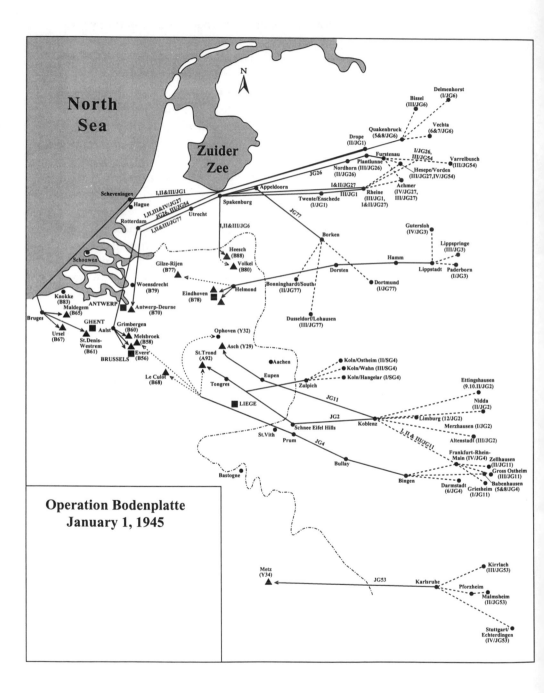

North Sea

Zuider Zee

Delmenhorst (I/JG6)

Bissel (III/JG6)

Vechta (6&7/JG6)

Quakenbruck (5&8/JG6)

Drope (II/JG1)

Furstenau

I/JG26, III/JG54

Varrelbusch (III/JG54)

Plantlunne

Nordhorn (III/JG26)

Hesepe/Vorden (III/JG27,IV/JG54)

JG26

I&II/JG27

Achmer (IV/JG27, III/JG27)

Appeldoorn

III/JG1

Rheine (III/JG1, I&II/JG27)

Scheveningen

I,II &III/JG1

Spakenburg

Twente/Enschede (I/JG1)

Hague

I,II,III&IV/JG27

JG77

Rotterdam

JG26, III/JG54

Utrecht

Gutersloh (IV/JG3)

I,II &III/JG77

I,II &III/JG6

Borken

Lippspringe (III/JG3)

Hamm

Schouwen

Heesch (B88)

Dorsten

Lippstadt

Paderborn (I/JG3)

Gilze-Rijen (B77)

Volkel (B80)

Bonninghardt/South (II/JG77)

Dortmund (I/JG77)

Woensdrecht (B79)

Eindhoven (B78)

Helmond

Knokke (B83)

ANTWERP

Antwerp-Deurne (B70)

Dusseldorf/Lohausen (III/JG77)

Bruges

Maldegem (B65)

GHENT

Grimbergen (B60)

Ursel (B67)

Aalst

Melsbroek (B58)

Ophoven (Y32)

St.Denis-Westrem (B61)

Evere (B56)

Asch (Y29)

St.Trond (A92)

BRUSSELS

Aachen

Koln/Ostheim (II/SG4)

Koln/Wahn (III/SG4)

Le Culot (B68)

Eupen

Koln/Hangelar (I/SG4)

Tongres

Zulpich

Ettingshausen (9.10.II/JG2)

JG11

Nidda (II/JG2)

LIEGE

JG2

Koblenz

Limburg (12/JG2)

Merzhausen (I/JG2)

Schnee Eifel Hills

Altenstadt (III/JG2)

St.Vith

Prum

JG4

I,II & III/JG11

Frankfurt-Rhein-Main (IV/JG4)

Zellhausen (II/JG11)

Bastogne

Bullay

Bingen

Gross Ostheim (III/JG11)

Babenhausen (5&8/JG4)

Darmstadt (6/JG4)

Griesheim (I/JG11)

Operation Bodenplatte
January 1, 1945

Metz (Y34)

JG53

Karlsruhe

Kirrlach (III/JG53)

Pforzheim

Malmsheim (II/JG53)

Stuttgart/ Echterdingen (IV/JG53)

OPERATION BODENPLATTE TARGETS

Target	Unit	Home Base
Asch	I/JG11	Darmstadt
	II/JG11	Zellhausen
	III/JG11	Gross-Ostheim
Deurne	I/JG77	Dortmund
	II/JG77	Bonninghardt
Eindhoven	I/JG3	Paderborn
	IV/JG3	Gutersloh
Evere	II/JG26	Nordhorn
	III/JG26	Plantlünne
Gilze-Rijen	III/JG3	Lippspringe
	III/JG27	Hesepe
	KG(J)51	Rheine
	Einsatzstaffel III/KG 76	Münster-Handorf
Grimbergon	I/JG26	Fürstenau
	III/JG54	Fürstenau
Heesch	I/JG6	Delmenhorst
	III/JG6	Bissel
Le Culot	I/JG4	Darmstadt-Greisheim
Maldegem	II/JG1	Drope
Melsbroek	I/JG27	Rheine
	II/JG27	Rheine
	IV/JG27	Achmer
	IV/JG54	Vörden
Metz	II/JG53	Malmsheim
	III/JG53	Kirrlach
	IV/JG53	St.Echterdingen
Ophoven	II/JG4	Babenhausen
St. Denis	III/JG1	Rheine
St. Trond	I/JG2	Merzhausen
	II/JG2	Nidda
	III/JG2	Altenstadt
	IVJG4	Rheine-Main
	III/SG4	Köln-Wahn
Ursel	I/JG1	Twente
Woensdrecht	III/JG77	Dusseldorf
Vokel	II/JG6	Quakenbrück

without a break in the freezing cold. Towards midnight, the flak fired and brought down an aircraft. At 0:300 hours the aircraft were finally ready."

So it was in the waning hours of 1944 when the *Gruppen* commanders first learned of the great operation. The role of each attacking wing was described, including approach routes, the low-altitude approach to avoid enemy radar and the strict policy of radio silence. However, given the sudden notice and lack of time for planning, Priller, like many other *Geschwader* leaders that morning would be happy just to give all his pilots a general idea of the operation. In the early morning after New Years, there were a number of blank stares. "Just follow me," several *Staffel* leaders told their inexperienced aircrew. Every healthy pilot, regardless of experience, was to take part. Each *Geschwader* was to receive assistance from two pathfinder aircraft of a night fighter unit— a telling indicator of the navigational capabilities in the *Jagdwaffe* at the close of 1944. "Look out for the golden rain," the pilots were told. These marker flares would be used to help mark their path as well as warn the German flak gunners in route that a low-level Luftwaffe air operation would be moving across their path that morning. Genmaj. Deutsch, the commander of the *16th Flak Division*, over which the German aircraft would fly, had received notice of the operation at his Arnhem headquarters only a short time before the German pilots would take off. That only a fraction of the fifty batteries had received these instructions by the early morning of January 1st would bring an extra element of danger to an already reckless operation.

The "Green Hearts" pilots were briefed by Maj. Borris of I/JG 26 who described how the Ju-88 night fighter out on the runway was to take the German pilots to their target. Due to the low level of navigation experience of the average pilot, much attention was paid to checkpoints, map coordinates and the use of *Goldregen* ("Golden Rain") flares to mark the front lines. The most important turning points within German territory, such as Spakenburg at the southern tip of the Zuider Zee, were to be indicated by ground markers— either red flares with orange smoke or green flares with white smoke. Marked on the maps were the compass headings, flying times and even airspeeds for each leg of the journey. Although the individual legs were comparatively short, checkpoints in the form of easily identifiable landmarks were often marked to help keep everyone on course. Even the cynical air veterans noted the thoroughness of the preparations— briefing cards were issued to each pilot telling them when to turn on their radios over the target, when to arm their guns, to note destroyed Allied planes and so on. Ground crews were to fit the 300-liter auxiliary tanks for the long trip and load each plane with a full issue of belt ammunition with incendiary rounds. Although some German pilots partied regardless of the edict forbidding this, most of the Luftwaffe aircrew used the opportunity to get a good night's sleep.

Dawn came early. Between 4 and 5 AM the air crews were awakened and received a magnificent breakfast and their last minute briefing. They were told that the operation could be called off if the attack force suddenly ran into numerous enemy fighters. The code word to call off the attack once everyone was airborne was to be *"Spätlese"*— "Late Harvest." But given the ambitious and thorough nature of the preparations, this possibility seemed rather remote. On the return from the air strike the pilots were instructed to follow a reciprocal path. That failing they were to follow a simple edict: "When in doubt, fly due East." A chain of German airfields running North to South in Western Germany would be standing by to receive any wayward or damaged aircraft.

Even after the terrible bloodletting of the past three weeks, morale of the German pilots receiving their orders was surprisingly high. Gefr. Werner Molge of *II/JG 26* had little combat flying under his belt, being assigned the job of ferrying FW-190D-9s for the unit. At 19 he was the youngest pilot in the *8 Staffel* and had become something of a mascot to its older pilots. But everyone was to fly in this operation and Molge was excited at no longer being left behind:

"Since the pilots were quartered in private homes in Nordhorn, enforcement of the order prohibiting alcohol was up to the self-discipline of each individual pilot, but most of us obeyed. We had to pack our flight bags so that they could be picked up in the morning. This in itself was unusual, but none of us knew what was up...I laid everything out, and was in bed by 2000. At 0500 the next morning, the *Gruppe* orderly went from house to house and awakened the pilots by ringing the doorbells. At 0600 breakfast was served in the pilot's mess at the Berning Hotel in Nordhorn. The bus which carried us daily to the field at Clausheide pulled out this morning at 0630. On the bus, the "weather frog" gave us the weather forecast for our mission area, as he did daily. For 1 January he predicted a cloudless sky, light winds from the southwest and a temperature of -5 degrees Centigrade. When we turned in at the field, a fantastic sight spread out in front of our eyes. The aircraft of all the *Staffeln* had been taxied from their dispersals by the ground crews and were lined up at the field, as if for parade inspection. Fifty FW 190D-9s in the last light of the moon. The mechanics had worked all night to get them ready; several were still being attended to. The bus did not take us to the readiness shacks at the various dispersals, as usual, but rather to the *Gruppe* command post. Inside, our three man band was playing hot rhythms to get us stirring. At the mission briefing we were finally informed of our orders and the target— "Low level attack on the airfield at Brussels-Evère." The maps we were given had the course from the German border to the target marked, as well as the return course to the border... Then we went out to our aircraft, which had their props turning over and their brakes applied. The crew chiefs helped buckle us in and left the engines running. Take-off was at 0800, into the reddish glare of the now rising sun. It was without incident, although the *Schwarme* of four aircraft threw up fountains of snow that greatly hampered visibility. Take-off at close spacing were always dangerous due to the prop-wash which threw us about unexpectedly. Also, there were four to six inches of snow on the ground which made things even more difficult."

Reveille for the jet men of *KG 51* was 0300hrs. The commanding officers and air crew were called into a briefing room and were given sealed envelopes with their targets. The mission was to hit British airfields near Eind-hoven. Every pilot received a detailed map with his route plotted. Take-off for Maj. Heinz Unrau's *I Gruppe* and Maj. Martin Vetter's *II Gruppe* was to be at 0745hrs with a rendezvous with *JG 3* where the entire mass would proceed to Brussels behind a Ju-88 pathfinder.[97]

The operation opened before dawn in the world's first night jet bomber operation. Four Arado 234s of *III/KG 76* dropped bombs on Brussels and Liège as part of armed reconnaissance to precede the main effort. The prime mission was to investigate the weather conditions for the coming attack, although the planes did carry bombs. Three were dropped on Brussels and its train station and the other in Liége. The operation went uneventfully, but so minuscule were the attacks that only the Germans really took note.[98] The Luftwaffe night fighters also put in their usual ghostly appearance. *NJG 3* shot up roads and railways south of Liège while *NJG 2* put in night attacks near Charleroi. The Ju-88s of *LG 1* along with the Me-110s of *NJG 1* strafed the cities of Huy and Hasselt, Belgium for good measure. But all this was normal; the Germans had been carrying on with these aggravation raids for weeks.

The attrition of the preceding two weeks was evident in the numbers available to Peltz for *Bodenplatte*. Rather than a force of 2,000, at dawn on January 1st some 900 German planes from eleven *Jagdgeschwader* with some 34 available *Gruppen* took to the air following their Ju-88 pathfinders. The strength was bolstered by staff flights and included twenty Me-262As of *KG(J) 51*. The more experienced pilots led the partly trained fliers towards the Allied air bases in Belgium and Holland. Between 9 and 10 AM the German fighters began to arrive over the American and British airfields. Most Allied aviators were still sleeping, some slumbering off the previous night's overindulgence. The German fighter groups struck the 19 airfields from a very low altitude— often only 160 feet off the ground.

Over the Netherlands that morning, the pilot of a lone Allied artillery observation plane blinked, looking intensely at a fantastic sight. Off in the distance was a huge armada of German aircraft. "At least two hundred Messerschmitts flying low on a course of 320 degrees!" he screamed into the radio. In Brussels, Belgians watched the Messerschmitts winging low against a pale sunlit sky while British soldiers took potshots at the Germans as they crossed overhead. Flt. Lt. E.J. Packwood flew tactical reconnaissance

---

97 *II Gruppe, KG 51*, was just becoming operational flying from Mülheim. The short runway there necessitated that its new Me-262-A2s use rocket assisted take-off.

98 More jet bomber missions were flown by *KG 76* on January 1st. Later that day, Oblt. Arthur Stark took six Ar-234s in an attack against Gilze-Rijen airfield with each jet carrying 33 light fragmentation bombs. As the bombers moved in to attack the airfield, they were joined by a small group of Me-109s and Fw-190s from *JG 3*. The airfield was the home of the Spitfires and Mustangs of the RAF's No. 35 Tactical Reconnaissance Wing. The attack went ahead, but only one P-51 was damaged. Although the British anti-aircraft claimed one downed jet, no losses were sustained. Another operation was flown at midnight against the docks at Antwerp by four Ar-234s, followed by an attack by five 234s against Liège on the morning of January 2nd.

for 35 Reconnaissance Wing at Gilze-Rijen airfield. Taking off in his Spitfire XIV at 8:29 AM, he headed for the Arnhem area. Then at 9:05 AM, Packwood spied a sight that made him look twice. Down on the deck were two Ju-88s with what he took to be an escort of some thirty German fighters. Dropping on the German formation from 5,000 feet, he closed to within 400 yards from astern and let loose a five-second stream of cannon fire into one of the Messerschmitts. The 109 took no evasive action, the cannon rounds chopping its right wing off; in seconds it was falling. Already, his wingman Flt. Lt. J.M. Young had sounded the warning. There was a big German raid coming!

At Asch, Belgium, *JG 11*'s surprise assault backfired. Asch, or Y-29, was home to the 366th Fighter Group, and was also the current station of the

TABLE 7

Organization of Luftwaffe Forces in Operation "Bodenplatte"		
Luftlotte West: (Genlt. Josef Schmidt); Limburg		
II Jagdkorps (Genmaj. Dietrich Peltz); Flammersfeld		
3 Jagddivision	**Gruppen**	**Targets**
JG 1	3	St. Denis-Westrem, Belgium
JG 3	3	Eindhoven, Holland
JG 6	3	Volkel, Holland
JG 26	3	Brussels-Evère, Belguim
III/JG 54	1	Brussels-Evère, Belgium
JG 27	4	Brussels-Melsbroek, Belguim
JG 77	3	Antwerp-Deurne, Belguim
Fighter Sector Middle Rhine		
JG 2	3	St. Trond, Belguim
JG 4	3	Le Culot, Belguim
JG 11	3	Asch, Belguim
Jagddivision 5		
JG 53	3	Metz-Frescaty, France
Other elements:		
SG 4 under JG 2		
KG(J) 51		
Einsatzstaffel III/KG 76		
Pathfinder aircraft:		
NJG 1, NJG 3, NJG 101		

TABLE 8

II Jagdkorps: Operation Bodenplatte January 1, 1945			
Unit	Aircraft	Home Base	Target (Effectiveness)
JG 1 (Obst. Ihlefeld) (~ 80)			
I Gruppe (Hptm. Hackbarth)	Fw-190 A-8	Twente	Ursel (D)
II Gruppe (Hptm. Staiger)	Fw-190 A-8	Drope	Maldegem (B)
III Gruppe (Hptm. Woitke	Me-109 G-14	Rheine	St. Denis (B)
JG 2 (Oblt. Bühligen) (~ 90)			
I Gruppe (Hptm. Hrdlicka)	Fw-190 A-8/A-9	Merzhausen	St.Trond (C)
II Gruppe (Hptm. Schröder)	Me-109 G-14/K-4	Nidda	St. Trond (C)
III Gruppe (Hptm. Lemke)	Fw-190 D-9	Altenstadt	St. Trond (C)
JG 3 (Oblt. Bär) (~ 70)			
I Gruppe (Hptm. Seidl)	Me-109 G-10/G-14	Paderborn	Eindhoven (A)
III Gruppe (Hptm. Langer)	Me-109 G-14/K-4	Lippspringe	Gilze-Rijen (D)
IV Gruppe (Lt. Müller)	Fw-190 D-9	Gutersloh	Eindhoven (A)
JG 4 (Maj. Michalski) (~ 50)			
I Gruppe (Hptm. Steinmann)	Me-109 G-14/K-4	Darmstadt-Greisheim	Le Culot (F)
II Gruppe (Maj. Schröder)	Fw-190 A-8	Babenhausen	Ophoven (D)
IV Gruppe (Hptm. Laube)	Me-109 G-14/K-4	Rheine-Main	St. Trond (C)
JG 6 (Obst. Kogler) (~ 70)			
I Gruppe (Hptm. Elstermann)	Fw-190 A-8	Delmenhorst	Heesch (D)
II Gruppe (Hptm. Naumann)	Fw-190 A-8	Quakenbrück	Volkel (D)
III Gruppe (Maj. Kühle)	Me-109 G-10/G-14	Bissel	Heesch (D)

JG 11 (Maj. Specht) (~ 65)

I Gruppe (Hptm. Kirchmayr)	Fw-190 A-8	Darmstadt	Asch (C)
II Gruppe (Hptm. Leonhardt)	Me-109 G-14/K-4	Zellhausen	Asch (C)
III Gruppe (Hptm. Fassong)	Fw-190 A-8	Gross-Ostheim	Asch (C)

JG 26 (Oblt. Priller) (~ 150)

I Gruppe (Maj. Borris)	Fw-190 D-9	Fürstenau	Grimbergen (C)
II Gruppe (Maj. Hackl)	Fw-190 D-9	Nordhorn	Evere (A)
III Gruppe (Hptm. Krupinski)	Me-109 G-14/K-4	Plantlünne	Evere (A)

JG 27 (Maj. Franzisket) (~ 60)

I Gruppe (Hptm. Schade)	Me-109 G-14/K-4	Rheine	Melsbroek (B)
II Gruppe (Hptm. Hoyer)	Me-109 G-14	Rheine	Melsbroek (B)
III Gruppe (Hptm. Clade)	Me-109 K-4	Hesepe	Gilze-Rijen (D)
IV Gruppe (Hptm. Dudeck)	Me-109 G-10	Achmer	Melsbroek (B)

JG 53 (Obstlt Bennemann) (~ 50)

II Gruppe (Maj. Meimberg)	Me-109 G-14/K-4	Malmsheim	Metz (B)
III Gruppe (Maj. Götz)	Me-109 G-14	Kirrlach	Metz (B)
IV Gruppe (Hptm Müer)	Me-109 G-14	St. Echter-dingen	Metz (B)

JG 54 (Obtl. Dortenmann) (~ 50)

III Gruppe (Oblt. Dortenmann)	Fw-109 D-9	Fürstenau	Grimbergen (C)
IV Gruppe (Maj. Klemm)	Fw-190 A-8/A-9	Vörden	Melsbroek (B)

JG 77 (Maj. Leie) (~ 105)

I Gruppe (Lt. Doppler)	Me-109 G-14	Dortmund	Deurne (D)
II Gruppe (Maj. Freytag)	Me-109 K-4	Bonninghardt	Deurne (D)
III Gruppe (Hptm. Köhler)	Me-109 K-4	Dusseldorf	Woensdrecht (D)

SG 4 (Oblt. Druschel) (~ 60)			
III Gruppe	Fw-190 F-8	Köln-Wahn	St. Trond (B)
Other Units (~ 30)			
KG (J) 51 (Hptm. Unrau)	Me-262A	Rheine	Gilze-Rijen (D)
Einsatzstaffel III/KG 76 (Hptm. Lukesch)	Ar-234	Münster-Handorf	Gilze-Rijen (D)
Key:			
A = Very successful attack			
B = Successful attack			
C = Limited success			
D = Minor damage			
F = Total failure			

352nd, the P-51 Mustangs that were on loan to the Ninth Air Force from the Eighth. The first morning of the new year had started off extremely cold. Even so, the ground crew and mechanics of the 352nd were up at 5:30 AM getting the aircraft ready for an escort mission scheduled for 11:00 AM. By 8:00 AM, all the aircraft were serviced and ready.

At about the same time that Lt. Col. John C. Meyer was trying to get his operational orders changed for January 1st, Gefr. Gerhard Böhm and his fellow pilots of the 9 *Staffel* of *JG 11* were getting their final briefing for *Operation Bodenplatte* at Gross Ostheim. Meyer's 352nd Fighter Group had been given the job of escorting a group of Eighth Air Force Bombers to targets near Kassel, Germany. But given the proximity of Asch airfield to the fighting front, Meyer thought this dangerous and asked to get his assignment changed to a combat patrol.

Some of the German pilots had known of the operation for some time. Just before the Ardennes Offensive had begun, Oblt. Hans Fiedler had learned of the planned attack from Hptm. Horst von Fassong, the 100-victory ace commander of *III Gruppe*. Fassong had held a secret briefing with his subordinate leaders to tell them of the upcoming operation. They had expected it to take place much sooner and had nearly forgotten the whole thing in light of the day-to-day struggle for survival over the Ardennes air space. *II/JG 11* was posted at Zellhausen; the pilots received the requisite briefing by Hptm. Leonhardt and marked maps of their planned course in the operation.

At 8:30 AM the 65 aircraft of the three *Gruppen* took to the air behind their Ju-188 pathfinder and formed up over Aschaffenburg. The German fighters flew very low at 150 feet until the front was reached when they climbed to 1,500. Meanwhile, at their target, Asch airfield, Col. Meyer was getting his twelve P-51 Mustangs ready to fly over to the St. Vith area to look for the

German fighters that could usually be found there. Over Frankfurt on Main, the Fw-190s of the *III Gruppe* took in the Me-109s forming up from Zellhausen. At the head of the fighter phalanx was Obstlt Günther Specht, the commander of the *Geschwader* and one of the outstanding leaders in the *Jagdwaffe*. A Knight's Cross recipient, Specht had been flying with the Luftwaffe since 1939, had been a *Gruppen* leader with *JG 11* since 1943 and had led the *Geschwader* since the previous April. His planes flew so low that they shook snow off the fir trees as the they crossed the Eifel.

When the fighters reached Aachen, flak began to burst around them. One of the first to go was the Fw-190 of Hans Fiedler. Oblt. Fiedler, the administrative adjutant for *III Gruppe* was experiencing a string of bad luck. On December 23rd, Fiedler had taken off from Gross Ostheim on a mission in which he developed engine trouble. He was forced to make an emergency landing at Göttingen and was grounded there for several days. He eventually made his way back to his unit, arriving on Sunday, December 31st. Von Fassong gave him a hard time for his extended absence. He heard rumors on his arrival of a possible operation the following day, but did not think that he would be expected to participate. Late that evening von Fassong entered his quarters, where Fiedler was catching up on paper work. The *Gruppenkommandeur* irately informed Fiedler that he would fly the following day. Fiedler still didn't believe he would be called on.

But at 8 AM he was roused to take part, flying a brand-new Fw-190A-8 as the wingman to Oblt. Grosser, the *Staffelkapitän* of *11./JG 11*. With virtually no idea of the nature of the mission, Fieldler took to the air with thirty others at 8:30 AM. They followed a Ju-88 pathfinder at a height of 400 feet and passed Koblenz. However, upon crossing into Allied territory, Fiedler sighted a single P-47 which made several strikes on his plane. Almost simultaneously, American AA guns opened up and Fiedler was hit badly, wounded in the head by shell splinters. The adjutant felt himself fainting as his aircraft dropped. He had no idea how his plane managed to crash land itself. When he came to, he was in British hands receiving medical treatment. Others were not as lucky; Uffz. Ernst Noreisch fell out of the sky over the same area. Still *JG 11* flew on in radio silence over the snow covered fields of Belgium.

Asch airfield was home to the 366th Fighter Group of the Ninth Air Force and the 352nd Fighter Group from the Eighth Air Force. Ophoven, just north of Asch, was home to the Spitfire XIVs of 41, 130, 350 and 610 Squadrons of the 2nd Tactical Air Force. The Mustangs of the 352nd were intended to provide top cover for the Ninth Air Force Thunderbolts. However, transferring from England, the flyers were unaccustomed to their crude accommodations. The only shelter at the frigid field were the tents; heating was minimal; everyone was allocated only one bucket of coal per day. Baths came from a bucket or were taken at a nearby coal mine using the miner's showers.

Headquarters, operations, intelligence and supply were all performed in a single tent with everyone taking turns warming their hands to use the single typewriter. Tech Supply consisted of a junked P-51 which everyone cannibalized for parts. Anything else had to come from England via Capt. Bill Stangel. Stangel, a veteran bush pilot from Minnesota, ran a ferry service from Y-29 to Bodney, UK. Even in impossible weather Stangel's C-47 carried everything from Merlin engines to Christmas turkeys and even a new jeep. For most of the men of the 352nd, Asch, Belgium was their first experience on the European continent. Most made trips to nearby Hasselt or Brussels where they found seemingly inexhaustible supplies of black market steaks, cognac, American-type beer, champagne and eager women. Like everyone else, the 352nd did their share of celebrating with the natives New Year's night.

For the regulars at Asch the end of the previous night's bacchanalia seemed painfully raw. The squinting airmen of the 390th Fighter Squadron of the 366th Fighter Group fed their headaches with a dubious breakfast of powdered eggs and black coffee. Red eyes were all over the mess. Then there was the usual briefing; it was still half light and dreadfully cold when the pilots walked out to the frozen airfield where the engines of their Thunderbolts were being warmed. The 391st Squadron under Capt. Eber E. Simpson had already taken to the air at 8:42 AM headed with 500 lb. bombs to blast German tanks near St. Vith in the Ardennes. They claimed several German tanks near Ondenval but lost one of the P-47s to light flak; the pilot belly landed south of Liège. Unbeknown to the others at Y-29 the squadron had run across two Me-109s while on their way home south of Malmédy. Lts. John F. Bathurst and Donald G. Holt claimed both destroyed. Back at Asch, the eight P-47s of "Red" and "Yellow" flights were airborne by 9:15 AM. Red flight was led by Capt. Lowell B. Smith who intended to fly an armed reconnaissance over the Ardennes area. Along with Smith in Red Flight were Lts. John Kennedy and Melvin R. Paisley and Flt. Off. Dave Johnson. "Yellow" flight included Lts. John Feeny, Robert V. Brulle, Currie Davis and Joe Lackey.

The P-47s of the 366th assembled over the field and set a course for the front. Just then, Capt. Smith received a strange message from his wingman, Lt. Jack Kennedy. He said there were flak bursts over the northeast edge of the field. With this, Smith led Red Flight to investigate. The P-47s saw an unusual sight, a group of German fighters strafing Ophoven, the British airfield about seven miles northeast of Asch. More important, however, was a collection of black dots headed their way on the horizon. More German fighters! Smith called for his P-47s to attack. They quickly jettisoned their bombs and armed their guns, diving to reach the Germans who were coming in "on the deck." The closer the Germans came, the bigger grew the eyes of the men in Red Flight. There were at least fifty enemy fighters in this gaggle!

But the Germans were totally surprised by the Allied fighters, intent, as they were, on striking the aircraft parked on the airstrip at Asch. Smith's P-47s sent machine gun bursts into several of the leaders in the German *Schwarm*. Some crashed, while others broke formation to counter the Thunderbolts. In moments the scene degenerated into an extremely confused affair of strafing German planes with P-47s on their tails, other bandits jockeying into position behind these while American AA gunners tried to identify friend and foe. One of the first pilots to score was Lt. Melvin Paisley:

> "...on the way in I jumped an Me-109. Instead of using my guns, I chose to initiate my attack with the rockets I was carrying. I missed him with the first two, but got him with the third."

Paisley quickly followed this unorthodox attack with machine gun fire, sending two more Fw-190s spinning into the ground. "As is always the case in a dogfight," Smith knowingly remembered, "the battles tend to boil down to individual combats where it is the fighting quality of the individual that makes the difference." Meanwhile, Capt. Smith and Lt. Bob Brulle took out more. Smith hit one German squarely in the cockpit with the enemy plane tumbling out of control and crashing into the ground. Brulle's victory came at almost exactly the same time.

> "I jettisoned my bombs and did a steep wing-over, getting into position on the tail of an Fw-190. I started firing and closed to 100 yards, observing many strikes. He exploded when he hit the ground. I then got on the tail of another Fw-190 and used up the rest of my ammo while firing at him. When I broke off I saw him trailing smoke, but never saw him hit the ground."

The chaos translated to added victories from the counter-punch of the 390th. Lts. Davis, Feeny and Flt. Off. Lackey all knocked out other enemy planes. But most importantly, the attack of the Thunderbolts had thrown a monkey wrench into the German assault plan— a key block for the P-51s of the base that were just at that moment trying to take off on their own mission. While Capt. Smith and the 366th Fighter Group was tangling with the enemy in the air, Lt. Col. John C. Meyer of the 487th Fighter Squadron in "Petie III" and his other eleven P-51s were moving down the runway to take off. Meyer pushed the throttles forward and watched the tarmac race by as his plane gracefully lifted into the air. It was 9:10 AM. Just then, however, the Meyer saw puffs of smoke from AA bursts. What the hell? Then he saw it— a Fw-190 racing straight at him. It was too late to put back down, so Meyer, with his landing gear not even retracted, instinctively opened fire with his guns. On the other side, Gefr. Böhm seems not to have seen Meyer and was concentrating on shooting up the C-47 transports parked on the airstrip. Suddenly Meyer's bullets struck home and Böhm's 190 cart-wheeled to the runway exploding beside one of the C-47s he had been strafing.

Asch was now under a full scale attack, but somehow some other P-47s from the 366th Fighter Group managed to make it into the air. Some German fighters ended up at Ophoven, just north of Asch. There a Spitfire from 610 Squadron had just made it into the air. The snowy field was still covered with fog and identification was difficult. As a few Luftwaffe fighters stumbled into the vicinity, an Australian, Flt. Lt. A.F.O. "Tony" Gaze, attacked. Soon, he felled a Fw-190 although himself came under fire from several mistaken P-51s. Fortunately, they recognized their error and Gaze flew on. The Germans did get to the Ophoven airfield, however, and shot up several Spitfires of 125 Wing in a largely unopposed action.

Meanwhile at Asch, the Germans stubbornly swooped down to shoot up the parked planes on the runway, even as the Allied pilots aloft picked off one attacker after another. Although a number of planes, buildings and facilities were shot up, JG 11 lost eight aircrew in a heartbeat. Obgefr. Karlheinz Sistenich, Fw. Harald Scharz, Fw. Herbert Kraschinski and Oblt. August Engel were all shot down and killed. Fw. Karl Miller crash landed and was severely burned. On the ground, the personnel at Asch were treated to a rare sight: here was the air war in Europe right on their doorstep! Many of the ground crew popped out of their foxholes and slit trenches to gawk at the display, cheering wildly when a "swastikaed bandit fell in flames," but darting quickly for cover whenever a low-flying fighter turned in their direction. But most of the enemy strafing runs that could get to the airfield were directed at the parked aircraft there and only one ground casualty was suffered. Meanwhile, the AA gunners stood swiveling their guns about without firing. The skies were full of both enemy and friendly planes; to shoot without positive identification was to invite disaster.[99] They were mostly forced to leave the job to the Allied fighters, although they would claim credit for the destruction of seven of the enemy destroyed that day. The total claimed for both fighter groups and the ground gunners amounted to 42 German planes with some double-counting likely. Bob Brulle:

"When I realized I was out of ammo and broke off, I high-tailed it west to get out of the area. It happened so fast that I flew right over our field and had all our AA gunners shooting at me! I rocked my wings violently and climbed to 3,000 feet, just below the cloud cover. I felt safe there, since I could duck into the clouds if any enemy aircraft came after me. From there I circled around and had a front seat to the battle below. While circling around and watching the battle, I observed a 109 heading back towards Germany, pursued by two P-51s about a 1,000 yards back. As the 109 started to go below my wing I started to roll over so I could keep an eye on him. He must have seen me and thinking I was going to dive on him, veered away. This allowed one of the P-51s to turn inside him and get close enough to shoot him down. When there was a lull in the battle I went in and landed. Just as I was turning off the runway, two Me-109s came over. I remember seeing them come right after me, and I shut off my engine and got out of my airplane and was running away from it as

---

99 There was at least one tragedy of this type at Asch. The Typhoon of Flt. Lt. Don Webber of 183 Squadron was accidently shot down by a zealous P-51 pilot in the heat of the battle.

they flew over. They strafed an aircraft on the other side of the field. The two 109s were being pursued by a Mustang. He had them in his sights, but was not firing since his fire would have raked across our field. The AA fire missed the two 109s, but hit the P-51s and the pilot dropped his gear and landed. I don't know who he was, but I'll bet he was mad!"

Lt. Col. Meyer was now serving as the deputy commanding officer of the group since the tragic death on Christmas Day of its former commander, Maj. George Preddy. During the frenzied dogfight at tree-top level his command shot down 13 Fw-190s and 10 Me-109s. Only one Mustang was damaged, and that from over-eager American anti-aircraft gunners. For its action, the 487th Squadron would receive the Distinguished Unit Citation— the only squadron in Doolittle's Eighth Air Force to be so honored. Meyer's after-action report:

"Immediately upon getting my wheels up I spotted 15 plus 190s headed toward the field from the east. I attacked one getting a two second burst at 300 yards, 30 degree deflection, getting good hits on the fuselage and wing roots. The E/A half-rolled, crashing into the ground. I then selected another 190 chasing it to the vicinity of northwest of Liège. On my first attack I got good hits at 10 degrees 250 yards. The E/A half rolled and recovered just on top of the trees. I attacked but periodically had to break off because of intense friendly ground fire. At least on three occasions, I got good hits on the 190, and on the last attack the E/A started smoking profusely and then crashed into the ground. Out of ammunition, I returned to the field, but could not land as the field was under attack. I proceeded west and was bounced twice by 109s and was able to evade by diving and speed..."

Six pilots of the 352nd claimed multiple victories in the encounter. Capt. William T. "Whiz" Whisner, one of George Preddy's drinking buddies, and Lt. Sanford K. Moats shot down four, Capt. Henry M. Stewart II and Lt. Alden P. Rigby got three and Lt. Col. Meyer and Lt. Ray Littge each claimed two. Bill Whisner's wingman, Lt. Walker G. Diamond bagged another as did Col. Meyer's wingman, Lt. Alex F. Sears. Of the twelve Mustang pilots aloft, eleven scored kills. Col. H. Norman Holt, the commander of the 366th Fighter Group described the scene:

"The famous all-out raid by the Luftwaffe against our strips arrived over our base in a force of approximately 50 Me-109s and Fw-190s. The enemy was engaged immediately by a flight of eight of our T-bolts that had just taken off and assembled. Jettisoning their bombs, they attacked the enemy planes and kept them from hitting our pitifully unprotected planes on the ground. The entire air circus took place at tree top level directly over the strip. Roaring engines, spitting machine guns and flaming planes going down to destruction had brought the war right to our door step! The onslaught lasted for fully 45 minutes. A couple of our planes, out of ammunition and low on fuel were forced to drop wheels and land in the midst of it. Alert Nazi pilots veered in on the tails of such juicy targets only to be shot down or scared away by our ack-ack gunners. One squadron commander in his eagerness, ran out and took off in his pajamas. Sleeping late on his day off, he had leaped out of the sack to get in on the kills. Me-109s and Fw-190s were flaming and auguring into the ground within sight of the entire group of officers and men."

"We hope at least one of their pilots got back to tell the story," Holt boasted, "They'd think twice about trying it again." Others of the 366th described their part of the battle. Capt. Smith's wingman, Lt. Kennedy, had suddenly disappeared and Smith "feared the worst." Kennedy told of a harrowing encounter:

"I don't know how many German planes there were, but I guess there were 50-60. We were in the midst of them in seconds— I don't know if I lost Capt. Smith or he lost me. With all of the aircraft just off the deck who could tell? I got on the tail of a 109, which at first I thought was a Spitfire. This 109 really filled the gunsight and I got off a few rounds when I was hit in the tail end. I found two Me-109s on my tail. I broke to the right and of course those guys followed me still firing away. I got hit again in the right wing and a hell of a fire broke out. I thought about jumping, but changed my mind because I didn't want to risk jumping through the fire. I broke to the left and flew past a slag pile with the 109s still firing away. Finally, two P-51s from the 352nd drove them off and I headed for a low cloud. By that time the fire was out and I headed in for a landing. Since my hydraulic fluid had burned away I had no flaps, so I came in kind of hot. I hit the strip at over 100 mph and then found I didn't have brakes either. I ran out of runway when the plane was still doing about 30 mph, but it finally came to a halt and I climbed out. When I got back to my tent I truly realized what a long night it had been. I had flown the mission with my flight suit pulled on over my pajamas."

Lt. Paisley shot down his fourth Fw-190 in an aerial confrontation in which the 366th and 352nd FGs fought together in a tag-team dogfight:

"An enemy plane then got on the tail of my wingman (F/O Johnson). I shot at it, noticed several strikes and shook him off. I then pulled a Fw-190 off the tail of a P-51 Mustang, knocking him down in one straight pass from above."

Meantime, Johnson tangled with two more German fighters, shooting down both, but sustaining serious damage from return fire. He bailed out and floated down near Asch in his parachute near the scene where one of his downed assailants had crashed. The Flight Officer borrowed a bicycle from a local farmer and rode to the scene of the crash. Johnson removed the dead German officer's papers and his pistol, riding back to Asch to announce his good fortune. Evidence would later show that Johnson had shot down the *Kommodore* of *JG 11*, Obstlt. Günther Specht.

The view at Asch from the German cockpit was reported by *Staffelkapitän* Lt. Georg Füreder, of *5./JG 11*, the only unit in *II Gruppe* to escape unharmed:

"Because of mist patches we took off later than planned, and I think that this did a lot to impair the success of the mission. The *Gruppe* joined the formation and set course for the target led by a couple of Ju-188 pathfinders... I did not notice whether any aircraft were hit by our own or enemy flak on the way in, but as we neared the target I remembered hearing on the radio that someone had been hit. Just short of the target we pulled up and fanned out to the left and right to look over the airfield, then we went into our firing runs. I pulled up and went straight into my attack. My approach was too steep to engage the Thunderbolts on the east side of the airfield, so I aimed at four or five twin-engined planes in the northwest corner. I started a sharp 180-degree turn to go for the Thunderbolts on the east side, when tracer rounds streaked past me. At first I thought it was flak, then to my surprise I saw two Thunderbolts behind me. One was firing at me with everything, but his aim was wild. I pulled sharply to port and his rounds passed astern of my plane. My pursuer and his No. 2 gave up the chase and headed off west. I started after them, then broke away for a final run at the airfield heading south. At this time I saw no other aircraft over or near the airfield. A pall of black smoke rose from the southern half of the airfield, coming from several burning aircraft. I made my firing run somewhat higher because of the smoke..."

III Gruppe finished the last strafing run, taking the worst losses of all. Having assaulted Asch for nearly 45 minutes, *JG 11* turned to the east to escape the hellish fire over the airfield. The ordeal was not over, however, as a number of the Allied fighters gave chase. Four more pilots were lost before the German border was reached. Uffz. Hermann Barion and Fw. Peter Reschke were killed and Ofw. Franz Meindl and Uffz. Kurt Nüssle were listed as missing. (Nüssle's remains have recently been excavated near Asch.) When the pilots reached Frankfurt, many were low on fuel and almost every aircraft showed signs of damage.

The German pilots would have been discouraged to know of the superficiality of their damage. At Ophoven, several buildings were shot up and seven fighters from Sqdn. Ldr. Leopold Collingnon's 350 Belgian Squadron were destroyed along with a few C-47 Dakotas. One P-47 was knocked out on the ground. At Asch, an additional four P-51s of the 352nd were shot down in dogfights although all the pilots survived; only one P-51 was damaged on the ground. Against this, *JG 11* lost at least 28 machines out of the 65 that attacked Asch that morning. Twenty five German pilots were killed including the leader of *JG 11*, Obstlt. Günther Specht. Hptm. von Fassong, the fiery leader of *III Gruppe*, was reported missing near Opglabbeek, last seen with two Thunderbolts on his tail. His ultimate fate has never been determined. In all, *III Gruppe* reported losing six pilots including Maj. Vowinkel of the *Gruppenstab*. Twelve of the lost pilots have never been traced. With Specht now gone, Maj. Jürgen Harder, an experienced commander left *I/JG 53* and took over the reins of *JG 11*. Harder was shocked to find how little was left of the once-proud command. Almost 40% of the brave Luftwaffe pilots from *JG 11* committed to *Operation Bodenplatte* were dead or captured.

Later that day the 366th would destroy another two Me-109s in a patrol south of Malmédy bringing their total claims up to 14 for the day. During the abortive German operation, the eight pilots of the 366th FG claimed 12 German fighters destroyed, two probably destroyed and six damaged for the loss of the aircraft of Flt. Off. Johnson. Lt. Melvin Paisley was the top gun of the 366th with four victories with Smith and Johnson each getting two others.

The leader of *JG 6*, Obstlt. Johann Kogler, was a long time Luftwaffe veteran. He had trained with the air force before the war and had flown an Me-110 with *ZG 76* during the campaign in the West in 1940. In 1942 he became the *Kommodore* of *ZG 101*, later becoming the leader of *ZG 26* during the summer of 1944. From the Me-110 *Zerstörer* (Destroyer) unit of *ZG 26* the fighter unit *JG 6* was formed, with Kogler becoming its first *Kommodore*. By the end of 1944, the 33-year-old Austrian commander had amassed 90 combat missions in the war with four victories and a number of awards. The most prestigious was the German Cross in Gold, which he earned for personally shooting the tail off a B-17 headed for Germany along the Baltic coast on April 11, 1944.

When the Ardennes Offensive began, Obstlt. Kogler already knew of *Operation Bodenplatte*. Although Kogler informed his *Gruppenkommandeure*, he kept the secret operation from his aircrew. He had no idea when it would begin, but knew that clear weather over German airfields was a prerequisite. Hitler's *Wacht Am Rhein* offensive on Saturday, December 16th came as a surprise to Kogler, but the proximity of his briefing at Altenkirchen two days before its start made him believe that it must come soon after. But as December wore on he offhandedly dismissed the operation from his mind. The clearing of the weather before Christmas came and went with no *Operation Bodenplatte*. But on December 31st the orders to execute the operation came, and although surprised, Kogler gave the briefing the night before. A model of Volkel airfield had been assembled, and this was used to describe the mission to the pilots. Maj. Kühle was confident that all preparations for the attack of his *III Gruppe* were thorough. He completed a preliminary briefing of the pilots at 9 PM. He then set about that evening to make sure that the Me-109Gs were properly serviced before the big day. Every available aircraft would be committed. The big worry would be the pilots. Kogler worried that many did not have the experience for such a demanding task.

In the early morning, he gave his fliers the specific objective: Volkel airfield. They were told to expect to find a hundred Allied aircraft. Each pilot was issued a detailed map of the flight route which was to be carried out at tree-top level. At 8:30 AM the seventy planes of *JG 6* took to the air behind their Ju-88 pathfinder. The losses began early. At Delmenhorst, Oblt. Eberhard Pfeiderer had trouble with his A-8 as he lifted from the airfield; he plunged to his death in a grove of trees just beyond the airfield. The formation queued over Quakenbrück and turned westward to Spakenburg on the southern shore of Holland's Zuider Zee. Spakenburg was reached in 30 minutes. From there they turned south towards Wegel. Theoretically they would arrive at Volkel from the West to enhance the surprise.

Meanwhile, the prey at Volkel were unknowing. The Tempest pilots of

No. 3 Squadron had been awakened for an early departure. They would be the first RAF pilots in the air that morning. Pilot Officer Ron W. Pottinger should not have been flying that Monday, his tour being up. He had become known as an ace against the V1 buzz bombs; he had shot down six during the summer of 1944. Pottinger had been on Christmas leave to England, but now found himself just back at 3 Squadron's barracks. Arriving late at the vacant seminary in Uden, some ten miles from Volkel airfield, all Pottinger wanted to do was go to bed. Unfortunately his contemporaries had other ideas and he was dragged along to a big New Year's party. There he mangled popular tunes of the day in a drunken sing-along with the others. Somehow, he managed to sneak out just after midnight. But early the next morning he was awakened. It seemed this Tasmanian chap was a bit under the weather from the night's festivities. Even with his tour expired he gamely agreed to fly for the fellow, but was designated as spare pilot before take-off when the squadron leader learned of his tour status. Just after 8 AM, K.F. "Jimmy" Thiele, the New Zealand CO of the squadron, led eight Tempest Vs out to the runway and into the morning sky. They were headed for an armed reconnaissance of the Paderborn area. Everyone having gotten airborne in one piece, Pottinger taxied his spare Tempest back to the dispersal area. Soon the squadron was joined by the Tempests of No. 56 Squadron and later by the New Zealanders of 486 Squadron over Hanover. Less than a hundred miles southwest of Volkel was the base at St. Denis-Westrem near Ghent. There the Polish pilots of 302, 308, and 317 Squadrons were preparing to take to the air. Group Captain Alexsander Gabszewicz's 131st Polish Wing took to the sky at first light with the intent of flying armed reconnaissance in Holland north of Arnhem. By 8:40 AM, all of the Spitfire XIVs were airborne. Heesch in the Netherlands was the northernmost airfield of the 2nd TAF. The Canadians of 402 squadron were just getting their Spitfire XIVs into a patrol in the skies over Volkel while 411 Squadron lifted to go hunting for German fighters in the air space between Osnabrück and Münster.

While Pottinger walked back to his quarters and the Poles and Canadians buzzed along towards their targets, the Germans planning their demise were knifing through the January sky. Hptm. Johannes Naumann lead the way for *II Gruppe*, followed by Maj. Helmut Kühle's *III* and Hptm. Ewald Trost's *I Gruppe*. According to the plan, the Knight's Cross holder, Hptm. Naumann would lead the first wave of the attack followed by Trost as the second wave. Maj. Kühle's fighters would provide top-cover protection for the other two.

The formation flew at only 500 feet to avoid detection heading over the Zuider Zee. In that vicinity the aircraft of Ofw. Walter Jung suddenly went down, possibly due to a mid-air collision. But another ominous development immediately placed the entire mission in jeopardy. Somehow, the trusted Ju-88 pathfinder had gotten lost. The pilot, Hptm. Bobsien made a navigational wrong turn and the whole group of planes flew too far to the west before the mistake was realized. This served to throw the entire operation into confusion. Only about nine aircraft from *JG 6* ever reached Volkel for which they had so carefully rehearsed their attack.[100]

Some of the misguided ended up at Eindhoven, but most stumbled onto Heesch airfield some ten miles northwest of their assigned objective. Heesch was the home of the five squadrons of the 126th Wing, RCAF: 402, 410, 411, 412 and 442. Luckily for the Canadians, most of these were already airborne when the Germans showed up. Some forty plus fighters of *JG 6* roared overhead at 9:14 AM just as 401 Squadron's planes were taxiing for takeoff. Meanwhile, the British AA gunners drew a bead on the assailing German fighters while 401 Squadron took straight off into the German attack. Miraculously, several Spitfires were able to get airborne and quickly shot down five German planes. Flg. Off. G.D.A.T. Cameron claimed three of these by himself. But the Germans were more numerous and methodically worked at sending each of the British fighters to the ground. As the Germans bombed and strafed, two of the squadrons from Heesch were busy performing their mission. While on a sortie, Winnepeg-native Flt. Lt. John MacKay managed to chase two German fighters into the ground in spite of being out of ammunition. 412 Squadron became embroiled with other German fighters over Venlo, while 411 Squadron was recalled to base. Flt. Lt. B.E. MacPherson of 412 Squadron shot down one Fw-190 and Flg. Off. V. Smith and Flt. Lt. J.P. Doak each destroyed another. Returning to the scene, 22-year old Flt. Lt. R.J. "Dick" Audet shot down two Fw-190s, one being "Blue 13," the mount of Uffz. Karl Fries which plowed into the ground near Nijmegen.

But most successful of the Royal Air Force that day were the pilots of 442 Squadron who pounced on the enemy as they returned from their earlier mission. Flt. Lt. R.C. Smith heard over his radio that his base at Eindhoven was under attack. Making his way back, he arrived to find a group of German fighters milling about and took on all them by himself. He shot up one badly enough to force the German pilot to his parachute. Flt. Lt. D.C. "Chunky" Gordon, returning to Heesch, downed two Me-109s only to be hit by Allied anti-aircraft fire and forced to crash land. Another section of the squadron ran into a whole pack of the Luftwaffe including some German jets west of Venlo. Flt. Lt. D.M. Pieri shot down two Fw-190s and Flt. Lt. N.A. Keene claimed another. The air battle resulted in claims of damage to two enemy Me-262s and three Fw-190s, although the squadron lost one of its Spitfires.

The Tempests of 486 Squadron had a field day after being recalled from their mission over Arnhem. Returning to the vicinity of Volkel-Eindhoven the New Zealanders felled five German fighters. Sqd. Ldr. A.E. "Spike"

---

100 It is certain that only three of the nine were even from *JG 6*; the remainder included an Me-262 jet and stray fighters from other formations attacking pell-mell whatever airfields they saw.

Umbers accounted for two, while Bill Trott, Gus Hooper and Jim Shedden each claimed singles. C.J. "Butch" Steadman ran across three Me-262s during the fighting, but in spite of expending all his ammunition was unable to hit one of the speedy planes. One of these was likely the jet bandit that crossed over Volkel at 9:25 AM from north to south at 5,000 feet. Another buzzed over an hour later, but in spite of a copious expenditure of Bofors ammunition, none could be brought down. In spite of this, the Tempests at Volkel had proven deadly to the Luftwaffe, shooting down eight German planes with the base virtually unscathed. This fact was underscored less than an hour after the German attack when Volkel sent aloft the Typhoons of 174, 175 and 184 Squadrons to bash German trains near Enschede and the Tempests of 274 Squadron dutifully went ahead with their planned mission to patrol the skies over Paderborn. When it was all over British records indicated a smashing rebuttal to the German surprise: 24 confirmed kills for 126 Wing versus only one lost Spitfire, that of Flg. Off. D. A. Brigden who died over Venlo.

The navigational error played a big part at Volkel; the crack 122 Wing (Tempests) of the British 2nd Tactical Air Force was almost missed entirely. That some did locate Volkel is certain, however. Ron Pottinger, the spare pilot for No. 3 Squadron, climbed down from his Tempest and was talking things over with the ground crews when German fighters suddenly roared overhead, their machine guns blazing. Everyone dashed for cover. Pottinger ran into a tent and pulled out a rifle; what he would do with this he wasn't sure. Two Australian pilots, Plt. Off. R.S. Adcock and Plt. Off. Bill Bailey were actually in their Tempest Vs when the Germans struck, having the distinctly unpleasant experience of climbing out of their aircraft while being strafed. Both ran for cover, while bullets stitched the frozen ground around them. Leading Aircraftman (LAC) Donald Macdonald was a fitter with 121 Wing. He was performing a major field overhaul on a "Rockphoon" when the Germans started strafing the field. Taken aback, he promptly jumped into a large ice-covered bomb hole going down to his waist in mud and slush. The German planes flew back and forth and Macdonald had to wait until they departed to leave his chilly sanctuary. "A short time after the attack," he recalled, "a strange airplane passed over, being engaged by our AA guns. We were informed that this was a German jet— the first one we had seen." LAC Dennis Brooks repaired instruments for 122 Wing at Volkel. That day the 22-year old airman was charging up oxygen cylinders out in the open while chatting with a friend who needed postage:

"...While we were talking about this he looked over my shoulder and said something like 'My God, a Jerry.' I said, 'Don't be stupid, it's a Tempest.' The Fw-190 that it actually was proved me wrong by opening fire on us both. We crashed to the ground and, with true survival of the fittest, tried to elbow each other out of a shallow depression that we were trying to get into. Some moments later all hell let loose when Me-109s and Fw-190s began attacking from different directions; the Bofors AA gun by us was firing non-stop, and our Tempests were jettisoning fuel tanks full of petrol all over the 'drome...Soon our own planes were overhead and the Germans were quickly shot down or driven off, and our Tempests were coming in to be re-armed, refueled and fitted with new oxygen bottles. I was kept really busy. Our pilots told us that the whole German air force was in the sky and they were shooting them all down..."

Many of the Tempests from Volkel were in the air and when returning from their missions fell upon the unsuspecting Germans in the vicinity. The homeward bound New Zealanders of 3 Squadron claimed two Me-109s, one each by Flg. Off. D.J. Butcher and Flt. Sgt. Maurice Rose. Plt. Off. D.E. Ness and Plt. Off. Artie Shaw of 56 Squadron shared the claim of another Me-109. Over the Paderborn-Bielefeld area, Flg. Off. J.W. Garland of 80 Squadron intercepted two Fw-190s headed for the airfields. Diving on the planes, he fired and both fell away and exploded.

A third of the planes from *JG* 6 were shot down, including Obstlt. Johann Kogler, its commander. All the detailed German plans had become so much miscalculation when Kogler realized that he was off course and far south of the target. The *Kommodore* was forced to follow the rail line from Helmond towards Volkel to try to even locate the airfield. He never made it. Some 14 miles south of Volkel, Kogler's Focke Wulf was hit by AA fire and his machine faltered. Over the radio Kogler passed the baton of command to Hptmn. Naumann with *II Gruppe* and belly-landed his Fw-190A-9 four miles west of Severum. As he popped his canopy and crawled out, he could see German fighters belonging to *I* and *II Gruppen* circling aimlessly overhead at only 500 meters. As far as they were from the airfield, he knew they would likely never find it. Soon Allied troops arrived on the scene and Kogler was taken prisoner.

The German attack had been a complete failure. Volkel and its dangerous Tempests remained nearly untouched, while the rest of *JG* 6 ambled over the Dutch countryside looking for airfields to strike. The three German planes, that did find Volkel were promptly shot down. These included Uffz. Rudolf Schlossborn, who knew little of the operation before taking off for a fellow flyer who was sick. Approaching the airfield with their small group of Me-109G-14s of 9 *Staffel*, someone shouted over the radio "Look out White 14!" just before strikes from two Tempests shattered his craft. Schlossborn took to his parachute, floating down close to Volkel airfield. Another, Uffz. Hans Joachim Rose suffered a similar fate. Taking off from Bissel at 8:30 AM, he followed the *Gruppe* leader, Maj. Kühle, flying towards the target at 300 feet. Presently, the aircraft arrived over Volkel and pressed home the attack, one *Staffel* following the other in turn. After two passes Rose's G-14 was engaged by a Spitfire at 450 feet and a dogfight ensued. Rose believed he had shot down the British fighter although not seeing it crash. On his way back for home, however, his engine sputtered and he was forced to make a crash landing some 5 miles east of Volkel. The other plane with Rose, that of Hptm. Willi Kindler was also shot down and the pilot killed. The entire German contingent was wiped out.

Some German pilots ended up joining the attack at Eindhoven. After being unable to find Volkel, Hptm. Ewald Trost, the 31-year old commander of 2 *Staffel*, spied an Allied field with some 40-50 aircraft and put in an attack. He made three circuits over the strip shooting up three Spitfires which burst into flame. In his last approach, his Fw-190A-8 was hit by AA fire and he was forced to make a crash landing some distance away, sustaining numerous injuries. Lt. Hans Wulff was also among the bewildered pilots unable to find Volkel. The 8 *Staffel* was loping over the area where the airstrip was supposed to be when the pilot spied some transport on the highway below. Deciding that attacking something was better than nothing, he opened fire on a column of trucks. However, as he turned away from his target of opportunity, he ran across a "superior number of Spitfires and Tempests." Wulff closed with these and claimed one before being drilled himself as he watched his kill spiral away. His A-8, "Blue 4," went out of control and he bailed out into captivity 24 miles east of Eindhoven.

The commander of the 5 *Staffel*, Hptm. Norbert Katz, plunged right into the airfield and Lt. Grabmeier and Uffz. Betz both fell to their death. JG 6 was badly scattered and returned to its bases helter-skelter. Many pilots were unaccounted for back at the bases of Delmenhorst, Vechta and Quakenbrück. Ten officers including some six unit leaders were missing. These included the head of JG 6, Obstlt. Kogler, and Hptm. Trost Of I *Gruppe* who were now Allied POWs. Maj. Helmut Kühle, the intrepid leader of III *Gruppe* had been killed. Volkel had hardly been attacked and Heesch was only lightly damaged. A third of the pilots taking part in the operation did not return.

In spite of all the confusion arising from the German blow, 412 Squadron managed to get off its planned fighter sweep at 9:30 AM, crossing the path of some thirty Fw-190s near Venlo. Four were shot down, with a second sortie at mid-day destroying a lone Ju-88 sighted in the Dortmund area. A final mission bagged three further German fighters near Osnabrück, although Flt. Lt. J.B. Doak was shot down and killed by an Fw-190. Ironically, earlier during the day Doak himself had shot down a Focke Wulf.

During the evening of December 31st, Obstlt. Heinz Bär, a Knight's Cross holder with 202 victories broke with protocol to brief the men of his JG 3 "*Udet*" Geschwader. Arguably, "Pritzl" Bär was the Luftwaffe's greatest ace. He had fought against the British in the early going, in North Africa, on the Russian front and now again in the West. Bär informed his *Gruppen* commanders of the operation and they in turn briefed their pilots the night before at Paderborn, Lippspringe and Gütersloh. Oblt. Seidel of I/JG 3 called all the available pilots to a meeting at 6 PM. Even though it was New Year's all passes were taken back and alcohol was forbidden. He told his pilots that this was "the big show" in which the entire *Geschwader* along with many others would finally give the Allies a real beating. That night, the snowy airfield teemed with activity to get the German fighters ready for the big attack. The security surrounding the operations was complete; ground crews even pulled from the Focke Wulfs and Messerschmitts the FuG 25 radar sets, the German equivalent of the RAF's IFF, identification friend or foe. At 7 AM, in the sleepy predawn, the pilots received the details. Lt. Mueller gave the briefing for the 28 participating pilots of *IV/JG 3* at Gütersloh, describing the target and passing out marked maps for the pilots. The course would be a direct one: Lippstadt to Dorsten in Holland to Eindhoven, Netherlands. Radio silence was the rule; pilots were not even to switch on their FuGe 16 radios until reaching the Rhine. More importantly, they were given their target: "This is the airfield west of Eindhoven. It is swarming with Spitfires. So watch out for any Spitfires which may already be airborne and over the target zone!" In fact, Eindhoven was home to three wings on January 1st: 124 and 143 Wings, both Typhoons, and 39 Reconnaissance Wing, flying Spitfires.

While Obstlt Bär planned their end, Typhoons of No. 137 Squadron took to the air from Eindhoven. Under the leadership of Flt. Lt. George Clubley, the rocket-laden fighter bombers were to paste the Germans over the Minden area. Similarly, Squadron Leader L.H. "Lennie" Lambert was preparing to put the Typhoons of 168 Squadron into the air:

> "I arrived back from England on the night of 31st December, having had to hitch-hike back because of weather. There was a bit of a party going on, but being tired I was in bed by midnight, but nobody was really in the mood for a big party, for everyone felt pretty tense about what was going on in the Bastogne salient. It was thought that the Germans might breakthrough unless the weather cleared and we could give the ground troops the air support we'd been able to give them from Normandy onwards...we were called at 4 AM and told that the weather was clearing. We had a very careful briefing because none of us had been to the attack area before owing to the fog. We were told where we would find an American liaison officer, and given radio frequencies etc, and prepared for take-off."

Little did Lambert know of the surprise *JG 3* had coming. At 8:30 AM Bär took off leading the twenty G-14s of *I Gruppe* from Paderborn along with Oblt. Seidel, the acting *Gruppekommandeur*. Lt. Mueller led *IV/JG 3*, being careful to avoid the filled bomb craters on the runway at Gütersloh during takeoff. By the time the swarm had assembled in over Lippstadt some 70 German fighters were in the van. Bär lead his attack force in a bee-line directly for Eindhoven; flying 140 miles at only 150 feet and 220 mph— just over the tree tops! The planes flew over the northern reaches of the Ruhr valley and crossed the Dutch border near Venlo. One pilot, Fw. Paul Fischer, was shot down by a lone Spitfire near Venlo after he strayed from the main formation with engine trouble. However, the mass of German fighters was still well organized and at nearly full strength as they sped for Eindhoven. It was only twenty minutes to the target. Near Sonse Heath, a small contingent broke off from the main body and headed for the airstrip at Gilze-Rijen where they joined fighters of *JG 27* along with a lone Me-262. Flt. Lt. A.D. "Dave" Mercer in his recon Mustang with 268 Squadron was flying over Utrecht at 9:15 AM when they spied three Ju-188s escorted by five Fw-190s on the deck. Mercer dove on the German planes and quickly accounted for one of the Ju-188s which caught fire and slashed into a woods below. Mercer warned the controllers at Gilze-Rijen that the Jerries were aloft. Then came a message "Action over base," calling the pilots back home to help. Mercer and his wingman John Lykes headed back at low altitude trying to avoid detection. They headed for a pall of smoke in the distance, which turned out to be Eindhoven. Mercer recalled the moment:

> "They were getting a real pasting, the airfield was covered in smoke, Bofors guns going full blast and Fw-190s buzzing like flies. I picked up a 190 and closed in on him. He still had his bomb on-board, but when I pressed the trigger nothing happened— used all my shells on the 188. He had not seen me and as I had excess speed I went alongside him and when he saw me I remember giving him the V-sign. He broke away and tossed his bomb off, harmlessly into a field; he probably never realized how near he had been to getting the chop."

At Gilze-Rijen, 16 enemy fighters made a determined, if poorly coordinated, attack. High-technology assistance for the operation was provided by the jets of *KG 51* and *KG 76*. In spite of intense flak the six Ar-234s of *9/KG 76* flicked their bombs onto the target and returned unscathed. These hit 124 Squadron; first the jets worked over the Typhoons, then came a wave of piston-powered fighters. But presently, Mercer and Lyke showed up over the field without ammunition although their mere presence sent three German fighters running. During a momentary lapse, they put down in the middle of the melee. Both escaped injury although Lykes' Mustang was peppered by enemy fire. The AA gunners were shooting away at German fighters. Three were claimed by the AA. The base sent a frantic warning to Eindhoven. The call was too late. The leader of 124 Wing, C.D. "Kit" North-Lewis, remembered:

> "The wing had moved up to Eindhoven from Brussels in September, 1944 and consisted of four squadrons: 181, 182, 137 and 247 each with 20 rocket Typhoons...The officers of 124 Wing had planned a big New Year's Eve party for the 31st December. However, when the party took place we were somewhat depleted as, during the German offensive in the Ardennes a few days before in which the wing had been heavily engaged, we lost the Group Captain— Charles Green— and three of the four squadron commanders! None had been replaced by 1 January and thus there was only one CO and myself to run the entire wing. Nevertheless, as far as my memory goes, a riotous time was had by all on New Year's Eve."

At the airfield, eight Typhoons of 438 Squadron were taxiing along the runway, ready to leave on their missions for the day. They were being led by Flt. Lt. Peter Wilson, who had just been assigned as the commanding officer of the squadron two days before. It would be his first mission leading his fellow Canadians. Just behind them were another eight Typhoons from 440 Squadron queued up to await take-off. And at the head of the entire group was Flt. Lt. H.P. "Gibby" Gibbons a 24-year old pilot of 168 Squadron who was to give a Typhoon its check-out flight that morning. They could not know that destiny was just seconds away.

A mass of German fighters made a wide sweep around Eindhoven and barreled in from the southwest. The Me-109s of *JG 3*, along with the armored Fw-190s *Sturmböcke* of *IV/JG 3*, swooped in for the attack. The German pilots were delighted to see that the British airstrip was tightly packed with aircraft parked wing-tip to wing-tip. The Typhoon fighter-bombers of 438, 439 and 440 Squadrons were taxiing out to the runway. The German fighters promptly blasted these. Wing Commander North-Lewis could not believe his eyes:

"Some time after nine o'clock I happened to look out of the window of my HQ and I saw eight to twelve strange aircraft in a line astern passing. As I registered that they did not belong to us, I realized that they were Me-109s. I remember wondering what in the hell they were doing at Eindhoven, for throughout the campaign from the beachhead in Normandy to Holland our airfields had never been attacked. Having realized that a German fighter force was over the airfield at low level, I dashed outside to see what was going on...I think there must have been some 20-25 German aircraft circling the airfield. They immediately started to make low-level attacks on the parked aircraft. The Canadian wing had their aircraft drawn up in lines outside the old German hangars. At the moment of the German attack they had one squadron fully bombed up and one squadron just getting ready to take-off. The Germans concentrated on these aircraft and few of those waiting to take-off escaped. The squadron leader made a brave attempt, but when I last saw him with his wheels still down, he had a couple of German aircraft queuing up behind him to shoot him down."

North-Lewis was watching the first pair of planes from 438 that were taxing down the runway when the Germans appeared at 9:10 AM. Flt. Lt. Gibbons was just lifting from the tarmac. Somehow, he managed to dodge the first German tracers and get behind the Fw-190 of Fw. Gerhard Leipholz and shoot it down before he himself was felled. The AA gunners went into action attempting to scatter the attackers away from the Typhoons on the runway. LAC Desmond C. Shepherd:

"After breakfast I was crossing the runway, going towards the armory and keeping a sharp look out for our aircraft, as some were already out on ops. and others were taking off. At that moment I heard gunfire. Looking up the runway I saw what looked like an Me-262 jet go streaking over my head. This was closely followed by several Fw-190s, and coming almost in the opposite direction were several Me-109s. I threw myself down onto the grass at the center of the runway, I saw what I think were the lead planes of each German section collide with each other. They burst into flames and locked together they came spinning down a few feet above my head, giving off tremendous heat. One of the pilots was struggling to get out, then the aircraft broke apart and exploded in the woods beyond the dispersal."

Several German fighters fell to the British fire. The guns were of all types; many of the pilots at the base ran outside to blast away with Sten guns. But the bigger Bofors guns were deadly; one of the first victims was Obfhr. Uwe Naumann of *11./JG 3* who plummeted to his death in his "Yellow 1."[101] Another, "Green 6" of Fhr. Friedrich Tatzreiter, was hit while approaching the airfield with the German pilot able to bail out, albeit with serious injuries. Awaiting his turn, Uffz. Helmut Reinecke in "Yellow 7" shot up an Allied fighter on the runway, which was already filled with flaming aircraft. However, in the process he observed another of his *I Gruppe* crash and explode just before he himself was hit by AA fire. He lost control of his Me-109G-14 which stumbled erratically away from the blazing air field. He was too low to bail out and somehow managed a crash landing in a vacant field. Having now fought in the Luftwaffe since February, 1943, Reinecke was tired of the war and happy to be alive. His Canadian captors found him completely cooperative. Seeing these losses, German flight leaders ordered their fighters to break formation. They were to strafe the airstrip singly to present a more difficult target for the British gunners.

But the Germans, sensing they had the upper hand, could not be distracted from the Canadian fighters attempting to take to the air. Another Typhoon, piloted by the new commanding officer, Flt. Lt. Peter Wilson, was hit repeatedly and the plane veered off the tarmac. Wilson climbed out of his crippled plane with a serious stomach wound; he died a few minutes later. Flg. Off. R.W. Keller in the second Typhoon also took to the air only to be pounced on by the Germans and sent to the ground in flames. Keller was later found in the charred hulk of his Typhoon. Flt. Sgt. L.A.V. Burrows of 137 Squadron was able to get through a hail of bullets to take off, only to be immediately trailed by a swarm of German planes as he struggled to climb. His aircraft exploded and plummeted to a grisly heap just beyond the end of the runway. Another pilot, Plt. Off. Don Campbell, was unable to get out of his plane; bullets were flying everywhere. He hunkered down in his cockpit and survived unscathed, running like hell after the German completed a strafing pass. Four other Canadians, waiting in the taxi line, bolted from their "Tiffies" after the first firing pass and fell to the ground or jumped into muddy slit trenches. Only Plt. Off. A.B. Harle was hurt when he was

---

101 Suffice it to say that shooting away at enemy aircraft with sidearms was less than safe. One man in the cookhouse at Eindhoven had the nickname of "Taffy." With everyone pinned on the floor by the German machine gun and cannon fire, Taffy lost patience. Jumping to his feet, he yelled "Who do they think they are?" Taffy grabbed a Sten gun and ran over to the window blazing away at the German fighters outside. Although surviving his heroics, Taffy was hit by return fire and taken to the hospital.

slashed by flying glass sent ballistic when a 1,000 lb. bomb exploded near the building to which he had run for cover.

The pilots of 439 Squadron were in their crew room when the Germans struck. Everyone dashed outside to see a German fighter headed straight for them. The airmen drew pistols and revolvers and began blasting away at the first German plane as it swept by. But there were more, and it was obvious that pistols would do little to stop them. Everyone ran for cover, with many crowding into an icy trench. Even the Squadron Leader R.G. "Bing" Crosby was chased from his jeep. Several of the men were wounded, although only one of 439's Typhoons was destroyed.

Many of the aircrew of 440 Squadron were in the ready room when the attack began. An exploding bomb blew out every window in the building and turned the quarters into a shambles. Meanwhile, eight of the pilots of 440 were out on the tarmac. Plt. Off. R.A. Watson of 440 managed to fire his plane's cannon from the ground and hit an enemy Fw-190 before his own aircraft was set aflame. Watson, along with the other seven pilots, jumped ship and in spite of running a gauntlet of fire, only one pilot was wounded. By the end of the attack 440 had only two aircraft left, both badly damaged and one pilot had been seriously wounded. Three airmen of the Typhoon squadrons were killed. 400 Squadron lost five of its reconnaissance Spitfires in the affair— one from a felled German fighter who plowed into the plane. 430 Squadron lost another four planes with three more badly damaged and two wounded pilots. Flg. Off. W.P. "Bill" Golden was hurt when a cannon shell exploded in the cockpit of his waiting Spitfire. Two Typhoons of 137 Squadron were destroyed by cannon fire, one of these being the ill fated Flt. Sgt. Burrows. The squadron's chief fitter, Flt. Sgt. R. Bazley, was killed when enemy fire mortally wounded him in his office. Several others were lucky to be alive as bullets bounced all over the place in their quarters. Des Shepperd of 137 was still lying on the ground taking in the sights:

> "Many pilots were jumping out of their aircraft and I saw a German aircraft crash in a row of parked Spitfires, causing more fires. Lorries were being shot up, including the 'breakfast special' resulting in LAC Norris, one of our armorers, dying from his wounds the following day. Many aircraft were burning, a petrol bowser exploded, huts and other buildings were shot up...Air battles were taking place around the airfield as more RAF planes joined in. German cannon shells were hitting the ground around me and one grazed my right knee cap, so I was unable to run for cover, although the main cause was that I was paralyzed with fear. I even tried to dig myself into the ground with my hands, but the ground was frozen hard. An empty German cannon shell case with links attached, fell onto my head. When it cooled off I put it inside my battle dress blouse thinking that if I survived this day I would keep it as a reminder of New Year's Day, 1945. I still have it."

181 Squadron did better than most with only one Typhoon lost. 182 Squadron was not as fortunate. Corp. Rabbitt was caught without cover and

shot down and LAC Hodges was badly wounded when a German cannon shell took one of his feet off. The Squadron Leader, C.J. Gray, ran for his life:

"We had just dressed on the second floor of a commandeered school just to the south of the airdrome when it started. I and five other pilots dashed in my jeep to the airfield. I remember my fitter beside my aircraft 'G', which he had started up, when a 190 came in very low and firing. He blew up two of my aircraft and shot the propeller boss and prop off my aircraft which caused it to rev up uncontrollably and seize..."

The losses were extensive. 438 Squadron reported only two of its aircraft undamaged. Nearly all the planes on the ground were destroyed. British records relate that the German planes "attacked the field in a well organized manner, being persistent and well led." This was true; JG 3 included a high percentage of veteran flyers such as Obstlt. Heinz Bär, its commander, who earned his 203rd and 204th kills in the attack. Fires blazed uncontrollably. A Mitchell bomber was shot up at the edge of the airfield while another German fighter hit a fuel storage truck which went up in a gushing orange boil of flame.

Presently, however, the Allied fighters that had been out on missions commenced to return. Sqd. Ld. Gordon Wonnacott, of 414 RCAF Squadron, spied some twenty Me-109s ending their run over the smoke filled skies around Eindhoven. The Canadians waded into the German fighters. Wonnacott picked out one which managed to outmaneuver him. Soon, however, he had locked onto an Me-109 at 100 yards. He loosed a stream of bullets, seeing strikes all over the German plane. Knowing a bad thing, the Luftwaffe pilot promptly popped his canopy and took to his silks. Quickly the Canadian was onto another in which a burst of gunfire from 250 yards set the airplane aflame. However, he had to break this combat off as three Fw-190s were darting along on his tail. Wonnacott turned into these three and loosed a burst which struck one before he ran out of ammunition. He successfully evaded his pursuers northeast of Helmond and managed to get back to base. One of the planes the Canadian officer had claimed as damaged was found on the ground with a dead German pilot aboard. Wonnacott was credited with three victories. One of these was Oblt. Graf von Treuberg, who was never found. Col. Rupert Preston witnessed one of Wonnacott's kills:

"I considered the best thing I could do was to return to Group HQ and report the situation to Air-Vice Marshal Broadhurst. On the way back I saw about 200 yards away from the road, a Spitfire chasing a German fighter around a haystack. The German crash landed about 100 yards from me. The pilot got out unhurt and surrendered to my driver. I put him in the back of my jeep and took him to the HQ. I gather he was second in command of the raid. I handed him over to Group Captain Paul Davoud. The German spoke English very well and said the war was over for them as far as he was concerned. I then knocked on Broady's door and went into his office. He was on the telephone to Air Marshal Coningham in Brussels and the conversation went something like this: 'They're flying down just above the houses here!" Broadhurst replied,

403

'Don't worry, they're flying below my window here!' and at that moment several did go by."

Ofw. Friedrich Hameister was one of the last German fighters to leave the scene at Eindhoven. On his first operational sortie with JG 3 and although with only 23 hours time in an Me-109G-14, Hameister was determined to make a good showing of himself.[102] In spite of blinding smoke during his strafing run, he claim to have strafed a petrol bowser and a twin-engined aircraft, sending both up in flames. Heading back home, he ran across a Spitfire just as it sent an Me-109 spinning to the ground. Hameister, in turn, shot down the RAF plane, only to be shot up himself by another Spitfire on his tail. His "Green 7" burst into flame, and Hameister was lucky to survive a severe crash landing. He wandered about during the rest of the day to be taken prisoner the following morning.

Several other German planes were lost when JG 3 ran afoul of other Typhoons of 439 Squadron, RCAF. The Typhoons were on their way back from a weather reconnaissance over the Ardennes near St. Vith under Flg. Off. Bob Laurence. The dogfight lasted only five minutes during which Uffz. Gerhard Schmidt downed the Typhoon flown by Flg. Off. S. Angelini, but was then himself hit in the exchange of fire. Schmidt managed a crash landing 20 miles east of Eindhoven where he informed his captors that he had destroyed two of their Spitfires on the ground. Angelini was found still in his mangled Typhoon two days later near Rips. It was only his 14th mission. But Bob Laurence, after some fancy footwork, managed to get on the tail of a Fw-190 and fired several bursts from 800 yards that crippled the German plane and forced its pilot to his parachute. Meanwhile, Laurence had a German plane on his own behind. He managed to shake loose his attacker and get behind another German plane. Two bursts of gunfire slammed into the canopy of the 190, probably killing the pilot, for the plane rolled slowly onto its back and slowly descended to its end. Unknown to Laurence at the time, Flg. Off. Hugh Fraser probably saved his life by shooting one 190 off his tail. The dogfight was a wild one and Fraser took hits on his Typhoon from another assailant before catching a long-nosed Fw-190 below him flying towards Venlo. Fraser closed to within 50 yards before opening fire. The close range cannon fire caused the D-9 to literally

---

102 Ofw. Hameister was a graduate of *Jagdschule Flensburg* where he trained during September and early October on Ar-96 and Me-109G aircraft. However, he amassed only about twenty hours time in both aircraft. He then moved to *Ergänzungs Jagdgruppe West* where he earned some additional experience with the Me-109. He was posted to JG 3 after Christmas. Of the fifty pilots finishing their training, there were four fatal accidents in the eight weeks he was at Stargard. Poor weather hampered much of the training— there were only 14 days in the whole period where flying was possible. Similarly, Uffz. Horst Tharann and fellow students received a lecture from Gen. Galland while training at Neuruppin in September. Galland warned the cadets that too many aircraft were being destroyed during training flights. According to the *Gen. der Jagdflieger*, for every 1,000 aircraft received by the schools, some 800 were damaged. This, he said, must cease so that the operational aircraft strength of the fighting units could be expanded.

disintegrate with the plane slamming into the ground in a huge explosion near a large windmill.

One of these German victims was Fw. Walter Rutowski. Rutowski was on his first operational mission before losing "Green 5" after making four strafing runs over Eindhoven. When he was shot down the *Feldwebel* had barely accumulated 55 hours flying the Me-109G including all of his training missions! Rutowski floated down into captivity at just after 9:30 AM.

The Typhoons of 168 Squadron was also coming back home after a strafing attack in the Ardennes under Sqd. Ldr. Lennie Lambert. As they made radio range, Lambert could hear that something serious was taking place. The messages were garbled, but according to the frantic calls they were under a massive German air attack. Lambert's "Tiffie" had been damaged by ground fire during his mission; he had to keep full right rudder just to keep the beast going straight— hardly combat worthy. But as they approached Eindhoven they suddenly ran across a swarm of German fighters seemingly chasing a P-51 Mustang! Lambert dove on the German group hoping to distract them from the Mustang:

> "There was no doubt about it, it was a Mustang. In retrospect I suppose I should have recognized what was happening before I dived, but thought he was being chased and we had very little fuel and ammo left anyway. We were told the following day that a Mustang had led the aircraft that had attacked Evère or Melsbroek and we had no reason to doubt it as this is what we had seen. After the war I understood the Germans themselves confirmed that one German pilot led quite a large force of fighters in a Mustang."

Flt. Lt. John D. Stubbs, with Lambert, also saw the P-51 with no markings, flying about 600 yards ahead of a pack of Me-109s. The P-51 made no attempt at evading the 109s, nor did the Messerschmitts attempt to close. It was a strange episode.[103] But after the Typhoons dove through the German formation, a wild dogfight broke out with much firing, but no claims by either side. The Germans continued on their way home. Meantime, 137 Squadron under Flt. Lt. George Clubley was also headed back for Eindhoven. After blasting trains near Steinheim, his Typhoons sighted a Me-262 over the Rhine area:

> "We turned towards him, but he left us standing with the greatest of ease. We then found an He-111 which we attacked. Although I had done about 140 operational flights with the Typhoon, this was my first attempt at shooting at an enemy aircraft and I suspect that my accuracy left much to be desired. However, when I came around again, the Heinkel was on the ground— possibly I had hit him or more probably the pilot felt it was the safest place."

When Clubley reached Eindhoven, he was shocked at the damage. Fires

---

103 The author can find no evidence that a German flown P-51 was involved in *Operation Bodenplatte*. However, two corroborating RAF witnesses seems to lend credence to the story.

were burning out of control and a pall of smoke reduced visibility. They were vectored to Volkel. According to the combat diary of Eindhoven it was "twenty-three minutes of hell that paralyzed everyone." Flt. Sgt. L.A.V. Burrows of 137 Squadron was killed and his unit ended the pasting with only 11 operational planes. The others were even less fortunate. 181 Squadron had eight left operational, 247 had five and 182 had none. At the end of the melee, the British 124th Wing could only muster 24 aircraft. A reconnaissance Mustang of 268 Squadron was damaged as it taxied for takeoff, although Flt. Lt. L.J. Packwood of 2 Squadron managed to destroy an Me-109. The British estimated that they had been attacked by 70 German planes before Spitfires and Tempests arrived to drive them off. The fighters and the busy Bofors gunners together claimed 44 of the enemy shot down— a claim approximately double that of the actual German losses. The AA men of Col. Preston's RAF Regiment had fired off some 2,750 rounds and were eventually credited with five shared victories. One memento made a certainty of one of their claims. The No. 8 gun position possessed the shattered cockpit canopy which it had blasted off one of the marauding Fw-190s.

The Germans would have been quick to acknowledge the cost. Heinz Bär himself claimed two Typhoons on the ground, likely the first two aircraft destroyed of 438 Squadron. Ten pilots were killed or missing and another six were taken prisoner— a loss rate of 22% of the German pilots taking part. That night ULTRA listened as *I/JG 3* reported that it was missing nine of its 22 aircraft which had taken part. Among the losses was Senior Warrant Officer Erich Kaiser, one of the most experienced of the jet bomber pilots with *KG 51* who was shot down near Lingen. Still, the German assault was a significant victory. By their own accounting, the Canadians lost some 144 aircraft on the ground with a further 84 damaged. These included 28 Spitfires, 11 Wellington bombers and many Typhoon fighter-bombers. Six pilots had been shot down in the melee and 40 officers and enlisted men were killed on the ground; a further 145 were wounded. It would be mid-January before the base was able to reequip and return to full service.[104] LAC Desmond Sheppherd eloquently describes the aftermath:

> "After the raid, at the bottom end of the airfield where the Canadians were, thick black smoke columns were rising and explosions, including the big one that sent a mushroom cloud up to great height, added to a very noisy morning...Some days before the raid, a four-engined USAAF bomber, badly shot up, force landed on the airfield and an American ground crew came and worked hard for many days repairing it and even changed its engines, completing the job on New Year's Eve. After the raid I saw the American crew chief standing with his men scratching his head, looking at the burned-out piece of twisted

---

104 The German attack also created a certain paranoia, with sometimes tragic results. Hoping to find better weather for operating against the Germans in the Ardennes, 164 and 183 Squadrons of the 2nd TAF were in the process of moving to the American airfield at Chievres when one of the Typhoons was shot down accidently by an American P-51 Mustang as it approached.

metal that was once his pride and joy. One of our 'Erks' stepped forward and said, 'Well, Chief, you really have something to repair now!" Later, during a visit to the sick bay for treatment of my knee, I saw the bodies of several German pilots lying outside with snow flakes slowly falling on them. They looked very young. Inside were more bodies covered by blankets, their boots were RAF and Army types..."

The 80 Me-109s and Fw-190s of *JG 1 "Oesau"* were to hit three Belgian airfields. *I* and *III Gruppen* would attack Maldegem and Ursel airfields, while *II Gruppe* would knock out St. Denis-Westrem. At the airfield of Twenthe, some ten miles from the German border with Holland, Hptm. Georg Hackbarth gave his pilots of *I/JG 1* the mission plan for *"Bodenplatte."* The presentation even included a pep talk at 4 PM the day before by the famous ace and leader of *JG 1*, Obstlt. Ihlefeld. Hptm. Staiger at Drope briefed the men of *II/JG 1* in the late afternoon of December 31st using a sand table model of the airfield they were to strike. *III Gruppe* at Rheine airfield received their briefing from their new commander, Hptm. Harald Moldenhauer the same afternoon. It was planned that each *Schwarm* would make five passes over the target, circling counter-clockwise between the attacks.

Staiger's pilots were awakened shortly before 6 AM. The group's 36 Fw-190A-8s were ready by the time they had finished a hearty breakfast. *I Gruppe* held its last minute briefing at 7 AM. The pilots were told they could expect to find Tempests, Spitfires and Mustangs on the ground at Maldegem airfield. Lt. Anton Guha with *III Gruppe* had been flabbergasted to find himself appointed the *Staffelführer* for *10./JG 1* when Oblt. Bilfinger failed to return from a mission a few days before. He only had ten sorties under his belt! Regardless, Guha stood down for *Bodenplatte* since his *Staffel* had more pilots than aircraft. But when New Year's morning came, Guha was unceremoniously awakened. It seems that one of his bunk mates scheduled to fly had a king-sized hangover. He took his former "friend"'s maps, but was so late to the strip that he had to push the throttles to catch up with the rest of the *Staffel*. His brand-new Me-109G-14 didn't even have markings!

Two Ju-88s of *I/NJG 2* served as pathfinders for the group, lifting from the airstrip at exactly 8:10 AM. The flight route was a long one, going straight across Holland at 300 feet to Spakenburg and then to the coast at The Hague from whence they would move southwest, hugging the water's edge before turning east towards their target over Bruges, Belgium. The twenty Fw-190A-8s of *I Gruppe* were soon joined by the 30 Me-109G-14s of *III Gruppe* which had taken off from Rheine at 8:15 AM. The combined formation assembled nicely, but after crossing the Zuider Zee and approaching the Hague, the 55 aircraft of *I Gruppe* suddenly found themselves under murderous anti-aircraft fire— friendly flak! Somehow the German gunners had not received the message regarding the operation and their marksmanship turned out to be deadly accurate. Uffz. Egon Comtesse and Jürgan Killian

407

were shot out the sky. Later, over Rotterdam, Fw. Heinz Böhmer was brought down by Allied guns.

Included in the losses was *Kommodore* Herbert Ihlefeld, himself, who was nailed while passing The Hague. He was lucky to be able to make a forced landing. Uffz. Killian was perhaps the most tragic loss. An ex-pilot of *III/JG 77*, Killian had flown in North Africa, Italy and Rumania. By the time he joined *JG 1*, he had some 80 combat flights, but not a single victory. Killian was not the typical Luftwaffe fighter pilot, being an artist and somewhat of a free spirit. In spite of these traits, the eccentric veteran was very popular with his fellow flyers. But after all this, Uffz. Heinz Jürgan Killian came to his end on the first day of 1945 at the controls of his Fw-190 A-8 "Yellow 6," an ironic victim of German flak guns!

Coming in over the cold gray waters of the North Sea, the fighter swarm made landfall near the historic town of Bruges where 4 *Staffel*'s small group of five aircraft, under Oblt. Gottfried Meinhoff, headed south looking for any promising targets on the airstrip between Knesselare and Ursel. This diversionary attack was a disaster. First, Uffz. Alfred Fritzsche was hit by AA before he even had a chance to fire his guns, suffering severe burns in a fiery crash landing. Then the swarm arrived over the airfield only to find that there were no targets. The twelve squadrons of Spitfires that had occupied the field had returned to England the day before, leaving only the 424 Re-arming and Refueling unit. Sgt. Peter Crowest:

> "We were positioned for duty at 9 AM and had barely time to judge the extent of our hangovers from the night before when we heard and saw a squadron of low flying fighters approaching. An inquiry from my CO as to whether we were expecting Spitfires was answered when I said that these were not Spitfires but Focke Wulf 190s! Movements later I was firmly gripping the ground..."

And LAC E.H. Green:

> "Suddenly, there was a very loud explosion and when I looked to see where it came from the first thing I saw was the Mosquito near the Control Tower going up in flames and black smoke. More gunfire and the B-17 Fortress was in flames, also the oil drums. Everyone started to take cover in a ditch and elsewhere. I saw three or four Fw-190s, with the sun on them, and flying along as if they were on a weekend trip with not a care in the world. With all this going on an RAF Sgt. Armorer came out of his store hut with a machine gun, got down in the ditch and had a go at the departing planes. What he was calling the Luftwaffe cannot be put in print!"

The only damage to Ursel was to destroy a B-17 that was in the process of being repaired (the repair crew was delighted to be done with it) and to knock out a Mosquito and two Lancasters. As final insult, on the return leg, Oblt. Meinhoff, the mission leader, died when his "Red 8" was shot down by Allied AA over Breda.

At Maldegem airfield, the New Zealanders of 485 Squadron had the assignment of taking their Spitfire IXs out on a patrol at 8:45 AM. However, this had been cancelled when the ice-covered airfield was judged unserviceable at daybreak. It was just as well, for had the operation gone forward, the pilots would have found themselves taxiing down the runway under German guns.

The main body of *III Gruppe* reached Maldegem airfield at just after 9 A.M, but a ground mist made it difficult to spot targets on the airfield although for once AA fire was not much of a problem; the guns had been withdrawn a few day before. The first run-in was a look-see at tree-top height to find targets. But on the next three passes the Me-109s ripped across the airfield with their guns blazing. Aircraft fitters arguing over whether the planes on the first pass were Mustangs or Thunderbolts resolved the issue face down in the nearby ditches! Even so, the lack of visibility, and the extensive dispersal of the RAF planes, was crippling to the German effort; a blind strafing run set 11 Spitfires aflame from the New Zealand 485 Squadron. Two more were so badly damaged as to be beyond repair. The squadron was left with only five serviceable Spitfires and 349 (Belgian) Squadron lost a further Spitfire LF IXe.

But there was no counting the German attack a success. So rebuffed, some of the *Gruppe* turned north and headed for home while others headed over to St Denis-Westrem. Two pilots went down over Maldegem. One was Lt. Anton Guha whose new G-14 developed engine trouble forcing the pilot to bail out six miles northeast of the airfield. Fhj-fw. Wilhelm Wichard was also taken prisoner by the RAF. Wichard was excited to be flying his first action as a pilot with *III/JG 1*— he only had about 30 hours in fighters. But when the novice pilot arrived over Maldegem, the airfield was covered with so much smoke from burning aircraft that he couldn't see a thing. In second and third passes he fired wildly at the ground hoping to hit something. On his way back home, however, his "White 19" was hit by AA fire over the Schelde and he was forced to make a crash landing. Wickard set fire to his Me-109G-14 and was taken prisoner shortly thereafter. His interrogators revealed that Wichard "feels sorry for himself, as he had the bad luck to be taken prisoner on his first action." But he should have counted himself fortunate; another pilot, Fw. Wilhelm Kräuter, crashed to his death on the way back, likely due to AA fire over the target. The "AA fire" had, in fact, been Sten gun and pistol fire directed at the German planes from the doorways and windows and billets of 485 Squadron as orchestrated by its leader J.G. Pattison, who blazed away with a German Mauser bolt-action rifle.

A little after 9 AM, Hptm. Staiger's *II Gruppe* roared over St. Denis-Westrem field near Ghent. The occupants of the field were three Polish squadrons of 131 Wing, RAF, all with the dreaded Spitfire Mk IX (302, 308 and 317 Squadrons). Unfortunately for the Germans, the birds had flown! All three squadrons were on a mission to Woensdrecht when they showed up looking for them. Even worse, for the low altitude Luftwaffe pilots, the Poles were already flying back to their nest. Just before the German arrival, 302 Squadron showed up nearly out of fuel and prepared to put down. The day had been frustrating for the Poles. They had already lost one of their number over the battle zone when Flt. Sgt. Stanislaw Celak was hit by Allied AA fire in another case of mistaken identity. And Flg. Off. Waclaw Chojnacki's two bombs had refused to release over their target. Still with the bombs, Chojnacki approached the airfield to land at 9:27 AM. He put his wheels down for the final approach at just the wrong moment. Suddenly, three German fighters appeared before him. Chojnacki instinctively raised his undercarriage and prepared to do battle. In spite of his plane's weight, he made a tight turn and got in behind the German fighters, firing a burst from 800 yards that blew its tail off. The German plane knifed through a tree, careened across the top of a building and plowed into a Flying Fortress that was on the ground. But now three more Luftwaffe fighters showed up and dove on Chojnacki's plane sending it plunging to the ground. The 27-year old Polish pilot, a veteran since February, 1944, died instantly. In the meantime, the German fighters got on with business and severely shot up the airfield. L.A. Simmons was scheduled to be taken to England in an Anson that morning. Instead, he had a brush with death:

"I got my bag out of the jeep, but when I tried the door of the Anson I found it jammed and it was five minutes before it could be gotten open. Two or three of my fellow passengers had rolled up while we were struggling with the door and when it was opened, two got in before me. I tossed my bag in and was halfway in myself when I happened to look over my shoulder and saw a mass of aircraft coming towards the 'drome from the north and while I yet looked, crowds of lights started coming from them— and a second later 'Tat-Tat-Tat-Pum-Pum' which developed into the most appalling clatter you ever did hear. I found myself flat on my face on the ground between the jeep, with my head buried under my hat. The Anson which I so nearly got into was a mass of flames within two minutes and the petrol tanks were due to go up. I glanced around the ground to my left. The cannon tracers were hitting the ground and bouncing off in graceful curves and there seemed to be hundreds of them. It was a free for all for the Jerry pilots as there were no ground defenses at all! They flew round and attacked and attacked till their ammunition was used up."

Presently, however, more of the Polish fighters commenced to reach St. Denis-Westrem, being forced to land amid their own AA fire and the strafing enemy fighters. While still on their way back Flt. Lt. Ignacy Olszeski, leading 308, attacked several Fw-190s he and Flt. Lt. Bronislaw Mach observed east of Ghent. Mach sent one German fighter to the ground near Termonde with the pilot bailing out.

Back at the airfield, the first AA fire was sporadic since the Bofors guns had been covered to protect them from snow. Soon they were back in action, managing to shoot down one Spitfire in error. Meanwhile, the Polish pilots began to collect over St. Denis looking to land or engage the Germans in combat. In all, *JG 1* claimed another nine attempting to touch down. But the gunfire of the AA and Spitfires was deadly.

Two German fighters plunged to the ground near the field. Hptm. Hackbarth, the commander of *I/JG 1* and a veteran with some thirty victories fell to his death near the St. Pieters railway station in Ghent. He was shot down by Flt. Sgt. Josef Stanowski who had just returned over the airfield. The Fw-190A-8 plowed into the back of the "Toebaert" flower shop and smashed through the front window with the crumpled body of Hptm. Hackbarth hideously thrown out into the street. Uffz. Karl Hahn was also shot down and killed, perhaps the first of Stanowski's two victims that day. Another Fw-190, "Blue 5," smashed into the ground near the village of Zwijnaarde. The pilot was Fw. Harry Klints, a 27-year old Latvian volunteer who had been assigned to the Luftwaffe in October, 1944. The group was told to make five strafing passes, but circumstances did not work out that way and German pilots returning reported "considerable confusion" in the operation. As the abuse went on at St. Denis-Westrem, the base called back their two other squadrons. When 308 Squadron was still 12 miles from Ghent they ran into the enemy fighters, promptly shooting down four. Presently, *II/JG 1* also showed up. Uffz. Edgar Ardner of the 5 *Staffel* was among this group. Since joining *II/JG 1* on 15 December he had seen at least twenty German aircraft destroyed and nearly as many pilots killed in the fighting around the Bastogne area where he had claimed one Thunderbolt for himself. But Ardner did not hesitate in opening fire on the parked Allied planes as soon as he reached the airfield. Soon all his ammunition was used up in a series of passes while he watched the aircraft burn on the airfield. Then, however, as he pulled out at 650 feet he was jumped by two Spitfires, most likely those of Flt. Lt. Waclaw Chojnacki and Sqd. Ldr. Marian Chelmecki. His cockpit was smashed and the controls went dead. He jumped from his stricken plane and was taken prisoner.

317 Squadron was coming back home as well. Arriving over Ghent Wt. Off. Stanislaw Piesik observed the enemy fighters strafing below. He dove on the planes sending one of the 190s slashing into the fields near the airfield. The Belgian civilians in Rosdambeek were in a foul mood. The shattered body of the 20-year old German native of Homberg was kicked by an angry woman in the neighborhood and his watch was stripped. Uffz. Fritz Hoffmann narrowly avoided a similar fate. He had just completed three strafing passes in which he shot up a Spitfire on the first and a bomber on another. Suddenly his craft was rocked by a hail of bullets while scarcely 300 feet off the ground. The "blast of fire" came from the Spitfire of Flt. Lt. Czeslaw Mroczyk of 317 Squadron who caught Hoffmann unware. The German pilot managed to gain height in his crippled A-8 before jumping. Swinging under a parachute was familiar to Hoffmann; he had been shot down on June 16th

411

over Falaise in France and again on Christmas Eve when a B-17 had hit his plane over the Eifel. But the third time was the bad-luck charm in this case; Hoffmann became an uncooperative POW near Ghent after evading an angry mob.

"When I was captured I was hit by civilians and the police. After spending two hours in a police station near Ghent, I was handed over to the British. I was examined for the first time at their airfield. There were many fires. The next day I was brought to an airfield near Brussels. I was questioned by two Captains of the British Secret Service, with a barrel in my back. They hit me, while I did not reveal any details. From Namur I boarded a twin-engined Douglas with ten friends who were shot down the same day. We were escorted by Spitfires to London, where we were questioned again until the end of January. Until March, 1945 I spent my days in a POW-camp at Marsh near Oxford."

But others were even less fortunate— Fw. Paul Mayr and Lt. Ernst von Johannides were killed. As the Spitfires arrived over the airfield the Luftwaffe was making another strafing run, shooting up six parked fighters belonging to 317 Squadron. Presently, the Spitfires appeared in increasing numbers with swirling dogfights sprouting up in the skies over Ghent. In the same aerial battle which brought down Uffz. Hoffmann, Sqd. Ldr. Chelmecki opened fire on a Fw-190 from 400 yards, getting hits but losing it in dark smoke from a B-17 burning on the field. But those on the ground saw its fate: spinning down in flames to smash into a building just beyond the rail line. Even with a poorly running engine Wt. Off. Zenobieuz Wdowczynski arrived over the airfield and shot down a 190 even though he was forced to crash land after the deed. Flt. Lt. Roman Hrycak brought down another. In these actions, one Polish pilot, Flt. Lt. Tadeusz Powierza was shot down and killed. Lt. Swoboda's 5 *Staffel* lost five aircraft in the vicious aerial combat. Soon after killing Hackbarth, Josef Stanowski felled another German fighter and Breyner, also of 308 Squadron, knocked out two more. But soon Stanowski ran out of gas and was forced to a belly landing northeast of town.

Olszewski and the remainder of 308 Squadron finally showed up nearly 3,000 feet above the airstrip. They could see the wasp-like German fighters attacking below, and Olszewski immediately singled out a Focke Wulf, dove to range and hammered it with cannon fire. Swatted, it flipped over and crashed east of Ghent. Meanwhile, Flg. Off. Tadesusz Szlenkier dove on another 190 observed attacking a Spitfire. Szlenkier's cannon fire ripped up the wing of the Focke Wulf, which promptly flicked over and slammed into the ground at high speed. The plane crashed near Zwijnaarde with Latvian pilot Harry Klints at the controls. But while, Szlenkier was busy destroying Klints, a Luftwaffe pilot had gotten the Pole in his sights and sent a stream of bullets cascading into his Spitfire IX. Szlenkier was lucky to be able to escape the clutches of his attacker to crash land a few moments later. At about the same time Plt. Off. Andrezj Dromlewicz chased down a 190 which took wild evasive maneuvers. Dromlewicz squirted off machine gun and cannon rounds spraying the air in his front. Finally, during one of these jogs the German fighter flew through the stream of his cannon fire. Pieces flew off the enemy right wing and the Luftwaffe pilot took to his parachute. Nearby, west of Terneuzen, Flt. Lt. Mach shot down another German pilot in a chase that went down to "zero feet." And Wt. Off. Stanislaw Bednarcyzk, the flight's number three man, also bagged another German fighter who had been attempting to shoot down Mach.

Meanwhile, at the church of St. Denis-Westrem a New Year's mass was being held at 9 AM. The church was crowded. It was the first free New Year's in the last four— an occasion to celebrate. But then a cacophony of noise drowned out the service. It sounded like gunfire and even bombs! Everyone in the congregation ran outside to see what was happening. Planes were diving and spitting fire through the skies and bombs and bullets were going off, seemingly everywhere. Two ugly columns of black smoke rose from Ghent itself. Just as soon as they saw what was happening over the airfield, they all ran inside to take refuge. Everyone prayed.[105]

Taking a terrible beating at the hands of the Poles, the Luftwaffe started back for home. But JG 1 suffered other losses on the way back. One was Uffz. Paul Wunderlich, forced to bail out over the Schelde estuary when he was brought down by AA fire. When the action was over, the records showed that JG 1 had destroyed or damaged 32 Spitfires, a B-17 and one Stirling of 295 Squadron— 18 of the fighters were plugged at St. Denis-Westrem. However, most of the destroyed planes had been on the ground and Allied aircrew casualties were very light; only two Polish pilots were killed. In contrast, the body count for JG 1 was macabre. A total of 24 pilots did not return; twelve were killed and another six became prisoners (the Poles claimed 20 German fighters destroyed). The members of 5 *Staffel* suffered most with five aircrew lost. They could only claim a single Spitfire destroyed by Lt. Hans Berger— hardly a reasonable exchange. The British counted the charred remains of some 19 German aircraft in the vicinity of Ghent. After making his way back to his command (he had been shot down by German flak before the approach!), Obstlt. Ihlefeld, the stormy commander of the *Geschwader*, made no secret of his bitterness. He had lost a third of his pilots including his new commander of I *Gruppe*, Hptm. Hackbarth. The enemy could easily replace its aircraft; Ihlefeld would end up with a former bomber pilot with no fighter experience, Maj. G. Capito, to take Hackbarth's place.

JG 2, the *"Richthofen" Geschwader*, was nestled in the Taunus hills north of Frankfurt. I *Gruppe*, JG 2 had been at Merzhausen base since October, 1944.

---

105 Today, a remembrance service is held at the church each New Year's for the Poles killed in defending St. Denis-Westrem on that cold first day of 1945.

Their leader, Kurt Bühligen, was highly revered, being one of the few pilots in the Luftwaffe to have amassed over a 100 kills over the Allies in the West, all achieved since joining *JG 2* in 1940. *II* and *III Gruppen* were situated close by at Nidda-Ettingshausen and Altenstadt. A few days before Christmas, the commanders of the *Gruppen* of *JG 2* were summoned to a meeting at Nidda where they were notified by Obstlt. Bühlingen that they would soon carry out a low-level air attack on St. Trond airfield. This was the old stomping grounds of the famous Luftwaffe night-fighter Maj. Heinz-Wolfgang Schnaufer, and *II/NJG I* the "Ghosts of St. Trond," But the quarry the Luftwaffe was stalking on the first day of 1945 was the American fighter-bombers who had taken over their old airfield. St. Trond was more recently the home of the U.S. 48th and 404th Fighter Groups. Bühligen stressed the importance of the mission and the need to carefully brief their subordinate pilots. It was still dark when the pilots were awakened for their drive to the airfield. The various fighter groups would assemble over Koblenz and then fly over the Schnee Eifel in the Ardennes before turning to the northwest to head for St. Trond.

The briefing by Hptm. Hrdlicka and the other group commanders was rushed although *II Gruppe* was given instruction on a sand-table model of the target airfield along with marked maps. Pilots also had time to look over reconnaissance photographs taken of St. Trond which showed some 130 fighters and half a dozen four-engined bombers parked on the airfield. Obstlt. Bühlingen told his young pilots to "Just follow and stay with me!" Disgruntled about missing the previous night's festivities, some pilots managed to sneak a sip of spirits into their cockpit. The ninety Fw-190s of the proud *Geschwader*, some of the D-9s so new that they lacked tactical markings, took off in billowing snow at just after 8 AM.

Bühlingen's was to rendezvous with *SG 4* over Aachen on the way to the target. Some pilots immediately had trouble with their untested machines. Only minutes after taking off, Uffz. Fritz Altpeter's Dora-9 spouted smoke and flames. His companions desperately wanted to signal the inexperienced pilot to bail from his "flaming crate", but could not. Orders forbade anyone to break radio silence during the operation regardless of the circumstances. Silently, and without protest, Altpeter crashed to his death. Meanwhile, "Yellow 17" took off for Fw. Karl Tschelesnig finding that his undercarriage would not retract. The 27-year old pilot landed and hastily had repairs made. Taking off he raced ahead at low altitude to catch up with others. However, just east of Verviers his Fw-190A-8 took light flak hits and the Feldwebel dove into a tree trying to evade the gunners. Amazingly, his aircraft emerged from the shrubbery whereupon he pulled the complaining machine up to a height of 600 feet and jumped ship. At the time he had 15 sorties under his belt with three victories. Reaching the ground he became a POW.

Obst. Alfred Druschel, had recently taken over as commander of *SG 4*.

Just short of his 28th birthday, Druschel was a Knight's Cross wearing Luftwaffe veteran of some 800 missions as an assault pilot since the beginning of the war. His record against the Russian ground forces in the east had been stellar and the first day of 1945 saw his promotion to Oberst and assignment of a new command. He was to lead the ground assault aircraft of *III Gruppe* to join in the attack on St. Trond with Obstlt. Bühligen. Druschel and his 12 Fw-190F-8s took off from Köln-Wahn and set a course to meet *JG 2* just southwest of Aachen. The ground attack group had been very busy during the Ardennes operations and due to the poor facilities at Kirtorf had been beset by technical difficulties with their aircraft. However, as the combined fighter formation approached Aachen from the south they came under heavy and accurate American anti-aircraft fire. German fighters fell out of the sky in numbers seldom seen. Four pilots of the *III/SG 4* went careening to the ground. One of these was the craft of Obst. Druschel, who fell south of the city, but whose ultimate fate still remains a mystery. Although shaken, Maj. Dörnbrack took over command of the group.

JG 2 was also riddled by the AA fire, Focke Wulfs and Messerschmitts falling like flies. Uffz. Otto Dost, Fw. Fritz Schuler, and Uffz. Friederich Optenhostert were shot down and killed. Uffz. Hans Wyssola, Uffz. Georg Wilkens and Obgefr. Willi Scherwadt abandoned their riddled machines to float down into Allied hands near Eupen. Uffz. Ernst Klein was less fortunate and plunged to his death in the same vicinity. Uffz. Helmut Breitweg was hit in the engine at low altitude and managed a successful crash landing into captivity. "Black 9," the Fw-190A-8 of Obgefr. Hubert Schyma, "Black 12" with Uffz. Michel Speiss and "Black 1," the D-9 of Uffz. Siegfried Binger were all hit by Allied AA fire just beyond the front and came down in the Malmédy-Verviers area. All three parachuted into American hands. Closer to the target, Lt. Christfried Clemens of *III/JG 2* was shot down and killed by AA fire near Sittard. But worst of all, Hptm. Georg Schröder, the leader of *II Gruppe*, and veteran of 108 missions, was forced abandon his Me-109 G-14 and to take to his parachute over Verviers before he could even lead his band of fighters to their objective.

Surprise for the 150 German planes of the two groups was less than complete since the base was alerted minutes before by radio from patrols already aloft. As the German fighters swooped in over the field the waiting AA guns opened a devastating fire. One pilot was surprised to see how similar was the tightly packed configuration of Allied planes to what he had seen in the briefing photos. Shooting up the parked planes was easy enough, he reported, it was the AA fire which made things rough. Several wild minutes ensued in which the Germans pumped bullets and cannon fire into the rows of Allied aircraft while the AA gunners doused the swarm of German fighters with a hail of bullets. Several spun into the ground. Uffz. Adolf Redlich perished as did Uffz. Helmut Bollwerk who fell at the controls of his Messerschmitt. Lt. Werner Edelhoff of the *Gruppenstab* lost his machine as well and was lucky to be able to parachute into captivity. The German fighters took additional losses when they passed once more over the thorny AA defenses around Aachen. Fw. Werner Hohenberg was a holder of the German Cross in Gold and a veteran of over 200 operational sorties in the war— he had already been shot down in the fighting in Russia. But the first day of 1945 would be his last of the war. Having participated in the gunnery over St. Trond, the Feldwebel was making his way back to Merzhausen when he was hit by AA fire. Too low to bail out, he managed to make a belly landing and had just gotten out when his Fw-190D-9 burst into flame. Uffz. Johann Jäger was not as fortunate, plunging to his death near Lontzen after being hit by the AA fire. When the *Geschwader* returned, the debriefing revealed a disastrous encounter. *JG* 2 had lost 33 pilots with 23 killed or missing. This represented nearly 40% of the German pilots involved; it was the death blow to the proud Luftwaffe unit.

SG 4 lost a further four of the thirty odd pilots which had taken off from Köln-Wahn airfield. Three flight leaders were missing. Ofw. Hans Schmieder, a veteran of the Luftwaffe campaigns in Italy and France, was hit by flak on the way to St. Trond. His Fw-190F-8 began to vibrate wildly as Schmieder turned back east. The 31-year old pilot bailed out at 400 feet and became a captive near Aachen. Two others, Fw. Richard Heinz and Fw. Rudolf Fye, were killed near Maasmechelen. For all this, the strike had managed to destroy less than a dozen P-47s. And against the German sacrifice, Allied aircrew casualties were virtually nonexistent. The view from the sidelines of the pilots of Nugent's XXIX TAC reflected more humor than anxiety:

"Officers and men of the 48th Fighter Group celebrated New Years in a unique and novel way. From midnight until the early hours of the morn Officers at their Club and Enlisted Men at the Fun Club could be found in various stages of inebriation at the aforementioned clubs. After drinking all there was to drink or more appropriately— all they could hold, they wended their way on a "beaucoup zig-zag" course home...Some managed to get there safely— others took longer routes. At approximately 0845 hours when some of the Group had taken their hangovers to work and most had just kept them in bed, an amazing thing happened. An unfamiliar drone of engines was heard— the first was immediately recognized as an Me-109. The plane was accompanied by five more of Göring's Groundhogs and they were busily preparing to clobber St. Trond/Brustem Airfield. Upon the alarm that enemy planes were attacking the field, offices and boudoirs were evacuated for more substantial dug-outs...By this time the MEs had made their pass and were preparing to take another one from the opposite direction. For awhile they were all over hell and gone and half of Belgium. They strafed the runways, they strafed the planes, they strafed everything that got in front of them. Later a pilot who was captured said that all he did was press the trigger every time the field swung in front of him. The ack-ack boys on the field made a good showing for themselves. They accounted for five enemy planes destroyed and one probable

416

that was smoking from the field when it left. Highlight for some of the personnel of the 493rd Squadron was when ack-ack hit a Fw-190 near the edge of the field. It caught fire and the pilot pulled up and bailed out. Half of the 493rd Squadron rushed out into an open field and formed a welcoming committee for the hapless pilot. He was not lacking in military escort when he was brought to the squadron area. There were at least nine carbines and three sub-machine guns stuck in his back. His plane crashed and burned...On the 492nd side of the field, ack-ack scored a direct hit on an Me-109; he crashed near one of the runways. The pilot earned a wooden cross rather than an iron one...Damage to our aircraft was negligible in spite of the amount of Nazi ammunition expended. We had two of our planes totally destroyed with 14 slightly damaged. Most of these were back in flying condition within the next few days..."

The captured German airman was interrogated at St. Trond. "This is just as the Führer said it would be," he scowled sarcastically, "Germany yesterday, Belgium today and United States tomorrow." It was too bad, the pilot said, that Hitler had neglected to tell them he would see all this from a POW camp.

At 6 PM on December 31st Maj. Schröder of *II/JG 4* called his pilots together at Babenhausen airfield to apprise them of the operation to take place the following day. They were first addressed by Obst. Handrick of *Jafü Mittelrhein*. He told them that this was the "Big Show" that Göring had hinted at during the recent conference with the *Geschwaderkommodore*. He claimed that 2,000 German fighters would participate. There would be little anti-aircraft fire or fighter opposition, he said, because the enemy would have been celebrating New Year's Eve. After the laughter faded, each pilot was given a slip of paper which must have cooled their ardor. It contained extracts from the Geneva convention; he told all the pilots that should they be unfortunate enough to be taken prisoner, they were to give no information other than rank, name, number and home address. Some followed the advice, but many others did not.[106] Maj. Gerhard Michalski then addressed the group. The Knight's Cross holder had shot down some 26 RAF fighters over Malta as part of his accumulated 70 victories. He warned his fledgling pilots that if the mission was not carried out with determination and success they would be sent out again to complete the job.

All the pilots of *II/JG 4* returned to the *Fliegerhorst* for further briefing by Maj. Schröder who provided further details before they were sent back to their barracks. They were to attack Le Culot, a Ninth Air Force base in Belgium. Radio silence was essential throughout the operation; the FuGe 16

---

106 The interrogations of the captured German fliers participating in the "Big Show" are quite enlightening. Some readily provided all requested information: "...security poor...confessed to being ashamed to have been shot down on his first operational flight..." while others were totally uncooperative: "...a typically arrogant and stupid type of Nazi who before joining the forces had been a bricklayer..." and others followed orders: "...very high morale and very security conscious. Information extracted with the greatest difficulty..."

wireless was to be switched on only as they approached the front but they were to say nothing more than listen for any instructions that he might give. Schröder recommended that pilots concentrate on keeping formation and follow him so they could keep out a careful watch for Allied fighters. They would be guided, he told them, by a special night fighter serving as a pathfinder for the *Gruppe*. To puzzled Luftwaffe pilots, the mystery of the lone Ju-88 twin-engined pathfinder at Babenhausen was finally revealed. He covered the route in detail; the aircraft were to all rendezvous over Bingen and then head straight to the west-northwest across Bullay to Prüm and finally Le Culot. Uffz. Horst Tharann, who was at the briefing, remembered that the fighter pilots were ardently enthusiastic about the mission— particularly those with little experience!

The armored Fw-190s of *IV/JG 4* with some 40 Me-109s were located at Rheine-Main airfield. During the night of the 31st, the ground crews had worked feverishly although by morning still only half of the fighters were serviceable. Maj. Steinmann's *I Gruppe* would be only able to contribute some ten aircraft. The pilots arrived from their billets in Sprendlingen and received their last minute flying orders from Maj. Michalski. Michalski used aerial photos which showed P-47s and medium bombers crowding the air field they were to strike. Detailed maps were passed out. The *Kommodore* told them this was to be "a maximum effort by the *Gruppe*."

At ten minutes after 8 AM, JG4 took to the air, forming up over Bingen. Fw. Günther Kotschote, flying the Ju-88G-1 pathfinder of *NJG 101*, lead the formation, being closely followed by Maj. Michalski. JG 4 flew to Bullay on the Moselle River and then to Prüm over the Eifel. As they crossed the wooded Eifel above the embattled Ardennes at 8:40 AM, the sun was just breaking through the haze. All seemed well. But contrary to Obst. Handrick's optimistic assessment several pilots were lost to AA fire as they passed over the front. Uffz. Günter Schwarzenau of *II/JG 4* was hit while he flew at tree-top level over Palenberg, managing to gain enough altitude in his Fw-190A-8 to bail out. Uffz. Horst Tharann was hit by AA as he passed over Hannut, Belgium forcing him into a crash landing. And over Heerlen, Holland the "seeing eye dog" was lost. Kotschote's Ju-88 was hit by light flak and the pilot was forced to drop away from JG 4 for a belly landing.

Perhaps this incident helps explain what became of JG 4. For, an explanation of the events from Prüm to Wavre, Belgium has never been satisfactorily resolved. What seems certain is that: the veteran Michalski and his entire *Geschwader* somehow lost their way. As a result, the attack on Le Culot ended up as a total failure. The 50 Me-109s and Fw-190A-8s could not guide themselves to A-89 some ten miles southeast of Brussels and wandered around looking for their target. Meanwhile, Le Culot held more than a hundred P-47s of the 36th, 363rd and 373rd Fighter Groups parked on the field. Many planes of *II Gruppe* mistakenly attacked the St. Trond airfield.

There Gefr. Walter Wagner was hit by AA fire which gave the German pilot the choice to land his "White 11" or crash. He put down in the middle of the airstrip and was taken prisoner only to find that this wasn't Le Culot after all! The Americans of the 404th Fighter Group were pleased; they now had possession of one slightly damaged Fw-190A-8. Other misguided Luftwaffe planes began haphazardly strafing American troops in the Bastogne area. German fighters of *IV/JG 4* stubbornly continued their search to the west running into a pack of P-47s and AA fire. They put in an attack on an airfield that turned out to be Melsbroek. In the assault Fw. Karl Berg was listed as missing in action and Obfhr. Horst Grüner was killed.

Obfhr. Hans Peschel arrived late over Melsbroek, having had trouble in starting the engine of his Fw-190A-8 in the morning cold. In arriving late, he virtually had the already damaged airfield to himself. In his first pass, he fired at the AA guns with unobserved results, but spied some five B-17s and a score of Thunderbolts parked on the strip. He blasted away at five of the Fortresses on his second pass. On his third and final strafing run he peppered the P-47s parked on the runway, but was suddenly struck by AA fire. He climbed to 1,600 feet and jumped from his A-8, being taken prisoner less than 200 yards from the Melsbroek airstrip. Uffz. Lothar Schmidt did not make it that far. His G-14 "Black 4" came under AA fire on the way out near the front and he was forced off course and lost the rest of *IV/JG 4*. He was struck by anti-aircraft fire once more and forced to a belly landing near Bütgenbach in the Ardennes. Obfhr. Arnulf Russow made two strafing runs over Melsbroek, but was hit by AA fire on the second. His "Yellow 13" was crippled. Russow nursed his aircraft east, but the engine sputtered and lost power. He made a belly landing at Ulbeek. Russow and the others ended their stint with the Luftwaffe as Allied prisoners. *JG 4* had become terribly scattered, with elements strewn about from Bastogne to Brussels. Some planes flew back over Aachen while others turned across Southern Holland. On the way back, American and German AA fire claimed planes in every *Staffel* in the wing. Fw. Franz Schneider, Uffz. Erich Keller and Hans-Gustav Diercks were all shot down by flak. Five more planes were felled over Holland.

For virtually no result, *JG 4* lost seventeen pilots killed or missing and six more captured after being shot down. Of the 60 aircraft taking part, half did not come back![107] In particular, *II Gruppe* lost many machines reporting only ten aircraft serviceable on the evening of January 1st. Maj. Schröder's *Sturmgruppe* was virtually wiped out.

JG 26 along with *III Gruppe*, *JG 54* was to obliterate the Brussels airfields with a whopping 170 Me-109s and Fw-190Ds. The briefing took place the

---

107 ULTRA overhead *JG 4* on New Year's evening mention having lost 31 aircraft of the 68 that had taken part in the operation; this figure is verified by the reports made by the unit the next day which shows the total serviceable aircraft down from 75 before the operation to 35 the following day.

evening before. Fw. Karlheinz Hartmann could barely contain his excitement. The old hands noted the "enormous enthusiasm" of the freshmen pilots like Hartmann. The *Feldwebel* had been with JG 26 only two weeks and this would be his first mission. At the morning briefing Maj. Borris described their role in *Bodenplatte*. Their mission was to hit Brussels/Grimbergen airfield. Take off was to be at 8:30 AM. Each pilot was to make three strafing passes over the target in sections of four. Willi Heilmann of *III Gruppe* recalled the electric atmosphere that morning:

> "We were woken at 3 o'clock in the morning and half an hour later all the pilots of JG 26 and III/JG 54 were assembled in the mess room. Hptm. Worner came in with the ominous envelope already open in his hand. 'To make it brief boys, we're taking off with more than 1,000 fighters at the crack of dawn to prang various airfields on the Dutch-Belgium border.' Then followed the details of take-off, flying order, targets and return flights. Brussels was the target for III/JG 54. The whole mission was to be carried out at less than 600 feet until we reached the targets so that the enemy ground stations could not pick us up. To this end, radio silence was the order until we reached the target. We were given a magnificent breakfast, cutlets, roast beef and a glass of wine. For sweets there were pastries and several cups of fragrant coffee. The last minutes before we were airborne seemed an eternity. Nervous fingers stubbed out half-smoked cigarettes. In the scarlet glow the sun slowly appeared above the horizon to the east. It was 8:25 AM. And then the armada took off..."

The 67 planes of I/JG 26 rose aloft at 8:14 AM just as the first rays of the feeble sun illuminated the snow-swept runways. Appropriately, Obstlt. Priller took off first. Maj. Borris would lead the first *Schwarm* of I *Gruppe* and III/JG 54 towards Grimbergen. II and III *Gruppen* under Maj. Hackl and Hptm. Krupinski also roared off from their bases at Nordhorn and Plantlünne with their objective the Brussels airfield at Evère. Evère was home to the Canadian 421 and 403 Squadrons with Spitfire XVIs. The large mass of some 170 aircraft traveled in three "vics," each composed of section of four in a line abreast. The formation flew dangerously low— only 150 feet off the ground headed for the turning point at Spakenburg and then on to Rotterdam, Holland where they were to turn south to reach their targets near Brussels. At tree-top level, radar would not detect them, but the need for radio silence almost immediately began to claim victims.

Although the *16th Flak Division* had been warned that strong friendly fighter formations would cross over their positions that morning, many batteries obviously did not get the message. Over a dozen planes were lost to friendly anti-aircraft fire over the V2 launching sites west of Rotterdam. The leader of 2 *Staffel*, Oblt. Franz Kunz fell over Polsbroek, severely injuring the experienced officer. Soon Uffz. Gerhard Kroll of III/JG 54, Obgefr. Niessen of 3 *Staffel* and Obfhr. Helmut Heuser of 6 *Staffel* suffered a similar fate and were forced to make belly landings. More were lost as the fleet passed over the Schelde and Walcheren Island. Oblt. Harald Lenz, Uffz. Leo Speer and Gefr. Horst Sengpiel were shot down by their own fire and fell to their deaths on the icy expanses of the Dutch coast. "White 11" with Obgefr. Hubert Lott was hit and his friends watched in horror as Lott flung himself from his stricken machine only to have his harness slip off with the shock of the opening parachute. Other pilots had to turn back due to mechanical problems. In spite of these alarming developments the procession flew on. Along the way, Dutch villages were suddenly awakened to a massive flock of German aircraft roaring only 500 feet over them.

As the German fighters made their final approach, however, some were set upon by RAF fighters of the Polish 308 Squadron. Over Waasmunster Polish pilot Flt. Lt. Zbigniew Zmigrodzki shot down Obgefr. Dieter Krägerloh's D-9 "Yellow 13." Krägerloh was a hard luck case having already been shot down in October winding up in the hospital after sustaining a fractured skull in the process. He had re-joined *JG 26* only on the last day of the year. Evidence of the skill level in the Luftwaffe at the opening of 1945 is illustrated by the fact that, even though the injured pilot had not been at the controls in two months, he became the prime wingman of Oblt. Heckmann, the leader of *3 Staffel*:

> "I was only 21 years old. We started early while it was still dark and were guided by a night fighter. Over the Schelde-estuary we were attacked by a British [sic] formation. My plane was hit several times. While I was flying further, my engine stopped and I attempted a crash landing. I was too low to bail out. The flaps did not respond, so I could not reduce my speed. It hit the ground very hard. My safety belts were torn and I smashed into the dashboard. I broke my back and my legs were pinned in the cockpit. I could only wait until a doctor gave me first aid before I could be moved from the wreckage."

A Belgian civilian, Mr. Jacques Reychler was one of the first people on the scene:

> "There were only seven or eight people around; one of them was an English officer. He tried to free the pilot, but in vain. He was crying in pain. We tried to make a hole in the fuselage, but it was very difficult. Meanwhile, Dr. De Loose returned from the church. He brought a syringe with morphine, but the German was afraid; he thought the doctor wanted to kill him. Finding a first aid kit in the fuselage, Dr. De Loose tried to help the pilots as much as he could. He asked for a cigarette, but would only smoke one after someone else smoked one. He kept asking where he was...He was taken away by an ambulance."

A few miles further west, Plt. Off. Dromlewicz shot down Fw. Paul Drutschmann's Dora-9. Drutschmann, a member of *9./JG 54* escaped to his parachute and plunked down into the frigid River Durme. The shivering pilot was promptly arrested by a Belgian policeman who demanded his gun. Drutschmann threw it in the river. Others were less fortunate. Flt. Sgt. Zygmunt Soszynski blasted the D-9 of Uffz. Heinz Schulz. Schulz died when his aircraft plunged into the streets of the village Sinai. Two other Fw-190s fell in the same village, destroyed by Sgt. S. Breyner, also of 308 Squadron.

In all the Polish wing claimed ten victories, including the other German aircraft it destroyed from *JG 1*.

In spite of these setbacks, at 9:20 AM the "long noses" of *I Gruppe* arrived over the Grimbergen airfield to a shocking sight: there were only six enemy planes on the ground! Equally shocked were the airfield tenders. Gp. Capt. Aleksander Gabszewicz had just flown from his base at St. Denis-Westrem the day before. Grimbergen was not operational at the time, but his wing was scheduled to move there and the group captain was understandably curious to see what it had to offer. Shortly after 9 AM he and his adjutant ambled over to the officers' mess. They heard the sound of approaching aircraft and wondered who was flying to base so early. Looking out, the Polish officer yelled, "They're bloody Focke Wulfs!" Everyone dove for cover. The six planes on the field— four B-17s, a Mustang and a twin-engined fighter— were quickly dispatched, but the operation cost the Luftwaffe a dozen planes shot down from anti-aircraft fire. One of these was "Yellow 8" of Fhr. Hans Joachim Werner who was hit as he made his second strafing pass. Thoughts of the Liberator and Fortress he had just brewed up faded as his aircraft shuddered; Werner pulled up and bailed out into captivity.[108] A Fw-190D-9 was suddenly sighted on the airfield, crash landing on its belly. It was one of the three unmarked Fw-190s of *11/JG 54*, piloted by Fw. Günther Egli. The ten Fw-190s of *4./JG 26* straggled behind the others to reach their target. According to Hans Kukla:

> "When we arrived over the field the other machines had already left. We saw from its white cross that the field was not operational. Since we could find no targets on the field, we made three attacks on the hangars, without great effect...At 1140 seven of us landed at Quakenbrück on our last drops of fuel."

Priller, himself had lost his group during one of the course changes in the morning mists and returned to Fürstenau early without combat damage. He had not flown a mission in several months and was relatively unfamiliar with his new Dora-9. Beyond that embarrassment, Priller was understandably livid about this costly wild-goose chase. A total of 12 aircraft from *I/JG 26* had failed to come back and *III Gruppe* suffered the worst— 12 of its 17 pilots did not return. The German planes made several runs against the facilities at the RAF base, but Bren guns and small arms fire claimed three fighters before the show was over. Each time one of the German planes went down, the Bren gunners cheered wildly.

One of these included the Fw-190D-9 of Lt. Theo Nibel of *10/JG 54* which was disabled, not by the Bren guns shooting at him, but by a partridge which punched a baseball-sized hole in its radiator. (One ecstatic villager claimed

---

108 This was 19-year old Fhr. Werner's second aerial escape in a little over a week. On December 23rd he was in an action over the Ardennes against the Marauders of the Ninth Air Force. He had shot down one B-26 when another hit his aircraft with a burst of fire. Werner parachuted to safety, making his way back to Fürstenau in five days. His seventh and last mission of the war was with 3 *Staffel*.

to have brought down the Focke Wulf with his shotgun!) Nibel made a controlled landing near the RAF air strip at Wemmel. The failure at Grimbergen seemed apparent to Nibel, the *Leutnant* having only seen two aircraft shot up on the field. He emerged from his Dora-9, to be taken captive. It was only his third combat mission. Nibel's "Black 12" immediately became an object of intense scrutiny— it was the first intact example of the high performance German piston fighter to fall into Allied hands.

> "I had the mission of silencing the flak of Grimbergen airfield. We flew a total of three attacks on the flak, which returned fire strongly. When I pulled up after the third attack, my engine quit, I suspected a flak hit on the engine. I had reached an altitude of 100 meters and had to decide quickly between a parachute jump and a crash landing. I lost height quickly, and was forced to make a belly landing. I found a freshly turned field beside a farmhouse, and made a perfect landing."

III/JG 54 had been slaughtered. Of the 17 aircraft which had taken off with *JG 26* to attack Grimbergen, only seven returned. Part of the losses occurred during the return flight where *III/JG 54* had the not uncommon misfortune of running into a group of Spitfires over Hasselt, Belgium. Five pilots were killed or missing including Hptm. Bottländer, the head of *11 Staffel*. Four others were known captured. At least three German aircraft came down over the built-up part of Brussels and five civilians were killed. Another German pilot, 24-year old Fw. Paul Steinkamp, found himself over the Schelde northwest of Antwerp "flying into the barrel of a 3.7 cm AA gun." One wing was nearly shot off and Steinkamp bailed out after he saw that his crippled machine would not make it back to German lines. Upon his capture near Hulst, his interrogators found the *JG 54* veteran of both the Russian front and the summer battles in France "very tough... his morale remained high to the last and his confidence in German victory was unshakable. 'The faith of the whole German nation was now in the Führer, who would find a way out to save Europe from Bolshevism; how and when the Führer knew'— P/W certainly didn't."

Maj. Borris's *I/JG 26* fared little better with six pilots failing to return to Fürstenau. Fw. Karlheinz Hartmann, a ten-day wonder with 4 *Staffel*, was hit by ground fire over the target after strafing Allied bombers at Grimbergen. Hartmann was so excited to be in the operation that he tried without success to report that he was hit and hurriedly took to his parachute. Only later did he realize that he had forgotten to switch on his radio. Made an immediate POW on the ground, the war was over for Hartmann after a single combat sortie.

The rest of *JG 26* had a better day at the Evère airfield which was a fully operational field for the British 2nd Tactical Air Force. The *II Gruppe* showed up at 9:30 AM to find the Spitfires of the famous 127 Wing (403, 416 and 421 Squadrons) of the Royal Canadian Air Force (RCAF). The planes were neatly lined up on the eastern edge of the airfield, some preparing to take off. All told there were at least 40 Spitfires on the eastern side of the airfield. On the western side were a number of B-17s, Austers, Ansons, a Beechcraft belonging to Prince Bernhard of the Netherlands and a luxurious VIP Dakota. The German "long noses" and "Gustavs" jettisoned their drop tanks to prepare for battle. As Spitfires of No. 416 Squadron taxied along the sanded runway, the sound of aircraft engines was heard in the distance. As the leaders prepared to take off, sixty German fighters suddenly roared across the airfield. Leading 416 was Flt. Lt. D.W.A. "Dave" Harling, a 23-year-old Canadian from Quebec. As the German aircraft approached, Harling pushed the throttles forward and zipped into the air, retracting his carriage immediately. Meanwhile behind him was chaos and destruction. The Luftwaffe fighters blasted one plane after another, the Canadian pilots jumping from their Spitfires and running for their lives. Flt. Lt. Harling, gained altitude and speed. He quickly ran across an Me-109 which he sent spiraling over Brussels. Then, however, he was overtaken and Harling was himself shot down. The gallant pilot died over the Belgian capital.

Down below, Gp. Capt. "Iron Bill" MacBrien and Wing Commander J.E. "Johnnie" Johnson could do little more than scream as the German fighters bashed their beautiful Spitfires. At the end of the runway was a small office where the duty controller and Flt. Lt. Frank Minton was trying to direct the chaotic goings-on overhead. As the Germans roared overhead, the phone rang. It was a staff officer warning Minton that there were Luftwaffe fighters in the area. "You're too late," Minton screamed over the din, "If I stick this phone outside you'll hear their bloody cannons!"

As this went on, several planes of 403 Squadron were already airborne having just left the field minutes before the Germans appeared. Responding to their radio, the Canadian pilots turned back in a hurry. Over Evère pickings were plentiful. Plt. Off. Steve Butte shot down two Messerschmitts and a Focke Wulf; Plt. Off. Mackenzie "Mac" Reeves claimed two 190s; Flt. Sgt. G.K. Lindsay knocked out another 109. One of these must have been the craft of Uffz. Wilhelm Schmitz who was fired upon during his second pass over the Evère and was probably killed or severely wounded, for his D-9 ambled on some 20 miles to the west crashing into a meadow near Aalst. The end of Schmitz was gruesome. His Fw-190D-9 smashed into a tree near Aalst, where the decapitated pilot was found amid the scattered wreckage rolled in his parachute. Plt. Off. Butte tells his story:

"I was Black 1 and I took off from B-56 with my No. 2 when enemy aircraft showed up over the base. I did not know of their presence until I was airborne. My first warning was the sight of a formation of aircraft on my port, flying approximately in the opposite direction and about 300 yards away. I recognized them immediately as Me-109s and passed the information to my No. 2 and ordered belly tanks to be dropped. Mine failed to come off, so I broke in the enemy formation and picked the nearest aircraft by closing from about 100-200 yards, firing several bursts and observing many strikes. The aircraft crashed in flames...Next I was on the tail of a Fw-190 and closed to approximately 100 yards. I saw strikes, the first one on the starboard wing, then on the port wing, then on the fuselage. The aircraft continued on a straight course and crashed behind the first row of houses after taking off part of a roof. Then I got behind the tail of an Me-109 and fired several bursts from a range of 175 yards and saw strikes on his wings and engine, causing black smoke and pieces to fall off...One of these pieces hit my drop tank; there was lots of smoke in the area and I could not locate myself. I broke away from the attack at approximately 500 feet and saw the aircraft practically on his back in a very steep dive. I had to break away and did not have time to see it crash. I got on the tail of another Me-109 and gave him a short burst from approximately 200 yards, when I ran out of ammunition...I had no more ammunition, so I headed west when I was bounced by two Fw-190s. I managed to get on one's tail, but could only take a picture...I broke away and flew under some factory smoke and when control gave me the "all clear" I pancaked at base."

However, all this did little to stop the Luftwaffe attack. While a portion of the attack *Schwarm* took on the AA defenses and another pumped cannon rounds into the parked planes, the rest of the German fighters pounced on the taxiing planes, destroying most before they could reach the end of the runway. The British pilots ran for their lives. The mission leader, Flt/Lt Davey, was able to take to the air, only to be immediately blasted apart before reaching altitude. Uffz. Lutz-Wilhelm Burkhardt, Oblt. Adolf Glunz, Maj. Anton Hackl and Lt. Siegfried Sy each sent one of the climbing Spitfires tumbling back to the ground.

After many of the British planes had been shot up, the German fighters strafed tanker trucks, barracks and hangars leaving the entire airfield ablaze. Ugly boils of flame consumed the densely packed runways sending big clouds of thick smoke mushrooming into the sky. 416 Squadron ended the day with only four serviceable aircraft; 421 Squadron did not even get into the air and lost five of its Spitfires. 127 Wing at Evère had lost a total of 11 aircraft destroyed on the ground and another dozen other severely damaged. The pall of black smoke from the devastation had reached 13,000 feet and was clearly visible to German pilots returning to their base at Nordhorn. The attack lasted for three quarters of an hour with *I* and *II/JG 26* making some dozen strafing runs over the wasted airfield. The RAF gunners at Evère claimed to have shot down three Luftwaffe planes over the field and other German aircraft were lost due to AA fire on their way back to Germany. Two of these included the D-9s from 5 and 7 *Staffel* of Uffz. Ernst Lamperhoff and Fw. Erich Ahrens, who were brought down over Beveland, Holland. But nothing could change the significance of the German victory at Evère airfield.

The destruction at Evère and Grimbergen was tremendous. Upon returning to Plantlünne in his own flak-damaged fighter, Hptm. Krupinski called all of the surviving pilots of *III Gruppe* together at lunch to offer congratulations on the operation. Of 29 taking off, only four had been lost with one other wounded. When tallies were totalled, they revealed that nearly 120 Allied aircraft were destroyed including 60 fighters and 32 heavy bombers against a total loss of 20 German pilots killed, missing or captured from *JG 26*.[109] Eleven pilots from *II Gruppe* were missing when the planes returned to Nordhorn, although three would eventually return. Uffz. Wilhelm Schmitz and Willi Sydow were killed during the strafing; a number of others were holed by the intense AA fire.[110] Lt. Gottfried Meier was found burned to death in the wreckage of his Me-109 near the village of Vrasene. He had only been with *JG 26* since December 22nd. In spite of Priller's stinging report to *OKL* that evening, the operation was perhaps the most successful operation of *'Bodenplatte.'*[111] That evening an *OKW* communique sounded praise for the strafing kills of *JG 26* that day: 20 B-17 and B-24 bombers, 24 twin-engined aircraft and another sixty odd fighters. Included in this total were Prince Bernhard's Beechcraft and the VIP Dakota. Nine aircrew on the ground were wounded and one was killed. Losses from 127 Wing at Evère totalled 12 Spitfires destroyed, including that of Dave Harling, and another 12 seriously damaged. One of the "missing German pilots" to return that night was Gefr. Werner Molge who had become lost on the way home:

> "I flew past my field at Nordhorn without seeing it. I landed after two hours and fifty minutes in the air, literally on my last drops of fuel on *III/JG 6's* airfield. I had to be towed in from the landing field by a half-track, as my engine had run dry. I was forbidden to take-off, because this was prohibited while enemy aircraft were over the Reich; also I had trouble getting fuel. Since this was a Bf 109 field, it only had B4 fuel. The FW 190D required C3 gasoline, which had to be brought in barrels. That afternoon I received 55 gallons of gasoline and flew back over Fürstenau to Nordhorn. I was pounced on in the Berning Hotel pilots' mess where New Year's was being celebrated belatedly. My comrades had already written me off as missing...So we had a proper celebration, but our spirits were not fully in it, as so many of our comrades had lost their lives in Unternehmen Bodenplatte. All of us were between 18 and 25 years old."

The *"Herzas"*— the "Red Hearts"— of *JG 77* was one of the most famous of the *Jagdgeschwadern*, having fought in every campaign from 1940 onwards. Its history was peopled with brilliant commanders, such as Maj. Johannes Steinhoff who had been with the *Geschwader* since March, 1943. However, in the fall his expertise was needed to take over the controls of the

---

109 The tally at Evère alone stood at a dozen B-17s and B-24s, 10 Wellingtons (69 Squadron), 9 Mosquitos, 4 Spitfires, and one each, Halifax, Dakota and Stirling.

110 Uffz. Norbert Risky of 6/JG 26 was hit in the engine of his D-9 during the second strafing run. Risky was able to baby his plane back over German lines, but was forced to take to his parachute over Zwolle when his Jumo engine burst into flame.

111 It was not, however, as successful as some German pilots believed. A number of Spitfires escaped unscathed and the Wing Commander and top-scoring RAF ace, Johnnie Johnson, would later observe that: "The shooting was atrocious, and the circuit at Evère reminded us more of a bunch of beginners on their first solos than pilots of front-line squadrons."

fledgling jet fighter unit, *JG 7*, at a time when the attrition on the proud fighter unit had beccome nearly intolerable. Just before the opening of Hitler's offensive, the Red Hearts had transferred their command to the Ruhr air bases coming under the wing of *II Jagdkorps*. At that time, Maj. Johannes Wiese had taken over the unit only to be shot down in the terrific battles over the Ardennes on Christmas Eve. Wiese had survived with serious injury and his place was taken over by Maj. Erich Leie on December 29th.

Erich Leie was another veteran, a Knight's Cross holder, with over 100 victories in the war. He had flown with the Luftwaffe since 1940 coming to *JG 77* from *I/JG51*. Hptm. Armin Köhler was in charge of *III Gruppe*. Unit pride showed at the airfields at Dortmund, Bönninghardt and Düsseldorf. At the end of the year, the *Geschwader* strength stood at 100 fighters— all Messerschmitts. The G-14s of the *I Gruppe* were designated as the *Sturmgruppe*, and would normally be assigned to assault enemy bombers; *II Gruppe*, also with G-14s was a straight fighter unit and *III Gruppe* with the new hot-rod K-4s was designed to provide high-altitude cover for the others. But tomorrow, all of the fighters, regardless of normal duties would be assigned to airfield strafing. The impressive strength of the "Red Hearts" was achieved through tremendous effort by the dedicated ground crews; a 300 liter drop tank was fitted to each that night.

The *Herzas Geschwader* stood as a potent and well-led command when *Operation Bodenplatte* was disclosed to its commanders on December 31st. The pilots learned that their objective would be the Antwerp-Deurne airfield some 200 miles away. Maj. Freitag provided the briefing to *II Gruppe* at 6 AM that morning. A photograph of the Antwerp/Deurne airfield was used to illustrate the attack plan, but some of the more attentive pilots noted that it could not have been a recent photo, as the trees around the airfield had all of their foliage. Soon maps were passed out along with the requisite orders. They would not fly a direct route, instead making a wide sweep to approach Deurne from Rotterdam. The pilots were to attack their target either singly or in pairs with each aircraft to make four separate strafing passes.

Deurne was home to the 145 and 146 RAF Wings. This included the Typhoon 1Bs of 193, 197, 257 and 263 Squadrons along with two French Spitfire units, 341 *"Alsace"* and 345 Squadrons. At Deurne, planning for the day's operations began before light with the pilots annoyed by a power failure that left everyone groping in the dark at the early morning briefing. Then more frustration. Take-off that morning was delayed due to the ice covering the runways, so the pilots hung around the briefing room waiting for the word to go. The Typhoons were clumped together at one end of the airfield due to the muddy state of the grassy areas on the field. They presented an inviting target.

In Germany, it was a cold crisp morning at Dortmund, Bönninghardt and

Düsseldorf when the hundred-plane flock of *I, II* and *III Gruppen* took to the skies. The three groups gathered over Borken flying across to Appeldoorn, Holland and then to Spakenburg before turning south at Rotterdam. However, as they approached the front line the German Navy flak sent a hail of anti-aircraft fire into the swarm of Messerschmitts. Almost immediately "White 13," the mount of Lt. Herbert Abendroth, fell away, the pilot managing to bail out to become a prisoner near Maeseyck. Two others were lost, Uffz. Johann Twietmeyer was captured near Rosendaal and another pilot was killed. As the formation crossed Antwerp the flak picked up once again, this time from the enemy. Lt. Heinrich Hackler, the CO of 11./JG 77, disappeared in the blink of an eye. His wingman, Lt. Wilhelm Mockel described how Hackler flew into the cables of a barrage balloon near Antwerp, ripping off his left wing. "Yellow 1" plunged to the ground near Moeren. The Luftwaffe veteran of 56 victories was dead.

JG 77 was now badly scattered: part of the raiding party was distracted into attacking the wrong airfield at Woendsrecht where, on closer inspection, not a single Allied fighter was seen. The two Spitfire squadrons there, 66 and 127, had lifted from the field at 9:10 AM to provide escort to RAF Mitchells on their way to bomb the Germans in the Ardennes. Even so, six German fighters buzzed the strip before continuing on their way.[112] Finally, however, the Germans collected themselves and the great dock areas of Antwerp hove into view with the cathedral spires of the city on the horizon. *II Gruppe* had trouble navigating itself to the final target, wandering aimlessly northeast of the city. They would be of little help in the final attack. The German strength was rapidly being frittered away, although *III Gruppe* continued on course. Presently, Deurne airfield hove into view. The remaining German fighters screamed in to attack. However, upon approaching for their strafing run the pilots were presented with a puzzling sight: Where were the Spitfires? The British fighters that had been the primary target at Woensdrecht were already airborne and those at Deurne were well dispersed and unseen at the other end of the field. The only target was a collection of British Typhoons from 266 Squadron on the ground. These the assailants clobbered; one was totally destroyed and more than a dozen others were severely damaged. 197 Squadron was also hurt with only six Typhoons left at the end of the encounter. Flt. Sgt. F. Eaton was with 257 Squadron:

> "It was full daylight with a clear, slightly hazy sky, when the roar of engines was heard and to our great surprise we saw a huge fleet of German fighters arrive, crossing the airfield from the embankment side. This enormous fleet seemed to be in complete disorder being a mixed bag of Me-109s and Fw-190s

---

112 The RAF gunners at Woensdrecht claimed two German fighters definitely shot down and another damaged that morning. Only the damaged Me-109 could have been from JG 77, however, which only flew Messerschmitts. The two destroyed aircraft were Fw-190s, which obviously came from other German units channelled through the vicinity.

[sic] flying like a great gaggle at heights from 150 to 300 feet. There was some firing at the attackers, but the embankment and perhaps the mixed gaggle, saved the Typhoon wing from large scale destruction. 257 Squadron lost two aircraft..."

The German attack looked distinctly amateurish to Flt. Lt. Ronnie E.G. Sheward of 263 Squadron:

"I was acting CO at the time...I remember getting the lads to bed early as we were on the first thing the next morning...I was down at dispersal for the early morning show— Army support east of Dordrecht— when the attack began. I remember standing on the bank with my pilots, and yelling at the Germans 'Weave you stupid bastards!' They were flying straight and level and being shot at by the ground forces. We couldn't take off at the time because of the ice on the runway. I later wrote in my logbook: 'Runway frozen— watched eight 190s and twelve 109s fly over 'drome. They strafed a few aircraft but put up a very poor show...'"

The entry in the 193 Squadron diary was even less complimentary: "They stooged across slow, like a Sunday picnic..." The 146 Wing Commander commentary was sardonic: "If any of my boys put on a show like that I'd tear them off a strip." The frustrated British and French pilots could only swear at the hung-over AA gunners. But if a bit late to start, the AA fire was heavy; Lt. Hans Schumacher belly-landed after being hit. So much for the idea of four strafing passes. Uffz. Heinrich Munninger was shot down and killed over Tilburg. Only thirty German planes in all had been able to even navigate themselves to Deurne and the RAF gunners there reported engaging only 16. Somehow, *II Gruppe* became lost and could not find the airfield at all; the others were turned away by enemy fighters closing in on their intrusion. Uffz. Alfred Hoffschmidt was running so low on fuel during the search for Deurne airfield that he was forced to turn back east. On the way to Aachen, Hoffschmidt vented his aggression on a freight train near St. Trond. But the engine of his Me-109G-14 began to miss badly and Hoffschmidt was forced to crash land near Eschweiler.

Others, like Uffz. Rolf Brabant, were brought down by AA fire while on the way back to Düsseldorf. Pilot inexperience also played a part. Gefr. Erwin Mannweiler, having only been with *JG 77* fighter pilot since early December, flew his "Blue 17" so low on the return flight that he struck a tree and crash landed. Although surviving the incident in good shape, he was shot while trying to escape the scene near Oosterhout and was hospitalized.

The "Red Hearts" were lucky to get back with the loss of only ten pilots. Four were killed, two more were missing and the other four were taken prisoner. Losses of *III Gruppe* were worst with six aircraft and their pilots not returning. While it was true that *JG 77* had suffered the lightest damage of any of the fighter units involved in *Operation Bodenplatte*, the damage to the enemy was pitifully small; in all, only 14 RAF planes were hit. 266 Squadron had one Typhoon totally destroyed and a few others were damaged, 197 wrote off three and 257 reported two others damaged.

The situation at Rheine airfield on December 31st had already cast doubts on *Operation Bodenplatte*. The commander in charge of *JG 27*, Maj. Ludwig Franzisket, was a holder of the Knight's Cross. He had amassed some forty victories against the Allies since joining the Luftwaffe in 1939. After the draining air battles over the last two weeks, *II Gruppe/JG 27*, under Hptm. Gerhard Hoyer, could only muster a dozen Me-109G-14s. At Hopsten, Hptm. Eberhard Schade's *I/JG 27* was in a similar way with only another 16. So paltry was the remaining strength that the two *Gruppen* were amalgamated at Rheine airfield. Unlike many of the other bases, the commanders did not brief their pilots until only an hour and a half before take-off.[113]

At 7 AM the aircrew poured over photos of Melsbroek airfield near Brussels— one pilot took the time to count 178 Allied planes in the photo. Maps were distributed and a short pep talk followed. They were instructed to open fire on 4-engined bombers on the ground from 300 meters, twin-engined aircraft from 200 meters and single engined fighters from 100 meters. The airfield, they learned, was home to a large group of medium bombers (three reconnaissance units: 16 Squadron with Spitfires, 69 with Wellingtons, 140 with Mosquitos and 98, 180 and 320 Squadrons with the B-25 Mitchell). As elsewhere, a Ju-88 night fighter would lead them as far as Utrecht with the planes forming over Rheine and then flying at a very low level until the target was reached. Each pilot was to fly three strafing runs over the airfield, destroying as many planes on the ground as possible. To increase the operation's muscle, Hptm. Emile Clade's *III/JG 27* from Hesepe and Hptm. Hans-Heinz Dudeck's *IV/JG 27* from Vörden would follow the other two *Gruppen*. The group of German fighters would fly almost due west until reaching Utrecht, just west of Spakenburg, Holland, where they would proceed south-west for Melsbroek.

Meanwhile, in the early hours of Monday morning the German quarry at Melsbroek, 34 Photo-Reconnaissance Wing and No. 139 Bomber Wing, were just getting started. From the latter, 98, 180 and 320 Squadrons were flagging their B-25 Mitchells into the air to put a bomb load on the German bridge over the Our River in the Ardennes at Dasburg. At 8:30 AM the 35 bombers lumbered off with a Spitfire escort from Woensdrecht. Only a few Mitchells remained behind. However, the majority of 34 Wing were on hand. These included the Spitfire XIs of 16 Squadron, 140 Squadron with Mosquito XVIs for day and night reconnaissance and 69 Squadron flying Wellington XIIIs on night reconnaissance missions. The squadron commander of the

---

113 The replacement pilots with *JG 27* were a bit better off than with many of the other fighter units since most consisted in December of ex-bomber and ferry pilots that at least had a reasonable level of experience in flying aircraft to begin with.

Wellingtons was M.J.A. "Mike" Shaw. Shaw had just returned to the base and was a bit under the sunny winter morning weather:

"I had flown back to Melsbroek on the 31st having spent Christmas at home in England. I wasn't on operations that night probably because of the bad weather— we had a lot of bad weather. The announcement of the award of my DSO came through that evening and so we had a bit of a party— to put it mildly!"

While the B-25 bombers motored towards Dasburg and Shaw nursed his hangover, the initial plans of *JG 27* proceeded without a hitch. The 85-odd aircraft thundered over Münster at 210 mph before crossing the border into Holland near Enschede. But as *JG 27* cruised over the icy southern expanse of the Zuider Zee, two squadrons of B-25 medium bombers were taking off from Melsbroek. Maj. Franzisket did not know it, but his quarry had escaped. At about the same time, the German force was suffering the fate that would kill dozens of German pilots from other *Geschwader*. Uffz. Heinrich Braun, Fw. Alfred Mannchen and Uffz. Heinrich Frickmann were all felled by "friendly" flak. So low were the planes, that none could bail out; all perished at the controls of their Me-109Gs. Approaching Breda, Holland the German fliers spied a distinctly unusual sight in the closing months of the war: many other friendly aircraft in the vicinity, probably planes from *JG 1* or *JG 26*. There was little time to look, however, and more AA fire, this time likely from the enemy, burst in a deadly pattern before them. This episode cost 2 *Staffel* its leader, Lt. Heinrich Weiss, whose K-4 smashed into the bank of the Waal River. In the same vicinity "Blue 30," the Me-109G-6 of Uffz. Karlheinz Berndt of *III/JG 26*, was hit forcing the pilot to a crash landing. Presently, the formation passed over an airfield, which numerous Messerschmitts peeled off to attack. This was not Melsbroek, however, but Gilze-Rijen, which had already been alerted by a group of attackers from *JG 3*. Correcting the mistake, *JG 27* continued on, buzzing low over the woods around Antwerp before reaching Brussels. Finally, their target loomed on the horizon.

At Melsbroek, the British observers spotted the gnat-like aircraft on the horizon. What were the B-25 Mitchells doing back now, they wondered? Soon they had an answer. Wing Commander Shaw continues:

"The morning following our party, we came out of the mess after breakfast when we saw these low flying aeroplanes beating up the place. We thought 'who on earth was doing that, thinking they were RAF until we saw the black crosses on them, and so we thought we'd better take cover, and dived into the nearest air raid shelter...One consolation was that the 139 Wing— Mitchells— which shared the airfield with us, were on ops. They always lined their Mitchells up on the disused runway in a lovely straight line. Luckily they had taken off before the Germans arrived, or there really would have been more of a shambles..."

R.D. Walton was leader for the night recce Mosquitos of 140 Squadron:

"I had been flying the night before and was in bed when the attack started. Hugh Tudor and Ian Ewing were scheduled to take one of our Mosquitos back to UK and they awoke me and my navigator, Bill Harper, to warn us of the attack. Our first reaction was that they were fooling, but the sound of cannon fire was enough to get us to the door of our billet and our first sight was that of a fighter at low level with its tailwheel down— an Me-109. We put on flying boots and greatcoats over our pajamas, and with our tin-hats and Smith & Wesson .38 pistols, went out to the sport field next to our billet...We had a grandstand view of the operation. We all popped off ineffectual shots at the aircraft with our .38s, at the ones that flew over us. One chap, I think it was Sqd. Ldr. 'Chunky' Brown, was blasting away with a double barreled shot gun..."

Some eighty planes— the 109s of *I* and *II/JG 27* and the 190A-8s of *IV/JG 54*, thundered over the airfield. The fighters poured cannon and machine gun rounds into the parked Wellingtons. AA fire was lighter than other airfield attacks, but still deadly nonetheless. Last to show up at the scene was Hptm. Dudeck with his *IV/JG 27*. Smoke already marked the target as the Me-109G-10s dove on the airfield out of the sun. Unlike the embarrassment of *JG 26* at Grimbergen, the German fighters found the airfield laden with targets— Spitfires, Mosquitos, Wellingtons, ancient Handley Page Harrows and one Stirling. The medium Mitchell bombers of 98 and 180 Squadrons had already flown the coop, being lucky enough to be out on a mission when the Germans struck. Regardless, the Luftwaffe fighters made strafing runs at roof-top height along the north-south runway systematically destroying the Allied planes. The British were not impressed with the German strafing skills which saw the enemy "firing indiscriminately and inaccurately." 34 Wing was hit hard, however, some 30-40 German fighters worked over the field for nearly 35 minutes in at least five strafing runs. Six of 16 Squadron's Spitfire XIs were blasted, 14 Wellingtons of 69 Squadron and six Mosquitos received the same treatment. The Mitchell wing lost a few B-25s: three from 180 Squadron, two from 320 and a single from 98. A few other odd B-17s and Liberators were also plowed up. The lone Stirling was also destroyed.[114] *JG 27's* Messerchmitts had actively sought out and attacked the AA gun emplacements leading to losses on both ends of the muzzle. The ground crews suffered from their lack of cover; five were killed and another 25 were wounded. On the other hand, several German aircraft were brought down (the RAF Regiment gunners claimed four), and a number of others were hit by AA fire as the Germans headed back to Rheine on the return leg.

Whether the cost was justified was a matter of judgement. Maj. Frankzisket, a German ace with some 40 kills, saw *JG 27* and the attached *IV/JG 54* lose 13 pilots killed or missing with another four captured. Against this calamity, they only had six Spitfires, six Mosquito night fighters and 24

---

114 To Mike Shaw, the CO of 69 Squadron, this was the best fortune of all; he was less than enthusiastic about test flying the recently repaired beast, scheduled for later in the day.

medium bombers to show for their sacrifice.[115] In the aerial battle over the airfield, three British planes were shot down at a cost of two German machines.

Hptm. Hans Dudeck, the commander of *IV/JG 27*, was too senior of a veteran at the beginning of 1945 to believe the war could still be won. The 28-year old commander had been with the Luftwaffe for ten years, having fought in the Battle of Britain and being shot down over the Channel near Le Havre. He had also covered the retreats of the army as a *Staffel* leader of *JG 77* and *JG 27* in Africa and Italy. But even if jaded and cynical, Hptm. Dudeck was pleased with the performance of his command over Brussels. He himself destroyed two bombers and a fighter on Melsbroek field. He was convinced that a considerable blow had been dealt the enemy as he headed back east at tree top level. However, near Venraij, Holland his Me-109G-10 was hit by light flak and burst into flame. Dudeck escaped his burning craft only to see his parachute ripped. As he fell to earth, he was certain he would die. Fortunately, for the *Gruppen* leader, he slammed through the branches of a tree which saved his life. Dudeck was lucky to find himself a prisoner in a British hospital the following day.

Uffz. Johannes Härtlein made four strafing passes over Melsbroek, but his compass failed on the way and he flew alone. Just after 10 AM over Thielen, Belgium he was hit by flak and forced to bail out. As he floated into captivity he could see his "White 7" burning on the ground. Fhr. Otto Theisen of *2./JG 27* was also claimed by the AA fire after his participation in the carnage. He was unable to parachute, however, and was badly burned in crash landing his maimed K-4. Even less fortunate were Lt. Joachim von Stechow, Fw. Gert Gabel, and Uffz. Karl Rehak who were all killed. The grim reaper's list for *JG 54* was despairingly long: 12 pilots did not return including Uffz. Werner Köpp; Uffz. Ohlenschläger was captured.

To the south of the Ardennes, the Ninth Air Force was bolstering its defenses. ULTRA had tipped the Allied high command that Hitler would soon open a new offensive— *Operation Nordwind*— in Alsace. Not to be caught with their pants down, Hoyt Vandenberg transferred his strength closer to the front there. Included were Ray Stecker's "Hell Hawks"— the 365th Fighter Group who moved to Metz-Frescaty airfield on December 27th. German intelligence was keeping track of all this through the poor Allied radio security. Neutralizing the P-47s at Metz was high on the priority list for *Operation Bodenplatte*. Hptm. Friedrich Müer transferred his *IV/JG 53* from Donaueschingen to Echterdingen airfield at the last moment. His Me-109G-14 had only recently been formed from the nucleus of *III/JG 76* during the chaotic autumn of 1944. Part of Obstlt. Helmut Bennemann's *"Pik*

---

115 Another count from a different source shows a bigger tally for the miscellaneous losses: one B-17 (34 BG), one B-24 (467 BG), 21 Spitfires, 9 Bostons and Mitchells, 4 Harrows, 3 Dakotas, 1 Anson and 1 Beechcraft.

As" or "Ace of Spades" *Geschwader*, their original mission had been to defend the airspace over Southern Germany. But Hitler's final offensives had changed all that. The 29-year old Bennemann was another successful Luftwaffe veteran, having amassed some ninety victories in his career. At 6 PM on Sunday evening, a briefing was held at the operations room at Malmsheim. All the available pilots of *II/JG 53* were present— a total of 22. The *Gruppenkommandeur*, Maj. Meimberg, was absent, having been hospitalized in the operations the day after Christmas. Instead Lt. Broo, the deputy commander, and a navigational officer gave them a briefing on the "Big Show" to take place the following day.

Also present was the crew of the lone Ju-88 at Malmsheim who would lead the pilots to their objective: Metz-Frescaty airfield. Marked maps were given out, although no current photographs of the airfield were available. Those passed around dated from the German occupation the previous summer. The Messerschmitt *Gruppen* were to rendezvous over Karlsruhe and then make a bee-line for Metz.

Early on the morning of January 1st, *II*, *III* and *IV/JG 53* stood ready. Just after 8 AM, the G-14s and K-4s roared off from the German bases at Kirrlach, Malmsheim and St. Echterdingen. At Malmsheim, the weather was clear with a bright sun; everyone considered this a good omen since their Ju-88 pathfinder had developed engine trouble and couldn't make the trip. Soon the fifty Messerschmitts formed up over Karlsruhe and headed straight over Piramasens where the opening ground assault of Hitler's *Nordwind* was underway. The German fighters cruised aloft in a long line of sections of four aircraft, the formation from which the ground attacks were to be made. Trouble erupted over the Pfalz Forest, however. A group of American P-47s jumped the 109s of *III Gruppe*. Due to radio silence there had been no warning and the Germans were forced to scrub their drop tanks and do battle. Nine of the *Gruppe's* aircraft were sent spinning to the ground between Kaiserlautern and Piramasens. Amazingly, all of the pilots escaped by parachute— even Uffz. Karl Göller who had rammed a Thunderbolt with his machine. And that was not the only problem. Hptm. Luckenbach, the CO of *12./JG 53* was flying a brand-new Gustav. During the heated air battle, the experienced officer put his machine through such torment that its engine "blew up around my ears." Cursing his luck, he bailed out from his smoking crate. But without their drop tanks *III Gruppe* was through for the day and turned back towards Kirrlach.

Although short of *III Gruppe* and with a number of other pilots floating down under parachutes, *JG 53* finally reached Frescaty airfield just two miles west of National Highway 37. Flying over the base, the *"Pik As"* pilots saw a long line of some forty yellow-nosed Thunderbolts parked tightly along the strip. Ofw. Kurt Opitz led his *Schwarm* of four fighters right up to the airfield as planned. Opitz saw his guns set three P-47s to blazing as he ran through a firing pass. But as the *Oberfeldwebel* pulled up from his run his Me-109G-14 shuddered from the impact of AA fire. Soon his engine began to smoke and Opitz smartly pulled up to 1,200 feet, popped the canopy and turned his aircraft over, dropping out under his parachute. As Opitz floated down he watched German fighters attempting to fire on the airfield as planes below him burned. The 24-year old pilot, had joined the Luftwaffe in 1939, flew for Rommel in 1942 and was a veteran of over 200 combat sorties. A prisoner on landing, for him the war was over.

Many pilots following the initial *Schwarm* never made it to firing range. Near Waldweisdorf, Gefr. Alfred Michel crash landed in "Blue 2" without even firing a shot. His Me-109G-6 had developed engine trouble! The 22-year old pilot had just come out of training school the day before Christmas and became a prisoner on his first and last combat mission. The Germans arrived over the target at about 9:30 AM shooting up several P-47s and bringing forth a deadly stream of AA fire. The aircraft of Uffz. Pechardscheck was hit, although the pilot managed to nurse his crippled ship back to base. Ofw. Stefan Kohl was hit by AA as he and Ofw. Ammon, his wingman with *13 Staffel*, approached the airfield from the southeast. Kohl had just returned from a hospital stay due to injuries he had received in August, but this time he was taken into captivity. Uffz. Rudolf Könitzer was brought down in his first firing pass over Frescaty in the tracer-filled sky. He made a forced landing south of the airfield.

The weather on New Year's at Metz airfield was distinctly unusual for the winter of 1944-45: it was clear with unlimited visibility. The "Hell Hawks," planned to fly as many missions as could be fit in between dawn and dusk. The first 11 aircraft got off at 8:28 AM, flying an armed reconnaissance against enemy rail targets near Norfelden. Many rail cars exploded from the impact of the 500 lbs bombs. As the pilots of the 387th Squadron turned to head back, the 388th Fighter Squadron under Capt. Jerry G. Mast roared aloft. They were to fly another armed recce in the Homburg area. However, when the 13 planes were about twenty miles east they received an urgent message from their controller, "Mudguard," that Frescaty airfield was under enemy attack! All bombs were jettisoned and Mast and his planes headed back; the 387th Squadron received the same message and throttled up to return in a hurry. Meanwhile, at the airfield the 386th Fighter Squadron was preparing for take off at 9:30 AM.

Suddenly, the ground crews heard the staccato banging of the AA guns. The airmen, who were performing the last minute checks on the Thunderbolts, looked up to see what the commotion was all about. What they saw looked like a dizzy swarm of hornets coming over the hills to the north. At first they thought the planes were British Spitfires; that's how they flew, someone said, all over the sky with little semblance of order. But then, things happened fast; jagged flames erupted from the rapidly closing hornets. They were Germans!

"Messerschmitts!" someone cried. Everyone ran like mad, scattering in all directions and looking for a place to hide. There were no foxholes so a number jumped into bomb craters; others pawed at the snow and frozen ground. Some hid behind guns; others splayed out on the snowy field trying to be small. Sixteen Me-109s roared overhead shooting like mad. To each man, alone on that icy field, it seemed as if the Germans were firing at him alone. For ten long minutes the planes made one pass after another with guns blazing. The airmen were pinned on the ground praying that they would not be hit.

Cpl. Lee F. Weldon was in his P-47 preparing for take-off when the Germans struck. The first machine gun burst hit his plane, wounding him in the thigh. Almost immediately his aircraft caught fire, but because of his wound he could not pull himself out. He was certain he would burn to death; the flames edged closer to the cockpit and the bomb racks. But then, in a true act of heroism, Cpl. Emanuel Catanuto saved his life. At first, Catanuto was cringing in the snow under the German fire, trying to look inconspicuous like everyone else. But when the German strafing hit the P-47 in front of him, he could see the pilot struggling to get out of its bubble canopy. He could also see the flames licking the machine; soon it would all explode. On adrenaline, Catanuto raced to the burning plane and despite choking smoke and the flames, he pulled Weldon from the plane, hauling him off the wing and onto the ground. The German planes were still buzzing the field. He hurriedly jerked the flyer along on the icy ground by his unwounded leg. The pair had only moved a short distance away from the burning P-47 when the bombs and fuel on the machine exploded. Catanuto and the corporal were thrown to the ground. Shrapnel whizzed eerily through the air. The plane was gone, only a burning pile of wreckage remained. Catanuto picked himself up; surprised to be alive. He pulled his wounded friend to safety. Catanuto received the Purple Heart.

Nine others of the 388th and 386th Squadrons were wounded by the gunfire, but, amazingly, no one was killed. There were many strange scenes. Cpl. Irving Wassermann was driving his BST trailer across the field hauling a dozen 500 lb. bombs when the bullets started to fly. He jumped off the truck while it was still moving and dove into the nearest foxhole, horrified to realize that his haven was next to the ammunition dump. But he dared not move until the strafing planes let up. Sgt. Donald J. Hutchins was in the latrine reading *Stars and Stripes* when the machine guns began chattering. Caught with his pants down, he could hear the bullets ricocheting into the latrine. Hutchins chose to jump into the latrine pit rather than take a bullet— a colorful vignette his war-time buddies would never let him forget.

Meanwhile, the AA gunners at the field drew a bead on the enemy. One

German fighter was hit by a volley of bullets that smashed its cockpit and killed the pilot. The plane slammed into the ground tearing itself to pieces over a 70 yard swath; another was hit, pinwheeling into a hangar and wounding an American pilot who had taken refuge nearby. In all, 22 of the "Hell Hawks" P-47s were destroyed on the ground; another eight were damaged beyond repair. The 386th Fighter Squadron was temporarily out of commission. By the time the Me-109s left the field, eight of them had been shot down by the AA gunners. One man, Lt. Samuel D. Lutz found himself "mad about the beautiful P-47s burning and blowing up." Lutz stood up, cocked his .45 calibre Colt and began firing at the Messerschmitt with his pistol. His own plane, an Alert ship, was hit in the cockpit while he fired. He watched as two Me-109s were shot down by AA fire, the enemy planes slamming into the ground with the German pilots' bodies being grotesquely strewn about the field. A number of American airmen unashamedly rushed over to pilfer the torn corpses. They were in search of souvenirs. Another 109 slammed into the ground near the 387th Squadron's headquarters, tearing itself to bits. The scene was particularly gruesome. The German pilot was decapitated, his legs were chopped off at the knees and someone had taken his watch. Lutz felt sick. An hour later, the Lieutenant was white and still shaking; when he flew the next day he could not but help think about the pitiful German pilots and their ignominious fate. What if he were shot down?

In all, three pilots of I/JG 53 were killed in the operation and four more were reported missing. Several ended up in captivity and others, like Fw. Johannes Müller, died in an American hospital after suffering severe burns. Others were killed outright: Fw. Ernst Nachotzky and Fw. Ernst Off were later found in their burned-out wrecks. IV Gruppe lost some eight pilots in the operation and the fate of another five has never been resolved. Typical of the likely fate of these was the discovery of the scattered remains of "White 13," the Me-109G-14 of Uffz. Herbert Maxis. On February 1st, exactly a month after Bodenplatte, the crash site was found near Saarlouis.

The German mission could be counted as no more than a limited success. Obstlt. Bennemann's JG 53 destroyed 22 P-47s on the ground at a cost of 14 pilots and some two dozen planes of his own. Two pilots of the no-shows in III Gruppe were wounded in the abortive scrap on the way to Metz. At sundown, only thirty Me-109s were still serviceable in the entirety of JG 53. Tragically, Hptm. Friedrich Müer, the commander of IV Gruppe would be killed in combat the following day with the fighter bombers he had attacked in Bodenplatte.

The P-47s of the 387th and 388th Squadron returned just after the enemy fighters departed the field. Although they gave chase they soon returned to base; the Germans were gone. They returned to Metz-Frescaty to a scene of smoking and wrecked planes and absolute chaos. What a day! But convincing evidence that the "Hell Hawks" were not taken out by the German assault was not long in coming. Later Monday afternoon, 44 of their "Jugs" were back in the skies east of the battle zone claiming four locomotives, 25 rail cars and eight rail cuts.

One of the German pilots shot down had bailed out to be captured at the edge of the airfield. He spoke excellent English and "was a very cocky person"— so insolent that the Luftwaffe pilot refused to be photographed until he had combed his hair and shined his boots. Maj. George R. Brooking, the commander of the just- devastated 386th Fighter Squadron, came over to headquarters where the pilot was being held. Brooking had been chased off the can from his morning constitutional when the fighters attacked. Pulling up his pants, he had crawled into an AA emplacement to direct the gun crew.

During his conversation with the Luftwaffe pilot the German strolled to the window and motioned to the still-burning planes on the airfield. "What do you think of that?" he asked. Brooking wanted to punch the German, but left the room instead. Over the next few days replacement planes quickly arrived at the Metz airfield. Maj. Brooking made a point of going back to visit the German pilot who was still being held at headquarters. Upon meeting, he motioned for the German pilot to look out the window. There sat ten new Thunderbolts where before had been smoldering wrecks of the burning aircraft. "What do you think of that?" Brooking pointed. The Luftwaffe pilot looked out and turned to Brooking, "That," he said thoughtfully, "is what is beating us."

A B-17 crew snapped this amazing photograph showing a partly crippled Flying Fortress at lower altitude being stalked by a German Fw-190 moving in for the kill. *(NASM)*

Ground crews remove snow from ordnance and Mitchell IIs of 320 (Dutch) Squadron at Melsbroek. *(Roba)*

Wing Commander J.E. "Johnny" Johnson, DSO and Bar, DFC and Bar. The distinguished leader of 127 "Canadian" Wing, Johnson was unimpressed with the German marksmanship of *Operation Bodenplatte*, which he described as a "bunch of beginners on their first flight." *(IWM)*

Spitfire of 302 (Polish) Squadron in action. *(NASM)*

Members of *JG 77* at Düsseldorf-Rathingen, December, 1944. From left to right, Lt. Hannes Renzow (*10./JG 77*), Hptm. Armin Köhler, (*Kommandeur III/JG 77*), Lt. Heinz Hackler (*Staffelführer 11./JG 77*) and Uffz. Hasso Fröhlich of *11./JG 77* with head bandaged. Fröhlich was wounded in the air battles on December 23rd. *(Fröhlich via Roba)*

ABOVE: Lt. Heinrich Hackler of *11./JG 77* seen in his Messerschmitt in November in Neuruppin. Hackler was killed in *Operation Bodenplatte* on January 1st, 1945. *(Böttner via Roba)*

LEFT: Crew chiefs and other support crew try to keep warm as P-47s taxi out for a mission. *(NASM)*

Operation Bodenplatte: January 1st, 1945

Destruction at Metz-Frescaty airfield. Destroyed American Thunderbolts after the surprise New Year's morning attack. *(Johnson)*

BELOW: Firefighters move into action to contain the damage from an accident involving a blazing P-38. (*HRC*)

Sgt. Ray N. Barclay makes a final check on a 500-pounder attached under the wing of a Republic P-47. (*HRC*)

After being shot down, this German pilot, captured on the edge of the Metz airfield, refused to be photographed until he had combed his hair and shined his boots! (*Johnson*)

Epitaph to failure. The tail of this Messerschmitt has literally been sawed off by bullet fire from an American P-47. (*NASM*)

The L-19 observation aircraft was a military adaptation of the Piper Cub. With clear weather over the German retreat, ski-footed planes like this one near Spa, Belgium, piloted by Maj. Jack Blohm of the 230th FA Battalion, directed a withering American artillery fire onto the hapless German columns. *(NA)*

"SNAFU" was an AA gun with the 410th Bomb Group in Coulommiers, France. *(NASM)*

German civilians labor to clear rubble from a shattered town east of the Ardennes. *(Unknown)*

M. Jules E. Pflough, a 61-year-old resident of Houffalize, Belgium, was the first citizen to re-enter the bombed out town after it was liberated by advancing American troops. More than any other location in the Ardennes, Houffalize bore the brunt of the Allied interdiction campaign against the German salient. The nightmare began on December 26th. During the weeks that followed, half of the approximately 400 civilians who remained in the town were killed. On the night of January 5th, a very heavy RAF raid killed over 100. In all, 192 died during the terrible winter bombardment in which the village was almost totally razed. *(NASM)*

An Accounting

In spite of the detailed planning for *Bodenplatte*, and the achievement of complete surprise, the results were not in keeping with the original intentions. In all, some 33 fighter groups and one ground attack group had participated— over 900 aircraft.[116] Of these, ten groups never located their targets and were forced to return to base without any accomplishment whatsoever. Two groups attacked a non-operational airfield and a further nine made attacks on airfields of only limited effectiveness. Only about one third of the Luftwaffe force executed the operation as planned and destroyed their intended targets. Then too, many German fighters returning from missions, both successful and not, were shot down by friendly anti-aircraft fire. Although flight leaders had done their best to call all of their fighters in after the strafing runs, some of the young German pilots simply got lost and ran out of fuel before reaching home; others disappeared without a trace. Even today, their ultimate fate remains a mystery.

To be sure, *Operation 'Bodenplatte'* destroyed at least 300 Allied planes on Allied airfields and shot down another 70 Allied aircraft in aerial combat. Listening in, ULTRA heard *Jagddivision 3* claim to have destroyed 398 aircraft on the ground with a further 93 damaged and another three shot down in aerial combat. However, the same communique ominously admitted their "considerable own losses" and later announced that a further 221 pilots had been posted to the Luftwaffe in the west to replace the attrition there. An *OKW* communique on January 2nd estimated 400 Allied aircraft destroyed on the ground and 79 shot down in the air. An *OKL* report on the same day put the totals at 402 and 87, respectively with a further 114 aircraft damaged. An aerial German photo reconnaissance mission, days after the raid and intercepted by ULTRA, revealed that 279 destroyed Allied aircraft were still visible on the ground (239 single engined, 21 twin-engined and 19 four engined planes) at eight airfields.

The quoted Allied losses appear greatly under-counted for reasons that to this day remain obscure. In a report dated January 3rd, the RAF recorded losses included 144 aircraft destroyed and another 84 seriously damaged. The USAAF acknowledged only 134 losses with 62 planes damaged beyond repair.[117] Whether this figure included the 40 admitted ground losses of the Eighth Air Force (16 B-17s, 14 B-24s, 8 P-51s, 2 P-47s) is unclear. Neither estimate includes the approximately 70 aircraft shot down by the Germans

---

116 The number of the German sorties varies by account. Dr. Percy Schramm, the *OKW* diary keeper, records a total of 1,035 aircraft sent on the *Bodenplatte* mission with some 300 missing thereafter.

117 Sources differ. SHAEF recorded losses of 122 operational aircraft on the ground, but noted that the RAF alone had written off another 168. The British 83 Group recorded 127 operational aircraft destroyed and 133 damaged. Inclusion of non-operational aircraft increased the totals as did addition of losses due to air combat.

during the operation. The documentary evidence suggests that overall Allied losses including machines damaged beyond repair and fighter combat losses amounted to over 300 aircraft. However, even with this tremendous loss of material, few Allied pilots perished in the fighting and their aircraft could be replaced in a week or two. In the less damaged Ninth Air Force, the losses, while disturbing, were quickly replaced. Within 24 hours sufficient replacement aircraft had arrived from the service command depots to maintain normal operations without diminution. And even had a large number of Allied pilots been killed, the results could not have been decisive, for by the beginning of 1945, so imposing was the advantage of the Allied air juggernaut, that they were no longer lacking in trained aircrew or aircraft.

The German side of the ledger was more serious. The losses sustained by the Luftwaffe in *Operation Bodenplatte* represented the greatest single losses to the German air force in any single day's action. Some 300 Luftwaffe planes were destroyed with about 85 of these shot down by their own flak. The overall loss rate was over 30%. However, with the current surplus of aircraft, more tragic was the devastating blow to the ranks of the German fighter crews. One hundred fifty-one pilots were killed or missing with another 63 taken prisoner.[118] Eighteen more were wounded. One out of every four pilots participating was gone. Some 137 German planes were claimed as being shot down over the Allied area of operations with 39 of these in the American zone. According to Allied counts, 57 of these were shot down by fighters and another 80 were claimed by AA defenses. By January 16th, some 96 of these were examined by RAF Technical Intelligence Officers. The pitiful carcasses of another 115 burned-out machines were inspected in the American zone. More were obviously lost over Germany. Ironically, many Luftwaffe planes had been lost to flak guns unaccustomed, as they were, to seeing their own planes. The destruction of the German aircraft was bad enough— over 20% of the fighter strength in the West.

Losses varied considerably from one fighter unit to the next. *JG 77* had the lowest casualty rate at 10% in its failed operation, while *JG 4* suffered the worst, losing 45% of the aircraft which took off that morning. But *III/JG 54* had the dubious honor of the highest losses of any one *Staffel*; 60% of its aircraft did not return from *Bodenplatte*. The loss of so many experienced pilots and carefully hoarded fuel was particularly crippling. In all six *Gruppe* and 11 *Staffel* commanders were lost in the operation. Three irreplaceable *Geschwader* commanders were lost: Obstlt. Johann Kogler of *JG 6* had been forced to bail out over enemy territory, and Obst. Alfred Druschel (*SG 4*) and Obst. Günther Specht of *JG 11* were dead. The "Great Blow" had not been applied as Galland had preached and it's feeble results would be of little

---

118 A total of 33 German bodies from 91 aircraft were recovered in the American area of operations with some 63 German pilots taken as POWs.

help to the Reich. Rather than a massive defensive fighter attack on the heavy bombers of the U.S. Eighth Air Force, the reserve had been exhausted in a surprise ground strafing mission for which its pilots were ill-trained.

On the other hand, many of the young pilots participating in *Operation Bodenplatte* had scarcely 15 hours of flight time. Committed to combat in the air, these *Nachwuchs* would have been clay pigeons for the skilled Allied fighter pilots. But on January 1, 1945 they could fire their guns well enough to at least claim some of the enemy on the ground. In the air they would have been sacrificed for less. In any case, the damage they wrought was not enough to change the course of the Luftwaffe's fate.

On the morning of January 3rd the citizens of Germany's capital opened their newspaper, the *Berliner Morgenpost*, to read a typically optimistic headline from Josef Goebbels' propaganda mill:

"**Attack on Dutch and Belgian Airfields**
A MAJOR SUCCESS FOR OUR FIGHTERS"

The article on the "Major Success" mentioned nothing of the 304 aircraft that failed to return. And of course, nothing was said of the pitiful fate of some 200 German pilots who had perished in the operation, their bodies strewn about the countryside along with their tattered machines, or augured deep into nameless heaths and marshes never to be found, or, even worse, burned beyond recognition. Only after the war would the truth would come out.

449

XXI

New Year Doubts: January 2nd

Göring had savored his attack on the Allied airfields. Jet reconnaissance had sighted 149 P-47 fighters and eight heavy bombers parked in the open at St. Trond airfield— ripe for attack. Hermann Göring had personally provided the orders for *Operation Bodenplatte* to begin. He had been sure that it would be easier to destroy the Allied planes on the ground than in the air. Originally, the German planes were to appear over their targets at 8:15 AM, but a number of factors, mostly the weather, had delayed the launch of the planes for over an hour. Göring was pleased to learn that the destruction to the Allied airfields had been significant, particularly to the British. But Göring knew the true score. The last great German air attack had resulted in the greatest single day'sloss of Luftwaffe pilots of the entire war. While the German pilots were out sacrificing the final flower of the Luftwaffe's fighter resources, Hermann Göring was sending out his stirring orders for New Year's Day. The exhortative was speedily decoded by ULTRA:

"Comrades of the Luftwaffe!
A year, heavy with fateful tests, has come to a close. In the teeth of all opposition and in spite of all our needs and worries, the year found us more than ever ready to fight steadfastly to do our duty. On the threshold of a new year, we turn our gaze, full of trust and hope to the future. At the present time, we see the first fruits of the hard and dogged work of the reconstruction of the Luftwaffe to maturity. With your new *Geschwader*, which have again risen, with exemplary paratroops, zealous flak gunners...our Air Force will continue to prove that it will continue in the old tried and true ways. We bow our heads in homage and proudly mourn our dead, who, at the front and at home, laid down their lives for Germany. Their sacrifice fills us with glowing faith..."

450

Given the loss of so many friends during the morning's operation, this encouragement must have rung hollow for the returning survivors. In spite of the Luftwaffe's pyrrhic victory, it buoyed, albeit temporarily, the miserable standing of Hermann Göring in Hitler's arena. The *Reichsmarschall* stayed on his luxurious train parked nearby Hitler's headquarters. There at night he ate sumptuous meals, drank cognac and smoked big cigars while reading trashy novels. Göring attended every meeting at *Adlerhorst* after New Years until January 10th. But as the German ground offensive withered and the Allies returned to their punishing ways in the air war, Hitler's attitude to Göring chilled to ice. On January 5th, Martin Bormann penciled in his diary, "*Reichsmarschall* summoned to the Führer on account of the air-war situation." When attending these meetings, Genfldm. von Rundstedt, in charge of German forces in the west, noted that while he was allowed to sit, the obese *Reichsmarschall* was made to stand. "Let's hope it's all over quickly so I can get out of this lunatic asylum," Göring announced to those around him. He remained on his luxurious train until January 11th, when he could take no more. "Three quarters of my shattered nerves are due not to the war," he shouted to Gen. Bodenschatz, nearly deaf since the July 20th bomb blast, "but to the Führer!" He departed to Karinhall.

Even worse than Göring's shattered pride, the failure of the operation to still the Allied air forces quickly became apparent. The weather on the afternoon of January 1st permitted all the Allied TACs as well as the Eighth Air Force to operate. The Allied air forces managed about a thousand sorties although many of these were not over the Ardennes.

The 366th FG meted out more punishment to the Germans near Mont-le-Ban and shot down two Me-109s near Malmédy. The 370th FG worked over the enemy near Büllingen. The view of the latter action was provided by the Germans who were attempting to move the big *Jagdpanthers* of the *560th s.Panzerjäger Battalion*. At daybreak, the detachment headed from Kall to assist the *12th SS Panzer Division* in Hitler's ordered vengeance attacks at Bastogne. As they passed through Buchholz, however, Gefr. Ernst Wulf watched in horror as a dozen fighter bombers bombed the column. In spite of near panic, when the dust cleared only the battalion kitchen had been damaged; the thick skinned hunting Panthers survived unscathed!

The pilots of the 367th FG, after drinking dark coffee to clear their hangovers, strode out to the runway to their waiting P-38s. Under their wings they carried bombs inscribed with "Happy New Year!" to hit German railway traffic near Frankfurt. The bombs found two locomotives and some 75 freight cars; an ammunition depot went up in a terrific explosion.

Recovering quickly from the shock of having Metz airfield blasted, the 365th FG responded with two missions to blast German rail facilities in the area around Sobernheim-Neunkirchen-Olsbrucken; and a further two to put up patrols around Metz in case the Germans decided to try another attack later in the afternoon. One of these ran into a suspicious group of P-47s over Blieskastel with orange tails and red noses. Although the controller, "Ripsaw," believed them to be enemy, the "Hell Hawks" pilots could not be sure and they were left alone and the incident remained a mystery.

Col. Wasem's intrepid 474th FG flew three armed recce missions in the La Roche-Malmédy-Prüm area, blasting road-bound transport between Bleialf and Schönberg. The high point of the day came at 9:30 AM when the group napalmed a German headquarters ensconced in a Belgian chateau east of La Roche near Samrée. The following day they would continue to strike the enemy in this area although losing two of their pilots to an "out of this world" concentration of enemy flak.[119] The remaining Thunderbolts of the 365th FG retaliated in the afternoon blasting 4 locomotives and 25 rail cars. The 48th FG from Nugent's XXIX TAC had a very active day, attacking Heimbach and Stemmln. The 404th FG reported 10 enemy tanks destroyed on the road to Schmidtheim and the 36th observed a huge fire after attack on a German fuel convoy in the northern reaches of the battle zone. Meanwhile the 373rd FG found 60 enemy vehicles on the St. Vith - Vielsalm road and left more than 25 of them burning.

The 368th FG flew an armed reconnaissance in the Sinzig area, bombing 50 German trucks observed in a woods north of Trier. Meanwhile the 354th FG bombed enemy positions in Grüfflingen, southwest of St. Vith and also attacked the positions of the *1SS Panzer Division* southeast of Bastogne near Lutrebois. Flak was heavy, however, and two pilots were lost in this operation.

The medium bombers of the Ninth Air Force renewed their attacks on the Ardennes traffic nodes at St. Vith, Salmchâteau, and La Roche. The following day they would blast the German-held railhead at Gouvy. According to reconnaissance the only line which remained open into the breakthrough area was the Moselle River bridge at Bullay, which was given priority for destruction. Accordingly, the 190 medium bomber sorties included the rail bridges at Ahrweiler, Konz-Karthaus and Bullay with a total of 343 tons of explosives. As this transpired ULTRA covertly listened in as Genfldm. Model of *Heeresgruppe B* ordered "ruthless seizing of motor transport to overcome the supply difficulties that had arisen from the temporary breakdown of the railways."

And of course the Eighth Air Force, in far off England was still to be reckoned with. 800 bomber mission paced by 700 fighters droned on to again hit the marshalling yards at Kassel and Limburg and blast the oil industry once more around Magdeburg. The strategic bombing returned to its relent-

---

119 Included in those killed were 2nd. Lts. "Greek" Zeece and James F. Hitchcock. Two weeks earlier, Zeece had nursed an "unflyable" P-38 back to base. Zeece was last heard from on January 2nd at 9:40 AM, reporting that his left wing was on fire. Hitchcock bailed out safely southeast of Vielsalm, but was later found to have been killed, likely after reaching the ground.

less campaign to lay waste to German transportation and to sap the very last drop of oil out of Germany's war machine. Meanwhile at the *I Jagdkorps* control center at Treuenbrietzen, the radar watchers waited to see how the attack was forming up before committing the limited fighter reserves of *JG 300* and *JG 301*. Finally, the home defense fighters were scrambled meeting the bomber stream near Bremen. The German fighters broached the P-51 fighter screen and were able to send a number of the bombers spiraling earthward. Near Hamburg, an arm of about 100 B-17s split off from the main force and made for the hydrogenation plant at Dollbergen east of Hanover. Near that location, some of Steinhoff's Me-262s of the embryonic *JG 7* made contact with Mustangs of the 336th Fighter Squadron and one of the jets fell over Fassburg with Lt. Heinrich Lönnecker at the controls. Meanwhile, the main bomber force seemed headed for Berlin and the entirety of *JG 301* was sent to halt the aerial column. Desperate air battles broke out over Stendal with a number of German fliers killed. But then the Americans changed course— their true target was Kassel. *I Jagdkorps* had been outfoxed! But so low on fuel were the German fighters that they had to return to base while the heavy bombers went on to pound their targets. And that was not all: RAF Bomber Command was again in action, hitting Dortmund/Ems with 560 tons by day and Osterfeld with 832 tons by night. The 2nd Bomb Division also lent a hand with the rail bridge interdiction effort, striking spans at Koblenz, Remagen and Neuwied. Nine German pilots had been killed, one was missing and another four were wounded in the failed intervention. They had knocked out some 16 Allied aircraft in the exchange. The British 2nd TAF was also out in force, flying some 409 aircraft on armed recce missions in the Osnabrück, Lingen and Paderborn areas. Against a loss of 13 aircraft, they claimed 72 planes shot down.

In his hometown of Limburg, Ofw. Kistier of the *15th Fallschirmjäger Regiment* witnessed the 40-minute bombing attack on the rail yards near his home. Later taken as a POW, Kistier described the local mood as "bitter with morale unlowered." Labor details with *Volkssturm* units and Hitler Youth set to work immediately after the raid while the womenfolk of the town prepared meals for the workers. The entire community pitched in to clear the rubble and repair the rails and by nightfall on January 3rd the first train departed from the town.

In spite of the heavy Luftwaffe opposition that day only eight bombers were lost and half as many fighters. Twenty-three German aircraft were claimed by the New Year's Day operations of the Eighth Air Force with some 17 of these coming from the escorting fighters. Five of the victories, including one destroyed Me-262, were credited to the 4th Fighter Group during a dogfight with Luftwaffe fighters around Ulzen, Germany. The only daytime offensive German air operations on January 2nd came from the ineffectual strikes by the jet bombers of *9./KG 76* which struck the rail yards in Liège again in the afternoon. The fighters of *JG 1* did take to the air in brief action on January 2nd near Oldenzaal and paid for their efforts with the loss of four more pilots, three being killed from 2 *Staffel* including Fw. Friedrich Steinborn who was killed in a non-combat mission.

In all, the American tactical air operations on January 1st had cost only six fighter-bombers lost, with another 19 damaged, most by enemy flak. And while according to the plan of Dietrich Peltz Allied air units should have been knocked out, the end of the day found those units submitting claims for a substantial booty: 22 armored vehicles, 320 trucks, 37 locomotives and 336 rail cars.

The German retribution using night fighters and ground attack bombers was ringing distinctly hollow. At 5 PM, just after dark on the cold evening of January 1st, Oblt. Werner briefed his 3 *Staffel* of *NSGr 1* of their upcoming nightly mission. They were to take ten of their geriatric Ju-87 Stukas and attack the Americans that they knew would be found at *Kampfraum Bastogne*. After this, they were to strafe whatever of the enemy they could see on the ground. An hour later the D-5s buzzed into to the air from Kirchhellen laden with 500 lb. and 1,100 lb. bombs. Flying at 2,000 feet, the Stukas found themselves in a thick cloudy soup. One aircrew, Gefr. Heinz Klinke and Obgefr. Wilhelm Knoblauch, lost their way in the mists and ended up north of Aachen and out of gas! They both bailed from their plane after the engine sputtered to a stop. Some of the others made it to Bastogne, but the desperation of the few scattered bombs now hardly made an impression on the resolute defenders there.

Of the succeeding days the claims of the Eighth Air Force fell off as poor weather returned. Meanwhile, the operations of Weyland's XIX TAC were back up to the old numbers— 407 successful sorties on January 2nd, and many over the battlefield. The 405th FG blasted a group of German tanks observed east of Clervaux and the 354th FG pummeled the enemy over the battle zone, finding flak, not the German air force, its worst enemy (four aircraft were lost to flak that day). Where the Ninth Air Force did find the enemy, the Germans often fled. Flying a fighter sweep over Bonn, the Mustangs of the 361st FG ran across five Me-109s which promptly headed east. The faster P-51s gave chase and shot down all five aircraft as they tried to land on a grass field. The Luftwaffe diary for Tuesday, January 2nd reflects their increasingly desperate position:

"2.1.45: Incursion by strong American bomber formations in western and southwestern Germany. Approximately 1,400 Allied fighters! Three *Gruppen* of *JG 4*, including the last nine operational aircraft of the former *Sturmgruppe*, *II/JG 4*, took off from airfields in the Palatinate to intercept. Heavy fighting against numerically far-superior enemy forces in the Kaiserlautern-Karlsruhe-Pirmasens triangle. Three killed: Uffz. Bojus (10 *Staffel*), Uffz. Hener (7 *Staffel*) and Oblt. Siller (Kapitän 6 *Staffel*). Three wounded: Uffz. Hässler (1 *Staffel*) forced landing, Obfhr. Meinke (1 *Staffel*) and Uffz. Henkel (3 *Staffel*) bailed out.

II and *IV/JG 53* engaged Allied fighter bombers in the Stuttgart area. Four pilots were killed: Gruppenkommandeur Hptm. Müer, (*IV/JG 53*) and Uffz. Ankelmann (*13 Staffel*). Gefr. Engel and Obfhr. Rubel, both of *II/JG 53*, were shot down and killed by Spitfires over Heimsheim as they were preparing to land at their airfield at Malmsheim."

However, *Operation Bodenplatte* had made an indelible impression on Allied air commanders. Noting a remarkable increase in German aircraft serviceability reports, the interpretations by ULTRA commentators did little to change this perception:

Heavy attack on 2nd TAF airfields morning 1/1 considered possible prelude to renewed German offensive. Intention may simply be to reduce Allied air superiority prior to expected thrust by *6th Panzer Army* towards Liège. On the other hand, may be prelude to opening of secondary offensive on northern sector of front aimed towards Antwerp...Similar attacks on Allied airfields and headquarters...should be anticipated..."

Later the same day, Eisenhower would see a new German offensive open up in Alsace near Bitche. Gen. Karl Henschel reported his *5 Jagddivision* would support the new offensive with fighter forces screening the new panzer spearhead in the Saar. And if all this wasn't enough to stoke the paranoia fires of Allied G-2s, the commander of the U.S. strategic air forces, Gen. Carl Spaatz, now estimated the war in Europe would not end before late summer and even longer if jet and V-weapon production could not be stopped.

Long an advocate for the oil campaign, Spaatz now found himself concerned with the jets and the German Air Force:

"...They have become increasingly aggressive, but not strikingly effective...The major portion of our fighter losses are still due to flak. The German air force is operating under Peltz, whom I consider the most competant commander the Germans have...On January 1, Peltz launched a full-out attack on our airdromes with some 800 fighters....On one airdrome, which Jimmy [Doolittle] and I visited the same day...a group of P-51s of the Eighth Air Force, which has been temporarily moved there, engaged the enemy on take-off..."

Spaatz was speaking of Asch airfield and the actions of Col. John Meyer. Later that day it became obvious that the Allied air leader was not the only one nervous. While flying with Doolittle the day of the Luftwaffe raid, their twin-engined aircraft was fired on by a trigger-happy anti-aircraft unit of the U.S. Third Army. Luckily the gunners' aim was poor, and the air commanders survived unscathed. Still, Gen. Patton was later informed, not only of the need for improved aircraft identification within his command, but also of better gunner practice. Still searching for the chimera of a knock-out blow, a deeply frustrated Spaatz would slowly be won over to Tedder's plan to wreck German communications under the codename of "Clarion." He would even begin to consider the continuing requests by the Air Ministry to obliterate Berlin in widespread area bombing. The Ardennes Offensive had been that troubling to Spaatz.

But in spite of the General's worries, *'Bodenplatte'* was really the last big German throw. From January 2nd through the end of the month the German air force seldom appeared in a strength greater than 150 sorties.[120] In spite of the brilliant strokes of German technological advance and the daring air attack— the largest single Luftwaffe operation of the war— the Allied air forces prevailed. And perhaps more importantly, the decisiveness of the Allied air victory had doomed Hitler's chances to successfully conclude his final desperate ground offensives to turn the tide. Like the German tanks broken and smoldering in the snows of the Ardennes, the air war to win the winter sky overhead had concluded, and Hitler had lost all.

The lack of fuel and transport had produced dire circumstances for the Germans still in the Ardennes. Petrol needs for the SS divisions had become so acute that regimental units were forced to send their organic transport as far to the rear as Blankenheim to secure 220 gallons of gasoline. Confirmation of the German lack of armored mobility came from all sides. The *9SS Panzer Division* reportedly had a dozen immobile tanks dug-in near Petit Langlir on the VII Corps front, with ten more as a static roadblock at Dochamps. According to POWs, supply trucks were proceeding to rear areas in two and threes with the lead truck towing the others to save fuel. The effects of the lack of mobility were translated into big troubles for the German gunners. One POW captured by the Third Army complained that he had been recently cut from six to five rounds per day because the fuel shortage had forced a total reliance on horse-drawn vehicles. Replacements for the *116 Panzer Division* were ordered to hitch-hike from Euskirchen to Houffalize. By 12 January the elite *1SS Panzer Division* would urgently request its needs be filled to haul out its operating tanks and damaged armor— 4,752 gallons of gasoline; the entire panzer regiment stocks on hand on that date totalled 264 gallons. And perhaps most pathetic of all, the *273 GHQ Flak Battalion* reported itself only able to acquire urgently need petrol by bartering its liquor ration to a neighboring unit.

On January 3rd the weather fogged back to its overcast ways. Although the IX TAC managed some 122 sorties, the 366th FG was particularly active (claiming 200 enemy vehicles destroyed) and a squadron of Typhoons of 123 Wing made successful rocket attacks on 30-40 German transport between St. Vith and Bastogne. The Eighth Air Force was also active, flying some 1,100 sorties and dropping 3,042 tons of explosives on Fulda, Koblenz and Hom-

---

120 The notable exceptions were on January 6th when approximately 175 sorties were essayed to support Hitler's ill-fated *Operation Nordwind* in Alsace, and ten days later when the Luftwaffe rose in numbers to oppose fighter bomber operations in the battle zone while the Germans were attempting to withdraw.

burg. Tactical targets in the Ardennes included St. Vith, Gemünd and Schleiden.

As the Germans attempted to withdraw from the Ardennes, the Luftwaffe found itself with fewer aircraft with which to help protect its armies. At least 280 aircraft had been drawn off with the *5 Jagddivision* to help provide a modicum of support to the new German offensive in Alsace. And so gaping were the ranks in the fighter *Gruppen* of *3 Jagddivision* after *Bodenplatte*, that a message on the 7th prohibited all operations over enemy territory until full operational readiness of its subordinate units could be restored.[121] Bereft of support, the German ground forces in the Ardennes were in a logistical tailspin. ULTRA intercepted messages from the *Sixth* and *Fifth Panzer Armies* reporting very low petrol stocks. The former was still trying to reopen its supply lines by getting the stalled vehicles off the road to its rear, while the later reported receiving no supplies at all on January 7th. The armor of the vaunted SS *Sixth Panzer Armee* was in a bad way. By the time Dietrich's army was ready to quit the Ardennes, it could only muster some 128 armored vehicles in its four tank divisions, where as this had been the established strength each of these formations when the offensive began.

On the other side, the headaches were also seeming without end for the Allied commanders. On January 1st the Germans had launched their new offensive, *Operation Nordwind*, in the Alsace region. It was a smaller version of *Wacht Am Rhein* and had been foreseen by ULTRA, but the fighting was fierce nonetheless. Although Lt. Gen. Jacob L. Devers' forces were stripped thin in that sector, the French demanded that Eisenhower not surrender Strasbourg, which would have otherwise been the logical thing to do. And while this transpired, such meager reconnaissance as could be flown in the poor weather indicated that the Germans might try to launch still another attack across the Moselle River just south of the Bulge and to the rear of the exposed Third Army right flank. In light of the severe fighting in both the Ardennes and Alsace, this could seriously undermine Allied efforts to turn back the enemy in both places.

Unfortunately, the return of the impenetrable winter weather meant that conventional intelligence would be unable to see whether the Germans were building up to cross the Saar River. The only way of getting the information was a low-level dicing mission, in which a photographic reconnaissance plane flew through the area with clicking cameras at tree-top level. The last time such a dicing mission had been attempted was before Normandy. Such missions were nearly suicidal. Regardless, Capt. Robert J. Holbury of the 10th Photo Recon Group volunteered to perform the mission on January 5th. The weather was bad; the ceiling was only 600 feet. Holbury took off in his

---

121 ULTRA revealed that the serviceable totals of aircraft in *3 Jagddivision*'s 21 *Gruppen* was 635 aircraft on January 4th.

Lockheed F-5 starting his low- level run from near Merzig where he flew north along the Saar to the Moselle River. It was a hair-raising 12 mile run in an unarmed P-38 aircraft:

> "It occupied my full attention to follow the river and at the same time avoid hitting obstacles. Hills were above me on either side most of the way and I concentrated on staying down as low as possible. Jerries were firing at me, but I was too busy to do anything but follow the river. Suddenly, red balls, about three quarters of the size of billiard balls were arching around me. I felt several sharp impacts as the wheel tried to jerk out of my hands and the right rudder went forward. It took heavy pressure to neutralize the controls, but they responded normally. I flew as close to the ground as possible while I looked for the damage. My left coolant gauge began creeping past the red line. A glance in the rear view mirror showed a stream of white vapor behind me. I immediately feathered the prop ... I was plenty frightened, but it soon changed to anger. As my speed dropped from 330 to 250 [mph] I saw several Jerries shooting at me and I would have given anything to have had some guns to dish out some lead myself. I received fire in several places, but as they didn't hit me I didn't consider it necessary to break away from the camera run. After I rounded a sharp bend intense flak again arched up. I felt my rudders jar and knew I had been hit again. The right engine was hot; the coolant radiator on it had been hit three times. I stayed on the deck till the last minute and pulled up over the hills with plenty of speed to spare. I got a vector to base and soon was circling the field at 300 feet...I landed okay, climbed out and patted that good right engine."

Holbury's F-5 had returned with a different air frame than the one with which he had started. The left rudder was nearly gone and the left vertical fin had been blown away. There were large ugly flak holes in the stabilizer and the entire fuselage was peppered as if it had metallic termites. However, Holbury did return with 212 informative photographs of the worrisome area. The photographic evidence showed no signs of a German build-up. The mission saved another Allied re-deployment and earned Holbury the Distinguished Service Cross.

The Ardennes offensive showcased the splintering relations between the Allied generals. Buoyed by his new position in charge of the British forces as well as the U.S. First and Ninth Armies, Field Marshal Montgomery continually pestered Eisenhower to make him overall ground forces commander. That would place Bradley under his heel. Eisenhower knew neither Bradley nor Patton would stand for that. In fact Bradley threatened to resign unless the First Army was returned to him when the Bulge was eliminated. Patton stuck with his friend and commander. Just before the close of the year, Montgomery had given alibis as to why First Army was not yet ready to attack the northern edge of the Bulge. "You disturb me," Eisenhower replied, referring to Montgomery's predictions of the offensive's "failure." And as for the matter of appointing him overall ground commander, "that in this matter I can go no further...It is you or it is me. If one of us has to give up his job, I do not think it will be me." Montgomery backed off, and more to the point he scheduled the First Army attack from the north for January 3rd.

Gen. Hodges, the plain-talking commander of the First Army, preferred a steady methodical attack for the offensive from the north. But the audacious Gen. Spaatz had other ideas. He recommended a carpet bombing of the German positions in the northern Ardennes as had been done for Cobra in Normandy. In spite of being shot at by Gen. Patton's anti-aircraft gunners, Spaatz arrived at Liège to ask Hodges if he could help him in this way. He reminded him that a carpet bombing had sprung George Patton loose in France.

But Hodges declined; he would stay on Montgomery's time line. Spaatz believed this a terrible mistake; they shouldn't allow the Germans to rebuild under bad weather. "The best time to attack is immediately." But Hodges could not be persuaded. By January 3rd the question was moot; the weather had reached its usual atrocious conditions. Spaatz called on Eisenhower. He informed the Supreme Commander of some other items to worry about. There were indications from intelligence, he said, that the Luftwaffe was developing some kind of secret "ray" which supposedly could stop aircraft engines. But more immediate was the threat of the jets. Eisenhower was unperturbed by the "secret ray," which he considered more of the general hysteria over the enemy's new found strength. But he was less inclined to dismiss the threat of the German jets. Unless their introduction could be slowed by blasting their factories, Spaatz warned, the Allies might lose air superiority. "Its going to take 10,000 tons of visual bombing to set jet fighter production back three months," he claimed. Eisenhower agreed, but added that at least for now, all the air forces must endeavor to defeat the enemy's latest attempt to regain the initiative.

And what of the jet menace that troubled the Allied commanders so? "*Edelweiss*," *KG 51*, continued it impuissant operations, although never gathering more than a handful of operational bombers. The single operational jet fighter unit, *III/JG 7*, upon which so much hope had been pinned, was still hardly a threat. Indeed, the training for units continued to be more dangerous than air combat. On December 15th Uffz. Wilhelm Schneller lost his life while on a training sorties; a similar fate killed Fw. Helmut Wilkenloh on December 23rd. On December 29th an experienced pilot, Fw. Erwin Eichhorn, was killed when his 262 stalled on landing approach to Lechfeld after an engine failure. The jet tumbled to the concrete in front of his horrified colleagues. Three days later, two Me-262s were lost, one jet overshooting the runway and another crashing when both engines faltered near Ulzen. There were a few victories, mostly against stray fighters over Lechfeld, but the losses were unacceptable. The "operational" status of the unit continued to slip into the future. Although *III Gruppe* reached its target of 40 pilots in the first week of January, the strength roster did not reach 19 262s until January

19th. Utilization of the few jets available created further dissention. "Initial operations with the Me-262 in the fighter role," read a candid Luftwaffe operations report, "brought negligible success as a result of incorrect tactical employment. Losses exceed victories. New tactics must be developed."

The direct result was that Obst. Johannes Steinhoff was dismissed, nominally due to his command's inability to bring the unit to successful operations in the six weeks allotted. Maj. Karl Weissenberger was appointed as his replacement with explicit instructions that the jets were only to be used against the heavy bombers and not their fighter escort. But the losses continued; two more pilots were killed during training flights on January 14th and 23rd and on the 19th Uffz. Heinz Kühn was shot down while in a conversion training flight near Ingolstadt.

Development of the new mass-produced jet, the He-162, was even more discouraging. Before his dismissal, Adolf Galland had pronounced the single-engined "Salamander" as unpromising. Galland's replacement, Obst. Gordon Gollob, was a technically experienced pilot. Following his appointment, he arrived in Vienna on February 12th along with Obstlt. Walther Dahl, the new Inspector of the Day Fighters. Gollob personally took the controls of an He-162M3 and although reaching a speed of 404 mph pronounced himself none too satisfied with its handling characteristics. Tests by the British after the war showed that the little beast could do little more than 450 mph and this only in the hands of a very experienced pilot due to the craft's dangerous instability. In any case, the plan for issuing the machine to untrained members of the Hitler Youth was quixotic and would have resulted in tremendous losses had it been seriously pursued.

While the Germans struggled with their new technology, the Allied air commanders were again drawing up plans to be executed when the weather cleared. The latest featured an expanded list of Rhine bridges including the Simmern span and four other bridges between Cologne and Koblenz. There was also a troubling assessment of the previous bridge campaign. Several of those assumed to be knocked out were still in service: Euskirchen, Koblenz, Neuwied, Morscheid and Konz-Karthaus. The new plan was to use the Eighth Air Force to take them out. Gen. Doolittle objected. During the course of the month, his heavy bombers dropped some 24,496 tons of explosives on bridges and communications centers. In particular, on January 1st and 2nd some 569 heavy bombers assaulted the Koblenz, Neuwied and Remagen bridges. On January 5th the IX BD, accompanied by P-38s of the 474th FG hit the bridge at Ahrweiler once more, while the Eighth Air Force put in big assaults with 900 sorties on Frankfurt, Hanau, Piramasens, Neunkirchen, Niederbreisig, Koblenz and Pronsfeld. And in spite of it all, a number of the target bridges continued in operation.

On the 6th another heavy bombardment was made on bridges at Bonn and Cologne. But the results on the latter seemed unsatisfactory and the bombing had to be repeated on January 7th and 10th. On the 7th the Eighth Air Force flew some 1,000 sorties with the 1st BD attacking Blankenheim, Kall, Gemünd, Bitburg and Euskirchen. But the rail bridges at Cologne and Koblenz were also on the list. The B-17s were often bombing through an overcast and Gen. Doolittle regarded this as a futile tactic for a precision target. He also professed that "the continued direction of Eighth Air Force against bridges was the result of undue enthusiasm where they had succeeded." Still, the effort drew the Luftwaffe away from the battle zone leading to the destruction of 315 German aircraft by their fighter escort that month. The bombers shot down another 41. Allied losses amounted to 93 bombers and some 44 fighters for the period.

On the ground, the Germans, both civilians and soldiers, were suffering terribly from the pounding. Uffz. Eduard Erlach was with a replacement company destined for the *989 Regiment* of the *277 Volksgrenadier Division*. On January 3rd, he arrived with another 110 men of the *Marsch Kompanie* at Koblenz. They had come from Bingen by train in a harrowing ride. Because of the frequent air raids, the men stayed in an underground air raid shelter by the railroad yard while waiting for transportation to the Ardennes front. On January 3rd the city experienced the most severe pounding yet by "50 waves of bombers" who blasted the city for nearly an hour. Erlach emerged from the shelter to see the railroad shelter obscenely wrecked, the twisted track, locomotives and disemboweled rail cars bound up in an ugly mass. A group of older civilians were dejectedly working to repair the mess. The morose workers spent their days in air raid shelters and going "home" to their cellars at 4 PM. In the shelters, Eduard listened to the civilians; their conversations revolved around their hope that the Americans would come soon. Then, the terrible bombing would end. They had not cleaned it up when Erlach left the town on foot on January 6th. The German company continued from Andernach to Gemünd— a journey which took four days due to the lack of transportation. However, upon arriving in Gemünd, near the front on the morning of January 10th, the group was attacked by thirty Allied aircraft. The men scattered and no one was hurt, but everyone saw all this as a bad omen.

Uffz. Erlach's predicament was hardly unique. On January 7th, SS Uffz. Heinz Pech was in the bombed out ruins of Houffalize. In the early morning hours four waves of Allied bombers blasted the town once more from a height of about 6,000 feet. The town was crowded with German personnel and equipment from the *9 SS Panzer Division*. Most of the vehicles in the town were wiped out and all of the mobile equipment including two assault guns of the *2 Battalion* of the *9 SS* were destroyed, much of it buried under collapsed houses. Casualties were severe and traffic through the shattered village was delayed by ten hours.

On January 6th the weather grounded all the fighter bombers of the Ninth although the Eighth Air Force continued to operate, putting up some 800 sorties who dropped 2,200 tons of explosives on rail and road bridges over or near the Rhine River. The only Ninth Air Force action was the bombing of Prüm. On January 7th it was again the Eighth Air Force who put up 1,000 sorties attacking the German towns in the Eifel: Blankenheim, Kall, Gemünd, Bitburg and Euskirchen as well as rail bridges at Cologne and Koblenz. On the 8th the Ninth was still grounded and the Eighth Air Force managed only 600 sorties, although these were again pointed at German communications targets east of the Ardennes: Wissembourg, Kyllburg, Schwiech, Speicher, Stadtkyll, Dasburg, Wittlich, Oudler, Clerf, Burg Reuland, Waxweiler and Lunebach. But the following day the weather in England soured and the Eighth Air Force did not fly. On the other hand, weather over the Ninth Air Force bases in France and Belgium improved. Although the IX and XXIX TAC were non-operational, by January 10th the XIX TAC was sending 325 sorties a day aloft to attack the Germans in the Ardennes.

Even top German generals were not exempt from the attention of the fighter bombers. On January 9th Gen. Josef Dietrich, in charge of the *Sixth Panzer Armee* was visiting the headquarters of the *2 SS Panzer Division* at the castle at Fme du Bois St. Jean north of Houffalize when American fighter-bombers struck. A number of vehicles were destroyed and the castle was set on fire by incendiaries. When the *IISS Panzerkorps* radioed to report the calamity at 11 AM, ULTRA was listening in:

> "Battle headquarters destroyed and completely burned out at 0900 hours in an attack by 12 Lightnings. Six to eight HE bombs fell near the target. Phosphorous containers dropped directly on the target. Estate St. Jean 4 kms SW of Les Tailles. Some slightly wounded, seven motor transport destroyed, baggage and equipment burned."

Although the SS generals were able to escape, the castle burned to the ground. The burned baggage belonged to Dietrich. Worse than the damage was the smart blow to his pride. "Sepp" Dietrich would later remark of the episode, "And the worst of it is that those damned *Jabos* don't distinguish between generals and anyone else— it was terrible!"

The damage wrought on the Germans from the air was relentless. On January 10th the fighter bombers hit a carefully camouflaged German petrol dump near Hillesheim containing some 15,000 gallons of the precious stuff. The cache went up in flames. Allied code breakers decrypted the news from German forces trying to escape the Ardennes that the bridge over the Our River had been hit by fighter bombers and that traffic was backed up. Covering III Corps, the 406th FG, bombed the town of Bras and destroyed most of the town including the German armor in the vicinity. Statistics for the day for XIX TAC comprised 325 sorties with claims of 246 motor vehicles, 14 tanks and 145 rail cars.

Over the following days ULTRA would eavesdrop as the Germans described escalating damage: on the 7th the *Organization Todt* reported the Hermann Göring Bridge at Neuwied had been smashed, the bridge at Düsseldorf was damaged on the 10th, and on the 13th came the terrible pummeling of Wiesbaden and the interruption of the railway from Kreuznach to Mainz. On the 15th *II Jagdkorps* reported the Hindenburg Bridge at Cologne out of commission. Meanwhile, the *Führer Begleit Brigade* in the Ardennes radioed on January 7th that:

> the fuel shortage dominates the conduct of operations...the main burden of the fighting is born by the infantry, because, in spite of all concentration of fuel supplies, our tanks have only been mobile in special circumstances...new allocation of six assault guns and four Hornisse...cannot be fetched as ordered because no fuel can be made available...bringing up of repaired tanks and removal of damaged tanks impossible as every drop of fuel is necessary for the battle.

Elsewhere, at Heppenbach on January 12th, assault guns with the 3 *Fallschirmjäger Division* were attacked by a quartet of fighter-bombers. The lead plane missed by 50 feet, but a rocket strike from the second blew the side off the gun and killed the crew. The surviving assault guns hid in the thick woods near Ondenval. The following afternoon, the armor tried to move once more towards Thirimont. Again, a swarm of fighter-bombers struck as the self-propelled guns emerged from cover. Only one of the guns was damaged, but the local cattle charged in a panic from the bombing, creating total chaos. "The cows were running around like wild," remembered Uffz. Albrecht Gollub who was charged with assisting the move. "We had to chase them away." Beginning on December 28th the men of the elite parachute division had received orders— some said they came from Göring himself— to raise their firearms wherever they saw the *Jabos* to fire at them. Although court martials was threatened to anyone disobeying the edict, the actual behavior under strafing fire was quite different. One soldier with the parachute division, Jg. Hans Bolten, related how after a low-level attack on Ondenval, the non-com in charge insisted that everyone fire away at the next wave of fighters with their side arms. However, when the American planes hove in and began strafing, the officer quickly retired to the cellar where he and his men had taken cover previously. "When the shooting began," one German officer related after the war, "the iron in their hearts turned to lead in their pants."

On Friday, January 12th while his paratroops ran for cover, Hermann Göring celebrated his 52nd birthday. The party at Karinhall was decidedly extravagant, particularly given the backdrop of unmitigated disaster unfolding for the Third Reich. With the sumptuous affair, the most splendid beverages were available: Polish vodka, choice claret, burgundy and brandy and the finest French champagne. While German soldiers foraged for what frozen scraps they might scavenge in the bombed out Ardennes farming villages, Hermann Göring enjoyed a *Reichsmarschall*-sized feast. There was fine Beluga caviar from Russia, duck and venison from the Schorfheide forests and the last of the *pâté de foie gras* from France. The irony of the snobbish occasion even elicited an ironic pre-meal grace from the *Reichsmarschall*. "The Göring family has always enjoyed a good table," he blustered without exaggeration, "This is no time to deny ourselves. We will all be getting a *Genickschuss* (a shot in the neck) very soon now." At the end of the gastronomic event, Göring quaffed a fine Napoleon brandy (his less privileged guests had to be content with cognac) and the toadish head of the table suddenly sprang to his feet in a toast. "Heil Hitler!" he bellowed with great bombast, "And God help Germany!"

The next day Göring entertained the Japanese Naval and Military attaches at Karinhall. The *Reichsmarschall* was in a chastened mood, as revealed by the deciphered reports sent back to the Emperor by the visitors from Imperial Japan. In speaking of the air war, the Japanese quoted Göring as relating "that he himself had thought that for large enemy bomber units to operate over Germany for an extended period of time was impossible, but this belief had been shattered...Moreover, he had not envisaged the enemy's ability to carry out accurately aiming bombing from above the clouds, due to the enemy having outstripped Germany in the development of radar" nor "the success of the enemy in building long-range fighter aircraft which accompanied the bombers..." The Japanese then waxed scornful of their pompous host: "At the present time the German Air Force is characterized by an extremely strong tendency towards dictatorship, with the result that suggestions put forward by staff officers are completely without effect...nothing can be accomplished without securing the direct approval of the *Reichsmarschall*." But the sounds of the war drew near from the East, and soon the annoying Japanese were gone.

Only a week later a huge Russian tank lumbered almost up to the gates of Karinhall before German anti-tank guns took it out. The *Reichsmarschall* promptly called in an entire Luftwaffe *Fallschirmjäger Division* to protect his estate. But the Russian tide was not to be denied. On January 31st, 1945, little Edda, her mother Emmy, and the housemaids and secretaries left the timbered walls of Karinhall for the last time. Göring stuck around long enough to supervise the packing of his cherished art collection: the priceless paintings, tapestries, crystal and rugs. It took four trucks just to transport the most valuable parts of the clandestine collection to Berchtesgaden. Before departing, he summarily shot his four favorite bison from his estate's preserve and cordially shook hands with the local foresters. This done, the *Reichmarschall* commanded the paratroopers defending his estate to lace the great palace with explosives. Under no circumstances was it to fall into the hands of the hated Russians. On his personal orders the engineers fired the charges: the great Karinhall was blown to bits.

XXII

The Bombs Fall: January 10th

E ven the birds are walking today," a weather officer glumly observed that first week in January. The mists and fog closed in once more with air operations virtually suspended over the battle zone. Close support missions for friendly ground units were few and far between and took place mainly in the Bastogne area. The weather was more conducive to air operations in the northern RAF zone, however. During the early afternoon of January 4th the 2nd TAF's 411 Squadron ran into seven Fw-190s over Henglo and managed to shoot down all but one. Almost simultaneously, 442 Squadron operating over the Lingen-Münster area fought a free-wheeling air battle with 15-20 enemy fighters and claimed one probable and another damaged. The New Zealand Tempest pilots had a number of encounters with the enemy on January 4th. 3, 80 and 56 Squadrons were also aloft. Flt. Lt. D.C. Fairbanks chalked up another Fw-190 and a total of five other German fighters were destroyed at no RAF loss. Spitfire pilots working to penetrate the murk to attack ground targets on January 6th suffered hard luck, however. Two pilots were shot down by flak during their missions.

On January 10th the weather cleared enough for limited operations. The Spitfires of 411 Squadron shot down three Fw-190s over Rheine-Münster. Meanwhile, 442 Squadron engaged enemy fighters over the Twente area. Flt. Lt. J.E.G. Reade, Flt. Lt. J.N.G. Dick and Flg. Off. A.J. Urquart each claimed an enemy plane, although the latter pilot was himself shot down and forced to parachute to safety. 401 Squadron found a group of

Fw-190s taking off and destroyed five, losing one of their own to enemy fire.

On the American side, the resolute survey of the 12th TAC R of the 10th PRG found a number of enemy vehicles moving through the village of Houffalize in the Ardennes. Coordinating their observations with American artillery batteries, Capt. Edward L. Bishop was able to direct very successful artillery fire adjustments. Most of the enemy column was destroyed. Then later that day Lts. Logothetis and Franklin encountered a German Me-262 over the Diekirch area. The jet made a firing pass and missed and Lt. Logothetis set chase for the plane which he followed through a series of dives and wing-overs until he was able to get shots of his own. He watched as shattered parts of the jet trailed by and the plane caught fire and fell out of control. The jet menace was also found elsewhere. During a raid on German transport coursing through the Ardennes village of Manderfeld on January 13th, one of the Mitchell bombers of the 2nd Group's 320 Dutch Squadron was seen to explode and crash following the sighting of one of the speedy jets. Walter Konantz with the 55th Fighter Group also encountered one of the 262s:

> "On January 13, 1945, the 338th Fighter Squadron was circling Giebelstadt airdrome in preparation for strafing it— the second time in a week. I noticed a couple of planes taxiing on the ground, then saw one take off...It was an Me 262 jet, not yet accelerated to high speed. We had the new K-14 gyro sight installed a week previously and I'd never fired the guns with this sight. It worked perfectly and I clobbered him all over with 40 strikes, setting his left engine on fire. He made no evasive action whatsoever, even after the first hit. He then spiraled into the ground and exploded."

486 Squadron Tempests suffered, however, in their armed reconnaissance in the skies over St. Vith. Very heavy and accurate German flak made the sky a minefield in the Euskirchen area. Three of the New Zealanders were knocked out of the air including Sqd. Ldr. A.E. Umbers. Fortunately, the squadron leader was able to bail out over the American held sector. Umbers was back at his unit a day later.

The 365th FG flew three missions over Trier-Bettendorf and Neunkirchen-St. Wendel, bombing and strafing German targets of opportunity in the Saar and southern Ardennes area. On January 11th the 474th FG hit an ammunition dump near Mayen and struck other German ground targets near St. Vith and Prüm while Anderson's medium bombers blasted Clervaux and Houffalize through which the Germans were attempting to pull back. Other strikes bombed the rail bridges at Simmern, Bullay and Annweiler and Ahrweiler. The attacks were less than perfect; the bombing of Simmern was completely ineffective and Bullay was also left serviceable, but the interdiction attacks in the Ardennes proper were more productive. On the ground, German artillery POWs being taken by the U.S. 90th Division southeast of Bastogne near Doncols told of an:

"acute shortage at the battery positions...attribute this to our bombing and strafing attacks on supply lines...communications completely disrupted yesterday...PW stated that in recent air attack on Brachtenbach, kitchen and QM stores were destroyed and a great number of solders were killed...chaos in the town."

On the 13th Weyland's XIX TAC flew some 546 sorties claiming multitudinous enemy vehicles (137 vehicles and 16 tanks). The 362nd Group was particularly active, flying eight missions against the Saar bridges near Trier and Konz-Karthaus and the 368th FG hit the Neunkirchen marshalling yards with such concussive force that pilots at 5,000 feet felt the strength of the explosions.

Once burned, twice cautious. Allied air commanders were still touchy after the Luftwaffe raid on their airfields on January 1st. The mysterious unfriendly P-47s in Luxembourg made for even greater concern. On January 13th Gen. Vandenberg's headquarters issued a warning:

"Information from various sources indicates strong possibility of recurrence of German air attacks upon our airfields within the next few days. It is desired that you take the necessary countermeasures to combat this threat..."

The next day Gen. Richard Nugent, with the XXIX TAC, convened a meeting to specifically deal with the prospect of a large scale raid by German jets on Allied airfields. In spite of a lengthy series of recommendations, more anti-aircraft guns and ammunition, more outposts and a general alert—nothing happened.

On January 14th the weather was clear and XIX TAC planes were out early in the hunt. Almost 750 sorties were flown in the "biggest day since summer." The Germans were hardly up to the challenge, although the jet bombers of *KG 76* were able to fly after two weeks of suspended operations due to persistent fog over Münster. Five of the speedy Ar-234s bombed American artillery concentrations in the Bastogne area, although Allied fighters made take-off and landing extremely risky. "Very strong fighter activity over the base with constant firing attacks," read the *Einsatzstaffel* situation report, "Own operations only possible with our fighters protecting takeoffs and landings (of 25 airfield protection fighters, only five reached our base, the others involved in dogfights on their way here."

The 474th FG had a frustrating experience. The group was assigned to escort a group of B-26s to bomb targets east of the Bulge. However, the Marauders never showed up at the assigned rendezvous point and the ground haze made it impossible to attack the enemy below. Two days later, however, they did find their bombers, which they accompanied to hit the important Rhine bridge at Neuwied. The P-38s were very unimpressed with the accuracy of the medium bombers who missed their target and expressed conviction that they could have done a better job had their own Lightnings been armed with bombs! Others did do better. The 386th BG damaged the railroad bridge at Bullay and the 323rd and 394th Bomb Groups plastered the wooden highway bridge over the Our River at Steinbruck.[122] The 394th completed the later mission in spite of losing the lead ship to the intense flak over the target; eleven of the 21 ships were damaged. Even though badly wounded and with his left engine and a good part of the its wing missing, Capt. Clifford Piper was able to nurse his stricken B-26 to Liège. Other IX BD missions hit Ahrweiler and Rinnthal with mixed results. West of St. Vith, other mediums of the Ninth blasted the village of Rodt. As usual, the indefatigable 365th FG was out again, this time for six missions. The P-47 fighter bombers flew an armed recce over Kaiserlautern with Capt. Joseph F. Cordner and 1st Lt. Ray L. Jones shooting down two Me-109s in the process. Other missions were flown strafing and chasing enemy transport over the Saar and southern Ardennes: Trier, Oberkirch, St. Ingbert, Grundstadt, Wittlich and St. Wendel. An additional six such missions would be flown the following day. The "Hell Hawks" attempted to intercede in the desperate battle around Bastogne, but so thick were the mists and so close was the fighting that identification proved impossible. To the north, the 48th FG flew missions, striking the villages of Wanne, Spineux and Maldingen in support of the U.S. 30th Infantry Division.

The 366th FG was scrambled to intercept bandits in the Düren area. The P-47s found twenty long-nosed Fw-190s in the vicinity, bouncing them at 4,000 feet. After the first firing pass, half of the enemy fighters took off for home, while the rest stayed to duke it out. In the resulting dogfight, the 366th claimed three shot down while losing two of their own. Later that afternoon the 366th returned to hammer the Germans between St. Vith and Houffalize. The villages of Mont-le-Ban and Baclain were hit after which the 3rd Armored Division moved in to claim the territory. Meanwhile, the 48th and 404th FGs pounded German troops assembling in the Prüm area, claiming over sixty vehicles destroyed.

---

122 The fighter-bomber advocates had a point. The Bullay bridge was not fully taken out until 10 February when the 395th Squadron of the 368th FG sent it into the water. Weyland sent a good-natured poke at Gen. Anderson, but Anderson was not to be outdone:

Dear Sam:

Here's the newest picture of that Bullay Bridge you were interested in for some time. Any time you find some little job that's too tough for the mediums, just call on us for a few of our P-47 heavy bombers.

Insultingly yours,

"Opie"

Dear Opie:

Congratulations on that Bullay job! In view of the fact that it had been severely weakened by medium bomber attacks on 14 and 16 January, I am not surprised that your pea-shooters were able to collapse the span. Also in view of the fact that O.R.S. tells me that your claims as to bridges destroyed and railroad cuts made are about 70% greater than actual damage, I can appreciate your elation over having one picture to prove one claim.

Equally insultingly yours.

"Sam"

The Bombs Fall: January 10th

Not only was the Ninth Air Force active once more, but January 14th marked the first time since January 1st that the Eighth Air Force had resumed its mission of devastation of the heartland of Germany. The weather was crystal clear with unlimited visibility. As usual, the Germans held back until believing they had divined the intentions of the 600 heavy bombers of the 2nd and 3rd Bomb Divisions that moved into Germany. Escorting B-17s of the Eighth Air Force, the 352nd FG was bounced by nine Fw-190s in the Lingen area. The P-51s claimed 5 without loss to themselves. Although the Luftwaffe fighter control thought another attack on Berlin was in the offing, the Eighth Air Force had other fish to fry. Their real objective was a large oil depot near Derben-Ferchland and other petrol facilities at Magdeburg. Another 400 bombers would hit the Cologne area to take out the Rhine bridges. The 357th Fighter Group paced the bombers, running head on into *JG 300* and *JG 301* been Havel and the Elbe.

The Luftwaffe struck back, launching some 189 aircraft— including a dozen Me-262s— aimed at repulsing the Eighth Air Force. The German fighters attempted to get at the bombers and the Mustangs picked them off as they did. At least five fighters went down in the wild aerial battles. A *Sturmböcke* unit with *JG 300* knocked out eight B-17s of the 390th Bomb Group which had become separated from the main formation. However, the results for the scale of the German effort was dismal: only 17 bombers and 11 fighters were destroyed. Returning USAAF aircrew of the 95th and 100th Bomb Groups commented on the obviously green German pilots, many had made only straight single head-on-passes on the B-17s which gave them little time to fire and exposed them to a deadly hail of bullets from the Fortresses. Although the 390th BG suffered their largest losses of the war (14 shot down), the German effort had backfired. The jet fighters of *9./JG 7* under Hptm. Georg Eder had little success against the bombers and Fw. Heinz Wurm was shot down by the Mustang of Lt. Col. Roland R. Wright near Prignitz. All the way to the target the German fighters sought to get at the bombers while the P-51 escort sent more German machines spiraling to their doom. Running interference for the bombers the P-51s of the 357th ran into a big party northwest of Brandenburg, Germany— more than a hundred German fighters of *JG 300* and *JG 301*. On that day, the 357th would experience the greatest single day score of an American fighter group in Europe in World War II. When all the claims were totaled, the group was credited with 56 1/2 German fighters shot down. Lt. Col. Andy Evans and Capt. John Kirla shot down four each. The exact number of confirmed victories is not exactly known. However, the two German fighter groups credited with defending the oil refineries admitted crushing losses on the 14th: 78 planes were lost and 69 Luftwaffe pilots were killed or wounded that Sunday. For the Reich home defense, it was their largest single day losses of the entire war.

The 355th Fighter Group shot down 11 Me-109s in a fighter sweep over the Münster area while the 20th Fighter Group (Col. Robert P. Montgomery) escorted the bombers of the 3rd Division towards Berlin. The group claimed 15 enemy aircraft at no losses. Similarly, the 78th Fighter Group was assigned to protect Eighth Air Force bombers moving on Cologne and was vectored against enemy fighters moving to oppose them. Meanwhile, the 356th FG uneventfully escorted B-24s to their target at Hallendorf. However, on the return leg around Dummer Lake the P-51s sighted 20 Fw-190s and shot down 13. Also participating were the P-47s of the 56th Fighter Group. Flying a sweep ahead of the bombers headed for Magdeburg, Germany, the "pack" came upon a huge gaggle of German fighters in combat with the 357th FG. The Thunderbolts waded into the fight, shooting down three of the enemy Me-109s.

The counterblow on January 14th was the last sustained assault on a heavy bomber unit of the Eighth Air Force in the entire war. The Luftwaffe losses dwarfed the Allied total with 140 aircraft lost. A great number of the 2,953 aircraft added to the rosters of the German air force during December were now consumed, along with the carefully hoarded fuel for support of the Ardennes Offensive.

Sunday, January 14th was the most disastrous day for *Luftflotte West* since *Operation Bodenplatte*. JG 1 tangled with British fighters in the Hengelo-Twente area losing a dozen pilots (7 killed, 2 missing and 3 wounded) in a confusing engagement in the fog in which many German fighters, unaccustomed to blind flying, became lost and landed pell-mell at bases all over Northern Germany. Without top cover the Spitfires caught the 1 and 2 *Staffeln* just as they took off and made quick work of the German fighters. Only two British machines were claimed, while wrecks and craters of the destroyed Luftwaffe fighters littered the environs around Twente airfield. Particularly damaging was the loss from I *Gruppe* of Uffz. Günter Sill, one of its more experienced pilots flying a new Fw-190D-9. Ihlefeld threatened Maj. G. Capito, the new commander of I *Gruppe* with court martials, but found it difficult to bring charges to bear as JG 1 was involved in the chaotic process of transferring its remaining planes to the Eastern Front.

Meanwhile over Münsterland, *IV/JG 54*, already bled white from the previous battle, was sent sprawling in combat with Allied fighters near the Mittelland Canal. Two *Staffel* commanders were killed, Oblt. Helmut Radke and Lt. Carl Resch, and a total of eight pilots were listed as killed or missing during the day. It was the final action of the *Gruppe* in the war. The poor luck extended to JG 3 who fenced with the Tempests of 3 and 486 Squadrons during the day, losing five pilots killed or missing in the process. A very large dogfight ensued in the Kaiserlautern area with Allied fighters attempting to rope off German fighters from the embattled Saar region. The combatants included JG 4, JG 11 and IV/JG 53. JG 4 continued its hard luck; two *Staffel* leaders fell: Oblt. Stark and Lt. Josef Kunz. JG 11 lost two pilots while *IV/JG*

4 lost one. *JG 26* was ordered to patrol the notorious Ardennes area and ran into a strong American fighter contingent over Cologne. Some 13 aircrew were killed or missing when the *Schlageter* pilots returned that evening. Included in these losses was Oblt. Gerhard Vogt, an experienced pilot with 48 kills to his credit. *IV/JG 53* ran into a hornet's nest near Karlsruhe, losing two pilots in the scrap that followed. Other German fighter groups also took their lumps: *JG 77* left nine pilots behind in the Dusseldorf area; *JG 2* lost four near Altenstadt and *JG 27* wrote off another two in battles over Ibbenburen.

If any day in the Luftwaffe's history was "Black Sunday," January 14th certainly laid its claim. The weather was ideal; the XIX TAC alone got off some 61 missions and 633 sorties. The 368th Fighter Group was hit hard by a surprisingly strong engagement with the enemy on January 14th. The 397th Squadron was jumped by nearly 50 Me-109s and Fw-190s four miles west of Neustadt at 10:30 AM. Six P-47s and their pilots were lost in the engagement in which the Germans had a tremendous numerical advantage. Two Fw-190s were shot down in retribution, although later in the day five German aircraft were shot down at no loss to the 395th Squadron who likewise ran into many German fighters south of Mainz. Two other aircraft each were lost to the 354th and 362nd FGs that day and the 405th lost one. Most of the later losses, however, came at the hand of enemy flak. By sunset, Weyland's P-51s and P-47s had claimed 161 total enemy fighters. The Germans themselves admitted the loss of some 107 pilots killed or missing on "Black Sunday" with another 32 pilots wounded. Five *Staffel* leaders had been killed.

The operations clearly broke the back of the Luftwaffe. After January 14th, the Eighth Air fighters seldom encountered the enemy over Germany in any strength. For instance, when the Flying Fortresses returned on January 16th to pound the German oil refineries at Magdeburg and Ruhland, the escorting 4th Fighter Group could not find any aerial opposition from the enemy and took out its frustration by strafing a German airfield at Neuhausen. The Luftwaffe had been virtually eliminated from the skies over Europe.

On the ground, German commanders in the Ardennes implored the Luftwaffe for help against their hellish bombardment:

> "0930 hours 14 January message believe to be from *5 Pz Army* stated that extraordinarily heavy fighter bomber activity brought all movements to a standstill. Fighter protection in Houffalize area urgently requested. Reply from *II Jagdkorps* at 1200 hours stated that up to 1100 hours 216 aircraft had been directed thither; no further forces were at the moment available."

The British 83 Group was also out in force, claiming a total of 23 victories. Six Typhoons of 184 Squadron made an armed reconnaissance of the Münster area, and sighted four enemy Me-109s. Wt. Off. A.J. Cosgrove gave chase to one of these, shooting until the German aircraft exploded. While on a fighter sweep over the Rheine-Achmer area, the 24 Spitfires of 331 and 332 (Norwegian) Squadrons ran into a gaggle of German fighters near

Osnabrück and shot down three, although losing one of their pilots, 2nd. Lt. J.P. Ditlev-Simonsen, who smashed into the ground in his enthusiasm to verify the kill of a Fw-190. The Tempests of 3 Squadron were assailed by a group of enemy fighters while blasting three locomotives in the Paderborn area. The indefatigable Flt. Lt. Fairbanks shot down another Fw-190 and Me-109 in the spat. A little later 486 Squadron destroyed another four German fighters near Münster, while 56 Squadron scored another two victories. In the afternoon, 3 Squadron returned to strafe Detmold airfield and claimed two Ju-52 transports destroyed on the ground.

On January 15th the *OKL* officers produced a sobering assessment of the air situation in the West. So grim were the conclusions, that the document was not to be distributed, but was instead committed to files. "Except for single recce machines, no German aircraft reached the front line over the last two weeks owing to the interception in the rear areas," the report revealed. "Artillery spotters very annoying. No apparent German fighter protection. Greatest danger low flying aircraft." The Luftwaffe officers further noted that diligent camouflage and dispersal were vital. The document went on to play a familiar and distressing tune, "Flak operations," it read, "only effective weapon against Allied air attacks...." They also ruefully called for a reduction in the number of army liaison units since most never had any fighter units to control. Furthermore, the air officers painted a critical portrait of the German ground units they met:

> "Large proportion of faults due to late briefing officers and fall in quality of leadership in ground troops...Need to save every minute of time and drop of petrol not sufficiently realized. Bomb damage not quickly enough cleared up to let supplies through. Traffic jams often due to lack of energy and leadership...Not enough attention paid to danger from air in locating headquarters, camouflaging motor transport and occupying villages. Too many men wandering about looking for their unit..."

At *Adlerhorst,* Hitler was packing. It was obvious that *Wacht Am Rhein* had failed. The Russian winter offensive had now opened, threatening to quickly engulf all of Eastern Germany in a fortnight. Reacting to pleas from Gen. Heinz Guderian on the Eastern Front, the German leader prepared to move back to Berlin to run the last stages of a war lost. At 7:15 PM, on Monday January 15th, Hitler boarded his special train bound for the German capital. On the way out an SS colonel remarked that "Berlin will be most practical as our headquarters. We'll soon be able to take the streetcar from the eastern to the western front!" Hitler heard the remark and glumly smiled along with the rest in his entourage. In his cabin, the curtains were carefully drawn. Before long, night mercifully came, hiding the scarred ruins of the countryside through which the train glided. The next morning he and his associates arrived at Grunewald Station in Berlin. As they made their way to the Reichschancellery, the snowdrifts mercifully hid much of the damage. But inside, the building showed its devastation. Snow filled craters pocked the once-tidy gardens. The building itself was nearly razed, save for the underground concrete bunker where he would now carry on the war. A war-torn chaos, the scene reflected the condition of the Third Reich at the curtain call of 1945.

The war went on over the January sky of Europe. The following day, the 365th Fighter Group continued its battle for control of airspace over the Saar. In the vicinity of Worms, its P-47s ran into two dozen Fw-190s and Me-109s at 3:25. 2nd. Lt. Earl D. Schank shot down one of these in cat-and-mouse chase through the clouds that ended down to the deck with the German pilot crashing into high-tension wires. 1st Lt. Robert L. Dickinson shot down another in a wild dogfight in which his wingman, Lt. James W. Burnett, Jr. was brought down. Burnett managed to bail out, although becoming a prisoner of war when he reached the ground. There were other "Hell Hawks" victories: Capt. Robert M. Fry shot down three German planes that day to become an ace and Lts. Fredrich W. Marling and Donald E. Kraman each bagged an enemy fighter. 2nd Lt. Henry Dahlen also took down an Fw-190 in spite of being severely shot-up himself. Lt. James F. Hensley scored two victories, but was himself shot down in a lone engagement with three Me-109s. Hensley bailed out to become a POW. In all, the 365th claimed 13 enemy planes shot down that day for the loss of two pilots. Returning that night to Metz, the pilots received their belated Christmas dinner, it having been delayed in the chaos surrounding the move from Chievres to Metz and then the New Year's strike on their airfield. Pilots the next day joked that they were so "stuffed with turkey" that they could hardly climb onto their wings.

On the same day, January 16, the 367th Fighter Group hit rail targets at Limburg. They caught and decimated two fully loaded troop trains near that town. Four days later the same fighter group sealed the portals of a railway tunnel although losing one of its most promising new pilots, Lt. Walter E. Bingham. Bob Dillion broke out of the clouds right behind him:

> "The first thing I saw as I came through the clouds was a German 40-mm or larger gun that stood out clearly against the snow. Its crew was shooting like hell and had just set Bingham on fire. I saw him go down. There was no chute: it all happened too quickly. I remember thinking that the crew had a lot of guts to stay there with all those airplanes in the sky..."

The German guns were deadly to British Commonwealth pilots as well. On January 16th an entire section of four planes from 412 Squadron were lost during an armed reconnaissance. The last heard of the flight was from a pilot who reported over the radio that he had been hit by German flak and was crash-landing. Other tragedy awaited the RAF Tempest pilots. While on a fighter sweep in the Oldenburg area, 56 Squadron observed a looming dogfight between a group of German Fw-190s and a group of P-51 fighters. The Tempests joined in to dispense with the enemy. They shot down one, but then had a Tempest hit by flak which was then destroyed by fire from an American P-51 in another case of mistaken identity.

On January 16th, Lt. John Tillet of the 10th PRG sighted an enemy convoy between Prüm and St. Vith. Word was passed on to a group of P-47s who finished off the job. But the more important mission for Patton's "eyes" was the state of the bridges over the Our River. The aerial reconnaissance of Lt. Howard Nichols provided the necessary information. It was obvious from this that the Germans were pulling out of the salient.

Under orders, the Germans made a determined attempt to intervene in the air battle on the 16th to assist the withdrawal of their armies. Their efforts, estimated at 175 sorties, cost some 14 fighters destroyed over the battle zone while only claiming five of the U.S. Ninth Air Force. The German attempt certainly backfired in regard to the 365th Fighter Group. The "Hell Hawks'" 388th Squadron was attacked by some 20 German Me-109s while on a patrol in the Worms area. Ten German fighters were shot down in the engagement at no loss to the 365th.

On the ground, important events transpired. Having attacked from the north for the last two weeks, the U.S. First Army was able to link up with Patton's forces advancing north. The historic occasion took place near the bombed-out ruins of Houffalize. Unfortunately, the bird in the bush had escaped. As at Falaise, the Germans had skillfully evaded the American pincers, and the coming together of the two armies was little more than a victory celebration. However, the event had special importance to Gen. Omar Bradley. Officially at midnight on January 17th, the First Army was returned to his command, ending the bitter dispute with Montgomery over its control. Simultaneously with the change on the ground, the IX TAC reverted to Gen. Vandenberg's command.

But Patton had his eyes focused on more than honor. Again, it was the deteriorating weather which remained such a problem for the anxious Third Army commander. He was worried that his quarry would escape altogether from the Ardennes. Critical to his plan to nail the Germans before they reached safe haven in Germany, was to capture or knock out the bridges over the Our River. But the weather was on the enemy side from January 17th to 21st. Patton's worst fears were being realized; the Germans fled the Ardennes en masse.

While the Allies schemed, the Luftwaffe feverishly transferred its fighters to the crumbling East. After the disasters of *Operation Bodenplatte*, Hitler rightfully believed that the fighters could no longer protect Germany from the heavy bombers. *JG 6* was pulled out first beginning on January 2nd. But the true straits of the Germans in Russia was illustrated by the hurried eastern shift of *JG 1* and *SG 4* on January 14th while the German army in the Ardennes suffered under a fantastic air bombardment. *JG 77* was also ordered off on January 17th and four days later *JG 3* and *JG 4* were ordered to leave on 90 minutes notice. When *JG 11* flew the same direction on January 23rd, half of the fighters in the West were gone. In particular, ULTRA attached great importance to the news that Dietrich Peltz was no longer in command of *II Jagdkorps*, the reins being turned over to Genmaj. Karl-Eduard Wilke. On January 27th, ULTRA estimated the following dispositions of serviceable aircraft in the Luftwaffe:

	Single Engine Fighters	Ground Attack Aircraft
Western Front	600	50
Eastern Front	850-900	450-500
Norway	90	nil
Defense of Germany	500	nil
Non-operational	360	170
Total:	2400-2450	670-720

The Luftwaffe threat in the West seemed over. Still, the American air commanders had other worries. Both Nugent and Quesada met that day to discuss the urgent problem with the replacement of P-47s. Neither TAC had enough of them. "Was today informed by A-4 that the supply of P-47s would probably be stopped for three months...If the report is correct, we will soon be cannibalizing groups and squadrons. Some action is essential."

At Florennes, Belgium, Lt. John C. Calhoun wrote home:

January 20th

"Dear Mother
I have seen what war has done to the women and children of Belgium, I know I fight that this may never happen to my mother and my little brother in America. At least the real sufferings of war have not reached our soil as yet, hard as it is for you civilians over there. I know you are lonely with your two oldest sons off in the services...But, at least you are not cold and hungry...Still slogging in mud, with the fog and snow, flying is like sailing in a bowl of soup. Some flying has to be done regardless, but for the most part we try to at least wait for good visibility. The Russian offensive has us hanging on the radio these days. Can it be possible that this offensive will settle things in the European area?...It's hard to be optimistic...Meantime, we are trying to make the Germans take a dim view of flying anywhere near us and doing a pretty darn good job of it.
—Your loving son   Jack"

Jack Calhoun would be shot down three weeks later over enemy territory. He was able to parachute from his stricken P-38 fighter-bomber and became a German POW. After the war, Calhoun received the Air Medal with five Oak Leaf Clusters. But until its end in May, his family would not know if he was alive or dead.

XXIII

Slaughter at Dasburg: January 22nd

Brig. Gen. Samuel E. Anderson was the commanding general of Vandenberg's IX Bomb Division. At 38, Anderson found himself in charge of a growing fleet of Marauders and Havocs which were absorbed into the Ninth Air Force to become the nucleus of the U.S. medium bomber offensive. Anderson was long on air experience, having earned his wings in 1929, going on to provide instruction at Kelly Field and later to Hawaii where he became an operations officer with the 5th Wing at Hickam Field. With the outbreak of war, Anderson was moved to the Headquarters of the Army Air Force and then later to the War Department General Staff. But in 1943 he got a field assignment when he was posted to the Ninth Air Force in England. Anderson relished his new command; a fact reflected in the enthusiasm of his medium bomber pilots.

Anderson knew the medium bombers as well as anyone; he had directed the medium bombardment attacks over Utah Beach on D-Day. The real challenge of the medium bombers in 1944 was choosing the most effective tactics for their use.

When first introduced, Anderson's B-26s were the brunt of jokes from the Flying Fortress pilots. The Glenn Martin aircraft had a very short wing span making the Marauder and the twin-engined bomber became the object of public scorn and even Congressional condemnation. Some took to calling them "Flying Prostitutes" since the scant wings showed "no visible means of support." for a twin-engined bomber; landing was tricky since the plane came in steep and landed fast. The favorite jab of the B-17 boys was this one:

"The Marauder is a beautiful piece of machinery— but it will never take the place of the airplane."

Although the proud B-26 flyers strongly resented such cracks, the plane did have a reputation of being difficult to fly, and the proper employment of the medium bomber was still a matter of conjecture.

Some had proposed that they strike from low altitude like big fighter-bombers to concentrate their meager bombing load squarely on the target. The first trial of this tactic over Ijmuiden, Holland ended up with the flight shot to pieces. Three days later the Marauders returned with ten planes to try the tactics again. Not one came back. Sam Anderson was not one to avoid an argument when he believed he was right. At the time, the commander of the Ninth Air Force was Lt. Gen. Lewis Brereton. Anderson was so upset about the formations Brereton was advocating for his mediums that he convened a meeting with Generals Weyland, Nugent and Quesada and the Ninth Air Force commander. Brereton wanted him to try other tactics that Anderson believed were flawed. "General," he explained, "I have tried those things and I know they don't work. I lost aircraft and crews." The argument ended in a Mexican stand-off. Anderson expected to find that he was fired. But instead, it was Brereton who was sent off; Hoyt Vandenberg took over the Ninth Air Force and Anderson was promoted to Major General. Anderson explained his views on tactics to Vandenberg. But to be sure of his ideas, Anderson flew a mission in the lead B-26, and then another in the tail plane to assess the new tactics. During the summer in France, the fortunes of Sam Anderson's B-26s flourished with the medium bombers opening the bomb bays from a medium altitude. Funny thing.

When the lighter A-20 "Havocs" were introduced, they were seen as too small for reasonable missions by some, and didn't have enough bomb carrying capacity or range. Their first missions were anything but successful. However, Anderson believed in the A-20, pointing out that the plane was much easier to fly and its smaller size might allow it to fly missions the B-26 could not. "The first thing I had to do, after I got those A-20s," Anderson remembered, "was train them. They were supposed to be trained in the States, but they couldn't navigate." One of the new commanders had missed the target on the first mission by 75 miles. Anderson replaced the commanders of the outfits with those with B-26 experience. He also set up a training center in Ireland and retrained the groups. By late 1944, these same under-achieving A-20 groups had become the most accurate medium bombers in Europe.

When the B-26 replacement, the nimble A-26 "Invader" became available, there was widespread talk about low level attack tactics for their pilots. The Invader was seen as a "big fighter bomber." At Anderson's request, Lt. Col. Leo C. Moon, the commanding officer of the 404th Fighter Group, had gone to the A-26 Group located at Bretigny to look into the matter. But before Moon arrived, the group had already been sent on a low-level mission at 1,500 feet. The entire formation had been riddled by flak. Col. Moon staged simulated dogfights with the A-26s and in some of the practice trials he had them fly on the deck and attempt to pinpoint targets called out from P-47s orbiting above. Based on these experiences, Moon ventured that the A-26 did have a low level speed exceeding the P-47s and also had equal climbing ability. However, steep dives and sharp pullouts exerted too much stress on the wings and visibility at low altitude was not nearly so great as a P-47. Col. Moon concluded that the A-26, while maneuverable, was not as nimble as a fighter and was very vulnerable to flak. Moreover, the ammunition load of the A-26 was comparatively small, so that the most effective use of the aircraft was as a medium bomber. That was that.

Anderson's attempts at improvement and innovation did not end with the A-20s. The most challenging target for the IX BD during the campaign were the constant requests to take out bridges. Rail or road bridges were maddeningly small targets for bombers dropping from altitude. But by carefully studying the statistical trail, Anderson discerned that a 12-plane box of bombers was a more efficient way of attempting to cut bridges than was the more conventional 18-plane box, since the third flight of six in the larger box rarely hit a target as small as a bridge. Better results were achieved by three 12-plane boxes hitting a bridge in waves than with two massive 18-plane formations.

The experience of the 386th Bomb Group under Anderson's command was typical of the low-rent conditions enjoyed by most American airmen that winter. The B-26 unit had moved to Beaumont-Sur-Oise (A-60) in October. The base was in terrible condition, having been on the receiving end of 386's own bombs before the "Crusaders" showed up. There were bomb craters all over, along with dummy canvas building the Germans had erected to make the airstrip look like a farming village. Unfortunately, the fake buildings were useless as accommodations. Instead of the snug huts they had enjoyed in Great Dunmow, England, Beaumont featured field erected tents with dirt floors. That the tents were drafty was good, since hygiene consisted of a sponge bath from a steel helmet; many wore the same clothes for weeks. Big rats were everywhere, some made off with shoes. The food was terrible, "whatever was being served was dumped into our mess kits along with bread and the ever-present fruit cocktail." Beds were folding cots and at first there was no electricity and certainly no hot water. Once winter came on, any heat at all was precious. Coal supplies were slim and the winter was the worst in Western Europe in 30 years. Trees around the tents disappeared as the thermometer dropped. Dick Denison was there:

> I remember the rain and mud and later the snow and cold...I will never forget sitting at makeshift tables on rickety benches eating a meal, wearing my trench

coat, with rain leaking down the back of my neck and into my mess kit...There was nothing like early morning rising at Beaumont. The snow was about a foot deep, there was no heat in the tent, the electricity usually wasn't working, dress in the dark and slog through the snow to the open 'John' where the nice layer of frost has to be removed before you can sit, then trudge through the snow to the jeep or weapons carrier, rake the snow off the seat before getting in and driving to the briefing. Great fun!...Weather terrible and the troops catching hell— we can't do anything to help. Christmas Day 1944, briefed for a mission, but repeated delays until just about the time we got our turkey dinner in our mess kits, we got the word to go. What a surprise to get flak at St. Vith, our fighter rendezvous, which was supposed to be in our hands. After the mission, back to the tent to face cold, congealed Christmas dinner. Digging a foxhole behind the tent when air raids were expected during the Bulge. I remember only one raid scare and we decided it was better to be hit in a warm tent than in a cold foxhole...

For the first week of the German offensive, the medium bombers of the 386th Bomb Group were grounded, but on December 23rd the weather cleared and the bomb group went out twice. During the next four days of good flying weather the group flew seven missions, mostly against railroad bridges as part of Gen. Anderson's interdiction plan. The 386th attacked ground targets at Blumenthal, Euskirchen and Nideggen, but it was the bridges that most veterans remembered. German rail bridges with strange names made an indelible impression on the crews, not only due to the drama of crossing over the bomb line into Germany, but the incessant briefing on each. Few 386th veterans can forget the German span at Konz-Karthaus. The bridge was attacked twice, but was briefed at least 15 times. There were others: Ahrweiler, Keuchengen, Bullay, Neuwied and Sinzig, the last being the roughest of all.

On Monday, January 22nd, the weather cleared, and Anderson's mediums expected to be back in business. Similar to the massive air operations on Christmas Eve, all of the Allied air forces operated in great strength. But it was the fighter-bombers who would achieve glory on January 22nd. The turkey shoot began in the early morning when Capt. Wilfred B. Crutchfield of the 362nd Fighter Group chanced upon an amazing "parking lot" of 1,500 German vehicles near Prüm. Crutchfield had sighted a portion of the SS *Sixth Panzer Armee* in the process of transferring to the Russian front to stem the tide there. He called his controller and told them to send all available groups. Further south, another massacre began when Lt. Howard Nichols of the 10th PRG sighted at least 400 German vehicles bunched up behind the Our River, waiting to get across the bridge at Dasburg. He too, called for a massive air strike.

Meanwhile, Anderson's IX Bombardment Division flung itself at German lines of communications. In all some 304 medium bombers of the command set out for six targets including the railhead for the *Sixth Panzer Armee* at Blankenheim and the marshalling yard at Gerolstein. Two of the bomb groups, the 387th and 394th, were essayed to hit the stuff Nichols had seen at Dasburg. Just after noon the 27 planes of the 387th arrived over the flak peppered skies over the Our River bridge and dropped 54 tons of bombs on the German traffic. Minutes later 1st Lt. K.F. Schmidt led the 394th, the "Bridge Busters" to the target. The Marauders loosed 42 tons of bombs from 12,000 feet landing squarely on the span rendering it useless. Shortly thereafter a liaison pilot flying an artillery adjustment mission radioed of the German traffic jams gathering at the bridge. Artillery fire was immediately brought to bear and word flashed to Weyland's XIX TAC that the Germans were sitting ducks. Soon, wave after wave of P-47 fighter-bombers showed up, blasting the road-bound Germans, destroying several hundred trucks, tanks and prime movers.

To the north, Quesada's IX TAC and other fighter bombers from Weyland's command pounded the enemy in the Prüm area. The weather was not so good in the vicinity of the hilly Schnee Eifel, however, and the A-26 Invaders of the 416th Bomb Group had to be called back. It was up to the fighter bombers with their ability to strike low. When the day was done, the 368th FG led in claims with 422 motor transport at Dasburg. The 362nd, who had discovered the prize at Prüm, claimed 312 motor vehicles and 11 tanks, another six armored vehicles, more than a dozen horse-drawn wagons and 44 gun positions.[123] Also, in the action at Prüm was the indefatigable 406th FG with claims of 119 trucks and 20 horse-drawn vehicles; its sister 405th added 179 blasted trucks to the score. The 367th Fighter Group operated in both areas and estimated 98 more enemy vehicles smashed by its actions. For all this, the XIX fighter bombers had only seven losses. At the same time, the 365th FG put up seven in the Saar area flying close support for the 94th and 95th Infantry Divisions. The day was only marred by a "comedy of errors" series of crashes at Metz. But beyond such mundane concerns, Weyland was obviously pleased with his command on the 22nd. His 550 sorties claimed 1,162 motor transport, 30 armored vehicles, 49 horse drawn wagons and 49 enemy gun positions wiped out.

The IX TAC totals for the day were also outstanding. Although only three of its five groups were aloft, Quesada's 350 sorties tallied the destruction of 409 enemy trucks, 28 armored vehicles, 8 horse-drawn vehicles and 13 gun positions. The 366th FG claimed 284 motor transport in the Prüm area and 16 armored vehicles, with the 404th FG hitting the enemy near Blankenheim area in the morning and the Prüm and Dasburg

---

123 Such close support operations were not without cost. The 362nd FG lost four pilots that day, all from the 379th Squadron. Lt. Chester B. Kusi was hit by flak and had to bail out over enemy territory. Three others were also hit by enemy guns, but were less fortunate: Capt. Carroll A. Peterson, Lt. John K. McMahon and 2nd Lt. Louis A. Bauer fell with their P-47s.

areas in the afternoon. Total losses to Quesada's command were six fighter-bombers.

Lt. William H. Lemley of the 394th Squadron knew nothing of all this as he prepared his P-38s for a mission that was to be a patrol of the area around Trier. Soon after take off Lem's ground controller changed their mission, vectoring them near Bitburg where they were to hit a congregation of German vehicles. The controllers were right, the pilots of the group stared in disbelief at the mass of enemy vehicles, many wrecked or in flames, in the vicinity. Lemley took his fighter bombers in an assault on two convoys that looked relatively unscathed. Soon some 60 enemy transports were smashed. However, as Lemley participated in the strafing run near Bollendorf, he received a hit from the intense local flak. As he pulled up to get away from the danger his Lightning burst into flames. Those with him, clearly heard their leader: "Boys, this is Lem. I've been hit, and there's smoke in the cockpit." Then a few second later, "Fellows, you're about to lose a good pilot...I'm bailing out. So long gang." Lemley was not heard from again. He was listed as missing until ground troops discovered his grave in Luxembourg some two months later. Lemley was not the only tragedy of that day; for all the destruction meted out to the Germans, the XIX TAC lost seven fighters in the conflagration.

Gen. Nugent's XXIX TAC to the north was also busy, blasting enemy rail traffic in the Düren area with some 163 sorties. Between them, the 36th and 373rd FG claimed 15 locomotives and 628 rail cars and four German planes on the ground, at a cost of two aircraft and twelve others damaged. Also, to the north, 168 Squadron of the 2nd TAF had two successful days, flying cover for the bomber units of 143 Wing. While on strafing missions to hit enemy locomotives and trucks in the Dorsten-Dulmen area, Flt. Lt. E.H.C. Vernon-Jarvis shot down an Me-109; a Ju-188 was blasted while on a landing approach near Twente. 421 Squadron flew an armed recce that morning over Münster and Rheine, their paths crossing with a score of German fighters. Five of these were shot down at a cost of one Spitfire. 411 Squadron claimed a further enemy fighter over Lingen. But the big news for the British was the action against the German jets by 401 Squadron at 10 AM. Observing Me-262s taking off from an air strip, the Spitfires bounced the jets before they could attain altitude. Three of the speedy aircraft were destroyed, likely including the Me-262A-2 of Oblt. Hans Holzwarth. This pilot of I/KG 51 was reported shot down near Hopsten that day. Just before noon, the squadron returned to the same vicinity looking for more action. Flt. Lt. Audet shot down a further Me-262 and destroyed another two on the ground although a Spitfire pilot was claimed by a group of Me-109s flying cover.

But the senior air commanders wanted more than claims on the enemy;

they wanted direct evidence of the damage they had inflicted along the Dasburg road. A "dicing" run was scheduled for the 31st Squadron of the 10th PRG. The idea of a "dicing run" was that an unarmed F-5 Lightning loaded with cameras looking down and from side to side would fly right over the target of interest while snapping hundreds of photographs. As always, the dicing missions were close to suicidal— they had to be made right down the throat of the enemy. Worse still, the P-47s that had put the kill on the Germans in Dasburg had reported intense flak during their attacks— several had already been shot down. Lt. Thair W. Best volunteered for the mission. He took off at 3:28 PM on the 22nd, circling the target once to get his bearings before running the photographic gauntlet. As he opened the throttle and dropped altitude, Best became aware of the enemy guns; there were at least 90 88mm flak guns protecting the bridge site. His F-5 was less than halfway through the run, when he took numerous hits from the enemy flak. His plane burst into flame and crashed. Best was presumed dead.[124] Later in the day Lt. Ray Krone was able to photograph the wreckage from 16,000 feet and confirm the blow dealt to the enemy. He and Lt. Clyde East also sighted more German vehicles— nearly 2,000 near the Gemünd bridge northwest of Vianden. They led a group of P-47s to the fruitful hunting grounds with East destroying four trucks of his own and watching the P-47s clobber 50 others before he departed.

By dusk, the slaughter in the Dasburg area had reached Normandy proportions. "Germans trying to evacuate the Bulge," Weyland jotted with relish in his diary on the 22nd, "worse than the Falaise pocket. Biggest day in TAC history of destructions..." Together his fighter groups (354th, 362nd, 365th and 368th) claimed 317 motor transports, six tanks, three armored vehicles and twelve gun positions destroyed. Gen. Hoyt Vandenberg relayed a special message to his airmen that he received from Carl Spaatz:

> "Operations of the Ninth Air Force today were most outstanding. Their effect on the enemy must have been terrific. My heartiest congratulations to all concerned."

Attempting to escape the Ardennes, the *Seventh* and *Fifth Panzer Armees* had piled up bumper-to-bumper in great traffic jams that were pinned against the Our River. The American fighter bombers were seemingly everywhere; not a single Luftwaffe plane was in evidence. The headquarters of the *LIII Armeekorps* took a direct hit, wounding almost everyone in the staff. And each time the *Jabos* swooped in for the kill, the rabble of foot soldiers, trucks, tanks and horse-drawn wagons went scurrying for cover.

---

124 Lt. Best was not killed. Amazingly, he rode down his crippled plane, survived the crash, and was captured by the Germans. The 31st Squadron did not learn he was alive until VE Day.

Slaughter at Dasburg: January 22nd

Gen. Bayerlein's *Panzer Lehr Division* had been desperately fighting to hold open an escape route across the Our River at the Gemünd bridgehead. Lack of gasoline was so pernicious at the time that he had been forced to leave behind 53 tanks in perfectly good operating condition. His men trudged through the knee deep snow to fight a series of bitter battles around Hoscheid. On the 22nd Bayerlein observed two huge formations of twin- and single-engined planes diving down to make attacks just to his north. The target, he later learned, was the bridge at Dasburg. The following day he drove a Volkswagen north to his CP at Eisenbach. He had to cross the one-way bridge at Gemünd to reach his post. The roads were stacked up with traffic all the way to Hosingen. At first light the bombs dropped on the traffic in a fury. Later when Bayerlein made his way back he had to pick his way carefully through the wreckage of vehicles, many still burning. He described an awful scene with dead horses, charred equipment and hundreds of smoldering hulks littering the road sides. The next day Bayerlein men were forced out of Hoscheid in desperate street fighting. His once proud *Panzer Lehr* pulled back across the Westwall at the German border with 18 tanks and 400 exhausted grenadiers. He reckoned on having lost 80% of his command.

In spite of the weather, on January 23rd the Air forces worked to keep up the pressure on the enemy at the Our bridging sites. The British 2nd TAF assisted the Ninth Air Force, claiming a total of 33 victories in numerous combats that day. The U.S. fighter-bombers put in a total of 750 sorties. The XIX TAC could only get four of its groups operating in the morning. In its 183 sorties, Weyland's 362nd, 368th and 354th FGs claimed another 317 enemy motor transport vehicles destroyed, most of them again in the Dasburg area. No American aircraft were lost. The IX TAC managed 408 total sorties with claims of 661 trucks and twenty enemy armored vehicles. The 48th, 370th and 404th FGs operated again in the lucrative Blankenheim area while the 366th and 474th FGs patrolled the enemy area to the south between Prüm and Dasburg. In the afternoon the 474th had very good hunting in the Gemünd-Hallschlag area shooting up some 75 German vehicles observed parked along the wooded roads near Stadtkyll. Five of Quesada's aircraft were lost.

Trying to find its way around the fiendish weather and get its share of the kills, Anderson's Ninth Bomb Division dredged up an old idea. With their faster speed and greater firepower, could they use their light and medium bombers like bigger P-47s? To find out, the IX BD dispatched its new medium A-26s in their first low-level mission since the disastrous raid on Ijmuiden on May 17, 1943 in which the 322nd Bomb Group lost all of its B-26 Marauders. It was unfortunate for Anderson that the commanders wanted to try this tactic again: the experience of the 416th Bomb Group attacking Dasburg on January 23rd was nearly catastrophic. The enemy flak was deadly; the lead bomber had its left engine blown away and it and another Invader were severely damaged. Somehow two of their crippled planes managed to crash land in friendly territory. None of the other five planes were successful in their mission and nearly all were hit by gunfire.

Later that afternoon six more A-26s from the 671st Squadron followed this failed attempt with similar results. Of the twelve aircraft sent out, only three had attacked ground targets. Most were damaged that made it to the enemy zone.

Of the six A-26s launched by the 409th BG, only one was able to hit the enemy. The six A-20s of the 410th BG had little more luck than the other two. Gen. Anderson, on hearing of the carnage of his medium bombers, would never again agree to such an inappropriate use of this command. The attempt by medium bombers at a low-level bombing and strafing at Dasburg had been disastrous, but the damage to the Germans had already been wrought the preceding day.

The weather on January 24th was closing fast. The Ninth Air Force managed to further damage what transport the Germans had left with a an additional 312 fighter-bomber sorties. Total claims for the 24th amounted to 359 enemy vehicles, 30 tanks or assault guns and numerous gun positions and horse-drawn vehicles. On the 25th the final blows were leveled at the enemy. A total of 581 fighter-bomber sorties struck the hapless Germans, with more activity in Nugent's sector which contributed 118 of the missions. Over the Eifel, the IX and XIX TACs shared in the destruction of 623 German vehicles, as well as some 40 armored vehicles. The IX TAC lost two fighters; the XIX lost one, although many others were damaged from enemy flak.

As always, even allowing for an exaggeration of claims versus actual destruction, the Allied punishment meted out to the Germans over the preceding four days had been tremendous. Beginning with the destruction of the Dasburg bridge on January 22nd, the three Tactical Air Commands had claimed staggering totals: 6,618 motor transport, 159 tanks, 237 other armored vehicles, 188 gun positions, 47 locomotives and 1,157 rail cars. Considering that the tables of organization for a German panzer division in 1944 had 2,700 motor vehicles for its organic transportation, most of the remaining armor in the Ardennes had lost the majority of whatever vehicles they still possessed in the great debacle from the 22nd - 25th. "For the first time," said Gen. Erich Brandenberger, the commander of the German *Seventh Armee*, "the situation in the air was similar to that which prevailed in Normandy."

But now, once more, the protective cloak of mist and overcast descended over the German Eifel. The airfields on both sides were socked in and inoperable. During the remainder of the month, air operations were impossible. For fledgling Luftwaffe pilots this was indeed fortunate. In the last 15 days of January the *Jagdflieger* had lost an additional 125 aircrew with much of the bloodletting moving with the *Geschwadern* to the East. The attrition rate in the four wings left to defend the unprotectable Reich soared to almost 30% of the sorties flown. The average new replacement pilot with *I Jagdkorps*— now redesignated *IX Fliegerkorps*— could scarcely expect to survive more than three missions! Against these losses, the Allies were daily plunking down four to six million pounds of bombs on Germany. Losses of Allied aircraft did not even amount to 0.2% of the sorties flown!

Allied air claims on the ground during Hitler's last great offensive from December 16th through the end of January reads like an epitaph to German failure: 11,378 motor transport, 1,161 tanks and armored vehicles, 507 locomotives, 6,266 rail cars, 472 gun positions, 974 rail cuts, 421 road cuts and 36 bridges. All across the Ardennes, burned out hulks of trucks, guns and tanks littered the roads, mute evidence of the impact of Allied air power. Hitler's final great offensive reserve was smashed. Attacking under a veil of bad weather, his armies had first been bled by the tough resistance of the American infantryman. Later, once the winter skies cleared, the merciless Allied air punishment doomed the enemy offensive to failure to failure. The Germans in the Ardennes were finished; the Luftwaffe had lost the battle for the winter sky.

Far away, along the frozen battlefields in Russia, the Soviets at last unleashed their dreaded winter offensive. It began on January 12th; by January 25th, the ULTRA seers strained to hear the enemy SS panzer divisions being ordered out of the Ardennes and to Russia. Almost simultaneously, *II Jagdkorps* was overheard grimly moving some of its fighter *Gruppen* to the debacle developing in the East. ULTRA dutifully reported as Göring was overheard dismissing the General of the Fighters:

> Order of the Day to the Fighters:
> After several years activity as AO of the fighters, Genlt. Galland is relieved of his appointment to be employed by the High Command after his health is restored. I express my sincere thanks and my particular appreciation...We stand in the hardest and most decisive hours of this war. In many places the *Volkssturm* has been called up for national defense. The last German is reaching for his weapons. The German fighters will not lag behind these men, but, inspired with sacred ardor and conscious of fighting for a just cause, will give its all.
> —Göring, *Reichsmarschall* of the Greater German Reich

It was finally official; Galland was gone, his place taken by Obst. Gordon Gollob.[125] But all of Göring's histrionics, calling for an even greater Luftwaffe effort fell on deaf ears. Bled white by their vain efforts to support Hitler's Ardennes Offensive, devastated by their tremendous losses in *Operation Bodenplatte* and the January battles, the Luftwaffe was *kaput*. Adolf Galland himself put it best after the war: "We sacrificed our last substance."

---

125 Obstlt. Walther Dahl, the hard-pressed commander of *JG 300*, replaced Galland's other responsibilities as *Inspekteur der Tagdjagd*.

Cost of the interdiction campaign. This B-17 crash landed in the Ardennes near Remagne, west of Bastogne. The photograph was taken on January 13, 1945. *(NA)*

Crew of a Douglas A-20 Havoc of the 410th Bomb Group heads for the debriefing room. *(NASM)*

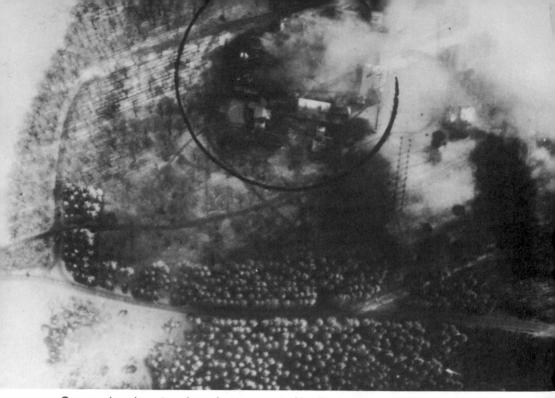

German headquarters in a chateau west of La Roche burns after being attacked on January 1, 1945. *(HRC)*

B-17s of the 92nd Bomb Group prepare to take to the air under less than favorable conditions. January 10, 1945. *(NASM)*

Havocs. Douglas A-20s of the 410th Bomb Group take off for another mission in spite of the Arctic conditions. January 11, 1945. *(NASM)*

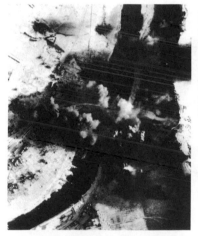

Hits crash all around the double-deck bridge at Bullay from a B-26 medium bomber attack by the 386th and 391st BGs on Sunday, January 16th. The bridge was important to interdict since it was a major traffic artery from Koblenz over the Moselle River to Trier. However, in spite of an imposing bomb tonnage, the span remained standing. *(NASM)*

The Bullay bridge, withstanding an on-slaught of attacks from medium bonbers, was finally brought down by a flight of four Republic P-47 fighter-bombers of the 368th Fighter Group on February 10, 1945. *(NASM)*

489

Zooming through a box of B-26 medium bombers at high speed, this Fw-190 narrowly misses the cascade of bombs dropping from a Marauder above. *(HRC)*

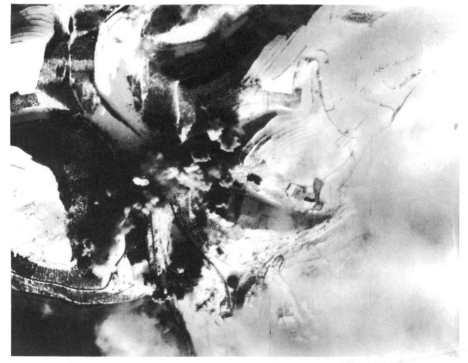

The 134 foot highway bridge over the Our River at Dasburg is shown under attack by the B-26 Marauders of the 387th and 394th Bomb Groups. Interdiction of the bridge trapped a massive log jam of German vehicles and armor attempting to escape the Ardennes back into Germany. *(NASM)*

ABOVE: Ninth Air Force fighter pilots of the 370th Fighter Group, 402nd Squadron, head for their P-38s and another mission at Florennes: Lt. W.E. Bates, Lt. W.D. Morgan and Lt. W. H. Bowers. *(NASM)*

RIGHT: Brig. Gen Samuel E. Anderson. Commander of IX Bomb Division, Ninth Air Force. *(HRC)*

Joys of mud. T/Sgt. Willie Beal-
mear shovels the stuff in front of
his tent accommodations at
Florennes, Belgium. *(HRC)*

Martin B-26. Ground crews remove snow and frost from this Marauder of the
323rd Bomb Group, 454th Squadron, Laon-Athies, France. Experience in Normandy had shown the medium bomber was ideal for attacking bridges. *(NASM)*

Slaughter at Dasburg: January 22nd

After the battle. Wrecks of German transport litter the road from Marnach to Dasburg. On January 22nd, the XIX TAC alone claimed some 1,179 enemy motor transport and 36 armored vehicles destroyed. *(NASM)*

In kinder days, Adolf Hitler awards Adolf Galland his third set of diamonds to the Ritterkreuz at Wolfsschanze in the company of other highly decorated wing commanders in 1942. To Galland's left is Obst. Dietrich Peltz, Obstlt. Günther Lützow, Maj. Karl-Eduard Wilke and Maj. Walter Oesau. *(NA)*

Reichsmarschall Hermann Göring in Allied captivity. Mondorf, Luxembourg, 1945. *(HRC)*

BELOW: How it all ended. A support crew member for a Northrop P-61 Black Widow, T/Sgt. Albert Wiederspiel of the Ninth Air Force's 422nd Night Fighter Squadron ("TheGreen Bats") takes a bit of well-earned relaxation in the May sunshine of victory, 1945. *(NASM)*

XXIV

Mutiny of the Aces

On the afternoon of Monday, January 22nd, 1945, while the Allied air forces were flattening the retreating German army in the Ardennes around Dasburg, a meeting convened at the Luftwaffe headquarters, the "*Haus der Flieger*," in Berlin. This gathering would henceforth become known as the "Mutiny of the Aces." The precipitating event was the dismissal of Galland. Under Gen. Dietrich Peltz, the Ardennes operations and *Operation 'Bodenplatte'* had proved major Luftwaffe fiascos. Rather than crippling the Allied bomber force as Galland had desired, these missions had operationally destroyed the last strength of the German air force; nearly 700 Luftwaffe pilots had been lost in these operations. Distinguished German airmen including Hermann Graf (202 kills), Günther Lützow (103), Gustav Rödel (98), Johannes "Macki" Steinhoff (149) and Hannes Trautloft (58) gathered to let their grievances be known. At the tense meeting, Obst. Lützow, the spokesman for the group, handed a memo to Göring and Gen. Koller. In part, it read:

1) The dismissal of General Galland was incomprehensible to the men of the fighter units. He was recognized by the fighter arm as its outstanding personality and leader despite the demands he made on those under him.

2) The frequent accusations of cowardice directed at the fighter men by the *Reichsmarschall*, and this despite the fact that their losses were probably higher than any arm of the Luftwaffe or Wehrmacht.

3) Although he is held in personal and professional respect, General Peltz can never gain the confidence of the fighter arm because: a) He held IX *Bomber Corps* back from operations (in the Ardennes) by imposing exaggerated training requirements, while at the same time committing the ill-trained day fighter pilots to battle with no thought of the consequences. b) He is not a fighter man. c) He was responsible both for the operation of January 1st, 1945 and for the losses that followed the

launching of the Ardennes Offensive which cost the Luftwaffe: 2 *Jag-dgeschwader* commanders, 14 *Gruppe* commanders and 64 *Staffel* commanders.

In the view of the fighter arm, these losses were basically attributable to command errors.

As Göring read, his chubby jowls reddened. He stared at his denouncers in rage. "I've never heard anything like it!" he charged, "Are you trying to accuse me of not having built a strong Luftwaffe?" Lützow said no; he agreed that the German air force had been plenty strong for the initial victories in Poland and France, "But since then, *Reichsmarschall*, you have been asleep!" Lützow was risking his life with this dangerous pronouncement. "What is this you are saying?" Göring roared, "This is a fine council of war! A ring of mutineers! I'll have the lot of you shot!" On this, Göring, red in the face, stormed out of the room.

None of them were shot. Lützow was exiled to a moribund fighter command in Italy. Trautloft was banished from an effective position. Galland, of course, had lost his post with the Luftwaffe, and although he and Steinhoff would fight in the closing months with an elite German jet fighter unit, *Jagdverbande 44*, neither man would lead again. Although the "mutiny of the aces" may have laid the group's collective consciences to rest, it did little to still the continuing slaughter of Luftwaffe pilots. Tragically, the sacrifice of men and flying machines would go on unabated until the end of the Reich in May.

The Sunday of the following week was January 30th, the twelfth anniversary of National Socialism's Third Reich. Adolf Hitler took to the airwaves over Germany once more to proclaim his defiance in the midst of total calamity. "What ever the crisis may be at the moment," he confided, "in the end it will be mastered by our unalterable will, by our readiness for sacrifice, and by our abilities. We will overcome this emergency also." It was another charismatic delivery by Adolf Hitler. Even amid total ruin, he remained beloved by many. Increasingly desperate and escapist talk always moved on to the usual bromide: the "secret weapons."

But the perception among his closest followers was splintering. Albert Speer, Hitler's architect, confidant and trusted manager of armaments and industry approached his beloved Führer with grave news. Delayed by the stubborn Allied defense on the ground and smashed from the air, Hitler's desperate counteroffensives in the Ardennes and Alsace had utterly failed. The Russians were inexorably advancing in the East and the Allied airpower had returned to its pounding of the remaining industry of the Third Reich. Within Germany all the utilities, telephone, gas, water and rail systems were out of operation and in total chaos. The British bomber command had now embarked on a frightful campaign to destroy the few German cities left standing, if for no other perverse reason than "that bombing anything in Germany is better than bombing nothing." The horror of Dresden loomed just ahead. But even now, the Allied bombing of German communications and industry was strangling coal output; now barely enough steel could be produced to only keep up with needs for munitions, much less future production for tanks, planes and other weapons. Along with the catastrophic destruction of oil production, these developments meant there was no way to continue. The game was up. Mustering all of his courage, Speer penned a concluding memorandum for his tenure. "The war," his parting statement concluded, "can no longer be pursued militarily."

Epilogue

On April 20th, 1945, Adolf Hitler emerged from his bunker for the final time. It was his birthday. With the German leader was Hermann Göring, his long-time friend, and leader of the Luftwaffe. The Führer made a solemn tour of the bombed out Reichschancellery above. Once intended as the starting point for the reconstruction of Berlin into a showcase of the Third Reich, the building was now a shattered ruin with fragments of concrete and marble strewn about. Most of the windows in the great building were shattered— it was a sad sight. Hitler was slowly escorted out to the garden with a heavy overcoat drawn about his frail-looking figure. The garden was scarred by shell craters; at mid-day the British and American air forces had executed their final massive air raids on the center of Berlin. Around the Reichschancellery stood ruins and great mounds of rubble. A group of very young Hitler Youth had been hurriedly assembled for the German leader to meet. Hitler smiled tiredly as he moved down the line shaking young hands and doling out medals. His colleagues and generals from the Führer bunker stepped forward perfunctorily to give him their best wishes on his birthday. "No one knew quite what to say," Albert Speer recalled. The booming of artillery filled the air like a nearing thunderstorm. The city streets were wrecked and smoking and the none-too-distant sounds of gunfire punctuated their speech. All of them knew that the Russians were at this moment encircling Berlin.

Soon the entourage moved back down into the musty confines of the bunker for Hitler's daily war conference. The usual situation map was present, with ugly red lines drawing a noose around the German capital. Hermann Göring seemed unusually pensive. Instead of his typical air force blue attire, the *Reichsmarschall* was wearing an olive green uniform. He almost looked American in appearance. Gone were the gaudy epaulets and medals. As the conversation moved to the situation at hand, Hitler told those assembled that he could see it would be a street-to-street battle. Several generals nervously pointed out to the Führer that it would be necessary to move the headquarters away from the fighting to Obersalzberg before they were completely surrounded. Göring, quickly agreed, pointing out that there was now but one route open to the south through which they might escape to Berchtesgaden. The Russians were almost on top of them!

But Hitler would have none of it. "How can I call upon the troops to undertake my decisive battle for Berlin if at the same moment I withdraw myself to safety? I shall leave it to fate whether I die in the capital or fly to Obersalzberg at the last moment!" The generals were stunned. Their leader seemed bent on dragging all down with him to a final *Götterdämmerung*. Göring vaguely motioned to Hitler. In a somber voice, he told Hitler he had "urgent tasks waiting for him in South Germany" and that either he or Gen. Koller should depart, ostensibly to manage the Luftwaffe's resistance from a new post. "You go, then," Hitler said quietly, "I need Koller here." Hitler looked dazed. Göring mumbled a few words of gratitude. He shook his leader's hands. He said he would leave Berlin that night. Albert Speer, who was among those present, had the sense that he was witnessing a historic moment. "The leadership of the Reich was splitting asunder." Before Göring left, Koller approached the *Reichsmarschall* with the expected news that Hitler "...is staying and will shoot himself at the last moment."

Late that night, at 1 AM on April 21st, 1945, Hermann Göring made his way out of the smoking ruins of Berlin for the last time. He left Hitler in his dreary concrete bunker, fully aware that the German leader would soon be dead. If there was any sadness at this departure, Göring seemed unfazed. He would be next in line. At last Hermann Göring the self-proclaimed Renaissance man would be the head of the Third Reich. Anyway, the Russians were now fighting in the streets! It was time for the would-be successor to Adolf Hitler to get while the getting was good. He headed to the south. Any professed objective of continued leadership seemed ludicrous, there was nothing left of his vaunted Luftwaffe to command. The once proud German city was utterly destroyed. Mosquito night-fighters hung in the air like wasps. As Göring made his way through the rubble of the former glory of Hitler's Reich, the Allied planes swooped in to bomb and strafe. The paunchy German leader fled to the local air raid shelter among a gaggle of refugees. "Let me introduce myself," Göring said reaching the entrance to the shelter, "my name is Meier."[126]

---

126 After the war, at the International Military Tribunal at Nuremberg, Hermann Göring was tried and found guilty of crimes against humanity. Sentenced to death, on October 15, 1946 he cheated the hangman by taking his own life with a hidden cyanide capsule in his prison cell.

References

Thanks to the following publishers and authors for graciously allowing quotation from published works:

Ultra in the West: The Normandy Campaign, by Ralph F. Bennett, published by Charles Scribner's, New York, 1980.

Castles in the Air: The Story of the B-17 Flying Fortress Crews of the U.S. 8th Air Force by Martin W. Bowman, published by Patrick Stephens Ltd., Wellingborough.

JG 26: Top Guns of the Luftwaffe by Donald W. Caldwell, published by Orion Books, New York, 1991.

Somewhere the Sun is Shining by Jack and Beryl Calhoun, published by Grossmont Press, San Diego, CA, 1976.

Patton: Ordeal and Triumph by Ladislas Farago, published by Dell Publishing Co., NY, 1970.

The Battle of the Airfields by Norman L. Franks, published by William Kimber Ltd., London, 1982.

Experiences of War: The American Airman in Europe by Roger A. Freeman, published by Motorbooks International, Osceola, WI, 1991.

The Mighty Eighth: The History of the Units, Men and Machines of the US 8th Airforce by Roger A. Freeman, published by Motorbooks International, Osceola, WI, 1991.

The Mighty Eighth: War Diary by Roger A. Freeman, published by Motorbooks International, Osceola, WI, 1990.

The First and the Last by Adolf Galland, published by Henry Holt and Company, NY, 1954.

The 362nd Fighter Group, History of WW II, by Dan Gianneschi, published by Aires Press, Chicago, IL, 1986.

Six Months to Oblivion by Werner Girbig, published by Schiffer Publishing, West Chester, PA, and Motorbuch Verlag, Stuttgart, 1989.

The Dynamite Gang: The 367th Fighter Group in World War II by Richard Groh, published by Aero Publishers, Fallbrook, CA, 1986.

Aces Against Germany: Vol. II by Eric Hammel, published by Presidio Press, Novato, CA, 1993.

Alert in the West by Willi Heilmann, published by William Kimber Ltd, London, 1955.

Zemke's Wolfpack by William N. Hess, published by Motorbooks International, Osceola, WI, 1992.

Fighters of the Mighty Eighth by William N. Hess and Thomas G. Ivie, published by Motorbooks International, Osceola, WI, 1990

Göring: A Biography, by David J.C. Irving, published by William Morrow and Sons, New York, 1989.

References

The 474th Fighter Group in WWII: An Enlisted Man's Observations, by Isham G. Keller, Privately Printed, Minneapolis, MN, 1988.

Panzer Battles by F.W. Mellenthin, published by University of Oklahoma Press, Norman, OK, 1956.

Master of Airpower: General Carl A. Spaatz by David R. Mets, published by Presidio Press, Novato, CA, 1988.

Defending the Reich: The History of Jagdgeschwader 1 "Oesau," by Eric Mombeek, published by JAC Publications, Norwich, Norfolk, U.K., 1992.

Thunder Monsters Over Europe: a history of the 405th Fighter Group, by Reginald G. Nolte, published by Sunflower University Press, Manhattan, KS, 1986.

The Last Year of the Luftwaffe: May 1944 - May, 1945, by Alfred Price, published by Motorbooks International, Osceola, WI, 1991.

The Ninth Air Force in World War II, by Ken C. Rust, published by Aero Publishers, Fallbrook, CA, 1967.

Arado 234 Blitz, by Richard J. Smith and Eddie J. Creek, published by Monogram Aviation Publications, Sturbridge, MA, 1992.

Inside the Third Reich, by Albert Speer, published by the MacMillian Company, NY, 1990.

The Final Hours, by Johannes Steinhoff, published by Nautical and Aviation Publishing Company of America, Baltimore, MD, 1977.

Kriegies, Caterpillars and Lucky Bastards, by Glenn A. Stevens, published by Robinson Typnographics, Anaheim, CA, 1991.

Intelligence at the Top, by Sir Kenneth Strong, published by Doubleday and Co., Garden City, NY, 1968.

Inside Hitler's Headquarters, by Walter Warlimont, published by Praeger Publishers, NY, 1964.

Stories of the Eighth: An Anthology of the 8th Air Force in World War II, by John L. Woolnough, ed., published by the Eighth Air Force News, Hollywood, FL, 1983.

The Story of the Crusaders: 386th Bomb Group in World War II edited by Barnett Young, published by the 386th Bomb Group Association, Ft. Meyers, FL, 1988.

"The Legend of Y-29," by Tom Ivie, published in *Air Classics*, August, 1987.

"Those People Could Shoot," by Jackson Granholm, published by *World War II*, May, 1988, p. 27-33.

Prologue

"Never before and never again did I witness," Galland, p. 162
"We were met with a shattering picture," Galland, p.163
"The prerequisite for that," Irving, 1989, p. 421
"I want no more planes produced at all," Speer, p. 519
"...a tirade against the Luftwaffe," P-069, Kreipe Diary
"Führer rages about Luftwaffe's failure," P-069, Kreipe Diary

Enemy Number One

"From 0600 hrs four operations were mounted," Price, 1991,p.68
"Enemy number one is the enemy air force," APWIU 28/1945
"...One must be clear," Heiber, 1962

Spaatz and the Allied Airborne Might

"You have, of course, noted," Mets, p. 251
"When I recovered the sky was empty," Freeman, 1991A, p. 94
"For the low-level job we had to do," Freeman, 1991A, p. 113
"We were very mobile in Europe," Hess, 1992

The Luftwaffe: In Hitler's Doghouse

"The enemy has struck us at one of our weakest points," Murray, p.258

"...it was rare for a single engine," Smith and Creek, p. 166

"This...was the only time I got into trouble," Smith and Creek, p. 165

"Our ground school lasted one afternoon," Price, 1991, p. 136

"The Ar-234 will, with all possible dispatch, P-069, Kreipe Diary

"Our strength lay in our enormous speed," Steinhoff, p. 47-48

"...north of Osnabrück," 357 FG History, November, 1944

"The effects of nearing the sound barrier," Smith and Creek, p. 179

"We simply went to the depot nearby," Price, 1991, p. 130

"...the monthly production," SRH-017, p. 328

Secret Weapons, False Hopes

"On the air and in the press," Baumbach, p. 206

"Living there was not the same," IX TAC HQ History, December, 1944

"Only once, as I was climbing," Steinhoff, p. 51

"We would have done much better," Speer, p. 468

"Belief in the imminent commitment," Speer, p. 521

"Allied bombers are dropping hay," C.S.D.I.C.(UK) SIR 1419

Adolf Galland and the "Big Blow"

"This was going to be the largest," Galland, p.241

"I must have 2,000 fighters," Price, 1991, p. 13

"...I've taken another fresh look," "That's a miserable result," and "This proves once and for all," Warlimont, p. 637-638

"The boys we are facing today," 352nd FG History, November, 1944

"...We were given large numbers," Steinhoff, p. 30

"I had almost completed my training," Price, 1991, p.15

"Each morning we pilots," Price, 1991, p. 130

"By reason of the strained fuel situation," SRH-017, p. 291

The War Below

"I said I have a plan," Weyland interview

"Almighty and merciful father," Farago, p. 661

Hitler Schemes: The Allies Unaware

"...The only thing which is not," Warlimont, p. 492

"Basic Idea of the cover plan," SHAEF, 1945A

"On many occasions we were prevented," Quesada interview, p. 4

"Allied losses high," SHAEF, 1945A

"supports other evidence," and "situation is now," SRS-1869, No. 779

"G-2 reports," 1st U.S. Army G-2 Estimate # 37, 10 Dec, 1944

Enter Dietrich Peltz

"Support through air units," OB West KTB, December, 1944, NARS, T-122

"Aim of operation," SHAEF, 1945A

"In the middle of November," Galland, p. 241

"I didn't suspect for a moment," Freeman, 1991A, p. 83

"The objection may be made," Warlimont, p. 489

"The final decisions have been made," Warlimont, p. 485

References

Support the Attack: December 16th
"...I picked up the heading," Groh, p. 110
"The hour of destiny has struck," Bennett, p. 208
"...we got rousted out of the sack," Nolte, p. 65

The Contested Sky: December 17th
"...our unhappy Officer of the Day," Unit History IX TAC, December, 1944
"Dear Parents, especially Dear Dad," APWIU (IX TAC) 84/1944
"Doc Whitner had big-dealed a lot of eggs," 422 NFS History, Dec., 1944
"We dropped our napalm bombs," Dorman letter, 406 FG Association
"Another halt is called," U.S. Ninth AF, Ground Forces Annexes, No. 19.
"It was morning 17 December, 1944," Mundt letter to author
"*II Jagdkorps* orders," SRS-1869, No. 780
"...Conditions of Meuse crossings," SRS-1869, No. 781

Achtung Jabos: 18 December
"Up to 1130 hours," Unit History IX TAC, December, 1944

Stormy Weather: December 19th
"The Führer himself," Strong, p. 214
"Each morning our gloom had deepened," Bradley, p. 469
"Twelve of us started out," NY Times, December 21, 1944
"Most of these targets," Thompson, 1950, December 20, 1944
"...already by 20 December," U.S. Strategic Bombing Survey, PW 2/26

War's Most Beautiful Sunrise: December 23rd
"On the morning of the 23rd," Park letter to author
"I was in a flight of six aircraft," Sledzick letter, 406 FG Association
"I got on the tail of the 109," 361 FG History, December, 1944
"The enemy was able to employ," OB West KTB, December 23, 1944
"As the group reached a location," Hess, 1992, p. 151
"Slightly above them," Hess, 1992, p. 154
"As the miles-long stream," Brewer, p. 80
"It appears that the enemy," Thompson, 1950, 23 December, 1944

The Greatest Air Battle: December 24th
"Today is clear," Nugent Diary
"Strikingly heavy employment," SRH-017, p. 305
"Shortly after take-off," Mombeek, p. 259
"Like children anxiously awaiting," Keller, p. 106
"In looking back on it," Groh, p. 118
"We were circling Arlon, Belgium," 362 FG History, p. 339
"We were in the vicinity," 361 FG History, December, 1944
"At the last minute," 361 FG, December, 44
"By this time," Hess and Ivie, 1990, p. 181
"Air attack on Cologne," SRH-017, p. 56
"I attacked a factory complex," Smith and Creek, p. 180
"The enemy air force employment," OB West KTB, 24, December, 1944

The Saddest Christmas: December 25th
"After bombing troop and supply," Freeman, 1991A, p. 90

"It was cold this morning," Freeman, 1991B, p. 405
"We were in the vicinity of Maastricht," 352 FG Press releases, Dec. 1944
"The enemy carried on," OB West KTB, 25 December, 1944
"I traveled in a jeep," Saturday Evening Post, Feb. 10, 1945
"...main task is protection," SRS-1869, No. 789
"As we went over the woods," Hess and Ivie, 1990, p. 182
"...The setting was *Stalag Luft* I," Woolnough ed, p.49

The War is Lost: December 26th
"Prevalent reports of strafing," XXIX TAC, Strawberry File
"Looking for the rest area," Ninth AF Ground Forces Annex No. 19
"Very cold," Girbig, p.89
"...I engaged in a turning battle," Caldwell, p. 318
"On the entire front," OB West KTB, 26 December, 1944
"The flow of supplies," Speer, p. 530

Sheer Hell: December 27th
"Air Force dominated the skies," SRH-017, p.306
"...many tracks out of operation," SRH-017, Appendix C
"Due to present situation," Ninth AF, Battle of the Ardennes, Chpt 3
"Our group of three," Park letter to author
"I wish to express to you," 406 Occupier, 1945, p. 24
"I set off for the *9th Panzer Division*," Mellenthin, p.409
"Take off of ten aircraft," War Diary of III/SG 4, p. 11

Black Friday: December 29th
"I was leading our squadron," Ruddel letter via Wyglendowski
"The *Staffel* and the *Stabsschwarm*," Caldwell, p. 320

Year's End: December 31st
"December 31 1944" and "We started for our rally point," Bowman, p. 178
"I don't believe they had seen us," Hess and Ivie, 1990, p.185
"I took off at 10:30 hours," Smith and Creek, p. 182
"Only the turn of the year," Hitler, Vital Speeches, 1/15/45, p. 201

Operation Bodenplatte: January 1st, 1945
"Maintaining complete radio silence," Girbig, p. 110
"On 31st December," Mombeek, p. 289
"Since the pilots were quartered," Caldwell, p. 332
"...on the way in," and "I jettisoned my bombs," Ivie, 1987
"When I realized I was out of ammo," Ivie, 1987
"Immediately upon getting my wheels up," 352nd FG History, Jan. 1945
"The famous all-out raid," Rust, p.138
"I don't know how many," and "An enemy plane," Ivie, 1987
"Because of mist patches," Price, 1991, p. 117
"...While we were talking," Franks, p. 39
"I arrived back from England," Franks, p. 29
"They were getting a real pasting," Franks, p. 48
"The wing had moved up," Franks, p. 55
"Some time after nine o'clock," and "After Breakfast," Franks, p. 58
"Many pilots were jumping," and "We had just dressed," Franks, 63

References

"I considered the best thing," Franks, p 70
"There was no doubt," Franks, p. 73
"We turned towards him," Franks, p. 75
"After the raid," Franks, p. 81
"We were positioned" and "Suddenly," Franks, p. 87
"I got my bag out of the jeep," Franks, p. 91
"When I was captured,"De Decker, p. 6
"Officers and men," 48 FG History, January, 1945, p. 6
"We were woken at 3 o'clock," Heilmann, 1955
"I was only 21 years old," De Decker, p. 6
"There were only seven," De Decker, p. 6
"When we arrived over the field," Caldwell, p. 330
"I had the mission," Caldwell, p. 328
"I was Black 1," De Decker, p. 9
"I flew past my field," Caldwell, p. 338
"It was full daylight," and "I was acting CO," Franks, p. 137
"I had flown back to Melsbroek," Franks, p. 26-27
"The morning following," and "I had been flying," Franks, p. 127

New Year Doubts: January 2nd
"Comrades of the Luftwaffe!" SRH-017, p. 308
"2.1.45: Incursion by," Girbig, p. 173
"Heavy attack on 2nd TAF," SRS-1869, No. 794
"...They have become increasingly aggressive," Mets, p.268
"It occupied my full attention," XIX TAC History, Jan, 1945, p. 7
"Battle headquarters destroyed," SRH-017, p. 311
"...the fuel shortage dominates," SRH-017, p. 62

The Bombs Fall: January 10th
"On January 13, 1945," Freeman, 1991A, p. 94
"acute shortage at the battery positions," XIX TAC History, p. 58
"Information from various sources," XXIX TAC, Strawberry file
"0930 hours 14 January," SRS-1869, No. 808
"Large proportion of faults," SHAEF, 1945A
"The first thing I saw, " Groh, p. 122
"Dear Mother," Calhoun, p. 59

Slaughter at Dasburg: January 22nd
"I remember the rain and mud," extract from Dick Denison, Young, p. 114
"Operations of the Ninth Air Force," XXIX TAC, Strawberry File
"Order of the Day to the Fighters," SRH-017, p. 319

Mutiny of the Aces
"The dismissal of General Galland," Girbig, p. 182

Bibliography

Unpublished Sources

AHB, "Luftwaffe Strength and Serviceability Statisitics, August 1938-April, 1945," Air Historical Branch, Air Ministry, G 302694/AR/9/51/50, Public Records Office, London.

Air Staff, SHAEF, 1945., "Report on Allied Air Force Operations from 17th to 27th December, 1944," Supreme Headquarters Allied Expeditionary Force Air Staff Office of the Assistance Chief of Staff A-3, 1945.

Anderson, Gen. Samuel E., 1976. "U.S. Air Force Oral History Interview: Gen. Samuel E. Anderson," U.S. Air Force Historical Research Center (USAF HRC), Maxwell AFB, AL.

"Bericht des Jagdgeschwaders 4 (January, 1945)," Bundesarchiv, RL 101/527, Freiberg.

A.D.I.(K), 1944-1945. "German POW Interrogations," RG 165, Box 740, 692/1944 - 215/1945, National Archives Records Service (NARS), Washington D.C., also at USAF HRC in Microfilm Rolls A5403-5405, Maxwell AFB.

A.P/W I.U., "Air P/W Interrogation Unit at IX Air Force (Advanced)," RG 165, Box 740-741, No. 71/1944 - 28/1945, NARS, Washington D.C.

Assistant Chief of Staff, HQ United States Air Forces in Europe, 1945. "The Contribution of Air Power to the Defeat of Germany: Vol. I Summary and Analysis," USAF HRC, Maxwell AFB, AL.

C.S.D.I.C.(U.K.), 1944-1945, "Combined Services Detailed Interrogations Center," RG 165, No. 179, various S.I.R. Nos. 1375 - 1996, RG 165, NARS, Washington D.C.

"Geschichte des Oberbefehlshabers West," NARS, Microfilm Roll T-122, Washington D.C.

Groehler, Olaf, "Starke, Verteilung und Verluste der Deutschen Luftwaffe in Zweiten Weltkrieg," *Militargeschichte*, Vol. 17, 1978.

HQ 12th Army Group, "PW Intelligence Bulletin: Effects of U.S. Strategic and Tactical Air Power," Mobile Field Interrogation Unit No. 4, G-2, 20 May, 1945, NARS, Washington D.C.

De Decker, Cynrik, 1993. "Operation Bodenplatte," unpublished study compiled for the author, Erembodegem, Belgium, October 1, 1993.

"48th Fighter Group, December 44," Capt. Emanual Bisher, Historical Officer, USAF HRC, Maxwell AFB, AL.

"406th Fighter Group, December 1944; January, 1945," USAF HRC, Maxwell AFB, AL.

"425th Night Fighter Squadron, December 1944 - January 1945," XIX TAC, 26th Statistical Control Unit, USAF HRC, Maxwell AFB, AL.

Grabmann, Walter, 1945. "Deutschen Luftverdeitigung 1937-1945, Band V: Jagdkräfte für die Ardennenoffensive Dezember 1944," USAF HRC, Maxwell AFB, AL.

Bibliography

Headquarters Bomber Command, Royal Air Force, 1945. "Bomber Command Quarterly Review, October - December, 1944" No. 11, London, NARS, RG 243, Washington D.C.

Hentschel, Genmaj. Karl, 1945. "5th Fighter Division," MS B-231, Foreign Military Studies, NARS, Washington D.C.

"History of the XIX Tactical Air Command: 1 July 1944 - 28 February, 1945," Pt. II Operations Narrative, USAF HRC, Maxwell AFB, AL.

"Historical Records and History of the Headquarters 67th Tactical Reconnaissance Group," USAF HRC, Maxwell AFB, AL.

National Security Agency, 1945A. "Ultra: History of U.S. Strategic Air Force Europe versus German Air Force," NARS, SRH-013, Washington D.C.

National Security Agency, 1945B. "Allied Strategic Air Force Target Planning," NARS, SRH-017, Washington D.C.

National Security Agency, 1945C. "Summary of Operational Activity of Detachment D, 12th Army Group, European Theatre of Operations," NARS, SRH-048, Washington D.C.

National Security Agency, 1945D. "Sunset Daily Intelligence Reports, December, 1944 - January, 1945," NARS, RG 457, SRS-1869, Washington D.C.

National Security Agency, 1981. "Post Mortem Writings on Indications of Ardennes Offensive, December, 1944," NARS, RG 457, SRH-112, Washington D.C., originally U.S. Army War College, "The ULTRA Study, 'The Battle of the Bulge,'" and "Communications Intelligence (COMINT) in the Prelude to the Battle of the Bulge," Lt. Col. Harry L. Dull, Jr., May, 1977, Carlisle, PA.

"9th Bomb Division and the Ground Forces," USAF HRC, Maxwell AFB, AL.

"The XIX Tactical Air Command in the European Theater of Operations, Operating Procedure and Functional Organization," Vol. III, Pt. 2, The Ninth Air Force and its Principal Commands in the European Theater of Operations, USAF HRC, Maxwell AFB, AL.

Ninth Air Force, 1945. *Counter-blow! A Photo History of the Ninth Air Force Tactical Operations during the German Ardennes Offensive*, USAF HRC, Maxwell AFB, AL.

Ninth Air Force, 1945. *The Ninth Air Force and Its Principal Commands in the E.T.O.*, USAF HRC, Maxwell AFB, AL.

Ninth Air Force, 1945. *Operational History of the Ninth Air Force: Book I: Battle of the Ardennes*, USAF HRC, Maxwell AFB, AL.

Ninth Air Force, 1945. *Operational History of the Ninth Air Force: Book III Across the Rhine, Two Sections and Statistical Annex*, USAF HRC, Maxwell AFB, AL.

Ninth Air Force, 1945. *Operational History of the Ninth Air Force: Book V, Ground Force Annexes*, USAF HRC, Maxwell AFB, AL.

Ninth Air Force, 1945. *Operational History of the Ninth Air Force: The IX Tactical Air Command*, USAF HRC, Maxwell AFB, AL.

Ninth Air Force, 1945. *Operational History of the Ninth Air Force: Tactical Annex*, 533.01-2, USAF HRC, Maxwell AFB, AL.

Ninth Air Force, 1945. *Operational History of the Ninth Air Force: Book IV Tactical Annex*, USAF HRC, Maxwell AFB, AL.

Ninth Air Force, 1945. *Operational History of the Ninth Air Force: Across the Rhine and Statistical Annex*, USAF HRC, Maxwell AFB, AL.

Ninth Air Force, 1945. "The IX Tactical Air Command in the European Theatre of Operations," USAF HRC, Maxwell AFB, AL.

Ninth Air Force, 1945. "The XIX Tactical Air Command in the European Theatre of Operations," USAF HRC, Maxwell AFB, AL.

Ninth Bomb Division, 1945. *Strikes!*, USAF HRC, Maxwell AFB, AL.

Ninth Bombardment Division, 1945. "Air-Ground Coordination: 9th Bombardment Division's Liason with the Ground Forces," Ninth Air Force, USAF HRC, Maxwell AFB, AL.

IX Tactical Air Command, 1945. "Unit History IX Fighter Command and IX Tactical Air Command Covering Period 1 December, 1944 - 31 December, 1944 and 1 January 1945 - 31 January 1945," USAF HRC, Maxwell AFB, AL.

IX Troop Carrier Command, 1945. "Operation Repulse: Resupply by Air, Belgium, December, 1944," USAF HRC, Maxwell AFB, AL.

XIX TAC, 1945. "Tactical Air Operations in Europe, 1 Aug, 1944 - 9 May, 1945," USAF HRC, Maxwell AFB, AL.

Nugent, Brig. Gen. Richard E., 1945. "Excerpts from Brig. General Richard E. Nugent's War Diary," 22 September, 144 - 31 March, 1945, USAF HRC, Maxwell AFB, AL.

Oberbefehschaber West, 1945. "Kriegstagebuch 1 - 31. December 1944," Bundesarchiv, RH-IV/2, Freiburg, Germany, also T-311, Roll 18 at NARS.

Oberkommando der Heeresgruppe B, 1944. "Operationsbefehl für den Angriff der Heeresgruppe B über die Maas auf Antwerpen," Anlage zu Ob.Kdo.H.Gr.B., Ia Nr. 0180/44 g.Kdos.Chefs., 11.11.44, Bundesarchiv, Freiburg, Germany.

Office of the Director of Intelligence, 1945. *Allied Air Power and the Ardennes Offensive: 15 December 1944 - 16 January 1945*, United States Strategic Air Forces in Europe, Coffin Report, U.S. Army Military History Institute, Carlisle, PA, also at USAF HRC.

"OKW Kriegstagebuch, 1 April - 18 December, 1944," NARS, Microfilm T-173, Roll 7, Washington D.C.

"Persönliches Kriegstagebuch des Generals der Flieger Kreipe," MS P-069, Foreign Military Branch, NARS, Washington D.C.

Quesada, Elwood R., 1975. "Interview by Lt. Col. Steve Long and Lt. Col. Ralph Stephenson at Army War College," Army War College, USAF HRC, Oral History Collection No. 838, Maxwell AFB, AL.

Roba, Jean Louis, 1993. "The Last Months of III/JG 77," unpublished manuscript, Charleroi, Belgium.

Second Tactical Air Force Operational Research Section, 1945. "Contribution of Air Forces to the Stemming of the Enemy Thrust in the Ardennes, December 16th - 26th, 1944," Report No. 19, AIR 37/1208, Second Tactical Air Force, 9 June, 1945.

SHAEF, 1945A. "Ardennes Offensive, December 1944. Plans, Scope and Inquest," Intelligence Party (OKL), Intelligence Report No. 22, Supreme Headquarters Allied Expeditionary Forces, July 23, 1945, USAF HRC, Maxwell AFB, AL.

SHAEF, 1945B. "G.A.F. Strength & Losses," Control Party (OKL), Intelligence Report No. 7, Supreme Headquarters Allied Expeditionary Forces, July, 1945, USAF HRC, Maxwell AFB, AL.

SHAEF, 1945C., "Report on Allied Air Operations from 17 to 27th December, 1944," A-3 Division Air Staff, USAF HRC, Maxwell AFB, AL.

Spaatz, Carl A., "Spaatz Papers," Manuscript Division, Library of Congress, Washington D.C.

Thompson, Royce L., 1950. "Tactical Air Phase of the Ardennes Campaign, Office of the Chief of Military History, NARS, Washington D.C.

Thompson, Royce L., 1952. "American Intelligence on the German Counterffensive," NARS, Washington D.C.

"352nd Fighter Group, December, 1944; January, 1945," Eighth Air Force, Eighth Fighter Command, USAF HRC, Maxwell AFB, AL.

"36th Fighter Group, Unit History, 1 Decmember to 31 December, 1944," USAF HRC, Maxwell AFB.

"354th Fighter Group, December 1944/January 1945," USAF HRC, Maxwell AFB, AL.

"357th Fighter Group, December 1944/January 1945," USAF HRC, Maxwell AFB, AL.

"361st Fighter Group, January, 1945," Eighth Air Force, USAF HRC, Maxwell AFB, AL.

"361st Fighter Group, December 1944," Eighth Air Force, USAF HRC, Maxwell AFB, AL.

XXIX TAC, 1945. "Strawberry File," USAF HRC, Maxwell AFB, AL.

508

Bibliography

U.S. Strategic Bombing Survey, 1945. "PW Intelligence Bulletins," RG 243, Mobile Field Interrogation Units, Nos. 1/29, 1/40, 2/23, 2/24, 2/26, 2/28, 2/29, 2/30, 2/31, 2/38, 2-39,
NARS, Washington D.C.

"War Diary of III/SG 4, December, 1944 - January, 1945," Bundesarchiv via Roba, translation
by J. Bowman.

Weyland, Maj. Gen. Otto P., 1945. "Excerpts from Weyland Diary," USAF HRC, Maxwell
AFB, AL.

Weyland, Maj. Gen. Otto P., 1988. "Historical Documentation General O.P. Weyland, Interview," USAF HRC, Maxwell AFB, AL.

Weyland, Maj. Gen. Otto P., 1945. "Interrogation of Generalfeldmarschall Gerd von Rundest-
edt," USAF HRC, Bad Kissingen, 2 July, 1945.

Wolter, Obst. i.G. von, 1945. "Die Luftwaffe im Zusammenwirken mit dem Westheer in der
Zeit von Ende September 1944 bis Mai 1945," NARS, RG 242, Microfilm T-122, Anlage 4,
Washington D.C.

Wyant, Joseph A., 1945. *Battle of the Ardennes, 1 December 1944 - 31 January, 1945*, Operational History of the U.S. Ninth Air Force, Book No. 1, USAF HRC, Maxwell AFB, AL.

Wyant, Joseph A., 1945. *Allied Effort During the Battle of the Bulge*, Ninth Air Force, Microfilm Roll B-5725, USAF HRC, Maxwell AFB, AL.

Wyant, Joseph A. "Material in Response to Telephone Request of September 1945 Concerning Allied Air Effort During the Battle of the Bulge," undated reply to Brig. Gen. R.C.
Candee, Office of Ninth Air Force History, USAF HRC, Maxwell AFB, AL.

Zimmermann, Genlt. Bodo et al., 1948. *Oberbefelschaber West, Pt 2*, NARS, RG-242, T-122,
Washington D.C.

Published Works

Air Ministry, 1983. *The Rise and Fall of the German Air Force, s 1939-1945.* Arms & Armour,
London; St. Martin's Press, NY.

Baumbach, Werner, 1960. *The Life and Death of the Luftwaffe*, Robert Hale, London; Coward-
McCann, New York.

Beck, Earl R., 1986. *Under the Bombs: The German Home Front 1942-1945*, University of Ken-
tucky Press, Lexington, KY.

Beck, Henry C., Jr., 1946. *The 397th Bomb Group: A Pictoral History*, Crane Howard, Cleve-
land, OH.

Bendiner, Elmer, 1980. *The Fall of the Fortress: A Personal Account of the Most Daring and
Deadly American Air Battles of World War II*, Putnam, NY; Sonvenir, London.

Bennett, Ralph F., 1979. *Ultra in the West: The Normandy Campaign*, Hutchinson, London;
1980, Scribner's, New York.

Blanco, Richard L., 1987. *The Luftwaffe in World War II: The Rise and Decline of the German Air
Force*, Messner, New York, NY.

Boehme, Manfred, 1983, *Jagdgeschwader 7, Die Chronick eines Me 262 Geschwader 1944/45*, Motorbuch Verlag, Stuttgart

Bowman, Martin W., 1984. *Castles in the Air: The Story of the B-17 Flying Fortress Crews of the
U.S. 8th Air Force*, Patrick Stephens, Wellingborough.

Bowyer, Michael J. F., 1974, *2nd Group R.A.F.: A Complete History, 1936-1945*, Faber and Faber, London.

Blumenson, Martin, 1974. *The Patton Papers 1940-45*, Houghton Mifflin Co., NY.

Brereton, Lt. Gen. Lewis H., 1946. *The Brereton Diaries: The War in the Air in the Pacific, Middle East and Europe*, Morrow, New York.

Brown, Anthony Cave, 1975. *Bodyguard of Lies*, Harper & Row, NY; W.H. Allen, London.

Brown, Arthur F., 1946. *History in the Sky: 354th Pioneer Mustang Fighter Group*, Newsfoto
Publishing, San Angelo, TX.

Caldwell, Donald L., 1991 *JG 26: Top Guns of the Luftwaffe*, Orion Books, New York; Airlife, Shrewsowy, England.

Calhoun, Jack and Beryl, 1976. *Somewhere the Sun is Shining*, Grossmont Press, San Diego, CA.

Cole, Hugh M., 1965. *The Ardennes: Battle of the Bulge*, U.S. Army in World War II, GPO, Washington D.C.

Constable, Trevor J. and Toliver, Raymond F., 1968. *Horrido!: Fighter Aces of the Luftwaffe*, Macmillan Company, NY.

Craven, Wesley Frank and Cate, James Lea, eds., 1951. *The Army Air Forces in World War II, Volume III, Europe: Argument to V-E Day*, University of Chicago Press, Chicago, IL.

Craven, Wesley Frank and Cate, James Lea, eds., 1951. *The Army Air Forces in World War II, Volume VI, Men and Planes*, University of Chicago Press, Chicago, IL.

Davies, A., 1948. *The 56th Fighter Group in World War II*, Infantry Journal Press, Washington D.C.

Dierich, Wolfgang, 1975. *Kampfgeschwader 'Edelweiss'*, Ian Allan, Shepperton.

Doolittle, James H. and Glines, Carrol V., 1991. *I Could Never Be So Lucky Again: An Autobiography*, Bantam Books, 1991.

Dornberger, Walter, 1954. *V-2*, Viking, NY; Hurst and Blockett, London.

Drop Zone Europe: The Story of the 440th Troop Carrier Group, 1946. Hollenbeck Press, Indianapolis, IN.

Duffy's Tavern: A Record of the Officer's Club of the IX Tactical Air Command, 1945., Ch. Vinche, Verviers, Belgium.

Eisenhower, Dwight D., 1948. *Crusade in Europe*, Doubleday, Garden City, NY.

Ellison, Bruce G. ed., n.d., *Orange Tails: The Story of the 358th Fighter Group and Ancilliary Units*, Rogers Printing Co., Chicago, IL.

Farago, Ladislas, 1970. *Patton: Ordeal and Triumph*, Dell, NY.

Fest, Joachim C., 1970. *The Face of the Third Reich*, Pantheon, NY; Weiderfeld, London.

Ford, Brian, 1969. *German Secret Weapons: Blueprint for Mars*, Ballantine, New York.

Franks, Norman L., 1982. *The Battle of the Airfields*, Kimber, London.

Freeman, Roger A., 1991A. *Experiences of War: The American Airman in Europe*, Motorbooks International, Osceola, WI; Arms and Armor, London.

Freeman, Roger A., 1991B. *The Mighty Eighth: The History of the Units, Men and Machines of the US 8th Airforce*, Motorbooks International, Osceola, WI; Arms and Armor, London.

Freeman, Roger A., 1990. *The Mighty Eighth: War Diary*, Motorbooks International, Osceola, WI; Arms and Armor, London.

Frischauer, Willi, 1951. *The Rise and Fall of Hermann Goering*, Houghton Mifflin, Boston; Odhams, London.

Galland, Adolf, 1954. *The First and the Last*, Henry Holt, NY; Methuen, London.

Gianneschi, Dan, 1986. *The 362nd Fighter Group, History of WW II*, 2nd edition, Aires Press, Chicago, IL.

Gilmore, Lawrence J. and Howard, J. Lewis, 1985. *History, 435th Troop Carrier Group, Ninth Troop Carrier Command*, Keys Print Company, Greenville, SC.

Girbig, Werner, 1989. *Six Months to Oblivion*, Schiffer Publishing, West Chester, PA.

Glines, Carroll V. 1980. *Master of the Calculated Risk*, Van Nostrand Rheinhold, NY.

Goralski, Robert and Freeburg, Russell W., 1987. *Oil and War*, William and Morrow, NY.

Green, William, 1970. *Warplanes of the Third Reich*, Macdonald, London; Doubleday and Co., NY.

Griehl, Manfred, 1988. *German Jets of World War II*, Arms and Armor, London.

Groh, Richard, 1983. *The Dynamite Gang: The 367th Fighter Group in World War II*, Aero, Fallbrook, CA.

Guild, Frank H., Jr., 1980. *Action of the Tiger, the Saga of the 437th Troop Carrier Group*, Battery Press, Nashville, TN.

Bibliography

Gunston, Bill, 1988. *Fighting Aircraft of World War II*, Salamardes, London; Arco Military Books, Prentice Hall, NY.

Gunston, Bill, 1992. *Allied Fighters of World War II*, Salamander, London.

Hallion, Richard P., 1990. *Strike from the Sky: The History of Battlefield Air Attack*, Smithsonian Institution Press, Washington D.C.

Hammel, Eric, 1993. *Aces Against Germany: Vol. II*, Presidio Press, Novato, CA.

Harris, Arthur T., 1947. *Bomber Offensive*, Macmillian, NY.

Hastings, Max, 1979. *Bomber Command*, Michael Joseph; London; Dial Press, New York.

Hecht, Heinrich, 1990. *The World's First Turbojet Fighter: Me 262*, Schiffer, Atglen, PA.

Heiber, Helmut (ed.), 1962. *Hitlers Lagebesprechungen: Die Protokollfragmente seiner militärischen Konferenzen 1942-1945*, Stuttgart.

Heilmann, Willi, 1955. *Alert in the West*, Kimber, London.

Hennessy, Juliette, 1952. *Tactical Operations of the Eight Air Force: 6 June 1944 - 8 May 1945*, USAF Historical Study No. 70, Washington D.C.

Hess, William N., 1977. *P-47 Thunderbolt at War*, Doubleday & Co., Garden City, NY.

Hess, William N. 1992. *Zemke's Wolfpack*, Motorbooks International, Osceola, WI; Airlife, Shrewsoum, England.

Hess, William N. and Ivie, Thomas G. 1990. *Fighters of the Mighty Eighth*, Motorbooks International, Osceola, WI.

Hess, William N. and Ivie, Thomas G. 1992. *P51 Mustang Aces*, Motorbooks International, Osceola, WI.

The History of a Bombing Outfit: The 386th Bomb Group, 1945. De Geneffe, St. Truiden, Belgium.

Irving, David J.C., 1973. *The Rise and Fall of the Luftwaffe: The Life of Field Marshal Erhard Milch*, William Morrow and Sons, New York.

Irving, David J.C., 1977. *Hitler's War*, Viking, New York; Hudder, London.

Irving, David J.C., 1981. *The War Between the Generals*, Congdon & Lattès, New York; Allan Lane, London.

Irving, David J.C., 1989. *Göring: A Biography*, Morrow, New York; Macmillan, London.

Ivie, Tom, 1981. *Aerial Reconnaissance: The 10th Photo Recon Group in World War II*, Aero, Fallbrook, CA.

Johnson, Charles R., 1975. *The History of the Hell Hawks*, Southcoast Typesetting, Anaheim, CA.

Jung, Hermann, 1971. *Die Ardennen Offensive*, Munsterschmidt Gottingen, Zurich.

Keim, Bill and Nan, 1990. *The 410th Book of Newsletters*, Avery Color Studio, Autrain, MI.

Keitel, Wilhelm, 1966. *The Memoirs of Field Marshal Keitel*, translated by David Irving, Stein and Day, NY.

Keller, Isham G., 1988. *The 474th Fighter Group in WWII: An Enlisted Man's Observations*, Privately Printed, Minneapolis, MN.

Ketchum, Carlton G., 1976. *The Recollections of Colonel Retread, USAAF, 1942-1945*, Hart Books, Pittsburg, PA.

Kober, Franz, 1990. *The World's First Jet Bombers: Arado 234 and Junkers 287*, Schiffer, West Chester, PA.

Koch, Horst Adalbert, 1954. *Flak: Die Geschichte der Deutschen Flakartillerie, 1935-1945*, H.H. Podzun, Bad Nauheim.

Lacey-Johnson, Lionel, 1991. *Pointblank and Beyond*, Airlife, Shrewsbury, UK.

Lee, Asher, 1972. *Goering: Air Leader*, Duckworth, London.

Lesage, Jean Marie, 1984. *Houffalize: Ville Martre*, Lesage Graphic, Houffalize, Belgium.

Link, Mae M. and Coleman, Hubert A., 1955. *Medical Support of the Army Air Forces in World War II*, Office of the Surgeon General, Washington D.C.

MacDonald, Charles B., 1985. *A Time for Trumpets: The Untold Story of the Battle of the Bulge*, Morrow, NY; Weidenfeld, London.

MacIsaac, David, 1976. *Strategic Bombing in World War II*, Garland Publishers, New York.

Manvell, Roger and Fraenkel, Heinrich, 1972. *Göring*, Ballintane Books, NY; Heineman, London.

McCrary, John R. and Scherman, David E., 1981. *The First of the Many: A Journal of Action with the Men of the Eighth Air Force*, Ariation Books, USA; Robson, London.

McFarland, Stephen L. and Newton, Wesley Phillips, 1991. *To Command the Sky*, Smithsonian Institution Press, Washington D.C.

McLachlan, Ian and Zorn, Russell, J. 1991. *Eighth Air Force Bomber Stories*, Patrick Stevens Ltd., Somerset, UK.

Meilinger, Philip S., 1989. *Hoyt S. Vandenberg: The Life of a General*, Indiana University Press, Bloomington, IL.

Mellenthin, F.W. von, 1956. *Panzer Battles*, University of Oklahoma Press, Norman, OK.

Mets, David R., 1988. *Master of Airpower: General Carl A. Spaatz*, Presidio, Novato, CA.

Miller, Kent D., 1989. *Seven Months Over Europe: The 363rd Fighter Group in World War II*, privately published, Hicksville, OH.

Mitcham, Samuel W., Jr, 1988. *Men of the Luftwaffe*, Presido, Novato, CA.

Moench, John O., 1989. *Marauder Men: An Account of the 32rd Bombardment Group*, Malia Enterprices, Longwood, FL.

Mombeek, Eric, 1992. *Defending the Reich: The History of Jagdgeschwader 1 "Oesau,"* JAC Publications, Norwich, Norfolk, U.K.

Morris, Danny, 1972. *Aces and Wingmen: Men, Machines and Units of the US Air Forces, Eight Fighter Command and the 354th Fighter Group*, Neville Spearman, London.

Mosley, Leonard, 1974. *The Reich Marshal: A Biography of Hermann Goering*, Doubleday, NY; Weidenfeld, London.

Murray, Williamson, 1985. *Luftwaffe*, Nautical and Aviation Publishing Company, Baltimore, MD.

Murray, Williamson, 1983. *Strategy for Defeat: The Luftwaffe, 1933-1945*, Air University Press, AL.

Nalty, Bernard C. and Berger, Carl, 1978. *The Men Who Bombed the Reich*, Elsevier-Dutton, NY.

Ninth Air Force, 1945. *United States Army Air Forces, Ninth Air Force*, Executive Liason Section.

XIX Tactical Air Command, 1945. *The Story of the XIX Tactical Air Command*, European Theater of Operations: Orientation Branch, Information and Education Division, ETOUSA, U.S. Military History Institute.

Noah, Joe and Sox, Samuel L. Jr., 1991. *George Preddy: Top Mustang Ace*, Motorbooks International, Osceola, WI.

Nolte, Reginald G., 1986. *Thunder Monsters Over Europe: a history of the 405th Fighter Group*, Sunflower University Press, Manhattan, KS.

Nowarra, Heinz J., 1993. *Heinkel 162 "Volksjäger"*, Schiffer, Atglen, PA.

Ong, Willaim A., 1981. *Target Luftwaffe: The Tragedy and Triumphs of the World War II Air Victory*, Lowell Press, Kansas City, MO.

Overy, R.J., 1984. *Göring, the "Iron Man,"* Routledge and Kegan Paul, London.

Parker, Danny, 1991. *Battle of the Bulge*, Combined Books, Philadelphia, PA; Greenhill, London.

Parton, James, 1986. *"Air Force Spoken Here:" General Ira Eaker and the Command of the Air*, Adler and Adler, Bethesda, MD.

Powell,Jr., Lewis F., 1987. *ULTRA and the Army Air Forces in World War II*, ed. Diane T. Putney, Office of Air Force History, Bolling Air Force Base, Washington D.C.

Powell, Robert H., Jr. and Ivie, Thomas, 1990. *The Bluenose Bastards of Bodney: A Commemorative History*, Taylor Publishing, Dallas, TX.

Price, Alfred, 1986. *The Luftwaffe Handbook*, Ian Allan, Shepperton, Surrey; Scribner's, NY.

Bibliography

Price, Alfred, 1991. *The Last Year of the Luftwaffe: May 1944 - May, 1945*, Motorbooks International, Osceola, WI; Arms and Armor, London.

Price, Alfred, 1991B. *Pictorial History of the Luftwaffe*, Motorbooks International, Osceola, WI.

Ring, Hans, and Girbig, Werner, 1971. *Jagdgeschwader 27*, Motorbuch Verlag, Stuttgart.

Rubel, George K., n.d. *Daredevil Tankers: 740th Tank Battalion*, Infantry Journal Press, Washington D.C.

Rust, Ken C., 1967. *The Ninth Air Force in World War II*, Aero, Fallbrook, CA.

Ryan, Cornelius, 1974. *A Bridge Too Far*, Simon & Schuster, NY; Hamish Hamilton, London.

Saied, Kemal, 1989. *Thunderbolt Odyssey, The P-47 War in Europe*, Stonewood Press, Tulsa, OK.

Saunders, Hilary St. George, 1975. *The Fight is Won: Royal Air Force 1939 - 1945*, Her Majesty's Stationery Service, London.

Schramm, Percy E., 1961. *Kriegstagebuch des Oberkommandos der Wehrmacht*, Vol. IV, Bernard and Graefe, Frankfurt.

Scutts, Jerry, 1992. *Jagdgeschwader 54 Grünherz: Aces of the Eastern Front*, Motorbooks International, Osceola, WI.

Shirer, William L., 1959. *The Rise and Fall of the Third Reich*, Simon & Schuster, N.Y; Seckes and Warburg, London, 1960.

Shores, Christopher F., 1970. *2nd TAF*, Osprey Publications, Reading Berks.

Smith, J. Richard and Creek, E.J., 1982. *The German Jets in Action*, Monogram Aviation Publications, Boylston, MA.

Smith, J. Richard and Creek, E.J., 1992. *Arado 234 Blitz*, Monogram Aviation Publications, Sturbridge, MA.

Speer, Albert, 1970. *Inside the Third Reich*, Macmillian, NY; Weiderfeld, London.

Steinhoff, Johannes, 1977. *The Final Hours*, Nautical and Aviation Publishing Company, Baltimore, MD.

Steinko, John T., 1986. *The Geyser Gang: The 428th Fighter Squadron in World War II*, Roma Associates, Minneapolis, MN.

Stevens, Glenn A., 1991. *Kriegies, Caterpillars and Lucky Bastards*, Robinson Typnographics, Anaheim, CA.

Stovall, Jack, D., Jr., 1991. *Wings of Courage*, Global Press, Memphis, TN.

Strong, Maj. Gen. Sir Kenneth, 1968. *Intelligence at the Top*, Cassel, London; Doubleday, Garden City, NY.

Tedder, Lord, 1966. *With Prejudice: The War Memoirs of the Marshal of the Royal Air Force*, Little, Brown and Company, Boston, MA.

Thomas, Lowell and Jablonski, Edward, 1982. *Doolittle*, Da Capo Publishers, New York.

Toland, John, 1977. *Adolf Hitler*, Doubleday, NY

Toliver, Raymond F., and Constable, Trevor J., 1978. *Fighter Aces of the Luftwaffe*, Aero Publishers, Fallbrook, CA.

Turner, Richard E., 1969. *Big Friend, Little Friend: Memoirs of a World War II Fighter Pilot*, Doubleday, Garden City, NY.

Walker, Hugh H., 1990. *391st Bombardment Group History of WWII*, n.p., 391st Bomb Group Association.

Warlimont, Walter, 1964. *Inside Hitler's Headquarters*, Praeger, NY; Weiderfeld, London.

Warren, Hoyt M., 1993. *Spy in the Sky*, Henry Co. Historical Society, Abbeville, AL.

Webster, Charles and Frankland, Noble, 1961. *The Strategic Air Offensive against Germany*, Vol. 2., Her Majesty's Stationery Service, London.

Whiting, Charles, 1984. *Ardennes: The Secret War*, Stein and Day, NY.

Wilson, Andrew F., ed., 1950. *Leap Off, 404th Fighter Group Combat History*, Newsfoto Publishing Co., San Angelo, TX.

Wolfe, Tom, 1979, *The Right Stuff*, Farrar, Straus and Giroux, New York.

Wood, Tony and Gunston, Bill, 1977. *Hitler's Luftwaffe*, Salamander, London; Crescent, NY.

Woolnough, John H., ed, 1983. *Stories of the Eight: An Anthology of the 8th Air Force in World War II*, 8th Air Force News, Hollywood, FL.

Young, Barnett, ed., 1988. *The Story of the Crusaders: 386th Bomb Group in World War II*, 386th Bomb Group Association, Ft. Meyers, FL.

Ziegler, J. Guy, 1949. *Bridge Busters: The Story of the 394th Bomb Group of the 98th Bomb Wing, 9th Bomb Division, 9th Air Force*, Ganis and Harris, NY.

Periodical Literature

"Again We Have Turned Fate Away," Hitler, Adolf, *Vital Speeches*, January 15, 1945.

"Air Power in the Battle of the Bulge: A Theater Campaign Perspective," Carter, Co. William R., *Airpower Journal*, Winter, 1989, p. 10 - 33.

"Allies Squeeze the German Bulge," *Life*, Vol. 18, No. 3, January 15, 1945.

"Americans Battle the German Big Push," Wertenbaker, Charles, C., *Life*, Vol. 18, No. 2, January 8, 1945.

"Another Tactical Triumph," *Impact* 3, No. 2, February, 1945.

"Back in Stride: Air Tactics of the U.S. Ninth Air Force," *Time*, January 15, 1945.

"Boss of the Heavyweights: Lt. Gen. Carl Spaatz," Middleton, Drew, *Saturday Evening Post*, May 20, 1944.

"Bulge Air Battle," *Life*, Vol. 18, No. 4, January 22, 1945.

"Flier, Downing 4 Foes, Says Nazis are Bold," Associated Press, *New York Times*, December 21, 1944.

"The 406th Occupier," Vol. 1, No. 13, Nordholz, Germany, September 28, 1945.

"Flying the World's First Jet Bomber," Joseph, Francis, *World War II Investigator*, November, 1988.

"Last Days of the Ardennes Salient," *Life*, Vol. 18, No. 6, February 5, 1945.

"The Last Prussian," Cort, David, *Life*, Vol. 17, No. 26, December 25, 1944.

"The Legend of Y-29," Ivie, Tom, *Air Classics*, August, 1987.

"Radar in ETO Air-Ground Operations," Galand, Blair E., *Signals 3*, No. 4, March-April, 1949.

"Rennaissance Man of Aviation," Wolk, Herman S., *Airpower History*, Winter, 1993.

"Smashing Windup to Ardennes Bulge Battle Was a Costly Experience for the Germans," *Impact 3*, No. 3, March, 1945.

"Strategic Air Wins in Europe," *Impact 3*, No. 7, July, 1945.

"Take Down That Damned Sign: Doolittle as Combat Commander, David, Robert G., *Airpower History*, Winter, 1993.

"Those People Could Shoot," Granholm, Jackson, *World War II*, May, 1988, p. 27-33.

"U.S. Tactical Air Power in Europe," *Impact 3*, No. 5, May, 1945.

"War's Most Beautiful Sunrise," Bess, Demaree, *Saturday Evening Post*, February 10, 1945.

Appendix

Tactical Air Sorties During the Ardennes Campaign Dec. 16, 1944 - Jan. 1, 1945			
Date	**Weather**	**Allied**	**German**
Dec. 16	Overcast	359[1]	170
17	Fog	1,053[2]	650[6]
18	Fog	519	849[6]
19	Overcast	196	290
20	Overcast	2	2
21	Overcast	100	0
22	Snow	943	100
23	Fog/Clear	6194	800
24	Clear	1,138	1,088
25	Clear	1,0665	600
26	Clear	937	404
27	Clear	1,294	415
28	Heavy Snow	23	15
29	Fog	460	340
30	Fog	690	150
31	Fog	700	613
Jan. 1	Clear	1,000	1,0357

1 None of these were battlefield sorties

2 647 of these were battlefield sorties

3 80 of these were 2nd TAF sorties

4 294 were battlefield sorties: total sorties for the day were 2,500

5 British 2nd TAF flew an additional 1,099 sorties, but only 371 were battlefield missions

6 A further 100-250 sorties were flown each night

7 Fewer than 100 sorties were over the battlefield; over 900 were associated with *Operation Bodenplatte*.

Sources for Table:

Thompson, Royce, 1950. "Tactical Air Phase of the Ardennes Campaign, Office of the Chief of Military History, NARS, Washington D.C.; Office of the Director of Intelligence, 1945. *Allied Air Power and the Ardennes Offensive: 15 December 1944 - 16 January 1945*, United States Strategic Air forces in Europe, Coffin Report, U.S. Army Military History Institute, Carlisle, PA; Jung, Hermann, 1971. *Die Ardennen Offensive*, Munsterschmidt Gottingen, Zurich; SHAEF Air Staff, 1945, "Report on Air Force Operations from 17th - 27th December, 1944," Operations Records, A-3 Division, SHAEF, USAF HRC, Maxwell AFB, Montgomery, AL.

Allied Air Mission Summary
December 16, 1944 - January 15, 1945

	Sorties	Bombs (Long Tons)	Aircraft Lost
United States			
9th AF	23,264	10,371	286
8th Af	28,330	36,326	128
British			
2nd TAF	5,636	1,418	190
RAF BC	6,511	23,072	43
TOTAL	63,741	71,187	647

Allied reports attribute enemy aircraft as the verified cause of their losses in only about 10% of cases. The actual number was certainly higher, although it does appear that German flak was responsible for most of the losses.

Summary of Allied Ground Air Attack Claims
December 16th, 1944 - January 15th 1945

Target	Destroyed	Probable	Damaged
Aircraft on the Ground	66	5	58
Gun Positions	299	-	157
Tanks and AFV	751	-	509
Motor Transport	6,037	-	3,178
Locomotives	584	-	657
Rail Cars	4,217	-	7,117
Tugs	4	-	-
Barges	27	-	57
Buildings	1,178	-	573
Fuel & Ammo Dumps	10	-	-
Oil Tanks	10	-	-
Bridges	18	-	10
Tunnels	7	-	2
Railway Cuts	-	-	654
Highway Cuts	-	-	161

This total represents results from more than 36,000 sorties flown by the Allied tactical air forces as well as some 5,600 missions by the Eighth Air Force which included ground targets. Examination of claims to actual destruction showed a ratio of at least 10 to 1 for armored vehicles, although probably a lower ratio for the softer targets such as motor transport. (see 2nd Tactical Air Force Operational Research Section, "The Contribution of the Air Forces to the Stemming of the Enemy Thrust In the Ardennes," Report No. 19, p. 5-6.

Attacks on German Airfields by Allied Air Forces
December 16, 1944 - January 16, 1945

German Airfield	Air Force	Number of Aircraft	Ordnance (Tons)	Days Unserviceable
December 24				
Babenhausen	8th	96	290	3 Days
Biblis	8th	100	290	12 Days
Darmstadt/Griesheim	8th	189	208	Little effect
Dusseldorf/Essen	RAF	164	791	6 Days
Mulheim	RAF	124	404	10 Days
Ettingshausen/Frankfurt	8th	43	95	2 Days
Rhein-Main	8th	143	441	Little effect
Giessen	8th	74	165	Little effect
Gross Ostheim	8th	60	200	No effect
Kirch Göns	8th	54	120	13 Days
Merzhausen	8th	198	442	6 Days
Nidda	8th	53	116	10 Days
Zellhausen	8th	85	279	2 Days
December 25				
Bonn/Hangelar	RAF	100	490	6 Days
December 31				
Nordholz	9th	9	22	Little effect
Stade	9th	13	38	No effect
Wensendorf	8th	62	182	16 Days
January 5				
Nieder-Breisig	8th	70	130	Little effect
January 10				
Gymnich/Köln	8th	83	94	No effect
Ostheim	8th	53	152	11 Days
Euskirchen/Odendorf	8th	98	182	20 Days
Bonn-Hangelar	8th	63	117	2 Days

Most attacks with more than 100 tons of bombs resulted in substantial non-serviceable periods for German airfields. However, a great may airfields were available to the Germans and a very substantial effort would have been necessary to significantly restrict the Luftwaffe air effort through such means. The length of time which some air fields remained serviceable was undoubtedly due to the time of year. The frozen ground made airfield craters difficult to fill by bulldozer. It is noteworthy, however, that all airfields which were heavily bombed on the day before Christmas participated in flying aircraft during the *Operation Bodenplatte* attack on January 1.

Luftwaffe Order of Battle in the West Luftflotte 3 January 10, 1945			
Unit	Aircraft	Total	Serviceable
NAGr. 1	Me-109	15	8
NAGr. 13	Me-109, FW-189	51	39
Kdo. Braunegg	Me-262	5	2
Kdo. Sperling	Ar-234	4	4
Kdo. Hecht	Ar-234	1	1
JG 1	Fw-190	112	91
JG 2	Fw-190	54	34
JG 3	Me-109, Fw 190	98	78
JG 4	Fw-190, Me 109	107	79
JG 11	Fw-190, Me-109	109	83
JG 26	Fw-190	183	109
JG 27	Fw-190, Me-109	109	91
JG 53	Me-109	135	89
JG 54	Fw-190	97	70
JG 77	Me-109	87	52
SG 4	Fw-190	152	101
NSGr. 1	Ju-87	44	37
NSGr. 2	Ju-87	39	26
NSGr. 20	Fw-190	28	21
LG 1	Ju-88	64	52
KG 51	Me-262	52	37
KG 53	He-111/Fi-103	101	79
KG 66	Ju-88	29	17
KG 76	Ar-234	12	11
TG 3	Ju-52	50	48
TG 4	Ju-52	51	46
Transportgruppe 30	He-11	10	5
Total		1,799	1,310

Summary of Allied Air Sorties
December 16, 1944 - January 16, 1945

Date	Bombers				Fighters			Total Day Sorties
	IX BD	2nd TAF	8th AF Bombers	RAF BC	8th AF Fighters	IX AF	2nd TAF	
December:								
16	0	0	115	108 (386)	106	280	0	609
17	0	0	0	0	0	1,101 (35)	251 (17)	1,352
18	172	9	389	0 (1119)	618	604 (21)	440 (132)	2,232
19	0	0	312	29 (279)	37	224 (10)	103 (179)	705
20	0	0	0	0	0	0	0 (2)	0
21	0	0	0	94	0	113	0	207
22	0	36	0	0 (415)	0	5 (5)	82	123
23	670	72	397	151 (283)	692	804	367 (56)	3,153
24	75	144	1,884	288 (148)	780	1,286 (8)	1,098 (104)	5,555
25	814	60	388	0 (269)	422	1,069 (25)	974 (184)	3,727
26	330	0	129	274	319	1,116 (43)	553 (53)	2,721
27	348	5	588	191	341	1,236 (37)	294 (10)	3,003
28	0	0	1,158	164 (386)	541	0 (23)	113 (61)	1,976
29	0	36	780	352 (552)	535	409	737 (93)	2,849
30	0	0	1,251	0 (547)	508	528 (12)	6 (2)	2,293
31	0	36	1,247	161 (693)	676	690	790 (9)	3,600
January:								
1	188	107	718	110 (322)	592	852 (19)	996 (225)	3,563
2	133	0	956	0 (550)	704	773 (17)	182 (99)	2,748
3	0	60	1,099	91 (1008)	609	0	60 (12)	1,919
4	0	0	0	0 (5)	0	0	393 (62)	393
5	191	144	869	151 (414)	528	750	373 (54)	3,006
6	26	10	771	0 (905)	501	0	72 (218)	1,380
7	0	0	1,016	0 (693)	629	0	5 (7)	1,650
8	0	0	595	0 (740)	219	0	0 (10)	814
9	0	0	0	0	0	0	0	0
10	0	0	912	0	260	375	25	1,572
11	118	0	0	0 (52)	0	33 (4)	0	151
12	0	0	0	0	0	0	0	0
13	95	0	909	0	270	664	371 (88)	2,309
14	279	14	841	0	712	841 (18)	711 (43)	3,398
15	16	0	619	0	632	472 (11)	0 (148)	1,739

Notes:

Does not include operations of the 1st Tactical Air Force; ( ) = night sorties.
Source: Office of the Director of Intelligence, 1945. *Allied Air Power and the Ardennes Offensive: 15 December 1944- 16 January 1945,* United States Strategic Air Forces in Europe, Coffin Report, U.S. Army Military History Institute, Carisle, PA.

Tons of Bombs Dropped by Allied Command and Target Type
December 17-27, 1944

Command	Cities	Oil	A/C Fact.	Airfields	Rail Targets	Close Support	Targets of Opp.	TOTAL
RAF BC	5,541	18	12	1,896	6,252	1,333	—	15,052
Eighth AF	166	—	—	2,870	7,404	—	690	11,130
Ninth AF	—	—	64	—	3,851	2,728	—	6,643
2nd TAF	—	—	—	268	282	—	550	—
TOTALS	5,707	18	12	4,830	17,775	4,343	690	33,375

Total Allied Claims of Enemy Aircraft and Ground Targets
December 17-27, 1944

Command	Enemy AC	AFV	M/T	Locos	R.R. Cars	Rd. & Rail Cuts	Bridges	Guns Positions
RAF BC	5	—	—	—	—	—	—	—
Eighth AF	240	—	—	1	—	—	—	—
Ninth AF	405	464	3147	44	597	184	6	167
2nd TAF	68	4	291	21	3	5	—	—
TOTALS	718	468	3438	66	600	189	6	167

Total Losses of Allied Aircraft in Combat – December 17-27, 1944

Type	RAF BC	Eighth AF	Ninth AF	Second TAF	TOTAL
Hvy. Bombers	0/47	18/54	0/0	0/0	18/101
Med. Bombers	0/0	0/0	37/8	0/1	37/9
Fighters	0/0	17/35	27/120	12/42	56/197
Total	0/47	35/89	64/128	12/43	111/307

First value In each column is the number of aircraft reported as shot down by enemy aircraft. Second column are losses due to all other causes. It is probable that some of these losses are attributable to enemy aircraft.

Index

521

Index

Index

525